Outback Australia

a Lonely Planet Australia guide

Ron & Viv Moon
Denis O'Byrne
Hugh Finlay

Rob van Driesum
Jeff Williams
Julian Barry

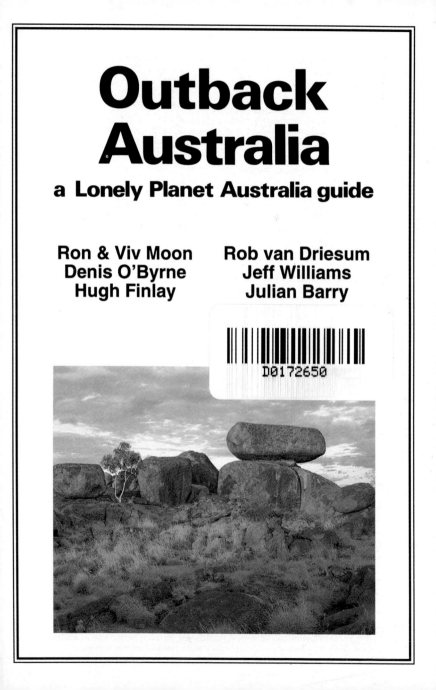

Outback Australia

1st edition

Published by
Lonely Planet Publications
Head Office: PO Box 617, Hawthorn, Vic 3122, Australia
Branches: 155 Filbert St, Suite 251, Oakland, CA 94607, USA
10 Barley Mow Passage, Chiswick, London W4 4PH, UK
71 bis rue du Cardinal Lemoine, 75005 Paris, France

Printed by
Singapore National Printers Ltd, Singapore

Photographs by

Mark Armstrong (MA)	Ross Barnett (RB)	John Chapman (JC)
Michelle Coxall (MC)	David Curl (DC)	Hugh Finlay (HF)
Richard I'Anson (RI)	Chris Klep (CK)	Mark Lightbody (ML)
Ron & Viv Moon (R & VM)	Jon Murray (JM)	Richard Nebesky (RN)
Denis O'Byrne (DO)	Ray Stamp (RS)	Paul Steel (PS)
Rob van Driesum (RvD)	Tony Wheeler (TW)	Jeff Williams (JW)

Northern Territory Tourist Commission (NTTC)

Front cover: Car on an outback road near Wittenoom, Western Australia, (The Photographic Library of
Australia Pty Ltd, Geoff Higgins)
Back cover: Sturt desert pea (Ron & Viv Moon)
Title page: Devil's Marbles at sunset, Northern Territory (Richard I'Anson)

First Published
November 1994

**Although the authors and publisher have tried to make the information as
accurate as possible, they accept no responsibility for any loss, injury or
inconvenience sustained by any person using this book.**

National Library of Australia Cataloguing in Publication Data

Ron Moon
    Outback Australia: Lonely Planet Australia guide.

    1st ed.
    Includes index.
    ISBN 0 86442 239 3.

    1. Australia – Guidebooks.
    I. Moon, Ron. (Series: Lonely Planet Australia guide)

919.40463

text & maps © Lonely Planet 1994
photos © photographers as indicated 1994
climate charts compiled from information supplied by Patrick J Tyson, © Patrick J Tyson, 1994

Ron & Viv Moon

Ron and Viv wrote the sections dealing with Cape York, the Kimberley and the Flinders Ranges, as well as the Canning Stock Route, Gunbarrel, 'Bomb Roads', Strzelecki, Silver City and Matilda Highway. They have spent much of their lives exploring and writing about Australia's wild and remote areas. They founded the magazine *Action Outdoor Australia*, where they were editor and assistant editor for a number of years. Ron is now well entrenched as editor of the national 4WD magazine *4X4 Australia*, and Viv is a freelance travel writer specialising in the more isolated and untamed places of Australia and overseas. Together they also write and publish their successful adventure guidebooks to Cape York, the Kimberley and the Flinders Ranges.

Denis O'Byrne

Denis wrote much of the material on central Australia, including the Oodnadatta and Birdsville tracks, MacDonnell Ranges, Finke Gorge, Simpson Desert and Plenty and Sandover highways, as well as the Gulf Track. Born and raised in country South Australia, Denis first ventured into the outback as an army surveyor. After a couple of years in Africa and Europe, he worked in Western Australia's Pilbara before arriving in Alice Springs on a round-Australia trip in 1978. He's lived in the Alice ever since, and currently struggles to keep up the mortgage payments by working as a freelance writer. Denis is a columnist and regular contributor of outback travel features to the national 4WD magazine *Overlander*.

Hugh Finlay

Hugh wrote the sections on the Stuart Highway and the Top End, the Tanami, Finke and Old Andado tracks, and the separate feature on Aboriginal art. Parts of the introductory chapters were based on *Australia – a travel survival kit*, of which Hugh is the coordinating author. While working his way around Australia, he spent two years driving through outback South Australia and the Northern Territory prospecting for diamonds (without success), and a further year in Western Australia's remote Mt Augustus region on a 1¼-million-acre cattle station. A half-year stint on an irrigation project in Saudi Arabia gave plenty of opportunities for sand-driving practice, while numerous safaris in East Africa have thrown up all sorts of driving challenges. He currently lives in central Victoria with Linda and their two daughters, Ella and Vera, trying to juggle the demands – and pleasures – of family life, restoring an old farmhouse, writing, rearing sheep, gardening, and lengthy phone calls from Lonely Planet editors!

Rob van Driesum

Rob was the coordinating author of this book and compiled the introductory chapters from material supplied by the authors. He grew up in several Asian and African countries before moving to Holland, where he studied Modern History at the University of Amsterdam and worked in a variety of jobs to finance his motorcycle travels. A round-the-world trip was cut short in Australia where he became editor of a motorcycle magazine, enabling him to pursue his passion for outback travel on the latest test bikes. Since joining Lonely Planet as editor in charge of its Europe guidebooks, he has contributed bits and pieces to several books and still dreams of finally marking the Tanami and Gibb River roads on his wall map of Australia.

Jeff Williams

Jeff wrote the sections on the Pilbara, the Eyre Highway and Gold Fields & Ghost Towns. More adept on a bicycle or in a pair of walking boots, Jeff drove some 16,000 km behind the wheel of Lonely Planet's 4WD researching his small part of this book. A co-author of the *New Zealand* and *Australia* travel survival kits, and *Tramping in New Zealand*, he is currently writing the *Western Australia* guide.

Julian Barry

Julian wrote most of the material on Aborigines and Aboriginal languages in the introductory chapters. He is an anthropologist and adult educator, and describes himself as a former refugee from Brisbane. He has spent 5½ years in central Australia and two years in the Top End. Most of Julian's time in central Australia has been spent living on Pitjantjatjara-speaking Aboriginal communities, including a number of years at Uluru National Park, where he currently lives. He says the park is an exciting a positive example of how Aboriginal and White Australians can live, work and learn together.

From the Authors

From Hugh Hugh Finlay wishes to thank the many people who gave generously of their time and knowledge. In particular, thanks to Peter Yates of the NTTC, Alan Withers of the NT Conservation Commission in Borroloola (did you ever get that croc?), Andrew Morley & Rowan of Milikapiti on Melville Island (NT) for arranging a visit there, Nick & Kerry Bryce for their hospitality in both Auburn (SA) and The Granites (NT), Ian Fox in Darwin (known far and wide for his bottomless fridge), and also to Linda, who accompanied Hugh for much of the time and gave many valuable insights.

From Jeff Jeff Williams would like to thank Rob van Driesum for getting him involved in this project, Helen & Albert Innes of Perth, Stef & Angela Frodshan of Fremantle, Jim & Collette Truscott of Karratha, and last but not least, Alison and Callum, who drove the 16,000 km with him.

From the Publisher

This book was edited by Rob van Driesum, Alison White, David Meagher, Alan Tiller and Katie Cody. The proofreader was Samantha Carew, who took the book through production and compiled the index, with assistance from Ann Jeffree. The maps, based on material supplied by the authors, were drawn by Indra Kilfoyle, with help from Chris Klep, Jane Hart, Adam McCrow and Maliza Kruh. Indra also handled the design and layout of the book. Jane designed the cover. Matt King coordinated the Aboriginal art section and Vicki Beale handled the design.

Special thanks to Tony Wheeler, for writing the introduction; to Jim Hart, for the sections on Flying Yourself and the Birdsville Races – a flying survival kit; to Peter 'Mr' Smith, for contributing his knowledge and wit to the Glossary; to Jon Murray, for his advice on cycling in the outback; to John Weldon, for his help on outback films; to Alex Cook from the Queensland Museum, for helping to organise the illustrations in the Palaeontology section; and to Jim Sinclair, for invaluable advice on outback radio. Additional thanks go to the authors for their cooperation and enthusiasm, making the project a particularly enjoyable one for all concerned.

Warning & Request

The outback is not to be treated lightly. The isolation, harsh climate and lack of water make it one of the few places in the world where survival can still depend completely on you – where you literally take your life into your own hands. If you are well prepared, outback travel is highly enjoyable and provides a great sense of achievement; if you prepare poorly, you may pay the ultimate price.

The outback infrastructure is highly volatile: waterholes dry up or become polluted; tracks that are fine one day could be washed away the next and may be abandoned as a result; new tracks are pushed through by the authorities and private individuals; and areas that have unrestricted access may suddenly become restricted to all but a select group of people. The outback is still a land of pioneers, which means that services, too, change all the time – farmers open up resorts or roadhouses, schedules change, prices go up, good places go bad, and bad places go bankrupt. So if you find things better or worse, recently opened or long since closed, please write and tell us and help make the next edition better.

Your letters will be used to help update future editions and, where possible, important changes will also be included in a Stop Press section in reprints.

We greatly appreciate all information that is sent to us by travellers. Back at Lonely Planet we employ a hard-working readers' letters team to sort through the many letters we receive. The best ones will be rewarded with a free copy of the next edition or another Lonely Planet guide if you prefer. We give away lots of books, but, unfortunately, not every letter/postcard receives one.

Contents

Map Legend

BOUNDARIES

.............International Boundary
.............State Boundary

ROUTES

.............Freeway
.............Highway
.............Major Road
.............Unsealed Road or Track
.............Abandoned Road
.............City Road
.............City Street
.............Railway
.............Disused Railway
.............Fence, with gate
.............Walking Tour
.............Ferry Route
.............Cable Car or Chairlift

AREA FEATURES

.............Aboriginal Land
.............Park, Gardens
.............National Park
.............Built-Up Area
.............Pedestrian Mall
.............Market
.............Cemetery
.............Reef
.............Rocks

HYDROGRAPHIC FEATURES

.............Coastline
.............River, Creek
.............Intermittent River or Creek
.............Lake, Intermittent Lake
.............Salt Lake
.............Swamp

SYMBOLS

✪ CAPITAL	.............National Capital	
◉ Capital	.............State Capital	
🌑 CITY	.............Major City	
● City	.............City	
● Town	.............Town	
● Village	.............Village	
■	.............Place to Stay	
▼	.............Place to Eat	
▮	.............Pub, Bar	
✉ ☎	.............Post Office, Telephone	
❶ ❽	.............Tourist Information, Bank	
⊖ 🅿	.............Transport, Parking	
🏛 ⛩	.............Museum, Youth Hostel	
🚐 ⅄	Caravan Park, Camping Ground	
† ☎ †	.............Church, Cathedral	
☪ ✿	.............Mosque, Synagogue	
⊥ ⚎	Buddhist Temple, Hindu Temple	

✪	★	.............Hospital, Police Station
✈	✝	.............Airport, Airfield
▭	✿	.............Swimming Pool, Gardens
❖	🐘	.............Shopping Centre, Zoo
✾	⊓	...Winery or Vineyard, Picnic Site
←	33	One Way Street, Route Number
	∴	.......Archaeological Site or Ruins
🏰	⚴	.............Stately Home, Monument
🞐	▣	.............Castle, Tomb
⌒	⌂	.............Cave, Hut or Chalet
▲	※	.............Mountain or Hill, Lookout
🗼	🗼	.............Lighthouses
)(	o—	.............Pass, Spring
★	10 ★	.............Distances, in kilometres
⟫	⊩	.............Rapids, Waterfalls
	⟸	.......Cliff or Escarpment, Tunnel
		.............Railway Station

Note: not all symbols displayed above appear in this book

Introduction

Out 'back of Bourke', way 'beyond the black stump', is Australia's outback. It may be hard to define but you'll certainly know it when you see it. It's the mythical Australia – the Australia of red dust, empty tracks, strange wildlife, endless vistas, tall tales and big thirsts. And, myth or not, it's ready and waiting for anyone with a spirit of adventure and some suitable transport.

Some of the routes that take you through the outback are modern sealed roads, like the east-west Eyre Highway or north-south Stuart Highway, but most of them are not. Some of them are not even maintained and it's only the passing of an occasional vehicle which keeps them open. Some of them are long and dreary, others provide a kaleidoscope of changes, but all of them traverse some of the most remote country on earth.

Improved equipment, from more reliable and readily available vehicles to better long-range radios, plus better track maintenance have made all the outback routes more accessible in recent years. Thirty years ago the Birdsville Track required a sturdy 4WD, and a breakdown in summer could easily be a prelude to disaster. Today, with a little care, you could drive the Birdsville in the same car you use for suburban supermarket runs, although breaking down in the heat of summer is still not recommended. Thirty years ago only Aborigines and a handful of explorers with camels had ever made it across the Simpson Desert. Today there's a steady trickle of 4WD parties crossing this awe-inspiring stretch of land. Even the Canning Stock Route, the three-week-long ultimate outback trip, is feasible for any well-equipped group to tackle.

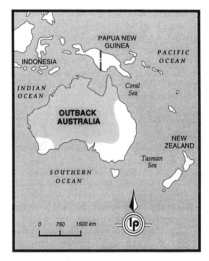

This book covers all the outback; it explores the easily accessible places like Alice Springs and Kakadu but it also comes to grips with the 'real' outback, the rough and tough tracks where you'd better be equipped with plenty of fuel, plenty of water and plenty of spare tyres. There are full details on when to go (many of the tracks are strictly for the cooler months), what vehicle to use (hardy travellers have even conquered some of the tracks on mountain bikes or on foot), equipment requirements (tools, radios, spare parts), supplies (on the Canning Stock Route it's even necessary to arrange a fuel drop) and safety (foolhardy travellers sometimes still pay with their lives).

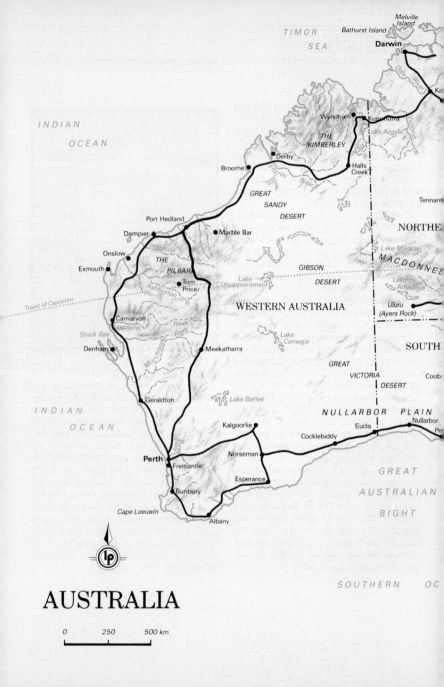

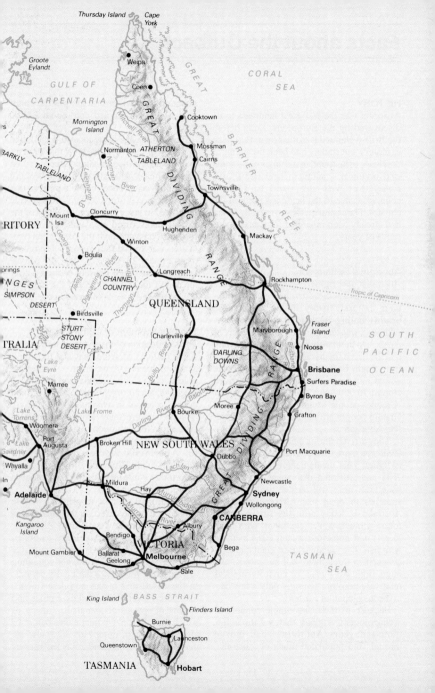

Facts about the Outback

HISTORY

Australia was the last great landmass to be discovered by the Europeans. Long before the British claimed it as their own, European explorers and traders had been dreaming of the riches to be found in the unknown – some said mythical – southern land *(terra australis)* that was supposed to form a counterbalance to the landmass north of the equator. The continent they eventually found had already been inhabited for tens of thousands of years.

Aboriginal Settlement

Australian Aboriginal (which literally means 'indigenous') society has the longest continuous cultural history in the world, with origins dating back to the last Ice age. Although mystery shrouds many aspects of Australian prehistory, it seems almost certain that the first humans came here across the sea from South-East Asia. Heavy-boned people whom archaeologists call 'Robust' arrived around 70,000 years ago, and more slender 'Gracile' people around 50,000 years ago. Gracile people are the ancestors of Australian Aborigines.

They arrived during a period when the sea level was more than 50 metres lower than it is today. This created more land between Asia and Australia than there is now, but watercraft were still needed to cross some stretches of open sea. Although much of Australia is today arid, the first migrants found a much wetter continent, with large forests and numerous inland lakes teeming with fish. The fauna included giant marsupials such as three-metre-tall kangaroos, and huge, flightless birds. The environment was relatively non-threatening – only a few carnivorous predators existed.

Because of these favourable conditions, archaeologists suggest that within a few thousand years Aborigines had moved through and populated much of Australia,

although the most central parts of the continent were not occupied until about 24,000 years ago.

The last Ice age came to an end 15,000 to 10,000 years ago. The sea level rose dramatically with the rise in temperature, and an area of Greater Australia the size of Western Australia was flooded during a process that would have seen strips of land 100 km wide inundated in just a few decades. Many of the inland lakes dried up, and vast deserts formed. Thus, although the Aboriginal population was spread fairly evenly throughout the continent 20,000 years ago, the coastal areas become more densely occupied after the end of the last Ice age and the stabilisation of the sea level 5000 years ago.

The Development of Culture Areas

The stabilisation of the sea level led to more stable patterns of settlement and the emergence of broad culture areas – Aboriginal groups who exhibited similarities in terms of language, social organisation, tools, art and the environment in which they lived. There is some disagreement among anthropologists about the definition of these areas, and their exact number. The Australian Institute for Aboriginal Studies recognises 11 regional subdivisions in Aboriginal Australia today, while individual anthropologists have identified up to 21.

Traditionally, most Aboriginal people either lived in the desert, in the inland non-desert areas, on the coast, or in Tasmania. Throughout the desert, Aborigines exhibited a similar foraging pattern, spreading out over large tracts of land after rain, and retreating to permanent waterholes during dry periods. In the desert and inland non-desert areas, they foraged on birds, various reptiles and dozens of species of mammals – many of which have become extinct either before or after the arrival of Europeans. They also ate many different fruits, and collected various seeds which were ground and mixed with water before being either baked in the coals to make damper, or eaten as a paste.

Coastal Aborigines ate roots, fruits, small game, reptiles, fish and shellfish. In Tasmania, where Aborigines were cut off from the mainland by the rise in sea level and were isolated for longer than any other society in human history, they developed a unique culture. Although they ate shellfish, they stopped eating fish about 3500 years ago. They also ate seals, small ground mammals and birds. In the Torres Strait Islands between Cape York and New Guinea, people ate (and continue to eat) fish, shellfish, dugong (a relative of the manatee and walrus), and a variety of fruits and yams. Many Aboriginal Australians today still eat a considerable amount of traditional foods.

Aboriginal Society

The Aborigines were tribal people living in extended family groups. Many today still live in clans, with clan members descending from a common ancestor. Tradition, rituals and laws link the people of each clan to the land they occupy. Each clan has various sites of spiritual significance on their land, places

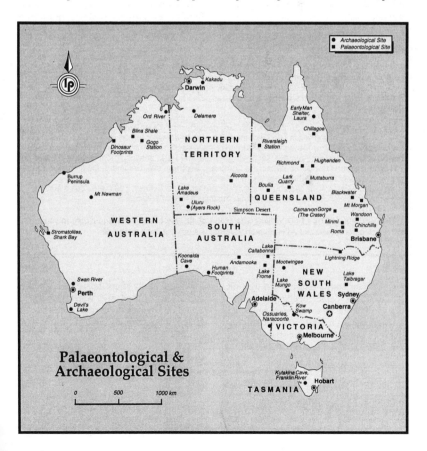

Palaeontological & Archaeological Sites

Archaeological Treasures

The early Aborigines left no stone buildings or statues to tickle our fancy, but archaeologists have unearthed many other treasures. The best known site by far is **Lake Mungo**, in the dry Willandra Lakes system in the south-west of New South Wales.

Mungo (the name is Scottish) is a living, evolving excavation. The archaeologists here are time and weather. This area was once a vast system of inland lakes, dry now for some 20,000 years. The embankment of sand and mud on the eastern fringe of the ancient lake system, named the 'Walls of China' by homesick Chinese workers, has been eroded by the wind in recent years, revealing human and animal skeletal remains, ancient campfires and evidence of inter-tribal trading.

The remains prove that ritual burial was practised here 15,000 years before the construction of the Egyptian pyramids. The fireplaces reveal that sophisticated, tertiary-chipped stone implements were fashioned by the dwellers at the edge of this now dry lake. The food they ate can be discovered in the fireplaces, and the long-extinct animals they preyed on are found in skeletal form on the dunes. This area is so important that the Willandra Lakes are now a World Heritage area.

Another fascinating area of study has been **Kow Swamp** in northern Victoria. This site has a rich collection of human remains which date from the late Pleistocene epoch. One body, buried 12,000 years ago, had a headband of kangaroo incisor teeth. In the lunette of **Lake Nitchie**, in western New South Wales, a man was buried 7000 to 6500 years ago with a necklace of 178 pierced Tasmanian-devil teeth.

The west and north of Australia have many significant sites. Groove-edged axes dating back 23,000 years have been found in the **Malangangerr** rock-shelter in Arnhem Land. Other rich sources of artefacts are **Miriwun** rock-shelter on the Ord River in the Kimberley; the **Mt Newman** rock-shelter in the Pilbara; and the **Devil's Lair** near Cape Leeuwin in the far south-west of the continent. Fragments and stone tools dating back 38,000 years were found in the nearby **Swan Valley**.

Ice-age rock engravings (petroglyphs) are found throughout the continent. Those in **Koonalda Cave**, on the Nullarbor in South Australia, are perhaps the oldest. Flint miners often visited the cave 24,000 to 14,000 years ago, and unexplained patterns were left on the wall – perhaps it is art, perhaps not. Other places where petroglyphs are easily seen are on the **Burrup Peninsula** near Dampier, Western Australia; **Mootwingee National Park**, between Tibooburra and Broken Hill in far western New South Wales; the **Lightning Brothers** site, Delamere, Northern Territory; and at the **Early Man shelter** near Laura in Queensland.

Josephine Flood's *Archaeology of the Dreamtime* (Collins, Sydney, 1983) provides a fascinating account of archaeological research into Australia's first inhabitants.

Warning: It might be OK in other parts of the world, but in Australia it is illegal to remove archaeological objects or to disturb human remains. Look but don't touch. ■

to which their spirits return when they die. Clan members come together to perform rituals to honour their ancestral spirits and the Dreamtime creators. These traditional religious beliefs are the basis of the Aborigines' ties to the land they live on.

It is the responsibility of the clan, or particular members of it, to correctly maintain and protect the sites so that the ancestral beings are not offended and continue to protect and provide for the clan. Traditional punishments for those who neglect these responsibilities can still be severe, as their actions can easily affect the wellbeing of the whole clan – food and water shortages, natural disasters or mysterious illnesses can all be attributed to disgruntled or offended ancestral beings.

Many Aboriginal communities were semi-nomadic, others sedentary, one of the deciding factors being the availability of food. Where food and water were readily available, the people tended to remain in a limited area. When they did wander, it was to visit sacred places to carry out rituals, or to take advantage of seasonal foods available elsewhere. They did not, as is still often believed, roam aimlessly and desperately in search of food and water.

The traditional role of the men was that of hunter, tool-maker and custodian of male law; the women reared the children, and gathered and prepared food. There was also female law and ritual for which the women were responsible. Ultimately, the shared effort of men and women ensured the continuation of their social system. This is still the view of many Aborigines in central Australia.

Wisdom and skills obtained over millennia enabled Aborigines to use their environment to the maximum. An intimate knowledge of the behaviour of animals and the correct time to harvest the many plants they utilised ensured that food shortages were rare. Like other hunter-gatherer peoples of the world, the Aborigines were true ecologists.

Although Aborigines in northern Australia were in regular contact with the farming and fishing peoples of Indonesia who came to Australian shores to collect trepang (bêche-de-mer, or sea cucumber), the farming of crops and domestication of livestock held no appeal. The only major modification of the landscape practised by the Aborigines was the selective burning of undergrowth in forests and dead grass on the plains. This encouraged new growth, which in turn attracted game animals. It also prevented the build-up of combustible material in the forests, making hunting easier and reducing the possibility of major bush fires. Dingoes assisted in the hunt and guarded the camp from intruders. (It's still unclear whether dingoes came with their prehistoric human masters from South-East Asia or were introduced later by Indonesians.)

Similar technology – for example the boomerang and spear – was used throughout the continent, but techniques were adapted to the environment and the species being hunted. In the wetlands of northern Australia, fish traps hundreds of metres long made of bamboo and cord were built to catch fish at the end of the wet season. In the area now known as Victoria, permanent stone dams many km long were used to trap migrating eels, while in the tablelands of Queensland finely woven nets were used to snare herds of wallabies and kangaroos.

Contrary to the common image, some tribes did build permanent dwellings, varying widely depending on climate, the materials available and likely length of use. In western Victoria the local Aborigines built permanent stone dwellings; in the deserts semi-circular shelters were made with arched branches covered with native grasses or leaves; and in Tasmania large conical thatch shelters were constructed that could house up to 30 people. Such dwellings were used mainly for sleeping.

The Aborigines were also traders. Trade routes crisscrossed the country, dispersing goods and a variety of produced items. Many of the items traded, such as certain types of stone or shell, were rare and had great ritual significance. Boomerangs and ochre were other important trade items. Along these trading networks, large numbers of people would often meet for 'exchange ceremonies', where not only goods but also songs and dances were passed on.

'Discovery' & Colonisation

Portuguese navigators had probably come within sight of the coast in the first half of the 16th century, and in 1606 the Spaniard Torres sailed through the strait between Cape York and New Guinea that still bears his name, though there's no record of his actually sighting the southern continent.

In the early 1600s, Dutch explorers began to map parts of the coastline, and the southern continent became known to the world as New Holland – a name that stuck until the second half of the 19th century when British settlers began using the more appropriate label 'Australia'. Traders first and foremost, the Dutch found little of value in this barren continent with its 'backward' inhabitants, and saw it mainly as an obstacle to be avoided on their hazardous sea voyages to and from the rich East Indies.

Heading east from the Cape of Good

Hope, Dutch captains intent on making time rode the Roaring Forties, the icy but powerful winds of the sub-Antarctic, for as long as they dared before changing course to the north. 'Dared' because longitude calculations were very much guesswork before the invention of the chronometer, and many of the more reckless captains smashed their ships into the empty Western Australian coast.

During the colonisation drive of the 18th century, French and British explorers began to take a stronger interest in New Holland. Captain James Cook 'discovered' the relatively fertile eastern coast that earlier explorers had overlooked, and the British government, to head off French claims, established a penal colony there in 1788 under the name of New South Wales.

Devastation of the Aborigines

When Sydney Cove was first settled by the British, it is believed there were about 300,000 Aborigines in Australia and around 250 different languages were spoken, many as distinct from each other as English is from Chinese. Tasmania alone had eight languages, and tribes living on opposite sides of present-day Sydney Harbour spoke mutually unintelligible languages.

In such a society, based on family groups with an egalitarian political structure, a coordinated response to the European colonisers was not possible. Despite the presence of the Aborigines, the newly arrived Europeans considered the new continent to be *terra nullius* – a land belonging to no-one. Conveniently, they saw no recognisable system of government, no commerce or permanent settlements and no evidence of landownership. (If the opposite had been the case, and if the Aborigines had offered coordinated resistance, the English might have been forced to legitimise their colonisation by entering into a treaty with the Aboriginal landowners, as happened in New Zealand with the Treaty of Waitangi.)

Many Aborigines were driven from their land by force, and many more succumbed to exotic diseases such as smallpox, measles, venereal disease, influenza, whooping cough, pneumonia and tuberculosis. Others voluntarily left their lands to travel to the fringes of settled areas to obtain new commodities such as steel and cloth, and experience hitherto unknown drugs such as tea, tobacco and alcohol.

The delicate balance between Aboriginal people and nature was broken, as the European invaders cut down forests and introduced numerous feral and domestic animals – by 1860 there were 20 million sheep in Australia. Sheep and cattle destroyed waterholes and ruined the habitats which had for tens of thousands of years sustained mammals, reptiles and vegetable foods. Many species of plants and animals disappeared altogether.

There was still considerable conflict between Aborigines and White settlers. Starving Aborigines speared sheep and cattle and then suffered fierce reprisal raids which often left many of them dead. For the first 100 years of 'settlement' very few Europeans were prosecuted for killing Aborigines, although the practice was widespread.

In many parts of Australia, Aborigines defended their lands with desperate guerrilla tactics. Warriors including Pemulwy, Yagan, Dundalli, Jandamarra (known to the Whites as 'Pigeon') and Nemarluk were feared by the colonists for a time, and some settlements had to be abandoned. Until the 1850s, when Europeans had to rely on inaccurate and unreliable flintlock rifles, Aborigines sometimes had the benefit of superior numbers, weapons and tactics. However, with the introduction of breach-loading repeater rifles in the 1870s, armed resistance was quickly crushed (although on isolated occasions into the 1920s, Whites were still speared in central and northern Australia). Full-blood Aborigines in Tasmania were wiped out almost to the last individual, and Aboriginal society in southern Australia suffered terribly. Within 100 years all that was left of traditional Aboriginal society consisted of relatively small groups in central and northern Australia.

First Contact in the Western Desert

The Anangu people of the Western Desert were the last Aborigines to have contact with non-Aboriginal people. The very last Anangu to abandon their autonomous hunting and gathering lifestyle were a small group of Pintupi, who in 1984 walked into Kintore, a small community 350 km north-west of Uluru (Ayers Rock).

First contact in other parts of the Western Desert is also relatively recent – even in the Uluru region where today over 250,000 tourists visit annually. Although Giles passed through the Western Desert region in the 1870s, during the following 50 years non-Aboriginal visitation was so infrequent that many Anangu didn't see a White person until the 1930s or 1940s – or even later.

By the early 1950s most Anangu were living permanently or semi-permanently on missions, or on pastoral properties where they often worked for no more payment other than food and clothing. Up until the late 1960s they continued to spend considerable periods travelling around on foot or on camels, in many cases still hunting with *kulata* (spear) and *miru* (spear thrower).

Up until the 1960s, government patrol officers searched out groups of Anangu, many of whom had experienced little or no contact with non-Aborigines, and trucked them from remote parts of the Western Desert to various settlements. This was part of a government policy which stated that Aborigines should be encouraged to abandon their traditions and become assimilated into mainstream White society. Also, in the Uluru area and on the roads leading to it, authorities claimed that Anangu were having a negative impact on the growing tourist industry.

In other parts of the Western Desert, Anangu were forcibly removed to make way for the testing of military hardware. In 1946 a guided-missile range was established at Woomera, within what was then the Central Desert Aboriginal Reserve. Until at least 1966, groups of Anangu were brought in from areas where testing had taken place. In some cases these people had been traumatised by rockets but had not experienced face-to-face contact with Whites.

As well as testing conventional weapons, in the 1950s the Australian government permitted the British to detonate atomic devices at Emu Junction 500 km south-west of Uluru, and at Maralinga a little further south. The authorities claimed that prior to detonation two patrol officers combed thousands of sq km, ensuring that no Anangu people were harmed by the tests. Anangu have another story: they say that as a result of these tests many people became sick and died.

Yami Lester is a Yankunytjatjara man who was a child at the time one of the British nuclear devices was detonated 180 km from his home. As a result of radioactive fallout, Yami saw many of his relatives sicken and die; some years later, he went blind. *Yami – The Autobiography of Yami Lester* (IAD Publications, Alice Springs) provides an excellent insight into many aspects of early Western Desert contact history, and the struggle for land rights which took place some decades later. ■

'Protection' & 'Assimilation' By the early 1900s, legislation designed to segregate and 'protect' Aboriginal people was passed in all states. The legislation imposed restrictions on the Aborigines' rights to own property and seek employment, and the Aboriginals Ordinance of 1918 even allowed the state to remove children from Aboriginal mothers if it was suspected that the father was non-Aboriginal. In these cases the parents were considered to have no rights over the children, who were placed in foster homes or childcare institutions. Many Aborigines are still bitter about having been separated from their families and forced to grow up apart from their people. An up-side of the ordinance was that it gave a degree of protection for 'full-blood' Aborigines living on reserves, as non-Aborigines could enter only with a permit, and mineral exploration was forbidden.

The process of social change was accelerated by WW II, and after the war 'assimilation' became the stated aim of the government. To this end, the rights of Aborigines were subjugated even further – the government had control over everything, from where Aborigines could live to whom they could marry. Many people were forcibly moved to townships, the idea being that they would adapt to European culture which would in turn aid their economic development. This policy was a dismal failure.

In the 1960s the assimilation policy came

under a great deal of scrutiny, and White Australians became increasingly aware of the inequity of their treatment of Aborigines. In 1967 non-Aboriginal Australians voted to give Aborigines and Torres Strait Islanders the status of citizens, and gave the national government power to legislate for them in all states. The states had to provide them with the same services as were available to other citizens, and the national government set up the Department of Aboriginal Affairs to identify the special needs of Aborigines and legislate for them.

The assimilation policy was finally dumped in 1972, to be replaced by the government's policy of self-determination, which for the first time enabled Aborigines to participate in decision-making processes by granting them rights to their land. See the Government section, later in this chapter, for more on Aboriginal land rights.

Although the latest developments give rise to cautious optimism, many Aborigines still live in appalling conditions, and alcohol and drug abuse remain a widespread problem, particularly among young and middle-aged men. Aboriginal communities have taken up the challenge to try and eradicate these problems – many communities are now 'dry', and there are a number of rehabilitation programmes for alcoholics, petrol-sniffers and others with drug problems. Thanks for much of this work goes to Aboriginal women, many of whom have found themselves on the receiving end of domestic violence.

All in all it's been a bloody awful 200 years for Australia's Aborigines. One can only be thankful for their resilience, which enabled them to withstand the pressures placed on their culture, traditions and dignity, and that after so many years of domination they've been able to keep so much of that culture intact.

White Exploration

Twenty-five years after the establishment of New South Wales, Blaxland, Lawson and Wentworth crossed the mountains west of Sydney Cove, and the White exploration of

inland Australia began. Already the coast was fairy well known, with Matthew Flinders making his great circumnavigation of the continent in 1803 and Phillip Parker King's voyages between 1817 and 1822 filling in most of the blanks.

By the 1840s Oxley, Hume, Hovell, Sturt and Mitchell had blazed their trails of exploration across the south-east of Australia, opening up the land between Sydney and the new settlements of Melbourne and Adelaide. Over in the west, explorers had set out from Perth to survey the land southwards close to present-day Albany and northwards to the Gascoyne River. In 1838 a group of men under Charles (later Sir) Grey landed on a rugged stretch of coast in the Kimberley at Hanover Bay and got nowhere, barely escaping with their lives in the forbidding terrain.

It is ironic that some explorers of inland Australia died of thirst and starvation in a land where Aborigines have survived for thousands of years. Rather than living with the land, they chose to conquer it the only way they knew: with weapons and supplies.

The 'Inland Sea' Edward John Eyre explored the Flinders Ranges in South Australia in 1840 while trying to find a way to the centre of the continent. A vast salt lake that he called Lake Torrens blocked his way, but in reality it was a number of lakes now called Torrens, Eyre and Frome, to name a few. It was this so-called impassable barrier that forced Sturt, a few years later, to head east and then north.

Giving up on his quest for the centre of Australia, Eyre, in an epic feat, crossed the continent from Port Lincoln in South Australia to Albany in the west. Although he was a little more successful than Grey and travelled a darn sight further, he too nearly died along the way, and one of the only things he proved was that it was not possible to drive cattle from Adelaide to Perth via the coast.

In 1844, Charles Sturt, already a well-known and respected explorer, set out from Adelaide on his greatest expedition, to find what many thought would be an 'inland sea'. Following the Murray and Darling rivers that he knew so well to a point near Menindee, his team struck north-west. Trapped by unbelievable heat and lack of water, the men spent months at Depot Glen, near present-day Milparinka, before pushing further inland, finally reaching a spot on Eyre Creek north of today's Birdsville. Forced back by the unrelenting conditions, it was thanks to Sturt's skills that only one man died on this 18-month journey into and out of hell. Sturt's health never fully recovered, and although he was welcomed back to civilisation a hero and promoted to government positions, he soon had to retire because of deteriorating eyesight.

The Tropics In south-east Queensland, the opening up of the Moreton Bay area to White settlement in 1842 soon led to pioneer pastoralists pushing further north and west. In 1846 the enigmatic Ludwig Leichhardt led his men from Brisbane to Port Essington (near present-day Darwin) in one of the great sagas of exploration, while Mitchell crossed the Darling River and pushed north into central Queensland. Mitchell went on to be knighted, but Leichhardt vanished without trace somewhere in central Australia a few years later.

In 1848 Edmund Kennedy set of from Rockingham Bay, just south of Cairns, and headed north towards the tip of Cape York through the mountains and jungles of northern Queensland. Forced to split his men and leave them at camps along the way, Kennedy met his death when he and his Aboriginal friend Jackey-Jackey were attacked by Aborigines near the headwaters of the Escape and Jardine rivers, just a few km south of where a boat was waiting for them. There were only two other survivors from the 14 people who had set out, and they owed their lives to Jackey-Jackey who led the ship and the crew back to where they had been left.

In the mid to late 1850s A C Gregory blazed a trail from the Victoria River, near the border of Western Australia and the Northern Territory, across the top of the continent and down the coast to Brisbane. A member of the team was Thomas Baines, an artist who had done extensive work in southern Africa, and his paintings of their adventures with crocodiles and hostile Aborigines in northern Australia still exist. Meanwhile, A C Gregory's brother Francis discovered good pastoral land in Western Australia between Geraldton and the De Grey River, 1000 km further north.

Burke & Wills In 1860 the stage was set for the greatest act in the White exploration of Australia. Some would say today that it was the greatest folly, but the Burke and Wills expedition was the largest, most lavish and best equipped expedition that set out to solve the riddle of inland Australia.

The lure of being the first to cross the continent was only part of the story. In 1859 the wonder of the telegraph line had reached India and was soon to head for Darwin. Depending on the route forged across the continent by an explorer, an overland telegraph line would finish either in Adelaide or Melbourne. Melbourne was the brashly rich capital of the colony of Victoria, where a gold rush fuelled the fires of progress. In South Australia, however, the government was offering £2000 to the first explorer who crossed the continent.

From Adelaide, John McDouall Stuart, who had been with Sturt on his central Australian expedition, was pushing his way further and further north in a series of small expeditions. The race was on!

With much fanfare Robert O'Hara Burke led the Victorian Exploring Expedition north out of Melbourne on 20 August 1860. Chosen by a committee of the Royal Society, Burke was neither an explorer nor surveyor, had no scientific training, had never led an expedition of any kind, had never set foot out of Victoria since arriving there just a few years previously, and was considered to be, if anything, a very poor bushman. He also ignored the advice of earlier explorers to enlist the help of Aboriginal guides. So much for committees.

Leaving most of his group at Menindee (then at the outer limits of civilisation), Burke and his new second-in-command,

William John Wills, pushed north to Cooper Creek where they set up a depot. From there Burke chose Wills, Charles Grey and John King to accompany him to the Gulf of Carpentaria, leaving the depot and the remainder of the expedition on 16 December 1860. At the height of summer, these men set out to walk 1100 km through central Australia to the sea! It says something of their fortitude and sheer guts that they made it, reaching the mangroves that barred their view of the Gulf of Carpentaria on 11 February 1861. Camp No 119 was their northernmost camp and can be visited today.

Turning their backs on the sea, the rush south became a life-and-death stagger with Grey dying at a place later called Lake Massacre, just west of the Cooper Creek depot. When Burke, Wills and King arrived at the depot they were astonished to find that the men there had retreated to Menindee that very morning! The famous 'Dig Tree', arguably the most historic site in inland Australia, still stands on the banks of Cooper Creek. The name relates to the message carved into its trunk by the departing men: 'DIG 3FT N.W. APR. 21 1861.'

Trapped at Cooper Creek the explorers wasted away, dying on the banks of this desert oasis. Only King, who had been befriended by some Aborigines, was alive when the first of the rescue parties arrived in September 1861.

These rescue expeditions really opened up the interior, with groups from Queensland, South Australia and Victoria crisscrossing the continent in search of Burke and Wills. Howitt, McKinlay, Landsborough and Walker were not only better explorers than Burke, but experienced bushmen who proved that Europeans, cattle and sheep could survive in these regions.

A little further west, Stuart finally crossed the continent, reaching Chambers Bay, east of present-day Darwin, in July 1862. So well planned and executed were his expeditions that the Overland Telegraph Line followed his route, as did the original railway line and road.

The Jardines Over in Queensland, the Jardine brothers battled their way north through the wilds of Cape York to the new settlement of Somerset in 1864. They took nine months to drive their mob of 300-odd cattle and 20 or so horses through plains wracked by the dry season in the southwestern Cape, across rivers flooded by the wet season in the central and northern Cape, while fighting with hostile Aborigines all the way. Frank Jardine, the leader of the small group, was to stay on at Somerset, where he died in 1919 after building an empire of cattle and pearl.

The 'Empty' West Between 1869 and 1875 John Forrest crossed from Perth to Fowlers Bay in South Australia and from Geraldton to the Overland Telegraph Line. Meanwhile, William Gosse, leaving from the telegraph station at Alice Springs, had discovered Ayers Rock while trying to find a route westwards.

Major John Warburton was also in the Alice around the same time trying to find a route to the west. Pushed north by the harsh deserts and finally existing on a spoonful of flour and water for breakfast, a tough strip of dried camel meat for lunch and whatever they could collect from bushes for dinner, his team finally made it to the Oakover River. At one stage they were forced to eat the hide of the camels as well. As Warburton wrote in his book, *Journey Across the Western Interior of Australia*, camel hide needed 'about forty hours continuous boiling and is then very good'!

Ernest Giles, one of Australia's most eloquent explorers, was also trying to be the first to cross the western half of Australia. He was the first White man to see the Olgas, naming them after the queen of Spain, and the lake that blocked his path, Lake Amadeus, after the king. Forced back after the loss and death of his companion, Alf Gibson, Giles crossed the deserts further south. A few months later he crossed the continent again, this time from the Gascoyne River in the west to the Olgas and the telegraph line in the east. The year was 1876 and Giles died

The Cattle Kings

More than any other enterprise, it was pastoral activity in general and the cattle industry in particular that led to White settlement in much of inland Australia. Given the vast distances, the often marginal country and the harsh climate, it was an arduous and often risky business to develop stations and rear cattle. Yet there was no shortage of triers prepared to give it a go, and some went on to make major contributions.

Sir Sidney Kidman Sid Kidman was the undisputed cattle king of Australia. He was born in Adelaide in 1857 and ran away from home at the age of 13. He headed north for the 'corner country' of north-western New South Wales where he found work on outback stations. Over the years he became an expert bushman and stockman.

It was in the latter part of the last century that the vast expanses of outback Australia were settled. The infrastructure was virtually nil and getting cattle to markets in good condition was a major problem. Kidman came up with a bold yet superbly simple solution: 'chains' of stations along strategic routes which would allow the gradual movement of stock from the inland to the coastal markets – in effect, splitting the entire outback into a number of paddocks.

Starting with £400 which he inherited at the age of 21, Kidman traded in cattle and horses, and later Broken Hill mines, and gradually built up a portfolio of land-holdings which gave him the envisaged 'chains'. Eventually he owned or controlled about 170,000 sq km of land (an area 2½ times the size of Tasmania, or about the size of Washington state) in chains, one which ran from the Gulf of Carpentaria south through western Queensland and New South Wales to Broken Hill and into South Australia, and another from the Kimberley into the Northern Territory and then down through the Red Centre and into South Australia.

Such was Kidman's stature as a pastoralist that at one time the north-western area of New South Wales was known as 'Kidman's Corner'. His life was potrayed, somewhat romantically, in Ion Idriess's book *The Cattle King*. Kidman was knighted in 1921, and died in 1935.

The Duracks Another name that is firmly linked with cattle and the opening up of inland Australia is the Durack family. Brothers Patrick (Patsy) and Michael Durack took up land on Cooper Creek in western Queensland in the 1860s, and were soon joined by members of their extended family.

With the discovery of good pastoral land in the Kimberley, the Duracks took up land in the Ord River in 1882. A huge cattle muster was organised and in June 1863 four parties of drovers with a total of 7500 head of cattle set off from the Cooper Creek area. On the map the trip was a neat 2500 km, but in 'drover's miles', meandering from water to water and grass to grass, it was much further. It took 28 months to make the journey, and men and cattle suffered greatly along the way – at one point they were held up for months at a waterhole waiting for the drought to break. Many cattle were lost to pleuropneumonia and tick fever.

Nevertheless, the party reached the Ord in September 1885 and still had enough cattle to establish three stations: Rosewood, Argyle and Lissadel.

Patsy Durack's granddaughter, Mary, became a popular author, and many of her novels were set in the Kimberley. Her most well-known work is *Kings in Grass Castles*, in which she describes the great trek.

Nat Buchanan Although Nathaniel Buchanan was not a great land-holder in the mould of the Duracks or Kidman, he was a great cattleman and drover, responsible for the settlement of huge areas of the outback.

Known as Old Bluey because of his shock of red hair, Buchanan led many drives through Queensland and the Northern Territory, and was responsible for what was probably the largest cattle drive ever to be undertaken in Australia: the movement of 20,000 head from Aramac in Queensland to Glenco Station near Adelaide River in the Northern Territory.

In 1896, at the age of 70, Buchanan set off from Sturt Creek, in northern Western Australia, trying to find a direct route across the Tanami Desert to Tennant Creek which was suitable for cattle, rather than having to take them much further north. Although the hoped-for route didn't eventuate, this was probably the first European crossing of the Tanami Desert.

Buchanan was accompanied on some his drives by his son, Gordon, who wrote about his experiences in the book *Packhorse & Waterhole*. ■

20 years later, unknown, in the gold-rush town of Coolgardie. His two-volume book, *Australia Twice Traversed*, is regularly reprinted as a facsimile.

By this stage the big picture of Australia was filled in. Some of the detail still needed completing, and during the 1890s the first of the 'scientific expeditions' sallied forth looking for minerals and studying the flora, fauna and the Aboriginal people who still lived their tribal ways in the vast interior.

The 1891 Elder Scientific Exploring Expedition, under David Lindsay, explored the area to the north-east of Coolgardie, and the 1894 Horn expedition explored south and west of Alice Springs. The Calvert Expedition, led by Lawrence Wells, met tragedy in the Great Sandy Desert of Western Australia in 1896, about the same time as a young gold prospector, David Carnegie, was blazing a trail north from Coolgardie to Halls Creek and back again. Carnegie died a few years later, not in the waterless wastes of Australia, but by a poisoned arrow in Nigeria.

In 1906 Alfred Canning, using the knowledge of these explorers, mapped and then constructed his famous stock route from Wiluna to Halls Creek. Today this line of wells is one of the greatest 4WD adventures left on the planet.

The 20th Century Around the turn of the century, Baldwin Spencer, a biologist, and Francis Gillen, an anthropologist, teamed up to study the Aborigines of central Australia and Arnhem Land. The results of their study are still one of the most detailed records of a vanished way of life. Other expeditions to northern Australia and Arnhem Land were led by the British polar explorer G H Wilkins (in 1923) and Donald Mackay (in 1928). Donald Thomson led his first expedition to Arnhem Land in 1935 and his work in northern Australia still receives accolades from anthropologists and naturalists.

In the 1930s, aerial mapping of the Centre began in earnest, financed by Donald Mackay. Surveys were carried out over the Simpson Desert, the only large stretch of the country still to be explored on foot. In 1939,

C T Madigan led an expedition that crossed this forbidding landscape from Old Andado to Birdsville; today the untracked route attracts a number of experienced adventurers.

In 1948 the largest scientific expedition ever undertaken in Australia was led by Charles Mountford into Arnhem Land. Financed by the National Geographic Society and the Australian government, it collected over 13,000 fish, 13,500 plant specimens, 850 birds and over 450 skins, along with thousands of Aboriginal implements and weapons.

During the 1950s the Woomera Rocket Range and the atomic-bomb test sites of Emu Junction and Maralinga were set up. This vast region, which had been seen by few Whites since Gosse, Giles and Canning, was opened up by the surveyor Len Beadell, widely regarded as the last Australian explorer. It was, as one of his books is called, the 'End of an Era'.

GEOGRAPHY

Australia is the world's sixth-largest country. Lying between the Indian and Pacific oceans, it measures about 4000 km from east to west and 3200 km from north to south, with a coastline 36,735 km long. Its area is 7,682,300 sq km, about 5% of the world's land surface and similar in size to the the 48 mainland states of the USA, and half as large again as Europe excluding the former USSR (Perth to Melbourne is the same distance as London to Moscow).

The landscape of this island continent is the result of gradual changes wrought over millions of years. Although there is still seismic activity in the eastern and western highland areas and in the central-southern Flinders Ranges, Australia is one of the most stable landmasses in the world. It is also one of the oldest geologically: for about 100 million years it has been free of the mountain-building forces that continue to shape huge mountain ranges elsewhere, and its mountains have eroded to the stage where many of them could be described as little more than glorified hills.

From the east coast a narrow, fertile strip merges into the almost continent-long Great Dividing Range, so called because it's the continent's main watershed – rivers flow either west or east from here, not across. These mountains are mere reminders of a once mighty range. Only in the section straddling the NSW/Vic border and in Tasmania are they high enough to have winter snow. The highest mountain is Mt Kosciusko in southern New South Wales at 2228 metres.

West of the range the country becomes increasingly flat, dry and inhospitable. This is the Central Lowland which stretches out to the middle of the continent. The endless flatness is broken only by salt lakes, occasional mysterious protuberances like Uluru (Ayers Rock) and Kata Tjuta (the Olgas), and some starkly beautiful mountains like the MacDonnell Ranges near Alice Springs. In places, the scant vegetation is sufficient to allow some grazing, so long as each animal has a seemingly enormous area of land. Graziers in south-west Queensland rely on summer floods, which, however, quickly evaporate.

The Great Artesian Basin lies under much of the Central Lowland. Water from the Great Dividing Range takes about 2.5 million years to seep westwards to one of the 7500 artesian wells that provide brackish and sometimes drinkable water. However, much of the Central Lowland is a barren land of harsh, stone deserts and dry lakes.

More than one-third of the continent lies north of the Tropic of Capricorn and is thus technically within the tropics, but only the extreme north – Cape York and the northern part of the Northern Territory (the so-called Top End) – lies within the monsoon belt. Although the annual rainfall there looks adequate on paper, it comes in more or less one short, sharp burst. This has prevented the Top End from becoming seriously productive agriculturally.

The western half of Australia consists mainly of a broad plateau, the so-called Western Plateau. In the far west are mountain ranges which herald the Indian Ocean, and in the south-west a fertile, forested corner that's home to over 95% of the Western Australian population. Further north the coast is less fertile; in the north-central part of Western Australia, the dry country runs right to the sea. The rugged Pilbara and Kimberley regions in the state's west and far north are spectacular worlds unto themselves.

CLIMATE

Australian seasons are the antithesis of those in Europe and North America. It's hot in December and many Australians spend Christmas at the beach, while in July and August it's midwinter. Summer starts in December, autumn in March, winter in June and spring in September.

The climatic extremes aren't too severe in most parts of Australia. Even in Melbourne, the southernmost capital city on the mainland, it's a rare occasion when the mercury hits freezing point, although it's a different story up in the mountains in Canberra, the national capital. The poor Tasmanians, further to the south, have a better idea of what cold is.

As you head north the seasonal variations become less pronounced until, in the far north around Darwin and up in Cape York, you're in the monsoon belt where there are just two seasons: hot and wet, and hot and dry. The centre of the continent has a typical desert climate – hot and dry during the day but often bitterly cold at night in the 'winter' months, when temperatures below freezing are not uncommon.

See the When to Go section in the Facts for the Visitor chapter for information on the best times to visit the outback. See also the Bicycle section in the Getting Around chapter if you want to take advantage of the prevailing winds, which can make a big difference in fuel costs.

FLORA

Australia's tropical north is largely covered with forest despite the fact that at least seven months of the year are hot and dry. The climate is much harsher in the arid inland, of course, but even the Simpson Desert is well

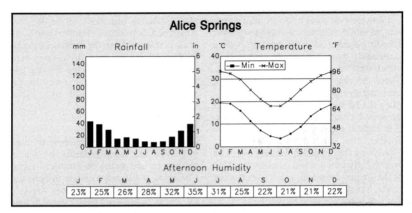

Alice Springs

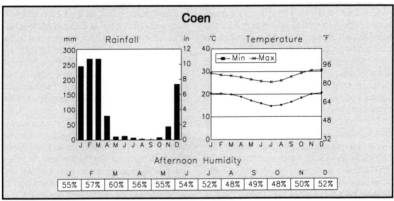

Coen

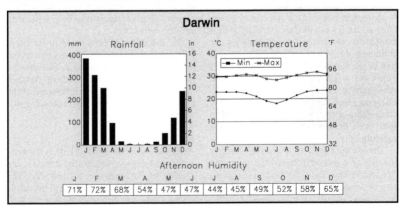

Darwin

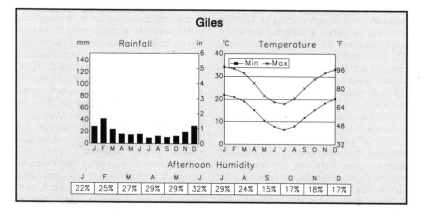

Giles

J	F	M	A	M	J	J	A	S	O	N	D
22%	25%	27%	29%	29%	32%	29%	24%	15%	17%	18%	17%

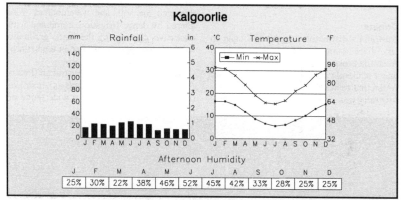

Kalgoorlie

J	F	M	A	M	J	J	A	S	O	N	D
25%	30%	22%	38%	46%	52%	45%	42%	33%	28%	25%	25%

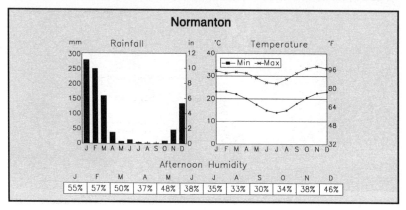

Normanton

J	F	M	A	M	J	J	A	S	O	N	D
55%	57%	50%	37%	48%	38%	35%	33%	30%	34%	38%	46%

vegetated, and tourists coming to Australia expecting to marvel at endless expanses of empty sand and rock will be disappointed. The MacDonnell Ranges near Alice Springs, close to the Simpson's north-west corner, contain nearly 600 native plant species, although many of them grow and flower erratically.

Plants have to be tough to cope with the harsh conditions, which might seem ideal for succulent plants such as the cactus. However, Australian deserts, unlike most of those overseas, have very few true water-holding plants and none are related to the cactus. This type of plant requires a reliable supply of water – even if it is scanty – and Australian deserts don't provide this.

Origins

Australia's distinctive vegetation began to take shape about 55 million years ago when Australia broke from the southern supercontinent of Gondwanaland, drifting away from Antarctica to warmer climes. At this time, Australia was completely covered by cool-climate rainforest, but due to its geographic isolation and the gradual drying of the continent, rainforests retreated, plants like eucalypts (gum trees) and wattles (acacias) took over and grasslands expanded. Eucalypts and wattles were able to adapt to warmer temperatures, the increased natural occurrence of fire and the later use of fire for hunting and other purposes by Aborigines. Now many species benefit from fire and even rely on it to crack open their tough seed casings.

The arrival of Europeans two centuries ago saw the introduction of new flora, fauna and tools. Rainforests were logged, new crops and pasture grasses spread, hoofed animals such as cows, sheep and goats damaged the soil, and watercourses were altered by dams. Irrigation, combined with excessive clearing of the land, gradually resulted in a serious increase in the salinity of the soil.

An interesting book on Australian flora is *Field Guide to Native Plants of Australia* (Bay Books). You can see a wide range of

Ghost gums (DO)

Australian flora at the all-native National Botanic Gardens in Canberra. Brisbane's Mt Coot-tha Botanic Gardens features Australia's arid-zone plants. Port Augusta's Australian Arid Lands Botanic Garden is under development and will be unique in Australia.

Eucalypts

Large eucalypts, or gum trees, are one of the most distinctive features of the Australian landscape, and the smell of burning eucalyptus leaves and twigs is guaranteed to make any expatriate Aussie homesick. The gum tree features in Australian folklore, art and literature. Many varieties flower, the wood is prized and its oil is used for pharmaceuticals and perfumed products.

There are around 560 species of the eucalyptus genus in Australia but only 60 or so are found in the arid zone, where, not surprisingly, most are rather stunted. However, some species can grow into huge trees that make a spectacular sight in their dry setting. **Mallee**, a multi-stemmed form of gum, is very common, and the roots of fallen mallees will burn seemingly forever in a campfire.

River red gums, usually called river gums or red gums, are generally confined to watercourses where their roots have access to a reliable supply of moisture. Given good conditions they can grow to 40 metres high and may live for 1000 years. This species is fairly easily identified from its habitat and its smooth, often beautifully marked grey, tan and cream bark. River gums are found throughout Australia, and in the outback wherever there is suitable habitat. They have a bad habit of dropping large limbs, so while they may be good shade trees it's certainly not wise to camp under them.

The **ghost gum** is a great favourite thanks to its bright green leaves and glossy white bark. Although these often majestic, spreading trees are common in tropical northern Australia, it's around Alice Springs where they've achieved most of their fame through the work of artists such as Albert Namatjira. In central Australia they're found on alluvial

Wattle in bloom (JM)

Parakelias (TW)

Sturt Desert Pea (R & VM)

Boabs (DO)

flats and rocky hills where they make a vivid contrast to their red surroundings.

Coolabahs are a common feature of watercourses, swamps and flood plains right through the outback's drier areas. They are typically gnarled, spreading trees with a rough, dark-brown bark and dull, leathery leaves. Coolabahs can grow to 20 metres high and often provide excellent shade. All eucalypts are hardwoods and this species is said to have the hardest timber of all. It is also very strong and termite-resistant, which made it extremely useful for building fences and stockyards in the days before steel became more readily available.

One of the dominant Top End gums is the **Darwin woollybutt**, which occurs on sandstone and lowland country from Broome right across to the east coast. This tall, spreading tree has rough, fibrous, dark-coloured bark on its lower trunk and a smooth white upper trunk and branches. Woollybutt is noted for its large clusters of bright orange flowers which occur from May to August.

Acacias

The Australian species of the acacia genus are commonly known as wattle – and they are common indeed. There are 660 species in Australia, but only about 120 are found in the arid zone. They tend to be fast-growing, short-lived and come in many forms, from tall, weeping trees to prickly shrubs. Despite their many differences, all wattles have furry yellow flowers shaped either like a spike or a ball. If you see a plant with a flower like this you'll know it's a wattle.

Most species flower during late winter and spring. Then the country is ablaze with wattle and the reason for the choice of green and gold as Australia's national colours is obvious. Wattle is Australia's floral emblem.

Mulga, probably the most widespread of the arid-zone wattles, occurs in all mainland states except Victoria. Although young mulga can look a little like small pines, the adults, which are 10 metres tall at their best, are more of an umbrella shape with a sparse crown of narrow grey leaves. Mulga sometimes forms dense thickets (the explorer

John McDouall Stuart complained how the scrub near Alice Springs tore his clothes and pack saddles to bits) but usually is found as open woodland. Mulga leaves are very resistant to water loss, and the tree's shape directs any rain down to the base of the trunk where roots are most dense. With these attributes mulga is a great drought survivor, but being good fodder for stock puts it at risk from overgrazing.

Spinifex

One of the hardiest and most common desert plants is spinifex, the dense, dome-shaped mass of long, needle-like leaves that you find on sandy soils and rocky areas. There are many species of spinifex but most share an important characteristic: in dry times their leaves roll into tight cylinders to reduce the number of pores exposed to the sun and wind. This keeps water loss through evaporation to a minimum, but even so, most plants will succumb during a really bad drought. Spinifex grasslands are very difficult to walk through – the explorer Ernest Giles called the prickly spinifex 'that abominable vegetable production'. They cover vast areas of central Australia and support some of the world's richest populations of reptiles.

Saltbush

Millions of sheep and cattle living in the arid zone owe their survival to dry shrubby plants called saltbush, which get their name from their tolerance to saline conditions. Saltbush – there are 30 species – is extremely widespread and can be dominant over vast areas. For example, on the Oodnadatta and Birdsville tracks you'll often see nothing else for considerable distances.

Desert Oak

Its height, broad shady crown, dark weeping foliage and the sighing music of the wind in its leaves make the desert oak an inspiring feature of its sand-plain habitat. These magnificent trees are confined to the western arid zone and are common around Uluru and Kings Canyon, near Alice Springs. You'll also see many along the Gunbarrel Highway. Young desert oaks resemble tall hairy broomsticks; they don't look anything like the adult trees and many people think that they're a different species altogether.

Wildflowers

After good autumn rains the normally arid inland explodes in a multicoloured carpet of vibrant wildflowers that will literally take your breath away. The most common of these ephemerals, or short-lived plants, are the numerous species of daisy. Others include docks (which came to Australia in camel-saddle stuffing last century), para-kelias, pussy tails and pea flowers.

In a miracle of nature, the seeds of desert ephemerals can lie dormant in the sand for years until exactly the right combination of temperature and moisture comes along to trigger germination. When this happens, life in the desert moves into top gear as the ephemerals hurry to complete their brief life cycles and woody plants likewise burst into bloom. The sandhills, plains and rocky ridges come alive with nectar-eating birds and insects, which adds up to a bumper harvest for predators as well. Everywhere the various forms of wildlife are breeding and rearing their young while food supplies are abundant. For nature lovers this is definitely the best time to tour the inland.

Water Lilies

Although the Top End can't match the visual spectacle of the desert in full bloom, it nevertheless has many spectacular wildflowers. One such is the water lily, which forms floating mats of large, roundish leaves on freshwater lagoons and swamps right across the tropical north. Its root stock is prized as a food by Aboriginal people, who dig it out of the mud and eat it either raw or cooked.

Boabs

The boab is Australia's most grotesque tree and is only found from the south-western Kimberley to the Northern Territory's Victoria River, where it grows on flood plains and rocky areas. Its huge, grey, swollen trunk topped by a mass of contorted branches make it a fascinating sight, particularly during the dry season when it loses its leaves and becomes 'the tree that God planted upside-down'. Although boabs rarely grow higher than 20 metres, their moisture-storing trunks can be over 25 metres around. The large, gourd-shaped fruits are edible and have a pleasant, fizzy taste similar to cream-of-tartar. Boabs are closely related to the baobab of Africa.

Weeds

By the 1920s the introduced **prickly pear** had choked millions of hectares of central Queensland before an effective biological control was found in the form of the cactoblastic moth. Today, in tropical Australia, weeds such as **mimosa bush** are threatening huge areas, while **salvinia** has begun to choke several waterways. In central Australia, the Finke River has been invaded by **athel trees** which threaten its entire ecosystem. Introduced weeds can destroy wildlife habitats as well as make pastoral and cropping land unusable. Australia-wide, their cost in environmental and economic terms is incalculable.

Preventing the Spread of Weeds Studies have shown that motor vehicles are a major culprit in the spread of weeds. In 1990, a check of 222 tourist vehicles entering Kakadu National Park revealed that 70% were carrying a total of 1511 seeds from 84 different species.

The implications of this are obvious when you consider the millions of vehicles that travel Australia's roads and tracks each year. The question is: How can you avoid being responsible for an outbreak?

First, you need to be able to identify the various weeds as well as their seeds and seed capsules. This is easy: get hold of a weeds pamphlet from a state department of primary production or shire office. Second, if possible avoid driving through weed infestations – pay particular attention to quarantine signs, which should be observed to the letter. Third, immediately after leaving an infested area give your vehicle a thorough check for seeds and pieces of plant which may propagate. It's a good idea to carry out such checks on a regular basis regardless of whether you think you've been near weeds. As well, always carefully check the dog, your clothing, tent and bedding for burs and seeds whenever you go walking or camping in the bush.

Seeds can become lodged in various places in the vehicle such as its undercarriage, engine compartment, radiator, wiper blades, gutters and around lights and doors. Don't forget the interior. For safety's sake, vehicles should only be washed on a proper wash-down area complete with sump and hard stand, not in places where weeds can grow.

If you find any seeds of noxious plants, seal them in a plastic bag and hand them in to the appropriate authorities for disposal; simply throwing them on the campfire is inadvisable as fire promotes the germination of some species. It's always a good idea to inform the authorities of isolated outbreaks in remote areas as they may not be aware of them. Take along a cutting – which ideally will include fruit, seeds or flowers – if you're uncertain about identification.

FAUNA

What can you say about the wildlife of an area with such a tremendous range of habitats and climates as the Australian outback? Obviously some areas are more rewarding than others when it comes to observing the local fauna. For example, the Top End rivers

Echidna (CK)

are like giant aviaries, particularly in early morning, and national parks inside the Dog Fence (see the following section on dingoes) seem inundated with kangaroos. Even the barren gibber plains of northern South Australia have much to offer those prepared to put some time and effort into their wildlife-watching.

It's fair to say that in most areas away from water the casual observer will wonder if anything lives there at all apart from bushflies and ants. This is because the birds tend to be small and secretive, and native outback mammals are mostly nocturnal as a means of avoiding heat stress and water loss. It's unusual to see reptiles in winter south of the Tropic of Capricorn as cold weather sends them into hibernation.

Until the introduction of foreign mammals by the Europeans, almost all Australian mammals apart from seals, bats, rodents and dingoes belonged to the order of **marsupials**. Marsupials are also found in Central and South America (opossums), but have had evolution to themselves in Australia where they were isolated from the rest of the world for 55 million years or so. Marsupials are a primitive order of mammals who lack a placenta; the young are born in an immature state, barely more than an embryo, climb through their mother's fur to her pouch (*marsupium*) and attach themselves to a teat to continue their development.

Australia is also home to the even more primitive order of **monotremes** (egg-laying mammals), which consists of only the platypus and echidna. The semi-aquatic platypus lives in eastern Australia and Tasmania, but within that area it can be found from near-freezing southern mountain streams to the sub-tropical rivers of Queensland; it has a duck-like bill and lays eggs in grass-lined nests. When the first reports of the platypus were sent back to England, the eminent scientists of the day thought they were a hoax.

The echidna, or spiny anteater, is a small, four-legged creature, covered on the back with long, sharp spines but on the underside by fur. It feeds on ants and termites, and is found in a great range of habitats, from hot, dry deserts to altitudes of 1800 metres in the Australian Alps, and also in New Guinea. The female carries her eggs in a pouch, and on hatching, the young remain there and suckle, only being evicted when their spines become too sharp for mum!

Kangaroos & Wallabies
Australia's national symbol and its smaller relative, the wallaby, generally spend the daylight hours in hidden places sheltering from the sun. For this reason they are seldom seen by most outback travellers except as road kills or as large shapes that suddenly appear in the headlights at night. Kangaroos tend to inhabit open woodlands and plains, while wallabies are more at home in dense scrub and forests.

There are six species of kangaroo, of which the red kangaroo is the largest with adult males weighing an average of 66 kg. Kangaroo numbers have exploded in many outback pastoral areas owing to the extermination of dingoes and the increase of watering points and grasslands for sheep and cattle. To the horror of many animal-lovers, about three million are shot each year as a means of population control.

Kangaroo meat is a favourite traditional food of Aboriginal people but is only just beginning to be accepted by other Australians. Until recently, it could only be sold as pet food in some states due to the lack of quality inspections.

Although kangaroos generally are not aggressive, males of the larger species, such as reds, can be dangerous when cornered. In

Dingo (JC)

the wild, boomers, as they are called, will grasp other males with their forearms, rear up on their muscular tails and pound their opponents with their hind feet, sometimes slashing them with their claws. Such behaviour can also be directed against dogs and, very rarely, people. It has also been said that kangaroos being pursued by dogs will sometimes hop into deep water and drown the dogs with their strong forearms.

Large kangaroos can be a hazard to people driving through the outback at night – hitting a two-metre kangaroo at 110 km/h is no joke.

Bandicoots
The small, rat-like bandicoots have been one of the principal victims of the introduced domestic and feral cats – a number of species have either been totally wiped out or are in danger of heading that way.

Bandicoots are mainly nocturnal, but can occasionally be seen scampering through the bush. They are largely insect eaters but do also eat some plant material. Their large claws are put to good use scratching for insects, including centipedes and scorpions, but also make them excellent fighters.

One of the most common varieties is the short-nosed bandicoot, which is found in eastern and western Australia. Others, such as the eastern-barred bandicoot, are these days found in very limited areas. The rare bilby or rabbit-eared bandicoot is found mainly in the Northern Territory and major efforts have been made to ensure its survival.

Dingoes
Whether they tagged along with early Abo-

Red kangaroo (DO)

rigines migrating from South-East Asia or were introduced fairly recently by Indonesian fishermen, the dingo, or wild dog, has been here long enough to be considered a native animal. (Perhaps one day they'll say the same about cats and rabbits.) Dingoes are found throughout the outback, where their eerie howling keeps many a new camper awake at night.

They differ from domestic dogs in various subtle ways – for example, dingoes breed only once a year while domestic dogs breed twice – but they can interbreed and this is the main threat to their survival as a pure strain. Dingoes are considered a threat to the sheep industry and in some areas have a price on their heads.

They are found north and west of the Dog Fence, the world's longest artificial barrier, designed to keep dingoes out of south-eastern Australia. Between 1.4 and 2.4 metres high, the fence runs for about 9600 km from near the Gold Coast in Queensland to the coast near Ceduna in South Australia. About 5500 km of fenceline is patrolled by inspectors who fix breaches in the wire, and set traps and poisoned bait. Any wild or runaway domestic dog that manages to get through the fence is liable to be shot instantly. Though this may seem cruel, the destruction these dogs can cause in a flock of sheep is not only heartbreaking but extremely expensive, and in days gone by, wild dogs drove many a grazier to bankruptcy. In some regions you're required by law to stay clear of the fence.

Introduced Animals

Soon after foxes and rabbits were introduced to Australia for sport in the mid-1800s it became apparent that a dreadful mistake had been made. Both spread far and wide with remarkable speed and it wasn't long before they became pests. **Rabbits** have had a devastating effect on native plants, particularly in the arid zone, while **foxes** – along with **domestic cats** gone wild – have chewed great holes in the populations of Australia's smaller marsupials. Feral cats are now found throughout the mainland but rabbits and

foxes have yet to successfully invade the tropical north (although in good seasons they push north into the Tanami Desert and up as far as Normanton on the Gulf of Carpentaria).

At least 18 introduced mammal species are now feral in Australia and many have become pests. Oddly enough, the **dromedary**, or one-humped camel, seems to have had the smallest impact even though it's the largest feral animal. Australia's estimated 100,000 wild camels are descended from those released by their owners when the camel trains that supplied the outback for 50 years were replaced by motor vehicles in the 1920s and '30s. Now forming the world's only wild populations of this species (the other 13 million or so in North Africa and the Middle East are domesticated), Australian camels are being exported to the Middle East to improve the local gene pool.

Other introduced animals include the pig, goat, donkey, water buffalo, horse, starling, sparrow, blackbird and cane toad. All are pests, and have multiplied rapidly through lack of natural enemies. Sparrows and starlings have yet to reach Western Australia – starling-shooters are employed on the Western Australian border near the coast to prevent them entering the state and posing a threat to agriculture in the wheat belt.

Crocodiles

There are two species: the large **saltwater**, or estuarine crocodile and the smaller **freshwater** variety. 'Salties' are found in northern coastal areas from Broome around to Mackay, though there have been sightings further south. Contrary to their name, salties aren't confined to salt water; they inhabit estuaries, and following floods may be found many km from the coast. They may even be found in permanent freshwater more than 100 km inland. Salties, which can grow to seven metres, will attack and kill humans.

'Freshies' are smaller than salties – anything over four metres should be regarded as a saltie. Freshies are also more finely constructed and have much narrower snouts and smaller teeth to suit their fish diet. Though

Freshwater crocodile

Saltwater crocodile

generally harmless to humans, freshies have been known to bite in defence of their nests, and children in particular should be kept away from them.

Both species of crocodiles were once hunted almost to extinction, but since they were proclaimed a protected species they have become prolific in northern Australia. So far, very few tourists have been killed by salties and attacks still make headlines.

There are simple rules to avoid being attacked and the most important one is to stay out of the water whenever you're in their territory. This can be rather difficult after a hot, muggy day's travel along a dusty track, but you'll just have to put up with it until the next safe bath. Observe the guidelines contained in park brochures and you'll be quite safe.

Snakes

Although only about 10% of Australia's 140 snake species are genuinely dangerous to humans, many of the world's most venomous snakes are Australian, which isn't a record to be proud of. The most toxic land snake in the world is the so-called fierce snake of south-western Queensland and north-eastern South Australia – one dose of its venom is enough to kill a quarter of a million mice. It's a relative of that other notorious snake, the taipan. The tiger snake is highly venomous too, and death adders, copperheads, brown snakes and red-bellied black snakes should also be avoided.

Many people spend months travelling in the outback without seeing a snake other than the occasional dead one on the road. Snakes tend to keep a low profile, but to minimise your chances of being bitten, always wear boots, socks and long, heavy-weight trousers when walking through undergrowth where snakes may be present. Walking in dry grass without shoes or long trousers in warm weather is inadvisable. Tramp heavily and they'll usually slither away before you come near. Don't put your hands into holes and crevices, and be careful when collecting firewood.

Always leave snakes alone – most people are bitten while doing something silly like trying to kill them, or stepping over them when they're asleep. In the unlikely event that you see a snake, the best approach is either to walk around it at a safe distance or to stand quietly until it's made its escape. In most cases it'll be as frightened as you, although if it feels cornered it may well strike in self-defence.

There are 30 species of sea snakes in Australian coastal waters. Although their venom can be 10 times as toxic as that of a cobra, they are shy creatures and won't attack if left alone.

First Aid Contrary to popular belief, snake bites do not cause instantaneous death. A snake bite is often shallow and will inject little venom – the snake's fangs may not penetrate the skin properly for many reasons

Stumpy-tailed lizard (TW)

Frilled-neck lizard (DC)

Sand goanna (DO)

(thick clothing, or the victim may have pulled away at the last moment), and a snake will rarely inject a full dose of the precious stuff anyway. Don't panic. Antivenenes are usually available but may not be close to hand. Tourniquets and sucking out the poison are now comprehensively discredited.

Instead, keep the patient calm and still. This is very important, as excitement and movement accelerate the spread of the venom. Wrap the bitten limb tightly, as you would for a sprained ankle. Start at the bite, work your way down to the fingers or toes, and then back up to the armpit or groin. Finally, attach a splint to immobilise the limb. This has the effect of localising the venom and slowing its spread. Then seek medical help, if possible with the dead snake for identification. Don't attempt to catch the snake if there is even a remote possibility of being bitten again. Ideally the patient should not be moved, but if you're in the middle of nowhere you may have no choice. Never leave the patient alone. If the bite is serious, the patient may experience breathing problems requiring artificial respiration, and you should be prepared for this.

Lizards

The outback hosts an amazing variety of lizards, from giant perentie goannas (Australian *iguanas* or monitor lizards) to tiny skinks and geckoes. The ones you're most likely to see are the various large goannas and dragons, which like to sun themselves in exposed situations such as bitumen roads. Unable to generate their own heat, most lizards need to lie in the sun on cool days until their blood reaches the desired temperature for hunting etc.

Goannas are sleek, heavily built lizards with longish, narrow heads. The perentie – the world's second-largest lizard – is found in the kinder habitats of central Australia and is easy to identify by the regular pattern of large yellow spots on its back. Perenties can grow to three metres long but you'd be most unlikely to see anything over two metres, which is still a big lizard. The large grey goannas found along the banks of northern rivers are water monitors.

Two of the more common **dragons** are the bearded dragon of arid Australia and the Top End's famous frilled lizard. Some people like to tease the latter to make its neck frill stand out (an attempt to make itself look large and fierce) but such behaviour is pretty thoughtless. You'll notice how the bearded dragon flattens its body when sunbaking so as to warm up in the shortest possible time.

Another unusual lizard is the **thorny devil**, or mountain devil. Found on the sandy plains of the western arid zone, this fat, brightly coloured little creature has an almost indescribably ferocious appearance thanks to its armour-plated coat of horns and spikes. However, it's quite harmless to humans as it lives entirely on tiny black ants.

Finches

Australia has 18 species of native finch of which most are found in the tropics – only two (the zebra finch and painted firetail) have adapted to arid conditions. **Zebra finches** are most commonly seen near permanent water as, being seed-eaters, they need to drink most days when it's cool and every day when it's hot. If you run out of water in hot weather and there are zebra finches around, you can be fairly sure there's a supply within a short distance.

The **Gouldian finch's** gorgeous colours make it one of Australia's most stunning birds. It was once common across the far north from the Kimberley to Cape York but is now scarce, largely because of its vulnerability to an introduced parasite that affects its respiratory tract. Trapping (both legal and illegal) may also have contributed to its decline.

Honeyeaters

Arguably the most common and widespread variety of bird in scrubland and timbered areas, Australia's 67 species of honeyeaters come in many shapes, sizes and colours, from large, drab, bald-headed friarbirds to the small, brilliantly coloured scarlet honeyeaters. They are generally active,

Brown falcon (DO)

noisy birds with longish curved bills designed for extracting insects and nectar from flowers. Their morning wake-up calls are a feature along inland watercourses, where they are often dominant.

Parrots & Cockatoos

There is an incredible assortment of these birds in the outback. With the exception of the galah, cockatoos tend to be large, loud

Emu (DC)

and not very colourful; their generally raucous screeching grates on the nerves, which makes you wonder why they're so popular as cage birds.

Parrots, on the other hand, are inoffensive and often very beautiful: the mulga parrot of the southern arid zone and the north's hooded parrot are typical examples. The latter, which nests in termite mounds, is now rare so it's a treat to see one. Budgerigars are extremely widespread and often occur in vast flocks as they follow the favourable seasons across the arid inland.

Birds of Prey

Being on top of the feathered food chain, the various eagles, goshawks, kites, harriers, falcons and kestrels are usually the most commonly seen of all outback birds. Largest of all is the **wedge-tailed eagle**, which you'll often notice feeding on road kills. With a wingspan approaching three metres they soar high on the thermals while scanning the ground for prey such as rabbits and young kangaroos. Their eyesight is so keen that they're thought to be able to see a rabbit quite clearly from a distance of 1.5 km. On remote coasts, watch for ospreys and white-bellied sea eagles.

Emus

The world's second-largest flightless bird, the emu is found in large numbers in less inhabited areas inside the Dog Fence. These birds tend to be mobile and will often create problems for cereal growers when drought forces huge numbers in from their outlying haunts. They are extremely curious and you can sometimes attract them right up to the vehicle by waving a handkerchief or flashing a mirror. Attempts are being made to farm them for their meat, hides and feathers. The emu features with the kangaroo in Australia's coat of arms.

Insects

It will come as no surprise to outback campers that Australia has by far the world's largest number and richest diversity of **ant** species. In fact, scientists come from all over the world to study them.

These do not include white ants, which are more correctly called **termites** and aren't related. Termite mounds (each mound is the upper part of a nest) are often a spectacular feature of the tropical north. One species builds a large tombstone-shaped mound that points north-south, as a means of regulating the temperature within the mound. Another builds an immense pillar-like mound over six metres high.

Bushflies can be an unbelievable nuisance and at such times your arm will feel like dropping off from giving the great Aussie salute. Why do they persist in crawling on you? The main answer is that they want to drink your sweat and tears to obtain protein, but they're also waiting for you to go to the toilet behind a bush. Flies lay their eggs in fresh animal droppings, which gives the maggots food to grow until they pupate. A single cow on good pasture can drop enough in one day for 2000 flies to develop. Bushflies become even more numerous after rain, and are at their worst during the warmest months.

Some shops sell the Genuine Aussie Fly Net (made in Korea), which is rather like a string onion bag but is very effective. Repellents such as Aerogard and Rid go some way to deterring the little bastards. Fortunately they disappear when it gets dark, which makes those outback nights around the campfire all the more enjoyable.

Mosquitoes can be a problem too, especially in the warmer tropical and subtropical areas. The risk of malaria is negligible but there may be a small risk of Ross River Fever, a potentially deadly disease with symptoms similar to glandular fever. Avoid bites by covering bare skin and using an insect repellent. Insect screens on windows and mosquito nets on beds offer protection. Mosquito coils give mixed results.

Most Australian **spiders** bite but very few are actually dangerous. Two spiders to keep away from are the red-back spider, a relative of the American black widow, and the Sydney funnel-web spider. The latter is

Red-back spider

found only in Sydney, while the former is more widespread and has a legendary liking for toilet seats. Both are extremely poisonous and have been lethal. Other nasties to look out for are the trap-door spiders that live in holes in the ground which are often fitted with trap-door lids. First-aid treatment is as for snake bite.

There are three species of **scorpion** in Australia, but they are not very venomous compared with overseas; so far only one human is recorded to have died as a result of an Australian scorpion sting. Scorpions often shelter in shoes or clothing – always give your shoes a good shake-out before donning them in the morning, especially when camping.

Fish

Best known of all the outback's fish is the mighty **barramundi** of northern Australia. See Barramundi Fishing under Activities in the Facts for the Visitor chapter for more about this prized catch.

Surprisingly, the arid zone also has its share of fish, although most are very small. The major exception is the **yellowbelly**, or golden perch, which can grow to over 20 kg if it lives long enough. Yellowbelly are found in the Cooper Creek and Diamantina River systems, both of which drain into Lake Eyre.

The outback's most widespread fish is the **spangled perch**, which grows to about half a kg and occurs in coastal and inland streams of all mainland states – it's one of the largest of the 10 species found in central Australia's Finke River. Among the least widespread are the three species known only from the hot pools of Dalhousie Springs, on the edge of the Simpson Desert.

Box Jellyfish

One sea creature you should be aware of is the box jellyfish, also known as the stinger or sea wasp. It inhabits coastal waters and estuaries north of the Tropic of Capricorn, and is particularly prevalent between November and mid-May. Its bell-shaped, translucent body is often difficult to spot, and its long, sticky tentacles discharge a highly potent venom that kills an average of one person a year and causes excruciating pain in many others.

If someone is stung, they are likely to run out of the sea, screaming, and collapse on the beach, with weals on their body as though they've been whipped. They may stop breathing, in which case artificial respiration is called for. Douse the stings with household vinegar (available on many beaches or from nearby houses); this will deactivate the tentacles, which can then be carefully removed with tweezers. Apply a compression bandage over the affected area to localise the venom as for snake bite, and seek medical help as soon as possible. Above all, stay out of the sea when the sea wasps are around – the locals are ignoring that lovely water in the muggy season for an excellent reason.

PALAEONTOLOGY

Australia has abundant evidence of earlier life forms, but the search is not easy as much of it is conducted in outback regions where conditions are harsh. Palaeontologists distinguish four main eras – Precambrian (2300-570 million years ago), Palaeozoic (570-225 million years), Mesozoic (225-65 million years) and Cainozoic (65 million years to the present) – and many more periods which are sub-divisions of the four eras.

The theory of continental drift says that the earth's landmass started as a supercontinent called Pangaea. About 200 million years ago, Pangaea broke into the northern and southern continents of Laurasia and Gondwanaland respectively; the latter consisted of what we now call Africa, South America, Australia, Antarctica and the Indian subcontinent. It broke apart too, and about 55 million years ago Australia finally separated from Antarctica and began its lonely journey northwards. (See the Palaeontological and Archaeological Sites map at the start of this chapter.)

In the Beginning...

The layered, mainly limestone deposits known as stromatolites, in the saline Hamelin Pool near Shark Bay in Western Australia, are still formed by the blue-green algae that are believed to have developed over three billion years ago, in the Archaean era, making them the oldest form of life on earth.

Australia also has some of the oldest rock on earth and embedded in it are some of the oldest fossils. Australia's most primitive vertebrate (back-boned) fish, *Arandaspis* from the Ordovician period (500-435 million years ago), were found in the Stairway sandstone deposits of the Amadeus Basin in the Northern Territory.

Australia is also known for its cornucopia of Devonian fish (395-345 million years ago). The Devonian Reef national parks of the Kimberley are a good source of fossils. Gogo Station, near Fitzroy Crossing, is the site of bony-plated placoderms such as the vertebrate *Rolfosteus canningenis*, which fed on fish and invertebrates in the ancient reef environment of the Devonian period.

In 240-million-year-old (Permian) coal deposits near Blackwater, central Queensland, curious fish with an upturned snout *(Ebenaqua ritchiei)* were uncovered in a large open-cut mine.

Amphibian life forms thrived during the Triassic period (230-195 million years ago). The Blina Shale of the Erskine Range, between Fitzroy Crossing and Derby, has revealed two interesting examples: *Deltasaurus kimberleyensis*, a fish predator similar to a crocodile in appearance; and *Erythrobatrachus noonkanbahensis*, another fish-eater with an elongated skull.

The first *dicynodont* ('two canine teeth') fossil was found in an area known as the Crater, near Carnarvon Gorge, Queensland. It was the first mammal-like reptile (theraspid) known to Australia, and became known as the 'Creature from the Crater'.

Dinosaurs & Friends

The Jurassic period (195-140 million years ago) was the heyday of the dinosaurs. There are possibly three groups: saurischians, ornithischians and a mixture of those two. In 1924 a fair amount of bone material of a

---

Stromatolites

The dolphins at Monkey Mia didn't contribute to the listing of Shark Bay as a World Heritage area; one of the main reasons was the existence of stromatolites at Hamelin Pool. These structures are several thousands of years old but are built by the oldest living things on this planet, the blue-green algae (one-celled plants) that evolved over 3.5 *billion* years ago.

Hamelin Pool is suited to the growth of stromatolites because of the clarity and hypersalinity of the water; the latter prevents other organisms from attacking the algae. In essence, each stromatolite is covered in a form of cyanobacterial microbe shaped like algae which waves around during daily photosynthesis. At night the microbe folds over, often trapping calcium and carbonate ions dissolved in the water. The sticky chemicals they exude adds to the concretion of another layer on the surface of the stromatolite.

These are the most accessible stromatolites in the world, spectacularly set amidst the turquoise waters of Hamelin Pool. Don't disturb them. ■

Muttaburrasaurus (Queensland Museum)

four-footed, long-necked, long-tailed reptile or sauropod known as *Rhoetosaurus brownei* was found near Roma in Queensland, the first Jurassic example in Australia.

Other creatures of the Jurassic period were the pliosaurs and plesiosaurs – marine reptiles. Remains of a freshwater pliosaur were found near Mount Morgan in Queensland and the remains of two plesiosaurs were recovered from the Evergreen formation, 70 km north of Wandoan in south-east Queensland.

One fascinating tale of the naming of bones relates to the opalised skeleton of Eric, a pliosaur from the Cretaceous period (140-60 million years ago) who tours the country feted like a celebrity. He/she was unearthed near Coober Pedy, South Australia, and after a national campaign, purchased for all Australians. Why 'Eric'? Well, the person who lovingly pieced together the jigsaw of bones was a John Cleese fanatic: the fish bones found in the plesiosaur's stomach contents were named Wanda, and the devourer of the fish, Eric.

The skeleton of a once bulky dinosaur, *Muttaburrasaurus langdoni*, was found in a cattle-mustering area on the banks of the Thomson River near Muttaburra, 100 km north of Longreach, Queensland. The bones surfaced in early Cretaceous marine deposits and before they were gathered up, cattle had trodden into the dust what local souvenir hunters had failed to gather.

After a public appeal the jigsaw began to take shape and the bone-detectives realised that they had chanced upon an ornithischian (bird-hipped) dinosaur of the Ornithopoda, or 'Bird-foot', suborder. What was more, it was closely related to the group of iguanodontids of the northern hemisphere. See for yourself when passing through Brisbane, as 'Mutta' is now displayed in the Queensland Museum (an artist's rendition in steel and plaster lives outside the general store-cum-petrol station in Muttaburra).

A spectacular Cretaceous reptile is *Kronosaurus queenslandicus*. Its first fragments were found near Hughenden, Queensland. It is thought to be the largest known marine reptile, and the name is derived from the Greek god Kronos who ate his children so they could not take over his throne. 'Krono' is a bulky pliosaur with its head making up for a quarter of its length.

Bones of Cretaceous ichthyosaurs have been found in a number of places; the broad-finned *Platypterygius australis* was found near Richmond, Queensland, and other sites throughout the Great Artesian Basin.

Only two specimens of Cretaceous sauropods have been found and one named: *Austrosaurus*. Their bone fragments were found in central Queensland. Two of the impressive carnivorous theropods, similar to the overseas *Allosaurus*, lived in the Cretaceous: *Rapator ornitholestoides*, found near

Lightning Ridge; and *Kakuru kujani*, found near Andamooka.

There is also evidence of where these huge creatures passed. Preserved footprints of a three-metre-high specimen are found at Gantheaume Point near Broome. More spectacular is the dinosaur stampede discovered at Lark Quarry south of Winton, Queensland. The prints were made when about 130 small dinosaurs were scared at a waterhole by a five-metre-long carnosaur dinosaur.

In the air, Australia boasted some mean-looking pterosaurs, or winged reptiles. In 1979, fossils were excavated near Boulia in west Queensland which occurred in early Cretaceous marine limestones, and more recently, jaws were discovered near Boulia and Richmond. The pterosaurs had a wingspan of two metres and were small sea-going fish-eaters.

During the Eocene (38-26 million years ago), the giant lungfish *Neoceradotus gregoryi*, known from central Australia and south-east Queensland, would have been crunching on water plants and freshwater snails. In the middle Miocene (16-14 million years ago), *rhabdosteids*, a type of river

Kronosaurus (Queensland Museum)

dolphin, inhabited the inland waterways. The bones of about six of them have been found in sediments in the Lake Frome district of South Australia.

There were huge flightless birds as well, such as 'giant emus' – the Mihirungs of Aboriginal mythology, which fossil evidence probably now substantiates. *Dromornis stirtoni* was probably the world's largest bird. At three metres in height and over 300 kg in weight it was much larger than Madagascar's extinct elephant bird; fossils from the Miocene were found at Alcoota Station near Alice Springs.

Alcoota has been a rich source of fossil material of the late Miocene (14-seven million years ago). It has provided information on the oldest known meat-eating thylacinids: a marsupial lion known as *Wakaleo alcootaensis*, and a cow-sized diprotodontid, *Plaisiodon centralis*.

Mammals

In Europe, mammals have been known for 200 million years (from the Triassic onwards), but in Australia they are relative newcomers. Australia's oldest fossil mammal is a relatively recent discovery; it is a monotreme, *Steropodon galmani*, found in Cretaceous opal near Lightning Ridge and believed to be 110 million years old. Until then, the oldest known monotreme was *Obdurodon insignis*, similar to a modern-day platypus, revealed from 15-million-year-old deposits from the Simpson Desert.

Marsupials that have long since become extinct include the Diprotodonta and related families – for example, *Ngapakaldia*, whose 14-million-year-old remains were retrieved from Riversleigh in north-west Queensland; or *Neohelos*, a browsing herbivore found in the Lake Eyre Basin, Bullock Creek in the Northern Territory and Riversleigh.

The biggest of the marsupials was *Diprotodon optatum*, three metres long and two metres high at the shoulder. This bulky creature ranged all over the continent and is thought to have disappeared between 25,000 and 15,000 years ago. Evidence of the largest of the wombats, *Phascolonus gigas*, from the

Pleistocene, has been found at Cooper Creek, Lake Callabonna and Lake Eyre.

Riversleigh Station is a treasure trove of fossils. The remains of *Wabularoo naughtoni* joins a number of other species of kangaroo found here. It is a type of rat-kangaroo which became extinct when browsing kangaroos evolved 10 to five million years ago.

Also found in recent times at Gag Site, Riversleigh, is an entirely new order of mammals, loosely named *Thingodonta* for a while but now known as *Yalkaparidon coheni*. The fossil remains of a seven-metre long snake were given the name *Montypythonoides*.

The Queensland Museum in Brisbane has the country's best collection of outback-related fossil and dinosaur material. Read more about this fascinating subject in *Prehistoric Australia* by Brian Mackness (Golden Press, Sydney, 1987); *The Antipodean Ark*, edited by Suzanne Hand & Michael Archer (Angus & Robertson, Sydney, 1987); and *Prehistoric Animals of Australia*, edited by Susan Quirk & Michael Archer (Australian Museum, Sydney, 1983). The latter two contain excellent illustrations by Peter Schouten.

NATIONAL PARKS & RESERVES

Australia has more than 500 national parks – non-urban protected wilderness areas of environmental or natural importance. Each state defines and runs its own national parks, but the principle is the same throughout Australia. National parks include rainforests, vast tracts of empty outback, strips of coastal dune land and long, rugged mountain ranges.

Public access is encouraged if safety and conservation regulations are observed. In all parks you're asked to do nothing to damage or alter the natural environment. Approach roads, camping grounds (often with toilets and showers), walking tracks and information centres are often provided for visitors.

Some national parks are so isolated, rugged or uninviting that you wouldn't want to do much except look unless you were an experienced, well-prepared bushwalker or climber. Other parks, however, are among Australia's major attractions and some of the most beautiful have been included on the World Heritage List – a United Nations list of natural or cultural places of world significance that would present an irreplaceable loss to the planet if they were altered.

The World Heritage List includes the Taj Mahal, the pyramids, the Grand Canyon and, currently, nine Australian areas: the Great Barrier Reef; Kakadu and Uluru national parks in the Northern Territory; the Willandra Lakes region of far western New South Wales; the Lord Howe Island group off New South Wales; the Tasmanian wilderness heritage area; the east-coast temperate and subtropical rainforest parks; the wet tropics area of Far North Queensland in the Daintree-Cape Tribulation area; Shark Bay on the Western Australian coast; and Fraser Island off the Queensland coast.

The Australian Conservation Foundation is one of a number of bodies lobbying to have further places listed. Currently these are Lake Eyre in outback South Australia, the Blue Mountains National Park near Sydney, the Nullarbor Plain, the mountain regions of south-west Tasmania not already listed, the Australian Alps, and Cape York Peninsula.

GOVERNMENT

Australia is a federation of six states and two territories. Under the written constitution, which came into force on 1 January 1901, the colonies joined to form the independent Commonwealth of Australia. The federal (central) government is mainly responsible for the national economy and Reserve Bank, customs and excise, immigration, defence, foreign policy and the post office. The state governments are chiefly responsible for health, education, housing, transport and infrastructure, and justice. There are both federal and state police forces.

Australia has a parliamentary system of government based on that of the UK, and the state and federal structures are broadly similar. In Federal Parliament, the lower house is the House of Representatives (with

147 members, divided among the states on a population basis), the upper house is the Senate. Elections for the House of Reps are held at least every three years; voting is by secret ballot and is compulsory for citizens aged 18 and over. Senators serve six-year terms, with elections for half of them every three years. Queensland does not have an upper house: it was abolished in 1922. The Commonwealth government is run by a prime minister; the state governments are led by a premier, and the Northern Territory by a chief minister. The party holding the greatest number of lower house seats forms the government.

Australia is a monarchy, but although Britain's king or queen is Australia's head of state, Australia is fully autonomous. The British sovereign is represented by the Governor-General and state governors, whose nominations for their posts by the respective governments are ratified by the monarch of the day. Increasing numbers of people feel that the continued constitutional ties with Britain are no longer relevant. There's still a deal of soul-searching to be done before the Governor-General is replaced by a president of a Republic of Australia, but change seems inevitable.

The Federal Parliament is based in Canberra, the capital of the nation. Like Washington DC in the USA, Canberra is in its own separate area of land, the Australian Capital Territory (ACT), and is not under the rule of one of the states. Geographically, however, the ACT is completely surrounded by New South Wales. The state parliaments are based in each state capital.

In Federal Parliament, the two main political groups are the Australian Labor Party (ALP) and the coalition between the Liberal Party and the National Party. These parties also dominate state politics but sometimes the Liberal and National parties are not in coalition. The latter was once known as the National Country Party since it mainly represents country seats. The only other political party of any real substance is the Australian Democrats, which has largely carried the flag for the ever-growing 'green'

movement. There are also two independent 'green' senators.

Aboriginal Land Rights

As we have seen, Britain founded the colony of New South Wales on the legal principle of *terra nullius*, a land belonging to no-one, which meant that Australia was legally unoccupied. The settlers could take land from Aborigines without signing treaties or providing compensation. The European concept of landownership was completely foreign to Aborigines and their view of the world in which land did not belong to individuals: people belonged to the land, were formed by it and were a part of it like everything else.

After WW II, Australian Aborigines became more organised and better educated, and a political movement for land rights developed. In 1962 a bark petition was presented to the federal government by the Yolngu people of Yirrkala, in north-east Arnhem Land, demanding that the government recognise Aboriginal peoples' occupation and ownership of Australia since time immemorial. The petition was ignored, and the Yolngu people took the matter to court – and lost. In the famous Yirrkala Land Case 1971, Australian courts accepted the government's claim that Aborigines had no meaningful economic, legal or political relationship to land. The case upheld the principle of *terra nullius*, and the common-law position that Australia was unoccupied in 1788.

Because the Yirrkala Land Case was based on an inaccurate (if not outright racist) assessment of Aboriginal society, the federal government came under increasing pressure to legislate for Aboriginal land rights. In 1976 it eventually passed the Aboriginal Land Rights Act (Northern Territory) – often referred to as the Land Rights Act.

Australian Land Rights Acts The Aboriginal Land Rights Act, which operates in the Northern Territory, remains Australia's most powerful and comprehensive land rights legislation. Promises were made to legislate for national land rights, but these were abandoned after opposition from mining companies and state governments. The act established three Aboriginal Land Councils, who are empowered to claim land on behalf of traditional Aboriginal owners.

However, under the act the only land claimable is unalienated Northern Territory land outside town boundaries – land that no-one else owns or leases, usually semi-desert or desert. Thus, when the traditional Anangu owners of Uluru (Ayers Rock) claimed traditional ownership of Uluru and Kata Tjuta (the Olgas), their claim was disallowed because the land was within a national park and thus alienated. It was only by amending two acts of parliament that Uluru-Kata Tjuta National Park was handed back to traditional Anangu owners on the condition that it was immediately leased back to the Australian Nature Conservation Agency (formerly the Australian National Parks & Wildlife Service).

At present almost half of the Northern Territory has either been claimed, or is being claimed, by its traditional Aboriginal owners. The claim process is extremely tedious and can take many years to complete, largely because almost all claims have been opposed by the territory government. A great many elderly claimants die before the matter is resolved. Claimants are required to prove that under Aboriginal law they are responsible for the sacred sites on the land being claimed.

Once a claim is successful, Aboriginal people have the right to negotiate with mining companies and ultimately accept or reject exploration and mining proposals. This right is strongly opposed by the mining lobby, despite the fact that traditional Aboriginal owners in the Northern Territory only reject about a third of these proposals outright.

The Pitjantjatjara Land Rights Act 1981 (South Australia) is Australia's second-most powerful and comprehensive land rights law. This gives Anangu Pitjantjatjara and Yankunytjatjara people freehold title to 10% of South Australia. The land known as the Anangu Pitjantjatjara Lands, is in the far north of the state.

Just south of the Anangu Pitjantjatjara Lands lie the Maralinga Lands, which comprise 8% of South Asutralia. The area, largely contaminated by British nuclear tests, was returned to its Anangu traditional owners by virtue of the Maralinga Tjarutja Land Rights Act 1984 (South Australia).

Under these two South Australian acts, Anangu can control access to land and liquor consumption. However, if Anangu traditional owners cannot reach agreement with mining companies seeking to explore or mine on their land, they cannot veto mining activity: an arbitrator decides if mining will go ahead. If the arbitrator gives mining the green light, he/she will bind the mining company with terms and conditions and ensure that reasonable monetary payments are made to Anangu.

In South Australia, other small Aboriginal reserves exist by virtue of the Aboriginal Land Trust Act 1966 (South Australia). This act gives Aboriginal people little control over their land.

Outside the Northern Territory and South Australia, Aboriginal land rights are extremely limited. In Queensland, only 1.85% of the state is Aboriginal land, and the only land that can be claimed under the Aboriginal Land Act 1991 (Queensland) is land which has been gazetted by the government as land available for claim. Under existing Queensland legislation, 95% of the state's Aborigines can't claim their traditional country.

Since the passing of the Nature Conservation Act 1992 (Queensland), Aborigines in the state also have very limited claim to national parks. If Aborigines successfully claim a Queensland park, they must permanently lease it back to the government without a guarantee of a review of the lease arrangement or a majority on the board of management. This is quite different to the arrangements at Uluru-Kata Tjuta National Park, where the traditional owners have a majority on the board, with a 99-year lease-back that is renegotiated every five years.

In Western Australia, Aboriginal reserves comprise about 13% of the state. Of this land about one-third is granted to Aborigines under 99-year leases; the other two-thirds are controlled by the government's Aboriginal Affairs Planning Authority. Control of mining and payments to communities are a matter of ministerial discretion.

In New South Wales, the Aboriginal Land Rights Act 1983 (New South Wales) transferred freehold title of existing Aboriginal reserves to Aborigines and gave them the right to claim a minuscule amount of other land. Aborigines also have limited rights to the state's national parks, but these rights fall short of genuine control and don't permit Aborigines to live inside parks. In Victoria and Tasmania, land rights are extremely limited.

Mabo & the Native Title Act Only in the last couple of years did the non-Aboriginal community, including the federal government, come to grips with the fact that a meaningful conciliation between White Australia and its indigenous population was vital to the psychological wellbeing of all Australians.

In May 1982, five Torres Strait Islanders led by Eddie Mabo began an action for a declaration of native title over the Queensland Murray Islands. They argued that the legal principle of *terra nullius* had wrongfully usurped their title to land, as for thousands of years Murray Islanders had enjoyed a relationship with the land that included a notion of ownership. In June 1992 the High Court of Australia rejected *terra nullius* and the myth that Australia had been unoccupied. In doing this, it recognised that a principle of native title existed before the arrival of the British.

The High Court's judgment became known as the Mabo decision, one of the most controversial decisions ever handed down by an Australian court. It was ambiguous, as it didn't outline the extent to which native title existed in mainland Australia. It received a hostile reaction from the mining and other industry groups, but was hailed by Aborigines and Prime Minister Paul Keating as an opportunity to create a basis of reconciliation between Aboriginal and non-Aboriginal Australians.

To define the principle of native title, the federal parliament passed the Native Title Act in December 1993. Contrary to the cries of protest from the mining industry, the act gives Australian Aborigines very few new rights. It limits the application of native title to land which no-one else owns or leases, and to land with which Aborigines have continued to have a physical association. The act states that existing ownership or leases extinguish native title, although native title may be revived after mining leases have expired. If land is successfully claimed by Aborigines under the act, they will have no veto over developments including mining. Despite (or because of) its complexity, it will no doubt take a number of years and court cases before the implications of the Native Title Act are fully understood.

ECONOMY

Australia is a relatively affluent, industrialised nation but much of its wealth still comes from agriculture and mining. It has a small domestic market and a comparatively weak manufacturing sector. Nevertheless, a substantial proportion of the population is employed in manufacturing, and for much of Australia's history it has been argued that these industries need tariff protection from imports to ensure their survival.

Today, however, tariff protection is on the way out and efforts are being made to increase Australia's international competitiveness. This has become more important as prices of traditional primary exports have become more volatile.

In the outback, where so much of the economy is dependent on wool, meat and mining, this volatility has resulted in a roller-coaster ride of boom and bust (more bust than boom). Alongside the huge cattle and wool enterprises and the billion-dollar mining conglomerates, there are thousands of struggling cow cockies, hard-partying opal diggers and reclusive gold-panning hermits. More often than not, these interesting characters fight a hard battle for survival in a harsh environment, but very few of them would dream of surrendering their freedom.

A typical cattle or sheep station in the outback covers tens of thousands of hectares, and the larger ones are the size of small countries – Anna Creek cattle station in South Australia is the size of Belgium! Large stations may have one or more semi-independent outstations. The headquarters of a station is the homestead, which is where the owner (or manager) and staff live. The livestock is often left to fend for itself, though the owner will ensure that there are sufficient watering points where additional fodder and salt may be left. Once or twice a year the livestock is mustered to check on their general welfare and take stock of births and deaths, but they may be mustered more often for sale or to move them to other paddocks. Sheep are sheared twice a year – the main shearing and then the stragglers; cattle are mustered once a year for ear-marking.

One of Australia's greatest economic hopes is tourism, with the numbers of visitors rising each year and projections for even greater numbers in the future. The other bright spot is the booming economies of South-East Asia. Australia is perfectly positioned to enter these markets, providing goods and services.

The government has sought to restrain real wages and is trying to stimulate new manufacturing and service industries. This policy has seen the creation of new jobs while many people employed in traditional sectors joined the dole queues, and unemployment is currently around 11%. However, prospects for the future are cautiously optimistic.

Although most non-Aboriginal Australians enjoy a high standard of living, the same can't be said for most of their Aboriginal counterparts. Many Aborigines still live in deplorable conditions, with infant mortality and outbreaks of preventable diseases running at an unacceptably high rate – higher even than in many Third World countries. Definite progress has been made with the recent Native Title legislation (see the previous Government section), but there's still a long way to go before Aborigines can enjoy the lifestyle of their choice.

POPULATION & PEOPLE

Australia's population is about 17 million. The most populous states are New South Wales and Victoria, each with a capital city (Sydney and Melbourne) with a population of around three million. Nationwide, the population is concentrated along the east-coast strip from Adelaide to Cairns and in the smaller coastal region of south-west Western Australia. The centre of the country is very sparsely populated.

Until WW II, Australians were predominantly of British and Irish descent with a sprinkling of Chinese settlers, but that has changed dramatically since the war. First there was heavy migration from Europe creating major Greek and Italian populations but also adding Germans, Dutch, Maltese, Yugoslavs, Lebanese, Turks and other groups.

More recently, Australia has had large influxes of Asians, particularly Vietnamese after the Vietnam war. In comparison to the country's population, Australia probably took more Vietnamese refugees than any other Western nation. On the whole these 'new Australians' have been remarkably well accepted and 'multi-culturalism' is a popular concept.

If you come to Australia in search of a real Australian you will find one quite easily – they are not known to be a shy breed. He or she may be a Lebanese cafe owner, an English used-car salesperson, an Aboriginal artist, a Malaysian architect or a Greek greengrocer. And you will find them in pubs, on beaches, at barbecues, mustering yards and art galleries. And yes, you may meet a Mick (Crocodile) Dundee or two telling the same tall stories – a popular activity in outback pubs.

Aboriginal Culture Groups

There are about 230,000 Aborigines and Torres Strait Islanders in Australia, most heavily concentrated in central Australia and the Top End. Because of the dynamic nature of Aboriginal groups, and the great changes that have occurred in Aboriginal culture since White settlement, it seems that the people who worry about these things will never reach agreement on the different culture groups.

However, by drawing on the work of a number of anthropologists one could recognise the following groups: the coastal Yolngu people of Coastal Arnhem Land; the Inland people of Arnhem Land; the people of the Kimberley Ranges in Western Australia; the South-Western people of Western Australia; the Far South-Western people of Western Australia; Western Desert Anangu people; Coastal South Australian people; the Central Australian people (including Arrente and Warlpiri people); Lake Eyre and Simpson Desert people; the people of Northern Cape York Peninsula; the North-Eastern Queensland Rainforest people; the North-Eastern Queensland dry-forest and grassland people; the Gulf people of Queensland and the Northern Territory; the Central and South-Eastern Coastal people; the Riverina people of New South Wales, Victoria and the Australian Capital Territory; and the Tasmanian Aboriginal people.

The 10,000 Torres Strait Islanders of the islands between Cape York and New Guinea comprise a cultural group distinct from Aboriginal Australia. They're mainly Melanesian people who speak one of two distinct Torres Straight Islander languages. The Western Torres Strait Islanders are semi-nomadic, whilst Eastern Torres Strait Islanders cultivate bananas, yams and taro in the rich eastern soils.

ARTS
Aboriginal Ceremonies
The perceived simplicity of the Aborigines' technology contrasts with the sophistication of their cultural life. Religion, history, law and art are integrated in complex ceremonies which depict the activities of their ancestral beings, and prescribe codes of behaviour and responsibilities for looking after the land and all living things.

Decorated coolamons, or bowls (RI)

The links between the Aborigines and the ancestral beings are totems, each person having their own totem, or Dreaming. These take many forms, such as caterpillars, snakes, fish and magpies. Songs explain how the landscape contains these powerful creator ancestors, who can exert either a benign or a malevolent influence. They tell of the best places and the best times to hunt, where to find water in drought years, and can also specify kinship relations and correct marriage partners.

Aborigines living an urban life in towns remain distinctively Aboriginal – they still speak their indigenous language (or a creolised mix) on a daily basis, and mingle largely with other Aborigines. Much of their knowledge of the environment, bush medicine and food ('bush tucker') has been retained, and many traditional rites and ceremonies are being revived.

See the later Religion section for more on Aboriginal ceremonies and sacred sites.

Outback Literature
For White Australian writers, a somewhat undelineated outback has always been an important source of inspiration, with its 'frontier' image. For Aborigines, however, the outback was not remote or dangerous: it was their life, and the focus of a rich oral

tradition; creeds and practicalities were passed on from generation to generation by word of mouth in songs, stories and accompanying rituals.

Aboriginal Song & Narrative These oral traditions are loosely and misleadingly described as 'myths and legends'. Their single uniting factor is the Dreamtime, when the totemic ancestors formed the landscape, fashioned the laws and created the people who would inherit the land. Translated and printed in English, these renderings of the Dreamtime often lose much of their intended impact. Gone are the sounds of sticks, dijeridu and the rhythm of the dancers which accompany each poetic line; the words fail to fuse past and present, and the spirits and forces to which the lines refer lose much of their animation.

At the turn of the century, Catherine Langloh Parker was collecting Aboriginal legends and using her outback experience to interpret them sincerely but synthetically. She compiled *Australian Legendary Tales: Folklore of the Noongah-burrahs* (1902).

T G H Strehlow was one of the first methodical translators, and his *Aranda Traditions* (1947) and *Songs of Central Australia* (1971) are important works. Equally important is the combined effort of Catherine & Ronald Berndt. There are 188 songs in the collection *Djanggawul* (1952), 129 sacred and 47 secular songs in the collection *Kunapipi* (1951), and *The Land of the Rainbow Snake* (1979) focuses on children's stories from western Arnhem Land.

More recently, many Dreamtime stories have appeared in translation, illustrated and published by Aboriginal artists. Some representative collections are *Joe Nangan's Dreaming: Aboriginal Legends of the North-West* (Joe Nangan & Hugh Edwards, 1976); *Milbi: Aboriginal Tales from Queensland's Endeavour River* (Tulo Gordon & J B Haviland, 1980); *Visions of Mowanjum: Aboriginal Writings from the Kimberley* (Kormilda Community College, Darwin; 1980); and *Gularabulu* (Paddy Roe & Stephen Muecke, 1983).

As you drive through the outback, realise that many of the features you see in the landscape have an oral history. They live, have a past and a present. You are, in effect, driving through the pages of the world's most ancient, illuminated manuscript!

Modern Aboriginal Literature Modern Aboriginal writers have fused the English language with aspects of their traditional culture. The result is often carefully fashioned to expose the injustices they have been subjected to, especially as urban dwellers. The first Aboriginal writer to be published was David Unaipon in 1929 *(Native Legends)*.

Aboriginal literature now includes drama, fiction and poetry. The poet Oodgeroo Noonuccal (Kath Walker), one of the most well known of modern Aboriginal writers, was the first Aboriginal woman to have work published *(We Are Going,* 1964). *Paperbark: A collection of Black Australian writings* (1990) presents a great cross-section of modern Aboriginal writers, including dramatist Jack Davis and novelist Mudrooroo Narogin (Colin Johnson). This book has an excellent bibliography of Black Australian writing.

There are a number of modern accounts of Aboriginal life in remote parts of Australia. *Raparapa Kularr Martuwarra: Stories from the Fitzroy River Drovers* (1988) is a Magabala Books production. This new company, based in Broome, energetically promotes Aboriginal literature. Autobiography and biography have become an important branch of Aboriginal literature – look for *Moon and Rainbow* (Dick Roughsey, 1971) and *My Country of the Pelican Dreaming* (Grant Ngabidj, 1981).

The Aborigine in White Literature The Aborigine has often been used as a character in White outback literature. Usually the treatment was patronising and somewhat short-sighted. There were exceptions, especially in the subject of interracial sexuality between White men and Aboriginal women.

Rosa Praed, in her short piece *My Australian*

Girlhood (1902), drew heavily on her outback experience and her affectionate childhood relationship with Aborigines. Jeannie Gunn's *Little Black Princess* was published in 1904, but it was *We of the Never Never* (1908) which brought her renown. Her story of the life and trials on Elsey Station includes an unflattering, patronising depiction of the Aborigines on and around the station.

Catherine Martin, in 1923, wrote *The Incredible Journey*. It follows the trail of two Black women, Iliapo and Polde, in search of a little boy who had been kidnapped by a White man. The book describes in careful detail the harsh desert environment they traverse.

Katharine Susannah Prichard contributed a great deal to outback literature in the 1920s. A journey to Turee Station in the cattle country of the Ashburton and Fortescue rivers, in 1926, inspired her lyric tribute to the Aborigine, *Coonardoo* (1929), which delved into the then almost taboo love between an Aboriginal woman and a White station boss. Later, Mary Durack's *Keep Him My Country* (1955) explored the theme of a White station manager's love for an Aboriginal girl, Dalgerie.

Outback Explorers When John Oxley published an account of his discoveries in 1820, he stimulated the myth of the 'inland sea', and others set about to find it. Charles Sturt gave the first written description of places in the interior such as the Simpson Desert.

Other accounts worth mentioning are the journals recalling Edward John Eyre's epic journey in 1841 across the Australian Bight; the account by Aboriginal Jackey-Jackey (Galmarra) of the death of Edmund Kennedy during an expedition to Cape York in 1848; and the writings of Ernest Giles from the period 1874 to 1876. Giles's matter-of-fact, unembellished descriptions of remote parts of Australia's arid heart, like the Gibson Stony Desert, are amongst the most literary and perceptive of explorers' writings.

You can find most of these accounts, either in full or in condensed form, in major public libraries.

Bush Ballads & Yarns The 'bush', in particular the outback, was a great source of inspiration for many popular ballads and stories. These were particularly in vogue at the turn of the century but they have an enduring quality.

Adam Lindsay Gordon was the forerunner of this type of literature, having published *Bush Ballads and Galloping Rhymes* in 1870. This collection of ballads included his popular *The Sick Stockrider*.

The two most famous exponents of the ballad style were A B 'Banjo' Paterson and Henry Lawson. Paterson grew up in the bush in the second half of the last century and went on to become one of Australia's most important bush poets. His pseudonym 'The Banjo' was the name of a horse on his family's station. His horse ballads were regarded as some of his best, but he was familiar with all aspects of station life and wrote with great optimism. *Clancy of the Overflow* and *The Man From Snowy River* are both well known, but The Banjo is probably most remembered as the author of Australia's alternative national anthem, *Waltzing Matilda*, in which he celebrates an unnamed swagman, one of the anonymous wanderers of the bush.

Henry Lawson was a contemporary of Paterson, but was much more of a social commentator and political thinker and less of a humorist. Although he wrote a good many poems about the bush – pieces such as *Andy's Gone with Cattle* and *The Roaring Days* are among his best – his greatest legacy are his short stories of life in the bush, which seem remarkably simple yet manage to capture the atmosphere perfectly. Good examples are *A Day on a Selection* (a selection was a tract of crown land for which annual fees were paid) and *The Drover's Wife;* the latter epitomises one of Lawson's 'battlers' who dreams of better things as an escape from the ennui of her isolated circumstances.

There were many other balladists. George

Essex Evans penned a tribute to Queensland's women pioneers, *The Women of the West;* Will Ogilvie wrote of the great cattle drives; and Barcroft Boake's *Where the Dead Men Lie* celebrates the people who opened up never-never country where 'heatwaves dance forever'.

Standing alone among these writers is Barbara Baynton. She is uncomprising in her depiction of the outback as a cruel, brutal environment, and the romantic imagery of the bush is absent in the ferocious depiction of the lot of *Squeaker's Mate* in *Bush Studies* (1902). Squeaker's mate, crippled whilst clearing her selection and powerless to do anything, has to endure the indignity of her husband flaunting his new mistress. More terrifying is the murder of a mother by a marauding swagman in *The Chosen Vessel*, also in *Bush Studies*.

Outback Raconteurs Many journalists and travel writers proudly proclaimed the outback to be the 'true' Australia. One of the least known is C E W Bean, Australia's official war historian of WW I. Two of his books, *On the Wool Track* (1910) and *The Dreadnought of the Darling* (1911), evocatively describe the outback of far western New South Wales.

Ion Idriess was an immensely popular writer in his time. His string of stories were eagerly awaited and their heroes were unashamedly outback: *Cattle King: Story of Sir Sidney Kidman, Flynn of the Inland* and *Lasseter's Last Ride*. In *Nemarluk: King of the Wilds* (1941) he chronicles the exploits of an Aboriginal resistance fighter in the Top End.

One of the best known travel writers was Ernestine Hill, whose *The Territory* (1951), it was said by the prolific Western Australian writer J K Ewers, 'ought to be in the swag of every Australian'. Her first publication, *The Great Australian Loneliness* (1937), described five years of travel through the outback.

Another writer in the vein of Idriess was Bill Harney. He married an Aborigine and was exposed to many aspects of Aboriginal culture. Much of his knowledge of the Top End was learned from the 'school of hard knocks', including a session in the Boorooloola lock-up for cattle-duffing. He later became a ranger near Ayers Rock for many years. His books, written in the 1940s and '50s, include *Tales from the Aboriginals, To Ayers Rock and Beyond, Songs of the Songmen: Aboriginal Myth Retold* and *Life among the Aborigines*.

George Farwell's *Ghost Towns of Australia* is a great source of outback yarns and history, and his travel books include *The Outside Track, Cape York to Kimberley* and *Traveller's Tracks*. Bill Wannan's *Hay, Hell and Booligal, A Dictionary of Australian Folklore* and *Bullockies, Beauts & Bandicoots* all have good titbits on the outback.

More recently, Patsy Adam-Smith covered the outback in her popular titles *The Shearers* (1982), *The Rails go Westward* (1969), *Across Australia by Indian Pacific* (1971) and her examination of famous and ordinary lives in *Outback Heroes* (1981).

Outback Novelists The author's name if not the content would have encouraged many overseas visitors to read D H Lawrence's *Kangaroo* (1923), which, in places, presents his frightened images of the bush. Later, Nevil Shute's *A Town Like Alice* (1950) would have been the first outback-based novel that many people read. Other Shute titles with outback themes were *In the Wet* (1953) and *Beyond the Black Stump* (1956).

Perhaps the best local depictor of the outback was the aforementioned Katharine Susannah Prichard. She produced a string of novels with outback themes into which she wove her political thoughts. *Black Opal* (1921) was the study of the fictional opal mining community of Fallen Star Ridge; *Working Bullocks* (1926) examined the political nature of work in the karri forests of Western Australia; and *Moon of Desire* (1941) follows its characters in search of a fabulous pearl from Broome to Singapore. Her controversial trilogy of the Western Australian gold fields was published separately as *The Roaring Nineties* (1946), *Golden Miles* (1948) and *Winged Seeds* (1950).

Xavier Herbert's *Capricornia* (1938) stands as one of the great epics of outback Australia, with its sweeping descriptions of the northern country. His second epic, *Poor Fellow My Country* (1975), is a documentary of the fortunes of a northern station owner. Herbert uses the characters to voice his bitter regret at the failure of reconciliation between the White despoilers of the land and its indigenous people.

One of the great non-fiction pieces is Mary Durack's family chronicle, *Kings in Grass Castles* (1959), which relates the White settlement of the Kimberley ranges. Her sequel was *Sons in the Saddle* (1983).

Australia's Nobel prize-winner, Patrick White, used the outback as the backdrop for a number of his monumental works. The most prominent character in *Voss* (1957) is an explorer, perhaps loosely based on Ludwig Leichhardt; *The Tree of Man* (1955) has all the outback happenings of flood, fire and drought; and the journey of *The Aunt's Story* (1948) begins on an Australian sheep station.

Kenneth Cook's nightmarish novel set in outback New South Wales, *Wake in Fright* (1961), has been made into a film.

Pictorial Art

Rock Art Petroglyphs, or rock drawings and engravings, are found widely in Australia, but western New South Wales, north-eastern South Australia and central Australia have many places of significance. These include such well-known sites as Ewaninga, south of Alice Springs; Chambers Gorge in the Flinders Ranges; Cooper Creek in the far north-east of South Australia; and Mootwingee in western New South Wales. All these locations can be visited by travellers, while other spots, such as at Sturt Meadows in New South Wales and Panaramitee near Yunta in South Australia are basically out of bounds.

The ancient art was pecked into the rock with simple tools, yet the designs at these remote places cover large areas of exposed rock. Thousands of engravings have been recorded at some sites: the Sturt Meadow engravings number over 14,000 separate designs, while the Yunta one contains over 8000. The designs consist mainly of concentric circles, other circles and animal tracks.

There are many variations on these themes, and each site is significant in that they are always slightly different to one another. In some areas the dominant footprints are those of the wombat, while in others it could well be the emu or kangaroo. Some of the designs seem to give glimpses into the recent past through what seem to be engravings of tracks made by recently extinct animals, such as diprotodonts and giant kangaroos. These animals lived when inland Australia was a wetter, more friendly place, and Aboriginal people lived side by side with these giant mammals.

At the Olary engravings in South Australia early this century, station children discovered what many believe is an engraving of a crocodile head. This large engraving is now in the South Australian Museum. The crocodile interpretation has added strength when you consider that one of the legends of the inland tribes was of an animal called Kadimakara that lived in the pools of the lakes and rivers and ate anyone that came too close.

Much effort has been put into dating these engravings. Although there seems to be little knowledge about this type of art among today's Aboriginal elders, the places are still of importance to them. Recent efforts at the Olary site and a breakthrough in dating the age of the 'desert varnish' (a natural substance that covers rocks in the desert country) have given an age of some of these engravings as 43,000 years, give or take a thousand years or so. That makes them by far the oldest art in the world!

Take the time and effort to visit these places, but please remember that these engravings are important to Aboriginal people and that all artefacts, including these ancient art sites, are protected by law. Take only photographs: leave no sign of your passing.

The South Australian Museum, North Terrace, Adelaide, has probably the best collection of Aboriginal artefacts in Australia. It's worth a look before you head north.

Recent Painting In the 1880s a group of young artists developed the first distinctively Australian style of watercolour or oil painting. Working from a permanent bush camp in Melbourne's (then) outer suburb of Box Hill, the painters of the so-called Heidelberg School captured the unique qualities of Australian life and the bush. In Sydney, a contemporary movement worked at Sirius Cove on Sydney Harbour. Both schools were influenced by the French plein-air painters, whose practice of working outdoors to capture the effects of natural light was very appropriate in capturing the fierce light and pastel hues of the Australian landscape. The main artists were Tom Roberts, Arthur Streeton, Frederick McCubbin, Louis Abrahams, Charles Conder, Julian Ashton and, later, Walter Withers. Their works can be found in most of the major galleries of the country and are well worth seeking out.

In the 1940s another revolution took place, when a new generation of young artists redefined the direction of Australian art. Included in this group are some of Australia's most famous contemporary artists, including Sir Sidney Nolan and Arthur Boyd. More recently the work of painters such as Fred Williams, John Olsen, Robert Juniper, Russell Drysdale, Lloyd Rees and Brett Whitely has also made an impression on the international art world. The Broken Hill-based painter Pro Hart continues to capture the images and spirit of the outback in his idiosyncratic work.

The pictorial art of the Aborigines is detailed in a colour section beginning on page 65.

Cinema

Many people overseas (and probably most Australians) have been introduced to the outback through films like *Crocodile Dundee* and the *Mad Max* series which depict the outback in all its glory, from the dry and dusty 'Red Centre' to the lush, tropical wetlands of the Top End.

Earlier and lesser known films like *The Chant of Jimmy Blacksmith* and *Walkabout* tell of the political and social problems faced by those who live in the outback. Both films deal with interracial relationships, but the spectre of the outback and how it affects one's survival and culture is ever present.

Some outback films have the 'pioneering' feel of a John Ford Western. Stories of conflict and struggle, of innocence and the loss of innocence abound. Look out for *Mr Electric*, about the effect of the first light bulbs on a very remote farm. *The Last Picture Show Man* tells the tale of a travelling projectionist who is constantly driven further up the road by the advance of technology. For outback horror, see *Razorback*, the story of a giant killer hog; for a psychological thrill, check *Wake in Fright* and see a man mysteriously unable to leave the eerie, sweltering town in which he finds himself marooned.

Music

Australia's participation in the flurry of popular music since the 1950s has been a frustrating mix of good, indifferent, lousy, parochial and excellent. However, even the offerings of the most popular acts have done nothing to remove the cultural cringe: the highest praise remains 'it's good enough to have come from the UK/USA'. And it's true that little of the popular music created here has been noticeably different from that coming from overseas. (One exception: the Birthday Party?)

Which is why the recent success of Aboriginal music, and its merging with rock, is so refreshing. This music really is different. The most obvious name that springs to mind is Yothu Yindi. Their song about the dishonoured White-man's agreement, *Treaty*, perhaps did more than anything else to popularise Aboriginal land-rights claims. The band's lead singer, Mandawuy Yunupingu, was proclaimed Australian of the Year in 1993.

Other Aboriginal names include Coloured Stone, Kevin Carmody, Archie Roach, Scrap

Metal, the Sunrise Band, Christine Anu (from the Torres Strait Islands), and the bands that started it all but no longer exist, No Fixed Address and Warumpi Band.

White outback music owes much to Irish heritage and American country influences, often with a liberal sprinkling of dry outback humour. Names to watch out for include Slim Dusty, Ted Egan, John Williamson, Chad Morgan, Lee Kernaghan, Neil Murray, Midnight Oil, the Gondwanaland Project and Smokey Dawson.

STATION LIFE

Life on remote station properties has been much improved by modern developments such as the Royal Flying Doctor Service, the School of the Air and the expanding national telephone network, but many White communities in the outback are still affected to a greater or lesser degree by the tyranny of distance. Not many city people can imagine living perhaps 500 km from the nearest doctor and supermarket, or their children sitting down in front of a high-frequency (HF) radio transceiver to go to school.

Flying Doctor

Established by the Reverend John Flynn with a single aircraft in 1928, the original Flying Doctor has grown into a national organisation, the Royal Flying Doctor Service (RFDS), which provides a comprehensive medical service to all outback residents. Where people once feared sickness and injury, even the most isolated communities are now assured of receiving expert medical assistance within two or three hours instead of weeks.

Almost as important is the social function of the RFDS's HF radio network, which allows anyone without a telephone to send

The Flying Doctor

Before the late 1920s the outback's far-flung residents had little or no access to medical facilities. The nearest doctor was often weeks away over rough tracks, so if you fell seriously ill or met with a bad accident, your chances of recovery were slim. Difficult pregnancies and illnesses such as rheumatic fever and acute appendicitis were almost a death sentence. If you were lucky you fell ill near a telegraph line, where your mates could either treat you or operate under instructions received in morse code. This pointed to another harsh truth of life in the outback: reliable and speedy communications over long distances were available to very few.

In 1912 the **Reverend John Flynn** of the Presbyterian Church helped establish the outback's first hospital at Oodnadatta. Flynn was appalled by the tragedies that resulted from the lack of medical facilities and was quick to realise that the answer lay in radios and aircraft. However, these technologies – particularly radio – were still very much in their infancy and needed further development.

Flynn knew nothing of either radios or aviation but his sense of mission inspired others who did, such as radio engineer **Alf Traeger**. In 1928, after years of trial and error, Traeger developed a small, pedal-powered radio transceiver that was simple to use, inexpensive and could send and receive messages over 500 km. The outback's great silence was broken at last.

Aircraft suitable for medical evacuations had become available in 1920 but it was the lack of a radio communication network that delayed their general use for this purpose. Traeger's invention was the key to the establishment of Australia's first Flying Doctor base in Cloncurry, Queensland, in 1928. Cloncurry was then the base for the **Queensland and Northern Territory Aerial Services** (Qantas), which provided the pilot and an aircraft under lease.

The new service proved an outstanding success and areas beyond the reach of Cloncurry soon began to clamour for their own Flying Doctor. However, the Presbyterian Church had insufficient resources to allow a rapid expansion. In 1933 it handed the aerial medical service over to 'an organisation of national character' and so the **Royal Flying Doctor Service** (RFDS) was born. Flynn's vision of a 'mantle of safety' over the outback had become a reality.

Today, 12 RFDS base stations provide a sophisticated network of radio communications and medical services to an area as large as western Europe and about two-thirds the size of the USA.

and receive telegrams and to take part in special broadcasts known as galah sessions. Like party lines, these open periods of radio time allow distant neighbours to keep in touch with each other and events around them in a way the telephone can never rival.

School of the Air

Until recent times, outback children living away from towns either attended boarding school or were educated through written correspondence lessons. In 1944, Adelaide Meithke recognised that HF radio transceivers could be used to improve the childrens' education as well as their social life by giving them direct contact both with trained teachers and their fellow students. Her idea for a classroom of the airwaves, using the RFDS radio facilities, became a reality when Australia's first School of the Air opened in Alice Springs in 1951.

Today there are 14 Schools of the Air scattered about the outback and most use the RFDS network as their classroom. The major education method is still correspondence lessons – materials and equipment are sent to students, who return set written and audio work by mail – which are supplemented by radio classes lasting 20 to 30 minutes. Students speak to their teachers daily and each has a 10-minute personal session with their teacher once a week. Although face-to-face contact is limited, students and teachers do meet at least once a year on special get-togethers, and teachers visit each of their students on patrols by 4WD vehicles and light aircraft.

With 14 teachers and eight support staff, the Alice Springs School of the Air teaches about 140 children in nine grades, from pre-school to year seven, over a broadcast area of 1.3 million sq km, the furthest student living 1000 km away. In 1992 the school broke new ground once again when it beamed 'live' lessons by satellite to its students.

Emergency evacuations of sick or injured people are still an important function, but these days the RFDS provides a comprehensive range of medical services, including routine clinics at communities that are unable to attract full-time medical staff. It also supervises numerous small hospitals that normally operate without a doctor; such hospitals are staffed by registered nurses who communicate by telephone or radio with their RFDS doctor.

The administration of RFDS bases is divided between seven largely independent sections, each of which is a nonprofit organisation funded by government grants and private donations.

Facts & Figures To get an idea of the scope of operations, let's take a look at the Central Section. The headquarters are in Adelaide and base stations are at Port Augusta and Alice Springs. This covers virtually the entire outback of South Australia as well as the Northern Territory's bottom half. It operates 10 sophisticated twin-engined aircraft and employs 77 staff, including 20 pilots, seven aircraft engineers, five doctors, 13 other medical staff and seven radio operators.

In the 1992-93 financial year the section's aircraft flew a total of 1.3 million hours on medical-related matters. These included 5302 medical evacuations, of which 3108 were transfers of patients from country hospitals to Adelaide. A total of 11,269 patients were treated at RFDS bush clinics, there were 90 consultations over its HF radio network and 5593 consultations by telephone. Over the same period, the emergency alarms were activated 323 times, mostly by callers seeking medical or other assistance. The two bases made a total of 12,737 radphone connections, in which persons calling in by HF radio were 'patched in' to the national telephone network.

So the service established by the Reverend John Flynn nearly 70 years ago is still a powerful force in the outback, enabling its residents to live secure in the knowledge that medical help is just a telephone or radio call away. However, there is talk of transferring the RFDS's HF radio network to a single OTC Maritime base on the eastern seaboard as a cost-cutting measure. This proposal is viewed with scepticism if not horror by many outback people, who appreciate the efficiency, local knowledge and experience of RFDS radio operators. They feel that such a radical change will degrade the service on which their lives and wellbeing often depend. ∎

Emergency evacuation by Flying Doctor (DO)

Shopping

Most stations are far from even the most basic facilities such as post offices, libraries and shops, and often neighbours can be 50 km or more apart. Most isolated communities receive mail and newspapers either weekly or fortnightly when the mail plane or mail truck does its rounds. Perishable groceries and minor freight can be sent out with the mail, but a major shopping expedition can mean a round trip of 1000 km or more to the nearest decent shops.

It's not all Bad

The outback presents its share of difficulties. Most of these can be attributed to isolation, but as the famous Australian poet A B (Banjo) Paterson wrote in *Clancy of the Overflow*, bush people do 'have pleasures that the townsfolk never know'. One of these is the ready accessibility of wide-open spaces untainted by air pollution, traffic noise and crowds. Another is the sense of self-reliance and independence that's still strong in the outback.

Being forced to make their own entertainment encourages people living hundreds of km apart to get together (usually on the RFDS radio network, although increasingly by telephone) to organise social functions such as horse-race meetings, camp drafts (rodeos) and gymkhanas. This strong sense of community spirit, even when the 'community' may be spread over a vast area, means that even neighbours who don't get on will more than likely assist each other in

a crisis. It's these aspects of outback life that help to make the hardships worthwhile.

RULES OF BEHAVIOUR

It's a hot, sweaty day out on the wide brown land and you're bouncing along a dusty road in your 4WD. You've never felt more in need of a bath, particularly after changing that last tyre back in the bulldust.

Then you spy a lonely windmill in the scrub beside the track. There's a large steel tank beside it and the thought of a bath brings instant good cheer. Off come your clothes, you climb onto the edge and with a glad cry leap into the water. To your horror the concussion bursts the wall and you escape fearful mutilation by clinging to the edge as the tank's precious contents gush out through the jagged hole.

This sort of thing doesn't happen very often (thank goodness) but it's an example of how people from an urban environment can come undone in the unfamiliar world of the outback. Most visitors want to do the right thing and here are some simple rules on how to avoid upsetting the people who live there:

Water

Most pastoralists are happy for travellers to make use of their water supplies, but they do ask that they be treated with respect. This means washing clothes, dishes and sweaty bodies in a bucket or basin, not in the water supply itself. Always remember that animals and people may have to drink it when you've finished.

School of the Air (R & VM)

Camping right beside watering points is also to be avoided. In the outback the stock is often half wild and will hang back if you're parked or have your tent pitched right where they normally drink. They'll eventually overcome their fear through necessity, which means you'll be covered in dust and develop grey hair as the thirst-crazed mob mills around your camp at midnight. If you must camp in the vicinity, keep at least 200 metres away and stay well off the pads that animals have worn as they come in to drink.

Much the same applies if you drive up to a bore or dam and find the stock having a drink. Stay well back until they've finished, then you can move in for your share. The thing to remember at all times is that this isolated pool or trough might be the only water in a radius of 30 km or more.

For more about water, see Health in the Facts for the Visitor chapter.

Gates

The golden rule with any gate is to *leave it as you find it*. You must do this even if a sign by an open gate says to keep it closed – it may have been left open for any number of reasons, such as to let stock through to water. It's fairly common for animals to perish because tourists have closed gates that a pastoralist left open.

Unfortunately, some home-made wire gates can seem like the work of the devil and on occasion will turn nasty, entangling you in barbed wire as you struggle to close them. When you arrive at one of these things, take careful note of how it works whilst opening it; closure should then be a relatively simple matter. Never throw up your hands in defeat and drive off leaving it either insecurely fastened or, worse, lying on the ground. Having opened it, you must persevere until you've worked out how to close it.

If you're driving in a convoy it's accepted procedure that, on coming to a gate, one of the lead vehicles remains on the spot until all others are through. That way, there won't be any mistakes with gates not being left as they were found.

Floods

Sometimes the outback receives a large part of its annual rainfall in a matter of days. When this happens, unsealed roads and tracks become extremely slippery and boggy. The correct thing to do in this event is either to get out before the rain soaks in or to stay put on high ground until the surface dries out. To do otherwise may see your vehicle gouging great ruts in the road surface, which of course won't endear you to the locals who must live with the mess you've made. Quite apart from that, you'll probably get well and truly stuck in some dreadful place far from anywhere. This is one of the reasons to carry plenty of extra stores on an outback trip. If a road is officially closed because of heavy rain, you can be fined for travelling on it – the norm is $1000 per wheel!

Fire

The outback usually experiences drought, during which time many grasses dry off to form standing hay. This, along with the foliage of trees and bushes, carries the stock through to the next rains. Under extreme weather conditions a careless camper can start a bushfire that might destroy the vegetation over many hundreds of sq km of grazing land. To avoid being responsible for such a disaster, always take care with your campfire by siting it at least five metres from flammable material, keeping it small and making certain it's out before you leave camp. The best way to guarantee the latter is to completely cover the ashes with soil.

For more about fire, see Dangers & Annoyances as well as Camping and Food in the Facts for the Visitor chapter.

Dogs

The tourist's best friend is a contentious issue in the outback at the best of times. There's no doubt that the best way to avoid dog-related hassles is to keep your pet on a leash at all times when in sheep and cattle country. If nothing else, this will save it from an untimely and unpleasant end.

First, dogs like to chase things. After a day cooped up in the back of a vehicle you'd probably want to chase something yourself, but the difference is that Rover might put a flock of sheep through the fence while he's trying to round it up. The distress caused through being chased and worried by domestic dogs is a major contributing factor in stock deaths each year. For this reason, pastoralists who find a strange dog on their properties tend to shoot first and ask questions later.

Second, dogs are great scavengers and no matter how well fed or bred they are they'll gobble up any old piece of meat or carcass they find lying around. Dingo poisoning is widely practised on station properties and the baits used can be bite-sized chunks of meat, small 'pellets' of processed meat as big as the end of your thumb, or the carcasses of animals killed by dogs. Rover won't be able to resist that one last meal.

Rubbish
The best way to dispose of all nonburnable rubbish is to store it in a heavy-duty plastic bag and carry it with you to deposit at an authorised dumping place. Many tourists believe they're doing the right thing by burying their garbage, but few dig a deep enough hole. Anything buried under less than a metre of soil will be dug up by goannas and dingoes, which are attracted by the food scraps. Crows will then scatter it everywhere and the end result is an unsightly mess. If you must bury your rubbish, any cans or other food containers should always be burned first to get rid of the tantalising smells.

See also Camping in the Facts for the Visitor chapter.

Courtesy
These days most outback pastoralists are on the telephone and it's a common courtesy to contact them before you invade their property. Straight-through travel on established roads is not a problem, but if you're thinking of going camping or fishing in some remote spot, the landholder will expect you to ask permission. You'll usually rise in the estima-tion of the more isolated people if you drop off some very recent newspapers or ask if there's anything they'd like brought out from town. Always remember to take-your-own-everything, as station folk seldom organise their shopping around the needs of ill-pre-pared visitors.

Cross-Cultural Etiquette
Many of the outback's original inhabitants lead lives that are powerfully influenced by ancient traditions, and the average tourist is almost entirely ignorant of Aboriginal social customs – let's face it, most of us have never met an Aborigine. Aborigines will make allowances for the ignorance of White people, but it does no harm to observe a few simple rules. One of the most important of these is to act naturally.

You won't go far wrong if you treat outback Aborigines as potential friends. Also, remember that Aborigines generally have great senses of humour and love a good laugh.

Paying a Visit You've arrived at a small Aboriginal community on a back road in the middle of nowhere. The front area outside each dwelling is the occupants' private space, a sort of outdoor living room. Park at a reasonable distance (say, 30 metres) so as not to intrude on this space, then get out of the vehicle and wait for someone to come over. That person will usually speak at least reasonable English and can point you in the right direction. If this approach yields no results, walk over to the nearest house or shelter and call out to attract attention.

Sometimes you'll find the residents sitting around in a circle, which usually indicates some sort of business in progress. Instead of barging in, stand a little way off – you may be beckoned over, or someone may come up. Don't hang around if it's obvious that your presence isn't wanted.

Most larger communities have a store staffed by White people, and this is the place to go first for information. The store is usually easy to find. If you're not sure, ask someone rather than head off on an unauthorised sightseeing tour that raises dust and could make you unpopular. One sure way to wear out a welcome is to drive around taking photographs without permission. Aborigines are people, not celebrities.

Many tourists feel extremely uncomfortable when visiting their first Aboriginal community, and this can find expression in rudeness. For example, there's a tendency for tourists to race down the road with their faces expressionless and eyes fixed straight ahead. Aborigines won't think you're immoral if you smile and wave; the fact is they'll generally appreciate it and you'll get a postive response.

People Skills Having got to first base, you need to watch your body language. For example, wrinkling your nose at someone else's odour is unlikely to win any friends. Desert dwellers naturally place washing well down on the list of priorities; people who eat a lot of kangaroo meat can also develop a distinctive and fairly strong body odour. To put a different perspective on this, the well-soaped White person can smell unpleasantly like a wet sheep to desert Aborigines. However, being invariably polite, they'll give no indication that they find your personal aroma to be anything other than what you imagine it to be.

Western society regards a firm handshake and eye contact as important in creating a favourable first impression – just ask any salesperson. However, both are signs of aggression in Aboriginal society. Their usual greeting is a soft clasp of the hands with little or no arm movement, and there may be no eye contact at all until a friendly relationship is established. The best approach to eye contact is to take it as it comes. If the other person isn't looking directly at you, it's polite not to look at them.

It's also unwise to rush or be pushy, as the usual Aboriginal way is to engage in sociable small talk before getting down to the matter at hand, even if this takes time. While they won't expect you to waffle on at length about the drought or scarcity of kangaroos, a pleasantry or two gets the conversation flowing

and establishes your unselfish interest in that person. This works well in White outback society too.

It's also important to remember that English is very much the second language on most remote communities and may not be spoken at all well. This doesn't mean you have to lapse into broken pidgin to make yourself understood. Not only is such behaviour demeaning to the audience, but they might think you're some sort of idiot. The correct approach is to speak distinctly and reasonably slowly, using straightforward English and a normal tone of voice. Don't make the mistake of addressing your audience as you would a slow learner with a hearing problem. See the Language section later in this chapter for more advice on communicating with Aborigines.

Purchasing A visit to an Aboriginal community presents an ideal opportunity to purchase traditional paintings or other works of art directly from the artist. However, bargaining such as takes place in an Indian bazaar is foreign to this society, and in any case the prices asked are usually very reasonable.

If you're tempted to drive the price down, remember that there's no sport in this as the seller's inherent politeness may force him or her to accept your unreasonably low offer rather than offend you. On the other hand, Aboriginal artists are waking up fast to the value of their work and the devious ways of many tourists.

Alcohol Many non-Aboriginal Australians claim that most Aborigines drink to excess. This assertion is hypocritical and inaccurate. In actual fact, a smaller percentage of Aborigines drink than do non-Aborigines.

However, Aborigines who consume alcohol are more likely than their non-Aboriginal counterparts to drink in public. One reason for this is the fact that Aboriginal councils have banned the possession and consumption of alcohol on many Aboriginal communities. As a result, many outback Aborigines have irregular access to alcohol, and only drink when they go to town.

Unforunately, this is the only time many non-Aboriginal people (and tourists) see Aborigines.

Throughout Australia, Aboriginal people are actively involved in the fight against alcohol. With the assistance of lawyers, they have persuaded some outback hotels and takeaway outlets not to sell alcohol to local Aboriginal people, and signs at such outlets explain that Aboriginal elders ask tourists to not buy alcohol for Aborigines. Also, some outlets may refuse to sell you alcohol if you're heading towards an Aboriginal community. Please respect such efforts to combat alcoholism.

RELIGION

A shrinking majority of people in Australia are at least nominally Christian. Most Protestant churches have merged to become the Uniting Church, although the Church of England has remained separate. The Catholic Church is popular (about a third of Australian Christians are Catholics), with the original Irish adherents boosted by the large numbers of Mediterranean immigrants.

Non-Christian minorities abound, the main ones in order of magnitude being Muslim, Buddhist and Jewish.

Aboriginal Religion

Traditional Aboriginal cultures either have very little religious component or are nothing but religion, depending on how you look at it. Is a belief system which views every event, no matter how trifling, in a non-material context a religion? The early Christian missionaries certainly didn't think so. For them a belief in a deity was an essential part of a religion, and anything else was mere superstition.

Sacred Sites Aboriginal sacred sites are a perennial topic of discussion. Their presence can lead to headline-grabbing controversy when they stand in the way of developments such as roads, mines and dams. This is because most other Australians still have great difficulty understanding the Aborigines' deep spiritual bond with the land.

Aboriginal religious beliefs centre on the continuing existence of spirit beings that lived on Earth during the Dreamtime, which occurred before the arrival of humans. These beings created all the features of the natural world and were the ancestors of all living things. They took different forms but behaved as people do, and as they travelled about they left signs to show where they passed. Most Australians have heard of rainbow serpents carving out rivers as they slithered from A to B. On a smaller scale you can have a pile of rocks marking the spot where an ancestor defecated, or a tree that sprang from a thrown spear.

Despite being supernatural, the ancestors were subject to ageing and eventually they returned to the sleep from which they'd awoken at the dawn of time. Some sank back into the ground while others changed into physical features including the moon and stars. Here their spirits remain as eternal forces that breathe life into the newborn and influence natural events. Each ancestor's spiritual energy flows along the path it travelled during the Dreamtime and is strongest at the points where it left physical evidence of its activities, such as a tree, hill or claypan. These features are sacred sites.

The ancestors left strict laws that determine the behaviour of people and animals, the growth of plants, and natural events such as rain and the change of seasons. Although all living things are considered to be conscious beings with their own language and way of life, they are still required to live in accordance with their ancestors' laws.

Every person, animal and plant is believed to have two souls – one mortal and one immortal. The latter is part of a particular ancestral spirit and returns to the sacred sites of that ancestor after death, while the mortal soul simply fades into oblivion. Each person is spiritually bound to the sacred sites that mark the land associated with his or her ancestor. It is the individual's obligation to help care for these sites by performing the necessary rituals and singing the songs that tell of the ancestor's deeds. By doing this, the order created by that ancestor is maintained.

However, the ancestors are extremely powerful and restless spirits and require the most careful treatment. Dreadful calamities can befall those who fail to care for their sites in the proper manner. As there is nowhere beyond the influence of an angry ancestor, the unpleasant consequences of either disrespect or neglect at a single site may stretch far and wide.

Some of the sacred sites are believed to be dangerous and entry is prohibited under traditional Aboriginal law. These restrictions often have a pragmatic origin. One site in northern Australia was believed to cause sores to break out all over the body of anyone visiting the area. Subsequently, the area was found to have a dangerously high level of radiation from naturally occurring radon gas. In another instance, fishing from a certain reef was traditionally prohibited. This restriction was scoffed at by local Europeans until it was discovered that fish from this area had a high incidence of *ciguatera*, which renders fish poisonous if eaten by humans.

Unfortunately, Aboriginal sacred sites are not like Christian churches, which can be desanctified before the bulldozers move in. Neither can they be bought, sold or transferred. Other Australians find this difficult to accept because they regard land as belonging to the individual, whereas in Aboriginal society the reverse applies. In a nutshell, Aborigines believe that to destroy or damage a sacred site threatens not only the living but also the spirit inhabitants of the land. It is a distressing and dangerous act, and one that no responsible person would condone.

Throughout much of Australia, when pastoralists were breaking the Aborigines' subsistence link to the land, and sometimes shooting them, many Aborigines sought refuge on missions and became Christians. However, becoming Christians has not, for most Aborigines, meant renouncing their traditional religion. Many senior Aboriginal law men are also devout Christians, and in many cases ministers.

LANGUAGE

Any visitor from abroad who thinks Australian (that's 'strine') is simply a weird variant of British or American will soon have a few surprises. For a start, many Australians don't even speak Australian – they speak Italian, Lebanese, Vietnamese, Turkish or Greek (Melbourne is said to be the third-largest Greek city in the world).

Those who do speak the native tongue are liable to lose you in a strange collection of Australian words. Some have completely different meanings in Australia than they have in English-speaking countries north of the equator; some commonly used words have been shortened almost beyond recognition. Others derive from Aboriginal languages, or from the slang used by early convict settlers.

There is a slight regional variation in the Australian accent but it's minute compared with variations in, say, the USA. The main difference between city speech and that in the country or outback, is speed.

Some of the most famed Aussie words are hardly heard at all – 'mates' and 'pals' are more common than 'cobbers'. Rhyming slang is used occasionally ('hit the frog and toad' for 'hit the road', 'Oxford scholars' for 'dollars'), so if you hear an odd expression that doesn't seem to make sense, see if it rhymes with something else that does.

If you want to pass for a native, try speaking slightly nasally, and shorten any word of more than two syllables and then add a vowel to the end of it (garbage contractors become 'garbos', worker's compensation becomes 'compo'). Make anything you can into a diminutive (the Hell's Angels become 'bikies'), and pepper your speech with as many expletives as possible. The Glossary in the back of this book will help.

Aboriginal Languages

Before the Europeans arrived, there were about 250 Aboriginal languages comprising about 700 dialects. It is believed that all the languages evolved from a single language family as the Aborigines gradually moved out over the entire continent and split into new groups. There are a number of words that occur right across the continent, such as *jina* (foot) and *mala* (hand), and similarities also exist in the often complex grammatical structures. Today there remain at least 100 distinct Aboriginal languages, many of which have a number of dialects. Some languages are actually growing as populations expand and dominant languages replace others.

Most Aboriginal languages have about 10,000 words – about the same number of words used by the average English speaker. Many words reflect the close relationship that Aboriginal people have with their environment. For example, the Western Desert Pintupi dialect has 18 words for 'hole': an ant burrow, a rabbit burrow, a goanna burrow, a small animal burrow etc. Traditionally, all Aboriginal adults could identify and name hundreds of plants and animals. This is still the case in many parts of outback and northern Australia, and one reason why Aboriginal people are central to much contemporary scientific research.

Dozens of Aboriginal words have been incorporated into Australian English: barramundi, boomerang, budgerigar, brolga, coolabah, corroboree, dingo, galah, jarrah,

Aboriginal Languages

0   500   1000 km

(The only languages shown are those spoken by 500 people or more)

kangaroo, kookaburra, mallee, mulga, perentie, quandong, wallaby and yakka, to name a few. Similarly, Aboriginal languages have absorbed many English words, which are invariably adapted to suit Aboriginal grammars and sound systems. For example, English words used by many Central Australian Aboriginal people include 'taraka' (truck), 'tiipii' (TV), 'riipula' (rifle) and 'ruuta' (road).

Aboriginal Kriol is a new language that has developed since European arrival in Australia. It is spoken across northern Australia and has become the 'native' language of many young Aborigines. It contains many English words but, once again, grammatical usage is along Aboriginal lines. For example, the English sentence 'He was amazed' becomes 'I bin luk kwesjinmak' in Kriol.

It is also interesting to note that within Aboriginal languages there are what linguists term 'speech registers', which use vocabulary not normally used in day to day life. Speech registers are a little like languages within languages. Some registers are employed during ceremony; others are used when talking to certain relatives.

Lonely Planet's *Australian Phrasebook* gives a detailed account of Aboriginal languages.

Pitjantjatjara As it's pointless to try and explain the many different languages, we'll focus on Pitjantjatjara (sometimes known as Pitjantjara). This is the best known dialect of Aboriginal Australia's largest language group, the Western Desert language. Western Desert dialects are spoken widely throughout central Australia, from 1000 km or so north-west of Alice Springs down almost to the Great Australian Bight, east almost to Queensland, and 1000 km or so west of the NT/WA border. Speakers of Western Desert dialects call themselves Anangu.

Pitjantjatjara is not the traditional language of Alice Springs, but it is often heard in Alice Springs and on some communities west of Alice. It is spoken extensively on Aboriginal communities from the NT/WA border, through Uluru National Park to the

eastern edge of the Simpson Desert, and throughout the Anangu Pitjantjatjara freehold Aboriginal lands of northern South Australia.

Pitjantjatjara means the dialect that has the word *pitjantja*, a form of the verb 'to come', and *tjara*, which means 'to have'. Other dialects use different words instead of *pitjantja* – for example Yankunytjatjara speakers use the word *yankunytja*. Despite these differences, Pitjantjatjara and Yankunytjatjara sound systems are identical, and most of their words are identical or very similar.

Aboriginal cultures are traditionally oral, and the languages were not written down until well after European contact; many languages were lost forever when their speakers were exterminated or died out. Pitjantjatjara was one of the first Aboriginal languages to be comprehensively transcribed, at Ernabella in South Australia in the 1930s in the context of Bible translation and bilingual education. Written Pitjantjatjara now has a standardised phonetic spelling system, which is an integral part of the signage at Uluru National Park.

Aspiring Pitjantjatjara-learners and those with a general interest in the language can buy the Pitjantjatjara/Yankunytjatjara-to-English dictionary. This is a well-illustrated publication available from the Institute for Aboriginal Development, PO Box 2531, Alice Springs, NT 0871. A number of other dictionaries of Central Australian languages are also available from the institute, as well as a range of language-learning tapes and manuals.

Pronunciation Like most Aboriginal languages, Pitjantjatjara has three vowels:

a – as 'u' in 'sun'
i – as 'i' in 'bin'
u – as 'oo' in 'look'

These vowels also have a long form – eg, kaanka (crow), nyii-nyii (zebra finch), and uulinanyi (to tease).

There are 17 Pitjantjatjara consonants: p, m, w, tj, ny, ly, y, t, n, l, r, t, n, l, r, k and ng. Consonants with lines under them (which can happen to t, n, l and r) are retroflexed, which means that when they are articulated the tongue is curled back. Thus when you pronounce the word 'miṉa' (arm) you must curl your tongue back when you pronounce the 'n'. If you fail to do so you will say 'mina', which means water.

Words & Phrases The following list will help you communicate with Aṉangu people in the south of the Northern Territory, the north of South Australia, and the south-east of Western Australia:

uwa	yes
wiya	no
munta	sorry
munta, ngayulu ngurpa	sorry, I don't (ie if someone asks if you smoke or for cigarettes)
palya	OK, no worries
nyuntu palya	are you OK?
kaapi yaaltji	where can we find water?
nyuntu kaapi kanyini	do you have any water?
nyuntu kaapi/petrol pulka-tjara	do you have a lot of water/petrol?
pikatjara	sick
yaalara	when
yaaltjingka	where

Communicating with Outback Aborigines

In many parts of outback Australia, including the Western Desert region and Arnhem Land, many Aborigines do not speak English regularly or fluently. There are many reasons for this. There are virtually no high schools on outback Aboriginal communities and many people emerge from school without basic English literacy or oracy. Many Aborigines seldom have to use English on their communities, and use their own languages when speaking to non-Aborigines with the expectation (or hope) that, with time and like other Aboriginal people, non-Aborigines will learn to understand and possibly speak their language. When they go to towns or shops, they can usually get by without speaking English. Many visitors to outback Australia see Aborigines in shops, selecting what they want and going through the checkout with eyes lowered, passing their money silently over the counter.

Because of all this, and the great differences between Aboriginal and English sound systems, many Aborigines have difficulty pronouncing English words. For example, many Aboriginal languages do not include the sounds 's', 'z', 'v', 'sh' or 'th' and do not distinguish between a 'b' and a 'p', or a 'd' and a 't'. Keep this in mind when you talk to Aboriginal people who have difficulty speaking English. Conversely, it is difficult for some English-speaking people to roll their r's, or to distinguish between the retroflexed and non-retroflexed sounds typical of most Aboriginal languages.

Most Aboriginal languages have no words for hello, please or thank you – these niceties are simply not part of traditional Aboriginal culture. However, these words have been adopted to some extent and people will appreciate you using them, as they show your friendly intentions.

People who come into contact with Aborigines should also be aware that Aboriginal people of mixed descent usually identify as Aborigines and don't like being referred to as half-castes. Refer to Aboriginal people as Aborigines, or Aboriginal people – words such as 'Abos' or 'coons' are grossly insulting.

However, many Aborigines have terms which they use to refer to themselves. For example, many Queensland Aborigines refer to themselves as Murris, many New South Wales and Victorian Aborigines call themselves Kooris, Western Desert speakers are Aṉangu, Warlpiri speakers Yappa, and northeast Arnhem Landers Yolngu. Nunga is used to refer to the people of coastal South Australia, and Nyoongah is used in the country's south-west. Aborigines appreciate non-Aboriginal people using these terms – provided that the correct term is used to refer to the appropriate group. If you call an Aṉangu from Uluru a Koori you will probably receive a blank stare.

See Cross-Cultural Etiquette in this chapter for general advice on meeting Aborigines.

Aboriginal Art

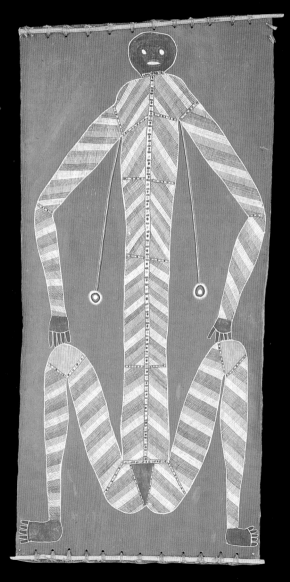

Namarrkon, Lightning Spirit by Curly Bardagubu, c. 1931-1987, Born clan; Kunwinjku language, Namokardabu, western Arnhem Land; earth pigments on bark; 156 x 75cm; 1987; purchased through the Art Foundation of Victoria with assistance from Alcoa of Australia Limited, Governor 1990; National Gallery of Victoria.

ABORIGINAL ART

Aboriginal art has undergone a major revival in the last decade or so, with artists throughout the country finding both a means to express and preserve ancient Dreaming values, and a way to share this rich cultural heritage with the wider community.

While the so-called dot paintings of the central deserts are the most readily identifiable and probably most popular form of contemporary Aboriginal art, there's a huge range of material being produced – bark paintings from Arnhem Land, wood carving and silk-screen printing from the Tiwi Islands north of Darwin, batik printing and wood carving from central Australia, and more.

The initial forms of artistic expression were rock carvings, body painting and ground designs, and the earliest engraved designs known to exist date back at least 30,000 years. Art has always been an integral part of Aboriginal life, a connection between past and present, between the supernatural and the earthly, between people and the land.

All early art was a reflection of the various peoples' ancestral Dreaming – the 'Creation', when the earth's physical features were formed by the struggles between powerful supernatural ancestors such as the Rainbow Serpent, the Lightning Men and the Wandjina. Not only was the physical layout mapped but codes of behaviour were also laid down, and although these laws have been diluted and adapted in the last 200 years, they still provide the basis for today's Aborigines. Ceremonies, rituals and sacred paintings are all based on the Dreaming.

A Dreaming may take a number of different forms – it can be a

Pampardu Jukurrpa by Clarise Poulson; acrylic on linen; 150 x 90cm; 1993; Warlukurlangu Artists Association, Yuendumu, NT; courtesy of DESART.

Left: Lightning Brothers rock art site at Katherine River; courtesy of the NT Tourist Commission.

Below: Ewaninga rock engravings, south of Alice Springs; courtesy of the NT Tourist Commission.

person, an animal or a physical feature, while others are more general, relating to a region, a group of people, or natural forces such as floods and wind. Thus Australia is covered by a wide network of Dreamings, and any one person may have connections with several.

CENTRAL AUSTRALIAN ART
Western Desert Paintings

The current renaissance in Aboriginal painting began in the early 1970s at Papunya (honey ant place), at the time a small, depressed community 240 km north-west of Alice Springs, which had grown out of the government's 'assimilation' policy. Here the local children were given the task of painting a traditional-style mural on the school wall. The local elders took interest in the project, and although the public display of traditional images gave rise to much debate amongst the elders, they eventually participated and in fact completed the *Honey Ant Dreaming* mural. This was the first time that images which were originally confined to rock and body art came to be reproduced in a different environment.

Other murals followed this first one, and before long the desire to paint spread through the community. In the early stages paintings were produced on small boards on the ground or balanced on the artist's knee, but this soon gave way to painting on canvas with acrylic paints. Canvas was an ideal medium as it could be easily rolled and transported, yet large paintings were possible. With the growing importance of art, both as an economic and a cultural activity, an association was formed to help the artists sell their work. The Papunya Tula company in Alice Springs is still one

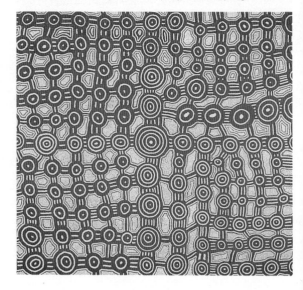

Untitled by Dini Campbell Tjampitjinpa; acrylic on linen; 182 x 152cm; 1993; Papunya Tula Artists Pty Ltd, Alice Springs, NT; courtesy of DESART.

of the few galleries in central Australia to be owned and run by Aborigines.

Painting in central Australia has flourished to such a degree that these days it is an important educational source for young kids, as they can learn aspects of religious and ceremonial knowledge. This is especially true now that women are so much a part of the painting movement.

The trademark dot-painting style is partly an evolution from 'ground paintings', which formed the centrepiece of traditional dances and songs. These were made from pulped plant material, and the designs were made on the ground using dots of this mush. Dots were also used to outline objects in rock paintings, and to highlight geographical features or vegetation. Over time the use of dots has developed, sometimes covering the entire canvas.

While the paintings may look random and abstract, they have great significance to the artist and usually depict a Dreaming journey, and so can be seen almost as aerial landscape maps. One feature which appears regularly is the tracks of birds, animals and humans, often identifying the ancestor. Various subjects, including people, are often depicted by the imprint they leave in the sand – a simple arc depicts a person (as that is the print left by someone sitting), a coolamon (wooden carrying dish) is shown as an oval shape, a digging stick by a single line, a camp fire by a circle. Males or females are identified by the objects associated with them – digging sticks and coolamons are always used by women, spears and boomerangs by men. Concentric circles are usually used to depict Dreaming sites, or places where ancestors paused in their journeys.

Liru Tjara by Mary Ungkaipai Forbes; watercolour on paper; 102 x 82cm; Kaltjiti Crafts, Fregon, SA; courtesy of DESART.

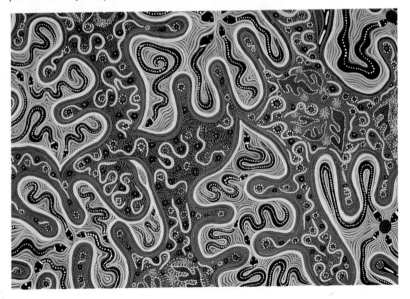

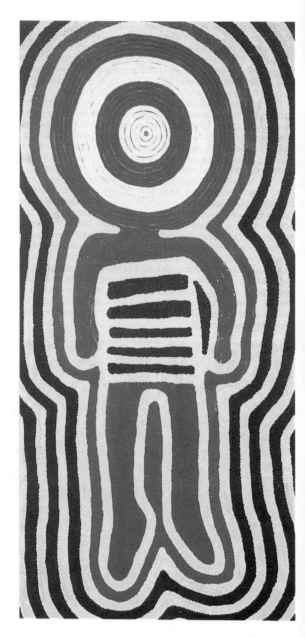

Kadaitja Man by
Ronnie Tjampitjinpa;
acrylic on linen;
122 x 61cm; 1993;
Papunya Tula Artists
Pty Ltd, Alice Springs,
NT; courtesy of
DESART.

While these symbols are widely used and are readily identifiable, their context within each individual painting is known only by the artist and the people closely associated with him or her – either by group or by the Dreaming – and different groups apply different interpretations to each painting. In this way sacred stories can be publicly portrayed, as the deeper meaning is not evident to any but those with a close association with the image.

The colours used in dot paintings from central Australia may seem overly vivid, and inappropriate to the land or story depicted. However, they are not meant to be true representations of the landscape, but variations in that landscape. The reds, blues and purples which often dominate the outback scenery, and which were so much a part of Albert Namatjira's painting (see below), feature prominently.

Albert Namatjira (1902-59) Australia's most well-known Aboriginal artist was probably Albert Namatjira. He lived at the Hermannsburg Lutheran Mission, about 130 km west of Alice Springs, and was introduced to European-style watercolour painting by a non-Aboriginal artist, Rex Batterbee, in the 1930s.

Namatjira successfully captured the essence of the Centre using a heavily European-influenced style. At the time his paintings were seen purely as picturesque landscapes. These days, however, it is thought he chose his subjects carefully, as they were Dreaming landscapes to which he had a great bond.

Namatjira supported many of his people on the income from his work, as was his obligation under tribal law. Because of his fame he was allowed to buy alcohol at a time when this was otherwise

Ngapa Manu Warna Jukurrpa (Water & Snake Dreaming) by Rosie Nangala Flemming; acrylic on linen; 180 x 120cm; 1993; Warlukurlangu Artists Association, Yuendumu, NT; courtesy of DESART.

illegal for Aborigines. In 1957 he was the first Aborigine to be granted Australian citizenship, but in 1958 he was jailed for six months for supplying alcohol to Aborigines. He died the following year aged only 57.

Although Namatjira died very disenchanted with White society, he did much to change the extremely negative views of Aborigines which prevailed at the time. At the same time he paved the way for the Papunya painting movement which emerged just over a decade after his death.

The Utopia Batik Artists

The women of Utopia, 225 km north-east of Alice Springs, have become famous in recent years for their production of batik material. In the mid 1970s the Anmatyerre and Alyawarre people started to reoccupy their traditional lands around Utopia cattle station, and this was given a formal basis in 1979 when they were granted title to the station. A number of scattered outstations, rather than a central settlement, were set up, and around this time the women were introduced to batik as part of a self-help program. The art form flourished and Utopia Women's Batik Group was formed in 1978.

Silk soon became the preferred medium for printing, and the batiks were based on the traditional women's designs which were painted on their bodies.

In the late 1980s techniques using acrylic paints on canvas were introduced to the artists at Utopia, and they have also become popular.

Other Central Australian Art

The making of wooden sculptures for sale dates back to at least early this century. In 1903 a group of Diyari people living on the Killalpaninna Lutheran Mission near Lake Eyre in South Australia

Handcrafted decorative central Australian carvings made from river red gum root; Maruku Arts & Crafts, Uluru (Ayers Rock), NT; courtesy of DESART.

were encouraged by the pastor to produce sculptures in order to raise funds for the mission.

The momentum for producing crafts for sale was accelerated by the opening up and settlement of the country by Europeans. Demand was slow to increase but the steady growth of the tourist trade since WW II, and the tourist boom of the 1980s, has seen demand and production increase dramatically.

The most widespread crafts seen for sale these days are the wooden carvings which have designs scorched into them with hot fencing wire. These range from small figures, such as possums, up to quite large snakes and lizards, although none of them have any Dreaming significance. One of the main outlets for these is the Maruku Arts & Crafts centre at the Uluru National Park rangers' station, where it's possible to see the crafts being made. Although much of the artwork is usually done by women, men are also involved at the Maruku centre. The Mt Ebenezer Roadhouse, on the Lasseter Highway (the main route to Uluru), is another Aboriginal-owned enterprise – and one of the cheapest places for buying sculpted figures.

Terracotta pots by the Hermannsburg Potters; 1992; represented by Alcaston House Gallery, Melbourne.

The Ernabella Presbyterian Mission in northern South Australia was another place where craftwork was encouraged. A 1950 mission report stated that: 'A mission station must have an industry to provide work for and help finance the cost of caring for the natives'. As the mission had been founded on a sheep station, wool crafts were the obvious way to go, and to that end the techniques of wool spinning, dyeing and weaving were introduced. The Pitjantjatjara (pigeon-jara) women made woollen articles such as rugs, belts, traditional dilly bags (carry bags) and scarves, using designs incorporating aspects of women's law (*yawilyu*). With the introduction of batik fabric dyeing in the 1970s, weaving at Ernabella virtually ceased.

The Arrernte people from Hermannsburg have recently begun to work with pottery, a craft which is not traditionally Aboriginal. They have incorporated moulded figures and surface treatments adapted from Dreaming stories.

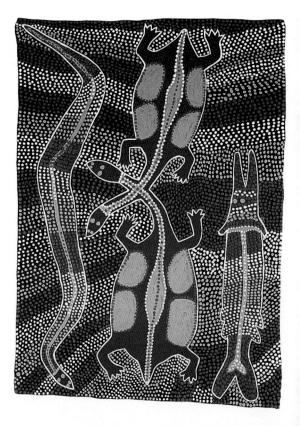

Old Man – Young Man – Very Big Story by Djambu Barra Barra, born about 1946; language group Wagilak related to Ritangu; domicile Ngukurr, NT; synthetic polymer paint on lanaquarelle paper; 63 x 67cm; 1992; represented by Alcaston House Gallery, Melbourne.

ARNHEM LAND ART

Arnhem Land, in Australia's tropical 'Top End', is possibly the area with the richest artistic heritage. It is thought that rock paintings were being made as much as 40,000 years ago, and some of the rock art galleries in the huge sandstone Arnhem Land plateau are at least 18,000 years old.

Although Arnhem Land is famous for its rock art, the tradition of bark painting is equally strong in the region. In fact in recent years, this portable art form has become very popular, probably because the boom in tourism has led to a high demand for souvenirs. As is the case in many communities throughout the country, producing art works for sale is an important form of employment in a place where there are generally few opportunities.

The art of Arnhem Land is vastly different from that of the central deserts. Here, Dreaming stories are depicted far more literally, with easily recognisable (though often stylised) images of ancestors, animals, and even Macassans – early Indonesian mariners who regularly visited the north coast long before the Europeans arrived on the scene.

Rock Art

The paintings contained in the Arnhem Land rock art sites range from hand prints to paintings of animals, people, mythological beings and European ships, constituting one of the world's most important and fascinating rock art collections. They provide a record of changing environments and Aboriginal lifestyles over the millennia.

In some places they are concentrated in large galleries, with paintings from more recent eras sometimes superimposed over older paintings. Some sites are kept secret – not only to protect them from damage, but also because they are private or sacred

Rock paintings, Nourlangie Rock, Kakadu National Park; courtesy of the NT Tourist Commission.

to the Aborigines. Some are even believed to be inhabited by dangerous beings, who must not be approached by the ignorant. However, two of the finest sites have been opened up to visitors, with access roads, walkways and explanatory signs. These are Ubirr and Nourlangie Rock. Park rangers conduct free art-site tours once or twice a day from May to October. (For more information see the Ubirr and Nourlangie Rock sections in the Northern Territory chapter.)

The rock paintings show how the main styles succeeded each other over time. The earliest hand or grass prints were followed by a 'naturalistic' style, with large outlines of people or animals filled in with colour. Some of the animals depicted, such as the thylacine (or Tasmanian tiger), have long been extinct in mainland Australia. Other paintings are thought to show large beasts which roamed the world and which were wiped out millennia ago.

After the naturalistic style came the 'dynamic', in which motion was often cleverly depicted (a dotted line, for example, to show a spear's path through the air). In this era the first mythological beings appeared – with human bodies and animal heads.

The next style mainly showed simple human silhouettes, and was followed by the curious 'yam figures', in which people and animals were drawn in the shape of yams (or yams in the shape of people/animals!). Yams must have been an important food source at this time, about 8000 years ago, when the climate was growing increasingly damp. As the waters rose, much of what is now Kakadu National Park became covered with salt marshes. Many fish were depicted in the art of this period, and the so-called 'x-ray' style, which showed the creatures' bones and internal organs, made its appearance.

By about 1000 years ago many of the salt marshes had turned into freshwater swamps and billabongs. The birds and plants which provided new food sources in this landscape appeared in the art of this time.

From around 400 years ago, Aboriginal artists also depicted the human newcomers to the region – Macassan fisherpeople and, more recently, the Europeans – and the things they brought, or their transport such as ships or horses.

Bark Paintings

While the bark painting tradition is a more recent art form than rock art, it is still an important part of the cultural heritage of Arnhem Land Aborigines. It's difficult to establish when bark was first used, partly because it is perishable and old pieces simply don't exist. European visitors in the early 19th century noted the practice of painting the inside walls of bark shelters. The bark used is from the stringybark tree (*Eucalyptus tetradonta*), and it is taken off in the wet season when it is moist and supple. The rough outer layers are removed and the bark is then dried by placing it over a fire and then under weights on the ground to keep it flat. Drying is complete within about a fortnight, and the bark is then ready for use. Most bark paintings made today have a pair of sticks across the top and bottom of the sheet to keep it flat.

The pigments used in bark paintings are mainly red and yellow (ochres), white (kaolin) and black (charcoal). Because these were

Kumoken (Freshwater Crocodile) with Mimi Spirits by Djawida, b.c. 1935, Yulkman clan; Kunwinjku language, Kurrudjmuh, western Arnhem Land; earth pigments on bark; 151 x 71cm; 1990; purchased 1990; National Gallery of Victoria.

the only colours available their source was an important place. The colour could only be gathered by the traditional owners, and it was then traded. Even today it is these natural pigments which are used, giving the paintings their superb soft and earthy finish. Binding agents such as birds' egg yolks, wax and plant resins were added to the pigments. Recently these have been replaced by synthetic agents such as wood glue. Similarly, the brushes used in the past were obtained from the bush materials at hand – twigs, leaf fibres, feathers, human hair and the like – but these too have largely been done away with in favour of modern brushes.

One of the main features of Arnhem Land bark paintings is the use of cross-hatching designs. These designs identify the particular clans, and are based on body paintings of the past. The paintings can also be broadly categorised by their regional styles. In the west the tendency is towards naturalistic images and plain backgrounds, while to the east the use of geometric designs is more common.

The art reflects Dreaming themes, and once again these vary by region. In eastern Arnhem Land the prominent ancestor beings are the Djangkawu, who travelled the land with elaborate dilly bags and digging sticks (which they used to create waterholes each time

Some Animals Have Secret Songs by Amy Johnson Jirwulurr, born about 1953; language group Wagilak; domicile Ngukurr, NT; synthetic polymer paint on cotton duck; 90 x 106cm; 1988; represented by Alcaston House Gallery, Melbourne.

Gabal Ritual by Willie Gudabi, born about 1916;
language group Alawa; domicile Ngukurr, NT;
synthetic polymer paint on lanaquarelle paper;
75 x 55cm; 1993;
represented by Alcaston House Gallery, Melbourne.

they stopped), and the Wagilag Sisters, who are associated with snakes and water holes. In western Arnhem Land the Rainbow Serpent, Yingarna, is the significant being (according to some clans), but one of her offspring, Ngalyod, and Nawura are also important. The *mimi* spirits are another feature of western Arnhem Land art, both on bark and rock. These mischievous spirits are attributed with having taught the Aborigines of the region many things, including hunting, food gathering and painting skills.

Fibre Art
Articles made from fibres are a major art form among the women. While the string and pandanus-fibre dilly bags, skirts, mats and nets all have utilitarian purposes, many also have ritual uses.

Hollow-Log Coffins
Hollowed-out logs were often used for reburial ceremonies in Arnhem Land, and were also a major form of artistic expression. They were highly decorated, often with many of the Dreaming themes, and were known as *dupun* in eastern Arnhem Land and *lorrkon* in western Arnhem Land.

In 1988 a group of Arnhem Land artists made a memorial as their contribution to the movement highlighting injustices against Aborigines – this was, of course, the year when non-Aboriginal Australians were celebrating 200 years of European settlement. The artists painted 200 log coffins – one for each year of settlement – with traditional clan and Dreaming designs, and these now form a permanent display in the National Gallery in Canberra.

Ngukurr Contemporary Painting
Since the late 1980s the artists of Ngukurr (nook-or), near Roper Bar in south-eastern Arnhem Land, have been producing works using acrylic paints on canvas. Although ancestral beings still feature prominently, the works are generally much more 'modern' in nature, with free-flowing forms and often little in common with traditional formal structure.

TIWI ISLAND ART
Due to their isolation, the Aborigines of the Tiwi Islands (Bathurst and Melville islands off the coast of Darwin) have developed art forms – mainly sculpture – not found anywhere else, although there are some similarities with the art of Arnhem Land.

The *pukumani* burial rites are one of the main rituals of Tiwi religious life, and it is for these ceremonies that many of the art

Tiwi art is derived from ceremonial body painting and the ornate decoration applied to funerary poles, *yimawilini* bark baskets and associated ritual objects made for the *pukamani* ceremony, which is held at the grave site approximately six months after burial. The ceremony marks the conclusion of formal mourning and the lifting of complex taboos associated with death.

Traditionally, the participants decorate themselves with a variety of ochre designs so as to conceal their true identity from the malevolent *mapurtiti*, the spirits of the dead. Tiwi art generally avoids specific reference to totems, dreamings or stories connected with the *palaneri* (Creation period).

Pukamani funerary poles and bark baskets installation; Milikapiti, Melville Island, NT; represented by Alcaston House Gallery, Melbourne.

works are created – *jimwalini* (bark baskets), spears and *tutini* (burial poles). These carved and painted ironwood poles, up to 2.5 metres long, are placed around the grave, and represent features of that person's life.

In the last 50 or so years the Tiwi islanders have been producing sculptured animals and birds, many of these being Creation ancestors. (The Darwin Museum of Arts & Sciences has an excellent display.) More recently, bark painting and silk-screen printing have become popular, and there are workshops on both islands where these items are produced. (For more information see the section on the Bathurst and Melville islands in the Northern Territory chapter.)

KIMBERLEY ART

The art of the Kimberley is most famous for its Wandjina images – a group of ancestor beings who came from the sky – but other styles also exist.

The Wandjina generally appear in human form, with large black eyes, a nose but no mouth, a halo around the head (representative of both hair and clouds), and a black oval shape on the chest. These beings were responsible for the formation of the country's natural features, and were also thought to control the elements. The images of the Wandjina are found on rock as well as on more

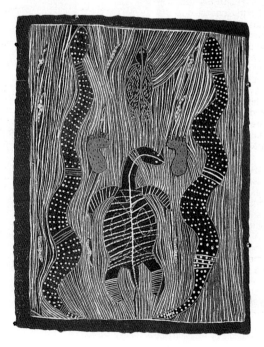

Walker River, NT by Djitjima Ngalandarra Wilfred, born about 1927; language group Ritangu; domicile Walker River, NT; synthetic polymer paint on lanaquarelle paper; 63 x 67cm; 1992; represented by Alcaston House Gallery, Melbourne.

recent portable art media, with some of the rock images being more than six metres long.

Another art form from the western Kimberley is the engraved pearl-shell pendants which come from the Broome area. It is believed that the Aborigines of the area were using pearl shell for decoration before the arrival of Europeans, but with the establishment of the pearling industry in Broome late last century the use of pearl shell increased markedly. Traditionally the shells were highly prized, and so were engraved and then used for a number of purposes – ceremonial, personal decoration and trade – examples of this art have been found as far away as Queensland and South Australia.

The designs engraved into the shells were usually fairly simple geometric patterns which had little symbolic importance. The practice of pearl-shell engraving has largely died out, although the decorated shells are still highly valued.

Art in the eastern Kimberley also features elements of the works of the desert peoples of central Australia, a legacy of the forced movement of people during the 1970s. The community of Warmun at Turkey Creek on the Great Northern Highway has been particularly active in ensuring that Aboriginal culture through painting and dance remains strong.

NORTH QUEENSLAND ART

In North Queensland it is once again the rock art which predominates. The superb 'Quinkan' galleries at Laura on the Cape York Peninsula, north of Cairns, are among the best known in the country. Among the many creatures depicted on the walls, the main ones are the Quinkan spirits, which are shown in two forms – the long and stick-like Timara, and the crocodile-like Imjim with their knobbed, club-like tails.

A number of ceremonial items were also traditionally produced in this area, with perhaps the best known being the men's decorated shields. These were mainly used for ritual purposes, but they were also put to practical use when fighting between clans occurred. Other items included clubs, boomerangs and woven baskets, many of which also carried painted designs.

URBAN ART

While the works of rural artists based on traditional themes is the high-profile side of Aboriginal art, another important aspect is the works produced by city-based Aborigines. As much of this work has strong European influences, it was often not regarded as an authentic form of Aboriginal art – this view has since changed.

A major impetus in the development of urban art was the Aboriginal land rights movement, which started to gain momentum in the 1970s. Images depicting the dispossession of the Aborigines and the racist treatment they had received became powerful symbols in their struggle for equality.

Although much of the work being produced still carries strong political and social comment, these days the range has become broader.

David Mpetyane paints and writes within the context of his joint ancestral background and his awareness of present and past. He lives and works in Alice Springs, and is influenced by the contemporary life of the community around him, while also using first-contact stories and his strong identification with the land. His imagination is fired by the anger and beauty of the natural environment, as he relives the Creation period journeys of his ancestors and weaves their stories into his present life. David's painting *Perfect Place for Philosophy and Waste* was inspired by the following poem.

Fertility

Alice lost her virginity
Witness by
The old man gum tree
While the dog sat confused
Patiently licking its wounds
She gave birth
To one stone room
Next a shed then a house

She then stepped one step south
Before the caterpillars knew
Alice grew
With the scenery so strong
The old man gum tree
Witness Alice lose her virginity
Long before me

David Mpetyane, 1992

Perfect Place for Philosophy and Waste by David Mpetyane, born 1963; language group Central/Western Aranda; domicile Alice Springs, NT; synthetic polymer paint on linen; 110 x 183cm; 1992; represented by Alcaston House Gallery, Melbourne.

DAVID MPETYANE
92

Facts for the Visitor

VISAS & EMBASSIES

Once upon a time, Australia was fairly free and easy about who was allowed to visit, particularly if you were from the UK or Canada. These days, only New Zealanders get any sort of preferential treatment and even they need at least a passport; they can get visas issued on the spot. Everybody else must apply for a visa in advance.

Visa application forms are available from travel agents or Australian diplomatic missions overseas, and you can apply by mail or in person. There are several different types of visas, depending on the reason for your visit.

Australian Diplomatic Representatives

Australian embassies and consular offices overseas include:

Canada
Suite 710, 50 O'Connor St, Ottawa K1P 6L2 (☎ (613) 236 0841)
– also in Toronto and Vancouver
China
15 Dongzhimenwai Dajie, San Li Tun, Beijing (☎ (1) 532 2331)
Denmark
Kristianagade 21, 2100 Copenhagen (☎ 3126 2244)
France
4 Rue Jean Rey, Paris, 15ème (☎ (1) 40 59 33 00)
Germany
Godesberger Allee 107, 5300 Bonn 1 (☎ (0228) 8 10 30)
– also in Frankfurt and Berlin
Greece
37 Dimitriou Soutsou St, Ambelokpi, Athens 11512 (☎ (01) 644 7303)
Hong Kong
Harbour Centre, 24th floor, 25 Harbour Rd, Wanchai, Hong Kong Island (☎ (5) 73 1881)
India
Australian Compound, No 1/50-G Shantipath, Chanakyapuri, New Delhi 110021 (☎ 60 1336)
– also in Bombay
Indonesia
Jalan Thamrin 15, Gambir, Jakarta (☎ (21) 323109)
– also in Denpasar

Ireland
Fitzwilton House, Wilton Terrace, Dublin 2 (☎ (01) 76 1517)
Italy
Via Alessandria 215, Rome 00198 (☎ (06) 832 721)
– also in Milan
Japan
2-1-14 Mita, Minato-ku, Tokyo (☎ (3) 5232 4111)
– also in Osaka
Malaysia
6 Jalan Yap Kwan Seng, Kuala Lumpur 50450 (☎ (03) 242 3122)
Netherlands
Carnegielaan 12, 2517 KH The Hague (☎ (070) 310 82 00)
New Zealand
72-78 Hobson St, Thorndon, Wellington (☎ (4) 73 6411)
– also in Auckland
Papua New Guinea
Independence Drive, Waigani, Port Moresby (☎ 25 9333)
Philippines
Bank of Philippine Islands Building, Paseo de Roxas, Makati, Manila (☎ 817 7911)
Singapore
25 Napier Rd, Singapore 10 (☎ 737 9311)
South Africa
4th Floor, Mutual & Federal Centre, 220 Vermeulen St, Pretoria 0002 (☎ (012) 325 4315)
Sweden
Sergels Torg 12, Stockholm C (☎ (08) 613 2900)
Switzerland
29 Alpenstrasse, Berne (☎ (031) 43 01 43)
– also in Geneva
Thailand
37 South Sathorn Rd, Bangkok 10120 (☎ (2) 287 2680)
UK
Australia House, The Strand, London WC2B 4LA (☎ (071) 379 4334)
– also in Edinburgh and Manchester
USA
1601 Massachusetts Ave NW, Washington DC, 20036 (☎ (202) 797 3000)
– also in Los Angeles, Chicago, Honolulu, Houston, New York and San Francisco

Tourist Visas

Tourist visas are issued by Australian consular offices; they are the most common and are generally valid for a stay of up to six months within a 12-month period. If you intend staying less than three months, the visa is free; otherwise there is a $30 processing fee.

When you apply for a visa, you need to present your passport and a passport photo, as well as signing an undertaking that you have an onward or return ticket and 'sufficient funds' – the latter is obviously open to interpretation. Like those of any country, Australian visas seem to cause their hassles, although the authorities do seem to be more uniform in their approach these days.

Working Visas

Young visitors from Britain, Ireland, Canada, the Netherlands and Japan may be eligible for a 'working holiday' visa. 'Young' is fairly loosely interpreted as around 18 to 26, and working holiday means up to 12 months, but the emphasis is supposed to be on casual employment rather than a full-time job, so you are only supposed to work for three months. Officially this visa can only be applied for in your home country, but some travellers report that the rule can be bent.

See the section on Working, later in this chapter, for details of what sort of work is available and where.

Visa Extensions

The maximum stay allowed to visitors in Australia, including extensions, is one year.

Visa extensions are made through Department of Immigration & Ethnic Affairs offices in Australia and, as the process takes some time, it's best to apply about a month before your visa expires. Any extension up to the first three months is considered 'short stay' and carries an application fee of $100; over three months is 'long stay' and the fee is $200 – and even if they turn down your application they can still keep your money! To qualify for an extension you are required to have medical insurance to cover the period of the extension, a ticket out of the country, and 'proof of funds'. Some offices are more strict in enforcing these conditions than others.

If you're trying to stay for longer in Australia, the books *Temporary to Permanent Resident in Australia* and *Practical Guide to Obtaining Permanent Residence in Australia*, both published by Legal Books, might be useful.

It's very difficult (some say impossible) to alter your status from visitor to resident while in Australia. In the past this was easier – especially if you married or entered into a de facto relationship with an Australian resident – but the rules were tightened considerably in the late 1980s, early 1990s. Now you'll probably have to go back home to reapply regardless of your personal circumstances.

Foreign Embassies & Consulates

The principal diplomatic representations to Australia are in Canberra. There are also representatives in various other major cities, particularly from countries with major connections with Australia like the USA, UK or New Zealand; or in cities with important connections, like Darwin which has an Indonesian consulate. Big cities like Sydney and Melbourne have nearly as many consular offices as Canberra has embassies, although visa applications are generally handled in Canberra. Look up addresses in the Yellow Pages phone book under 'Consulates & Legations'.

Embassies and high commissions in Canberra (telephone code 06) include:

Austria
    12 Talbot St, Forrest (☎ 295 1533)
Canada
    Commonwealth Ave, Yarralumla (☎ 273 3844)
Germany
    119 Empire Court, Yarralumla (☎ 270 1911)
Indonesia
    8 Darwin Ave, Yarralumla (☎ 273 3222)
Ireland
    20 Arkana St, Yarralumla (☎ 273 3022)
India
    3 Moonah Place, Yarralumla (☎ 273 3999)
Japan
    112 Empire Circuit, Yarralumla (☎ 273 3244)
Malaysia
    7 Perth Ave, Yarralumla (☎ 273 1543)

Netherlands
    120 Empire Circuit, Yarralumla (☎ 273 31₄1)
New Zealand
    Commonwealth Ave, Yarralumla (☎ 270 4211)
Norway
    17 Hunter St, Yarralumla (☎ 273 3444)
Papua New Guinea
    Forster Crescent, Yarralumla (☎ 273 3322)
Singapore
    Forster Crescent, Yarralumla (☎ 273 3944)
South Africa
    State Circle, Yarralumla (☎ 273 2424)
Sweden
    Turrana St, Yarralumla (☎ 273 3033)
Switzerland
    7 Melbourne Ave, Forrest (☎ 273 3977)
Thailand
    111 Empire Circuit, Yarralumla (☎ 273 1149)
UK
    Commonwealth Ave, Yarralumla (☎ 270 6666)
USA
    21 Moonah Place, Yarralumla (☎ 270 5000)

TRAVEL PERMITS

If you intend to travel through the outback on your own, see the Getting Around chapter for the permits you may need if you wish to enter Aboriginal land or camp in national parks.

CUSTOMS

When entering Australia you can bring most articles in free of duty provided that Customs is satisfied they are for personal use and that you'll be taking them with you when you leave. There's also the usual duty-free quota per person of one litre of alcohol, 250 cigarettes and dutiable goods up to the value of A$400.

With regard to prohibited goods, there are two areas you need to pay particular attention to. Number one is, of course, dope – Australian Customs have a positive mania about the stuff and can be extremely efficient when it comes to finding it. Unless you want to make first-hand investigations of conditions in Australian jails (not very good), don't bring any with you. This particularly applies if you are arriving from South-East Asia or the Indian Subcontinent.

Problem two is animal and plant quarantine. You will be asked to declare all goods of animal or vegetable origin – wooden spoons, straw hats, the lot – and show them to an official. The authorities are naturally keen to prevent weeds, pests or diseases getting into the country – Australia has so far managed to escape many of the agricultural pests and diseases prevalent in other parts of the world. Fresh produce is also unpopular, particularly meat, sausages, fruit, vegetables, flowers and flower bulbs (there are even restrictions on taking fruit and vegetables between states within Australia).

Weapons and firearms are either prohibited or require a permit and safety testing. Other restricted goods include products (such as ivory) made from protected wildlife species, non-approved telecommunications devices and live animals.

When it is time to leave, there are duty-free stores at the international airports and their associated cities. Treat them with healthy suspicion. 'Duty-free' is one of the world's most overworked catch phrases, and it is often just an excuse to sell things at prices you can easily beat by a little shopping around.

MONEY
Currency

Australia's currency is the Australian dollar, which consists of 100 cents. The dollar was introduced in 1966 to replace the old system of pounds, shillings and pence. There are coins for 5c, 10c, 20c, 50c, $1 and $2, and paper notes for $5, $10, $20, $50 and $100. There are also nasty little indestructible plastic versions of the $5 and $10 notes, which are far more common than the good old paper ones these days – the old $5 notes have all but disappeared, and the old $10 notes are rapidly heading that way.

There are no notable restrictions on importing or exporting currency or travellers' cheques except that you may not take out more than A$5000 in cash without prior approval.

Exchange Rates

In recent years the Australian dollar has fluctuated quite markedly against the US dollar, but it now seems to hover around the 70c mark – a disaster for Australians travelling overseas but a real bonus for inbound visitors.

C$1	=	A$0.99
DM 1	=	A$0.86
HK$10	=	A$1.77
NZ$1	=	A$0.82
UK£1	=	A$2.11
US$1	=	A$1.37
¥100	=	A$1.38

Changing Money

Changing foreign currency or travellers' cheques is no problem at almost any city bank. It's done quickly and efficiently and never involves the sort of headaches and grand production that changing foreign currency in the USA always entails.

However, banks in small outback towns aren't always geared up for complicated transactions and it can be a long way between banks. Make sure you have sufficient Australian funds before you head into the bush, or carry a mixture of travellers' cheques, credit cards and cash. Add a Commonwealth Bank passbook (see below) and you'll have money at your disposal almost anywhere.

Travellers' Cheques

As long as you remember that there aren't many banks in the outback, travellers' cheques are the most straightforward option if your stay is limited, and they generally enjoy a better exchange rate than foreign cash. American Express, Thomas Cook and other well-known international brands are all widely used. A passport will usually be adequate for identification; it would be sensible to carry a driver's licence, credit cards or a plane ticket in case of problems.

Commissions and fees for changing foreign currency travellers' cheques seem to vary from bank to bank and year to year. It's worth making a few phone calls to see which bank currently has the lowest charges, as they can add up.

Buying Australian dollar travellers' cheques is an option worth looking at. These can be exchanged immediately at the bank cashier's window without being converted from a foreign currency or without incurring commissions, fees and exchange-rate fluctuations.

Credit Cards

Credit cards are widely accepted in Australia, even in the outback. The most common credit card is the purely Australian Bankcard system, but Visa and MasterCard are also well established. Diners Club and American Express may not be as successful as you would hope.

Cash advances from credit cards are available over the bank counter and from many automatic teller machines (ATMs), depending on the card. If you're planning to rent cars while travelling around Australia, a credit card is looked upon with much greater favour by rent-a-car agencies than nasty old cash; many agencies simply won't rent you a vehicle if you don't have a card.

Local Bank Accounts

If you're spending a few months in Australia, it's worth considering other ways of handling money that give you more flexibility and are more economical. This applies equally to Australians setting off to travel around the country.

Most travellers these days opt for an account which includes a cash card, which you can use to access your cash day or night from ATMs found all over Australia (though hardly in the outback yet). Westpac, ANZ, National and Commonwealth bank branches are found nationwide, and it is possible to use the machines of some other banks: Westpac ATMs accept Commonwealth Bank cards and vice versa; National Bank ATMs accept ANZ cards and vice versa. A card takes about a week to issue and you'll need an Australian address.

Many businesses, such as service stations, supermarkets and convenience stores, are linked into the EFTPOS system (Electronic Funds Transfer at Point Of Sale), and at places with this facility you can use your bank cash card to pay for services or purchases direct, and sometimes withdraw a

Old cart (MC)

Cattle yard (HF)

limited amount of cash as well. Bank cash cards and credit cards can also be used to make local, STD and international phone calls in special public telephones found in many towns.

Opening an Account Opening an account at an Australian bank is not all that easy these days. A points system operates and you need to score a minimum of 100 points before you can have the privilege of letting the bank take your money. Passports, driver's licences, birth certificates (with a certified translation if they're not in English) and other 'major' IDs earn you 40 points; minor ones such as credit cards get you 20 points. Just like a game show really! Foreigners need only a passport to open a bank account within six weeks of arriving in Australia, but after that, the same rules apply.

If you don't have an Australian Tax File Number, 48% of interest earned from your funds will be collected by our old mate, the Deputy Commissioner of Taxation.

Passbook Account The easiest way of obtaining cash in the outback is with a Commonwealth Bank passbook. This is one of those old-fashioned booklets that you may have had when you were a kid, where your transactions are typed in. The Commonwealth Bank is largely government-owned and all post offices or post-office agencies throughout the country are also agencies for the bank. Not all post-office agencies have the electronic facilities to handle cards but every one of them will handle a passbook, which makes this option particularly useful.

A Passbook Account can be opened on the spot at any Commonwealth Bank branch. Make sure you get a passbook with a black-light signature or you may not be able to use it everywhere. You usually have to return to the same branch to close the account when the time comes to leave Australia, but many people don't worry about that last dollar.

Costs

Compared to the USA, Canada and European countries, Australia is cheaper in some ways and more expensive in others. Manufactured goods tend to be more expensive if they're imported, and if they're locally manufactured they suffer from the extra costs entailed in making things in comparatively small quantities. Thus you pay more for clothes, cars and other manufactured items. On the other hand, food is both high in quality and low in cost; accommodation is also very reasonably priced.

The biggest cost in any trip to Australia is transport, simply because it's such a vast country. If there's a group of you, buying a second-hand car is probably the most economical way to go. Fuel is cheap, though more expensive than in the USA and you'll need lots of it.

Freight charges increase the cost of everything in the outback, adding 20% to 30% to city prices even in a major centre like Alice Springs. Fuel is also more expensive, not just because of freight but because most roadhouses and the like have to produce their own electricity using diesel generators. Another problem is the difficulty of attracting reliable labour, as relatively few people who aren't intent on escaping something (whether it be the law, their spouse or personal problems) are interested in leaving the comforts of town life to work in the bush. Tourists who complain at the high prices charged by remote roadhouses seldom have any appreciation of what it costs to provide the service.

Tipping & Bargaining

Tipping isn't entrenched in Australia the way it is in the USA or Europe. It's only customary to tip in more expensive restaurants and only then if you want to. If the service has been especially good and you decide to leave a tip, 10% of the bill is the usual amount. Taxi drivers don't expect tips (of course, they don't hurl it back at you if you decide to leave the change). In many parts of the outback the old egalitarian attitude persists, and tipping may still be considered slightly offensive, especially in pubs.

Bargaining is not at all common, and in the outback in particular it may be considered offensive. In markets and second-hand shops in the bigger cities, however, you could sometimes give it a try ('These three books cost $4 each. How about 10 bucks for the lot?').

WHEN TO GO

Roughly speaking, January-February is the middle of summer in the lower three-quarters of Australia and July-August is the middle of winter (see Climate in the Facts about the Outback chapter). Up in the monsoon belt, where the temperature remains relatively constant all year, 'summer' is the wet season and 'winter' is the dry season. The best time to visit either the Centre, the Kimberley, the Top End or Cape York is May to October. July is ideal, but everyone knows that and the popular spots fill up fast.

Some people visit the Centre in January, and this is indeed possible if they're well prepared, carry plenty of water, and stick to the busy routes – every year several travellers die of exposure when their vehicles break down in remote areas. Daytime temperatures may hover around 40°C at the height of summer and often reach the mid-40s in the hotter parts of central Australia; add the blazing sun – which seems to shine much brighter in Australia than elsewhere – and physical activities such as cycling and walking are pretty much out of the question. Motorcyclists should take great care with dehydration; car drivers may find the going uncomfortable without air-conditioning.

There's really not much point visiting the Centre in summer unless you're out to prove something. You'll be pretty much confined to the air-conditioned cocoon of your car and roadhouse; when you brave the furnace outside, the fauna is in hiding, the flora seems quite dead but the bushflies are a nightmare. You'll enjoy the Centre much more from May to October, when the climate is more agreeable and nature comes to life, especially after a burst of rain – the wildflowers in particular are worth going a long way to see.

The wet season in the Top End and Cape York occurs somewhere between November and May. The rains can be late or early and their unpredictability is a popular topic of discussion, though everyone seems relieved when they finally begin. Unsealed roads turn to bottomless mud, dry creeks become raging torrents, low-lying areas become vast, shallow lakes, and whole regions are cut off from the rest of the world for weeks at a time.

However, an increasing number of tourists are discovering that the wet season can also be a good time to visit the Top, the Kimberley or the Cape: there's no dust, the tropical vegetation is lush, the fauna is active, the many waterfalls are at their most spectacular, and you'll never forget those fierce electrical storms. If you can handle hot and humid conditions and don't plan on driving (or can stick to sealed roads that haven't been cut by floods), you'll find quiet tourist facilities and bargain package deals. The biggest drawback about visiting the north in the Wet is that you can't cool off in the sea because of the dreaded 'stingers', or box jellyfish (see the Fauna section in the Facts about the Outback chapter).

Another consideration when travelling anywhere in Australia is school holidays. Australian families take to the road (and air) en masse at these times and many places are booked out, prices rise and things generally get a bit crazy. Holidays vary somewhat from state to state, but the main holiday period is from mid-December to late January; the other two-week periods are roughly early to mid-April, late June to mid-July, and late September to early October.

TOURIST OFFICES

There are a number of information sources for visitors to Australia and, in common with a number of other tourist-conscious Western countries, you can easily drown yourself in brochures and booklets, maps and leaflets.

Local Tourist Offices

Within Australia, tourist information is handled by the various state and local offices. Most states and the ACT and Northern Territory have a main office in the capital cities, as well as regional offices in main tourist centres and also in other states. (The exception is Victoria, where Tourism Victoria has its head in the corporate clouds and refers common people to the state automobile association, the RACV.)

As well as supplying brochures, price lists, maps and other information, the state offices will often book transport, tours and accommodation for you. Unfortunately, very few of the state tourist offices maintain information desks at the airports and, furthermore, the opening hours of the city offices are very much of the 9-to-5 weekdays and Saturday-morning-only variety. Addresses of the main state tourist offices are:

Australian Capital Territory
    Canberra Tourist Bureau, Jolimont Centre, Northbourne Ave, Canberra City, ACT 2601 (☎ toll-free 1800 026 166)
New South Wales
    NSW Government Travel Centre, 19 Castlereagh St, Sydney, NSW 2000 (☎ (02) 231 4444)
Northern Territory
    Darwin Regional Tourism Association, 31 Smith St, Darwin, NT 0800 (☎ (089) 81 4300)
Queensland
    Queen St Mall Information Centre, corner Adelaide and Albert Sts, Brisbane, Qld 4000 (☎ (07) 229 5918)
South Australia
    Tourism South Australia Travel Centre, 1 King William St, Adelaide, SA 5000 (☎ toll-free 1800 882 092)
Tasmania
    Tasmanian Travel Centre, 80 Elizabeth St, Hobart, Tas 7000 (☎ (002) 30 8250)
Victoria
    RACV Travel Centre, 230 Collins St, Melbourne, Vic 3000 (☎ (03) 650 1522)
Western Australia
    Western Australian Tourist Centre, Forrest Place, Perth, WA 6000 (☎ (09) 483 1111)

A step down from the state tourist offices are the local or regional tourist offices. Almost every major town in Australia seems to maintain a tourist office or centre of some type or other, and in many cases these have a great deal of local information not readily available from the larger, state offices. In the outback, it's worth checking the pamphlets and other information at police stations, park ranger offices and roadhouses.

Tourist offices will be happy to provide bookings and put you on to tour operators, but usually know very little about independent outback travel. The automobile associations (see Useful Organisations below) are a better bet; their head offices are often well stocked with maps and brochures of the outback in their own state.

Tourist Offices Abroad

Overseas, tourist promotion is handled by the Australian Tourist Commission (ATC). ATC offices have a useful free magazine-style booklet called *Travellers' Guide to Australia* which is a good introduction to the country, its geography, flora, fauna, states, transport, accommodation, food and so on. They also have a handy free map of the country. This literature is intended for distribution overseas only; if you want copies, get them before you come to Australia. Addresses of the ATC offices for literature requests are:

Australia
    80 William St, Woolloomooloo, Sydney, NSW 2011 (☎ (02) 360 1111)
Germany
    Neue Mainzerstrasse 22, D6000 Frankfurt/Main 1 (☎ (069) 274 00 60)
Hong Kong
    Suite 6, 10th floor, Central Plaza, 18 Harbour Rd, Wanchai (☎ 802 7700)
Japan
    8th floor, Sankaido Building, 9-13, Akasaka 1-chome, Minato-ku, Tokyo 107 (☎ (03) 3582 2191)
    4th floor, Yuki Building, 3-3-9 Hiranomachi, Chuo-Ku, Osaka 541 (☎ (06) 229 3601)
New Zealand
    Level 13, 44-48 Emily Place, Auckland 1 (☎ (09) 379 9594)
Singapore
    Suite 1703, United Square, 101 Thomson Rd, Singapore 1130 (☎ 255 4555)
South Africa
    c/o Mrs Dee Mets, 6th floor, Petrob House, 343 Surry Ave, Randburg 2125, Johannesburg (☎ (011) 787 6300)
UK
    Gemini House, 10-18 Putney Hill, London SW15 (☎ (071) 780 2227)

Henley-on-Todd Regatta (NTTC)

Bar of the pub at McKinlay (Queensland), the scene of Crocodile Dundee's 'Walkabout Creek Hotel' (R & VM)

USA
> Suite 1200, 2121 Ave of the Stars, Los Angeles, CA 90067 (☎ (213) 552 1988)
> 31st floor, 489 Fifth Ave, New York, NY 10017 (☎ (212) 687 6300)

Canadians should contact the Los Angeles or New York office; from Ireland, France or the Netherlands, contact the London office.

USEFUL ORGANISATIONS
Automobile Associations

Australia has a national automobile association, the Australian Automobile Association, but this exists mainly as an umbrella for the various state associations and to maintain international links. The day-to-day operations are all handled by the state organisations who provide breakdown service, literature, excellent maps and detailed guides to accommodation and campsites. Some of the material they produce is of a very high standard, and is relatively cheap or often free.

The state organisations have reciprocal arrangements amongst the various states in Australia and with similar organisations overseas. So, if you're a member of the National Roads & Motorists Association (NRMA) in New South Wales, you can use the facilities of the Royal Automobile Association of South Australia (RAA). Similarly, if you're a member of the AAA in the USA or the RAC or AA in the UK, you can use any of the state organisations' facilities. But bring proof of membership with you and, if you come from overseas, a letter of introduction.

The most useful state offices are:

New South Wales
> NRMA, 151 Clarence St, Sydney, NSW 2000 (☎ (02) 260 9222)

Northern Territory
> Automobile Association of the Northern Territory, 79-81 Smith St, Darwin, NT 0800 (☎ (089) 81 3837)

Queensland
> Royal Automobile Club of Queensland (RACQ), 300 St Pauls Terrace, Fortitude Valley, Qld 4006 (☎ (07) 361 2444)

South Australia
> RAA, 41 Hindmarsh Square, Adelaide, SA 5000 (☎ (08) 202 4500)

Tasmania
> RACT, corner Patrick and Murray Sts, Hobart, Tas 7000 (☎ (002) 38 2200)

Victoria
> RACV, 422 Little Collins St, Melbourne, Vic 3000 (☎ (03) 607 2137)

Western Australia
> Royal Automobile Club of Western Australia (RACWA), 228 Adelaide Terrace, Perth, WA 6000 (☎ (09) 421 4444)

National Parks Organisations

The Australian Nature Conservation Agency (ANCA), formerly the Australian National Parks & Wildlife Service, is a commonwealth body which is responsible for Kakadu and Uluru national parks in the Northern Territory, other offshore areas such as the Cocos (Keeling) Islands and Norfolk Island, and also international conservation issues such as whaling and migratory bird conventions.

The individual national park organisations in each state are state-operated, not nationally run. They tend to be a little hidden away in their capital-city locations, although if you search them out they often have excellent literature and maps on the parks. They are much more up-front in the actual parks where, in many cases, they have very good guides and leaflets to flora and fauna, geology, bushwalking, nature trails and other activities. The state offices are:

Australian Capital Territory
> Australian Nature Conservation Agency, GPO Box 636, Canberra, ACT 2601 (☎ (06) 250 0200)

New South Wales
> National Parks & Wildlife Service, 43 Bridge St, Hurstville, NSW 2220 (PO Box 1967, Hurstville, NSW 2220)

Northern Territory
> Conservation Commission of the Northern Territory, PO Box 496, Palmerston, NT 0831 (☎ (089) 89 5511)
> Australian Nature Conservation Agency, Smith St, Darwin, NT 0800 (GPO Box 1260, Darwin, NT 0801, ☎ (089) 81 5299)

Queensland
> National Parks & Wildlife Service, 160 Ann St, Brisbane, Qld 4000 (PO Box 155, North Quay, Qld 4002)

South Australia
    Department of Environment & Natural
    Resources, 77 Grenfell St, Adelaide, SA 5001
    (GPO Box 667, Adelaide, SA 5001)
Tasmania
    Department of Parks, Wildlife & Heritage, 134
    Macquarie St, Hobart, Tas 7000 (PO Box 44A,
    Hobart, Tas 7001)
Victoria
    Department of Conservation & Natural
    Resources, 240 Victoria Parade, East Melbourne,
    Vic 3002 (PO Box 41, East Melbourne, Vic 3002)
    (☎ (03) 412 4011)
Western Australia
    Department of Conservation & Land Manage-
    ment, 50 Hayman Rd, Como, Perth, WA 6152

Australian Conservation Foundation

The Australian Conservation Foundation
(ACF) is the largest nongovernment
organisation involved in conservation. Only
about 10% of its income is from the government; the rest comes from memberships and
subscriptions, and from donations (72%),
which are mainly from individuals.

The ACF covers a wide range of issues,
including the greenhouse effect and deple-
tion of the ozone layer, the negative effects
of logging, preservation of rainforests, the
problems of land degradation, and protection
of the Antarctic. It frequently works in conjunction with the Wilderness Society and
other conservation groups.

The ACF (☎ (03) 416 1455) is based at
340 Gore St, Fitzroy, Vic 3065.

Wilderness Society

The Tasmanian Wilderness Society was
formed by conservationists who were determined to prevent the damming of the
Franklin River, one of Australia's first major
conservation confrontations. In 1983, after
the High Court decided against the damming
of the Franklin, the group changed its name
to the Wilderness Society because of its Australia-wide focus on wilderness issues, such
as forest management and logging. There are
Wilderness Society shops in all states (not in
the Northern Territory) where you can buy
books, T-shirts, posters, badges etc. The
society's head office (☎ (002) 34 9366) is at
130 Davey St, Hobart, Tas 7000.

Australian Trust for Conservation Volunteers

This nonpolitical, nonprofit group organises
practical conservation projects for volunteers to take part in, such as tree planting,
track construction and flora and fauna
surveys. Travellers are welcome and it's an
excellent way to get involved with the conservation movement and, at the same time,
visit some interesting areas. Past volunteers
have found themselves working in places
such as Finke Gorge, Kakadu, Broken Hill
and many other parts of the country.

Most projects are either for a weekend or
a week and all food, transport and accommodation is supplied in return for a small
contribution to help cover costs. Most travellers who take part in ATCV activities join
a Banksia Package, which lasts four weeks
and includes six different projects. The cost
is $500, and further weeks can be added for
$120.

Contact the head office (☎ (053) 33 1483)
at PO Box 423, Ballarat, Vic 3350, or the
following state offices:

New South Wales
    23-33 Bridge St, Sydney, NSW 2000
    (☎ (02) 228 6461)
Northern Territory
    52 Temira St, Darwin, NT 0800
    (☎ (089) 81 3206)
Queensland
    Qld Government House, QUT Grounds, George
    St, Brisbane, Qld 4000 (☎ (07) 210 0330)
South Australia
    TAFE College, Brookway Dve, Campbelltown,
    Adelaide, SA 5000 (☎ (08) 365 1612)
Victoria
    13 Duke St, South Caulfield, Vic 3162
    (☎ (03) 532 8446)

WWOOFing

WWOOF (Willing Workers On Organic
Farms) is a relatively new organisation in
Australia, although it is well established in
other countries. The idea is that you do a few
hours' work each day on a farm in return for
bed and board. There are about 350
WWOOF associates in Australia, mostly in
the more developed farming areas, but a

handful would certainly qualify as 'outback'.

As the name says, the farms are supposed to be organic but that isn't always so. Some places aren't even farms – you might help out at a pottery or do the books at a seed wholesaler. There are even a few straight commercial farms which use WWOOFers as cheap harvest labour, although these are rare. Whether they have a farm or just a vegetable patch, most participants in the scheme are concerned to some extent with alternative lifestyles.

To join WWOOF (☎ (051) 55 0218), send $20 (A$25 from overseas) and a photocopy of your passport data page to WWOOF, Mt Murrindal Co-op, Buchan, Vic 3885, and they'll send you a membership number and a booklet listing WWOOF places all over Australia.

ANZSES

The Australian & New Zealand Scientific Exploration Society is a nonprofit organisation which undertakes scientific expeditions into wilderness areas of Australia. Each year over 100 volunteers are sent into the field, always under the guidance of an experienced leader.

The organisation offers volunteers the opportunity to participate in the collection of scientific data and the experience of living and working in remote areas of Australia which are generally not accessible to the average traveller.

Recent studies have included flora and fauna-gathering west of Coober Pedy and in Witjira National Park, Eungella National Park, Cedar Bay National Park, Fraser Island and Sturt National Park. ANZSES (☎ (03) 690 5455) can be contacted at PO Box 174, Albert Park, Vic 3206.

Disabled Travellers

There are a few organisations that can supply advice to disabled travellers, but many of them only operate within a single state. The office of the National Industries for Disability Services (ACROD) (PO Box 60, Curtin,

ACT 2605, ☎ (06) 282 4333) produces information sheets for disabled travellers, including lists of state-level organisations, specialist travel agents, wheelchair and equipment hire and access guides. It can also sometimes help with specific queries, and would be grateful if enquirers could send at least the cost of postage.

BUSINESS HOURS & HOLIDAYS
Business Hours

Most shops close at 5 or 5.30 pm weekdays, and either noon or 5 pm on Saturdays. In some places Sunday trading is starting to catch on, mainly in the major cities. In many cities there are one or two late-shopping nights – usually Thursday and/or Friday – when the doors stay open until 9 or 9.30 pm.

Banks are open from 9.30 am to 4 pm Monday to Thursday, and until 5 pm on Friday. Some large city branches are open from 8 am to 6 pm Monday to Friday; some are also open to 9 pm on Fridays. Of course there are exceptions to Australia's unremarkable opening hours. Some places stay open late and all weekend – particularly milk bars, but also some convenience stores, supermarkets and city bookshops.

In the outback, late-shopping nights and weekend hours are rare, and shops in remote outback towns often open and close when they please.

Holidays

The Christmas holiday season is part of the long summer school vacation and the time you are most likely to find accommodation booked out and long queues – except in the centre of the country (when it's the hottest time of the year) and in the north (when it's the wet season). There are three other, shorter school-holiday periods during the year but they vary by a week or two from state to state, falling from early to mid-April, late June to mid-July, and late September to early October.

Like school holidays, public holidays vary quite a bit from state to state. The following is a list of the main national and state public holidays:

New Year's Day
    1 January
Australia Day
    26 January
Labour Day (Vic)
    first or second Monday in March
Labour Day (WA)
    second Monday in March
Easter
    Good Friday and Easter Saturday, Sunday and
    Monday (and Tuesday in Victoria)
Anzac Day
    25 April
Labour Day (Qld)
    first Monday in May
May Day (NT)
    1 May
Adelaide Cup (SA)
    third Monday in May
Foundation Day (WA)
    first Monday in June
Queen's Birthday (Qld, NT, Vic)
    second Monday in June
Bank Holiday (NSW)
    first Monday in August
Picnic Day (NT)
    first Monday in August
Queen's Birthday (WA)
    first Monday in October
Labour Day (NSW, ACT & SA)
    first Monday in October
Melbourne Cup (Vic)
    first Tuesday in November
Christmas Day
    25 December
Boxing Day
    26 December

CULTURAL EVENTS

Some of the most enjoyable Australian festivals are, naturally, the ones that are most typically Australian – like the outback rodeos and race meetings, which draw together isolated townsfolk, the tiny communities from the huge stations and more than a few eccentric bush characters.

The following is just a brief overview of some of the more famous 'cultural' events in the Centre and Top End. Check the track descriptions later in this book for more events, and contact the relevant state tourist

Climbing Ayers Rock (TW)

authorities for exact dates, which tend to vary a bit from year to year:

July
    NT Royal Shows Agricultural shows in Darwin,
    Katherine, Tennant Creek and Alice Springs
August
    Darwin Rodeo – NT. This includes international
    team events between Australia, the USA, Canada
    and New Zealand
    Darwin Beer Can Regatta – NT. Boat races for
    boats constructed entirely out of beer cans, of
    which there are plenty in the world's beer-drink-
    ing capital
    Shinju Matsuri (Festival of the Pearl) – WA.
    Held in the old pearling port of Broome, this
    week-long festival is a great event and includes
    Asiatic celebrations
September
    Birdsville Cup – NSW. The tiny town of Birds-
    ville hosts the country's premier outback horse-
    racing event on the first weekend in September
October
    Henley-on-Todd Regatta – NT. A series of races
    for leg-powered bottomless boats on the
    (usually) dry Todd River

POST & TELECOMMUNICATIONS
Post
Australia's postal services are relatively efficient. It costs 45c to send a standard letter or postcard within Australia, while aerogrammes cost 70c. Air-mail letters/postcards cost 75/70c to New Zealand, Singapore and Malaysia, 95/90c to Hong Kong and India, $1.05/95c to the USA and Canada, and $1.20/$1 to Europe and the UK.

Post offices are open from 9 am to 5 pm Monday to Friday, but you can often get stamps on Saturday mornings from post-office agencies that operate from local newsagencies or general stores, or from the Australia Post shops found in large cities.

Receiving Mail All post offices will hold mail for visitors and some city GPOs have very busy poste restante sections. You can also have mail (but not parcels) sent to you at the American Express offices in big cities if you have an Amex card or carry Amex travellers' cheques. Although Australia Post's delivery speed compares favourably with that in many other countries, you may have to add one or two weeks for mail to/from isolated outback towns – always specify air mail.

Mail Runs One of the great traditions of the outback is the weekly mail run. For many people living and working in the vast expanses of inland Australia, their visit from the mailman (or woman) may be the only regular contact with other people for weeks or even months on end. Even with the rapid advances in communication technology, the mailman is still an important link in the spread of information – not to mention gossip – in the outback.

Some mail runs cover thousands of sq km by light plane. During the wet season in the Top End, when roads are often cut for weeks and long-distance travel by vehicle is not possible, the weekly mail plane becomes the only traffic in and out of many stations.

Other mail runs are done by truck, usually along hundreds of km of often dusty and bumpy roads. The arrival of the mail truck is a keenly awaited event, for not only does it bring the mail, but also much needed station supplies – everything from groceries to vehicle spare parts to a new refrigerator come with the mail.

Joining a mail run is a great way to experience the outback. See the Getting Around chapter for details.

Telephone
The Australian phone system used to be wholly run by government-owned Telecom, but the market has been deregulated with a second player, Optus, offering an alternative in the profitable cities, but so far only on long-distance and international calls. This has caused some resentment in the outback, since it undermines Telecom's policy of using profitable calls to subsidise an affordable telephone service for all Australians no matter where they live.

The system is efficient and, equally important, easy to use. Australia has been at the forefront of satellite communication technology, and the outback is remarkably well covered with public telephones, often solar-powered.

Local phone calls cost 40c for an unlimited amount of time. You can make local calls from gold or blue phones (often found in shops, hotels, bars etc) and from payphone booths (often solar-powered in the outback).

It's also possible to make long-distance (STD – Subscriber Trunk Dialling) calls from virtually any public phone. Many public phones accept the Telecom Phonecards, which are very convenient. The cards come in $2, $5 and $10 denominations, and are available from retail outlets such as newsagents and pharmacies which display the Phonecard logo. You keep using the card until the value has been used in calls. Otherwise, make sure you have plenty of 20c, 50c and $1 coins, and be prepared to feed them through at a fair old rate. STD calls are charged by distance and are cheaper in off-peak hours – see the front of a local telephone book for details.

Some public phones are set up to take only bank cash cards or credit cards, and these too are convenient, although you need to keep an eye on how much the call is costing as it can quickly mount up. The minimum charge for a call on one of these phones is $1.20.

Many businesses and some government departments operate a toll-free service, which means it's a free call no matter where you are ringing from around the country. These numbers have the prefix 1800 or the old toll-free prefix 008. Phone numbers with the prefix 018 are mobile or car phones. Many companies, such as the airlines, have six-digit numbers beginning with 13, and these are charged at the rate of a local call. Often they'll be Australia-wide numbers but sometimes are applicable only to a specific STD district; unfortunately there's no way of telling without actually ringing the number.

Other weird numbers you may come across are nine-digit numbers starting with 0055. These calls, usually recorded information services and the like, are provided by private companies, and your call is charged in multiples of 25c (40c from public phones) at a rate selected by the provider (Premium 70c per minute, Value 55c per minute, Budget 35c per minute).

New Numbers Australia is running out of telephone numbers, and since June 1994, AUSTEL (the Australian Telecommunications Authority) has begun adding one or two digits to numbers so that all numbers will have a total of eight digits by 1999. The campaign began in Sydney's Mona Vale area and will probably take a while to affect outback regions.

In metropolitan areas an extra digit will be added to the front of a seven-digit number to form a new eight-digit number. In regional areas the last two digits of the present area code will be added to the front of the local number to the same effect. By 1999, the nation's 54 area codes will be merged into just four: 02 will cover New South Wales and the ACT, 03 will cover Victoria and Tasmania, 07 will cover Queensland, and 08 will cover Western Australia, the Northern Territory and South Australia.

There will be a six-month period when both the old and new numbers will be accessible, followed by a further three-month period when a recorded message will refer the caller to the White Pages phone book information section. The change will not alter the cost of calls: long-distance calls will still be charged as such, even if they're within the same area code.

International Calls From most STD phones you can also make ISD (International Subscriber Dialling) calls, and if your call is brief it needn't cost very much.

All you do is dial 0011 to get out of Australia, then the country code (44 for Britain, 1 for the USA or Canada, 64 for New Zealand etc), the city code (71 or 81 for London, 212 for New York etc), and finally the subscriber number. Have a Phonecard, credit card or plenty of coins to hand.

To use Optus rather than Telecom, which is only possible from private phones and may or may not be slightly cheaper (the two are constantly trying to undercut one another), you may have to dial 1 or 1456 before the ISD country code or STD area code. In 1994, telephone subscribers in the larger cities were asked whether they wanted Telecom or Optus as their 'main carrier'. Those who chose Optus can just dial normally (0011 etc); those who chose Telecom will have to dial 1456 before any other codes if they want a particular call to go through Optus. Those who haven't yet had a ballot – and this includes most of outback Australia – should dial 1 for Optus, though many of the older exchanges in the outback don't allow calls through Optus at all.

Overseas calls are relatively cheap by international standards. Off-peak times, if available, vary depending on the destination – see the front of any telephone book for more details. Weekends are often the cheapest times to ring.

Country Direct Country Direct is a service that gives travellers in Australia direct access to operators in 42 other countries. You can talk to an operator in your home country in your own language and make collect (reverse-charges) calls, have calls charged to your phone-company credit card or perform other credit feats. For a full list of the countries hooked into this system, check the local telephone book or ring international directory enquiries. Some of them include: Canada (☎ 1800 881 150), Germany (☎ 1800 881 490), Japan (☎ 1800 881 810), New Zealand (☎ 1800 881 640) and the UK (☎ 1800 881 440 for BT and 1800 881 417 for Mercury). To the USA, you can go through AT&T (☎ 1800 881 011), IDB WorldCom (☎ 1800 881 212), MCI (☎ 1800 881 100) or Sprint (☎ 1800 881 877).

Radio Communications

Radio communications play an important role in the outback. Most travellers manage perfectly well without a radio, but in the more remote areas it can be an important safety feature. When travelling in convoy, the ability to communicate with each other on the move can make the trip more enjoyable too.

CB Radio CB radio comes in two forms, working in two frequency bands. The cheaper of the two is AM in the 27MHz frequency range, while the dearer is UHF in the 477MHz band. Both bands have 40 channels to choose from; channel 9 is reserved for emergency contact on the 27MHz band, and channel 5 on the UHF sets.

The cheapest sets on the market are the pure AM sets (from under $100), but these are pretty limited in what they can do and are built to a price. The better 27MHz set is an AM/SSB (single sideband) unit ($250 to $300), and while both units can talk to one another and are good for inter-vehicle communication, the SSB facility gives a longer range. This function may be unreliable and completely unpredictable, but is of some use as a safety feature.

The UHF sets can be expensive ($500 to $800), and while they give good and clear inter-vehicle communication, they are really only a line-of-sight communication device. In the more settled areas of Australia their

Ruins near Flinders Ranges (PS)

range has been improved by the use of repeater towers, but you need to know the required channels in the respective areas.

For anybody travelling with another vehicle, a CB radio is a great boon. You can yarn to one another, tell the second vehicle of the need to close a gate, of a large dip in the road, or whatever.

All CB radios need to be licensed (though you don't have to study for this) and a callsign is issued to each set registered with the Spectrum Management Agency. The agency has offices in each state capital as well as some major regional centres.

Callsigns use the radio alphabet, ie callsign 7VAB would be spoken as 'Seven Victor Alpha Bravo'.

HF Outpost Radio For those travelling the remote areas of Australia, an HF (high-frequency) radio is the way to go. 'Outpost' refers to any building or vehicle that doesn't have direct contact with the normal telephone service. People without radio qualifications can get units that are set up for the Royal Flying Doctor Service (RFDS) or the government-controlled Telstra (OTC) frequencies, or several other professional safety organisations. For emergency situations an RFDS HF set will be your best choice.

These radios are expensive: a reliable second-hand unit can cost at least $1000, while a new unit is up to $3500. However, they can be hired from the RFDS or from a number of good radio outlets in the capital cities for about $50 a week. Whether you buy one or hire one, you'll need a Mobile Outpost Station Licence issued by the Spectrum Management Agency, though this doesn't require study.

These sets are mainly meant for long-distance communication up to 3000 km. You can talk from one mobile unit to another or from a mobile to a base, or to an RFDS base or a Telstra base.

The RFDS system provides emergency medical aid right throughout the outback and is on call, for an emergency, 24 hours a day, 365 days a year. Its bases also provide a radio-telephone (radphone) service where, for a small charge, you can call the base and have a call put through to the telephone service. This service operates during business hours, five days a week.

Telstra operates from its six bases around the Australian coastline. It provides a number of communication services including a radphone service. This is available 24 hours a day, 365 days a year. In the future it is probable that Telstra will take over the running of the RFDS bases as the RFDS drops its communications function and concentrates on its core function of providing medical aid, but at this stage they are running in parallel.

Each base operates a number of channels and these are detailed in the individual track descriptions later in this book. With the RFDS, each individual station you intend to communicate with must be contacted beforehand, an account raised, and then you can use that station for radphone calls. With Telstra you only need to register with one base, once, and you are away. For more information on Telstra, call ☎ 1800 81 0023.

If you are planning to travel a particular track, it's always a good idea to contact the relevant RFDS or Telstra base beforehand to ask whether there's anything you need to know (channel changes, road closures etc). The RFDS in particular is usually very up-to-date with its road information.

Calling a Station Before using the radio, spend a couple of hours just listening so you become familiar with what's normal for each channel. Though you need to use callsigns and the like, there is no great drama about this and nobody is going to get mad at you for saying something not quite correct. Select the RFDS or Telstra station closest to you, choose the 'primary' or 'on call' channel, tune the antenna to that channel and listen before making your call. This is important. You will be told, generally in no uncertain terms, if the channel is busy and you call over the top of whoever is talking. If the channel is busy, wait until the channel is clear or select another.

When it is free, make a voice call such as, if calling the Telstra base in Sydney, 'Sydney Radio this is Seven Victor Alpha Bravo calling. How do you read? Over.' If calling an RFDS base, such as Broken Hill, include its callsign by saying something like 'VJC Broken Hill this is Seven Victor Alpha Bravo calling. How do you read? Over.' Once you have established contact, ask for whatever you require.

Tonecall facilities (basically a distress signal) should be available on any HF set worth its salt. Selcall (a more complex version of Tonecall, which allows the base to call *you)* is available on the better sets and this does make it easier to call the required station.

If you don't succeed first time, try again. If you have no luck on one channel, try another. The time of day and other cyclic factors (seasons, sunspot cycles etc) affect radio communication. Remember the rule of thumb: the higher the sun, the higher the channel number (or frequency). Longer distances also mean higher frequencies so you may have to try a few. You'll soon get the hang of it.

The Future HF radio will be a part of the communication scene for a long time to come and will get better with such facilities as AutoRadphone coming into service by the end of 1994.

Cellular phone services cover 85% of the population in Australia but only 4% of the landmass, which makes them pretty useless in the outback.

Mobile satellite phone services came into operation at the beginning of 1994, and if you can afford to buy one ($15,000 to $20,000) and to operate it (around $2.30 a minute), they are pretty good. However, you still can't talk mobile to mobile, and as you need to aim the antenna at the satellite, you can't do a phone call while you're mobile.

TIME
Australia is divided into three time zones: Western Standard Time (Western Australia) is plus eight hours from GMT/UTC, Central

Standard Time (Northern Territory, South Australia and the Broken Hill area in New South Wales) is plus 9½ hours, and Eastern Standard Time (Tasmania, Victoria, New South Wales, Queensland) is plus 10. When it's noon in Western Australia it's 1.30 pm in the Northern Territory and South Australia, and 2 pm in the rest of the country. During the summer, things get slightly screwed up as daylight-saving time (when clocks are put forward an hour) does not operate in Western Australia or Queensland, and in Tasmania it lasts a month longer than in the other states. In 1995, Victoria and South Australia plan to join Tasmanian time, and New South Wales could be the odd one out...

ELECTRICITY
Australia runs on 240 V, 50 Hz AC. The plugs are three-pin, but not the same as British three-pin plugs. Sockets often come with their own power switch, so if your appliance doesn't work, try turning on the power at the socket. Buy your adapter before coming to Australia; the ones available locally are intended for Australians going overseas and won't be of any use to you. You can bend US plugs to a slight angle to make them fit, but beware of the difference in voltage.

WEIGHTS & MEASURES
Australia went metric in the early 1970s. Petrol and milk are sold by the litre, apples and potatoes by the kg, distance is measured by the metre or km, and speed limits are in km per hour (km/h). Many people in country areas and the outback still think in miles and (imperial) gallons and pints. Australia-wide, fuel consumption is still often referred to in miles per gallon (29 mpg is roughly 10 km per litre), and almost everybody still quotes tyre pressures in pounds per square inch (28 psi is roughly two kg per sq cm).

For those who need help with metric, there's a conversion table at the back of this book.

BOOKS & MAPS
In almost any bookshop in the country you'll

find a section devoted to Australiana with books on every Australian subject you care to mention. The outback features prominently, especially among the coffee-table books; Penny van Oosterzee's *The Centre – The Natural History of Australia's Desert Regions* is one of the more affordable and informative; the two-volume *Australia's Wilderness Heritage*, published by Angus & Robertson, is quite affordable in its paperback version and is filled with stunning photographs. At the Wilderness Society shops in each capital city and the Government Printing Offices in Sydney and Melbourne you'll find a good range of wildlife posters, calendars and books.

Aborigines

The Australian Aborigines by Kenneth Maddock is a good cultural summary. The award-winning *Triumph of the Nomads* by Geoffrey Blainey chronicles the life of Australia's original inhabitants, and convincingly demolishes the myth that the Aborigines were 'primitive' people trapped on a hostile continent – the book's an excellent read.

For a sympathetic historical account of what happened to the original Australians since Whites arrived, read *Aboriginal Australians* by Richard Broome. *A Change of Ownership* by Mildred Kirk covers similar ground to Broome's book, but does so more concisely, focusing on the land rights movement and its historical background.

The Other Side of the Frontier by Henry Reynolds uses historical records to give a vivid account of an Aboriginal view of the arrival and takeover of Australia by Europeans. His *With the White People* identifies the essential Aboriginal contributions to the survival of the early White settlers. *My Place*, Sally Morgan's prize-winning autobiography, traces her discovery of her Aboriginal heritage. *The Fringe Dwellers* by Nene Gare describes just what it's like to be an Aborigine growing up in a White-dominated society.

Don't Take Your Love to Town by Ruby Langford and *My People* by Oodgeroo Noonuccal (Kath Walker) are also recommended reading.

History

For a good introduction to Australian history, read *A Short History of Australia*, a most accessible and informative general history by the late Manning Clark, the much-loved Aussie historian, or *The Fatal Shore*, Robert Hughes' best-seller account of the convict era.

Geoffrey Blainey's *The Tyranny of Distance* is an engrossing study of the problems of transport in this harsh continent and how they shaped the pattern of White settlement: transporting produce 100 miles by bullock cart from an inland farm to a port cost more than shipping it from there around the globe to Europe – a handicap that only wool and later gold were profitable enough to overcome.

Finding Australia by Russel Ward traces the story of the early days from the first Aboriginal arrivals up to 1821. It's strong on Aborigines, women and the full story of foreign exploration, not just Captain Cook's role. There's lots of fascinating detail, including information about the appalling crooks who ran the early colony for long periods, and it's intended to be the first of a series.

The Exploration of Australia by Michael Cannon is coffee-table book in size, presentation and price, but it's a fascinating reference book about the gradual European uncovering of the continent.

Cooper's Creek by Alan Moorehead is a classic account of the ill-fated Burke and Wills expedition which dramatises the horrors and hardships faced by the early explorers.

The Fatal Impact, also by Moorehead, begins with the voyages of Captain James Cook, regarded as one of the greatest and most humane explorers, and tells the tragic story of the European impact on Australia, Tahiti and Antarctica in the years that followed Cook's great voyages of discovery. It details how good intentions and the economic

Road sign near Broome (RI)

imperatives of the time led to disaster, corruption and annihilation.

To get an idea of life on a Kimberley cattle station last century, *Kings in Grass Castles* and *Sons in the Saddle*, both by Dame Mary Durack, are well worth getting hold of. Other books which give an insight into the pioneering days in the outback include *Packhorse & Waterhole* by Gordon Buchanan, son of legendary drover Nat Buchanan who was responsible for opening up large areas of the Northern Territory; *The Big Run*, a history of the huge Victoria River Downs cattle station in the Northern Territory; and *The Cattle King* by Ion Idriess, which details the life of the remarkable Sir Sidney Kidman, the man who set up a chain of stations in the outback early this century.

Fiction

There's no shortage of excellent Australian fiction with an outback theme. See Literature under Arts in the Facts about the Outback chapter.

Travel Accounts

Accounts of travels in Australia include the marvellous *Tracks* by Robyn Davidson. It's the amazing story of a young woman who set out alone to walk from Alice Springs to the Western Australia coast with her camels – proof that you can do anything if you try hard enough. It almost single-handedly inspired the current Australian interest in camel safaris.

Quite another sort of travel is Tony Horwitz's *One for the Road*, an often hilarious account of a high-speed hitchhiking trip around Australia (Oz through a windscreen).

Travel is also possible while standing still, as described in *Our Year in the Outback* by Michael & Susan Cusack, published by Australian Geographic. It chronicles their experiment of living in complete isolation on the Kimberley coast, and contains some fascinating insights into human relationships in adversity, illustrated with stunning photographs. Unfortunately it's out of print, but most libraries will have it.

The late Bruce Chatwin's *The Songlines* tells of his experiences among central Australian Aborigines and makes more sense of the Dreamtime, sacred sites, sacred songs and the traditional Aboriginal way of life than 10 learned tomes put together. Along the way it also delves into the origins of humankind and throws in some pithy anecdotes about modern Australia.

The journals of the early European explorers can be fairly hard going but make fascinating reading. The hardships that many of these men (and they were virtually all men) endured is nothing short of amazing. These accounts are usually available in the main libraries. Men such as Sturt, Eyre, Leichhardt, Davidson, King (on the Burke and Wills expedition), Stuart, Jardine and many others all kept detailed journals.

Travel Guides

Burnum Burnum's Aboriginal Australia is subtitled 'a traveller's guide'. If you want to explore Australia from the Aboriginal point of view, this large and lavish hardback is the book for you.

The track descriptions in this book mention literature relevant to the particular tracks. For more general reading, the late Brian Sheedy's *Outback Australia on a Budget* includes lots of practical advice and anecdotes. By the same author, *Outback on your Doorstep* describes the more accessible outback tracks within one or two days' drive from Sydney, Melbourne and Adelaide. Malcolm Gordon's *Outback Australia at Cost* focuses on the Centre, Top End and Kimberley; it's full of practical information but is a bit unwieldy.

Peter & Kim Wherrett's top-selling hardback, *Explore Australia by Four-Wheel-Drive*, is beautifully laid-out with a wealth of illustrations and maps (including a detailed road atlas of Australia), and offers solid advice on planning and vehicle preparation. However, this book omits quite a few of the tracks, and the information on the tracks it does cover is at times inaccurate.

Jeff & Mare Carter's *The Complete Guide to Central Australia* has some beautiful photographs and provides lots of knowledgeable background on flora & fauna, but has little practical information and is not very up-to-date.

Safe Outback Travel by Jack Absalom is a practical little book with basic advice on vehicle preparation and troubleshooting, general rules of outback travel, and the most important survival skills.

There are a number of other books about vehicle preparation and driving in the outback, as well as survival skills and general bushcraft. In the latter category, *Stay Alive* by Maurice Dunlevy gives practical advice on survival techniques and first aid. *The Outdoor Companion* by Q & J Chester, Paddy Pallin's *Bushwalking & Camping* and Lex Lannoy's *The Australian Bushcraft Handbook* (endorsed by the Scout Association) are all good but mainly aimed at bushwalkers and cross-country skiers. The Western Australian police force produces an excellent book titled *Aids to Survival*, which

Snow gum (TW)

covers map reading, first aid and survival techniques.

For general travel, Lonely Planet's *Australia – a travel survival kit* covers the whole country and has become an essential guidebook for most do-it-yourself travellers. LP's *Bushwalking in Australia* describes 23 walks of different lengths and difficulty in various parts of the country, though only a few of them are in 'outback' areas. LP also has guidebooks to the states of *Victoria* and *New South Wales*, city guides to *Melbourne* and *Sydney*, and an *Australian phrasebook* with detail on Aboriginal languages.

The *Outback Australia Handbook* by Moon Publications is a bit of a misnomer: apart from a few of the main sights in the Centre, west and Top End, it offers little coverage of the outback proper. There are also state-by-state Reader's Digest guides to coasts and national parks, and Gregory's guides to national parks.

Maps

Maps are absolutely essential on any outback trip. The more you carry the better, as they often contradict one another. The maps in this book will give you a good overview of the various tracks but may not show all the detail you want. The individual track descriptions list some of the most appropriate maps on a case-by-case basis, and you'd be well advised to try and get hold of them.

There's no shortage of maps available, although many of them are of pretty average quality. The various oil companies – Shell, BP, Mobil etc – publish road maps that are available from service stations. They're quite good for major roads but begin to let you down off the beaten track.

The state motoring organisations (see Useful Organisations, earlier in this chapter, for addresses) produce maps that are often free (if you're a member) or cheaper than the oil company maps. Their maps and track-note sheets of outback regions in their own states can be very good indeed. Don't forget the state tourist offices listed earlier in this chapter either: they sometimes have lovingly produced outback maps that are virtual works of art, though they won't be free.

Westprint maps produced by John Deckert are excellent and provide copious detail on points of interest, tracks and historical and tourist information. Unfortunately the Westprint catalogue of 16 outback maps is limited to southern and central Australia, but this is expanding. They're available in specialist map shops and local information centres, or through Westprint Heritage Maps (☎ (053) 91 5233, fax 91 5221) at RMB 33, Nhill, Vic 3418.

The Hema regional maps of Cape York, the Kimberley and central Australia look good and are full of useful information for travellers but aren't always as accurate as they seem. They're often available at local outlets, or contact Hema Maps (☎ (07) 290 0322, fax 290 0478) at PO Box 724, Springwood, Qld 4127.

If you want the best, get the topographic sheets put out by the national mapping agency, the Australian Surveying & Land Information Group (AUSLIG). They may be several years out of date, with indicated tracks long since abandoned and new ones formed, but their detail is staggering. Many of the more popular sheets are available over the counter at shops that sell bushwalking gear and outdoor equipment. AUSLIG also has special interest maps showing various types of land use such as population densities or Aboriginal land. For more information, or a catalogue, contact AUSLIG (☎ (06) 201 4300), Department of Administrative Services, PO Box 2, Belconnen, ACT 2616.

In every state capital there is at least one good shop that specialises in maps and guidebooks. All run a mail-order service. In Adelaide there is the Map Shop (☎ (08)231 2033), Brisbane has Hema Maps (☎ (07)221 4330), while Melbourne has the Melbourne Map Centre (☎ (03) 569 5472) and Bowyangs Map Centre (☎ (03) 853 3526). In Perth there is the Perth Map Centre (☎ (09) 322 5733), while in Sydney the Rex Map Centre (☎ (02) 428 3566) has four outlets.

MEDIA

Australia has a wide range of media, although a few big companies (Rupert Murdoch's News Corporation and Kerry Packer's Consolidated Press being the best known) own an awful lot of what there is to read and watch.

Newspapers & Magazines

Once upon a time, virtually every Australian town of any significance had its own newspaper; some still do, and these are worth reading if you want to know what's happening locally. The *Sydney Morning Herald* and the Melbourne *Age* are two of the most respected daily newspapers, but they become harder to get as you move into the outback. There's also the Murdoch-owned *Australian*, the country's only national daily, which you may be able to pick up in outback newsagencies (sometimes even on the day); it has reasonable coverage of international events. In the west the *West Australian* does a good job too.

Weekly newspapers and magazines include an Australian edition of *Time* and a combined edition of the Australian news magazine the *Bulletin* with *Newsweek*. The *Economist* and *Guardian Weekly* are sometimes available and are excellent for international news. Newsagencies also stock a wide variety of special-interest magazines.

Radio & TV

The national advertising-free TV and radio network is the ABC. In most state capitals there are a couple of ABC radio stations and a host of commercial stations, both AM and FM, featuring the whole gamut of radio possibilities, from rock and talkback to 'beautiful music'. There's also a wide variety of community radio stations that rely on volunteers and listener subscriptions.

In Sydney and Melbourne there are the ABC, three commercial TV stations and SBS, a government-sponsored multicultural TV station that beams to the state capitals and a small number of regional centres. Around the country the number of TV stations varies from place to place; there are regional TV stations but in some remote areas the ABC may be all you can receive.

Imparja is an Aboriginal-run TV station that operates out of Alice Springs and has a 'footprint' that covers one-third of the country. It broadcasts a variety of programmes, ranging from soaps to pieces made by and for Aborigines.

FILM & PHOTOGRAPHY

Australian film prices are not too far out of line with those of the rest of the Western world. Including developing, 36-exposure Kodachrome 64 or Fujichrome 100 slide film costs from around $25, but with a little shopping around you can find it for around $20 – even less if you buy in quantity.

There are plenty of camera shops in all the big cities and standards of camera service are high. Developing standards are also high, with many places offering one-hour developing of print film. Melbourne is the main centre for developing Kodachrome slide film in the South-East Asian region.

When taking photographs in the outback, allow for the exceptional intensity of the light. Best results are obtained early in the morning and late in the afternoon, when colours are 'warmer' and shadows make the different shapes in your picture stand out better. As the sun gets higher, colours appear washed out, which can be compensated to some extent with a polarising filter. You must also allow for the intensity of reflected light. Especially in the summer, you should allow for temperature extremes and do your best to keep film as cool as possible, particularly after exposure. Other film and camera hazards are dust and, in the tropical regions of the far north, humidity.

As in any country, politeness goes a long way when taking photographs – ask before taking pictures of people. Note that many Aborigines do not like to have their photographs taken, even from a distance.

HEALTH

Australia is a remarkably healthy country considering that such a large portion of it lies in the tropics. Tropical diseases such as malaria and yellow fever are unknown, diseases of insanitation such as cholera and typhoid are unheard of, and even some animal diseases such as rabies and foot-and-mouth disease have yet to be recorded. However, there are some venomous creatures in Australia that you need to beware of – see the Fauna section in the Facts about the Outback chapter.

So long as you haven't visited an infected country in the past 14 days (aircraft refuelling stops do not count) no vaccinations are required for entry. There are, however, a few routine vaccinations that are recommended worldwide whether you're travelling or not, and for the outback you might want to check whether your tetanus booster is still up to date.

Medical care is first-class and only moderately expensive. A typical visit to the doctor costs around $35. If you have an immediate health problem, contact the casualty section at the nearest public hospital or outback medical clinic. For those equipped with an HF radio able to reach the nearest Flying Doctor base, expert medical advice is available 24 hours a day via the radio's emergency call button.

Travel Insurance

Ambulance services in Australia are self-funding (ie they're not free) and can be frightfully expensive in the outback, so you'd be wise to take out travel insurance. Make sure the policy specifically includes ambulance, helicopter rescue and a flight home for you and anyone you're travelling with, should your condition warrant it. Also check the fine print: some policies exclude 'dangerous activities' such as scuba diving, motorcycling and even trekking. If such activities are on your agenda, you don't want that policy.

Medical Kit

Doctors and hospitals are few and far between in the outback. At least one person in your party should have a sound knowledge of first-aid treatment, and in any case you'll need a first-aid handbook and a basic medical kit. Some of the items that should be included are:

- Aspirin or Panadol – for pain or fever
- Antihistamine (such as Benadryl) – useful as a decongestant for colds, allergies, to ease the itch from insect bites or stings or to help prevent motion sickness. Antihistamines may cause sedation and interact with alcohol so care should be taken when using them
- Kaolin preparation (Pepto-Bismol), Imodium or Lomotil – for stomach upsets
- Antiseptic such as Betadine, which comes as impregnated swabs or ointment, and an antibiotic powder or similar 'dry' spray – for cuts and grazes
- Calamine lotion or old-fashioned Tiger Balm – to ease irritation from bites or stings
- Eye drops
- Sterile gauze bandages (50 and 75 mm)
- Triangular bandages – to support limbs and hold dressings in place
- Assortment of other bandages and Band-aids – for minor injuries
- Adhesive tape, cotton wool, tissues
- Elastic or crepe bandages – for sprains and snake bite

- Scissors, tweezers, safety pins and a thermometer (note that mercury thermometers are prohibited by airlines)
- Insect repellent, sunscreen, suntan lotion, chapstick, perhaps water purification tablets
- Pencil and note pad

Optional items include:

- Cold and flu tablets
- Mylanta tablets, or similar, for indigestion
- Ear drops (Aquaear if you're heading for the tropics)
- Rubber-pointed eye probe, eye wash
- Vinegar for jellyfish stings
- Temporary tooth-filling mix to replace fillings, loose caps
- Toothache drops
- Burn cream
- Cream/ointment for bruises and swelling due to injury
- Strepsils or similar
- Methylated spirits
- Airsplint – for broken limbs, or immobilising limbs after snake bite

St John Ambulance Australia has a selection of first-aid kits for car drivers, motorcyclists and bushwalkers, ranging in price from $45 to $85. They include a first-aid handbook and are well worth considering as a base kit to which you can add some of the above items. They're available at St John offices and at the motoring organisations.

Don't forget any medication you're already taking, and include prescriptions with the generic rather than the brand name (which may not be available locally).

Health Precautions

Travellers from the northern hemisphere need to be aware of the intensity of the sun in Australia. Those ultraviolet rays can have you burnt to a crisp even on an overcast day, so if in doubt wear protective cream, a wide-brimmed hat and loose-fitting cotton clothing that gives maximum skin coverage. Loose clothes allow the air to circulate around your skin and you'll find cotton to be much more comfortable and cooler than synthetics. Smother all exposed areas of skin with a sunscreen (protection factor 15 or higher). Australia has the world's highest incidence of skin cancer, a fact directly connected to exposure to the sun. Be careful.

Good sunglasses are a must, but make sure they're treated to absorb ultraviolet radiation – if not, they'll actually do more harm than good by dilating your pupils and making it easier for ultraviolet light to damage the retina.

If you wear glasses or contact lenses, take a spare pair and your prescription. A Medic Alert tag is worth having if your medical condition is not always easily recognisable (heart trouble, diabetes, asthma, allergic reactions to antibiotics etc).

The contraceptive pill is available on prescription only, so a visit to a doctor is necessary. Doctors are listed in the Yellow Pages phone book or you can visit the outpatients section of a public hospital. Condoms are available from chemists, many convenience stores and often from vending machines in the toilets of pubs.

Basic Rules

Heat You can expect the weather to be hot throughout the outback between October and April, and travellers from cool climates may feel uncomfortable even in winter. 'Hot' is a relative term depending on what you're used to. The sensible thing to do on a hot day is to avoid the sun between mid-morning and mid-afternoon. Infants and elderly people are most at risk from heat exhaustion and heat stroke (see below).

Water People who first arrive in a hot climate may not feel thirsty when they should; the body and 'thirst mechanism' often need a few days to adjust. The rule of thumb is that an active adult should drink at least four litres of water per day in warm weather, more when walking or cycling. Use the colour of your urine as a guide: if it's clear you're probably drinking enough but if it's dark you need to drink more. Remember that body moisture will evaporate in the dry desert air with no indication that you're sweating.

Coober Pedy wall art (TW)

Tap water is safe to drink in the settled parts of Australia, but in the outback it may be bore water that's unfit for human consumption – check with the locals. Bore water is often OK even if it tastes unpleasant, but children's stomachs in particular may have trouble coping with the high mineral content. (Note how soap often won't lather in outback showers.) There's nothing you can do short of actually distilling the water – or carrying your own supply of drinking water. Outback residents normally save valuable rainwater for drinking and use bore water for other purposes.

Always beware of natural water, as it may have been infected by cattle or wildlife. The surest way to disinfect water is to boil it thoroughly for 10 minutes. Simple filtering won't remove all dangerous organisms, so if you cannot boil water, treat it chemically. Chlorine tablets (Puritabs, Steritabs or other brand names) will kill many but not all pathogens. Iodine is very effective and is available in tablet form, such as Potable Aqua, but follow the directions carefully and remember that too much iodine can be harmful. If you can't find tablets, tincture of iodine (2%) can be used. Two drops per litre or quart of clear water is the recommended dosage, and the treated water should be left to stand for 30 minutes before drinking. Flavoured powder will disguise the taste of treated water and is a good idea if you're travelling with children.

Salt Sweating will also lead to loss of salt. Excessive salt loss manifests itself in headaches, dizziness and muscle cramps. Salt tablets are not a good idea as a preventative, but will quickly restore the balance if you show symptoms of salt loss. Add salt to your food to prevent this happening – a teaspoon a day should normally be enough in hot climates. If you're on a low-salt diet, check with your physician before you leave.

Food If you don't vary your diet, are travelling hard and fast and therefore missing meals, or simply lose your appetite, you can soon start to lose weight and place your health at risk, just as you would at home.

If you rely on fast foods dished out by roadhouses and local takeaway shops, you'll get plenty of fats and carbohydrates but little else. Remember that overcooked food loses much of its nutritional value. If your diet isn't well balanced, it's a good idea to take vitamin and iron pills. Fruit and vegetables are a good source of vitamins and they're more readily available throughout the outback than you'd expect.

Health Problems
Prickly Heat Prickly heat is an itchy rash caused by excessive perspiration trapped under the skin. It usually strikes people who have just arrived in a hot climate and whose pores have not yet opened sufficiently to cope with greater sweating. Keeping cool, bathing often, using a mild talcum powder or even resorting to air-conditioning may help until you acclimatise.

Heat Exhaustion Dehydration or salt deficiency can cause heat exhaustion. Take time to acclimatise to high temperatures and make sure you get sufficient (nonalcoholic) liquids. Think of your salt level too.

Anhydrotic heat exhaustion, caused by an inability to sweat, is quite rare. Unlike the other forms of heat exhaustion it is likely to strike people who have been in a hot climate for some time, rather than newcomers.

Heatstroke This serious, and sometimes fatal, condition can occur if the body's heat-regulating mechanism breaks down and the body temperature rises to dangerous levels. Long, continuous periods of exposure to high temperatures can leave you vulnerable to heatstroke. You should avoid excessive alcohol or strenuous activity when you first arrive in a hot climate.

The symptoms are feeling unwell, not sweating very much or at all and a high body temperature (39°C to 41°C). When sweating has ceased, the skin becomes flushed and red. Severe, throbbing headaches and lack of coordination will also occur, and the sufferer may become confused or aggressive. Eventually the victim will become delirious or convulse. Hospitalisation is essential, but meanwhile get patients out of the sun, remove their clothing, cover them with a wet sheet or towel and fan them continually.

Fungal Infections Hot-weather fungal infections are most likely to occur on the scalp, between the toes or fingers (athlete's foot), in the groin (jock itch or crotch rot) and on the body (ringworm). You get ringworm (a fungal infection, not a worm) from infected animals or by walking on damp areas, like shower floors.

To prevent fungal infections, wear loose, comfortable clothes, avoid artificial fibres, wash frequently and dry carefully. Always wear plastic sandals or thongs in showers you can't completely trust. If you do get an infection, wash the infected area daily with a disinfectant or medicated soap and water, and rinse and dry well. Apply an antifungal powder like the widely available Tinaderm. Try to expose the infected area to air or sunlight as much as possible, wash all towels and underwear in hot water and change them often.

Motion Sickness Eating lightly before and during a trip will reduce the chances of motion sickness. If you are prone to motion sickness, try to find a place that minimises disturbance – near the wing in aircraft, near the centre in cars and buses. Fresh air and looking at a steady reference point like the horizon usually help, whereas reading or cigarette smoke don't. Commercial antimotion-sickness preparations, which can cause drowsiness, have to be taken before the trip commences; when you're feeling sick it's too late. Ginger is a natural preventative and is available in capsule form.

Diarrhoea Two major causes of diarrhoea in the outback are drinking mineralised bore water and stopping at places that have been frequented by travellers with a poor understanding of hygiene. Knowing where the flies have been before they crawl over your face and food is enough to make you find somewhere else to camp. It's always a good idea to carry plenty of safe drinking water in the car, particularly if you have little children in tow – adults can usually cope better with changes in water. Various forms of gastroenteritis sometimes occur in the outback, and one of the more common ways by which it is passed around is on contaminated money.

Worms These parasites are common in outback animals. The steak that you buy at the butcher's or get served in the roadhouse will be perfectly safe, but kangaroo or wild goat that hasn't been checked by the proper authorities can be risky, especially if undercooked. Worms may also be present on unwashed vegetables, and you can pick them up through your skin by walking in bare feet.

Infestations may not show up for some time, and though they are generally not serious, if left untreated they can cause severe health problems. A stool test is necessary to pinpoint the problem, and medication is often available over the counter.

Sexually Transmitted Diseases The outback is generally a bastion of sexual conservatism, but there's a lot of alcohol about and a lot of short-term residents who don't mind partying on. Take care. Abstinence is the only 100% preventative, but using condoms is also effective (though not against pubic lice known as crabs).

Gonorrhoea and syphilis are the most common of these diseases; sores, blisters or rashes around the genitals, discharges or pain when urinating are common symptoms. Symptoms may be less marked or not observed at all in women. Syphilis symptoms eventually disappear completely but the disease continues and can cause severe problems in later years. The treatment of gonorrhoea and syphilis is by antibiotics.

Unfortunately there is no cure for herpes and there is also currently no cure for HIV/AIDS. Remember that it is impossible to detect the HIV-positive status of an otherwise healthy-looking person without a blood test.

There are numerous other sexually transmitted diseases, for most of which effective treatment is available. If you suspect anything is wrong, go to the nearest public hospital or medical clinic.

Cuts & Scratches Skin punctures can easily become infected in hot climates and may be difficult to heal. Treat any cut with an antiseptic solution and Mercurochrome. Where possible, avoid bandages and Band-aids, which can keep wounds wet. Coral cuts are notoriously slow to heal, as the coral injects a weak venom into the wound. Avoid coral cuts by wearing shoes when walking on reefs.

Women's Health
Poor diet and even contraceptive pills can lead to vaginal infections when travelling in hot climates. Maintaining good personal hygiene, and wearing skirts or loose-fitting trousers and cotton underwear will help to prevent infections.

Yeast infections (thrush), characterised by a rash, itch and discharge, can be treated with a vinegar or even lemon-juice douche or with yoghurt. Nystatin suppositories are the usual medical prescription. Trichomonas is a more serious infection; symptoms are a discharge and a burning sensation when urinating. If a vinegar-water douche is not effective, medical attention should be sought. Flagyl is the prescribed drug. In both cases, male sexual partners must also be treated.

Some women experience irregular periods when travelling because of the upset in routine. Don't forget to take time zones into account if you're on the pill. If you run into intestinal problems, the pill may not be absorbed. Ask your physician about these matters before you go.

WOMEN TRAVELLERS
Australia is generally a safe place for women travellers, although it's probably best to avoid walking alone late at night in any of the major cities. Sexual harassment is unfortunately still second nature to some Aussie males, and it's generally true to say that the further you get from 'civilisation' (ie, the big cities), the less enlightened your average Aussie male is going to be about women's issues. Outback women tend to give as well as they get, and the unenlightened outback male will show great respect for creative swearing.

Female hitchhikers should exercise care at all times. See the section on Hitching in the Getting Around chapter.

DANGERS & ANNOYANCES
Fortunately, Australia is free of carnivorous wild mammals that tear you to shreds at night, but it does have its fair share of potentially dangerous creatures such as crocodiles and snakes, and more annoying flies than you ever thought possible. See the Fauna section in the Facts about the Outback chapter.

Other dangers include the climate and the extreme isolation if something goes wrong in a remote area. Plan your outback trips carefully. Beware of abandoned mine shafts when walking in mineral-rich areas; they're often very deep and can be difficult to spot as they tend to be surrounded by ridges of excavated ore.

On the Road
Collisions with cattle, sheep and kangaroos are all too common (as the many carcasses by the side of the road will attest) but there's a simple solution: don't drive at night. Unfortunately, other drivers are even more dangerous, particularly those who drink – which happens a lot in the outback. See the Getting Around chapter for more on driving hazards.

Bushfires
Bushfires happen every year in Australia. Don't be the idiot who starts one. In hot, dry, windy weather, be extremely careful with any naked flame – no cigarette butts out of car windows, please. On a Total Fire Ban Day (listen to the radio or watch the billboards along the roads), it is forbidden even to use a camping stove in the open. The locals will not be amused if they catch you breaking

The results of a bushfire (RvD)

this particular law; they'll happily dob you in, and the penalties are severe.

If you're unfortunate enough to find yourself driving through a bushfire, stay inside your car and try to park off the road in an open space, away from trees, until the danger has passed. Lie on the floor under the dashboard, covering yourself with a wool blanket if possible. The fire front should pass quickly.

Bushwalkers should take local advice before setting out. On a Total Fire Ban Day, don't go – delay your trip until the weather has changed. Chances are that it will be so unpleasantly hot and windy, you'll be better off anyway in an air-conditioned pub sipping a cool beer.

If you're walking in the bush and you see smoke, even at a great distance, take it seriously. Bushfires move very quickly and change direction with the wind. Go to the nearest open space, downhill if possible. A forested ridge is the most dangerous place to be. Eucalypts burn easily because of their high content of volatile oil and may literally explode into flame. Heat radiation is a big killer, so cover yourself up, preferably in a less flammable material such as wool.

Fires are a part of nature, and many Australian trees and plants have come to rely on it for reproduction. In outback areas in particular, the authorities will often leave bushfires to burn themselves out if there's no immediate danger to humans.

EMERGENCY
In the case of a life-threatening situation, dial 000. This call is free from any phone and the operator will connect you with either the police, ambulance or fire brigade. To dial any of these services direct, check the inside front cover of any local telephone book.

For other telephone crisis and personal counselling services (such as sexual assault, poisons information or alcohol and drug problems), check the front pages of the local telephone book.

If you have a CB or HF radio, see Radio Communications in the Post & Telecommunications section earlier in this chapter.

SURVIVAL

The key to safe travel anywhere is preparation, and the only way you can be prepared is to research your destination. For the outback you need to find out such things as: what the temperature is likely to be; the availability of drinking water; which maps give the best coverage; and whether your vehicle is suitable for the conditions. If you're unsure, seek expert advice from local police, park rangers and the like; you may not like what they say but you would be foolish to ignore it.

There are plenty of books on bushcraft and survival, and they're all pretty good. It's well worth buying one in advance and reading it – you never know when one of those neat little tricks may save your life. See the earlier Books & Maps section.

There are a number of general survival tips to remember regardless of whether you're driving or bushwalking – and despite the outback's fierce reputation, there is plenty of excellent walking on offer.

Water

See the earlier Health section about your water needs and sources. The main thing is to carry sufficient water to get you through to the next resupply point and still have plenty in reserve for emergencies – don't forget additional supplies for washing purposes and for refilling the vehicle's radiator. If you're planning a trip, allow four to five litres' drinking water per day per person. On most tracks, around 20 litres per person is a sensible amount to carry, provided you top it up when you can, and store it in more than one container. Food is less important – the space might be better allocated to an extra spare tyre.

If your vehicle breaks down and you run out of water, use the water in your radiator only if it's free of chemical additives. When walking, it's wise to carry at least one full canteen per person even on a short walk – you never know when you might need it. Army-style canteens that can withstand hard knocks are ideal, while flimsy plastic bottles such as fruit-juice containers are not.

Register Your Intentions

In the remoteness of the outback you should always let a responsible person know details of your proposed activities so that the police will come looking for you if need be. Generally the best person to use as your insurance policy is someone who cares about you rather than a casual acquaintance – though obviously you'd register your intentions with a ranger if walking in a national park. Leave a map showing where you're going, how you're getting there and how long you expect to take. Always check in as arranged, otherwise you may spark an unnecessary search and rescue operation. This will be very expensive for you.

Safety in Numbers

It's better to travel in company, firstly for the social advantages of sharing experiences and secondly for safety. The minimum recommended number when bushwalking is three people: if someone is hurt, one person can stay to assist while the other goes for help. The silliest thing to do is to go bushwalking by yourself and not tell anyone your plans.

Getting Lost or Breaking Down

The best way to avoid getting lost is to have current large-scale maps of the area and to keep track of where you are at all times. When walking in unfamiliar terrain, always take note of the landmarks around you (including behind in case you want to return by the same route) and the direction of the sun; use a compass if you can't tell north any other way.

It's a good idea to keep a detailed running log when driving on remote tracks. Simply note each point of interest (for example a track intersection, windmill, gate or any obvious feature) and its distance from your starting point. Running logs enable you to backtrack with confidence and can also be used to advise fellow travellers.

If you do get hopelessly lost or your vehicle breaks down beyond repair it's essential not to panic, as this will more than likely make things worse. You will have told someone where you're going so the best idea is to sit quietly in the shade and conserve water supplies until the search party arrives. If you call for help on the radio, remember that the most protracted searches are often for people who confidently claim to be where they are not; only report an approximate position of which you can be absolutely sure.

To assist aerial searchers, you can lay out a large 'V' (the recognised ground-to-air visual signal for requiring help) in an open area using any material of contrasting colour to the ground. As a general rule, *never* leave your vehicle and wander off to seek help: the car is much larger than you and will more easily be seen by searchers.

WORK

If you come to Australia on a 12-month 'working holiday' visa you can officially only work for three out of those 12 months. Working on a regular tourist visa is strictly *verboten*. Many travellers on tourist visas do find casual work, but with a national unemployment rate of around 11%, and youth unemployment as high as 40% in some areas, it's becoming more difficult to find a job – legal or otherwise. In outback areas, however, the difficulty of attracting labour means that there's still a fair bit of casual work available and potential employers won't ask too many questions about your background.

To receive wages in Australia, you must have a Tax File Number issued by the Taxation Department. Forms are available from post offices and you'll need to show your passport and visa.

The best prospects for casual work in the outback include bar work, waiting on tables or washing dishes, other domestic chores at roadhouses, and nanny work. Cooks, welders, carpenters, electricians, plumbers and mechanics are also in demand.

Still, short-term work is not as easy to find as it once was, even in the outback, and many travellers who have budgeted on finding work return home early. If you are coming to Australia with the intention of working, make sure you have enough funds to cover you for your stay, or have a contingency plan if the work is not forthcoming.

The Commonwealth Employment Service (CES) has over 300 offices around the country, and the staff usually have a good idea of what's available and where. Try the classified section of the daily papers under Situations Vacant, especially on Saturday and Wednesday.

The various backpackers' magazines, newspapers and hostels are other good information sources – some local employers even advertise on their notice boards. Also keep an eye out for notices posted in shop windows, and it doesn't hurt to ask around in pubs and at roadhouses.

If you've worked legally, it may be worth filing a tax return when you leave Australia; you could be pleasantly surprised by your refund.

ACTIVITIES

There are many fantastic walks in the various national parks. If you're interested in surfing, you'll find great beaches and surf in most states – in particular the southern and south-western coast, and the eastern coast south of the Great Barrier Reef. There's great snorkelling and scuba diving at a number of places around the coast but particularly along the Great Barrier Reef.

In northern Queensland you can ride horses through rainforests and along sand dunes and swim with them in the sea, but you can hire horses at any number of places in the outback. Camel riding has taken off in a big way in the Northern Territory. If you've done it in India or Egypt or you just fancy yourself as the explorer/outdoors type, then here's your chance.

You can cycle anywhere in Australia; for the athletic there are long, challenging routes and for the not so masochistic there are plenty of great day trips, with many places where you can hire bikes. In most states there are helpful bicycle societies with lots of maps and useful tips and advice.

Windsurfing, paragliding, rafting, canoeing, hot-air ballooning and hang-gliding are among the many other outdoor activities. For more information, see the Activities sections in the track descriptions in this book or contact any of the state tourist bureaus.

Two activities that draw many people to the outback are fossicking (hunting for gemstones and gold, in a wide range of areas) and barramundi fishing (in the north). In fact, they're so popular that we'll deal with them separately:

Fossicking

The best places to fossick for gemstones are in areas where mountain-building has taken place. The rocks of such areas are often formed under conditions that are ideal for the development of large crystals.

Most important of these are pegmatites, which are the major hosts for a whole range of gemstones such as aquamarine, tourmaline, garnet, quartz and topaz. Pegmatites originate as molten, mineral-rich material which is injected into cracks in the earth's crust. Being resistant to erosion they often form wall-like structures across the landscape.

Also important are rocks, particularly limestone, which have been chemically changed through coming into contact with an invading body of super-heated material – a process known as contact metamorphism. Rocks altered in this way are also major hosts for many types of gems including sapphire, ruby, aquamarine, garnet, epidote, sphene and zircon.

About 30% of Australia's land area consists of basins which have been filled with sediments; with the notable exception of precious opal, these are poor in gemstones. Only about 15% has potential for fossickers and this lies in three interrupted zones that run roughly north-south across the continent. The western zone includes the Kalgoorlie gold fields, the Pilbara and the Kimberley. The central zone runs from Kangaroo Island off South Australia to Darwin and includes the northern Flinders Ranges, the Harts Range in central Australia and the Top End gold fields; an offshoot from this zone covers the Broken Hill area. The eastern zone runs up the eastern highlands from Tasmania to Cape York.

Research A successful fossicking trip is usually dependent on good research. If you've never been to an area before and don't know anyone who has, its potential is best discovered in your armchair with large-scale geological maps, mines-department reports and any other literature you can find. The most popular areas are likely to be written about in the various fossicking guides available from mines departments and bookshops.

State-produced geological maps – the larger their scale the better – are essential as they show the types of surface rock and thus give a hint of the kinds of gems and minerals you may find there. They also show roads, homesteads, watercourses and the locations of old mines, prospecting areas and any interesting mineral occurrences. Make sure to get hold of the explanatory booklet that

Panning for gold (RB)

accompanies each map as this will contain additional information.

Fossicking Tools Successful fossicking doesn't require a trailerful of equipment, but you must have some basic tools. These should be easy enough to fit among your normal travelling luggage, and as a minimum would include: a small spalling hammer or sledgehammer; a pick and shovel; nest of aluminium sieves; prospecting dish; large basin or cut-down drum to wash gravel in; and a small crowbar. Most of these will earn their keep in other ways. If you can fit in a pry bar, a selection of rock chisels, a magnifying glass and a gardening trowel, so much the better. A book on mineral identification is essential, of course.

Prospecting dishes come in a range of sizes and can be either metal or plastic; the best ones have a groove around the edge which is designed to catch heavy particles such as gold as material is washed out of the pan. A shiny metal pan should be blackened first so that the gold stands out – turning it upside down on a burning spinifex clump is an ideal way to do this. You need water to use a pan effectively, but unfortunately few outback gold deposits have a supply next to them. This is where the cut-down drum or large basin comes in handy.

Sieves are essential when fossicking for gems in dirt or gravel. The most convenient ones are the small round aluminium sieves that can be fitted together to form a combination – three sieves of 12 mm, six mm and three mm mesh fitted together are ideal for most purposes. Fossickers who are really serious and want to move a lot of material usually prefer a large wooden-framed sieve mounted on a tripod. The sieved material needs to be washed so that any gems will be easily seen.

Where to Look River deposits are the best places to fossick as running water and gravity have already done the hard work of collecting nature's treasures and concentrating them in one spot. Any situation that causes a drop in flow rate, hence deposition

Newman gums and waterhole (RI)

of heavier materials, should be checked. These include the inside of bends and the downstream side of obstacles such as trees and boulders. Rock bars often yield exciting finds as gold and gems, being heavy, move along the bottom during a flood and may become trapped in potholes or crevices in the bar. If necessary use your crowbar to gain access to crevices, which should be cleaned out using your trowel and a brush. All material obtained should be either panned or sieved depending on whether it's gold or gems you're after.

The use of a prospecting dish is straightforward but requires some practice with ball bearings or lead shot to perfect the art. First, the dish must be submerged in water as it is water that helps concentrate the heavy particles on the bottom. Second, grasp the rim of the dish with both hands (one on either side) and tilt it slightly, the groove being downwards. Third, agitate the contents by gently shaking the dish sideways and back and forth so that the backwash carries the lighter material over the edge – don't be too vigorous or you'll lose the gold. As you progress you can sweep the larger stones out with your hand. Eventually all that remains will be heavy particles, which you concentrate further by slowly rotating the dish so that the gold forms a tail. To remove the gold, you simply moisten the end of a finger and press it on the specks, which you then transfer to a jar of water – just dip your finger in the water and the gold will drop off.

Digging and sieving around the base of suitable rock outcrops, particularly pegmatites, is worth trying as you can often be rewarded with a variety of interesting minerals. Generally, finding crystals in the rock itself is only slightly less difficult than extracting them in one piece. Often it's best not to try as pegmatites can be extremely tough and all you may succeed in doing is smashing the crystal. There are some outstanding areas of gem-yielding pegmatite in the outback, including the Pilbara region near Marble Bar, the Harts Range near Alice Springs and the northern Flinders Ranges.

Mine dumps that date from last century –

or at least no later than the 1930s – are fruitful sources of all kinds of secondary minerals, including gemstones. High costs and the inefficient methods used during the early days often meant that only high-grade ore was worth mining, so anything of poorer grade, including fine specimens, was thrown out with the waste. As well, other minerals that occurred with the one being sought were also usually discarded. A good example is Harts Range, where the mica miners heedlessly tossed magnificent gems onto the dumps because they had no monetary value. On the opal fields, precious opal with orange fire was out of favour late last century so the gougers threw most of it away.

The best way to fossick on old dumps is to either sieve material from untouched areas (you'd do this on the opal fields) or drag down the sides with a rake. You can also find gemstones by closely examining the surface without necessarily disturbing it. This is best done soon after rain when the dust has been washed away leaving the gems readily visible.

Abandoned mines are dangerous. *Never* enter workings where the roofs are held up by old timbers or where there are signs of rock falls, and always stand well back from old shafts as your weight may trigger a collapse. Stay out of old mines.

Mining Law Mining law differs between the states and territories but all have one thing in common: a fossicker must be in possession of a miner's right or fossicking permit to search for gems and minerals on crown land. Permission to fossick on freehold land and mineral leases must usually be obtained from the owner or leaseholder. A miner's right may allow access to pastoral leasehold, but this should be checked with the relevant authority. Sadly, the actions of the thoughtless minority in trespassing and abuse of property has brought the hobby into disrepute in many areas and fossickers are no longer always welcome.

Information Contact the following state departments for information on mining law and the availability of geological maps, reports and fossicking guides:

New South Wales
Department of Mineral Resources, PO Box 536, St Leonards 2065 (☎ (02) 901 8888)
Northern Territory
Department of Mines & Energy, PO Box 2901, Darwin 0800 (☎ (089) 89 5511)
Queensland
Department of Minerals & Energy, QMEC Building, 61 Mary St, Brisbane 4000 (☎ (07) 237 1435)
South Australia
Department of Mines & Energy, PO Box 151, Eastwood 5063 (☎ (08) 274 7500)
Western Australia
Department of Minerals & Energy, Minerals House, 100 Plain St, East Perth (☎ (09) 222 3333)
Victoria
Department of Energy & Minerals, PO Box 98, East Melbourne 3002 (☎ (03) 651 7799)

Barramundi Fishing

For many visitors to the northern regions of Australia, one of the primary motivations for getting off the beaten track is to find the perfect spot to fish for Australia's premier native sport fish, the barramundi. It seems that every other 4WD you come across has a 'tinny' (aluminium dinghy) on the roof.

The 'barra' is such a highly prized fish mainly because of its great fighting qualities: once it takes a lure or fly, it fights like hell to be free. As you try to reel one in, chances are it will play the game for a bit, then make some powerful runs, often leaping clear of the water and shaking its head in an attempt to throw the hook. Even the smaller fish (three to four kg) can put up a decent fight, but when they are about six kg or more you have a battle on your hands which can last several minutes.

Landing the barra is a challenge, but it's only half the fun; the other half is eating it! The barramundi is a prized table fish, although the taste of the flesh does depend to some extent on where the fish is caught. Those caught in saltwater or tidal rivers are generally found to have the sweetest flavour; those in landlocked waterways can have a muddy flavour and soft flesh if the water is a bit murky.

Naturally, everyone has their own theory as to where, when and how barramundi are most likely to be caught. The fish is found throughout coastal and riverine waters of the Kimberley, Top End, Gulf Country and Cape York. The best time to catch them is the post-Wet, ie around late March to the end of May. At this time the floods are receding from the rivers and the fish tend to gather in the freshwater creeks which are full of young fish. The best method is to fish from an anchored boat and cast a lure into a likely spot, such as a small creek mouth or floodway.

The period from June to September is the Dry. While it's not the best season for barra, many roads and tracks which are impassable at other times of the year are open, and so the opportunities of finding a good spot are much enhanced. Trolling close to banks, snags or rock bars with lures is best at this time as the barra tend to stay deep and are relatively inactive as the water is cool.

The build-up to the Wet, from October to late December, is another good fishing time. The water temperature is on the rise, so the fish are more active. Coastal inlets and tidal rivers offer the best fishing at this time, and trolling lures is the best method, although live bait also gets good results.

During the Wet, from January to March, fishing is generally done from boats as many tracks and roads are flooded, making access by vehicle difficult. Casting lures into floodwater run-off or channels is the best method, but even fishing from a river bank or into large channels which feed the rivers is often successful.

In tidal rivers the barra seem to strike most during the last hour or so of the ebb tide, particularly if this is late in the day. The same applies to saltwater areas, although the first couple of hours of the rising tide are also good.

Life Cycle of the Barramundi Early in the Wet, the female barras spawn around the river mouths. The high tides wash the eggs into the coastal swamps. At the end of the Wet, juvenile fish migrate up the rivers to the freshwater areas. By the end of the first year, a barra weighs around half a kg and measures around 30 cm. Here they stay until they are three to four years old (around 3.5 kg and 65 cm), when they head for the tidal waters. Maturing males start to head downstream at the beginning of the Wet, and once in the open water, mature males undergo an amazing transformation as they turn into females and start spawning! By the time the fish are about seven years old they weigh upwards of seven kg (around 90 cm), and fish of up to 20 kg are not uncommon.

Bag & Size Limits It's in everyone's interest to follow the legal restrictions when fishing for barra. In the Northern Territory, the minimum size limit is 55 cm, and the bag limit is five fish in one day. They may not be retained on a tether line at any time. Certain areas of the Northern Territory are closed to fishing between 1 October and 31 January. In Queensland, the closed season lasts from 1 November to 31 January, the minimum size is 50 cm and there's also a bag limit. While there is no size limit in Western Australia, there is a bag limit.

Good Fishing Practices Apart from following the legal restrictions, there are a number of things you can do to enhance the quality of barra fishing for yourself and others who follow.

When releasing undersized fish or those you don't need, try to remove the hook while the fish is still in the water, use a net to land the fish for dehooking and weighing. Where it's necessary to handle the fish, grip it firmly by the lower jaw ensuring your fingers don't get under the gill cover.

To store fish in top condition, they should be killed and bled as soon as possible. Bleeding by cutting the gills or throat is the best method, and if the fish is then placed in ice water this reduces clotting and aids bleeding. Rapid cleaning also preserves the quality, and it's helpful if you can avoid cutting into the flesh surrounding the gut region or rupturing the intestines. Chill the cleaned fish as soon as possible, as this slows the rigor mortis process; when rigor mortis takes place rapidly, violent muscle contractions result in loss of natural juices and the flesh has a tendency to fall apart when filleted.

Clean and rinse fish in a container if possible; doing so in the river may attract crocodiles.

Information The following addresses may be useful:

Amateur Fishermen's Association of the Northern Territory, PO Box 41512, Casuarina, NT 0810 (☎ (089) 89 5096)

Northern Territory Game Fishing Association, GPO Box 128, Darwin, NT 0801 (☎ (089) 89 5605)

Fisheries Service of the Queensland Department of Primary Industry, Cairns (☎ (070) 35 1580)

Fisheries Department of Western Australia, Broome District Office (☎ (091) 92 1121)

Western Australian Department of Fisheries, 108 Adelaide Terrace, East Perth (☎ (09) 220 5333)

Organised Fishing Trips There are a host of commercial operators offering fishing trips for barra and other sporting fish. Some of them include:

Alligator Airways
    PO Box 10, Kununurra, WA 6743
    (☎ (091) 68 1575)
Arafura Safaris
    GPO Box 3304, Darwin, NT 0801 (☎ (089) 27 2372). Fishing year round along the Arnhem Land coastline
Big Barra Fishing Tours
    11 Bailey Circuit, Driver, NT 0830 (☎ (089) 32 1473). One-day trips to the Mary River system east of Darwin, or extended tours in north-western Arnhem Land (one of only two operators to have permission to fish in Arnhem Land)
Birri Fishing Resort
    Mornington Island, Qld 4871 (☎ (077) 45 7277)
Budget Barra Tours
    GPO Box 671, Darwin, NT 0801 (☎ (089) 27 2572). Barra fishing safaris to Daly River, Roper River and Shady Camp (near Kakadu)
Carpentaria Safaris
    Seisia, PO Bamaga, Qld 4876 (☎ (070) 69 3254)

Croc-Spot Fishing Tours
 PO Borroloola, NT 0854 (☎ (089) 75 8722). Day trips along the tidal waters of the McArthur River for barra and other sports fish, or extended off-shore trips to Barranyi National Park for ocean fishing
Escott Lodge
 c/o P O Burketown, Qld 4830 (☎ (077) 45 5108)
Kimberley Charter Co
 PO Box 192, Wyndham, WA 6740
 (☎ (091) 611 023)
Kimberley Sport Fishing (☎ (091) 68 2752), or the 'Bush Camp' on the Ord River (same phone)
Wimray Safaris
 PO Box 1634, Darwin, NT 0801 (☎ (089) 45 2755). Day trips to the Mary River system east of Darwin

HIGHLIGHTS

In a country as broad and geographically diverse as Australia the list of highlights is virtually endless, although one person's highlight can easily be another's disappointment. There are, however, a number of features in each state which shouldn't be missed.

In **northern Queensland** there's the Cape York Peninsula, a rugged country that may not be as lushly tropical as you'd expect, but which has tracts of rainforest along the east coast that run right down to the beach, with the Great Barrier Reef just offshore. In **central Queensland**, the Stockman's Hall of Fame in Longreach is a moving testimony to the explorers and settlers who opened up the outback.

The **Northern Territory** has the obvious attraction of Uluru (Ayers Rock), probably Australia's most readily identifiable symbol after Sydney's Opera House. There's also the World Heritage-listed Kakadu National Park with its abundant flora and fauna and superb

Uluru (Ayers Rock) (RI)

wetlands. The Territory is also where Australia's Aboriginal cultural heritage is at its most accessible – the rock-art sites of Kakadu, and Aboriginal-owned and run tours of Arnhem Land, Manyallaluk (near Katherine) and King's Canyon are just a few of the possibilities.

Then there's **Western Australia** with its vast distances and wide open spaces. The Kimberley region in the far north of the state is as ruggedly picturesque as any you'll find – the Bungle Bungles (Purnululu) National Park here is unforgettable. The 1700-km Canning Stock Route is the longest 4WD trip in the country and a true adventure.

South Australia's big drawcards are the Flinders Ranges, which offer superb bushwalking and stunning scenery. In the northern areas of South Australia you can get a real taste of the outback along famous tracks such as the Strzelecki, Oodnadatta and Birdsville, while the opal-mining town of Coober Pedy, where many people not only work underground but also live in subterranean houses, is unique.

New South Wales has the outback mining town of Broken Hill, once the largest silver-lead-zinc mine in the world and now a convenient base for outback excursions, including to the treasure trove of early Aboriginal history at Mungo National Park.

ACCOMMODATION

A typical town of a few thousand people will have a basic motel at around $40/45 for singles/doubles, an old town centre hotel with rooms (shared bathrooms) at, say, $25/35, and a caravan park – probably with tent sites for $8 to $15 and on-site vans or cabins for $25 to $30 for two. If the town is situated on anything like a main road or is bigger, it'll probably have several of each. Some surprisingly small and seemingly insignificant towns also have backpackers' hostels these days. If there's a group of you, the rates for three or four people in a room are always worth checking; often there are larger 'family' rooms or units with two bedrooms.

For comprehensive accommodation list-ings, the state automobile clubs produce directories listing hotels, motels, holiday flats, caravan parks and even some backpackers' hostels in almost every city and town in the country. They're updated every year so the prices are generally fairly current. They're available from the clubs for a nominal charge if you're a member or a member of an affiliated club enjoying reciprocal rights. Alternatively, some state tourist offices (notably Western Australia) also put out frequently updated guides to local accommodation.

Camping

The camping story in Australia is partly excellent and partly rather annoying. The excellent side is that you can camp almost anywhere out in the bush for free, or at national park campsites for free or next to nothing. Roadhouses and service stations often have showers free of charge or for a nominal fee; they're meant for truck drivers but other people often use them too. If you prefer hot showers and laundry facilities when camping, there's a great number of caravan parks where you'll almost always find space available.

One of the drawbacks is that professional campsites are often intended more for caravans (house trailers for any North Americans out there) than for campers, and the tent campers get little thought in these places. The fact that in Australia most of the sites are called 'caravan parks' indicates who gets most attention.

Equally bad is that campsites in most big cities are well away from the centre. This is not inconvenient in small towns, but in general if you're planning to camp around Australia you really need your own transport. Still, it's not all gloom. Australian caravan parks tend to be well kept and excellent value. Many sites also have on-site vans which you can rent for the night. These give you the comfort of a caravan without the inconvenience of actually towing one of the damned things. On-site cabins are also widely available.

Bush Camping Camping in the bush, either freelance or at designated spots in national parks and reserves, is for many people one of the highlights of a visit to Oz. Nights spent around a campfire under the stars are unforgettable.

You won't even need a tent – swags are the way to go in the outback. Another option is a stretcher (camp bed), as follows: park your vehicle about three metres from a small tree or shrub; between the two, erect the stretcher and roll out your sleeping bag, string up a mosquito net and tuck it in under the bag. This way you'll sleep off the ground, safe from creeping insects, mosquitoes and early-morning flies, and you can still look at the blazing stars as you doze off.

There a few basic rules to camping in the wild:

- Most of the land in Australia belongs to someone, even if you haven't seen a house for 100 km or so. They own it – it is their back yard. You need permission before you are allowed to camp on it. In national parks and on Aboriginal land, you will need permits. On public land, observe all the rules and regulations.
- Select your camping spot carefully. Start looking well before nightfall (which will be very sudden at these latitudes) and choose a spot that makes you invisible from the road. You'll notice any number of vehicle tracks leading off the main road into the bush: explore a few and see what you find.
- Keep to constructed vehicle tracks – never 'bush bash'. Avoid areas that are easily damaged, such as swamps and vegetated sand dunes.
- Some trees (for instance, river red gums and ironwood) are notorious for dropping limbs. Know your trees, or don't camp under large branches.
- Ants live everywhere, and it's embarrassingly easy to set up camp on underground nests. Also beware of the wide variety of mean spiny seeds on the ground which can ruin your expensive tent groundsheet with pinprick holes – sweep the ground first, and erect your tent on a layer of thick agricultural plastic sheeting.
- Carry out all the rubbish you take in, don't bury it. Wild animals dig it up and spread it everywhere.
- Observe fire restrictions. Where and when you can light a fire, make sure it is safe – use a trench and keep the area around the fire clean of flammable material.
- Don't chop down trees or pull branches off living trees to light your fire. Don't use dead wood that's

become white-ant habitat (it won't burn well either). If the area is short of wood, go back down the track a little and collect some there. If that is not possible, use a gas stove for cooking.
- Respect the wildlife. This also means observing crocodile warnings and keeping away from suspect river banks.
- Don't camp right beside a water point. Stock and wildlife won't come in while you are there, and if it is the only water around they may die of thirst.
- Don't camp close enough to a river or stream to pollute it. In most parks the minimum distance is 20 metres.
- Don't use soap or detergent in any stream, river, dam or any other water point.
- Use toilets where they are provided. If there isn't one, find a handy bush, dig a hole, do the job and then fill in the hole. If you're staying a few days, dig a trench (long, narrow and deep) and use that as a toilet pit for everyone, with each individual covering their waste with a little dirt. Burning used toilet paper before burying it is also a good idea, but make sure you don't burn the bush down in the process. Alternatively, do what the majority of the world's population does and use water and your left hand. Bury all human waste well away from any stream.
- If you have young kids, disposable nappies are anything but disposable and are becoming a major item of pollution in the bush. They are hard to burn completely and difficult to bury as they take up so much room and are easily dug up by wild animals. Use cloth nappies or let your kids run naked (with sunscreen!). Alternatively, carry used disposables away with you in a heavy-duty plastic bag on the roof rack (they don't smell much if rolled up tight anyway).

If you're doing your own cooking, see Campfire Cooking in the following Food section.

Youth Hostels

Australia has very active state Youth Hostel Associations (YHAs) and you'll find hostels all over the country, including the major centres in the outback. YHA hostels provide basic accommodation, usually in small dormitories or bunk rooms although more and more of them are providing twin rooms for couples. The nightly charges are rock bottom (usually between $8 and $15 a night) and there are no age limits – in fact, the YHAs are campaigning actively to attract an older clientele.

Stretcher set-up: off the ground and safe from mosquitoes (RvD)

Many take non-YHA members, although there may be a small 'temporary membership' charge. To become a full YHA member in Australia costs $24 a year (there's also a $16 joining fee, although if you're an overseas resident joining in Australia you don't have to pay this). You can join at a state office or at any youth hostel.

YHA hostels are affiliated with Hostelling International (HI), formerly known as the International Youth Hostel Federation (IYHF), so if you're already a member of the YHA in your own country, your membership entitles you to use the Australian hostels. Hostels are great places for meeting people and often function as travel centres where you can sign up for good-value tours. The annual *YHA Accommodation Guide* booklet, available from any YHA office in Australia and from some YHA offices overseas, lists all the YHA hostels around Australia, with useful little maps showing how to find them.

You must have a regulation sheet sleeping bag or bed linen – for hygiene reasons a regular sleeping bag won't do. If you don't have sheets they can be rented at many hostels (usually for $3), but it's cheaper, after a few nights' stay, to have your own. YHA offices and some larger hostels sell the official YHA sheet bag.

All hostels have cooking facilities and 24-hour access, and there's usually a communal area where you can sit and talk. There are usually laundry facilities and often excellent notice boards. Accommodation can usually be booked directly with the manager or through a Membership & Travel Centre. The YHA handbook tells all.

The Australian head office (☎ (02) 565 1699) is in Sydney, at the Australian Youth Hostels Association, 10 Mallett St, Camperdown, NSW 2050. If you can't get a YHA hostel booklet in your own country, write to them, but otherwise deal with the following Membership & Travel centres:

New South Wales
422 Kent St, Sydney, NSW 2001
(☎ (02) 261 1111)
Northern Territory
Darwin Hostel Complex, 69A Mitchell St, Darwin, NT 0821 (☎ (089) 81 3995)
Queensland
Westpac Bank Building, corner George and Herschel Sts, Brisbane, Qld 4000 (☎ (07) 236 1680)
South Australia
38 Sturt St, Adelaide, SA 5000 (☎ (03) 231 5583)
Tasmania
1st floor, 28 Criterion St, Hobart, Tas 7000
(☎ (002) 34 9617)
Victoria
205 King St, Melbourne, Vic 3000
(☎ (03) 670 9840)
Western Australia
65 Francis St, Northbridge, Perth, WA 6003
(☎ (09) 227 5350)

Not all of the 140-plus hostels listed in the handbook are actually owned by the state YHAs. Some are 'associate hostels', which generally abide by hostel regulations but are owned by other organisations or individuals. You don't need to be a YHA member to stay at an associated hostel. Others are 'alternative accommodation' and do not totally fit the hostel blueprint. They might be motels which keep some hostel-style accommodation available for YHA members, caravan parks with an on-site van or two kept aside, or even places just like hostels but where the operators don't want to abide by all the hostel regulations.

Backpackers' Hostels

In recent years the number of backpackers' hostels has increased dramatically, though they have yet to penetrate the outback to the same extent as the YHA hostels. Some are run-down hotels where the owners have tried to fill empty rooms. Others are purpose-built as backpackers' hostels; these are usually the best places in terms of facilities, although sometimes they are simply too big and lack any personalised service. The best places are often the smaller, more intimate hostels where the owner is also the manager. These are usually the older hostels that were around long before the 'backpacker boom'.

Prices at backpackers' hostels are generally in line with YHA hostels, typically $10 to $12, although the $7 bed is still alive and well in some places.

As with YHA hostels, the success of a hostel largely depends on the friendliness and willingness of the managers. One practice that many people find objectionable – in independent hostels only, since it never happens in YHAs – is the 'vetting' of Australians and sometimes New Zealanders, who may be asked to provide a passport or double ID which they may not carry. Some places will actually only admit overseas backpackers. This is because the hostel in question has had problems with locals treating the place more as a dosshouse than a hostel – drinking too much, making too much noise, getting into fights and the like. If you're an Aussie and encounter this kind of reception, the best you can do is persuade the desk people that you're genuinely travelling the country and aren't just looking for a cheap place to crash for a while.

Hotels & Pubs

For the budget traveller, hotels in Australia

Silverton Hotel, Silverton (TW)

Whim Creek Pub, near Port Hedland (JW)

Railway Hotel, Oodnadatta (TW)

Exchange Hotel, Kalgoorlie (JW)

are generally older places – new accommodation usually means motels or Hilton-style hotels. To understand why Australia's hotels are the way they are requires delving into the history books a little. When the powers that be decided Australia's drinking should only be at the most inconvenient hours, they also decided that drinking places should also be hotels. So every place which in Britain would be a 'pub' in Australia was a 'hotel', but often in name only.

The original idea of forcing pubs to provide accommodation for weary travellers has faded into history and not every place called a hotel will necessarily have rooms to rent, although many still do. If there's nothing that looks like a reception desk or counter, or if it doesn't appear to be staffed, just ask at the bar. A 'private hotel', as opposed to a 'licensed hotel', really is a hotel and doesn't serve alcohol. A 'guesthouse' is much the same as a 'private hotel'.

You'll find hotels around the town centres in smaller towns while in larger towns the hotels that offer accommodation are often close to the train stations. In historic centres like the gold-mining towns, the old hotels can be magnificent. The rooms themselves may be pretty old-fashioned and unexciting, and will rarely come with private facilities, but the hotel façade and entrance area will often be quite extravagant. In isolated outback towns the hotel is often a place of real character – the real 'town centre' where you'll meet all the local eccentrics.

A bright word about hotels (guesthouses and private hotels, too) is that the breakfasts are usually excellent – big and 100% filling. A substantial breakfast is what this country was built on and if your hotel is still into serving a real breakfast you'll probably feel it could last you until breakfast comes around next morning. Generally, hotels will have rooms from around $20 or $30. When comparing prices, remember to check if breakfast is included.

Motels

If you have transport and want a more modern place with your own bathroom and other facilities, then you're moving into the motel bracket. Motels cover the earth in Australia, just like in the USA, but they're usually located away from the city centres. Roadhouse accommodation along the major (sealed) outback roads generally falls in this category, though many roadhouses also have camping facilities of some sort.

Prices vary, and with the motels, unlike hotels, singles are often not much cheaper than doubles. The reason is quite simple: in the old hotels many of the rooms really are singles, relics of the days when single men travelled the country looking for work. In motels, the rooms are almost always doubles.

You'll sometimes find motel rooms for less than $30, and in most places will have no trouble finding something for $45 or less. Most motel rooms have tea/coffee-making facilities and a small fridge, and often a TV. Many motels will deliver breakfast to your room for a fee, but very few do main meals as well.

Stations

The outback is a land of large sheep or cattle farms ('stations') and one of the best ways to come to grips with Australian life is to spend a few days on one. With commodity prices falling daily, mountainous wool stockpiles and a general rural crisis, tourism offers the hope of at least some income for farmers, at a time when many are being forced off the land. Some stations have switched almost entirely to tourism. Many offer accommodation where you can just sit back and watch how it's done, while others like to get you more actively involved in the day-to-day activities.

Accommodation can range from campsites and dormitories to four-star bungalows, and prices are pretty reasonable. Many stations that take guests are listed in the track descriptions later in this book, and the state tourist offices can also advise you on what's available.

Other Possibilities

One organisation that sometimes offers

accommodation is the Country Women's Association (CWA), but this is usually for women only. The CWA is a powerful institution in country and outback Australia, with strong input into local legislation and community projects.

If you want to stay somewhere for more than a few days, it might be worth sharing a holiday unit or serviced apartment with a few travelling companions, though in the outback this sort of accommodation is only available in the major tourist centres like Alice Springs, Darwin and Broome. For longer term accommodation, the first place to look for houses to share or rooms to rent is the classified ad section of the local newspaper; notice boards in hostels, supermarkets and certain popular bookshops and cafes are also good places to look.

FOOD

Australia's food (mighty steaks apart) used to have a reputation for being like England's, only worse. Miracles happen and Australia's miracle was immigration. The Greeks, Yugoslavs, Italians, Lebanese and many others who flooded into Australia in the 1950s and '60s brought, thank God, their food with them. More recent arrivals include the Vietnamese, whose communities are thriving in several cities.

In the larger outback towns you can have Greek moussaka, Italian saltimbocca and pastas, German dumplings, or maybe even Middle Eastern treats. The Chinese have been sweet & souring since the gold-rush days, while more recently Indian, Thai, Vietnamese and Malaysian restaurants have been making their way into the Australian interior.

Australian Food

Although there is no real Australian cuisine, there is some typically Australian food. For a start there's the meat pie – every bit as sacred an institution as the hot dog is to a New Yorker. Some places make this classic dish on their premises and do a good job of it, but the standard factory pie is an awful concoction of anonymous meat and dark

gravy in a soggy pastry case. A 'vegetarian' alternative is the pasty – pastry folded over a vegetable filling that sometimes contains meat as well (ask if you want to be sure).

Even more central to Australian eating habits is Vegemite. This dark-coloured yeast-extract substance looks like tar and is spread on bread. It's similar to Marmite or Promite but tastes less salty. Empty Vegemite jars make handy wine glasses – as you may discover in many an outback household.

Bread lovers will be horrified to discover that Australian tastes have hardly progressed beyond white and the occasional wholegrain, especially in the outback, though they may be lucky and stumble upon a German bakery.

Everybody knows about good Australian steaks. They may be a bit tough in the outback (like the cattle) but they taste terrific and you'll never complain about the size. Fish like John Dory and the esteemed barramundi are often available far inland, as are superb lobsters and other crustaceans like the engagingly named Moreton Bay bugs! Yabbies are delicious crayfish that often thrive in outback dams.

Vegetarians will find their options limited in the outback, although most roadhouses and many pubs will have a vegetarian dish on the menu. Australia grows almost all its own food, and even in the outback a salad will usually be fresh.

Where to Eat

Eating options are obviously more limited in the outback than in the big cities. Some towns will have a Chinese restaurant, and in the larger towns there may be other nationalities too. Many restaurants allow you to bring your own wine or beer, for which you may be charged a small 'corkage' fee.

For a quick meal, roadhouses and local takeaway shops offer straightforward fish and chips, and many different sandwiches that might be a more wholesome alternative. A 'hamburger with the lot' comes with egg, cheese and salad and provides a filling meal for under $5 – ask them to hold the beetroot if you don't share the Australian fetish for this red vegetable.

For a 'proper' meal, roadhouses will oblige but better value is to be found in the pubs. Look for 'counter meals', so called because they used to be eaten at the bar counter. Some places still are just like that, while others are fancier, almost restaurant-like, with serve-yourself salad tables where you can add as much salad, French bread and so on as you wish. Most pubs have a 'lounge' area where you can sit at a table. Good counter meals are hard to beat for value for money, and although the food is usually of the simple steak-salad-chips variety, the quality can be excellent.

Counter meals are usually served as counter lunches or counter teas, the latter a hangover from the old northern English terminology where 'tea' meant the evening meal. One catch with pub meals is that they usually operate fairly strict hours. The evening meal time may be just 6 to 7.30 or 8 pm. Pubs doing counter meals often have a blackboard menu outside but sometimes not – just ask at the bar. Counter meals vary enormously in price but in general the better class places with good serve-yourself salad tables will be in the $6 to $16 range for all the traditional dishes: steak, veal, chicken, fish and so on.

Preparing Your Own

Roadhouse and pub meals can get a bit boring after a while, and many people prefer to prepare their own food. Most outback shops have a reasonable range of fairly expensive supplies. Perishable products (meat, milk etc) can be kept good for a few days in an ice container known as an 'esky' after a leading Australian brand; ice is often available at service stations and general stores, and of course at pubs.

The fruit-fly blocks are always a problem when carrying supplies. Movement of fruits, vegetables, plants and even honey is

Bush food: bush bananas, mulga nuts and witchetty grubs (NTTC)

restricted in many states and there are a number of fruit-fly block inspection stations around Australia to police quarantine regulations; or there may be an 'honesty pit' where you're expected to dump all fruit and vegetable matter. The Department of Primary Industries & Energy, Australian Quarantine & Inspection Service has produced an informative booklet called *Traveller's Guide to Plant Quarantine*. To obtain a copy, write to or phone the appropriate state department. Stiff penalties apply for not obeying the rules.

Cooking in the Bush Cooking over an open fire need not be a daunting prospect. It is in fact quite easy, though there are a few basic rules. Firstly you need a good-quality camp oven (a cast-iron pot with a lid) and a fire grate to place over the fire. Next you need plenty of coals if you are baking or roasting in your camp oven, and the wood available will determine the heat you are going to get out of your coals. Allow plenty of time to get a good bed of coals going.

Dig a trench in which to lay your fire. The width and length will depend on your own cooking needs and size of your fire grate, but it should be about 30 cm (1 foot) deep.

Don't rely on always being able to cook over an open fire though, as there are many times when a fire is not possible – such as on Total Fire Ban days, and in areas where open fires are not permitted, as is the case in many national parks. As well, many councils and shires have their own fire bans in force during the summer months when open fires are prohibited. Bring a gas stove and bottle as a standby.

Bush Cooking in Style by Gayle Hughes explains all you need to know about bush cooking, including planning and packing. For a good range of basic recipes, get hold of *Rabbit on a Shovel* by Herb ('Lummo') Lummis. Jack & Reg Absalom's *Outback Cooking in the Camp Oven* has exotic recipes like kangaroo, and gives all the details on how to use a camp oven.

See the Checklists in the back of this book

Campfire cooking (note the fly hat) (R & VM)

for general cooking equipment and campfire cooking items.

DRINKS

In the nonalcoholic department, Australians knock back Coke and flavoured milk like there's no tomorrow and also have some excellent mineral water brands. Tea and coffee in the outback invariably mean teabags and instant, though many places now also have espresso machines.

Beer

Beer plays an integral role in the social fabric of the outback. Australian beer will be fairly familiar to North Americans and is similar to what's known as lager in the UK. It may taste like lemonade to the Continental beer addict, but don't say this out loud in an outback pub. It's always chilled before drinking.

Foster's is, of course, the best known international brand with a worldwide reputation, but its share of the home market is in decline. Each Australian state has its own beer brand and there will be someone to sing the praises of each: XXXX (pronounced 'fourex') and Power's (Queensland), Swan and Emu (Western Australia), Tooheys (New South Wales), and VB (Victoria Bitter, Victoria). Although most big-name beers are associated in particular with one state, they are available across the country. The smaller breweries generally seem to produce better beer – Cascade (Tasmania), Coopers (South Australia) and Matilda Bay (Western Australia) being three examples; Coopers Sparkling Ale is similar to some Belgian Trappist beers, including the sediment.

A word of warning to visitors: Australian beer has a higher alcohol content than British or American beers. Standard beer is generally around 4.9% alcohol, although most breweries also produce 'lite' beers with an alcohol content of between 2% and 3.5%. And another warning: people who drive under the influence of alcohol and get caught lose their licences (unfortunately, drink-driving is a real problem in Australia). The maximum permissible blood-alcohol concentration for drivers in Australia is 0.05% (0.08% in the Northern Territory).

All around Australia, beer, the containers it comes in, and the receptacles you drink it from are called by different names. Beer comes in stubbies, long necks, bottles, tinnies and twisties, depending on where you are. Tinnies are cans, bottles contain 750 ml, and stubbies, long necks and twisties are small bottles (375 ml), usually with a handy twist-off cap.

Ordering at the bar can be an intimidating business for the newly arrived traveller. A 200-ml beer is a seven in Queensland (seven ounces); a 285-ml beer is a pot or a tenner in Queensland, but a middy in New South Wales and Western Australia; in New South Wales they also have the 425-ml schooner, but in South and Western Australia a 425-ml glass is called a pint. In New South Wales they're likely to ask if you want new or old, 'new' being ordinary beer and 'old' being stout. A low-alcohol beer is called a light, while regular strength beer can be called a

heavy. If in doubt, take local advice, which will readily be offered!

Australians are generally considered to be heavy beer drinkers, but per capita beer consumption even in the notoriously hard-drinking Northern Territory has been falling faster than in any other developed country.

Wine

If you don't fancy Australian beer, then turn to wines like many Australians are doing. Australia has a great climate for wine-producing and makes some superb wines that are cheap and readily available.

Wine is sold in bottles or two- and four-litre 'casks'; the two-litre glass 'flagons' are on their way out in the cities but still alive and well in the outback.

It takes a little while to become familiar with Australian wines and their styles, especially since the manufacturers are being forced to delete generic names from their labels as exports increase; the biggest victim is 'champagne', which will have to be called 'sparkling wine'. White wines are almost always drunk chilled, and in the outback many people chill their reds too.

Australia also produces excellent ports (perfect at a campfire) but only mediocre sherries.

THINGS TO BUY

There are lots of things definitely *not* to buy: plastic boomerangs, fake Aboriginal ashtrays and T-shirts, and all the other terrible souvenirs that fill the tacky souvenir shops. Most of them come from Taiwan or Korea anyway. Before buying an Australian souvenir, turn it over to check that it is actually made here!

Often the best souvenirs are the ones that have special meaning: the fly-net hat bought at Urandangi when the flies were driving you insane, the beautiful shell from the beach on the Gulf of Carpentaria, the gold nugget found near Kalgoorlie, or the 'antique' glass insulator picked up along the old Overland Telegraph Line north of Alice.

Aboriginal Art

Top of the list for any real Australian purchase would have to be Aboriginal art. Nobody captures the essence of outback Australia better than the Aborigines. It's an amazingly direct and down-to-earth art that has finally gained international appreciation. If you're willing to put in a little effort, you can see superb examples carved or painted on rocks and caves in many parts of the outback. Now (and really just in time) skilled Aboriginal artists are also working on their art in a more portable form. Have a look at the spectacular Aboriginal artworks hanging in the respected art galleries before you make your choice.

Prices of the best works are way out of reach for the average traveller, but among the cheaper artworks on sale are prints, baskets, small carvings and some very beautiful screen-printed T-shirts produced by Aboriginal craft co-operatives – and a larger number of commercial rip-offs. It's worth shopping around and paying a few dollars more for the real thing. See Cross-Cultural Etiquette in the Facts about the Outback chapter if you want to purchase works of art on Aboriginal communities.

Australiana

The term 'Australiana' is a euphemism for souvenirs that are supposedly representative of Australia and its culture, although many are extremely dubious. Some of the more worthwhile items are wool products such as hand-knitted jumpers, sheepskin products, and jewellery made from opal. The seeds of many of Australia's native plants are on sale all over the place; try growing kangaroo paws back home. Australian wines are well known overseas, but why not try honey (leatherwood honey is one of a number of powerful local varieties), macadamia nuts (native to Queensland), or Bundaberg rum with its unusual sweet flavour – a 'Bundy & Coke' is a popular mixed drink in the outback.

Aussie Clothing

While you're here, fit yourself out in some local clobber – made in Australia for Australian conditions. Start off with some Bonds undies and a singlet, a pair of Holeproof Explorer socks and Blundstone elastic-sided boots. Slip on a pair of Stubbie shorts, slap on an Akubra hat and you've got the complete Aussie outback labourer's working uniform. If this is totally impractical for the cold, wet climate back home, invest in a Driza-bone waxed-cotton overcoat.

Opals

The opal is Australia's national gemstone, and opals and jewellery made with it are popular souvenirs. It's a beautiful stone, but buy wisely and shop around – quality and prices can vary widely from place to place.

Gold and silver follow world prices and aren't as cheap as you would expect in a country that mines so much of the stuff.

Getting There & Away

Getting to or from Australia means flying, although it is sometimes possible to hitch a ride on a yacht to/from Australia.

AIR

The basic problem with getting to Australia is that it's a long way from anywhere. Coming from Asia, Europe or North America there are lots of competing airlines and a wide variety of air fares, but there's no way you can avoid those great distances. Australia's current international popularity adds another problem: flights are often heavily booked. If you want to fly to Australia at a particularly popular time of year (the middle of summer, ie Christmas time, is notoriously difficult) or on a particularly popular route (like Hong Kong-Sydney or Singapore-Sydney), then plan well ahead.

Australia has a large number of international gateways. Sydney and Melbourne are the two busiest international airports with flights arriving from everywhere. Perth also gets many flights from Asia and Europe and has direct flights to New Zealand and Africa. Other international airports include Hobart in Tasmania (New Zealand only), Adelaide, Port Hedland (Bali only), Darwin, Cairns, Townsville and Brisbane. One place you can't reach directly from overseas is Canberra, the national capital.

Although Sydney is the busiest gateway, it makes a lot of sense to avoid arriving or departing there. Sydney's airport is stretched way beyond its capacity and flights are frequently delayed on arrival and departure. Furthermore, the customs and immigration facilities are too small for the current visitor flow, so you may face further delays after you've finally landed. If you can organise your flights to avoid Sydney, it's a wise idea. Unfortunately many flights to or from other cities (Melbourne in particular) still go via Sydney. If you're planning to explore the outback, then starting at a quieter entry port like Cairns or Darwin can make a lot of sense.

Discount Tickets

Buying airline tickets is like shopping for a car, a stereo or a camera: five different travel agents will quote you five different prices. Rule number one if you're looking for a cheap ticket is to go to an agent, not directly to the airline. The airline can usually only quote you the official regular fare. An agent, on the other hand, can offer all sorts of special deals, particularly on competitive routes.

Airlines would rather have a half-price passenger than an empty seat, so if they can't fill seats, they will either let agents sell them at cut prices, or occasionally make one-off special offers on particular routes – watch the travel ads in the press.

Of course what's available and what it costs depends on what time of year it is, what route you're flying and who you're flying with. If you're flying on a popular route (like from Hong Kong) or one where the choice of flights is very limited (like from South America or Africa), then the fare is likely to be higher or there may be nothing available but the official fare.

Similarly, the dirt-cheap fares are likely to be less conveniently scheduled, to go by a less convenient route or to be with a less popular airline. Flying London-Sydney, for example, is most convenient with airlines like Qantas, British Airways, Thai International or Singapore Airlines. They have flights every day, operate the same flight straight through to Australia, and are good, reliable, comfortable, safe airlines. At the other extreme you could fly from London to an Eastern European or Middle Eastern city on one flight, switch to another flight from there to Asia, and change to another airline from there to Australia. It takes longer, there are delays and changes of aircraft along the way, the airlines may not be so good and furthermore, the connection only works once a week and that means leaving London at 1.30 on a Wednesday morning. The flip side is it's cheaper.

To/From the UK

The cheapest tickets in London are from the numerous 'bucket shops' (discount ticket agencies) that advertise in magazines and papers like *Time Out*, *City Limits*, *Southern Cross* and *TNT*. Pick up one or two of these publications and ring round a few bucket shops to find the best deal. The magazine *Business Traveller* also has a great deal of good advice on air-fare bargains. Most bucket shops are trustworthy and reliable but there's the occasional sharp operator – *Time Out* and *Business Traveller* give useful advice on precautions.

Trailfinders (☎ (071) 938 3366) at 46 Earls Court Rd, London W8, and STA Travel (☎ (071) 581 4132) at 74 Old Brompton Rd, London SW7, and 117 Euston Rd, London NW1 (☎ (071) 465 0484), are good, reliable agents for cheap tickets.

The cheapest London to Sydney or Melbourne bucket-shop (not direct) tickets are about £310 one-way or £572 return. Cheap fares to Perth are around £330 one-way and £583 return. Such prices are usually only available if you leave London in the low season – March to June, which ties in well with the outback season. In September and mid-December fares go up about 30% while the rest of the year they're somewhere in between. Average direct high-season fares to Sydney or Melbourne are £527 one-way, £957 return; to Perth, £478 one-way and £865 return.

Many cheap tickets allow stopovers on the way to/from Australia. Rules regarding how many stopovers you can take, how long you can stay away, how far in advance you have to decide your return date and so on, vary from time to time and ticket to ticket, but recently most return tickets have allowed you to stay away for any period between 14 days and one year, with stopovers permitted anywhere along your route.

From Australia, you can expect to pay around A$1200 one-way and A$1800 return

to London and other European capitals, with stops in Asia on the way. Prices increase 20% to 30% in the European summer and at Christmas.

To/From North America

There is a variety of connections across the Pacific from Los Angeles, San Francisco and Vancouver, including direct flights, flights via New Zealand, island-hopping routes and more circuitous Pacific rim routes via nations in Asia. Qantas, Air New Zealand and United all fly USA-Australia; Qantas, Air New Zealand and Canadian Airlines International fly Canada-Australia.

One advantage of flying Qantas or Air New Zealand rather than United is that on the US airlines, if your flight goes via Hawaii, the west coast-Hawaii sector is treated as a domestic flight. This means that you have to pay for drinks and headsets – goodies that are free on international sectors. Furthermore, when coming in through Hawaii from Australasia, it's not unknown for passengers who take a long time clearing customs to be left behind by the US airline and to have to take the next service!

To find good fares to Australia, check the travel ads in the Sunday travel sections of papers like the *Los Angeles Times*, *San Francisco Chronicle-Examiner*, *New York Times* or *Toronto Globe & Mail*. The straightforward return excursion fare from the USA west coast is around US$1090, and from the east coast the return fare ranges from US$1185 to US$2100. The costs vary seasonally, but plenty of deals are available. You can typically get a one-way ticket from the west coast for US$800, or US$1050 from the east coast. At peak seasons – particularly the Australian summer/Christmas time – seats will be harder to get and the price will probably be higher.

In the USA, good agents for discounted tickets are the two student travel operators, Council Travel and STA Travel, both of which have lots of offices around the country. Canadian west-coast fares out of Vancouver will be similar to those from the

US west coast. From Toronto, fares go from around C$1650 return.

The French airline Air France has an interesting island-hopping route between the US west coast and Australia which includes the French colonies of New Caledonia and French Polynesia (Tahiti etc). The Air France flight is often discounted and is very popular because of its multiple Pacific stopover possibilities. Los Angeles-Sydney on Air France costs around US$830 one-way and US$1000 return. Polynesian Airlines has a similar route (Los Angeles-Sydney via Hawaii and Apia in Western Samoa) which costs between US$800 and US$1000 return.

If Pacific island-hopping is your aim, several other airlines offer interesting opportunities. One is Hawaiian Airlines which flies Honolulu-Sydney via Pago Pago in American Samoa once a week. Qantas give you Fiji or Tahiti along the way, while Air New Zealand can offer both and the Cook Islands as well. See the Circle Pacific section for more details.

One-way/return fares available from Australia include: San Francisco A$1000/1650, New York A$1150/2000 and also Vancouver $1150/1800.

To/From New Zealand

Air New Zealand and Qantas operate a network of trans-Tasman flights linking Auckland, Wellington and Christchurch in New Zealand with most major Australian gateway cities. You can fly directly between a lot of places in New Zealand and a lot of places in Australia.

Fares vary depending on the cities and the season, but from New Zealand to Sydney you're looking at around NZ$520 one-way and NZ$650 return, and to Melbourne NZ$600 one-way and NZ$720 return. There is a lot of competition on this route, with United, British Airways, Qantas and Air New Zealand all flying it, so there is bound to be some good discounting going on.

Cheap fares to New Zealand from Europe will usually be for flights via the USA. A straightforward London-Auckland return bucket-shop ticket costs around £950.

Coming via Australia you can continue right around on a Round-the-World (RTW) ticket which will cost from around £1050 for a ticket with a comprehensive choice of stopovers.

To/From Asia

Ticket discounting is widespread in Asia, particularly in Singapore, Hong Kong, Bangkok and Penang. There are a lot of fly-by-nights in the Asian ticketing scene so a little care is required. Also, the Asian routes have been particularly caught up in the capacity shortages on flights to Australia. Flights between Hong Kong and Australia are notoriously heavily booked, while flights to or from Bangkok and Singapore are often part of the longer Europe-Australia route so they are also sometimes very full. Plan ahead.

Typical one-way fares to Australia from Asia include from Hong Kong for around HK$4400 or from Singapore for around S$540. These fares are to the east-coast capitals; Brisbane, Perth or Darwin are sometimes a bit cheaper.

You can also pick up some interesting tickets in Asia to include Australia on the way across the Pacific. Air France was first in this market but Qantas and Air New Zealand are also offering discounted trans-Pacific tickets. On the Air France ticket you can stop in Jakarta, Sydney, Noumea, Auckland and Tahiti.

From Australia, return fares from the east coast to Singapore, Kuala Lumpur and Bangkok range from A$700 to A$900, and to Hong Kong from A$900 to A$1300.

The cheapest way out of Australia is to take one of the flights operating between Darwin and Kupang (Timor, Indonesia). Current one-way/return fares are A$198/330.

To/From Africa & South America

The flight possibilities from these continents are not so varied and you're much more likely to have to pay the full fare. There is only a handful of direct flights each week between Africa and Australia and then only between Perth and Harare (Zimbabwe) or

Johannesburg (South Africa). A much cheaper alternative from East Africa is to fly from Nairobi to India or Pakistan and on to South-East Asia, then connect from there to Australia.

Two routes now operate between South America and Australia. The long-running Chile connection involves a Lan Chile Santiago-Easter Island-Tahiti flight, from where you fly Qantas or another airline to Australia. Alternatively there is a route which skirts the Antarctic circle, flying Buenos Aires-Auckland-Sydney, operated by Aerolineas Argentinas in conjunction with Qantas.

Round-the-World Tickets

Round-the-World (RTW) tickets have become very popular and many of these will take you through Australia. The airline RTW tickets are often real bargains, and since Australia is pretty much at the other side of the world from Europe or North America, it can work out at the same price, or even be cheaper, to keep going in the same direction round the world than to do a U-turn.

The official airline RTW tickets are usually put together by a combination of two airlines, and permit you to fly anywhere you want on their route systems so long as you do not backtrack. Other restrictions are that you (usually) must book the first sector in advance and cancellation penalties then apply. There may be restrictions on how many stops you are permitted and usually the tickets are valid from 90 days up to a year. A typical price for a South Pacific RTW ticket is around £816 or US$1900.

An alternative type of RTW ticket is one put together by a travel agent using a combination of discounted tickets from a number of airlines. A UK agent like Trailfinders can put together interesting London-to-London RTW combinations including Australia for between £750 and £930.

Circle Pacific Tickets

Circle Pacific tickets use a combination of airlines to circle the Pacific – combining Australia, New Zealand, North America and Asia. Examples would be Qantas/Northwest Orient, Canadian Airlines International/Cathay Pacific and so on. As with RTW tickets, there are advance purchase restrictions and limits to how many stopovers you can take. Typically, fares range between US$1750 and US$2180. Possible Circle Pacific routes are Los Angeles-Bangkok-Sydney-Auckland-Honolulu-Los Angeles, or Los Angeles-Tokyo-Kuala Lumpur-Sydney-Auckland-Honolulu-Los Angeles.

BOAT

Forget it. Every now and then someone will try and set up a regular passenger service between Indonesia and Darwin, but so far such attempts have been short-lived. You could, however, hitch a ride on a yacht if you're lucky. See Boat in the following Getting Around chapter for details about crewing on yachts.

ARRIVING & DEPARTING

Arriving in Australia

Australia's dramatic increase in visitor arrivals has caused some severe bottlenecks at the entry points, particularly at Sydney where the airport is often operating at more than full capacity and delays on arrival or departure are frequent. Even when you're on the ground it can take ages to get through immigration and customs.

First-time travellers to Australia may be alarmed to find themselves being sprayed with insecticide by the airline stewards. It happens to everyone. Beware of the strict rules relating to the importation of plant and animal matter, including food.

Leaving Australia

When you finally go, remember to keep $25 aside for the departure tax. This will increase to $27, but rather than being collected at the airport on departure, it may be added on to your ticket, similar to the US system. Check with your travel agent.

Warning

This chapter is particularly vulnerable to

change – prices for international travel are volatile, routes are introduced and cancelled, schedules change, rules are amended, and special deals come and go. Airlines and governments seem to take a perverse pleasure in making price structures and regulations as complicated as possible and you should check directly with the airline or travel agent to make sure you understand how a fare (and ticket you may buy) works.

In addition, the travel industry is highly competitive and there are many lurks and perks. The upshot of this is that you should get opinions, quotes and advice from as many airlines and travel agents as possible before you part with your hard-earned cash. The details given in this chapter should be regarded only as pointers and cannot be any substitute for your own careful, up-to-date research.

Getting Around

AIR

There are only two main domestic carriers within Australia – Qantas (Australia's international carrier, which took over the domestic Australian Airlines) and Ansett – despite the fact that the airline industry is deregulated. For 40-odd years, Australian and Ansett had a duopoly on domestic flights, charged virtually what they liked, and operated virtually identical schedules. All this meant that domestic airline travel within Australia was expensive and the choices of flights limited, particularly on the low-volume routes to places like Alice Springs and Darwin.

With deregulation came another player, Compass, and a fierce price war – proof that in this business it took three to tango. The net result was that Compass folded (twice) and for all intents we're back to a two-airline industry. The only difference is that travellers have come to expect some discounting,

and the two airlines are doing more of this than in the past.

Note that all domestic flights in Australia are nonsmoking. Because Qantas flies both international and domestic routes, its flights can leave from either the internatioinal or domestic terminals at Australian airports. Flights with flight numbers from QF001 to QF399 operate from international terminals, and flight numbers QF400 and above, from domestic terminals.

Cheap Fares

Random Discounting The airlines sometimes offer substantial discounts on selected routes. Although this seems to apply mainly to the heavy-volume routes, it's not always the case.

To make the most of the discounted fares, you need to keep in touch with what's currently on offer, mainly because there are usually conditions attached to cheap fares –

Getting around a cattle station, Northern Territory (PS)

such as booking 14 or so days in advance, only flying on weekends, or between certain dates and so on. Also the number of seats available is usually fairly limited. The further you can plan ahead the better. Because the situation is so fluid, with special deals coming and going all the time, booking through a travel agent who knows what's on offer will usually get you a better fare than doing it yourself direct with the airline.

Some Possibilities If you're planning a return trip and have 14 days up your sleeve, you can save 45% to 50% by travelling Apex. You have to book and pay for your tickets 14 days in advance and you must stay away at least one Saturday night. Flight details can be changed at any time, but the tickets are nonrefundable. If you book seven days in advance, the saving is 35% to 40% off the full fare.

For one-way travel, if you can book three days in advance a saving of 25% to 30% is offered; for immediate travel on off-peak flights the discount is 15% to 20%.

University or other higher education students under the age of 26 can get a 25% discount off the regular economy fare. An airline tertiary concession card (available from the airlines) is required for Australian students. Overseas students can use their International Student Identity Card.

All nonresident international travellers can get a 30% to 40% discount on internal Qantas flights simply by presenting their international ticket when booking. It seems there is no limit to the number of domestic flights you can take, it doesn't matter which airline you fly into Australia with, and it doesn't have to be on a return ticket. However, the discount applies only to the full economy fare, and in many cases it will be cheaper to take advantage of other discounts offered. The best advice is to ring around and explore the options before you buy.

There are also some cheaper deals with regional airlines such as East-West (see Other Airline Options below) or a number of

Queensland operators. On some lesser routes these operators undercut the big two.

Another thing to keep your eyes open for is special deals at certain times of the year. January and early February, May and early June, and November and the first half of December are slack periods during which the airlines will try and lure passengers. When the Melbourne Cup horse race is on in early November and when the Aussie Rules football Grand Final happens (also in Melbourne) at the end of September, lots of extra flights are put on. These flights would normally be going in the opposite direction nearly empty so special fares are offered to people wanting to leave Melbourne when everybody else wants to go there. The Australian Grand Prix in Adelaide in late October or early November is a similar one-way-traffic event.

Air Passes

With discounting, air passes do not represent the value they did in pre-deregulation days, so much so that Qantas doesn't even offer them.

Ansett still has its Kangaroo Airpass, which gives you two options: 6000 km with two or three stopovers for $949 ($729 for children) and 10,000 km with three to seven stopovers for $1499 ($1149 for children). A number of restrictions apply, but the pass can be a good arrangement if you want to see a lot of country in a short period of time. You don't need to start and finish at the same place: you could start in Sydney and end in Darwin, for example.

Other Airline Options

There are a number of secondary airlines apart from the two major domestic carriers. East-West Airlines connects the Queensland coast with the rest of eastern Australia, and Kendell Airlines services country areas of Victoria, South Australia and Tasmania, as well as Broken Hill and Ayers Rock. There are numerous other, smaller operators. See the track descriptions in this book for details.

Outback Air Tours

Scenic flights are available in small aircraft at the more popular outback destinations. Prices are very reasonable, sometimes including pick-up and drop-off from where you're staying, and the experience is unforgettable – nothing beats the sight of Ayers Rock or the Bungle Bungles from the air. See the track descriptions in this book for more information, or contact the state or local tourist offices.

If you have a bit of money to burn, there are tour operators who will take you to the highlights of the outback in six-seater Piper Aztecs or 10-seater Piper Chieftains. Itineraries range from four-day trips to Ayers Rock from around $1500 per person, to two-week, six-state outback tours for $5000 to $6500. Accommodation is included, and you may even have some input into the itinerary. The state tourist offices can provide details. Two operators who have been around for a while are: Aviatour (☎ & fax (03) 589 4097), 524 Balcombe Rd, Beaumaris, Vic 3193; and Air Adventure Australia (☎ 008 03 3160, fax (055) 72 5979), PO Box 339, Hamilton, Vic 3300.

Other Tour Options

See the Mail Runs section later in this chapter for details on mail planes. At most outback airfields there will be someone who will take you flying, enabling them to get their hours on the board while you cover the costs. Just ask around.

Flying Yourself

If you are a pilot, flying yourself can be an interesting option and a fairly efficient way to cover large distances.

Many flying schools and clubs hire out planes for private use, and are the best places to meet other pilots and find out about local flying conditions. They are listed in the Yellow Pages phone book or you can just go out to the local airport and ask around. Most capital cities have a separate suburban airport for general aviation, such as Bankstown Airport in Sydney or Moorabbin in Melbourne.

Typical single-engine hire charges start at around $85 an hour for a Cessna 152, or $95 for a Cessna 172 or a Piper Warrior. From there they increase roughly in proportion to cruising speed. If you want a twin, a Seminole is about $180 an hour. Rates at the lower end are usually 'wet VDO', ie engine hours inclusive of fuel and oil. You get a credit for any fuel you buy along the way, but only at the operator's local price, not what you paid for it. If you want to take the aircraft away overnight the operator will probably expect a minimum average usage.

Flying Conditions

Anyone planning to fly in Australia will need more information than can be covered in these general comments, and any flying school or hire company will have instructors who are qualified to explain everything you need to know about local conditions and current regulations. They will also brief you on current airspace classifications which are in the process of being reviewed to bring them into line with international standards.

Australia has a fairly low level of air traffic, especially compared with North America and Europe, and it is mainly concentrated around a few cities and a couple of tourist areas. Elsewhere the sky is pretty empty but unfortunately navigation facilities are equally sparse. Radar coverage is limited to regions around the major cities and much of the country is outside the range of VOR transmitters so you have to rely on dead reckoning and the ADF for cross-country flying, especially in the outback. The use of GPS equipment is increasingly common but is not yet approved as a primary means of navigation.

Much of central Australia is classified as a 'Designated Remote Area' because of its inaccessibility or being beyond the range of VHF communications, and flights here must carry a higher level of on-board equipment, such as HF radio or an ELB. Similar restrictions apply over smaller mountainous areas in the south-east and in Tasmania.

Australia generally uses metric measurements but some imperial units are used in aviation for consistency with other countries. The result is a mixture, with altitudes in feet, winds and airspeeds in knots, long distances in nautical miles, short distances like runway lengths in metres and fuel in litres. Don't worry, it's not as confusing as it sounds.

Flight Planning Charts and other planning documents can be obtained from the Civil Aviation Authority (CAA) Publications Centre in Melbourne (☎ (03) 342 2000, fax 347 4407, toll-free ☎ 1800 33 1676) or from aviation supply shops at the larger general aviation airports.

Most large country towns have a local airport with sufficient facilities for regional

Bamaga, Queensland (R & VM)

commuter airlines. Many smaller towns offer a licensed aerodrome, even if it's only a gravel strip, a windsock and (with luck) a public phone. The CAA's *En Route Supplement – Australia* (commonly known as *ERSA*) has details of all licensed aerodromes, including runway diagrams, navaids and fuel availability.

There are also a number of private and unlicensed aerodromes (some of them mentioned in *ERSA*), and further down the scale numerous private strips and landing areas. Prior permission to land at these is usually required from the owner of the plane and also from the landowner if it is private property.

Avgas is widely available but prior notice may be required in some places. The price varies from around 75 cents a litre in the cities, increasing with distance to almost double in remote outback towns. Expect to pay a call-out fee (typically $20) to refuel outside normal hours.

Licences Licensing and all other regulations are controlled by the CAA, which has regional offices at airports in most capital cities and larger regional centres. The head office (☎ (06) 268 4393, fax 268 4729) can be contacted at GPO Box 367, Canberra, ACT 2601.

If you have a current foreign licence, the CAA will issue a Certificate of Validation which allows you to fly for up to three months. This costs $46 and is available over the counter from any regional office. No medical or flying test is required for visual flying but you must be able to speak English.

For longer periods a Special Pilot Licence is available for private operations for a fee of $37. Again there is no theory exam or flight test for VFR operations but you do need a current overseas medical certificate and to have had a flight check within the previous two years. You can apply at any CAA regional office, and the licence is then mailed to you from Canberra.

With either method, if you have an instrument rating you will generally need to pass a written exam and a flight test before flying IFR in Australia.

Gravel road, Northern Territory (PS)

In addition to the CAA's legal requirements, any company hiring you an aircraft will require a check flight with an instructor to get you familiar with local conditions. Instructor rates are usually around $55 an hour on top of the normal hire cost.

Airport Transport

There are private or public bus services at almost every major town in Australia, but at smaller airports you may have to rely on taxis, and at outback airstrips, on friendly locals. If you've booked a motel or other accommodation, they might come and pick you up. Quite often a taxi shared between three or more people can be cheaper than the bus.

BUS

Bus travel is generally the cheapest way from A to B, other than hitching of course. The bus networks are far more comprehensive than the rail system, though they tend to stick to the main, sealed highways (there once was a bus from Perth to Ayers Rock via the Lav-

erton-Warburton road, but unfortunately it no longer operates). The buses all look pretty similar and are similarly equipped with air-conditioning, toilets and videos. See the track descriptions later in this book for specific bus services.

There is only one truly *national* bus network: Greyhound Pioneer Australia, which consists of the former Greyhound/Pioneer and Bus Australia. All were once separate companies, and in fact the buses are still done out in their original paint-jobs.

McCafferty's, operating out of Brisbane, is probably the next biggest, with services all along the east coast as well as the loop through the Centre to Adelaide, Alice Springs and Darwin to Townsville.

There are many smaller bus companies operating locally or specialising in one or two main intercity routes. These often have the best deals. In South Australia, Stateliner operates around the state including to the Flinders Ranges. Westrail in Western Australia operates bus services to places the trains no longer go.

Bus Passes

Greyhound Pioneer Australia has a variety of passes, so it's a matter of deciding which suits your needs.

Set-Distance Version The Greyhound Getaway Pass is probably the most flexible as it gives you 12 months to cover the distance you select along any of the Greyhound Pioneer routes. The main advantage of these passes is that they give you the flexibility to put your own itinerary together. Getaway Passes are valid for 12 months and can be used on any Greyhound Pioneer service. The passes are issued in multiples of 1000 km (minimum 2000 km, no maximum) and the cost is $180 for 2000 km, $360 for 4000 km, $480 for 6000 km and $750 for 10,000 km.

Many travellers find that to make proper use of the passes they have to travel faster than they would wish. This particularly seems to apply to people who buy their passes before they arrive in Australia.

Set-Route Version Another option is the set-route Aussie Explorer Pass, which gives you six or 12 months to cover a set route. You don't have the go-anywhere flexibility of the set-km bus pass but if you can find a set route which suits you – and there are 20 to choose from – then it generally works out cheaper than the set-km pass.

The main limitation with this kind of pass is that you can't backtrack, except on 'dead-end' short sectors such as Darwin to Kakadu, Townsville to Cairns, and Ayers Rock to the Stuart Highway.

Aussie Highlights allows you to loop around the eastern half of Australia from Sydney taking in Melbourne, Adelaide, Coober Pedy, Ayers Rock, Alice Springs, Darwin (and Kakadu), Cairns, Townsville, the Whitsundays, Brisbane and Surfers Paradise for A$690. The same trip on a set-km pass would cost you $840. Or there are one-way passes, such as the Go West pass from Sydney to Cairns via Melbourne, Adelaide, Ayers Rock, Alice Springs, Katherine, Darwin (and Kakadu) and Townsville for $590; or Across the Top, which goes from Cairns to Perth via the Top End and Kimberley, for $490. There's even an All Australia pass which takes you right around the country, including up or down through the Centre, for $1235.

Set-Duration Version The set-duration pass is known as the Aussie Pass. This allows travel on a set number of days during a specified period. There are no restrictions on where you can travel. The passes range from $343 for seven days of travel in one month up to $2100 for 90 days of travel in six months (what a nightmare!). It's hard to see what advantages these passes have over the others already mentioned.

TRAIN

Before Australia became independent it was governed as six separate colonies, all administered from London. When the colony of Victoria, for example, wanted to build a railway line it checked not with the adjoining colony of New South Wales but with the colonial office in London. When the colonies were federated in 1901 and Australia came into existence, by a sheer masterpiece of misplanning not one state had railway lines of the same gauge as a neighbouring state! The immense misfortune of this inept planning has dogged the railway system ever since.

In 1970 a standard-gauge rail link was completed between Sydney and Perth and the very popular Indian-Pacific run was brought into operation. The old Ghan railway line between Adelaide and Alice Springs was only replaced by a new standard-gauge line in 1980. See below for more details about these famous trains.

Apart from different gauges there's also the problem of different operators. The individual states run their own services, or a combination of them for interstate services. Australian National Railways is an association of the government-owned systems in Queensland, New South Wales, Victoria and Western Australia, and this body goes some way to coordinating the major services.

Train travel in Australia today is something you do because you really want to – not because it's cheaper (especially now with cheap bus and reduced air fares), and certainly not because it's fast. The train is generally the slowest way to get from anywhere to anywhere. On the other hand, the trains are comfortable and you see Australia at ground level in a way you wouldn't be able to otherwise.

Rail Passes

There are a number of passes that allow unlimited rail travel either across the country or just in one state. With the Austrail Pass you can travel anywhere on the Australian rail network, in either 1st class or economy. The cost is $725/435 in 1st/economy class for 14 days, $895/565 for 21 days, $1100/685 for 30 days, $1535/980 for 60 days and $1765/1125 for 90 days.

The Austrail Flexipass differs in that it allows a set number of travelling days within a specified period. While this pass offers greater flexiblity, it cannot be used for travel between Adelaide and Perth or Alice Springs. The cost is $530/320 in 1st class/economy for eight days of travel in 60 days, or $750/475 for 15 days' travel in 90 days.

Surcharges are payable on sleeping berths in both classes, and on certain trains, such as the Ghan and the Indian-Pacific, there are compulsory meal charges as well ($31 and $113 respectively).

For travel within a limited area, the passes that just cover travel in one state may be more suitable. These are available for Victoria, Queensland and Western Australia. They can be purchased at major train stations and from travel agents. For details of passes and conditions, contact Rail Australia on ☎ (08) 217 4479.

As the railway booking system is computerised, any station (other than on metropolitan lines) can make a booking for any journey throughout the country. For reservations, contact ☎ 13 2232 during office hours; this will connect you to the nearest mainline station.

The Ghan

History The Ghan saga started in 1877 when the authorities decided to build a railway line from Adelaide to Darwin. They took more than 50 years to reach Alice Springs, and are still thinking about the final 1500 km to Darwin more than a century later. The basic problem was that they made a big mistake at the start of the project: they built the line in the wrong place.

Because all the creekbeds north of Marree were bone dry, and because nobody had seen rain, the authorities concluded that there wasn't going to be rain in the future. So they laid the initial stretch of line right across a flood plain, and when the rain came the line was simply washed away. In the century or so that the original Ghan railway line survived, this was a regular occurrence.

The wrong route was only part of the Ghan's problems. At first it was built as a broad-gauge line to Marree, and then extended using narrow gauge to Oodnadatta in 1884. Travellers went from Adelaide to Marree on the broad-gauge line, changed there to narrow gauge as far as Oodnadatta, then had to make the final journey to Alice Springs by camel train. The Afghani-led camel trains pioneered transport through the outback, and it was from these Afghanis that the Ghan took its name.

It was a jerry-built line: the foundations were flimsy, the sleepers were too light, the grading was too steep and it meandered hopelessly. It was hardly surprising that the top speed of the old Ghan was a flat-out 30 km/h!

Finally, in 1929, the line was extended from Oodnadatta to Alice Springs. At the best of times the Ghan was slow and uncomfortable as it bounced and bucked its way down the badly laid line. It was unreliable and expensive to run, and worst of all, a heavy rainfall could strand it. Parachute drops of supplies to stranded train travellers became part of outback lore, and on one occasion the Ghan rolled in 10 days late.

By the early 1970s the South Australian state railway system was taken over by the federal government, and a new line to Alice

Old Ghan track sleepers near Finke (TW)

Advance-purchase fares are available for 1st-class travel only, and these cost $305.

The train departs from Adelaide on Thursday at 2 pm, arriving in Alice Springs the next morning at 9.25 am. It departs from Alice Springs on Friday at 2 pm, arriving in Adelaide the next day at 11 am. From April to December there's a second departure from Adelaide on Monday and Alice Springs on Tuesday. You can also join at Port Augusta, the connecting point on the Sydney-Perth route. Fares between Alice Springs and Port Augusta are $139 coach, $180 holiday and $310 1st class.

You can transport cars between Alice Springs and Adelaide for $195, or between Alice Springs and Port Augusta for $185, but only between April and December. Double-check the times you need to have your car at the terminal for loading: it must be there several hours prior to departure for the train to be 'made up'. Unloading at the Adelaide end is slow so be prepared for a long wait.

Bookings can be made from anywhere in Australia by phoning ☎ 13 2232 during business hours.

The Indian-Pacific

Along with the Ghan, the Indian-Pacific run is one of Australia's great train journeys: a 65-hour trip between the Pacific Ocean on one side of the continent and the Indian Ocean on the other. Travelling this way, you really appreciate the immensity of the country (or, alternatively, are bored stiff).

From Sydney, you cross New South Wales to Broken Hill and then continue on to Adelaide and across the Nullarbor. From Port Augusta to Kalgoorlie, the seemingly endless crossing of the virtually uninhabited centre takes well over 24 hours, including the 'long straight' across the Nullarbor Plain – at 478 km the longest straight stretch of railway line in the world.

Springs was planned. The $145 million line was to be standard gauge, laid from Tarcoola, north-west of Port Augusta on the Indian-Pacific line, to Alice Springs – and it would be laid where rain would not wash it out. In 1980 the line was completed ahead of time and on budget.

In the late 1980s the old Ghan made its last run and the old line was subsequently torn up. One of its last appearances was in the film *Mad Max III*.

The old train took 140 passengers and, under ideal conditions, made the trip in 50 hours. The new train takes twice as many passengers and does it in less than half the time. It's still the Ghan, but not the trip it once was.

Fares The Ghan costs $139 in coach class (no sleeper or meals); holiday class gives you a sleeper with shared facilities and no meals for $229; 1st class costs $435, which includes meals and a self-contained sleeper.

History
The promise of a transcontinental railway link helped to lure gold-rich Western Australia into the Commonwealth in 1901. Port Augusta in South Australia and Kalgoorlie in Western Australia were the

existing state railheads in 1907, when surveyors were sent out to map a line between the two. In 1911 the Commonwealth legislated to fund north-south (Ghan) and east-west (Indian-Pacific) routes across the continent.

The first sod was turned in Port Augusta in 1912 and, for five years, two self-contained gangs, a total of 3000 workers, inched towards each other. They endured sandstorms, swarms of blowflies and intense heat as they laid 2.5 million sleepers and 140,000 tonnes of rail. The soil and rock was removed with pick and shovel and the workers were supplied by packhorse and camel. The whole job was completed with a minimum of mechanical aids, one of the few machines being the Roberts track-layer.

As Australia was embroiled in WW I, there was no great opening celebration when the track gangs met in the sand hills near Ooldea. The first Transcontinental Express pulled out of Port Augusta at 9.32 pm on 22 October 1917, heralding the start of 'the desert railway from Hell to Hallelujah'. It arrived in Kalgoorlie 42 hours 48 minutes later after covering 1682 km.

The participants in the struggle to get the railway started are reflected in the names of the stations along the straight stretch: Forrest, Deakin, Hughes, Cook, Fisher, O'Malley and Barton; Bates commemorates Daisy Bates, who devoted herself to the welfare of Aborigines and for a time lived alongside the line near Ooldea; Denman was the governor-general who turned the first sod in 1917.

A good read is Patsy Adam Smith's *The Desert Railway*, which has many photographs of the building of the line. The line's history is covered exhaustively in *Road through the Wilderness* by David Burke.

Fares To Perth, one-way fares from Adelaide are $337 for an economy sleeper, $566 for a 1st-class sleeper or $170 in an economy seat with no meals; from Melbourne they're $444 economy sleeper, $715 1st-class sleeper or $215 seat only; and from Sydney, $495 economy, $850 1st class or $230 seat

The New Ghan line (TW)

only. Caper (advance-purchase) fares offer reductions of around 30%.

Melbourne and Adelaide passengers connect with the Indian-Pacific at Port Pirie. Cars can be transported between Adelaide and Perth for $290, a good option for those not wishing to drive the Nullarbor in both directions.

The distance from Sydney to Perth is 3961 km. You can break your journey at any stop along the way and continue later as long as you complete the one-way trip within two months; return tickets are valid for up to six months. Westbound, the Indian-Pacific departs Sydney on Thursday and Monday. Heading east, the train departs Perth on Monday and Friday. Book at least a month in advance.

The main difference between economy and 1st-class sleepers is that 1st-class compartments are available as singles or twins, economy as twins only. First-class twins have showers and toilets; 1st-class singles have toilets only, with showers at the end of the carriage. In the economy-seating compartments, the showers and toilets are at the end of the carriage. Meals are included in the fare for 1st-class only; economy-berth and economy-seat passengers have the option of purchasing meals from the restaurant car. First-class passengers also have a lounge compartment with piano.

Between Adelaide and Perth you can also travel on the weekly Trans-Australian. Fares are the same as the Indian-Pacific fares, and the trip takes 38 hours.

Reservations are made with Australian National in Adelaide and Port Augusta, both on ☎ 13 2232.

TRAVEL PERMITS

If you wish to travel through the outback on your own, you may need special permits to pass through or visit Aboriginal land or to camp in national parks.

Aboriginal Lands

A glance at any up-to-date land-tenure map of Australia shows that vast portions of the north, centre and south are Aboriginal land. Generally this has either government-administered reserve status or it may be held under freehold title vested in an Aboriginal land trust and managed by a council or corporation. With either format, the laws of trespass apply just as with any other form of private land, but the fines attached can be somewhat heftier.

In some cases permits won't be necessary if you stay on recognised public roads that cross Aboriginal territory. However, as soon as you leave the main road by more than 50 metres, even if you're 'only' going into an Aboriginal settlement for fuel, you may need a permit. If you're on an organised tour, the operator should take care of any permits, but this is worth checking before you book.

Applications To make an application, you have to write to the appropriate land council or government department, as outlined below, enclosing a stamped, self-addressed envelope and giving all details of your proposed visit or transit. In general, the following information is required: the names of all members of the party; the dates of travel; route details; purpose of the visit; and contact address and telephone number. The Northern Territory's Central Land Council and Northern Land Council, and the Aboriginal Areas Planning Authority in Western Australia, also require the make, model and registration number of the vehicle.

Allow plenty of time: the application process may take one or two months as the administering body generally must obtain approval from the relevant community councils before issuing your permit. Keep in mind also that there is no guarantee that you'll get one. It may be knocked back for a number of reasons, including the risk of interference with sacred sites, or disruption of ceremonial business. As well, some communities simply may not want to be bothered by visitors.

Specific permit requirements are explained in the track descriptions in this book. However, the general requirements are as follows:

Western Australia The Aboriginal Affairs Planning Authority is responsible for all Aboriginal land. People wishing to travel on these lands, including transit on the Giles-Laverton road, should write to the Permits Officer (☎ (09) 483 1222, fax 321 0990) at PO Box 628, West Perth, WA 6005.

South Australia Outside the Woomera Prohibited Area, virtually the entire region bordered by the Transcontinental Railway, the Stuart Highway, and the Northern Territory and Western Australia borders is Aboriginal-owned. The northern portion of this region is taken up by the Anangu-Pitjantjatjara Lands while to the south are the Maralinga-Tjarutja Lands. The two are separated on the map by a line drawn east-west through Mt Willoughby on the Stuart Highway about 230 km south of the Northern Territory border.

Private tourist traffic is not permitted in the Anangu-Pitjantjatjara Lands. If you want to take a look at this area and meet the people, you can do so only on a guided tour with

Desert Tracks, based in Alice Springs. For information on Desert Tracks, see the Organised Tours section later in this chapter.

Permits to visit the Maralinga-Tjarutja Lands, which include access to the Unnamed Conservation Park and tracks in the Emu Junction area, can be obtained from the Administration Officer, Maralinga-Tjarutja Inc (☎ (086) 25 2946) at PO Box 435, Ceduna, SA 5435.

Northern Territory The Central Land Council administers all Aboriginal land in the southern and central regions of the Territory. Write to the Permits Officer (☎ (089) 51 6320/6321, fax 53 4345) at PO Box 3321, Alice Springs, NT 0871.

A transit permit is required for the Yulara-Docker River road, but not for either the Tanami Road or the Sandover Highway where these cross Aboriginal land. Travellers may camp overnight without a permit within 50 metres of the latter two routes. On the Tanami Road, you can call in to Yuendumu and fuel up without a permit.

Arnhem Land and other northern mainland areas are administered by the Northern Land Council. Write to the Permits Officer (☎ (089) 20 5172, fax 45 2633) at PO Box 42921, Casuarina (Darwin), NT 0811.

Queensland There is no formal permit system for entry onto Aboriginal land in Queensland. Instead, you obtain permission directly from the community, as you would with most other land-holders. Addresses and telephone numbers for the various community councils can be obtained from the Aboriginal Coordinating Council (☎ (070) 31 2623) at PO Box 6512, Cairns Mail Centre, Qld 4870.

National Parks

You usually need a permit to camp in a national park or sometimes even to visit, and such a permit must be obtained in advance. It often includes maps and other useful information. Details of required permits are provided in the individual track descriptions in this book. If you're spending a lot of time in a particular state's national park, it also pays to check if there's an annual pass system in operation, what it covers and how many parks it is valid for. It could save you money.

Desert Parks Pass For example, to visit the parks and regional reserves in the north of South Australia, you must have what is called a Desert Parks Pass. The parks included in this system are the Simpson Desert Conservation Park, the Simpson Desert Regional Reserve, Witjira National Park, Innamincka Regional Reserve and Lake Eyre National Park. The Pass not only permits you to visit and camp in these parks, but also provides a full package of information on local travel, history and nature. Included also are some excellent maps.

The Pass is available from a number of outlets in northern South Australia, as well as good map shops Australia-wide. For more information, contact the South Australian National Parks & Wildlife Service, Far Northern Region (☎ (086) 48 4244), based in Hawker in the Flinders Ranges.

In 1994 the Pass cost $50 a vehicle, and while that may sound expensive, it's good value if you are staying for a few nights in the northern region of South Australia. Special passes are available for single-night stops at Dalhousie Springs, one of the most popular spots in this area.

CAR

Public transport is almost nonexistent in most parts of the outback, and for this reason alone having your own transport is the way to go. Buying or hiring a car need not cost a fortune if there are three or four of you, and provided you don't have a major mechanical problem the benefits are great.

Inexperienced drivers conquer some of the most difficult tracks in unsuitable vehicles, but they just happen to do so under perfect conditions and have more than their fair share of luck (or help from passers-by). Other keen souls never make it and some even perish. Everyone needs a bit of luck now and then; just be aware that your life is

Road train on the move – give them plenty of leeway! (R & VM)

at stake if your luck runs out. There's simply no substitute for careful planning.

Road Rules

Driving in Australia holds few real surprises. Australians drive on the left-hand side of the road just like in the UK, Japan and most countries in south and east Asia and the Pacific. There are, however, a few basic rules to keep in mind.

The main one is 'give way to the right'. This means that if you're driving along a main road and somebody appears on a minor road on your right, you must give way to them – unless they are facing a give-way or stop sign, or are coming out of a driveway. This rule caused so much confusion over the years that most intersections in the more populated parts of the country are signposted to indicate which is the priority road (usually the main one). But it's wise to be careful because stop signs elsewhere are few and far between and the old give-way rules will apply.

The general speed limit in built-up areas in Australia is 60 km/h and out on the open highway it's usually 100 or 110 km/h depending on where you are. In the Northern Territory there is no speed limit outside of built-up areas, although you might still be booked for driving at a 'speed inappropriate to the prevailing conditions' (for instance 160 km/h at dawn/dusk/night). The police everywhere in Australia have radar speed traps and speed cameras, and they often use them in carefully hidden locations. On the

other hand, when you get far from the cities and traffic is light, you'll see a lot of vehicles moving a lot faster than 100 km/h. Oncoming drivers who flash their lights may be giving you a friendly indication of a speed trap ahead.

Australia was one of the first countries in the world to make the wearing of seat belts compulsory. All new cars in Australia are required to have seat belts back and front and if your seat has a belt then you're required to wear it. You're liable to be fined if you don't. Small children must be belted into an approved safety seat.

The average Aussie considers driving a right rather than a privilege, and because there's no compulsory driver training as such (merely a 'Learner Period'), driving standards aren't exactly the highest in the world. Drink-driving is a real problem too, especially in country areas. Serious attempts have been made in recent years to reduce the road toll – random breath tests are not uncommon in built-up areas. If you're caught with a blood-alcohol concentration of more than 0.05% (0.08% in the Northern Territory), then be prepared for a hefty fine, a court appearance and the loss of your licence.

Although overseas licences are acceptable for genuine overseas visitors, an International Driving Permit in conjunction with your overseas licence is even more acceptable.

On the Road

You can now drive all the way round Australia on Highway 1 or through the middle all the way from Adelaide to Darwin on tarred roads, but that hasn't always been so. The Eyre Highway across the Nullarbor Plain in the south was only surfaced in the 1970s, the final stretch of Highway 1 in the Kimberley region of Western Australia was done in the mid-1980s, and the final section of the Stuart Highway from Port Augusta up to Alice Springs was finished in 1987. But you don't have to get very far off the beaten track to find yourself on dirt roads.

If you've ever travelled on unsealed roads in Africa or South America, however, you'll be pleasantly surprised by their counterparts in the outback. The major roads are graded fairly regularly, and because of the low volume of traffic they tend to last quite well between gradings. You may not even need a four-wheel-drive (4WD) vehicle – a well-prepared, conventional 2WD car with sufficient ground clearance is usually quite suitable on the more established tracks. The individual track descriptions in this book give an indication of the type of vehicle required.

Signposting on the main roads between cities is quite OK, and even on outback tracks you'll often find signposts where they matter. Be careful, though, as what matters to you may not matter to an outback road crew, and a missed turn-off can have serious consequences. This is all the more reason to keep a running log when travelling in the outback (see Survival in the Facts for the Visitor chapter) and to have plenty of maps.

Cattle, sheep and kangaroos are common hazards on outback roads, and a collision is likely to kill the animal and seriously damage your vehicle. Kangaroos tend to seek shade during the day but are active at night, especially at dawn and dusk when they come to feed on luscious grass in road ditches. They move in groups, so if you see one hopping across the road in front of you, slow right down – its friends are probably close behind. If one hops out right in front of you, hit the brakes and only swerve to avoid the animal if it is safe to do so. The number of people who have been killed in accidents caused by swerving to miss an animal is high. Many Australians avoid travelling altogether between 5 pm and 8 am, even though the night is 'cooler for the engine'.

Roads often pass through private property and usually aren't fenced off (which is why you see so many cattle and sheep on the road). Instead, station boundaries are marked by cattle grids. Slow down when you come to one of these, not only to save your tyres and suspension but also to help prolong the life of the grid-well.

The bitumen (asphalt, tar) on some outback roads is only wide enough for one

Old petrol bowser (RN)

vehicle, which begs the question what to do when someone comes towards you. First of all, slow down. Tourists (Australian or otherwise) move the left half of their vehicle off the edge and expect the oncoming vehicle to do the same. Wrong, because this gives either party the worst of both worlds. Outback residents usually wait and see what the other vehicle does: if it moves off the edge they'll stay on the bitumen and risk a broken windscreen from flying gravel; if it stays on the bitumen they'll move off the edge and wear out their suspension and tyres. Everyone moves off the edge for an oncoming truck or road train.

Finally, if an oncoming vehicle throws up so much dust that you can't see the road ahead, slow down (and turn on the lights) or stop, and don't pass in dust clouds.

Fuel

Service stations generally stock diesel, super and unleaded, although the more remote ones may not stock unleaded. Liquid petroleum gas (LPG, Autogas) is often unavailable, even at larger service stations along the main sealed roads (check current availability with the state's automobile association). Prices vary from place to place and from price war to price war, but generally they're in the 75c to 85c-a-litre range and $1 a litre is not uncommon (diesel sometimes costs a few cents more, and LPG significantly less). In the more remote outback the price can soar, and some service stations are not above exploiting their monopoly position (then again, their costs are high too).

Distances between fill-ups can be long, and in some really remote areas deliveries can be haphazard – it's not unknown to finally arrive at that 'nearest station x hundred km' only to find there's no fuel until next week's delivery! Ring ahead if you want to be sure.

The track descriptions in this book will give an indication of the required fuel ranges. There are a few tracks where your vehicle will need a long-range fuel tank, but on many others you'll be able to scrape by on your vehicle's standard tank with, say, one or two 20-litre jerry cans as backup. Don't carry fuel in the passenger compartment or on the roof.

Popular Tracks

There are many tracks to choose from, and this book describes most of them. To help you narrow down your choice, here are a few of the more popular ones:

Birdsville Track Running 517 km from Marree in South Australia to Birdsville just across the border in Queensland, this is one of the best-known routes in Australia and these days is quite feasible in a well-prepared conventional vehicle.

Strzelecki Track This track covers much the same territory, starting south of Marree at Lyndhurst and going to Innamincka, 460 km north-east and close to the Queensland border. From there you can loop down to Tibooburra in New South Wales. The route has been much improved due to work on the Moomba gas fields. It was at Innamincka that the hapless early explorers Burke and Wills died.

Oodnadatta Track This runs parallel to the old Ghan railway line to Alice Springs. It's 429 km from Marree to Oodnadatta and another 216 km from there to the Stuart Highway at Marla. There are many historical sites, and it's worth taking your time to see them. So long as there's no rain, any well-prepared vehicle should be able to manage this route, which used to be a secret and much smoother alternative to the heavily corrugated Stuart Highway before that was sealed.

Simpson Desert Crossing the Simpson Desert from the Stuart Highway to Birdsville is becoming increasingly popular but this route is still a real test. Four-wheel drive is definitely required and you should be in a party of at least three or four vehicles equipped with long-range two-way radios. There are several routes: the French Line or a couple of easier but longer alternatives. The many sand dunes, the silence and 'space' are the main attractions.

Warburton Road/Gunbarrel Highway This route runs west from Ayers Rock via the Aboriginal settlements of Docker River and Warburton to Laverton in Western Australia. From there you can drive down to Kalgoorlie and on to Perth. A well-prepared conventional vehicle can complete this remote route through the typical red desert landscape of central Australia, although there are a few sandy sections and ground clearance can be a problem. For 300 km near the Giles Meteorological Station, the Warburton Road and the Gunbarrel Highway run on the same route. Taking the old Gunbarrel north past Warburton all the way to Wiluna in Western Australia is a much rougher trip requiring 4WD. The Warburton Road is now commonly but incorrectly referred to as the Gunbarrel – just to make life simple.

Tanami Track Turning off the Stuart Highway just north of Alice Springs, the Tanami Track goes north-west across the Tanami Desert to Halls Creek in Western Australia. It's a popular short-cut for people travelling between the Centre and the Kimberley. The road has been extensively improved in recent years to

he WA border and conventional vehicles are quite
OK, although there are occasional sandy stretches on
he WA section. Be warned that the Rabbit Flat road-
ouse in the middle of the desert is only open from
riday to Monday.

Canning Stock Route This old stock trail runs
south-west from Halls Creek to Wiluna in Western
Australia, and is one of the great 4WD adventures in
Australia. It crosses the Great Sandy and Gibson
deserts, and since the track has not been maintained
or over 30 years it's a route to be taken seriously. Like
he Simpson Desert crossing, you should only travel
n a well-equipped party, and careful navigation is
equired.

Plenty & Sandover Highways These two
outes run east from the Stuart Highway north of Alice
springs to Boulia or Mount Isa in Queensland.
Though often rough, they provide an interesting and
significantly shorter alternative to the sealed road
leading east above Tennant Creek, and are usually
uitable for conventional vehicles.

Cape York The Peninsula Development Road up to
he tip of Cape York, the northernmost point in mainland Australia, is a popular route through a unique part
of the country. There are a number of rivers to cross,
and the track can only be attempted in the dry season
when the water levels are low. The original Cape York
Track along the old telegraph line definitely requires
4WD. Conventional vehicles can take the new
Heathlands' road to the east beyond the Wenlock
River, which bypasses the most difficult sections, but
he Wenlock itself can be a formidable obstacle that
often blocks conventional vehicles even at the driest
ime of year.

Gibb River Road This is the 'short cut' between
Derby and Kununurra, and runs through the heart of
he spectacular Kimberley in northern Western Aus-
ralia. Although very rough and badly corrugated in
places, it can sometimes be negotiated by conven-
ional vehicles in the dry season.

Buying a Car

Australian cars are not cheap to buy. Locally
manufactured cars are made in small, uneco-
nomical numbers and imported cars are
heavily taxed so they won't undercut the
local products. If you're buying a second-
hand vehicle, reliability is all important.
Mechanical breakdowns in the outback can
be dangerous and at least very inconvenient
– the nearest mechanic can be a hell of a long
way down the road.

Shopping around for a used car involves
much the same rules as anywhere in the
Western world. For any given car you'll
probably get it cheaper by buying privately
through newspaper private ads or youth-
hostel notice boards than through a car
dealer. Buying through a dealer does give the
advantage of some sort of warranty, but a
warranty is not much use if you buy a car in
Sydney and set off for Perth via the outback.
Used-car warranty requirements vary from
state to state – check with the local automobile organisation.

An important consideration when choos-
ing a particular make and model is the
availability of spares. When your fancy
German car goes kaput somewhere back of
Bourke, it's likely to be a long wait while the
new bit arrives fresh from Stuttgart. In the
4WD category, Toyotas and (to a lesser
extent) Nissans are a dime a dozen and
there's usually a local mechanic who knows
how they work, or a dealer not too far away.
Old Toyota Landcruisers in particular are
common outback workhorses and are easier
to repair than the newer models. Not so
common in the backblocks are Mitsubishi
Pajeros, Holden Jackaroos and the like,
although parts are generally available in
major towns. Older Land Rovers and smaller
Suzuki Sierras can be found in the most
out-of-the-way places, but later versions
aren't so common.

The further you get from civilisation in a
two-wheel-drive vehicle, however, the better
it is to be in a Holden or Ford. New cars can
be a whole different ball game of course, but
if you're in an older vehicle, something that's
likely to have the odd hiccup from time to
time, then life is much simpler if it's a car for
which you can get spare parts anywhere from
Bourke to Bulamakanka. When your rusty
old Holden goes bang there's probably
another old Holden sitting in a ditch with a
perfectly good widget waiting to be
removed. Every scrap yard in Australia is full
of good ole Holdens and Ford Falcons.

Expect to pay $1000 to $3500 for an old
Holden or Ford, and $3000 to $10,000 for an
old 4WD. Obviously the closer you get to the

lower figures, the more you need to know about cars and how to fix them. For a 4WD, about $15,000 should get you something reasonably new (five years old) and reliable enough to take you to remote areas.

Depending on which Australian state you're in, registration can cost $250 to $400 a year for a conventional car and $350 to $800 for a 4WD, so it's worth checking how much registration is still left when you buy second-hand. Note that third-party personal injury insurance is included in the registration cost. This ensures that every vehicle (as long as it's currently registered) carries insurance for hospital expenses inflicted on other road users. But you're wise to extend that minimum to at least third-party property insurance as well – minor collisions with Rolls Royces can be amazingly expensive.

When you come to buy or sell a car there are usually some local regulations to be complied with. In Victoria, for example, a car has to have a compulsory safety check (Road Worthiness Certificate – RWC) before it can be registered in the new owner's name – usually the seller will indicate if the car already has an RWC. In New South Wales and the Northern Territory, on the other hand, safety checks are compulsory every year when you come to renew the registration. Stamp duty has to be paid when you buy a car, and, as this is based on the purchase price, it's not unknown for buyer and seller to agree privately to understate the price. It's much easier to sell a car in the same state in which it's registered otherwise it has to be re-registered in the new state and the authorities may want to take a closer look.

Finally, make use of the automobile organisations – see the Facts for the Visitor chapter for details. They can advise on local regulations you should be aware of, give general guidelines about buying a car and, most importantly, for a fee (around $70) will check a used car and report on its condition before you agree to purchase it. They also offer car insurance to their members.

Old abandoned Holden (RvD)

Buy-Back Schemes One way of getting around the hassles of buying and selling privately is to enter into a buy-back arrangement with a dealer. The main advantage of these schemes is that you don't have to worry about selling the vehicle quickly at the end of your trip, and the dealer can usually arrange insurance, which short-term visitors may find hard to get. However, the cars on offer may have been driven around Australia a number of times, often with haphazard or minimal servicing, and are generally pretty tired. Dealers will often find ways of knocking down the price when you return the vehicle, even if a price has been agreed in writing – often by pointing out expensive repairs that allegedly will be required to pass the dreaded safety check.

A company that specialises in buy-back arrangements on cars and motorcycles, with fixed rates, is Car Connection Australia. Also known as Bike Tours Australia, it has been organising motorcycle adventure holidays in the outback for over 10 years and has recently branched into this sideline. Its programme is basically a glorified long-term rental arrangement where you put down a deposit to the value of the vehicle and in the end you get your money back, minus the fixed 'usage' fee.

The bottom line is that a second-hand Ford station wagon or Yamaha XT600 trail bike will cost you a fixed sum of $1950 for any period up to six months; a Toyota Landcruiser, suitable for serious outback exploration, is $3500, also for up to six months. Prices include a limited 5000 km warranty on engine and gearbox. The company will pick you up at Melbourne Airport, throw in a night's accommodation in Castlemaine (Victoria) to help you acclimatise, and send you on your way with touring maps and advice. You can also rent camping equipment (no sleeping bags). Car Connection Australia (☎ (054) 73 4469, fax 73 4520) is at RSD Lot 8, Vaughan Springs Rd, Glenluce (near Castlemaine), Vic 3451. Information and bookings are handled by its European agent: Travel Action GmbH. Contact them on ☎ (++49-2764) 7824, fax 7938, Einsiedeleiweg 16, 57399 Kirchhundem, Germany.

Renting a Car

If you have the cash, there are plenty of car-rental companies ready and willing to put you behind the wheel. The track and city descriptions in this book provide details.

Competition in Australia is pretty fierce so rates tend to be variable and lots of special deals pop up and disappear again. Whatever your mode of travel on the long stretches, it can be very useful to have a car for some local travel. Between a group it can even be reasonably economical. There are some places – like around Alice Springs – where there's no public transport and the distances are too great for walking or even cycling.

The three major companies are Budget, Hertz and Avis, with offices in almost every town that has more than one pub and a general store. The second-string companies that are also represented almost everywhere are Thrifty and National. Then there is a vast number of local firms or firms with outlets in a limited number of locations. The big operators will generally have higher rates than the local firms but not always, so don't jump to conclusions. In many cases local companies are markedly cheaper than the big boys, but in others what looks like a cheaper rate can end up quite the opposite if you're not careful.

One advantage with the big operators is that they're more amenable to one-way rentals – pick up a car in Adelaide and leave it in Sydney, for example. There are, however, a variety of restrictions on these. Usually it's a minimum-hire period rather than repositioning charges, and only certain cars may be eligible for one-ways. Check the small print before deciding on one company rather than another. One-way rentals are generally not available into or out of the Northern Territory or Western Australia, and special rules may also apply to one-ways into or out of other 'remote areas'.

The major companies offer unlimited km rates in the city, but in country and 'remote' areas it's a flat charge plus so many cents a km. On straightforward city rentals they're all pretty much the same price. It's on special deals, odd rentals or longer periods that you find the differences. Weekend specials – usually three days for the price of two – can be good value. If you just need a car for three days around Alice Springs, make it the weekend rather than midweek. 'Stand-by' rates and other special deals are also worth investigating.

Daily rates are typically about $70 for a small car (Ford Laser, Toyota Corolla, Nissan Pulsar), about $90 for a medium car (Holden Camira, Toyota Camry, Nissan Pintara) or about $100 to $110 for a big car (Holden Commodore, Ford Falcon), all including insurance. See the following section for 4WD rentals.

There's a whole collection of other factors with this rent-a-car business. For a start, if you're going to want it for a week, a month or longer, then they all have lower rates. If you're in the really remote outback (Darwin and Alice Springs are only vaguely remote), then the choice of cars is likely to be limited to the larger, more expensive ones. You usually must be at least 21 to hire from most firms.

And don't forget the 'rent-a-wreck' companies. They specialise in renting older cars – at first they really were old, and a flat rate like '$10 a day and forget the insurance' was the usual story. Now many of them have a variety of rates, typically around $35 a day. If you don't want to travel too far out, they can be worth considering.

Many car-rental companies, including some of those renting 4WDs, may have serious misgivings about their cars being taken onto dirt roads. A well-maintained dirt road leading to a major tourist site is usually not a problem, but if you engage in more serious stuff you may well find that you're breaking the rental terms in the small print. Cairns rental agencies, for instance, often forbid you taking their vehicles up to Cape Tribulation, and they have been known to check with paid informers. Tell the rental company about your plans before signing the agreement; if you let sleeping dogs lie, you could well find yourself in serious financial trouble if something goes wrong.

4WD Rentals Renting a 4WD vehicle is within the budget range if a few people get together. Something small like a Suzuki or similar costs around $100 a day; for a Toyota Landcruiser you're looking at around $150 which should include insurance and some free km (typically 100 km). Check the insurance conditions, especially the excess, as they can be onerous.

Hertz has 4WD rentals, with one-way rentals possible between the eastern states and the Northern Territory. Budget also rents 4WD vehicles from Darwin and Alice Springs. Brits: Australia (☎ 1800 331 454) rents 4WD vehicles fitted out as camper vans. These have proved extremely popular in recent years, although they are not cheap at $155 a day with unlimited km, plus Collision Damage Waiver ($12 a day). Brits has offices in all the mainland capitals, as well as Cairns and Alice Springs, so one-way rentals are also possible. In Western Australia, South Perth 4WD Rentals (☎ (09) 362 5444) has a large range of vehicles and provides information and maps, as well as extra equipment. See the track and city descriptions later in this book for rental companies closer to your chosen destinations.

Four-wheel-drive hire vehicles tend to be pretty basic. You'll probably have to organise extra equipment if you want to do a Simpson trip, but then again you shouldn't be doing such a hard, remote trip if you don't have any experience. If you're travelling with a tour operator (see Organised Tours at the end of this chapter), they may be able to organise a self-drive vehicle for you.

Trailers & Caravans

These come in all shapes and sizes, and what you prefer will depend on your wallet and personal preferences. There are many places where you cannot take a caravan (house trailer), but a well-constructed luggage trailer designed for off-road work will go virtually anywhere – with a few big provisos.

First, the trailer must be well made. Every

year, dozens fall apart on the tracks up to Cape York or through the Kimberley. Axles bend, springs and spring hangers break, tow couplings snap, chassis fall apart and, if that is not enough, they can make you lose control easier. Second, trailers will slow you down and get you stuck. Third, they are banned in some places, such as Finke Gorge and Gurig national parks. At times they are simply not worth the trouble.

Car Preparation

A well-prepared vehicle is of paramount importance, though you can easily go overboard in setting it up. There are a host of accessories for 4WDs, some of them next to useless. But if you intend to keep your vehicle for a long time, or are planning some of the harder trips in this book, then the following advice becomes useful.

Good driving lights will let you see the cattle and wildlife on the road at night, and if you don't, a bull bar will help protect you and your machine. An aftermarket suspension helps carry the loads you end up with on these long trips, and a long-range fuel tank takes the worry out of carrying fuel inside the cabin or on the roof (neither of which are recommended). Roof racks are useful for carrying light, bulky items such as tents and sleeping gear. Good racks can carry a bit more, including a spare tyre.

A dual battery (with isolating switch) under the bonnet is a great help to keep the fridge running, for starting your vehicle when the main battery goes flat, or for some emergency welding.

Radios are an important accessory – see Radio Communications under Post & Telecommunications in the Facts for the Visitor chapter.

Items such as spare parts, tools and recovery gear are included in the Checklists in the back of this book, and depend to some extent on your trip. It goes without saying that someone in your group should know how to use them. You don't have to be a qualified mechanic or Camel Trophy veteran, but someone with knowledge and experience is

a great help; the more remote tracks demand a good amount of both.

If your tyres are on their last legs, buy new ones before you set out – six-ply or eight-ply if you can afford them. Stick to common brands, preferably with solid, narrow profiles – wide-profile 'desert' tyres are more fragile and tend to damage easily. Buying them in the bush is always expensive.

Spare tyres and tubes? As a rule of thumb, if you travel for a day without passing a supply point, you'll need to carry more than one complete spare. For hard trips like the Simpson you'll also need a tyre/tube repair kit.

Have your vehicle well serviced before you go. Thoroughly check the cooling system, engine, the complete drive train, suspension and brakes. There are 4WD specialist service centres in each state capital and major regional centres, and many specialise in trip preparation.

We could write a whole book on setting up and preparing your vehicle for the outback, but there are any number around, as well as specialist magazines such as *4X4 Australia* and *Overlander* that are a useful source of up-to-date information on not only where to go, but also what the conditions are like, what preparation you need for a trip, and who to see for specialist advice.

4WD Techniques

Driving a 4WD properly, and to the vehicle's capability, is a skill that needs to be learnt and practised. It's certainly not something that can be explained here in a few paragraphs. There are more detailed books and instructional videos around. Above all, take your time to learn, and remember to tread lightly wherever you go.

Most of the older vehicles (pre-1984) don't have power steering or great brakes. Their suspension is very truck-like, giving a fairly harsh ride, a touch or more of understeer, and on rough roads a fair amount of bump steer. Later-model 4WDs are a lot better, getting progressively more car-like as you get closer to the present crop of expensive, well-set-up and very capable vehicles.

The Basics You should understand the operation of such things as free-wheeling hubs and the transfer-box gear selection. On bitumen or hard dirt surfaces, the vehicle should be in 2WD, high ratio, or if it's a constant 4WD vehicle such as a Range Rover, leave it in normal without the centre diff locked.

Once the road or track gets sandy, muddy or just slippery, you can engage 4WD high ratio, or lock the centre diff of a constant 4WD vehicle. When the going slows and it is rough, sandy, or muddy, you can engage 4WD low ratio, or low ratio with the centre diff locked in a constant 4WD machine. This will give you the ultimate in traction and power.

It should be made clear that a 4WD won't guarantee that you won't get bogged, but it will help you get bogged less often. The down side of a 4WD is that when you do get bogged it is normally deeper and further into the quagmire than a normal car.

Corrugations These are one of the things you will begin to hate on dirt roads. They can be so bad they will seem to be vibrating the vehicle to pieces. Going too fast can be dangerous as well as detrimental to you and your car, while going too slow might not be as dangerous but it will certainly be tiring on you and wearing on your vehicle. In most cases a speed around 80km/h is the optimum, as at that speed the vehicle will tend to 'float' across the hollows, giving a smoother ride. Mind you, what sort of ride you will get will all depend on how good your suspension is: poor shock absorbers will make you feel every bump.

In the Bush If you are unsure of the ground ahead, especially if there is mud or water, get out and check.

Keep thumbs outside or on the edge of the steering wheel. Irregularites in the track can suddenly make the steering wheel turn with incredible force, bruising or even breaking a thumb in the process.

Trailers sometimes aren't worth the trouble (RvD)

Don't change gear in the middle of a tricky section, and if in doubt, always choose the lower gear.

Tyre pressures play a very important part in four-wheel driving. Too hard and the drive will be uncomfortable and you will get bogged more often; too soft and you will destroy tyres. The load you are carrying will determine what pressure you use, but for general touring, pressures between 210 and 280 kPa (30 to 40 psi) are a sensible average.

Cross small ridges square-on; ditches should be crossed at a slight angle.

Steep Hills Low second or third gear is generally best for going uphill, while low first is best for steep downhills. Use the foot brake sparingly and with caution and keep your feet well away from the clutch. Don't turn a vehicle sideways on a hill, and if you stall going uphill, don't touch the clutch or accelerator. See the later Stall Start section for what to do.

Sand Speed and flotation are the keys to success, and high ratio is best, if possible.

Tyre pressures are important here. Generally 140 kPa (20 psi) is a good starting point, but if you are heavily loaded this may be too low and 175 kPa (25 psi) could be more appropriate. If you are lightly loaded, 105 kPa (15 psi) may be the way to go.

Stick to existing wheel tracks, avoid sudden changes in direction and tackle dunes head-on. When descending a dune, avoid braking at all costs, keep the nose pointing downhill, and don't travel too fast but don't go so slow that the wheels stop turning.

If you do get stuck in sand, rock the vehicle backwards and forwards, building up a small stretch of hard-packed sand that you can move off from. Don't spin the wheels or you'll only dig yourself in deeper.

Water Crossings Always check the crossing before you plunge in. Walk through it first if you're unsure. A 4WD should be able to tackle a crossing of around 60 cm deep without any problems or preparation, but a

Deep ruts make life interesting (R & VM)

soft sandy bottom or a strong current flow can change all that.

Spray electrical components with WD40, loosen the fanbelt unless the fan has an auto clutch, and in deep water, fit a canvas blind to the front of the vehicle.

Enter the water at a slow, steady pace – low second gear is generally best – and keep the engine running even if you stop.

Don't forget to dry your brakes out once through the water crossing, and if you were stuck, check all your oils for contamination.

Mud Speed and power are essential, and in deep mud, low second or third are probably best. Keep a steady pace and if possible keep out of ruts.

Stall Start or Key Start When you stop on a steep hill, don't panic; think and stay calm. Engage both the handbrake and the footbrake. Switch the engine off if it hasn't already stalled, ease the clutch in, select low-range reverse gear, and ease the clutch out. Check to see if the track is clear and the wheels are pointing straight ahead, take the handbrake off and the footbrake, but keep your foot close to the brake just in case. Keeping your feet away from the clutch or the accelerator, start the engine and slowly back the vehicle down the hill. Slight feathering of the brake is possible but take care.

MOTORCYCLE

Much of the previous Car section also applies to motorcycles. One of the major differences is that most of the 4WD tracks don't require an off-road motorcycle. True, the going will be much easier on an enduro or motocross machine, especially in sand, but you won't be able to carry the gear you need. On a motorcycle it's much easier to pick your way through or around an obstacle, and if you get stuck, you can always get off and push.

Many bikers travel the outback alone, but for obvious reasons that's not something we can recommend. The ideal setup for serious outback travel is a small group of bikes with one or two follow-up vehicles for fuel, water and luggage; make sure one of the vehicles can also carry a broken-down bike.

You'll need a rider's licence and a helmet. Some motorcyclists in New South Wales have special permission to ride without a helmet, ostensibly for medical reasons.

Unfortunately there's no motorcycling organisation that can help with touring advice. The Auto Cycle Council of Australia (ACCA, with state-based Auto Cycle Unions) deals exclusively with sport, while the various state Motorcycle Rider's Associations busy themselves with legislation issues and social get-togethers; there's no all-encompassing national organisation like the American AMA. The state automobile associations are your best source of information, though they usually don't know much about motorcycles.

Which Motorcycle?

The ideal motorcycle is a large-capacity dual-purpose machine, one that will handle the long distances to and from your chosen track with ease and won't be too disturbed by the track itself. Good choices available in Australia include the Yamaha XT500/550/ 600 or Ténéré models (the 'Land Rovers' of motorcycles – rugged, simple and proven) and the Super Ténéré; Honda XL600, XLV650 Transalp or NX650 Dominator (one of the best machines for the outback, but let down by a small tank); Suzuki DR600/650/750; Kawasaki KLR600 or Tengai 650; Moto Guzzi NTX650; Cagiva 750/900 Elefant; Triumph Tiger; and last but certainly not least, BMW 800/1000/1100 GS.

You'll probably meet a few motorcyclists, often Japanese, on small-capacity dual-purpose bikes, proof that size isn't all-important. A 250 cc may be a bit tedious over the long approach roads though – especially if you're carrying gear and aren't lightweight yourself. A sturdy, uncomplicated road bike from the 1970s or '80s with a large front wheel (18 inch or preferably 19 inch) will generally be OK too.

Important points to consider are fuel consumption and tank size. Few bikes have a fuel range of more than 300 km in favourable conditions, just enough to get you around and straight through the continent on the sealed roads but not sufficient for many outback tracks.

An electric start will make life a lot easier: a stalled bike is often reluctant to start, and the engine usually floods when you drop it. Water-cooling is fine, but if you're faced with the choice, go for a simpler and less sensitive air-cooled engine. The bike ideally should have spoked wheels as these absorb shocks and corrugations better than cast wheels (which have been known to crack under Australian conditions).

Obtaining a Motorcycle

Bringing your own motorcycle into Australia will require a *carnet de passages*, and when you try to sell it here you'll get less than the market price because it doesn't have Australian approval markings (less of a problem in the Northern Territory and Western or South Australia). Shipping from just about anywhere is expensive, but may be worth looking into if you're serious.

With time up your sleeve, you can easily buy a motorcycle thanks to the chronically depressed market. The start of the southern winter is a good time to strike – perfect timing for the outback season. Australian newspapers and the lively local bike press have extensive classified advertisement sections where $2500 will easily take you around the country if you know a bit about bikes. The main drawback is that you'll have to sell the bike again afterwards.

An easier option is a buy-back arrangement with a large motorcycle dealer in a major city – Elizabeth St in Melbourne is a good hunting ground. They're keen to do business, and basic negotiating skills allied with a wad of cash (say, $4000) should secure a decent second-hand road bike with a written guarantee that they'll buy it back in good condition minus $1500 to $2000 after your four-month, round-Australia trip. (Don't be surprised if they'll haggle about what constitutes 'good condition' when you return the bike, so it helps if you don't tell them about your Gunbarrel trip.) Popular brands for this sort of thing are BMWs (cheap ones) and large-capacity, shaft-driven Japanese bikes. Dual-purpose bikes go for a bit less, but the problem is that very few dealers are willing to buy them back. See the earlier Buying a Car section for a company that does buy-backs on Yamaha XT600s.

Preparation & Spares

The owner's manual for your bike often specifies oils of different viscosity for different conditions; use the highest ('thickest') viscosity listed.

Road-going tyres will generally see you through but dual-purpose tyres are a much better proposition. Off-road 'knobbies' are great on chewed-up tracks with deep ruts like the Cape York telegraph track and are less susceptible to punctures than other types of tyre, but you'll probably wear them out before you get to the start and they're hair-raising in wet weather on bitumen. Tubeless tyres are manageable if they're fairly narrow

and you carry at least six carbon-dioxide cartridges in the appropriate repair kit (buy cheap soda-water cartridges and tap the threads or have that done). A tubeless tyre will never seat properly with a hand pump and you'll be pumping forever. Replace the gas in the tyre with air at the earliest opportunity.

The different ways of carrying luggage could fill a separate chapter. Carry your heaviest stuff (tools etc) in a tank bag, which puts the weight between the wheels. Lighter, more bulky gear can be carried over the rear wheel, preferably not high over the rear end but in panniers, or bags, that lower the centre of gravity. Luggage racks should be quite solid and if necessary braced to withstand corrugations. Aluminium racks tend to crack and aren't easy to weld. Take plenty of elastic straps (octopus or 'ocky' straps) to tie down your gear, and bring a few spare.

Outback dust, especially the powdery bull dust, has a habit of getting everywhere you don't want it. Most motorcyclists stop oiling their chains in the outback, and if you have an O-ring chain this is probably a good idea. Make sure the air intake is completely sealed: apply silicone sealant to the outside of any connections, and grease the contact areas of the air filter and cover.

If you're travelling in sandy or muddy regions, a small steel plate welded to the bottom of the sidestand prevents it sinking, though a flattened can or small wooden plank kept to hand in the tank bag also works.

Ensure that the brake and clutch levers can twist around the handlebars in case of a fall – if you do the clamps up tight they'll break off. A headlight protector (plastic cover or steel grid) is a good idea to protect the expensive lens against stones thrown up by oncoming traffic.

It's worth carrying some spares and tools even if you don't know how to use them, because someone else often does. If you do know, you'll probably have a fair idea of what to take. The basics include:

a spare tyre tube (front wheel size, which will fit in the rear but usually not vice versa); you must know how to fix a tyre

- puncture repair kit with levers and a pump, or tubeless tyre repair kit with a pump and enough carbon dioxide cartridges to fix two or three flats (at least two cartridges per flat)
- a spare tyre valve, and a valve cap that can unscrew same
- the bike's standard tool kit for what it's worth (aftermarket items are better); some extra tools – talk to a friendly bike shop if you don't know
- spare throttle, clutch and brake cables
- tie wire, cloth tape ('gaffer' tape) and nylon 'zip-ties'
- a handful of bolts and nuts in the usual emergency sizes (M6 and M8), along with a few self-tapping screws
- one or two fuses in your bike's ratings, and a few metres of electrical wire
- a bar of soap for patching-up tank leaks (knead to a putty with water and squeeze into the leak)
- most important of all, a workshop manual for your bike – even if you can't make sense of it, the local motorcycle mechanic can

Minimum clothing requirements are sturdy boots, gloves, trousers and jacket, and a helmet, ideally with a peak to cut out the sun early and late in the day. Knee and elbow protectors are seriously worth considering, and should be worn under your clothes for best results. Pick up a cheap sheepskin and throw it over the seat to ease the sore-bum syndrome – very effective.

Always carry water – at least two litres on sealed roads where someone is bound to come along soon, much more off the beaten track. Beware of dehydration in the dry, hot air: force yourself to drink plenty of water even if you don't feel thirsty, and keep checking that urine.

Finally, learn something about first aid and carry a first-aid kit. Graze wounds are common in bike get-offs, and your kit should contain some special gauze for this.

Riding Techniques

If you've never ridden on unsealed roads, the outback could be a bad place to start because of the serious consequences if something

It can be done – in this case along the Gunbarrel Highway (R & VM)

goes wrong. If you're in a group with a few experienced riders, however, it could be great fun.

The first mistake that beginners make is to 'freeze' and lock solid onto the handlebars as soon as they see dirt. Wrong. The bike will want to 'wander' a bit and find its own way – let it. Move your weight slightly back on the seat, keep the power on, and guide the bike loosely. If things seem to get out of control, stand on the footpegs a bit; this will lower the centre of gravity and calm things down, and if you grip the tank with your knees at the same time, you'll be surprised how well you can 'steer' the bike. Look reasonably far ahead on the track, not immediately ahead of the front wheel or you'll get nervous.

If a sandy patch comes up, the above techniques are mandatory. It's important to keep the power on; move back on the seat, maybe shift down a gear and open the throttle a bit further. You don't have to accelerate as such; the important thing is to keep enough power onto the rear wheel and maintain momentum. This will help move the centre of gravity to the rear and prevent the front wheel sliding sideways or digging into the sand, twisting sideways and spitting you over the bars – the latter result is guaranteed if you close the throttle and thereby transfer weight to the front. Don't try to 'jump ruts' unless they're shallow; choose a particular rut and try to ride it out. Great fun once you get the hang of it!

The same techniques apply to deep gravel, often encountered on freshly levelled ('graded') roads. Car drivers love these, but to motorcyclists the loose surface can be bad news – a bit like riding on marbles. Keep the power onto the rear wheel, but be careful not to overdo it because the rear will break sideways more easily than in sand; better to shift back on the seat a bit. The less 'off-road' your tyre tread, the more of a problem you'll have with gravel.

You can fight against sand and gravel, but mud is a much more formidable adversary. In theory the same riding principles apply, but unless you're on an enduro machine with knobby tyres, mud requires a delicate balancing act with the throttle: if the front wheel doesn't slide out from under you the rear wheel will, especially in the slippery red or black soil usually encountered in the outback. 'Soften' the power delivery by selecting a higher gear than you normally would for that speed. Take it slowly with your feet out if things are really wet, or look for harder surface off the side of the road. Also beware of mud build-up under the rear mudguard (and the front if it sits low on the wheel): the rear wheel could well lock up, and if you try to keep going you'll burn the clutch. All you can do is stop and clear out the mud, which may be necessary every few hundred metres in blacksoil.

On corrugated roads, car drivers tend to sit on relatively high speeds so they skim over the top and make life more comfortable for themselves and their suspension. The drawback is that the tyres lose grip, which is fine so long as the road is flat and there aren't any corners. But a motorcycle has less inherent stability, and you could well find yourself drifting sideways out of control if you don't slow down. See how you go, but if the corrugation is really bad you may have to slow right down and ride on the side of the road or off the road altogether.

Beware that road sides and ditches often contain nails, bits of glass and other meanies that lie in wait for unsuspecting tyres.

BICYCLE

Whether you're hiring a bike to ride around town or wearing out your chain-wheels on a Melbourne-Darwin marathon, you'll find that Australia is a great place for cycling. It has always been popular, and not only as a sport: some shearers would ride for huge distances between jobs, rather than use less reliable horses. There are bike tracks in most cities, and in the country you'll find thousands of km of good roads which carry so little traffic that the biggest hassle is waving back to the drivers. Especially appealing is that in many areas you'll ride a very long way without encountering a hill.

Bicycle helmets are compulsory wear in all states and territories.

If you're coming specifically to cycle, it makes sense to bring your own bike. Check your airline for costs and the degree of dismantling/packing required. Within Australia you can load your bike onto a bus or train to skip the boring bits. Note that bus companies require you to dismantle your bike, and some don't guarantee that it will travel on the same bus as you. Trains are easier, but supervise the loading and if possible tie your bike upright, otherwise you may find that the guard has stacked crates of Holden spares on your fragile alloy wheels.

You can buy a reasonable steel-framed touring bike in Australia for about $400 (plus panniers), but if you want quality fittings or a good mountain bike, costs rise sharply. It may be possible to rent touring bikes and equipment from a commercial touring outfit. A touring bike is better than a mountain bike if you're staying on the tar.

Planning

There are two approaches to seeing the outback by bike. The first is to stay on the few sealed roads. Although these are usually highways, they carry little traffic and offer very good riding. Distances between sources of food and water can be long, though, so plan carefully. Much of eastern Australia seems to have been settled on the principle of not having more than a day's horse ride between pubs, so until you get to the back of beyond it's possible to plan even ultra-long routes and still get a shower at the end of the day. Most people do carry camping equipment, but, on the east side of the continent at least, it's feasible to travel from town to town staying in hotels or on-site vans most nights.

The other approach involves planning a trip on one of the unsealed routes. You'll probably need a mountain bike, not necessarily because of the rough terrain but because the wider tyres will help with the loose road surface. Some roads might be impossibly deep in sand or dust and the only sure way to find out is to talk to another cyclist. Allow plenty of time and be prepared

to change your plans. Riding on dirt roads can be very slow, so don't underestimate the time it will take to reach the next water supply.

The major unsealed routes are technically highways and are regularly graded, so they should be in reasonable condition. A local council or shire will be able to tell you about this. The police are another good source of information, but they will have to deal with the results if something goes wrong and may try to dissuade you. Don't dismiss their advice lightly: they often know the local conditions better than anyone else.

Always check with the locals if you're heading into remote areas, and notify the police if you're about to do something particularly adventurous. That said, don't rely too much on local knowledge of road conditions: most people have no idea of what a heavily loaded bike needs. What they think of as a great road may be pedal-deep in sand or bull dust, and flooded roads which are closed to cars might not be a problem for bikes. Then again, they might be!

If you're determined to do some cycling on minor outback tracks but don't necessarily want to get from point A to point B, consider riding in one of the big national parks, where the ranger will have plenty of information on conditions.

You can get by with standard road maps, but one of the government series (either from AUSLIG or the CMA series put out by the New South Wales government) showing topography and handy features such as farm buildings helps you plan routes and gives a better appreciation of the surrounding country. The 1:250,000 series is the most suitable (although these maps are becoming outdated) but you'll need a lot of maps if you're covering much territory. The next scale up, 1:1,000,000, is adequate. If you're travelling off the main roads, have a look at smaller scale maps.

Spares

It's rare to find a reasonably sized town that doesn't have a shop stocking at least basic bike parts, although whether they will be ompatible with exotic machines is another matter. It might be worth talking with a specialist bike shop in a major city before you et out. They may be able to courier spare arts to you in case of emergency.

Compulsory spares include: puncture epair kit, tubes and tyres (hot roads wear vres quickly, and Michelin World Tours start) get pretty thin after about 2000 km), brake nd gear cables, spokes (about 10, in the orrect gauge), bearings and lubricants plus ll the tools required to strip down and clean earings, and perhaps a spare chain (if you're oing a long way) and crank. You obviously hould know how to perform routine repairs.

On the Road

Intil you get fit, be careful to eat enough to eep you going – remember that exercise is n appetite-suppressant. It's surprisingly asy to be so depleted of energy that you end p camping in the spinifex just 10 km short f a shower and a steak.

No matter how fit you are, water is vital. Death by dehydration is a real possibility on remote track. Inland Australia can be npossibly hot in summer, and spring and utumn may not be much cooler. Take it easy, vear a hat and plenty of sunscreen, and drink *ts* of water. Six litres a day isn't an unreaonable amount if you're working hard, and ou may well need more – check the colour f your urine. Heat exhaustion can also kill, nd you need to be aware of how you body s coping. Obtain good medical advice perhaps from a sports medical clinic) and earn to recognise the onset of dehydration nd heat exhaustion.

The first time you're passed by a road train vill be an interesting experience, but if you tick to sealed roads the most dangerous ehicles are buses, which use a lot of road nd are surprisingly quiet. When you haven't een another vehicle for a few hours it's easy o be on the wrong side of the road when the lice Springs express blasts through.

In the eastern states, be aware of the blistering 'hot northerlies', the prevailing winds hat make a northbound cyclist's life very ncomfortable in summer. In April, when the south-east's clear autumn weather begins, the Southerly Trades prevail, and you can have (theoretically at least) tailwinds all the way to Darwin. If you're travelling across the Nullarbor, don't try cycling from east to west against the westerlies: they're pretty strong all year and can soon wear you out. It's not uncommon for trans-Nullarbor trucks to use 30% more fuel heading west rather than east.

Information

In each state there are touring organisations that can help with information and put you in touch with touring clubs:

Australian Capital Territory
Pedal Power ACT, PO Box 581, Canberra, ACT 2601 (☎ (06) 248 7995)
New South Wales
Bicycle Institute of New South Wales, 82 Campbell St, Surry Hills, NSW 2010 (☎ (02) 212 5628)
Queensland
Bicycle Institute of Queensland, The Web, 142 Agnew St, Norman Park, Qld 4101 (☎ (07) 899 2988)
South Australia
Bicycle Institute of South Australia, 11 Church Rd, Mitcham, SA 5062 (☎ (08) 271 5824)
Tasmania
Pedal Power Tasmania, c/o Environment Centre, 102 Bathurst St, Hobart, Tas 7000 (☎ (002) 34 5566)
Victoria
Bicycle Victoria, 29 Somerset Place, Melbourne, Vic 3000 (☎ (03) 328 3000)
Western Australia
Cycle Touring Association, PO Box 174, Wembley, WA 6014 (☎ (09) 349 2310)

HITCHING

Quite a few travellers hitch rides in the outback. The locals are generally pretty easy-going and friendly, and often pick up hitchers for company. The drawback is that they may deposit them at the track leading to their property, usually a long way from anywhere. Also, many car drivers in the outback are engaged in long-distance travel themselves and aren't able to pick up hitchers. For these reasons, hitching in the outback is really only feasible along the main sealed

A convoy on the Sandy Blight Junction Road (R & VM)

roads, where rides take you from town to town or roadhouse to roadhouse.

Hitching is never entirely safe in any country, and it's not a form of travel we can recommend. People who decide to hitch should understand that they are taking a small but potentially serious risk, also in Australia. They will be safer if they travel in pairs and let someone know where they are going. University and hostel notice boards are good places to look for hitching partners.

Just as hitchers should be wary when accepting lifts, drivers who pick up hitchers or cost-sharing travellers should also be aware of the possible risks involved.

Two people is the ideal number for hitching, any more makes things very difficult. Ideally those two should comprise one male and one female – two guys hitching together can expect long waits. It is not advisable for women to hitch alone, or even in pairs.

The ideal appearance for hitching is a sort of genteel poverty – threadbare but clean. Don't carry too much gear – if it looks like

it's going to take half an hour to pack your bags aboard you'll be left on the roadside. A sign announcing your destination can be useful, and if you're visiting from abroad, a nice prominent flag on your pack will help.

Trucks often provide the best lifts but they'll only stop if they are going slowly and can get started easily again. Thus the ideal place is at the top of a hill where they have a downhill run. Truckies often say they are going to the next town and if they don't like you, will drop you anywhere. As they often pick up hitchers for company, the quickest way to create a bad impression is to jump in and fall asleep.

BOAT

Not really. Once upon a time there was quite a busy coastal shipping service but now it only applies to freight, and apart from specialised bulk carriers, even that is declining rapidly. In inland Australia, long-distance freight used to go by river – as evidenced by the admiralty office in the outback New South Wales town of Bourke – but modern rail and road transport have taken over completely. There are still a few ferries in outback regions, such as along the Birdsville and Cape York tracks and up at Thursday Island, and details are provided in the relevant track descriptions.

It is, however, quite possible to make your way round the coast by hitching rides or crewing on yachts. Ask around at harbours, marinas or yacht or sailing clubs – anywhere where boats call. It obviously helps if you're an experienced sailor, but some people are taken on as cooks (not very pleasant on a rolling yacht). Usually you have to chip in something for food, and the skipper may demand a financial bond as security. A lot of boats move north to escape the winter, so April is a good time to look for a berth in the southern harbours.

If you know your way around a commercial fishing boat, there's often temporary work available on the many small trawlers operating the remote north-eastern and northern coastline. The pay can be excellent or lousy depending on the catch, but it's quite an experience and you visit parts of the coast that can't be reached by anybody else. Ask around at fishing ports. Trawler crews are often amenable to hiring female cooks, and women who pursue this option report good and bad experiences.

MAIL RUNS
It's possible to get a first-hand idea of what a mail run means to the people of the outback by going along for the ride (see Post & Telecommunications in the Facts for the Visitor chapter for an explanation of mail runs). In Coober Pedy, the mail truck leaves on Monday and Thursday along 600 km of dirt roads as it does the trip round Coober Pedy, Oodnadatta and William Creek. There's a backpackers' special price of $49, or the standard fare including lunch is $59. You can stay at Oodnadatta or William Creek and return to Coober Pedy on the next mail truck. For details, ring toll-free on ☎ 1800 802 074, or contact Underground Books

(☎ (086) 72 5558) at 1 Post Office Hill Rd, Coober Pedy.

Another possibility is the mail planes, and there are a few you can ride, although they're not that cheap. In Port Augusta, Augusta Airways (☎ (086) 42 3100) does a run on Saturday to Boulia in western Queensland, via Innamincka and Birdsville; the cost is $325. In Cairns, Cape York Air Services (☎ (070) 35 9399), the local mail contractor, does mail runs to remote outback stations on weekdays. Space permitting, you can go along on these runs, and the cost is $140 to $275, depending on the length of the trip. Air Mount Isa (☎ (077) 43 2844) does mail runs and supply flights to isolated mines, and takes tourists for negotiable fees.

ORGANISED TOURS
There are many operators who offer outback tours in a variety of vehicles and even on foot. Some 4WD safaris go to places you simply couldn't get to on your own without a vehicle and large amounts of expensive equipment. See the individual track descriptions for details.

YHA tours are good value – find out about them at YHA Travel offices in capital cities. In major centres like Darwin and Cairns there are many tours aimed specifically at backpackers – good prices, good destinations, good fun.

Tag-Along 4WD Tours
If you already have a 4WD and want to experience the remote country safely, easily

(HF)

and in the company of others, there are a number of guiding services or 'tag-along' operators well worth considering. They may be able to set you up with a 4WD hire vehicle if necessary, and a few may even take a passenger or two.

Some provide a catering service and can really produce wonderful meals in the scrub, including wine with the evening meal. Most of these operations expect a little help preparing the food, washing dishes and carrying some of the tucker, usually on an informal roster basis.

Other operations only provide a guiding service. Of course these are much cheaper but you need to provide your own food and the enthusiasm and expertise to cook it in the bush.

All the tag-along services provide experienced guides who are experts with driving and recovery, and who will give you all the hints necessary to get you through. Full radio gear and recovery equipment are also carried. As well, many of the operators have areas opened to them that are not open to the private traveller. Of course they know where all the worthwhile attractions are as well as the best camping spots. Where permits are required, they look after all that.

Once you've decided where you'd like to go, contact the operators servicing that area. Details are provided in the individual track descriptions in this book.

Motorcycle Tours

There are several operators offering outback motorcycling tours, either tag-along or (more often) on bikes supplied by them. Some are mentioned in the track descriptions in this book.

Bike-tour operators tend to come and go. One that has been in business for over 10 years is Bike Tours Australia, offering long-distance tours on Yamaha XT600 trail bikes. These include a variety of outback tours (such as a five-week adventure diagonally across Australia from Perth to Cape York for $5400) for which you have to be a reasonably good rider. Most of Bike Tours' clients

are Continental Europeans (often German); other nationalities are welcome, but Aussies may have trouble fitting in. The company also operates a car and motorcycle buy-back scheme under the name Car Connection Australia; see the earlier Buying a Car section for contact details.

Aboriginal Culture Tours

Aboriginal involvement in the tourist industry has increased greatly in the last few years. Considering that outback Aborigines are faced with few employment opportunities, and that Aboriginal culture is of major interest for most people who visit outback Australia, this trend is likely to continue.

Such tours often give an introduction to traditional Aboriginal law, religion and lifestyle, all of which remain strong in many parts of outback Australia. These tours often describe how, during the creation period (the 'Dreaming'), Aboriginal creation ancestors travelled the face of the earth, creating the landforms that we see today. Aborigines have also built up an encyclopaedic knowledge of useful plants and animals over the past 50,000 years; 'bush tucker' still forms an important part of the diet of many communities, and you can find out about that too.

If you do go on any of these tours, please respect any requests that Aboriginal guides make about appropriate behaviour.

Northern South Australia Desert Tracks (☎ (089) 56 2144) is an Anangu-owned organisation that offers an eight-day tour of the Aboriginal-owned and administered Anangu-Pitjantjatjara Lands. Few if any other tours offer such a deep insight into traditional Aboriginal culture. Desert Tracks' tours seem expensive – $1825 for seven days or $680 for two – but they are very good. Costs include payment to Anangu elders as guides and teachers. Contact Desert Tracks well in advance of your preferred date of departure. Desert Tracks departs from Ayers Rock Resort, 20 km from Uluru.

Northern Territory – south & centre
Uluru-Kata Tjuta (Ayers Rock-the Olgas) National Park's Liru Walk is an excellent insight into Anangu culture. It leaves three days a week. Advance bookings are essential on ☎ (089) 56 2299. The park's Mala Walk is often hosted by Anangu, but not always. Both walks take 1½ hours and are free.

Uluru Experience (☎ 008 80 3174) sometimes has Anangu along on its walks. It also offers an Anangu guided tour to part of the Petermann Ranges, 250 km west of Uluru.

The Ayers Rock Resort Visitors Centre (☎ (089) 56 2240) also keeps abreast of new tourist initiatives and will assist you where it can. At the time of writing, local Anangu were trying to establish a camel safari on a homeland just outside the park.

At Watarrka (King's Canyon) National Park, various tours are offered by Anangu-owned and operated Kurkara Tours (☎ (089) 56 7442). Oak Valley Day Tours (☎ (089) 56 0959) is also Aboriginal-owned and operated – it offers day tours south of Alice Springs.

West of Alice Springs, Wallace Rockhole Aboriginal Community (☎ (089) 56 7415) offers a 1½-hour walk and talk about Aboriginal culture, including rock engravings; Sahara Outback Tours (☎ (089) 53 0881) will also take you to Wallace Rockhole for this purpose as part of a two-day tour. The Ipolera Community (☎ (089) 56 2299) offers a two-hour walk and talk about Aboriginal culture. Also of interest is the Ntaria (Hermannsburg) Aboriginal Community (☎ (089) 56 7402), which offers a self-guided tour of the historical community.

In Alice Springs, Rod Steinert Tours (☎ (089) 55 5000) offers a corroboree (ceremonial dance) and a culture and bush-tucker tour. Pitchi Richi (☎ (089) 52 1931) is an eclectic establishment that offers Aboriginal guided tours.

In Tennant Creek between March and November, you can take the Walala Bush Tucker Tour (☎ (089) 62 3388/1353) with Aboriginal women.

Northern Territory – Top End Outback NT Air Safaris and Kakadu Parklink (☎ (089) 79 2411) in conjunction with the Manilakarr people offer excursions to Mikiny Valley, in which various aspects of Aboriginal culture are covered. Umorrduk Aboriginal Safaris (☎ (089) 48 1306) flies and drives tourists to Kakadu and north-west Arnhem Land for culture tours that include stunning old rock art. Adventure Terra Safari Tours (☎ (089) 41 2899) offers a trip to the Kakadu region. It is also worth ringing Australian Frontier Holidays (☎ (089) 75 4727) to enquire about Bill Harney's Jankangyina Tours. Aussie Safaris (☎ (089) 81 1633) will take you west for a day in the life of Peppimenarti Aboriginal Community. Tiwi Tours and Australian Kakadu Tours (☎ (089) 81 5144) will introduce you to Melville and Bathurst islands north of Darwin.

From Katherine, Travel North (☎ (089) 72 1044) will arrange for you to see a corroboree at Springvale Homestead. Manyallaluk and Travel North (☎ (089) 72 1044) together can organise for you to meet Jawoyn traditional owners and go on a number of tours. Wilderness Experience (☎ (089) 412899) offers an eight-day experience of the area with Aboriginal guides.

Western Australia Karijini Walkabouts offers six backpacking expeditions with Aboriginal guides in the Pilbara's Karijini National Park; for details and bookings, ring John the Travel Broker (☎ (09) 309 1395) in Perth. By ringing Contact Point Inbound Tours (☎ (09) 388 2210), also in Perth, you can arrange a trip to either the Pilbara or the Kimberley with former Aboriginal Artist of the Year Shane Pickett.

In Derby, by ringing the Derby Tourist Bureau (☎ (091) 91 1426), you can arrange to go on a Geikie Gorge boat cruise with some of its Bunuba traditional owners. From Broome, Flack Track Tours (☎ (091) 92 1487) offers a visit to an Aboriginal community.

Queensland In Rockhampton, you can go on guided tours of the Dreamtime Aboriginal Cultural Centre (☎ (079) 36 1655).

In Far North Queensland, at Kuranda, the

Camels (TW)

Rainforestation (☎ (070) 93 7251) organises Aboriginal guided walks and performances. From Cairns, you can fly to Quinkan in Cape York Peninsula for a Quinkan Rock Art Safari and Bush Camp; for details, ring Tresize Bush Guides (☎ (070) 55 1865), also for 4WD tours out of Cairns. The Ang-Gnarra Aboriginal Corporation (☎ (070) 60 3214) at Laura offers guided tours of Split Rock Gallery near Laura, as well as tours of other rock galleries in the area by prior arrangement. Ku Ku Yelangi woman Nalba (Hazel) Douglas will take you on an excellent one-day 4WD culture/adventure tour –

contact the Port Douglas Dive Centre on ☎ (070) 99 5327.

The Far North Queensland Travel Centre (☎ (070) 51 3588) can help to arrange various tours in the area. These include a Munbah Aboriginal Culture Tour (☎ (070) 60 9173) organised by the Hopevale Aboriginal community, 50 km north of Cooktown, where you can sleep in traditional Aboriginal huts; a six-day Torres Strait Island Cruise at the tip of Cape York, operated by Jardine Shipping (☎ 008 81 0634); or a Kuranda Rainforest and Dreamtime tour operated by Tropic Wings Tours (☎ (070) 35 3555).

The Central Deserts

Alice Springs

Population 20,500

Alice Springs, a pleasant, modern town with good shops and restaurants, is an access point for the many tourist attractions of central Australia.

Alice Springs's growth has been recent and rapid. When the name was officially changed in 1933 (it was previously called Stuart) the population had only just reached 200! Even in the 1950s, Alice Springs was still a tiny town with a population in the hundreds. Until WW II there was no sealed road leading there, and it was only in 1987 that the old road south to Port Augusta and Adelaide was finally replaced by a new, shorter and fully sealed highway.

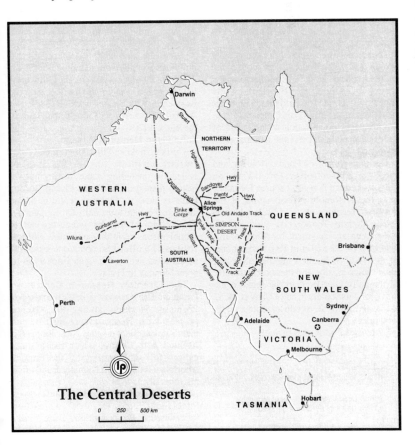

The Central Deserts

0   250   500 km

THE CENTRAL DESERTS

Information

The tourist office, the Central Australian Tourism Industry Association (☎ (089) 52 5199), is on the corner of Hartley St and Gregory Terrace in the centre of town. The staff here are very helpful and they have a range of brochures and maps.

The Northern Territory Conservation Commission has a desk at the tourist office, and has a comprehensive range of brochures on all the parks and reserves in the Centre. The main office (☎ (089) 51 8211) is just off the Stuart Highway, about five km south of town.

The main post office is at 33 Hartley St (☎ (089) 52 1020), and there's a row of public phones outside. The telephone area code for Alice Springs is 089.

There are three good bookshops. The Arunta Gallery on Todd St, just south of the mall, Dymocks in the Alice Plaza, and a branch of Angus & Robertson in the Yeperenye Centre. The Arid Lands Environment Centre (☎ 52 6782) on Gregory Terrace is a nonprofit organisation which is full of information on both local and national environmental issues.

The Department of Lands, Housing and Local Government office (☎ 51 5743) on Gregory Terrace is a good source for maps, as is the Automobile Association of the Northern Territory (☎ 53 1322), which is also on Gregory Terrace.

For camping equipment, try Alice Springs Disposals (☎ 52 5701) in Reg Harris Lane, off the Todd St Mall. A number of people make swags locally, and these are generally substantially cheaper than the brand-name ones found nationally. Centre Canvas (☎ 52 2453), 9 Smith St, produces some really good ones.

Other useful addresses include:

Medical Facilities
  Alice Springs Hospital, Gap Rd (☎ 51 7777)
Permits
  Central Land Council, 33 Stuart Highway, PO Box 3321, NT 0871 (☎ 52 3800)
Police
  Parsons St (☎ 51 8888)

Royal Flying Doctor Service
  Stuart Terrace, PO Box 2210, NT 0871 (☎ 52 1033)

Things to See

Alice Springs has plenty of attractions, and it's worth putting aside a couple of days to see some of the more interesting ones.

The 1870s **Telegraph Station**, one of a string through central Australia, is two km north of the town; it has a small museum which is open daily. The **Alice Springs** here (from which the town takes its name) are a great spot for a cooling dip and a picnic.

Anzac Hill is at the northern end of Todd St; it offers fine views over modern Alice Springs and down to the MacDonnell Ranges.

There are a number of interesting old buildings around town including: the Stuart Town Gaol built in 1907-08, the Old Courthouse, which was in use until 1980; the Residency, which dates from 1926-27; and Adelaide House on the Todd St Mall, built in the early 1920s and now preserved as the **John Flynn Memorial Museum**.

Upstairs in Alice Plaza, the **Central Australian Museum** has a fascinating collection, including some superb natural history displays. The **Royal Flying Doctor Base** is close to the town centre in Stuart Terrace; there are tours daily except Sunday. The **School of the Air**, which broadcasts school lessons to children on remote outback stations, is on Head St, about one km north of the town centre. It's open from 9 am to noon Monday to Friday.

The **Strehlow Research Centre** on Larapinta Drive commemorates the work of Professor Strehlow among the Arrente people of the Hermannsburg district, and there's an excellent display. Next door is the **Araluen Arts Centre**, which has a small gallery full of paintings by the famous Aboriginal artist Albert Namatjira, and often has other displays as well.

South of the Heavitree Gap causeway is **Pitchi Richi** ('gap in the range'), a miniature folk museum. Every morning there's billy tea and damper, and an interesting and lively

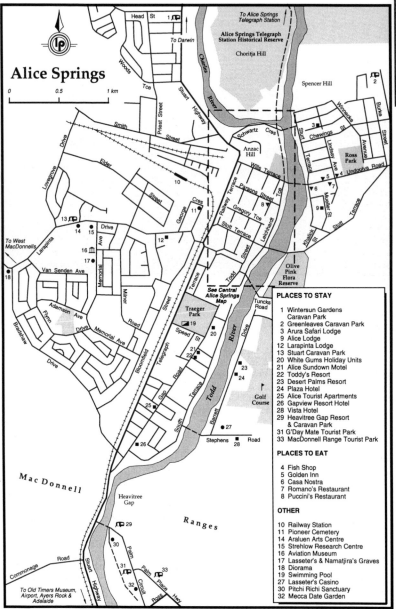

Alice Springs

0   0.5   1 km

PLACES TO STAY

1 Wintersun Gardens
  Caravan Park
2 Greenleaves Caravan Park
3 Arura Safari Lodge
9 Alice Lodge
12 Larapinta Lodge
13 Stuart Caravan Park
20 White Gums Holiday Units
21 Alice Sundown Motel
22 Toddy's Resort
23 Desert Palms Resort
24 Plaza Hotel
25 Alice Tourist Apartments
26 Gapview Resort Hotel
28 Vista Hotel
29 Heavitree Gap Resort
   & Caravan Park
31 G'Day Mate Tourist Park
33 MacDonnell Range Tourist Park

PLACES TO EAT

4 Fish Shop
5 Golden Inn
6 Casa Nostra
7 Romano's Restaurant
8 Puccini's Restaurant

OTHER

10 Railway Station
11 Pioneer Cemetery
14 Araluen Arts Centre
15 Strehlow Research Centre
16 Aviation Museum
17 Lasseter's & Namatjira's Graves
18 Diorama
19 Swimming Pool
27 Lasseter's Casino
30 Pitchi Richi Sanctuary
32 Mecca Date Garden

View of Alice Springs (NTTC)

chat on Arrente Aboriginal lore and traditions.

At the MacDonnell Siding, off the Stuart Highway 10 km south of Alice Springs, is the **old Ghan**, a collection of restored Ghan locomotives and carriages on a stretch of disused siding from the old narrow-gauge Ghan railway track. The **Chateau Hornsby** winery, 15 km south of town, produces some decent wines.

Organised Tours

There are literally dozens of tours available from Alice Springs. Listed here are some of the more interesting ones. See also the Organised Tours sections in the individual track descriptions and the Getting Around chapter.

Rod Steinert (☎ 55 5000) operates a variety of tours including his popular $42 Dreamtime & Bushtucker Tour. It's a half-day trip in which you meet some Aborigines and learn a little about their traditional life.

You can have a short camel ride for a few dollars at the Frontier Camel Farm (☎ 53 0444), or take longer overnight or two to seven-day camel treks costing from $385 to $800. Noel Fullerton's Outback Camel Safaris (☎ 56 0925) is another operator.

Sunrise balloon trips are also popular; these cost from $88, which includes breakfast and a 30-minute flight. Outback Ballooning (☎ toll-free 1800 809 790) and Ballooning Downunder (☎ 52 8816) are two companies that operate balloon trips.

Events

The Camel Cup, a series of camel races, takes place in July. In August there's the Alice Springs Rodeo.

In late September there's the event which probably draws the biggest crowds of all: the Henley-on-Todd Regatta. The boats are all bottomless, the crews' legs stick out and they simply run down the (usually) dry riverbed! The Verdi Club Beerfest is held early in October, at the end of the regatta.

Places to Stay

Camping Alice Springs's caravan parks and their rates are:

G'Day Mate Tourist Park (☎ 52 9589), Palm Circuit, near the date garden and Pitchi Richi Sanctuary – camping ($12, $15 with power) and cabins ($45)

Greenleaves Caravan Park (☎ 52 8645), two km east of the town centre on Burke St – camping ($15, $17.50 with power) and on-site vans ($34)

Heavitree Gap Caravan Park (☎ 52 2370), Palm Circuit, four km south of town – camping ($14, $16 with power) and on-site vans ($37)

MacDonnell Range Tourist Park (☎ 52 6111), Palm Place, five km from town – camping ($13, $16 with power) and on-site cabins ($32 to $50)

Stuart Caravan Park (☎ 52 2547), two km west of the town centre on Larapinta Drive – camping ($12, $15 with power), on-site vans ($35) and cabins ($45)

Wintersun Gardens Caravan Park (☎ 52 4080), two km north of the town centre on the Stuart Highway – camping ($11, $15 with power), on-site vans ($30) and cabins ($38)

Hostels & Guesthouses There are plenty of hostels and guesthouses in Alice Springs. Popular ones include: the *Melanka Backpackers* (☎ toll-free 1800 815 066) at 94 Todd St, with a variety of rooms, ranging from eight-bed dorms at $9 to singles/doubles for $20/24; the relaxed *Alice Lodge* (☎ 53 1975) at 4 Mueller St, with nightly rates of $9 in the dorm, $23 for a single or $13 per person in a double; *Toddy's Resort* (☎ 52 1322) at 41 Gap Rd, where it costs $10 for dorms with shared facilities, $12 with TV and bathroom, $28 for doubles and $39 for doubles with bathroom; and the *Gapview Resort Hotel* (☎ 52 6611), about one km south of the town centre, which charges $6.80 for a bed in an eight-bed room, $10.50 in a six-share, $12.60 in a four-share, or there are twin rooms for $36.75.

Hotels, Motels & Holiday Flats Right by the river at 1 Todd St Mall is the *Old Alice Inn* (☎ 52 1255). This pub gets noisy when there are bands playing on weekends, but otherwise it is quite a reasonable place to stay. Room rates are $40 for singles/doubles, some with bath.

At 67 Gap Rd, there's the *Swagman's Rest Motel* (☎ 53 1333) with singles/doubles for $52/62. The units are self-contained and there's a swimming pool.

The *Alice Tourist Apartments* (☎ 52 2788) are also on Gap Rd and have one and two-bedroom, self-contained, air-con apartments from $55 to $95. There's a communal laundry and the obligatory swimming pool.

On Barrett Drive, next to the Plaza Hotel, the *Desert Palms Resort* (☎ 52 5977) has spacious rooms, each with a small kitchen, at $65. There's a swimming pool, and if you have a car this is one of the best value motels in the Alice.

Motels include: the *Alice Sundown Motel* (☎ 52 8422), 39 Gap Rd, with self-contained rooms from $52/63 to $63/74 for singles/doubles; *Desert Rose Inn* (☎ 52 1411), 15 Railway Terrace, with rooms at $71/79, or larger rooms at $95; and the *Larapinta Lodge* (☎ 52 7255), 3 Larapinta Drive, with singles/doubles for $55/67. There's a communal kitchen and a laundry for guests' use.

Places to Eat

Snacks & Fast Food There are numerous places for a sandwich or light snack along Todd St Mall. Several of them put tables and chairs outside – ideal for a breakfast in the cool morning air.

The *Jolly Swagman* in Todd Plaza off the mall is a pleasant place for sandwiches and light snacks. Off the mall on the other side, *Thai Kitchen* offers similar fare as well as Asian food. *La Cafeteriere*, at the southern end of the mall, is open for breakfast, burgers, sandwiches etc.

The big Alice Plaza has three lunch-time eating places. *Fawlty's* and *Doctor Lunch* have snacks, light meals, sandwiches and a salad bar, while *Red Centre Chinese* has Chinese fast food to eat there or take away. Across the mall, the Springs Plaza has *Golly It's Good*, with more sandwiches and snacks.

In the Yeperenye shopping centre on Hartley St there's the *Boomerang Coffee Shop*, the *Bakery*, another *Fawlty's* outlet and a big *Woolworths* supermarket.

THE CENTRAL DESERTS

Central Alice Springs

0   150   300 m

PLACES TO STAY

1	Desert Rose Inn
3	Old Alice Inn
16	YHA Pioneer Hostel
23	Diplomat Motel
31	Alice Springs Pacific Resort
34	Melanka Backpackers
35	Melanka Lodge & Bus Centre
36	YHA Alice Springs Hostel

PLACES TO EAT

11	Puccini's Restaurant & Ansett Airlines
14	Thai Kitchen & Le Cafeteriere
17	Flynn's on the Mall
19	Jolly Swagman
21	Overlander Steakhouse
24	La Casalinga
25	Eranova Cafeteria
28	Bojangles
33	Oriental Gourmet Chinese Restaurant

OTHER

2	Alice Plaza
4	Spring Plaza
5	Police
6	Stuart Town Gaol
7	Old Courthouse
8	Yeperenye Shopping Centre
9	CAAMA
10	The Residency
12	General Post Office
13	John Flynn Memorial Museum
15	Qantas & Gallery Gondwana
18	McCafferty's
20	Tourist Office
22	Hertz
26	Panorama Guth
27	Papunya Tula Artists & Avis
29	Automobile Association of the Northern Territory
30	Library & Civic Centre
32	Billy Goat Hill
37	Royal Flying Doctor Service Base
38	Alice Springs Hospital

Across the river on Lindsay Ave, near the corner of Undoolya Rd, the *Fish Shop* is a good and reasonably cheap fish & chip shop.

Pub Meals Far and away the most popular place for pub food is the *Todd Tavern* in the Old Alice Inn. The food is good and cheap, and there are special nights when you can get a meal from $5 to $8, including unlimited attacks on the vegetable bar. There's also the slightly more formal *Fishcaf* here, with meals from $8 to $15.

Upstairs in the Alice Plaza on Todd St Mall, the *Stuart Arms Bistro* does straightforward meals from $7 to $12, and you can add a salad plate for a couple of dollars.

Restaurants The *Eranova Cafeteria* at 70 Todd St is a comfortable place with a good selection of excellent food. It's open for breakfast, lunch and dinner from Monday to Saturday. Meals range from $7 to $15.

Around the corner at 105 Gregory Terrace, *La Casalinga* has been serving up pasta and pizza for many years; it's open from 5 pm to 1 am every night. Meals cost from $10 to $15, and it has a bar.

Across the river from the town centre, on the corner of Undoolya Rd and Sturt Terrace, the *Casa Nostra* is another pizza and pasta specialist. You can also get good pasta at the *Al Fresco* at the northern end of the mall. *Rocky's* on the Stuart Highway is another pizza place.

Also in the town centre is the licensed *Flynn's on the Mall*, opposite the John Flynn Memorial Museum. It's a popular place, with meals in the $13 to $17 range. Meats such as crocodile and kangaroo are featured here, and at quite a few restaurants around town.

There are a number of Chinese restaurants around the Alice. The *Oriental Gourmet* is on Hartley St, near the corner of Stott Terrace. *Chopsticks*, on Hartley St at the Yeperenye shopping centre, is said to be good, and so is the bright yellow *Golden Inn* on Undoolya Rd, just over the bridge from the town centre. Aside from the usual items, you can sample some Malaysian and Sichuan dishes.

Of course the Alice has to have a steakhouse, so you can try the *Overlander Steakhouse* at 72 Hartley St. It features 'Territory food' such as beef, buffalo, kangaroo and camel – a carnivore's delight! It's quite popular, but not that cheap with main courses from $17 to $25.

For something a little different, there's *Keller's Swiss & Indian Restaurant* on Gregory Terrace, which gives you the chance to try two vastly different cuisines in the one place. It's open for dinner nightly, and main courses start from around $10. *Puccini's*, an Italian restaurant on Todd Mall, serves excellent food.

Out-of-town dining possibilities include the daily barbecue lunches at the *Chateau Hornsby* winery, or a late breakfast, lunch or tea at the *White Gums Park*, opposite the Simpson's Gap National Park turn-off 17 km west of town.

Another interesting possibility is an evening meal combined with a ride on the old Ghan train at MacDonnell Siding (☎ 55 5047). It operates twice weekly from April to October, and weekly at other times. The cost is $49, and the meal is actually provided by the *Camp Oven Kitchen* (☎ 53 1411); it consists of soup and damper, and a roast, all cooked in 'camp ovens' – cast-iron pots which are buried in coals from a fire. It's also possible to do the meals without the train ride for $45. They take place on Monday, Wednesday and Saturday evenings. It's a popular and good-value evening.

Entertainment

At the *Old Alice Inn*, by the river on the corner of Wills and Leichhardt Terraces, the Jam Session has live bands on Monday nights, and sometimes features better known bands.

Bojangles is a restaurant and nightclub on Todd St, and the *Alice Junction Tavern* off Ross Highway has a disco on Friday and Saturday nights. The *Overlander Steakhouse* is the home of a good local bush band, Bloodwood.

If you want to watch the Australian gambling enthusiasm in a central Australian setting, head for *Lasseter's Casino*, but dress up. Outback 'character' Ted Egan puts on a performance of tall tales and outback songs three nights a week at *Chateau Hornsby* for $15, or $33 with dinner.

There are all sorts of events at the *Araluen Arts Centre* on Larapinta Drive, including temporary art exhibits, theatre and music performances and regular films.

Things to Buy

Alice Springs has a number of art galleries and craft centres. If you have an interest in central Australian art or you're looking for a piece to buy, there are a couple of places where you can buy direct from the artists. The Papunya Tula Artists shop is on Todd St just south of the mall, or there's Jukurrpa Artists at 35 Gap Rd. Both of these places are owned and run by the art centres which produce the work.

The Central Australian Aboriginal Media Association (CAAMA) shop on Hartley St, by the Yeperenye shopping centre, is another very good place, and prices are reasonable.

There are plenty of other, generally more commercial outlets for Aboriginal art. Two of the better ones are Gondwana Gallery and the Original Aboriginal Dreamtime Gallery on the mall.

Getting Around
To/From the Airport The Alice Springs airport is 14 km south of town, about $20 by taxi.

There is an airport shuttle bus service (☎ 53 0310) which meets flights and takes passengers to all city accommodation and to the train station. It costs $9.

Car Rental Five car-rental companies including Hertz, Avis and Brits have offices in Alice Springs. All have 4WD vehicles ranging from Suzuki Sierras, which seat from two to four people, to Toyota Troopcarriers, which seat 11. Competition is fierce and different packages are available, but the cheapest rates are usually offered by Territory Rent-a-Car and Centre Car Rentals, the two home-grown firms.

Alice Springs is classified as a remote area so car hire can be expensive, particularly if you want to drive down to Uluru (Ayers Rock) or further afield. Territory, for instance, charges $28 per day plus $0.28 per km for its cheapest vehicle without air-con. Avis and Budget also have 4WDs for hire. You're looking at around $85 per day for a Suzuki, including insurance and 100 km free per day. For a Toyota Landcruiser or similar, the price jumps to around $155 per day. Discounts apply for longer rentals (more than four to seven days, depending on the company).

The outback specials offered by Hertz are worth investigating if you're flying into Alice Springs and want to do a camping trip. Its Troopcarriers cost $165 per day with unlimited km for seven days or more, and you can hire a full set of camping equipment for four people for an additional $40 per day.

Brits has fully equipped 4WD bush campers accommodating three adults, starting at $160 per day for a trip of seven to 20 days. You need the company's written permission before tackling many of the tracks described in this book.

It pays to read the conditions carefully particularly when it comes to insurance matters. For example, Centre advises that its vehicles aren't insured once they leave the bitumen. Although its rates are relatively cheap, this condition means that you can't visit Chambers Pillar, Palm Valley, Kings Canyon and many other scenic attractions around Alice Springs. The insurance excess for a single-vehicle accident with Hertz is $4000 while with Brits it's $5000. However, you can reduce the excess with Brits to $1000 by taking its collision damage waiver package.

Avis, Budget, Hertz and Territory all have counters at Alice Springs Airport. In town, Avis (☎ 52 4366) is at 78 Todd St, Hertz (☎ 52 2644) is at 76 Hartley St, Budget (☎ 52 8899) is at 10 Gap Rd, Thrifty (☎ 52 2400) is at 94 Todd St, Brits (☎ 52 8814) is at the corner of the Stuart Highway and Power St about four km north of town, Territory Rent-a-Car (☎ 52 9999) is at the corner of Stott Terrace and Hartley St and Centre Car Rentals (☎ 52 1405) is at the corner of Wills Terrace and Todd St Mall.

Bicycle Alice Springs has a number of bicycle tracks; a bike is a great way of getting around town and out to the closer attractions, particularly in winter. The best place to rent a bike is from the backpacker hostels. Typical rates are $10 per day.

Stuart Highway

The 2708-km-long Stuart Highway traverses the heart of Australia from the south coast at Port Augusta to Darwin on the north coast. It is one of the most important arteries in the country's highway system, providing the

Top End of Australia with a direct link to the south.

While it is no longer a true outback track now that all of it is sealed and there's a well-developed network of roadhouses, it does go straight through the heart of outback Australia. It also gives access to many of the tracks described elsewhere in this book and has a number of worthwhile sights of its own. If you are spending any amount of time travelling in Australia's harsh interior, it's almost guaranteed that some of that time will be spent on 'The Track', as the Stuart Highway is affectionately called.

HISTORY

The highway takes its name from John McDouall Stuart, who, in 1862, was the first European to cross Australia from south to north. The road itself is obviously a modern creation. In the early days travellers heading off into the interior were very much dependent on the availability of water, and so the route which initially developed was what is known today as the Oodnadatta Track, some distance to the east of the current highway, where water supplies were more reliable.

With the decline of vehicle traffic along the Oodnadatta Track due to the completion of the railway line to Alice Springs, the discovery of opals in Coober Pedy in 1915 and later the development of the Woomera Rocket Range, the main road developed further west along today's route. Surfacing work on the section from Port Augusta to the NT border was only completed in 1987.

From Alice Springs to Darwin the highway basically follows the route of the Overland Telegraph Line, which was built in 1872 largely along the route which Stuart had taken a decade before.

INFORMATION

As you would expect on such a major road, there are no special requirements for travelling on the Stuart Highway. It's two-lane bitumen all of the way, there's fuel and accommodation at regular intervals and you're never more than half a day's drive from the nearest pub – civilised indeed! The

Flower bed with a difference (HF)

main thing you need to be aware of is that from Woomera (169 km north of Port Augusta) to Glendambo (a distance of 115 km) the highway skirts the southern edge of the Woomera Prohibited Area, and from Glendambo to Coober Pedy (251 km) it cuts right through. Travelling off the main road and into this area is prohibited without a permit from the Area Administrator in Woomera.

Should you strike mechanical trouble, it's unlikely that you'd have to wait more than an hour or two for another vehicle to pass by. For those with HF radios, the Royal Flying Doctor base at Port Augusta (callsign VNZ) monitors the following frequencies from 6 am to 9 pm daily: 2020, 4010, 6890 and 8165 kHz. From Alice Springs (VJD) there's 24-hour emergency coverage on 5410 MHz, or the following frequencies are monitored from 7.30 am to 5 pm weekdays: 2020, 5410 and 6950 kHz. Darwin is covered by the

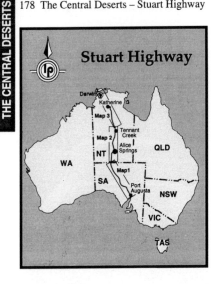

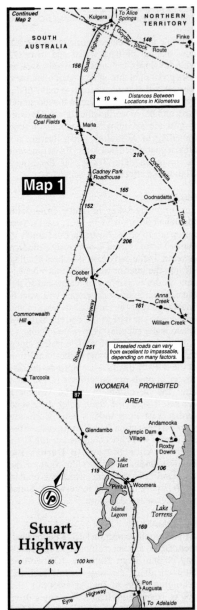

Aerial Medical Services (VJY) on 2360, 4010, 6840 and 7975 kHz daily.

The NT Tourist Commission and Tourism South Australia have got together and published a series of sectional strip maps, entitled *A Traveller's Guide to Australia's Stuart Highway*, and these give excellent information on both practical and historical subjects. They are sporadically available from tourist offices along the way.

If you have a cassette player, it might be worth getting hold of the taped 'guidebook' produced by Take a Tour Guide. The Stuart Highway is covered in four cassettes: Port Augusta to Alice and Alice to Darwin, and the same sections in reverse direction (because you can't listen to a tape backwards). The tapes cost $20.95 each and come with a booklet of discount vouchers for goods and services along the way – the discounts alone will easily offset the purchase price. The tapes are available at some service stations and caravan parks along the highway, or by mail order from TATG (☎ (03) 555 8419), PO Box 109, Highett, Vic 3190; include $2 for postage and handling.

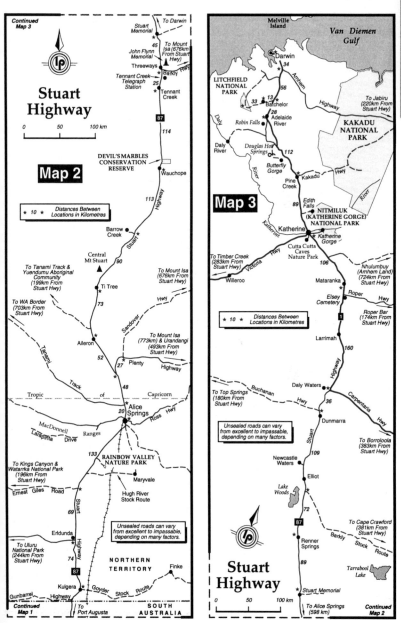

THE ROUTE
Port Augusta
The Stuart Highway starts the long haul north from the crossroads town of Port Augusta (population 14,600) at the head of Spencer Gulf. Some useful addresses in Port Augusta include:

Medical Facilities
    Port Augusta Hospital (☎ (086) 48 5500)
National Parks
    McKay St (☎ (086) 48 5310)
Police
    Commercial Rd (☎ (086) 48 5020)
Post Office
    (☎ (086) 42 2789)
Royal Flying Doctor Service
    4 Vincent St (☎ (086) 42 2044)
Tourist Office
    Wadlata Outback Centre, 41 Flinders Terrace
    (☎ (086) 42 4511)

Port Augusta to Coober Pedy
The first stretch is 169 km to the scruffy little settlement of **Pimba**, which sits on a virtually treeless plateau and, despite its accessibility, is one of the most desolate places imaginable. The township of **Woomera** (population 1600) lies five km north of the highway and in itself is hardly worth the detour, although you can pass through if you intend visiting the opal-mining settlement of Andamooka or the huge Olympic Dam mining project (see Detours, later in this section). Woomera had its heyday in the 1950s and '60s when it was the base for military and civil personnel involved in rocket-launching experiments. These days it has something of a ghost-town feel, not unlike Canberra on a Sunday afternoon! There's a small museum in the centre of town.

From Pimba the highway swings west for the 115 km run to **Glendambo**, along the way passing the usually dry salt lakes of Island Lagoon and Lake Hart. The road once again swings north for 251 km until it reaches the opal-mining town of Coober Pedy.

Coober Pedy
Coober Pedy (population 2500) is as close as Australia gets to a having a frontier town. The name is Aboriginal and means 'white fellow's hole in the ground', which aptly describes the place, as a large proportion of the population live in dugouts to shelter from extreme temperatures. The most dominant landmark is the **Big Winch**, which is a lookout over the town and has an extensive display of cut and uncut opal. The **Old Timers Mine** and the **Umoona Mine & Museum** are also worth a look. Several dugout homes are open to visitors – all you have to do is create an eccentric enough abode and you can charge admission! A must-see is **Crocodile Harry's**, an interesting dugout home about four km from town which has featured in a number of documentaries and movies, including *Mad Max III*. Not far either side of the Stuart Highway at Coober Pedy you have the world's largest sheep station (Commonwealth Hill at 10,567 sq km) and its largest cattle station (Anna Creek at 30,113 sq km).

Some useful addresses in Coober Pedy include:

Medical Facilities
    Coober Pedy Hospital (☎ (086) 72 5009)
Police
    (☎ (086) 72 5056)
Post Office
    (☎ (086) 72 5062)

From Coober Pedy, rough and dusty dirt roads lead east to **William Creek** (161 km) and north to **Oodnadatta** (206 km), both on the Oodnadatta Track. A short distance out of Coober Pedy, the road to Oodnadatta crosses the Dog Fence, and then traverses a flat, eerie and almost lifeless plain known as the Moon Plain (also featured in *Mad Max III*).

Coober Pedy to Alice Springs
The highway continues north from Coober Pedy through fairly unchanging country, passing through **Cadney Park Roadhouse** after 152 km, from where a good dirt road strikes out east to Oodnadatta (165 km), an attractive route which passes through the

colourful mesa hills known as the **Painted Desert**.

The next settlement on the highway is the small town of **Marla** (population 250), 83 km north of Cadney Park, and the head of the Oodnadatta Track (see the Oodnadatta Track section). The opal-mining fields of **Mintabie**, 35 km to the west, are worth a quick visit, although permits need to be arranged from the Marla police station.

From Marla it's just a hop, skip and a jump (156 km to be exact) to the **Northern Territory border**, and a further two km to where one of the most famous outback tracks, the **Gunbarrel Highway**, heads off into the vastness of the western deserts (see the Gunbarrel Highway section).

Kulgera is next, and from here you can strike out east along a dirt road (which can be treacherous in the wet) to **Finke**, from where there are a number of possibilities: east to Old Andado and then south to Mount Dare and Oodnadatta or north to Alice Springs, or head north to Alice Springs along the Finke Track, also known as the Old Ghan Track (see the Finke & Old Andado Tracks section).

From **Erldunda**, 74 km north of Kulgera, you can head west along the bitumen road to **Uluru** (Ayers Rock, 250 km) and **Kata Tjuta** (the Olgas, 287 km), from where the dirt takes over once again for the 188-km journey to the settlement of **Docker River**, on the Western Australia border.

The turn-off for Kings Canyon is 69 km north of Erldunda, and from here the final stage into Alice Springs is 133 km, passing en route the **Outback Camel Safaris** camel farm in the James Ranges.

Alice Springs (see the earlier Alice Springs section), set in the heart of the rugged and spectacular MacDonnell Ranges, is an oasis – a place to rest, restock, eat out and make repairs before heading bush again. It's a lively town with plenty of things to see, and most people find that a few days here are well spent. Being the biggest population centre in the outback, the Alice is also the

Crocodile Harry's (HF)

best place for mechanical repairs and spare parts.

Alice Springs to Tennant Creek

Twenty km north of Alice Springs is the **Tanami Track** turn-off, and the signboard here indicates it's a long and lonely 703 km to the Western Australia border. This road gives direct access to the Kimberley and is becoming increasingly popular. Conventional vehicles can pass with care (see the Tanami Track section for details).

The **Plenty Highway** turn-off is a further 48 km north, and this road heads east to the Queensland border and on to Mount Isa (773 km). The **Sandover Highway**, which leaves the Plenty Highway 27 km east of the Stuart Highway, is an alternative to the Plenty, and it heads north-east into outback Queensland, with connections to Camooweal and Mount Isa (see the Plenty Highway and Sandover Highway sections).

Continuing north you pass through the settlements of **Aileron** (52 km north of the Plenty Highway turn-off), **Ti Tree** (a further 73 km), **Barrow Creek** (90 km) and **Wauchope** (113 km). It's about here that you pass the last sand dune of the Centre, and start the transition from the red country of the centre of Australia to the more densely vegetated and generally greener Top End. This part of the highway crosses the very eastern edge of the Tanami Desert, and so spinifex grass, which explorer Ernest Giles called 'that abominable vegetable production', dominates.

The **Devils Marbles Conservation Reserve**, just a few km north of Wauchope in the Davenport Ranges, consists of unusual spherical boulders scattered haphazardly over a surprisingly extensive area. Aboriginal mythology has it that they were laid by the Rainbow Serpent.

Tennant Creek

The town of Tennant Creek (population 3500), 114 km north of Wauchope, is, along with Katherine, the only town of any size between the Alice and Darwin. Known as Jurnkurakurr by the local Aborigines, the town has an interesting history. It was on the Overland Telegraph route; it had a station here and was also the site of a small gold rush in the 1930s. There's an information centre and a museum and you can also visit the **Tennant Creek Battery**, where gold was crushed; guided tours are held daily in winter. Some useful addresses in Tennant Creek include:

Medical Facilities
   Tennant Creek Hospital, Schmidt St
   (☎ (089) 62 4399)
National Parks
   Conservation Commission (☎ (089) 62 2140)
Police
   Paterson St (☎ (089) 62 1211)
Post Office
   (☎ (089) 62 2196)
Tourist Office
   Visitor Information Centre, Transit Centr
   (☎ (089) 62 3388)

Tennant Creek to Katherine

Twenty-five km north of Tennant Creek **Threeways** marks the junction of the Stuart Highway and the Barkly Highway, which is the only bitumen connection between Queensland and the Northern Territory. At this major road junction a stone **memorial** commemorates the Reverend John Flynn, the founder of the Royal Flying Doctor Service.

About 45 km north of Threeways there's a **memorial** to Stuart at Attack Creek, where the explorer turned back on the first of his attempts to cross Australia from south to north, after his party was attacked by a group of hostile Aborigines. The party was running low on supplies and this incident was the final straw. Just a few km further north, and four km off the road along the old Stuart Highway, is **Churchill's Head**, a large rock said to look like Britain's wartime prime minister.

Back on the Stuart Highway, a large rock known as **Lubra's Lookout** overlooks **Renner Springs**, 89 km north from the Stuart Memorial. This is generally accepted as the dividing line between the seasonally wet Top End and the dry Centre, and the ighway also divides the Tanami Desert on ne west side from the Barkly Tableland on ne east. Seventy-two km after Renner prings there's the turn-off to the east of the **Barkly Stock Route**, a dirt road which joins p with the Carpentaria Highway.

The next intersection is 109 km up the tuart Highway, where the **Buchanan Highway**, named after the great cattleman Jat Buchanan, heads north-west to **Top prings**, **Victoria River Downs** and **Timber Creek** on the Victoria Highway. **Daly Waters**, 36 km north of the Buchanan Highway junction and three km off the ighway, was an important staging post in ne early days of aviation – Amy Johnson anded here. The **Daly Waters Pub** is an tmospheric place, dating from 1893; it's aid to be the oldest pub in the Territory. There's good food available here.

Just south of Daly Waters, the single-ane, sealed **Carpentaria Highway** heads ff east to **Borroloola**, one of the best arramundi fishing spots in the Northern erritory, 383 km away near the Gulf of Carpentaria.

About 160 km north of Daly Waters, the **Roper Highway** branches east from the tuart Highway. It leads 174 km to **Roper Bar**, near the Roper River on the edge of Aboriginal land – an area mainly visited by shing enthusiasts. All but about 40 km of ne road is sealed. About five km south of the Roper junction is the turn-off to the **Elsey Cemetery**, not far off the highway. Here are ne graves of characters like 'the Fizzer' who ame to life in *We of the Never Never*, Jeannie Gunn's classic novel of turn-of-the-century utback life.

Mataranka is on the Stuart Highway, nother seven km north of the Roper Highway turn-off. The attraction is **Mataranka Homestead**, seven km east of ne highway along the turn-off just south f the small town. The crystal-clear hermal pool here, in a pocket of rainfor-st, is a great place to wind down after a ot day on the road – though it can get crowded.

From Mataranka the highway curves to the north-west and reaches Katherine after 106 km.

Katherine

Katherine has long been an important transit point, since the river it's built on and named after is the first permanent running water if you're coming north from Alice Springs. The town includes some historic old buildings, such as the **Sportsman's Arms**, featured in *We of the Never Never*. Interesting features of the town include the old **railway station** (owned by the National Trust), the small **Katherine Museum** in the old airport termi-nal building, and **Springvale Homestead**, eight km south-west of town (turn right off the Victoria Highway after 3.75 km), which claims to be the oldest cattle station in the Northern Territory. Today, it's also a tourist accommodation centre, but free half-hour tours around the old homestead are given once or twice daily.

Katherine is also where the **Victoria Highway**, part of National Route 1 around Australia, joins from the west, connecting the Northern Territory with Western Aus-tralia.

Some useful addresses in Katherine include:

Medical Facilities
    Katherine Hospital, Gorge Rd (☎ (089) 72 9211)
National Parks
    Conservation Commission , Giles St
    (☎ (089) 73 8770)
Police
    Stuart Highway (☎ (089) 72 011)
Post Office
    Stuart Highway (☎ (089) 72 1439)
Tourist Office
    Katherine Region Tourist Association, Stuart Highway (☎ (089) 72 2650)

The main interest here, however, is the spec-tacular **Katherine Gorge**, 30 km to the north-east along a bitumen road – a great place to camp, walk, swim, canoe, take a cruise or simply float along on an air mat-tress. Strictly speaking, Katherine Gorge is 13 gorges, separated from each other by rapids of varying length. The gorge walls

Thermal pool in Mataranka (RvD)

Katherine Gorge in the dry season (TW)

ren't high, but it is a remote, beautiful place. It is 12 km long and has been carved out by the Katherine River, which rises in Arnhem Land. Further downstream it becomes the Daly River before flowing into the Timor Sea, 80 km south-west of Darwin.

Katherine to Darwin

From Katherine it's 89 km to **Pine Creek**, an interesting little former gold-mining centre and the turn-off for the southern route into **Kakadu National Park** along the recently sealed Kakadu Highway (see the Kakadu section in the Tropics chapter).

North of Pine Creek, a sealed section of the old Stuart Highway makes a loop to the north-west before rejoining the main road 52 km on. It's a scenic trip and leads to a number of pleasant spots, but access to them is often cut in the wet season. To reach **Douglas Hot Springs**, turn south off the old highway just after it branches from the Stuart Highway and go about 35 km. The nature park here includes a section of the Douglas River and several hot springs – a bit hot for bathing at 40°C, but there are cooler pools, and a pretty camping area.

Butterfly Gorge National Park is about 15 km beyond Douglas Hot Springs along a 4WD track. True to its name, butterflies sometimes swarm in the gorge.

The turning to **Daly River** (109 km from the Stuart Highway) is 27 km further on. There's a **Catholic mission** (the ruins of an 1886 Jesuit mission) and the **Daly River Nature Park** where you can camp. Bird life is abundant at some times of the year, and quite a few saltwater and freshwater crocodiles inhabit the river.

The beautiful 12-metre **Robin Falls** are a short walk off the old highway, 18 km along. The falls, set in a monsoon-forested gorge, dwindle to a trickle in the dry season, but are spectacular in the Wet.

The old highway rejoins the Stuart Highway at the small settlement of **Adelaide River**, which has a cemetery for those who died in the 1942-43 Japanese air raids. The whole stretch of the highway between here and Darwin is dotted with a series of roadside WW II airstrips.

Twenty-eight km north of Adelaide River is the turn-off to the regional centre of **Batchelor**, which is the main access point for **Litchfield National Park**. (See the Litchfield National Park section in the Tropics chapter.) The highway then continues north through cleared farmland for the final 90 km stretch into Darwin. The only feature of note along this section is where the **Arnhem Highway**, the access road to Kakadu National Park and Arnhem Land, branches off the Stuart Highway 34 km south of Darwin.

See the Darwin section in the Tropics chapter for information on the capital of the Top End.

DETOURS

While most of the detours off the Stuart Highway are tracks in themselves, there's an interesting trip you can make from Woomera to Andamooka and the huge Olympic Dam mine at Roxby Downs. **Andamooka** (population 470) is a small opal-mining community, similar in many respects to Coober Pedy, but on a much smaller scale. However, due to its isolation, it is much less visited. It is 106 km north of Woomera, the last 30 km being on a well-maintained dirt road.

The **Olympic Dam** uranium, gold, silver and copper mine was established in the early 1980s. It is the world's largest copper-uranium mine, and is currently one of only three uranium mines in the country. There are mine tours daily from the BP station at Roxby Downs township.

FACILITIES

Facilities along the Stuart Highway are excellent all the way; the longest stretch without a fuel stop is 251 km between Glendambo and Coober Pedy.

There are roadhouses with fuel (all types), food, accommodation and mechanical repairs at most centres along the way. While some roadhouses in the larger towns have 24-hour fuel, the smaller places are typically open from early morning to late evening. Details of accommodation along the Stuart Highway include:

Port Augusta

No shortage of hotels, motels and campsites.

Woomera

Woomera Eldo Hotel (☎ (086) 73 7867), Kotara Crescent, has single/double rooms from $33/45. The *Woomera Tourist Village* (☎ (086) 73 7800), Wirruna Ave, has camp sites for $5 per person and on-site caravans from $25.

Glendambo

Glendambo Tourist Centre (☎ (086) 72 1030 (motel) and ☎ (086) 72 1035 (caravan park)) has rooms for $75/85, accommodation in a bunkhouse for $15, on-site vans from $30 a double and camp sites from $12.50 for two people.

Coober Pedy

No shortage of hotels, motels and campsites.

Cadney Park

Cadney Homestead Motel & Caravan Park (☎ (086) 70 7994) has rooms at $65/72 and camp sites from $6 per person. One-bedroom cabins are also available for $35.

Marla

Marla Travellers Rest (☎ (086) 70 7001) has rooms from $49/59, cabins for $25/36 and camp sites from $4 per person.

Kulgera

Kulgera Motel & Caravan Park (☎ (089) 56 0973) has rooms from $38 and camp sites from $3 per person.

Erldunda

Desert Oaks Motel & Caravan Park (☎ (089) 56 0984) has rooms for $61/72, cabins for $26/36 and camp sites from $6 per person.

Alice Springs

See the earlier Alice Springs section.

Ti Tree

Ti Tree Roadhouse Motel & Caravan Park (☎ (089) 56 9741) has rooms from $45/55 and camp sites from $4 per person.

Barrow Creek

Barrow Creek Hotel & Caravan Park (☎ (089) 56 9753) has rooms and cabins for $20/35 and camp sites from $6.

Wauchope

Wauchope Well Hotel & Caravan Park (☎ (089) 64 1963) has rooms from $25/50 and camp sites from $5.

Tennant Creek

No shortage of hotels, motels and campsites.

Threeways

Threeways Roadhouse Motel & Caravan Park

(☎ (089) 62 2744) has rooms from $45 and camp sites from $4 per person.

Renner Springs

Renner Springs Motel (☎ (089) 64 4505) ha rooms from $35/45.

Elliott

Elliott Hotel (☎ (089) 69 2069) and the *BP Road house* (☎ (089) 69 2018) have rooms from around $25/35. The *Midland Caravan Park* (☎ (089) 69 2037) has camp sites from $8 for two people.

Daly Waters

The *Daly Waters Pub Hotel & Caravan Park* (☎ (089) 75 9927) on Stuart St, three km west of the Stuart Highway, has rooms from $25/35 and camp sites from $6. The *Hi-Way Inn & Caravan Park* (☎ (089) 75 9925) has rooms from $40/6 and camp sites at $3 per person.

Larrimah

Larrimah Wayside Inn & Caravan Park (☎ (089 75 9931) has rooms from $25/40 and camp sites from $5. The *Green Park Tourist Complex* (☎ (089) 75 9937) has camp sites from $8 for two people.

Mataranka

The *Territory Manor Motel* (☎ (089) 75 4516) Martin Rd, has rooms from $37/41. The *Old Elsey Inn* (☎ (089) 75 4512), Stuart Highway, ha rooms for $45/55. The *Mataranka Homestead* (☎ (089) 75 4544), nine km south-east of town costs around $60 for a double room. You can also camp at the Mataranka Homestead from $14, and at the *12 Mile Yards Camping Area* (☎ (089) 7 4767) on John Hauser Drive for $5 per person.

Katherine

No shortage of hotels, motels and campsites.

Pine Creek

Pine Creek Motel & Caravan Park (☎ (089) 76 1288 (hotel) and (089) 76 1217 (caravan park)) Moule St, has rooms from $60/70 and camp site from $5.

Adelaide River

Adelaide River Inn & Caravan Park (☎ (089) 76 7047) has rooms from $30/50 and camp site from $6 for two people.

ALTERNATIVE TRANSPORT

As you'd expect on such a major highway there are daily scheduled bus services all the way from Port Augusta to Darwin with both Greyhound Pioneer Australia (☎ toll-free 1800 13 2030) and McCafferty's (☎ (08) 21 5066). You can also take the Ghan train from Port Augusta to Alice Springs (see the separate entry on the Ghan in the Getting Around chapter).

MacDonnell Ranges

The timeless MacDonnell Ranges sweep in a rugged red barrier from east to west for 400 km across the vast central Australian plain, with Alice Springs situated conveniently in the middle. The ranges consist of a parallel series of long, steep-sided ridges that rise between 100 and 600 metres above the intervening valley floors. Scattered along its entire length are deep gorges carved by ancient rivers that flowed south into the Simpson Desert. Here also you find the four highest peaks west of the Great Dividing Range: Mt Zeil, the highest, is 1531 metres above sea level and 900 metres above the surrounding plain.

Although arid, the ranges are covered with a huge variety of plants, including many tall trees, with the majestic ghost gum an outstanding feature. In hidden, moist places are relics of the rainforest flora that covered this region millions of years ago. Wildlife enthusiasts will be delighted by the chance to observe 167 species of birds, 85 reptiles, 23 native mammals, 10 fish and five frog species; a number of the mammals are rare or endangered elsewhere in the arid zone.

Tourism is big business in Alice Springs, with over 350,000 international and interstate visitors to the town each year. Many of the most spectacular landscapes and most important biological areas are now included in national parks and reserves, most of which are readily accessible by conventional vehicle. The largest of these, the new 2100-sq-km West MacDonnells National Park, stretches 160 km from the outskirts of Alice Springs. To the east, a string of generally small parks lies scattered through the ranges for nearly the same distance.

All parks in the MacDonnell Ranges have basic picnic facilities, and there are many excellent walks and superb scenic highlights. However, good opportunities for vehicle-based camping are rather limited and most bush camping grounds bulge at the seams during the cooler months. There are

just two commercial facilities outside Alice Springs: Glen Helen Homestead 135 km to the west and Ross River Homestead 80 km to the east. These holiday resorts offer a range of services, including meals, motel-style accommodation and fuel.

INFORMATION
Tourist Offices
The best place to get general information on all aspects of the MacDonnell Ranges is the Central Australian Tourism Industry Association's (CATIA's) information centre (☎ (089) 52 5199), on the southwest corner of Gregory Terrace and Hartley St in Alice Springs. The Conservation Commission of the Northern Territory (☎ (089) 51 8211), PO Box 1046, Alice Springs, NT 0871, is a source of practical advice on the parks of the area. Alternatively, contact the rangers direct at:

Simpsons Gap (☎ (089) 55 0310) for the eastern half of the West MacDonnells National Park
Ormiston Gorge (☎ (089) 56 7799) for the western half of the West MacDonnells National Park
Alice Springs Telegraph Station (☎ (089) 52 1013) for Emily & Jessie Gaps Conservation Reserve
Trephina Gorge (☎ (089) 56 9765) for Corroboree Rock Conservation Reserve, N'Dhala Gorge Nature Park and Trephina Gorge Nature Park
Arltunga (☎ (089) 56 9770) for the Arltunga Historical Reserve and the Ruby Gap Nature Park

Emergency
In the event of a medical emergency, you can always obtain assistance at any park ranger station. These are located at Simpsons Gap and Ormiston Gorge west of Alice Springs, and Trephina Gorge and Arltunga to the east. The resorts at Glen Helen and Ross River also have staff trained in first aid and, like the ranger stations, are in telephone contact with the outside world. In more remote areas, hail one of the tourist coaches, which are invariably fitted with HF radios and first-aid kits.

Books
Sadly, there are no good books on the MacDonnell Ranges, although Jeff & Mare

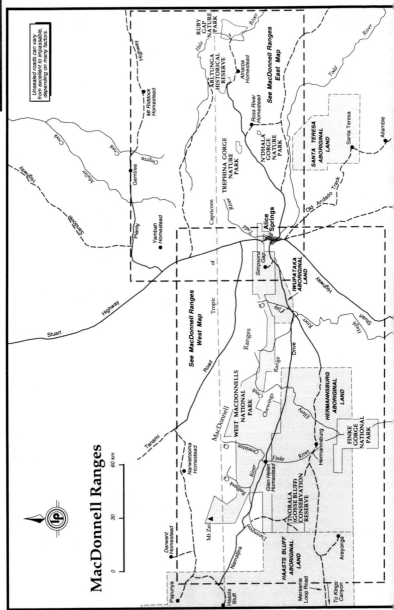

MacDonnell Ranges

Carter's *The Complete Guide to Central Australia* (Hodder & Stoughton, Sydney, 1993) does have a fair-sized section devoted to touring the area. This comprehensive, well-written book is a worthwhile purchase, particularly if you're travelling further afield in the Red Centre.

Those keen on science may enjoy Penny van Oosterzee's *The Centre – the Natural History of Australia's Desert Regions* (Reed Books Pty Ltd, Sydney, 1991), as it contains interesting material on the central ranges.

Maps

For detailed topographic information, you'll need at least the Hermannsburg and Alice Springs 1:250,000 sheets. For bushwalkers, a 1:50,000 series of orthophoto maps covers the ranges east of Serpentine Gorge. These can be purchased from the Department of Lands, Housing & Local Government (☎ (089) 51 5737), 21 Gregory Terrace, Alice Springs, or order them through any AUSLIG sales outlet.

The map-cum-guide entitled the *MacDonnell Ranges*, by Westprint Heritage Maps, is a useful planning and touring reference. It's available from numerous outlets around Alice Springs, including some news-agencies, service stations and the Department of Lands, Housing & Local Government.

Radio Frequencies

As the main roads of the MacDonnell Ranges are fairly busy most of the year, an HF radio isn't usually considered necessary. The major exception would be a visit to remote Ruby Gap in the off-peak season (October to April), when a radio could prove useful. The Alice Springs RFDS base (callsign VJD – Victor Juliet Delta) can be reached on 5410 and 6950 kHz between 7.30 am and 5 pm Monday to Friday, excluding public holidays. For after-hours emergency calls, use 2020 and 5410 kHz. Further information can be obtained by ringing the base (☎ (089) 52 1033).

WEST FROM ALICE SPRINGS

Spearing between high ridgelines, the road west from Alice Springs through the West MacDonnells is sealed for the first 135 km, to the Finke River crossing near Glen Helen. From here the final 37 km past Redbank Gorge to the road between Haasts Bluff and Hermannsburg is rough dirt. There are a number of spectacular red gorges and several deep waterholes along the way, with all but Standley Chasm located within the new West MacDonnells National Park. In dry conditions, all the main attractions along this route are accessible to conventional vehicles.

Simpsons Gap

Heading west on Larapinta Drive you pass the site of a proposed desert flora & fauna park on the outskirts of Alice Springs before arriving at the grave of Dr John Flynn, founder of the RFDS and the Australian Inland Mission. Sited on a low rise with ghost gums and a magnificent view of nearby **Mt Gillen**, the great man's last resting place is just outside the eastern boundary of the West MacDonnells National Park.

Twenty-two km from town is **Simpsons Gap**, where Roe Creek has gouged a red gorge with towering cliffs through Rungutjirba Ridge. The area is popular with picnickers, and also has some nice walks, as well as a world-class cycle path that winds through the bush from Flynns Grave to the gap itself (see Activities, later in this section). Early morning and late afternoon are the best times to see the rock wallabies that live among a jumble of huge boulders right in the gap. Simpsons Gap is open between 8 am and 8 pm daily.

Standley Chasm

From the Simpsons Gap turn-off, you cross Aboriginal land for the next 29 km to Standley Chasm, which is owned and managed by the nearby community of **Iwupataka**. This narrow cleft has smooth vertical walls and is famous for its midday light display – for a brief period at noon, reflected sunlight causes the rocks to glow red. The 15-minute walk up the rocky gully

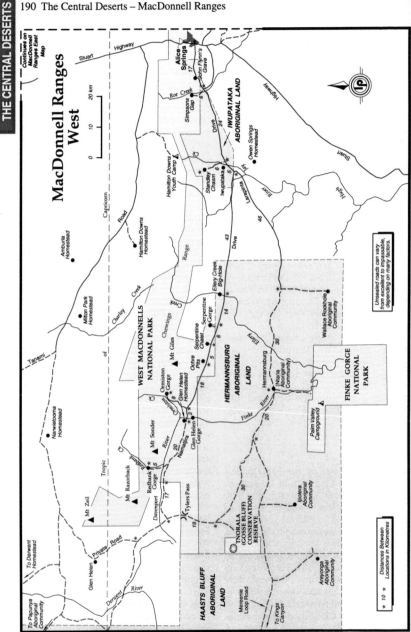

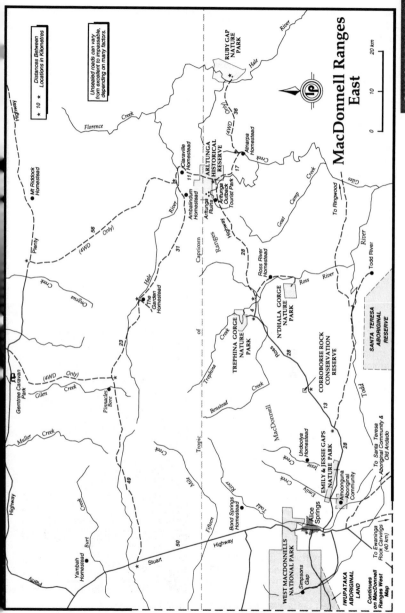

MacDonnell Ranges East

Distances Between
Locations in Kilometres
* 10 *

Unsealed roads can vary
from excellent to impassable,
depending on many factors.

0   10   20 km

RUBY GAP
NATURE PARK

River

Hale

Highway

Florence Creek

Mt Riddock Homestead

Plenty Creek

56
(4WD Only)

Ongeva Creek

Hale River

The Garden Homestead

23

31

Claraville Homestead

Ambalindum Homestead

11

ARLTUNGA
HISTORICAL
RESERVE

Arltunga Ruins

Arltunga Outback Tourist Park

(4WD Only)

36

Atnarpa Homestead

17

Giles Creek

Coot Camp Creek

To Ringwood

28

Capricorn

Ranges

of

Ross River Homestead

Ross River

Todd River

Gemtree Caravan Park

(4WD Only)

Gilen Creek

Pinnacles Bore

Muller Creek

TREPHINA GORGE
NATURE PARK

Trephina Creek

Benstead Creek

Ross Creek

28

N'DHALA GORGE
NATURE PARK

CORROBOREE ROCK
CONSERVATION RESERVE

Todd

SANTA TERESA
ABORIGINAL
RESERVE

MacDonnell

Tropic

Milk River

Fifteen Creek

Emily Creek

13

Undoolya Homestead

EMILY & JESSIE GAPS
NATURE PARK

Jessie Creek

28

Amoonguna
Aboriginal
Community

To Santa Teresa
Aboriginal Community &
Old Andado

Yambah Homestead

Burt Creek

Plenty Creek

49

50

Bond Springs Homestead

Todd River

Stuart Highway

Alice Springs

WEST MACDONNELLS
NATIONAL PARK

Simpsons Gap

IWUPATAKA
ABORIGINAL
LAND

To Ewaninga Rock Carvings
(40 km)

Continues
on MacDonnell
Ranges West
Map

Highway

from the refreshment kiosk to the chasm is crammed with moisture-loving plants such as river gums, cycad palms and ferns, creating an unexpected lushness in this arid world of craggy bluffs. It's one of the nicest walks in central Australia but most visitors are in too much of a hurry to notice. For a real walking challenge with many rewards, you can return to Alice Springs along the Larapinta Trail (see Activities). Standley Chasm is open daily between 7.30 am and 6 pm and charges an entry fee of $2.50 per adult or $2 concession.

Ellery Big-Hole & Serpentine Gorge

Leaving the Standley Chasm turn-off, you pass through a scenic gap in the Heavitree Range before swinging right onto Namatjira Drive. Larapinta Drive continues straight on to Hermannsburg and Palm Valley, and you can come back this way after exploring the West MacDonnells (see Alternative Routes, later in this section).

Ten km from the intersection you cross the **Hugh River**, with its large river gums, before entering a steep-sided valley that takes you all the way to Glen Helen, 75 km further on. It was the Hugh River that provided the explorer John McDouall Stuart with a route through the MacDonnell Ranges on his expeditions to the north between 1860 and 1862. Stuart named the ranges after the then governor of South Australia.

Ellery Creek Big-Hole, 93 km from Alice Springs, is a popular swimming hole in summer but, being shaded by the high cliffs of Ellery Gorge, is generally too cold for comfort most of the year. There's a small camping ground here (see Camping), and the rangers recommend that you do the 20-minute **Dolomite Walk**. An information shelter at the carpark explains the area's fascinating geological history, which is exposed in the creekbanks downstream from the waterhole.

Continuing on from Ellery Creek you soon arrive at the Serpentine Gorge carpark. From here it's a one-km walk to the main attraction, and this makes a nice introduction to the area. Most times a waterhole blocks

the gorge entrance, but if you swim through (brrr), you can walk up the rocky creek past large cycads to a second water-filled cleft. There is some stunning scenery here, which can also be enjoyed from a lookout located a short scramble above the main entrance. Section eight of the Larapinta Trail (see Activities) starts at the carpark and takes you via Counts Point Lookout to Serpentine Chalet dams and Inarlanga Pass, then on to the Ochre Pits.

Ochre Pits

Six km past Serpentine Gorge is the turn-off to the old Serpentine Chalet, where concrete slabs are all that remain of a 1950s tourist venture. The access track, which is rough and best suited to 4WD vehicles, takes you past a number of bush campsites suitable for winter use (see Camping). For details of walks in the area, see the brochure for section eight of the Larapinta Trail.

Serpentine Gorge with rare cycad palms (DO)

Ormiston Gorge (RI)

The nearby Ochre Pits, with extensive parking and picnicking areas, has some interesting information signs relating to ochre and its importance to Aborigines. Except for a small deposit of yellow ochre, which is still used today, the material at this minor quarry site is of poor quality. Nevertheless, the swirls of red and yellow ochre in the walls of this little ravine make an attractive picture in the afternoon sun. From here a walking track takes you to a gorge in the main range (see Activities).

Ormiston Gorge

From the Ochre Pits it's a further 26 km to Ormiston Gorge, where soaring cliffs, tall gums, rich colours and a deep waterhole combine to form some of the grandest scenery in the central ranges. Most visitors congregate at the gorge entrance, but for those who want to explore further afield there are several recommended walks (see Activities) that start and finish at the infor-

mation centre. Ormiston Gorge is a good spot for wildlife enthusiasts, thanks to the variety of habitats (mulga woodland, spinifex slopes, rock faces, large river gums and permanent water) that you find in close proximity to each other. Its small camping ground (see Camping) makes an ideal base for exploring the western half of the West MacDonnells.

Glen Helen Gorge & Homestead

Motel accommodation, a restaurant, a bar, fuel sales, limited camping and scenic flights are available at Glen Helen homestead, 135 km from Alice Springs (see Facilities). Nearby Glen Helen Gorge, where there is another large waterhole, has been carved out by the Finke River as its floodwaters rush south to the Simpson Desert; a major flood in 1988 backed up so high that it flooded the nearby tourist accommodation. A 10-minute stroll takes you from the resort down to the gorge entrance, but if you want to go further you'll have to either swim through the waterhole or climb around it. Bush camping is permitted in the Finke River upstream from the crossing on Namatjira Drive (see Camping).

Redbank Gorge

The bitumen ends at Glen Helen, and for the next 20 km to the Redbank Gorge turn-off you're on rough dirt with numerous sharp dips.

From Namatjira Drive it's five km to the Redbank carpark, from which the final stage is a 20-minute walk up a rocky creekbed to the gorge. Redbank Gorge is extremely narrow, with polished, multihued walls that close over your head to block out the sky. You normally need an air mattress to get through, as its deep pools are freezing, but it's worth doing – the colours and cathedral atmosphere inside are terrific. Redbank Gorge is the usual starting point for a walk to nearby Mt Sonder (see Activities).

EAST FROM ALICE SPRINGS

The road from Alice Springs to Arltunga is extremely scenic for the most part, taking you through a jumble of high ridges and hills drained by gum-lined creeks. Along the way you pass several parks and reserves where you can explore a variety of attractions such as rugged gorges, Aboriginal culture and abandoned mining areas.

The Ross Highway from Alice Springs is sealed for the 71 km to the Arltunga turn-off, where it changes to a good dirt road for the final nine km to Ross River Homestead. Arltunga is 32 km from the Ross Highway, and this unsealed road can be quite rough, as can the alternative return route via Clara-ville, Ambalindum and The Garden homesteads to the Stuart Highway (see Alternative Routes). Access to John Hayes Rockhole (in Trephina Gorge Nature Park), N'Dhala Gorge and Ruby Gap is 4WD only, but other main attractions east of Alice Springs are normally accessible to conventional vehicles.

Emily & Jessie Gaps

Leaving the town centre you head south along the Stuart Highway through Heavitree Gap, then turn east after two km onto the Ross Highway. Parallelling a high quartzite ridge to the north, the road heads out through the South Alice tourist area, with its caravan parks and various attractions – including the **Mecca Date Farm** and the **Frontier Camel Farm** – before, finally, you're in the bush.

Ten km from the Stuart Highway you arrive at Emily Gap, a beautiful spot with **Aboriginal rock paintings** and a deep waterhole in the narrow gorge. Local drunks have caused numerous problems here over the years, particularly on weekends, so check the situation before leaving your car to go walking or sightseeing. Jessie Gap, eight km further on, is equally scenic, and normally a much quieter and safer place to enjoy nature. The walk along the ridge between the two is worth doing (see Activities).

Corroboree Rock

Past Jessie Gap you drive over eroded flats, the steep-sided Heavitree Range looming large on your left, before entering a valley between red ridges. Forty-three km from Alice Springs you arrive at Corroboree Rock, one of a number of unusual tan-coloured dolomite hills scattered over the valley floor. A small cave in this large dog-toothed outcrop was once used by local Aborigines as a storehouse for sacred objects.

Trephina Gorge

About 60 km from Alice Springs you cross the sandy bed of **Benstead Creek**, with its lovely big gums. The thousands of young river gums that line the road germinated in the mid-1970s, when the Alice Springs region received unusually high rainfall. This delightful scenery, which is totally at odds with the common perception of central Australia, continues for the six km from the creek crossing to the Trephina Gorge turn-off.

Three km north of the Ross Highway, Trephina Gorge Nature Park offers some magnificent gorge, ridge and creek scenery, nice walks (see Activities), deep swimming holes, abundant wildlife and low-key camping areas (see Camping). The main attractions are Trephina Gorge, Trephina Bluff and **John Hayes Rockhole**. The rockhole, a permanent waterhole, is reached by a rough track that wanders for several km up the so-called **Valley of the Eagles** (you'll be lucky to see one) and is often closed to conventional vehicles.

Trephina Gorge has a restful atmosphere and some grand scenery, so it's a great spot for a quiet picnic. It also boasts a colony of black-footed rock wallabies on the cliff above the waterhole – wander down first thing in the morning and you'll usually spot them leaping nimbly about on the rock face. The final three km from the park entrance to the Trephina Gorge Road is unsealed, and is closed to all traffic during flooding.

N'Dhala Gorge & Ross River Homestead

The sealed road ends at the Arltunga turn-off, 71 km from Alice Springs, leaving nine km of mainly good dirt to the Ross River homestead. Shortly before the resort you come to the 4WD track to N'Dhala Gorge Nature Park, where hundreds of ancient **rock carvings** decorate a deep, narrow gorge about 20 minutes' walk from the carpark. The 11-km access track winds down the picturesque **Ross River valley**, where a number of sandy crossings make the going tough for conventional vehicles. As the sign says, towing is costly. You can continue on downstream past N'Dhala Gorge to the Ringwood Road, then head west to rejoin the Ross Highway about 30 km from Alice Springs.

Originally the headquarters for Loves Creek station, the Ross River homestead resort has a pretty setting under rocky hills beside Ross River. It offers a range of services, including camping, bunkhouse and motel-style accommodation, meals, liquid refreshments of all kinds, and fuel sales. Boomerang-throwing, horse and camel rides, a small swimming pool (guests only) and some beaut opportunities for bushwalkers feature on the list of activities. For more details, see Facilities, later in this section.

Arltunga

Leaving the Ross Highway, the first 12 km of the Arltunga Road passes through scenic **Bitter Springs Gorge**, where rumpled red quartzite ridges tower high above dolomite hills. This was the route taken by the early diggers as they walked from Alice Springs to the gold fields at the turn of the century. The road can be quite rough at times and is impassable after heavy rain.

Located 103 km from Alice Springs, the **Arltunga Historical Reserve** features significant evidence of the gold-mining activity that took place in its arid hills between 1887 and 1913. The major attraction is a partially restored ghost town that contains the remains of a treatment plant and several stone buildings, including a police station and gaol. Walking tracks take you past **old mines**, now complete with bat colonies – one mine is open to visitors, so make sure to bring a torch (see Activities).

The richest part of the gold field was **White Range**, but in a remarkable feat of short-sightedness, almost all the ruins and small mines that once dotted this high ridge were destroyed during a recent short-lived mining operation. Joseph Hele, who is credited with the discovery of gold at White Range in 1897, is buried in the nearby cemetery. For details on the various points of interest, see the reserve's informative brochure.

Arltunga is a fascinating place for anyone interested in history. To get some idea of what life was like for the early diggers, call in to the information centre, which has interesting displays of old mining machinery and historic photographs. The rangers regularly hold slide shows during the winter months, and these are also worth attending.

Fossicking is not permitted at Arltunga, but there is a **fossicking reserve** in a gully just to the east where you may (with luck) find some gold. A permit is required, and you can obtain one from the Department of Mines & Energy, 58 Hartley St, Alice Springs.

Ruby Gap

Leaving Arltunga you head east towards Atnarpa homestead. Turn left immediately before the gate at 11 km from the Claraville turn-off. The road now deteriorates and is restricted to 4WD vehicles thanks to its sandy creek crossings and sharp jump-ups. Twenty-five km beyond the gate you arrive at the **Hale River**; follow the wheel ruts upstream (left) along the sandy bed for about six km to the turn-around point, which is through Ruby Gap and just short of rugged **Glen Annie Gorge**. If you're first on the scene after a flood, always check that the riverbed is firm before driving onto it, otherwise you may sink deep in quicksand.

Ruby Gap Nature Park was the scene, in 1886, of a frantic ruby rush that crashed overnight when it was found that the rubies were worthless garnets. The park's gorge and river scenery is some of the wildest and most attractive in central Australia, and being remote and hard to get to, it doesn't have the crowds that often destroy the atmosphere at more accessible places. Camping is allowed anywhere along the river. The park is managed by the rangers at Arltunga (☎ (089)56 9770), so check road conditions with them before continuing on.

ALTERNATIVE ROUTES
Gosse Bluff
An alternative return route to Alice Springs once you reach Redbank Gorge is to continue west on Namatjira Drive, then turn south over Tylers Pass on the normally rough dirt road to Hermannsburg and Larapinta Drive. En route you pass Gosse Bluff, the fascinating remnant of a huge crater that was blasted out when a comet plunged into the ground 130 million years ago. The Aboriginal name for it is Tnorala, and in the local mythology it's a wooden dish belonging to some star ancestors that crashed down from the sky during the Dreamtime. The area is covered by a conservation reserve managed by the rangers at Ormiston Gorge; check with them about access and the suitability of Tylers Pass for conventional vehicles.

From Gosse Bluff you continue on to Hermannsburg, where diesel, super and unleaded petrol are available. For details on this historic mission station, see the chapter

on Finke Gorge. Gosse Bluff is about 40 km from the Redbank Gorge turn-off, and it's 54 km from the bluff to Hermannsburg.

A detour to Gosse Bluff can also be made from the newly opened Mereenie Loop Road between Ipolera and Kings Canyon. For information on this road, see Detours in the Finke Gorge section, later in this chapter.

Arltunga Tourist Drive
The rough, 123-km station road from Arltunga via Ambalindum and The Garden stations meets the Stuart Highway 50 km north of Alice Springs and makes an interesting alternative to the Ross Highway. En route you can detour to the **Harts Range gem fields** via 4WD tracks that turn off about five km past Claraville homestead and 23 km past The Garden – fuel is available at the Gemtree Caravan Park (☎ (089) 56 9855) on the Plenty Highway (see the section on the Plenty Highway for details). You'll need a range of at least 400 km to drive from Ross River homestead to Alice Springs with side trips to Arltunga and Ruby Gorge. Check with the rangers at Arltunga for an update on road conditions before continuing on.

ACTIVITIES – WEST OF ALICE SPRINGS
Walks
The Larapinta Trail When completed in the late 1990s, 220 km of walking tracks through many of the park's remoter areas will link Alice Springs to Mt Razorback, at the western end of the West MacDonnells National Park. The following stages were open in 1994:

* Alice Springs Telegraph Station to Simpsons Gap (25 km)
* Simpsons Gap to Jay Creek (24 km)
* Jay Creek to Standley Chasm (15 km)
* Serpentine Gorge to the Ochre Pits (19 km)
* Ormiston Gorge to Glen Helen (13 km)

Each section has its own distinctive highlights: wildlife, rare plants, high lookouts, gorge scenery, deep waterholes or shady creeks. Experienced enthusiasts will enjoy

Corroboree Rock (TW)

them all, but if you're a beginner, you'll probably find the Alice Springs to Simpsons Gap and Ormiston Gorge to Glen Helen sections more suitable. The separate stages are covered by detailed brochures available for $1 from the CATIA information centre in Alice Springs, from the Alice Springs Telegraph Station and from the rangers at Simpsons Gap and Ormiston Gorge.

Ranger-guided overnight walks operate on alternate weekends from May to September on the two sections between Jay Creek and Alice Springs. These cost $25 per person and are truly excellent value. The rangers arrange for your swag and food to be trucked in to the campsite, so all you need to carry is a day pack and canteens. Book at the Alice Springs Telegraph Station (☎ (089) 52 1013).

Simpsons Gap There are many opportunities for good walking here, with the short track up to the Cassia Hill lookout recommended for starters. You can do day walks on the Larapinta Trail – peaceful Bond Gap (to the west) and Wallaby Gap (to the east) are both worthwhile – or take the Woodland Trail to Rocky Gap. This track continues on to Bond Gap via the Larapinta Trail, but it's hard walking through rough hills and won't appeal to many. The flatter wooded country south-east of Simpsons Gap between Rungutjirba Ridge and Larapinta Drive has plenty of potential for off-track walks.

Ochre Pits A three-hour return walk takes you to scenic Inarlanga Pass at the foot of the Heavitree Range. Although the track passes through uninspiring country, the gorge is most interesting, as is the old Serpentine Chalet dam, an hour's walk to the east along the Larapinta Trail. For details, see the brochure on section eight of the Larapinta Trail.

Ormiston Gorge One of the best short walks in the MacDonnell Ranges is the three-hour loop from the information centre into remote Ormiston Pound and back through Ormiston Gorge. Do it first thing in the morning in an anticlockwise direction so you can enjoy a

THE CENTRAL DESERTS

sunlit view of the big cliffs. Two other excellent but much longer cross-country excursions are mentioned in the *Walks of Ormiston Gorge and Pound* brochure – the walk up Ormiston Creek to Bowmans Gap takes at least one day while the **Mt Giles** route is a two-day affair. If you're an experienced bushwalker, do yourself a favour and spend a night on Mt Giles, as the dawn view across Ormiston Pound to Mt Sonder is sensational. Section 10 of the Larapinta Trail winds over rocky hills and along gum-lined creeks from Ormiston Gorge to Glen Helen, with fine views to Mt Sonder en route.

Mt Sonder The full-day return walk along the ridgetop from Redbank Gorge to the summit of Mt Sonder will appeal to the well-equipped enthusiast. The route is unmarked and the trek itself is nothing to rave about (it's rather monotonous and seems never-ending), but the view from Mt Sonder and the sense of achievement are ample reward. As on Mt Giles, the atmosphere and panorama of timeless hills at sunrise makes it worth camping out on top. The rangers at Ormiston Gorge, who can give you sound advice on the route, suggest that you register with them before doing this walk.

Cycling

Simpsons Gap The 17-km sealed cycling path between Flynns Grave and Simpsons Gap wanders along timbered creekflats and over low rocky hills, with occasional kangaroos to keep you company. There are many bush picnic spots en route, and beaut views of Mt Gillen, Rungutjirba Ridge and the rugged Alice Valley. The path is suitable for novice cyclists, but don't go too fast: there are some sharp corners. Flynn's Grave is seven km from the town centre, and you do this part along Larapinta Drive. For the best views (not to mention comfort), cycle out in the early morning and return in the afternoon. Carry plenty of drinking water in warm weather: there is none along the way.

ACTIVITIES – EAST OF ALICE SPRINGS

Walks

Emily & Jessie Gaps For a minor challenge the eight-km walk along the high, narrow ridgetop between these two gaps has much to recommend it. You get sweeping panoramas all the way and there's usually wildlife such as euros, black-footed rock wallabies and wedge-tailed eagles, to see. The idea is to get someone to drop you off at Emily Gap then have them continue on to Jessie Gap to get the picnic ready. Allow at least 2½ hours for the walk, which isn't marked.

Trephina Gorge There are several good walks here, ranging from 30 minutes to five hours, each offering its own attraction. A examples, you can enjoy a relaxing stroll among the big gums along Trephina Creek take the short, scenic rim walk around Trephina Gorge or, for a rewarding challenge, try the marked route over the main range from Trephina Gorge to John Haye Rockhole. For details, see the *Walks of Trephina Gorge* brochure.

Arltunga Four interesting walks of under one hour give access to various old mining areas. One track leads to the MacDonnell Range Reef mine, where you can climb down steel ladders and explore about 50 metres of tunnels between two shafts. The adjoining walk to the nearby Golden Chance mine is also worth doing for its varied content.

Ruby Gap There are no marked walks here but for the enthusiast a climb around the craggy rim of Glen Annie Gorge features superb views of this beautiful spot. You can climb up on the southern side and return from the north along the sandy floor, or vice versa. The grave of a ruby miner is located at the gorge's northern end.

ORGANISED TOURS

One and two-day tours of the MacDonnell Ranges are very popular and there are numerous operators and styles to choose from – contact the CATIA information centre

☎ (089) 52 5199) for details. Costs vary, but expect to pay around $65 for a day tour and $170 for a two-day camping safari – discounts usually apply during the off season. Extended camping safaris incorporating places such as Palm Valley and King's Canyon are also available. Ask about off-season standby rates.

For something entirely different, you can take a 2½-day camel safari through the wilds of the West MacDonnells with Frontier Camel Tours. This unique experience includes one night in a swag at the gum-studded Davenport River and one night at Glen Helen homestead. The cost is $385 per person.

FACILITIES – WEST OF ALICE SPRINGS
Glen Helen Homestead
A high red cliff provides a dramatic backdrop to this resort (☎ (089) 56 7489), which is built on the site of an early homestead of Glen Helen station. One of the nice things about it is its comfortable lounge area, where you can drink bottomless cups of tea and coffee and enjoy the relaxed atmsophere.

The resort offers dormitory-style accommodation ($10 per person), self-contained motel rooms ($80/92/120 a double/triple/family) and limited powered caravan sites. For meals there's a choice of takeaway, restaurant and bistro. Guided bushwalks, camel and horse rides, and helicopter scenic flights feature on the list of activities.

Camping
Ellery Gap There's a small, usually crowded camping area with wood-burning barbecues (no wood provided), tables, pit toilet and limited shade within easy reach of the waterhole. Fees (honesty box) are $1 per person and $3 per family.

Serpentine Chalet Eleven sites scattered through the mulga and mallee along the track to the old Serpentine Chalet site have wood-burning fireplaces (collect your own wood) and a sense of isolation. These are ideal for winter camping but are too exposed in hot weather. The first five sites are accessible to conventional vehicles, the last six to 4WD only. No fees are charged.

Ormiston Gorge This relatively up-market camping ground almost in the shade of Ormiston Gorge features hot showers, toilets, picnic furniture and gas barbecues, but there is no room for caravans. Fees are $4/10 per person/family. Water supplies become severely limited in drought times, when restrictions may apply.

Finke River Free bush camping is available among big river gums along the Finke River upstream from Namatjira Drive. There are no facilities but the views and atmosphere are first class.

Redbank Gorge A small but pleasant camping ground on a creekflat with shady coolabahs has wood-burning barbecues (no wood provided), picnic tables and pit toilets. Fees are $1/3 per person/family, payable at the honesty box. An early morning stroll downstream beside the Davenport River, with the sun softly lighting the river gums, is a nice way to start the day.

FACILITIES – EAST OF ALICE SPRINGS
Ross River Homestead
Set beside one of the region's most attractive rivers, the resort (☎ (089) 56 9711) has a good range of accommodation styles and meals, plus fuel sales (diesel, super and unleaded), a bar, a landing strip and various activities (of which boomerang-throwing and damper-eating are extremely popular).

A large camping area down on the river bank has unpowered sites ($4 per person), powered sites ($15 per site) and bunkhouse accommodation with linen supplied ($12 per person). Shade is limited, but there is a small, rustic-style bar in the camping ground where you can enjoy a cold drink. The old homestead on the other side of the river has cosy timber cabins accommodating up to five people each. Rates are $100 (twin-share room only) – add $15 per extra person over 14 years (anyone under is free). B&B costs $120 per person or $170 per couple. You can

Mt Sonder at sunrise (RI)

get buffet, carvery, bistro and barbecue meals, all at reasonable prices and with plenty of food.

For something out of the ordinary, the resort puts on an overnighter with either horses or camels. This involves a two-hour ride to a bush campsite in the hills, where you enjoy a three-course campfire meal before unrolling the swag under the stars. In the morning you eat breakfast before returning to the resort. It's extremely good value: $45 per adult and $20 for children.

Camping

Trephina Gorge Small camping grounds at Trephina Gorge, The Bluff and John Hayes Rockhole offer a variety of camping experiences, and all are cheap: $1/3 per person/family (payable into honesty boxes). You can collect firewood from a heap just before the first Trephina Creek crossing on the Trephina Gorge access road.

The *Trephina Gorge camping area* is in a timbered gully a short stroll from the main attraction, and has running water, pit toilets, wood-burning barbecues and tables. It is suitable for caravans, unlike *The Bluff campground*, which is only about five minutes' walk away. The Bluff has similar facilities (the barbecues are gas) but a more spectacular creekbank setting under tall gums in front of a towering red ridge. *John Hayes Rockhole* has two basically appointed sites beside a rocky creek just down from the waterhole. The most obvious thing about this restricted area is its large population of ants.

N'Dhala Gorge There are three sites at the gorge entrance. Facilities are limited to wood-burning barbecues (collect your own wood), tables and a pit toilet; shade is limited. Camping fees are $1/3 per person/family, payable into the honesty box.

Arltunga Camping is not permitted within the historical reserve, but the nearby Arltunga Tourist Park has unpowered sites

Gold-mining relics at Arltunga (DO)

for $4 per person. The facilities are basic and the setting is dusty.

Ruby Gap Free camping (without facilities) in a beautiful gorge environment is a major attraction of this area. The park is remote and visitors should be self-sufficient in everything. Please take your rubbish with you.

Finke Gorge

The historic Hermannsburg mission, on the banks of the Finke River 135 km west of Alice Springs, is the gateway to two 4WD tracks that take you south to Palm Valley and Boggy Hole in 46,000-hectare Finke Gorge National Park. These tracks run through Finke Gorge itself, where central Australia's largest river has carved a long meandering passage through the James Ranges. For much of the time you're actually driving in the sandy riverbed, so a 4WD vehicle and experience in using it are essential. The latter particularly applies to the Boggy Hole track, which continues on to join up with Ernest Giles Rd to Watarrka (King's Canyon) National Park.

Famous for its rare palms, Finke Gorge National Park is one of central Australia's premier wilderness areas, with plenty to offer those who enjoy bushwalks and remote camping without facilities. The landscape is spectacular and colourful. The main gorge features high red cliffs, stately river gums, cool waterholes, plenty of clean white sand and clumps of tall palms. Combine this tremendous natural beauty with the area's fascinating history and you have an excursion that's packed with interest.

Anyone intending to drive out from Alice Springs to Hermannsburg, visit Palm Valley, then continue on to Watarrka via Boggy Hole and Illamurta Springs should have a minimum fuel range of 650 km, allowing for heavy going in the Finke River. If you can't do this, plan to buy fuel at Hermannsburg, as the only other outlet between here and Watarrka is at King's Creek, 35 km before

Watarrka. Most maps show a refuelling stop 100 km east of Watarrka, but this facility no longer exists.

HISTORY

For thousands of years, the Finke River formed part of an Aboriginal trade route that crossed Australia, bringing goods such as sacred red ochre from the south and pearl shell from the north to the central Australian tribes. Far from being desert, the area around Hermannsburg had an abundance of game animals and food plants. It was a major refuge for the Western Arrente people in times of drought, thanks to its permanent water, which came from soaks dug in the Finke River bed. An upside-down river (like all others in central Australia), the Finke flows beneath its dry bed most of the time. As it becomes saline during drought, the Western Arrente call it *Lhere pirnte* (hence Larapinta), which means salty river. It was their comprehensive knowledge of its freshwater soaks that enabled them to survive in the harshest droughts.

The explorer Ernest Giles arrived on the scene in 1872, when he travelled up the Finke on his first attempt to cross from the Overland Telegraph Line to the west coast. To his amazement he found tall palms growing in the river, which had been named 12 years earlier by John McDouall Stuart, and went into raptures over the beauty of the scenery that he saw there. Giles later briefed the Lutheran Church of South Australia on the country he'd visited at the northern end of Finke Gorge. The Lutherans were keen to start missionary work among Aboriginal people in central Australia, and after talking to Giles they applied for a lease over the area.

In 1876, fresh from the Hermannsburg Mission Institute in Germany, pastors A H Kempe and W F Schwarz left Adelaide bound for central Australia with a herd of cattle and several thousand sheep. Eighteen months later they finally arrived at the new mission site, having been held up by drought at Dalhousie Springs for nearly a year. It was a nightmarish introduction to the harsh central Australian environment, but the pastors were committed to the task of bringing Christianity and 'civilisation' to the Aborigines.

Despite incredible hardships and difficulties, including strong opposition from White settlers to their attempts to protect the Aborigines from genocide, the missionaries successfully established what became the first township in central Australia. At one time Hermannsburg had a population of 700 Western Arrente people, a cattle herd of 5000 and various cottage industries, including a tannery. The mission continued to operate until 1982, when the Lutheran Church handed its lease back to the Western Arrente. Since that time most of its residents have left Hermannsburg and established small outstation communities on traditional clan territories. There are now 35 such outstations on the old mission lease. Although about 200 Aborigines still live at Hermannsburg, its main function is to provide support and resources for the outlying population.

INFORMATION
Tourist Offices

The best source of information on Finke Gorge National Park is the Conservation Commission's Alice Springs office (☎ (089) 51 8211), open Monday to Friday from 8 am to 4.20 pm. Outside these hours, ring the Palm Valley ranger (☎ (089) 56 7401).

Brochures on Hermannsburg, Ipolera and Wallace Rockhole and details of tours from Alice Springs are available from the tourist information centre (☎ (089) 52 5199) on the corner of Hartley St and Gregory Terrace in Alice Springs. For an update on track conditions between Hermannsburg and Ernest Giles Rd, contact the rangers at either Watarrka National Park (☎ (089) 56 7460) or Palm Valley.

Emergency

In the event of a medical emergency, you can obtain assistance at the Hermannsburg health clinic, which has registered nursing staff. The rangers at Palm Valley and most bus drivers have training in first aid, and their

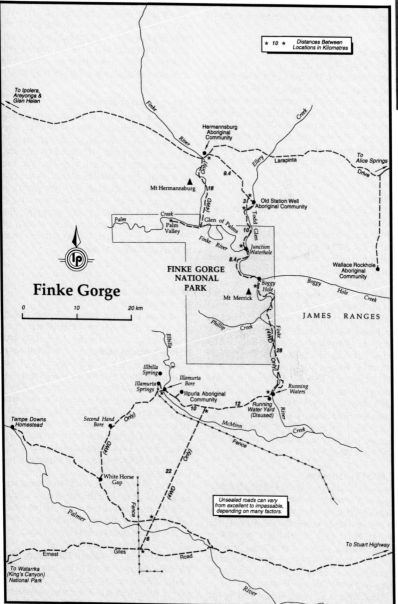

Finke Gorge

★ 10 ★ Distances Between Locations in Kilometres

To Ipolera, Areyonga & Glen Helen

Finke River

Hermannsburg Aboriginal Community

Ellery

Larapinta

To Alice Springs Drive

9.4

Mt Hermannsburg

18

3

Old Station Well Aboriginal Community

Palm Creek

Glen of Palms

Todd Glen

10

Palm Valley

Finke River

Junction Waterhole

8.4

FINKE GORGE NATIONAL PARK

Mt Merrick

Boggy Hole

Boggy Hole Creek

Wallace Rockhole Aboriginal Community

JAMES RANGES

0   10   20 km

Phillip Creek

Illbilla Ck

25

Finke River (4WD Only)

Illbilla Spring

Illamurta Bore

Running Waters

Illamurta Springs

Illpurla Aboriginal Community

12

Running Water Yard (Disused)

Tempe Downs Homestead

Second Hand Bore

(4WD Only)

10   7

McMinn

Fence

Creek

White Horse Gap

(4WD Only)

22

Palmer

Fence

Unsealed roads can vary from excellent to impassable, depending on many factors.

6

To Watarrka (King's Canyon) National Park

Ernest

Giles

Road

To Stuart Highway

River

vehicles are generally equipped with HF radios.

Permits

The Boggy Hole track crosses Aboriginal land for the 16 km from Hermannsburg to the national park boundary. Although there is no requirement for a permit to use the road, camping is not allowed in the area and visitors must stay on the main route. Likewise, you can visit the commercial facilities and historic mission at Hermannsburg without a permit but residential areas are out of bounds.

Maps

The Conservation Commission's brochure *Finke River 4WD Route* covers the Boggy Hole track from Hermannsburg to Ernest Giles Rd, including the detour to Illamurta Springs. The brochure is available on request from the rangers at Palm Valley and Watarrka.

Much better topographic detail is shown on the Henbury 1:250,000 map sheet, available from the Department of Lands, Housing & Local Government office in Gregory Terrace, Alice Springs, and from AUSLIG sales outlets in all capital cities. The final 28 km of the Boggy Hole track isn't shown on the Henbury 1:250,000 map, but it's easy enough to draw it in: the missing section is dead straight, leaves the Running Waters-Illamurta Bore track 12 km west of Running Water Yard and meets Ernest Giles Rd on the eastern side of the fence-crossing at grid reference KN6281.

Radio Frequencies

As Palm Valley is a popular tourist attraction, you won't require an HF radio (except possibly in summer, when visitor numbers drop to a few vehicles per day). Likewise, the Boggy Hole track is relatively popular in winter, though there can be a week between vehicles when the weather is hot. It would be a good idea to carry an HF radio if you're intending to do this trip in summer.

The Finke Gorge area is serviced by the Alice Springs RFDS base (callsign VJD – Victor Juliet Delta), which operates on 5410 and 6950 kHz between 7.30 am and 5 pm Monday to Friday (except public holidays). Use 2020 and 5410 kHz for after-hours emergency calls. For further information on services, contact the base (☎ (089) 52 1033).

SPECIAL PREPARATIONS

The track from Hermannsburg to Ernest Giles Rd is definitely not suitable for low-clearance 4WD vehicles. Even experienced off-road drivers can get bogged on this one, so make sure to pack a high-lift jack and base-plate, long-handled shovel, tyre-pressure gauge and good-quality tyre pump. A winch (or at least a strong tow rope) might also come in handy. Anyone attempting the track in summer should carry plenty of drinking water and travel in company with at least one other vehicle.

THE ROUTE

Hermannsburg

Shaded by tall river gums and date palms, and with a view over the Finke River's normally dry, shimmering bed, the **old Hermannsburg mission** is a fascinating monument to the skill and dedication of the early Lutheran missionaries. The group of 11 low, whitewashed stone buildings includes a church, a school and various houses and outbuildings. Dating from 1882, the buildings are probably as good an example of traditional German farmhouse architecture as you'll find anywhere outside that country. They were fully restored with a federal government grant in 1988.

About 20,000 tourists visit Hermannsburg each year and explore the mission on a self-guided tour. Admission costs $2.50 per adult and $1.50 per child and includes a guided tour of the **art gallery**. Run by arrangement only, the latter provides an insight into the life and times of **Albert Namatjira**, the Western Arrente artist who opened the world's eyes to the striking landscapes around Alice Springs. The gallery contains examples of the work of 39 Hermannsburg water colourists, including three generations of the Namatjira family.

Hermannsburg to Palm Valley (18 km)

The Palm Valley track turns off Larapinta Drive on the Finke River's western bank about one km west of Hermannsburg, and keeps to the riverbed for most of the next 11 km. Deep corrugations and soft sandy sections are normal conditions here, while a flood can close the track for days. However, the major hazards are large 4WD tourist coaches, which have right of way on the narrow track – when you see one of these monsters heading towards you, either pull right over or reverse back until you can get off the track without bogging yourself. With 65,000 tourists visiting Palm Valley each year, the track can be fairly busy in peak holiday periods (July and September).

Finke River Floods About a km downstream from the Palm Valley turn-off, the track enters the red-walled confines of Finke Gorge and hits the first patch of soft sand – this is where visitors in conventional vehicles who've ignored the warning signs invariably come to grief. For the next 10 km the track dives in and out of the river, passing occasional small waterholes and tall river gums that make a cool contrast to the arid hills on either side.

There were many more big gums in the river until 1988, when one of the greatest floods in centuries roared down from the MacDonnells and swept most of them away. The debris piled against surviving trees gives you an idea of the river's force when it's in full flood. Take one look at the scars high up on the trunks and you quickly appreciate that Finke Gorge is no place to be when heavy rain sets in. The river comes down on average about once a year in the gorge but relatively few floods reach the Stuart Highway bridge south of Alice Springs. Eventually even the largest floods simply vanish into the sands of the Simpson Desert, which if you count every twist and turn in the

Old Hermannsburg mission (DO)

river is 650 km from the MacDonnell Ranges.

Palm Valley

Leaving the Finke at its junction with Palm Creek, you head west past the old ranger station (the houses were flooded in 1988 and are now abandoned), and a km further on arrive at the Kalarranga carpark. En route there's a small information bay that gives you an introduction to the area and to some of the walks you can do (see Activities). Kalarranga, more usually known as the **Amphitheatre**, is a semicircle of striking ochre-coloured sandstone formations sculpted by a now-extinct meander of Palm Creek. Be there in early morning or late afternoon for the best views.

Continuing on from the Amphitheatre, the track becomes extremely rough and rocky for the final three km to Palm Valley. Along the way you pass the camping ground and picnic area before arriving at **Cycad Gorge**, where a chocolate-coloured cliff towers over a clump of tall, slender palms. The gorge is named for the large number of shaggy cycads found growing on and below the cliff face. Lending a tropical atmosphere to their barren setting, the palms and cycads are leftovers from much wetter times in central Australia. They only survive here because a reliable supply of moisture within the surrounding sandstone means they can escape the harsh realities of drought.

Just past Cycad Gorge you come to the Palm Valley carpark, with the first oasis of palms just a stone's throw away. The valley is actually a narrow gorge that in places is literally choked with lush oases of waving **red cabbage palms** up to 25 metres high. Found nowhere else in the world, the species *(Livistona mariae)* grows within an area of 60 sq km and is over 1000 km from its nearest relatives. There are only 2000 mature individuals in the wild, so the rangers ask that you resist the temptation to enter the palm groves – the tiny seedlings are hard to see and are easily trampled underfoot. This is probably why there are hardly any young ones near the Palm Valley carpark. A botanist's paradise, the gorge is home to over 300 plant species, of which about 10% are either rare or have a restricted distribution.

Hermannsburg to Boggy Hole (31 km)

Heading out along Larapinta Drive from Alice Springs, you come to the Boggy Hole track on your left just 50 metres or so before the signposted turn-off to Hermannsburg. For the first 12 km the track is graded but rough, spearing across a red sandy plain as it takes you past small outstation communities on what was the old mission lease.

The graded section stops abruptly at the entrance to **Todd Glen** on Ellery Creek; ignore the track on the left and continue on into the gorge. From this point the track is simply a pair of wheel ruts winding along the mainly stony creekbed. Although the going is often rough, the colourful scenery and the sense of discovery make it all worthwhile.

Ten km after entering the gorge you arrive at **Junction Waterhole**, where Ellery Creek meets the Finke River. When full, the hole makes a picture to gladden any eye, and as a bonus there are some good camp sites under the gums that line its banks. Unfortunately, however, the waterhole is empty as often as not. A few years ago you could drive down the Finke from Palm Valley to Junction Waterhole, but the rangers closed the track when they found they were spending too much time pulling hire cars out of bogs.

Boggy Hole

At Junction Waterhole you re-enter Finke Gorge for the slow 8.4-km slog to Boggy Hole. A haven for migratory waterbirds such as swans and pelicans, Boggy Hole stretches for 2.5 km after a flood but shrinks to only about 300 metres during extreme droughts. It's one of only a handful of permanent waterholes in the Finke south of the Mac-Donnell Ranges and so has immense conservation value – believe it or not, 10 species of mainly small fish live here. The bank is rocky and the river gums suffered badly in the 1988 flood, so good camp sites with shade are in short supply near the water.

In the 1880s, Boggy Hole was the site of

a police camp from which Mounted Constable William Willshire and his Aboriginal troopers rode the ranges, quelling Black resistance to White settlement. Their method of doing this was to shoot as many Aborigines as possible, prompting a Hermannsburg missionary to write in 1885: 'In ten years time there will not be many Blacks left in this area and this is just what the white man wants.'

A year later the missionaries were protesting vigorously at the alarming decrease in the Aboriginal male population. It was thanks largely to their efforts that the police were moved to Illamurta Springs in 1893 and the murderous Willshire brought to trial for his excesses. He wasn't convicted, but the trial meant the end of his career in the Northern Territory. The stone remains of the police camp (not to be confused with those of a more recent safari camp) can still be seen on the waterhole's eastern bank.

Boggy Hole to Ernest Giles Rd (68 km)

The river's character changes continuously in the 28 km from Boggy Hole to the old Running Water cattle yards. One minute you're driving along a broad valley or through red sandhills, the next you're hemmed in with cliffs on either side. These narrow sections act as dams when the river is in flood, the water banking up to submerge the flats on either side under metres of water. At one point, about eight km past Boggy Hole, scars eight metres or more up in the river gums show where flood-borne debris, including huge trees, has bashed against their trunks. Looking around at the normally parched surroundings, it's difficult to imagine that such things can happen here.

Running Waters Twenty km from Boggy Hole you pass through a gate in a grove of desert oaks and enter Henbury station. Five km further on, at the southern end of Finke Gorge, a couple of metal shelters off to the left mark the site of an Aboriginal outstation at Running Waters. Here the Finke is littered by tree trunks that were either snapped off or plucked from the riverbed during the 1988 flood. A solitary palm rises from the bulrushes that line the waterhole, which although permanent is quite shallow, in contrast to others in the river. The track continues downstream for a short distance to a set of old timber yards, where you turn right (west) along the southern foot of the James Ranges.

Picturesque clumps of ghost gums are the major scenic highlights of the 12 km to the turn-off to Ernest Giles Rd – continue straight on if you want to visit the Illamurta Springs Conservation Reserve (see Detours). From the turn-off the track heads south-west across red sandhills covered with desert oaks, the going soft in parts and so badly corrugated in others it'll make your teeth rattle. Twenty km later you arrive at a claypan that heralds the start of the **Palmer River flood plain**. Although devastated by rabbits and cattle over the past century, the flood plain's desolate claypans, scattered crimson dunes and skeletons of dead trees do give it a certain awful beauty.

Two km onto the flood plain you cross the Tempe Downs Rd, then it's about the same distance to the Palmer River's broad, sandy bed. The crossing point, which is extremely soft, is usually the track's worst obstacle, and you can tell from the holes and broken branches that many vehicles get bogged there. Still, the river gums are very beautiful, so there are worse places to be stuck. Once past the river it's only about three km to the intersection with Ernest Giles Rd. The Stuart Highway is 63 km to the left, while Watarrka National Park is 130 km to the right.

DETOURS
Wallace Rockhole

The Arrente community of Wallace Rockhole, off Larapinta Drive about 30 km east of Hermannsburg, offers **rock-art tours** (four tours daily) and a chance to sample traditional bush tucker in season. Kangaroo tail cooked in the ground is a speciality. Wallace Rockhole has a pleasant camping area and caravan park, and the general store sells ice and locally produced Aboriginal

THE CENTRAL DESERTS

crafts. Ring the community office (☎ (089) 56 7415) for details of rates and activities.

Ipolera

Cultural tours for men and women (yes, they're separate) with Arrente guides are the major attraction at Ipolera, a small community 58 km west of Hermannsburg. Here you're the guests of the Malbunka family, who proudly claim their camping ground to be one of the most scenic in central Australia. Tours are conducted on Monday, Wednesday and Friday and cost $60/25/10 per family/adult/child (five to 14 years). Visits to Ipolera must be prearranged (☎ (089) 56 7466, fax 56 7316). The community is definitely worth a visit, firstly because the Malbunkas are such nice people and secondly because you'll get a fascinating insight into both traditional and contemporary Aboriginal lifestyles.

Nearby is rugged Gosse Bluff, a spectacular remnant of a comet crater, best reached from the Hermannsburg to Glen Helen road (see the MacDonnell Ranges section). For an update on access to the bluff, which is within a conservation reserve, call the rangers at Ormiston Gorge (☎ (089) 56 7799).

Mereenie Loop Road

Opened to the general public in 1994, the Mereenie Loop Road between Ipolera and Kings Canyon makes an excellent short cut to the latter from Glen Helen and Hermannsburg. In fact, it provides an exciting opportunity for a complete circuit of the western central ranges taking in the West MacDonnells National Park, Gosse Bluff, Palm Valley, Kings Canyon and the Boggy Hole Track. The circuit, which covers 800 km or more including side trips, will appeal to the more adventurous 4WD traveller with time to appreciate the attractions en route. This means allowing at least seven days for the trip.

The Mereenie Loop Road passes through inspiring and varied semidesert wilderness, but is generally only suitable either for

Red cabbage palms in Palm Valley (DO)

4WDs or conventional vehicles with heavy-duty suspension and good ground clearance. To use it you need a permit called the Mereenie Tour Pass, which doubles as a visitor information guide. The pass is available free of charge at the Glen Helen Homestead, Hermannsburg (the Ntaria Council office), Kings Canyon Resort and the CATIA tourist information office in Hartey St, Alice Springs.

You'll need a fuel supply to cover at least 350 km betwen Hermannsburg (the last fuel stop) and Kings Canyon, including detours to Gosse Bluff and Ipolera. Note that camping is not permitted past Ipolera.

Illamurta Springs

At the foot of the James Ranges 22 km west of Running Water yard, this fascinating but little-visited spot is excellent for bird-watching, thanks to its permanent spring and the variety of habitats nearby. Hidden away in thick mallee a stone's throw from the spring are the evocative stone remains of what must have been one of the Northern Territory's loneliest police outposts. It makes you wonder what crimes the constables were guilty of to be posted there. The station opened in 1893 and closed in 1912. You can camp at the boundary fence, but there are no facilities apart from drinking water, which is usually available at nearby Illamurta Bore. From the fence it's only a short walk to the spring.

Watarrka (King's Canyon)

Ernest Giles Rd terminates in Watarrka National Park, one of the major scenic drawcards of central Australia. The park includes a range of environments, from permanent springs with delicate ferns and cycads to red sandhills covered by desert oaks and spinifex. Best of all, however, are the colourful 300-metre-high cliffs that line King's Canyon – you get two perspectives of this spectacular landform from walking tracks at both the top and bottom of the gorge. For information on the park, contact the rangers (☎ (089) 56 7460) and ask them to send you a brochure.

Garden of Eden, Kings Canyon (TW)

Accommodation within the park is confined to the *King's Canyon Frontier Lodge* (☎ 008 89 1101), which has up-market hotel rooms with private facilities at $142 for a twin room. Rooms with share facilities cost $60 a twin and $80 for four people. For meals you have the choice of an à la carte restaurant or cafe-style meals. The latter are good value at $10 for a choice of three main courses with salads and sweets. The complex includes a well-stocked minimarket, which also sells fuel (diesel, super and unleaded) from 7 am to 7 pm seven days a week.

The *Frontier Lodge camping ground* won't be everyone's cup of tea, as the idea seems to be to get as many into a given space as possible. It's also rather pricy, at $10/8 per person with/without power. For something friendlier, cheaper and more akin to a bush experience, try *King's Creek station*, on Ernest Giles Rd just outside the national park's eastern boundary. The very pleasant camping ground is set among large desert oaks and costs start at $5 per person. Fuel, ice and limited stores are available seven days a week at the shop.

ACTIVITIES
Walks

There is excellent potential for bushwalking in Finke Gorge National Park, although few visitors do more than short walks in the Palm Valley area. One good day or overnight walk with plenty of variety is a loop from the Palm Valley camping ground south to Little Palm Creek, then down to the Finke River and back to the camp. If you're camped at Boggy Hole, a walk to the top of Mt Merrick, which is about 300 metres above the Finke River, is recommended for the view. A quiet stroll along the Finke also has much to offer in the way of colourful scenery and wildlife, particularly in the Glen of Palms between Palm and Little Palm creeks.

Unfortunately there are no large-scale topographic maps of Finke Gorge National Park, which is shown in broad detail on the Henbury 1:250,000 sheet. Before doing any long walks, ask the ranger (☎ (089) 56 7401) for advice on conditions and preparation.

Palm Valley Walking Tracks There are three walking tracks in the Palm Valley area, all of them suitable for family use and each with its own particular attractions. The most popular is a five-km loop through Palm Valley and back over the top to the carpark. It offers nice views down the gorge and shows you how the availability of water determines plant life in the area.

A second five-km track starts and finishes at the Kalarranga carpark and takes in the Finke River, Palm Bend and the rugged Amphitheatre. It leads you in the footsteps of a mythological hero from the Aboriginal Dreamtime, whose adventures are explained by signs along the way. The third track, a relatively short one, takes you up to a lookout on a sandstone knob; the view over the Amphitheatre is striking.

FACILITIES
Hermannsburg

The best place to start a visit to the historic precinct is the *Hermannsburg Tea Room* (☎ (089) 56 7402) in the old missionary house. Open seven days a week from 9 am to 4 pm, the tea room has a marvellous olde-worlde atmosphere in which, for a very reasonable price, you can relax with a light lunch, or a bottomless cup of tea or coffee and a large slice of delicious home-baked cake – the traditional apple strudel is highly recommended. If you're making a special trip out from Alice Springs in the summer months, call first to check that they'll be open.

The tea room sells a good range of traditional and watercolour paintings, artefacts and pottery, all items being the work of local Aboriginal people. The quality is generally very good, and you'll find the prices more appealing than in most souvenir outlets in Alice Springs.

Supermarket shopping is available at the Mission Store near the historic precinct, and at the Ntaria Supermarket at the main entrance to town. The former has by far the best variety of foodstuffs on offer, and also sells hardware items and motor accessories such as electric air pumps. Both are open from 8.30 am to 5.30 pm Monday to Friday and from 8.30 am to 11.30 am on Saturday.

Diesel, super and unleaded petrol is sold seven days a week between 8.30 am and 5.30 pm at the garage next door to the Ntaria Store. These fuels are also available from the Tjuwanpa Outstation Resource Centre, opposite the Palm Valley turn-off on the river's western bank. The latter is open from 8 am to 5 pm Monday to Friday and from 8 am to 1 pm on Saturday. Both can help you in the event of a mechanical breakdown.

Palm Valley

A small camping area beside Palm Creek has shady trees, hot showers and gas barbecues, as well as numerous friendly birds that are always on the lookout for a free feed. You have to keep your food under cover, but otherwise it's a very pleasant place in a scenic setting of red sandstone ridges – the spectacular Amphitheatre is just a few minutes' walk away. Overnight charges are

$4 per adult or $10 per family, paid into the honesty box; day-trippers have free use of the nearby picnic area and its shade shelters, flush toilets and gas barbecues. Dead timber cannot be collected past the park entry sign in the Finke River, so if you want a fire, make sure to collect your firewood in advance.

Bush Camping

You'll find many magnificent campsites with shade, clean sand, firewood and beautiful gorge scenery along the Finke River between Junction Waterhole and Running Waters. The most popular spot (though by no means the best) is Boggy Hole, which attracts many Alice Springs residents on weekends. As waterholes in the Finke are vital to the survival of many wildlife species, the rangers ask that you do your washing in a bucket and camp well back from the water's edge. All rubbish should be carried out.

The Tanami Track

The Tanami Track cuts right through the heart of the Tanami Desert and some of Australia's least populated country. It connects Alice Springs in the Centre with the Kimberley's Halls Creek in the country's far north-west. Despite the remoteness, or perhaps because of it, the Tanami Track is becoming an increasingly popular route for those seeking to get off the beaten track, and it can save hundreds of km spent backtracking if you want to visit both the Top End and the Kimberley from Alice Springs. It's also possible to leave the Tanami Track at the Tanami Mine and head north for Lajamanu and Kalkaringi on the Buchanan Highway, from where there are a number of possibilities: north-east to Katherine and the Stuart Highway, west to Halls Creek or north along the Delamere Rd to Victoria River Downs and on to Timber Creek on the Victoria Highway. The Lajamanu Road is best attempted with a 4WD, although the local Aborigines manage OK with their trusty

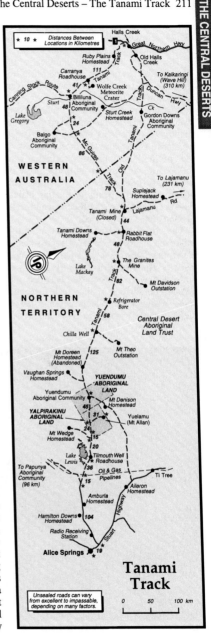

Tanami Track

Unsealed roads can vary from excellent to impassable, depending on many factors.

0   50   100 km

Ford Falcons. (See Alternative Routes below for more details on the Lajamanu Road.)

The Tanami Track is officially called the Tanami Road in the Territory and McGuires Track in Western Australia but it is universally known as the Tanami Track.

Apart from the sense of achievement which crossing the Tanami Desert gives, the highlights of the track are the Wolfe Creek Meteorite Crater and the sheer vastness of the spinifex plains liberally sprinkled with millions of red **termite mounds**, many of which are over three metres high. The country is mainly gently undulating plains, with occasional low rock outcrops and areas of sand dunes.

The 1000-km track has been much improved in recent years; it's possible to cover the track in a well-prepared 2WD vehicle. The Northern Territory section is wide and well graded, but between the WA/NT border and Halls Creek there are some sandy patches which require care – a high-clearance vehicle is advisable. After rain (rare), sections of the track can become impassable.

In the cooler months there is quite a bit of traffic – up to 40 vehicles a day pass through Rabbit Flat – so a breakdown need not be cause for alarm if you are well prepared with food and water. In summer the heat can be extreme – days where the temperature hits 50°C are not uncommon – so think carefully before setting off at this time.

The Tanami Desert is the traditional homeland of the Walpiri Aboriginal people, and for much of its length the Tanami Track passes through Aboriginal land.

HISTORY

The first European exploration of the Tanami Desert was undertaken by the surveyor and explorer A C Gregory (later Sir) in 1855. His party headed south from the Victoria River to what is now Lajamanu, then headed west until they came to a dry watercourse near the present WA/NT border, which Gregory named Sturt Creek, after the explorer. He

One of the many giant termite mounds along the Tanami Track (R & VM)

followed the creek south-west to a lake south-west of Balgo, which he humbly named after himself, before returning to his Victoria River base.

The first White crossing of the desert was probably in 1896 when the pioneering cattle driver Nat Buchanan crossed from Tennant Creek to Sturt Creek. Buchanan was responsible for some amazing cattle drives from Queensland, and he hoped to find a route suitable for stock so they didn't have to detour so far north. Although he crossed the desert without undue difficulty, no sources of permanent water were found and the hoped-for stock route never eventuated.

Allan Davidson was the first European to explore the Tanami Desert in any detail. In 1900 he set out looking for gold, and mapped, with amazing accuracy, likely-looking areas. Gold was discovered at a couple of sites in the Tanami and for a few brief years there was a flurry of activity as hopefuls came in search of a fortune. The extremely harsh conditions and small finds deterred all but the most determined, and there were never more than a couple of hundred miners in the Tanami. The biggest finds were at Tanami and The Granites, and after many years of inactivity, the latter was reopened in 1986 and is still being mined today; the Tanami Mine closed in 1994.

Pastoral activity in the area has always been a precarious proposition, although some areas are suitable for grazing. Suplejack ('soo-pull-jack') Downs and Tanami Downs, respectively 60 km north and south-west of Rabbit Flat, are two which have survived. Suplejack is one of the few pieces of non-Aboriginal land in the Tanami Desert, while Tanami Downs is owned by the Mangkururrta Aboriginal Land Trust.

During the 1920s Michael Terry, a geologist, led a number of expeditions across the northern half of Australia in vehicles as well as on camels, searching for minerals. During his 1928 expedition, when he used a couple of Morris six-wheel trucks on what were the first motorised trips through this part of the continent, he travelled from Broome, via Halls Creek (Old Halls Creek today) down to Tanami and then south-east to Alice Springs. His book, *Hidden Wealth and Hiding People*, recounts the adventures he and his men had and what life was like for the prospectors and the natives at this time.

Some of the facts and figures he states regarding his vehicles make interesting reading less than 70 years later. Oil consumption was down to 250 miles to the gallon(!), while fuel consumption was down to less than five miles to the gallon. Mind you, that was across country, as all there was to follow was a camel pad. He also states, regarding tyres, '...the Australian Dunlops stood up very well...,' even though he recorded 57 punctures and tyre pressures of 80 psi! It must have been a hard trip.

INFORMATION

Permits are not required for travel on the Tanami Track, although if you want to venture more than 50 metres either side of the road, a permit is required. This does not apply to the settlement of Yuendumu, which lies two km off the road.

Although it is not compulsory to register with the police at either end of the Tanami Track, remember that travel in this area is no Sunday-school picnic and you should at least notify someone reliable of your travel plans.

The best map for the track is the Westprint Tanami Track map. It is available in Alice Springs at the Automobile Association of the Northern Territory office (☎ (089) 53 1322) at 105 Gregory Terrace.

The Tanami Track is covered by the RFDS in Alice Springs (☎ (089) 52 1033) and Derby (☎ (091) 91 1211); Alice Springs (VJD) monitors 2020, 5410 and 6950 kHz from 7.30 am to 5 pm weekdays, while the Derby (VJB) frequencies are 2020, 2792, 5300 and 6925 kHz, and these are monitored on weekdays from 7 am to 4 pm, and on Saturday from 9 to 9.30 am.

THE ROUTE
Alice Springs to Rabbit Flat

The Tanami Track starts at the Stuart Highway, 19 km north of Alice Springs. Here the somewhat daunting sign informs you that it's 703 km to the Western Australia border, the first 118 km of which are sealed.

The first point of interest is the masts of the Defence Department's **radio receiving station** off to the north of the road (entry prohibited). On the south side of the road is the rugged northern face of the **Western MacDonnell Ranges**.

Shortly after passing the receiver station the road crosses the **Hamilton Downs station** boundary fence, and the turn-off to the Apex youth camp at the foot of the ranges. The station was established early this century and named by the explorer John McDouall Stuart. The road then enters Amburla station (and crosses the Tropic of Capricorn) and, 104 km from the Stuart Highway, there's the turn-off to the Aboriginal community of **Papunya**, 96 km to the west along a good dirt road (permit required).

A further 15 km brings you to the crossing of the underground **oil and gas pipelines**, which takes the oil and gas from the fields near Palm Valley all the way to Katherine and Darwin. It's then another 36 km to the first fuel and supply stop along the track, the modern **Tilmouth Well Roadhouse** on the banks of the (usually) dry Napperby Creek.

On from Tilmouth the track passes through the **Stuart Bluff Range**, one of the few outcrops of rock seen along the track, before coming to the turn-off to Mount Wedge homestead after 20 km. The boundary of the **Yalpirakinu Aboriginal land** is reached after 15 km, and a further 24 km brings you to the turn-off to the **Yuelamu Dreaming Art Gallery & Museum**, 31 km north of the track at Mt Allan in the Ngalurbindi Hills. Although permits are officially required, if you phone ahead (☎ (089) 51 1520) to let them know you are coming, they can give permission to enter over the phone. Apart from selling arts & crafts (mainly acrylic paintings), there's also fuel and food available.

Back on the main track, it's another 45 km before you reach the turn-off to the Aboriginal community of **Yuendumu**, which lies two km north of the track. Visitors are welcome to buy fuel or provisions from the store, but permits are required to visit elsewhere, and alcohol is prohibited. Yuendumu has a thriving art community, and the work put out by the Warlukurlangi artists is highly regarded. It's not possible, however, to visit the artists without a permit. The town also has the highly sophisticated Tanami Network, a satellite TV conference network which can link Yuendumu with Darwin, Alice Springs and even overseas.

From Yuendumu the track crosses into **Mount Doreen station** and soon skirts the southern edge of the **Yarunganyi Hills**. On the northern side of the hills and close to the road is the site of the abandoned Mount Doreen station. Although originally built in the 1920s, it was later abandoned due to the unreliable water supply. These days the station is run from **Vaughan Springs station**, which lies about 80 km west of the track at this point.

The track then enters the vast expanses of the **Central Desert Aboriginal Land Trust**. The spinifex grass and anthills often stretch as far as the eye can see, and there's little to break the monotony – just the occasional acacia tree and the ubiquitous Telecom microwave towers at 50-km intervals.

The turn-off to **Mount Theo Outstation** and **Chilla Well** is reached 125 km northwest from Yuendumu, and from there it's 58 km to **Refrigerator Bore**, off to the right (north) of the track. Up until the early 1970s there was a stock route which went from Refrigerator Bore, passing through Tanami Downs (then Mongrel Downs) and on to Balgo and Halls Creek. This route had been pioneered in the early 1960s and a series of wells dug along its length to supply the cattle. Once trucks took over from droving as the main way to shift cattle, the route was no longer used.

Just before the new gold mine of The Granites, a low rocky outcrop on the left of the road and a couple of **old ruins** can be seen. These are worth exploring as they are the original buildings dating back to the workings during the 1930s.

A rough vehicle track winds up to the top

of the hill, about 500 metres from the road. It's best to leave the vehicle here and from this vantage point the new mine can be seen away to the west, while a huge new working can be seen at the base of the rise. Watch out for exploratory trenches and the like which seem to spring up with gay abandon around this area.

If you wander down the southern flank of the hill, you can see older relics, the most important of which is an old ore stamper, or battery. It is a beauty! Elsewhere there is the ruin of an old truck, a number of cyaniding tanks and a few other buildings. The site has long been picked over for small relics, but it is still worth stopping and soaking up the atmosphere of this place. What the old miners went through is vastly different to what the present workers experience, flying in and out from Alice Springs on their weekly shift.

The Granites Gold Mine is the next major point of interest, 82 km along the track from Refrigerator Bore, although there is no public access or facilities. Although small-scale mining had been carried out in the area since the early 1900s, the mine site was first pegged in 1927, and the mine itself operated until 1947. The returns were small, however, with a yield of only about 1000 ounces per year. In 1986 the mine reopened after exploratory drilling by North Flinders Mines proved gold reserves were still there. Production is currently running at around 170,000 ounces of gold per year, from both The Granites site and the area known as Dead Bullock Soak, 45 km to the west. The ore from Dead Bullock Soak is carted to The Granites site for treatment along a new bitumen road (definitely the only one for hundreds of km!) on huge four-trailer road trains, each carting well over 100 tons of ore. These monsters travel at great speed and require at least one km to stop.

It's just 48 km from The Granites to the most famous place in the Tanami, the **Rabbit Flat Roadhouse**, a km or so off to the north of the track. The roadhouse was established by Bruce Farrands and his French wife Jacqui in 1969 and has been serving travel-

lers on the Tanami Track ever since. It's certainly not an attractive place – just a couple of breeze-block buildings and a few fuel tanks – but it's the social centre of the Tanami, not least because it's the only place for hundreds of km where Aborigines can buy a drink. On Friday and Saturday nights it can get pretty lively with all the workers in from the mines.

Rabbit Flat to Halls Creek

From Rabbit Flat the track continues north-west for 44 km to the **Tanami Mine**. The story here is much the same as at The Granites – early interest and small yields followed by a period of inactivity from the 1930s to the 1980s, when modern techniques made the prospect viable once again. In 1987 Zapopan NL commenced operations and between then and March 1994, when the mine was once again shut down, around 380,000 ounces of gold were taken from the earth. There are no tourist services or public access to the mine site.

Just a km or so past the Tanami Mine, the **Lajamanu Road** heads off north (see Alternative Routes below). After the turn-off, the Tanami Track swings due west for the 80-odd km run to the Western Australia border and beyond. In the days of the area's minor gold rush, the track continued north-westerly, passing through Gordon Downs station and on to Halls Creek, but this route was abandoned once the rush was over. The route the current track takes between the Tanami Mine and **Billiluna Aboriginal Community** was established in the 1960s by Father McGuire from what was then the Balgo Aboriginal Mission.

It is 78 km from the roadhouse to the WA/NT border, and another 86 km will see you at the junction of the road to **Balgo Aboriginal Community**, nearly 40 km to the south. A fainter track heads north from this point across Aboriginal land to Sturt Creek homestead and finally to the **Duncan Highway**, 70 km east of Halls Creek. This 170-km trip north to the highway requires a permit.

From near the junction the occasional

Old stamper and cyanide tanks at the Granites gold mine (R & VM)

Wolfe Creek meteorite crater (TW)

sand ridge can be seen from the track, which now becomes a little sandier. A car with low clearance could easily become bogged. The track begins to swing north the further west you travel, and 24 km from the junction a second road heads south to Balgo.

The track continues to be sandy in places for the next 48 km to the crossing of **Sturt Creek**. Here is one of the few reasonable spots to camp along this route, with a couple of pleasant spots on the western bank, just north of the road crossing.

Sturt Creek occasionally flows, its flood-waters ending up in **Lake Gregory**, 100 km south of the Tanami Track. When this occurs, the lake becomes one of the great bird habitats in inland Australia. During one bird surveying expedition more than 240,000 waterbirds of 57 species were counted, including cormorants, pink-eared ducks, plumed whistle-ducks, coots, darters, egrets and brolgas, to name just a few.

Just a km past the crossing a track comes in from the south. This leads a short distance to Billiluna Aboriginal Community and is the start (or the end, depending on which way you are travelling) of the **Canning Stock Route**.

From here the road improves and swings almost due north, and the sand ridges slip away to the south-west. **Carranya Roadhouse** comes up on the right 41 km north of the Sturt Creek crossing; you can sometimes get fuel and limited supplies here, as well as turn off to travel the 20-odd km to Wolfe Creek Meteorite Crater and the small national park that surrounds it. This station track leads 16 km east to the nearly deserted Carranya homestead which you pass close to, before continuing on another five km to the small parking area at the base of the crater walls.

Wolfe Creek Meteorite Crater This crater is the second-largest of its type in the world. Known to the Aboriginal people as the place where some of their Dreamtime ancestors originated, early explorers and then the first aviators across this vast desert region knew of it, long before its significance was recorded by geologists in 1947. It was first gazetted as a reserve in 1969.

The rim of the crater is about 850 metres across and up to 35 metres above the surrounding sand plain. While the outer walls of the crater are relatively steep, the inner walls are much more so and descend, in places, via sheer cliffs, over 50 metres to the crater floor. Once it would have been much deeper, but sand has filled the crater in.

When was it formed? Sometime within the last two million years, and possibly within the last 500,000 years. Scientists tell us that to create such a crater the meteorite would have had to weigh many thousands of tonnes and be travelling at around 900 km per minute!

There are no facilities at the crater, not even a tree to cast a patch of shade, but it is worth looking at. The view from the crest of the rim is worth the short walk, and with care you can clamber down into the crater and explore the flat interior. The centre of the crater is a natural water trap and shrubs have grown up in profusion where the water is closer to the surface.

Halls Creek

Back on the main road, there is still another 111 km of dirt before the major T-intersection with Highway 1 and the bitumen. You are just 16 km west of Halls Creek and all the facilities of this small but major town. There is a choice of fuel outlets, repair places, a supermarket, police station, hospital and more. For more information on the facilities, see the section on the Canning Stock Route in the North-West chapter.

ALTERNATIVE ROUTES
Lajamanu Road

The Lajamanu Road heads north off the Tanami Track at the Tanami Mine, although it's not even marked on many maps. It's generally kept in very good condition, although it does get sandy towards Lajamanu, and there are numerous creek-bed crossings and the occasional washout. Even so, it is negotiable in the dry by 2WD with care.

The road offers an interesting alternative to the Tanami Track and takes you through country which has very little tourist traffic. It passes through the Central Desert Aboriginal Land and the Lajamanu Aboriginal Land. A permit is not required to traverse the road, or to get fuel and supplies at Lajamanu.

From the Tanami Mine it's 231 km to **Lajamanu**, and the trip takes around four hours. The road goes through some very pretty countryside, especially around Suplejack Downs station, and is generally more interesting than the Tanami Track itself.

The *Lajamanu Service Station* (☎ (089) 51 1573) sells fuel (super, unleaded, diesel), and there's a supermarket and takeaway food counter. The hours for fuel sales are 10 am to noon and 3 to 5 pm weekdays, and 10 am to noon on Saturday (closed Sunday). The takeaway food shop is open from 10 am to 5 pm Monday to Friday.

Heading north from the small Aboriginal settlement of Lajamanu, the road passes through typical spinifex plains until suddenly, about 10 km before the road hits the Buchanan Highway, the countryside changes from the red of the Centre to grassed and lightly treed cattle country. The change is quite dramatic – like a line has been drawn delineating the desert and the grazing land.

The Lajamanu Road joins the single-lane bitumen Buchanan Highway at an unmarked T-junction eight km east of **Kalkaringi**, which has a pleasant location on the banks of the Victoria River. At Kalkaringi there's a police station (☎ (089) 75 0790), caravan park, service station (☎ (089) 75 0788) with fuel (super, unleaded, diesel), takeaway food and very limited provisions. There is also the famous *Frank's Bar & Grill*, a fine establishment which should not be missed.

From Lajamanu it's 105 km to the Buchanan Highway and the journey takes about 1½ hours.

ORGANISED TOURS

A couple of tour companies offer the Tanami Desert as part of a wider tour taking in the Kimberley and the Top End from Alice Springs. Contact Austour (☎ toll-free 1800 335 009) or Australian Bushman's Tours (☎ toll-free 1800 800 260). With Austour you have the option of travelling in your own vehicle.

FACILITIES

Fuel supplies are well spaced out along the eastern end of the Tanami Track, but be warned that Rabbit Flat is only open from Friday to Monday, and that supplies at Carranya Roadhouse are unreliable. The longest stretch without fuel is nearly 500 km from Halls Creek to Rabbit Flat, including a 50-km round-trip detour to Wolfe Creek Meteorite Crater and assuming there is no fuel at Carranya Roadhouse. If there is fuel at Carranya then it's only 321 km between there and Rabbit Flat.

Although there are a number of bores quite close to the track along the way, the water in some of these is undrinkable so don't rely on them for your own consumption.

Tilmouth Well Roadhouse

At the modern *Tilmouth Well Roadhouse* (☎ (089) 56 8777) there's fuel (super, unleaded, diesel), basic spare parts and accessories. The restaurant should be open by now, and there's takeaway tucker as well. Out the back there's a basic campsite for $5 per person, and dongas for $20. The roadhouse is open daily from 7 am to 9 pm.

Yuendumu

The *Yuendumu Store* (☎ (089) 56 4006) has fuel (super, unleaded, diesel) and a fairly well-stocked supermarket. It's open on weekdays from 8 am to 5 pm, and on weekends from 2.30 to 4.30 pm. Permits are not required if you just want to get fuel and provisions; however, to visit anywhere else in the town a permit is required.

The other option here is the *Yuendumu Mining Company* store (☎ (089) 56 4040). It is well-stocked and has all types of fuel. Opening hours are from 9 am to 5 pm daily.

Yuelamu

At *Yuelamu* (Mount Allan) (☎ (089) 51 1520) you can get fuel (super, diesel), basic provisions and takeaway food. No permit is required but you must phone ahead.

Rabbit Flat

The quirky *Rabbit Flat Roadhouse* (☎ (089) 56 8744) stocks fuel (super, unleaded, diesel) and oil. Although your attention will be drawn to it, note that the somewhat antiquated fuel bowsers can only register prices up to 99 cents per litre. As the fuel costs at least $1.20 per litre (possibly and not surprisingly the most expensive in the country), the displayed price is only half that and the final price is doubled. The Farrands also sell basic provisions and beer ($53 for a carton!), and there's a bar. It's also possible to camp here, and there's no charge for this. Be warned also that the roadhouse is only open from Friday to Monday, and that business is conducted on a cash-only basis.

Carranya Roadhouse

The Carranya Roadhouse (☎ (091) 68 8927) is a relatively new establishment on the Tanami but it rarely has anything to offer. If you are lucky it will have fuel and a cool drink or two. Don't expect anything else – in fact don't even rely on that!

Plenty Highway

Leaving the Stuart Highway 70 km north of Alice Springs, the 742-km-long Plenty Highway spears across a semiarid plain on the fringe of the Simpson Desert, terminating at Boulia in western Queensland. Isolation is almost guaranteed on the Plenty Highway – even in winter you can drive the entire route and see fewer than a dozen vehicles. Signs of human habitation are rare and facilities are almost nonexistent – there are none whatsoever in the final 456 km to Boulia. In other words, anyone deciding to take this good short cut to Queensland from the Centre must be self-sufficient in everything.

The first 103 km from the Stuart Highway are sealed, but after that the road can be extremely rough and corrugated; large bulldust holes usually pose a hazard on the Queensland side, which is not so well maintained and is often more like a track than a road. Once past the bitumen, the highway is suitable for use only in dry weather and is definitely not recommended for caravans. Diesel, super and unleaded fuel are available at the Gemtree Caravan Park (140 km from Alice Springs), Jervois homestead (356 km) and Boulia (812 km). The Atitjere Aboriginal Community (215 km from Alice Springs) sells diesel fuel and super only.

HISTORY

The disappearance of the eccentric German explorer Ludwig Leichhardt and his large, well-equipped party is one of Australia's great unsolved mysteries. Leichhardt vanished somewhere in the interior on his final expedition, in 1846, and it's possible that he crossed the area of the Plenty Highway while attempting to return to civilisation. The evidence that this actually happened is largely based on the discovery of marked trees in central Australia and far west Queensland.

In 1886 the surveyor David Lindsay, of Simpson Desert fame, found trees in the Harts Range that had been carved with Leichhardt's distinctive mark. Many years later, more such trees were discovered along the Georgina River on Glenormiston station. Also of interest is the fact that the bones of several unknown White men had been found by a waterhole near Birdsville in the early 1870s, before the area was settled.

Leichhardt had intended to cross northern Australia from east to west, but he may have been forced south by the waterless scrub west of the Roper River. Judging by the location of the carved trees, he reached the MacDonnell Ranges, headed east around the top of the Simpson Desert and then, on striking the Georgina, had turned south once more. Reaching the junction of the Georgina and Diamantina rivers, he managed to upset the local Aborigines, who killed him and his remaining companions. No-one knows if the bones found by that lonely waterhole belonged to Leichhardt and his men, but the theory is a fascinating and plausible one.

H Vere Barclay was one of the next Europeans on the scene. In 1878, while engaged in carrying out a trigonometric survey from Alice Springs to the Queensland border, he was north-east of the Harts Range when he was faced with a critical water shortage. He dug into a sandy riverbed – this being the usual method of finding water in dry outback rivers – and found ample supplies of the precious fluid flowing beneath the surface. That is how the Plenty River got its name, and it's why the present beef road, which was first upgraded from a two-wheel track during the 1960s, is called the Plenty Highway.

INFORMATION
Tourist Offices
The Gemtree Caravan Park (☎ (089) 56 9855) can advise you on fossicking in the western Harts Range area, while the Boulia Shire Office (☎ (077) 46 3188) is the best source of information on Boulia and the road east of the border. For road reports, contact the Alice Springs police (☎ (089) 51 8888) or the Boulia Shire Office.

Emergency
In the event of a medical emergency, you can obtain assistance from the health clinic at Atitjere, where a registered nurse is in charge. The Boulia hospital is under the control of a matron, and an RFDS clinic is held there on a weekly basis. Apart from that,

you'll have to call in to the nearest homestead and ask for help. Lack of medical facilities is a compelling reason to carry a comprehensive medical kit on all remote outback roads.

Books & Maps
Many of the fascinating reminiscences contained in *A Son of the Red Centre*, by Kurt Johannsen, involve the Plenty Highway area. Johannsen, who is regarded as the father of modern road-train transport, mined copper near Jervois and hauled huge loads from his mine to Mount Isa before there was a road. The book will appeal to anyone interested in Australian pioneering history and is available from bookshops and newsagents in Alice Springs, and also from the author, at 2 Stephen's Place, Morphettville, SA 5043.

If you're intending to look for gems in the Harts Range, you'll need *A Guide to Fossicking in the Northern Territory*, by the Northern Territory Department of Mines & Energy (Darwin, 1986). This publication has details on many of the range's fossicking areas and its old mines, including maps, although much of the information about access is out of date, it's still an essential reference. Most areas mentioned are accessible either on foot or by 4WD vehicle only, as tracks within the range tend to be too rough for conventional vehicles.

At a scale of 1:1,000,000, the map/guide entitled *Plenty Highway*, by Westprint Heritage Maps, makes a useful planning and touring reference for this road. As a bonus, it includes the short cut from the Plenty Highway to Mount Isa via Urandangi, and the direct route from Boulia to Birdsville. The guides are on sale at numerous outlets around Alice Springs and in map shops everywhere.

Radio Frequencies
The highway west of the border is served by the Alice Springs RFDS base (callsign VJD – Victor Juliet Delta), which operates on 5410 and 6950 kHz between 7.30 am and 5 pm Monday to Friday (public holidays excepted). Use 2020 and 5410 kHz

Mitchell-grass plain (DO)

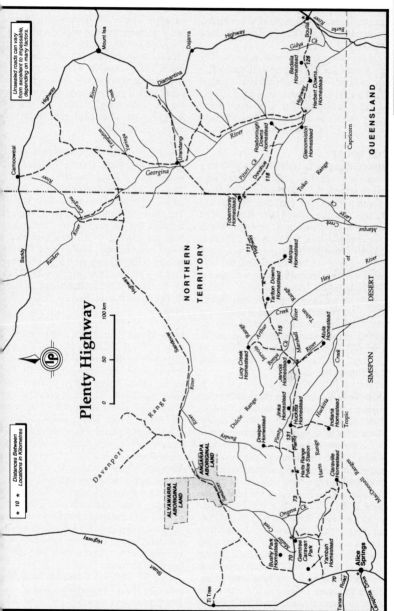

Plenty Highway

for after-hours emergency calls. For further information on services, contact the base (☎ (089) 52 1033).

In the east you enter the zone serviced by the Mount Isa RFDS base (callsign VJI – Victor Juliet India), which can be reached on 2020 and 5110 kHz between 8 am and 5 pm Monday to Friday. For after-hours emergency calls, use 5110 kHz. Ring the base (☎ (077) 43 7887) for an update on services.

THE ROUTE
Stuart Highway to Harts Range (143 km)
From the Stuart Highway to the Harts Range police station, the road parallels the rugged northern flanks of first the Strangways Range and then the Harts Range. The scenery is attractive almost throughout, with several picturesque creeks in the 103 km to Ongeva Creek. Most of these are well worth stopping at if you feel like boiling the billy under a river gum and relaxing with nature, although you'll generally need a 4WD vehicle to get away from the road. There's also good potential for quiet walks in the bush, and the chance of finding minerals such as zircon, quartz, garnet and staurolite. The road is single-lane bitumen as far as Ongeva Creek; beyond that it's wide, formed dirt to the police station.

Mud Tank Seventy km from the Stuart Highway you come to the Gemtree Caravan Park, on the gum-lined banks of Gillen Creek. This is the only tourist facility of note on the Plenty Highway. Among its services, it offers guests the chance to hire fossicking equipment and search for gems at the nearby **Mud Tank zircon field**. Advice on how to use the hired equipment is included in the price.

Alternatively, for a fee of $25, you can take the park's accompanied trip to the zircon deposit (equipment provided) and get some practical experience with an expert. The top 80 cm of soil conceals zircons of various colours (including yellow, light brown, pink, purple and blue), ranging in size from small chips to large crystals. Provided they put their backs into it, even novices have an excellent chance of finding gem material with nothing more complicated than a shovel, a couple of small sieves (minimum mesh size seven mm) and some water in a drum. There is usually a cut-down drum or two lying around that you can use, but don't count on it. If you find anything worth faceting, the caravan park's gem-cutter can turn your find into a beautiful stone ready to be set in gold or silver.

The turn-off to the zircon field is on the right (south) at the big windmill about seven km east of Gemtree, and the fossicking area is nine km in along the track. Deposits of gem-quality garnet also occur in the general area – ask about these at the caravan park. The zircon field and one or two of the garnet deposits can be reached by conventional vehicles (driven with care), provided it hasn't been raining. Don't forget that fossicking is illegal unless you hold a Northern Territory Miners Right, which costs $20 and can be obtained at the Department of Mines & Energy office in Hartley Street, Alice Springs.

Mica Mines The Harts Range starts at Ongeva Creek, where a track on the right takes you to the ominously named Blackfellows Bones mica mine. (Apparently, back in the 1870s, a large group of Aborigines from the Sandover River country were slaughtered nearby in reprisal for an attack on settlers.) From 1888 to 1960, mica was mined from pegmatites throughout the Harts Range, with literally dozens of small mines being developed on a front of about 100 km. Because of its remoteness, the rugged terrain, lack of water and uncertain markets, the field was never rich but the miners (most of whom were Italians after the 1920s) persevered until cheaper imports eventually put them out of business. Now the old dumps are a popular target for visiting fossickers, who come in search of the gems that were thrown out with the waste.

One of Australia's premier fossicking areas, the Harts Range yields a host of interesting gems and minerals, including mica, smoky and rose quartz, aquamarine, black

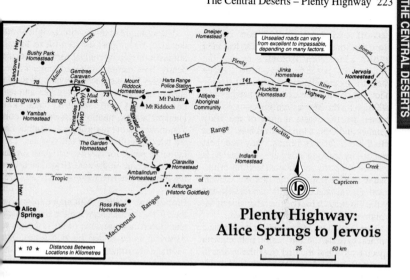

Plenty Highway:
Alice Springs to Jervois

and green tourmaline, sphene, garnet, sun-stone, ruby, iolite and kyanite. Among the many magnificent stones found here is the world's largest known specimen of sphene. However, the area is extremely rugged and the best fossicking spots are hard to get to – high-clearance 4WD vehicles are required for most tracks. It's also essential to carry plenty of water at all times.

Seven km past Ongeva Creek you come to a signposted 4WD track that leads to garnet deposits en route to Ambalindum station and the Arltunga Road, 60 km to the south. Then a massive ochre-coloured ridge looms on your right, its steep flanks of bald rock issuing an invitation to keen hill climbers. It's a tough scramble to the top of **Mt Riddoch**, the highest point, but the view is well worth the effort. Before setting out on the walk, you can park your vehicle at Kong Bore, the turn-off to which is about 16 km past Ongeva Creek. The dumps of abandoned mica mines in the near vicinity yield various minerals, such as black tourmaline, quartzes, hornblende and epidote.

Harts Range

High ridges and mountains keep you

company for the next 40 km to the Harts Range police station, where a road turns off to the right to give access to the Harts Range racecourse. The two police officers based here have the awesome task of preserving law and order over a sparsely populated area of 120,000 sq km – apart from constant travel, they do everything from investigating murders to issuing driving licences. By all accounts they're kept busy controlling revellers during the annual Harts Range races, which take place over the first weekend in August. This is a good weekend's entertainment, with a barbecue and bush dance on the Saturday night, but you need to get there early to find a campsite reasonably handy to the action.

The road continues on past the racecourse, but soon deteriorates to a 4WD track that gives access to a number of old mica mines both on and around the rocky slopes of **Mt Palmer**. At 600 metres above the northern plain, this is one of the highest points in the Harts Range and has many large cycads growing on its southern flank. It's well worth climbing – the atmosphere and the sweeping panorama from the top are magnificent.

Mt Palmer first becomes visible past the

turn-off to Mount Riddock station, 117 km from the Stuart Highway. Like a retreat for a goblin king from Tolkien's books, the mountain's jagged, misty-blue outline makes a spectacular sight as it rises steeply above the plain. The two white patches you see high up on the western slopes as you get closer are the waste dumps of the Billy Hughes and Oolgarinna mica mines. Two of the field's largest mines, they are best reached by walking along the old camel pads that wind up the mountainside from primitive mining camps at the bottom. Camels were used as beasts of burden, both here and at the Disputed mine (on the other side of Mt Palmer), right up until mining ceased.

The Disputed is famous in mineralogical circles because of the many fine mineral specimens it has yielded over the years. In the 1930s, miners opened a cave-like cavity in the pegmatite and found it to be lined top and bottom with huge crystals of black tourmaline, mica, feldspar, quartz and beryl. Apparently the tourmaline crystals stuck up from the floor like fence posts. Known as the Jeweller's Cave, this sparkling wonderland was permanently sealed off by a mine collapse not long after its discovery. A 4WD track takes you from the racetrack to the old Disputed camp, after which it's a half-hour walk along the camel pad to the dumps high above on the mountainside. En route you pass the Spotted Dog mine, where two miners died in a rock fall in the late 1920s. Their simple grave is nearby, although hard to find.

Harts Range to the Queensland Border (357 km)

The road is wide and formed all the way from Harts Range to the border, but it can still be quite rough, depending on when it was last graded. The first 50 km is extremely scenic, with attractive tall woodlands of whitewood and weeping ironwood fronting the ragged Harts Range to the south. Later, mulga and gidgee become dominant and only flat-topped hills, scattered low ranges and occasional, beautiful gum-lined creeks break the monotony of the endless plain.

The highlight of this section is right beside the road, 50 km past the turn-off to Jervoi homestead. Here a conical **termite mound** nearly five metres high and three metres thick rears like a breaching whale above the surrounding sea of stunted mallees and spinifex. It makes an extraordinary sight, like a giant prehistoric monument soaked in blood. The mound is the highest point around, and the white splashes on top tell you that it's a favourite perch for hawks. You pass similar termite mounds in the next 10 km but few of these rise above two metres.

Pioneers & Poison Although explored in the 1870s, the area between the Harts Range and Queensland was one of the last parts of Australia to be settled by Europeans. The shortage of permanent surface water kept the pastoralists at bay until bore-drilling equipment became readily available in the late 1940s. Indiana, Jervois, Atula, Lucy Creek, Tarlton Downs and Marqua stations were all first taken up for cattle grazing between 1950 and 1960. Atula, on the Simpson Desert fringe, was recently purchased by the federal government and handed back to its Aboriginal occupants.

Near Mount Riddock homestead you begin to notice clumps of gidgee beside the road. A tough acacia, this generally low gnarled tree with dark-brown bark and dense grey foliage is the dominant species past Arthur Creek. Although a valuable fodder plant in some areas, gidgee is extremely poisonous to cattle in others. At certain times its pods and young leaves carry a powerful toxin that causes any beast grazing on them to have a heart attack immediately after drinking – the unfortunate animal literally drops dead at the trough. In the early days stations in this area often suffered devastating stock losses due to gidgee poisoning, but better fencing has brought the problem under control.

Queensland Border

At the Queensland border, the road changes its name and becomes known as the Donohue Highway. Crossing the border

The five-metre termite mound near Jervois homestead (DO)

grid, you'll also usually notice a dramatic change in road conditions – the Boulia Shire does its best, but it only takes a few road trains to break the surface and form deep bulldust holes. After the first few shattering experiences with these nasties, you soon learn to identify them and take due care. If it starts raining steadily while you're in this area, either head for Boulia fast or make for the nearest stony or sandy ground and make camp.

Queensland Border to Boulia (244 km)

For virtually the entire way to Boulia, you pass through a mix of gidgee scrub and open **mitchell-grass country**, with variety provided by occasional stony undulations and coolabah creeks. Mitchell-grass habitats, which occur in a great arc from southern Queensland through the Territory's Barkly Tableland to the Kimberley, are the arid zone's most productive in terms of stock grazing. As you'll see along the Plenty and Donohue highways, Queensland has a much greater share of these rich grasslands than

does the Territory. They are the best places to see the endangered bustard, a large, rather haughty bird that often gathers in flocks to feed on grasshoppers and other insects in the mitchell grass.

Georgina River At 118 km from the border you come to the Georgina River, and other than the vast expanses of empty space, this waterway is the highlight on the Queensland section of the highway. The main channel features shady coolabahs, good camp sites and abundant bird life – you'll often see brolgas, emus and bustards as well as large flocks of budgies, cockatiels, galahs and corellas in the immediate area. If there's a down side, it's the **Noogoora burr** that infests the banks. This introduced noxious weed has prickly, cigar-shaped seeds which can easily hitch a ride on your clothing. If you stop here, make sure you're not carrying any unwanted passengers before driving on.

Fed by summer monsoon rains, the Georgina River rises on the Barkly Tableland north-west of Camooweal and heads southwards to join the Diamantina River near Birdsville. A large enough flood will eventually reach Lake Eyre, which is quite a journey by the standards of Australian rivers. The crossing is normally dry, but any flooding causes it to be closed until conditions improve, which can take many days.

Boulia

Eight km from Boulia you meet the bitumen and joyous relief from the bulldust and corrugations. By the time most travellers reach this point, they're ready to kill for a cold beer in the pub.

Straggling down to a large waterhole in the **Burke River**, which the ill-fated Burke and Wills visited on their dash across Australia in 1861, Boulia is the administrative centre for the vast Boulia Shire. The shire covers about 60,000 sq km and has a population of 250,000 sheep, 75,000 cattle and about 600 people, 300 of whom live in Boulia. There are a few minor tourist attractions in the town, including a **folk museum** and the last known **corroboree tree** of the Pitta Pitta tribe. About 10 km out on the Coorabulka Road is a rare stand of endangered **waddy trees**, which are known only from three scattered locations around the margins of the Simpson Desert (the other two are near Birdsville and Old Andado homestead).

If you're camped on a dark night in the Boulia area, you may be lucky enough to see the famous **Min Min Light**, a ghostly luminous glow like a fluorescent football that floats through the air as if someone is carrying a lantern in a mist. Many people have seen the light but no-one has ever managed to get close enough to catch it. Apparently it was first noticed many years ago above the graveyard at the old Min Min Hotel on the Winton Road. There is no scientific explanation for the phenomenon, and outsiders tend to scoff that a few ales are necessary before a sighting. However, few people living in the region doubt that the Min Min Light exists.

ALTERNATIVE ROUTE
Mount Isa via Urandangi (280 km)

The road to Urandangi, which turns off the Plenty Highway 493 km from the Stuart Highway, makes an excellent short cut to Mount Isa, provided the bulldust holes aren't too bad and the conditions are dry. Gidgee scrub and open mitchell-grass plains keep you company for the 96 km from the highway to the Georgina River crossing, after which tiny Urandangi is only a minute or two away.

A faded shadow of a more prosperous era (the town died when the droving teams gave way to road transport), Urandangi's main attraction is an interesting old pub (☎ (077) 48 4988), where fuel, meals, basic accommodation and camping facilities are available. Leaving the town, you endure similar road conditions for a further 110 km, then turn onto the bitumen for the final 73 km to Mount Isa.

FACILITIES
Gemtree Caravan Park

Conveniently located close to deposits of gem-quality zircon and garnet, the Gemtree Caravan Park (☎ (089) 56 9855) offers good shade, a kiosk, public telephone, fuel sales (diesel, super and unleaded) and a range of accommodation options. On-site caravans cost $37 for two people, while powered/unpowered sites cost $16/12 for two. These rates increase by $5 for each additional adult and $3 for each child. Bush camping (with access to shower and toilet facilities) costs $6 per person. Games of paddymelon bowls, with tea and damper to follow, provide some light-hearted entertainment on Saturday nights in the cooler months. Paddymelons, whose fruits look like small round watermelons, often occur in large patches beside roads and on other disturbed areas.

Atitjere

The Atitjere Community Store (☎ (089) 56 9773) sells basic food requirements and cold drinks, as well as diesel and super. Aboriginal art and interesting gemstones from the nearby Harts Range are also on offer most of the time. The store is open between 9 am and 5 pm Monday to Friday and from 9 am to noon on Saturday.

Jervois Homestead

You can buy diesel, super and unleaded fuel at the Jervois homestead (☎ (089) 56 6307) during daylight hours, seven days a week. Shower and toilet facilities are also available. Camping isn't permitted at the homestead itself, but you can stop either at the turn-off, where there is a lay-by, or along the homestead access road between the highway and the first gate (about one km in). The many magnificent ghost gums growing along the nearby Marshall River make a beautiful setting for a bush camp.

For something different, you can inspect the huge rocket-proof shelter that was built at the homestead during the 1960s, when Blue Streak rockets were fired in this direction from Woomera in South Australia. Instead of huddling inside as they were supposed to, the stationfolk preferred to stand on top to watch the fireworks. Similar shelters were provided for all the stations in this area. It all seems to have been a waste of taxpayers' money, although a couple of rockets did come down near the highway.

Boulia

This isolated township has a good range of facilities, including a hospital, police station, post office, all-weather aerodrome, hotel, caravan park, two garages, a cafe and a handful of other shops. The Min Min Store in the main street sells hardware items and has a minisupermarket. Banking facilities are limited to a Commonwealth Bank agency in the post office, which takes passbooks only.

The *Australian Hotel* (☎ (077) 46 3144) has air-conditioned accommodation for 45 people. There are four motel-style rooms with en suites and TV, costing $45/55 per single/twin. Single/twin/triple rooms in the hotel cost $30/35/45; there are two rooms sleeping four people ($55) and one room sleeping six ($72). The dining room serves breakfast, lunch and dinner, all meals being country-style in quality and quantity. A cooked breakfast costs $12 and a two-course evening meal is $15.

It's usually quite peaceful down at the grassy *Boulia Caravan Park* (☎ (077) 46 3144) beside the Burke River at the eastern end of town. Powered caravan sites cost $12 for two people plus $2 per additional person. Powered/unpowered campsites cost $4/3 per person. The nearby waterhole was visited by the ill-fated Burke and Wills on their dash across Australia from Cooper Creek in 1860.

Bush Camping

There are numerous good camping sites in the mulga and gidgee scrub that line the Plenty Highway, although you'll generally need a 4WD vehicle to reach them. If you are so equipped, the soft, sandy beds of Annamurra Creek (80 km), the Plenty River (270 km) and Arthur Creek (322 km) have excellent camp sites among large, colourful river gums. The best sites in Queensland are found along the Georgina River, where coolabah trees offer good shade and firewood. Roadside stops with small shade shelters, wood-burning barbecues and water tanks are located at the turn-offs to Jervois homestead and Urandangi.

Sandover Highway

Leaving the Plenty Highway 96 km from Alice Springs, the Sandover Highway heads north-eastwards across flat semidesert for 552 km to terminate at Lake Nash homestead, near the Queensland border. Getting its name from the Sandover River, whose course it follows for about 250 km, this long, wide ribbon of red dirt is an excellent short cut for adventurous tourists wishing to drive between central Australia and north-west Queensland.

The Sandover Highway offers a memorable experience in remote touring. For almost the entire distance the only signs of human achievement are occasional Telecom communication towers, signposted turn-offs to a handful of isolated homesteads and Aboriginal communities, and the road stretching endlessly ahead. There is light traffic as far as the Ammaroo turn-off, 218 km from the

Plenty Highway, but beyond that it's usually a novelty to see another vehicle, even in winter.

Tourist facilities are nonexistent along the road but you can buy fuel and supplies at the Arlparra Store (250 km from Alice Springs) and the Alpurrurulam Aboriginal Community (643 km from Alice Springs).

Road conditions depend to a great extent on the weather: prolonged rain creates bogs that can keep the highway closed for days. In the late 1980s the road was closed to all traffic for several months after exceptionally heavy rains caused long sections to be washed away. Although often rough, the road is normally suitable for conventional vehicles with high ground clearance and heavy-duty suspensions.

HISTORY

For most of its distance the Sandover Highway crosses the traditional lands of the Alyawarra people, whose lives until recent times focussed on the relatively rich environment of the Sandover River. White people arrived in Alyawarra country in the 1880s, when Lake Nash and Argadargada stations, near the Queensland border, were established for sheep and cattle grazing. The country to the south-west wasn't permanently settled by Europeans until 40 years later; Ooratippra was the last station to be taken up, being leased in the late 1940s. As elsewhere in the outback, the loss of food resources and the fouling of precious water supplies by cattle caused bloody conflicts between pastoralists and Aborigines. The so-called Sandover Massacre of the 1920s resulted in the deaths of about 100 Alyawarra, who were either shot or poisoned after committing the grievous crime of cattle-spearing.

Atartinga station, about 140 km north-east of Alice Springs, was taken up by R H (Bob) Purvis, father of the present owner, in 1920. Known as the Sandover Alligator because of

River red gums (DO)

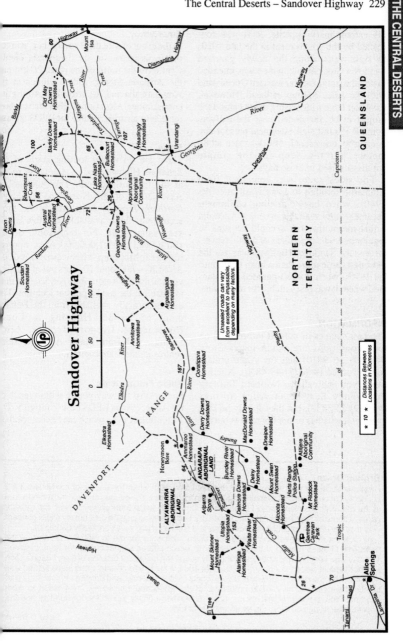

his extraordinary appetite, R H was contracted by the government in the late 1920s to sink wells along the newly gazetted Sandover Stock Route, which was intended to link the stations of far western Queensland with the Alice Springs railhead. However, the water table's increasing depth caused the project to be abandoned near the halfway point. R H's last well, sited near present-day Ammaroo homestead, struck water at 80 metres, far too deep for the simple windlasses used in those days.

The stock route was continued from Ammaroo through to Lake Nash after the 1940s, when heavy drilling equipment became readily available in central Australia – this meant that bores could be sunk at regular intervals regardless of depth. Nevertheless, the Sandover Highway was, for the most part, little more than a bush track until the 1970s, when it was upgraded to a standard where it was just suitable for road trains.

INFORMATION

The best sources of current information on road conditions are the Arlparra Store (☎ (089) 56 9910) and the Alpurrurulam council office (☎ (077) 48 4800). Alternatively, you can call the Northern Territory Emergency Service in Alice Springs (☎ (089) 52 3833), but they'll only be able to tell you whether or not the road is open.

Emergency

In the event of a medical emergency, you can obtain assistance at the Urapuntja Health Centre (to the north of the road, 21 km past the Arlparra Store), and at clinics at the Ampilatwatja and Alpurrululam Aboriginal communities. Most (if not all) homesteads en route have airstrips suitable for RFDS aircraft.

Maps

There are no useful touring maps of the Sandover Highway and its alternative routes at the Queensland end. The Automobile Association of the Northern Territory's *Northern Territory* road map is the most accurate of those available, but this is at a very small scale. For reasonable detail you'll need the 1:1,000,000 Alice Springs topographic map sheet produced by AUSLIG – it's about 20 years out of date but you can use the Automobile Association map to establish the road's present location. The map is normally available from the Department of Lands, Housing & Local Government, Gregory Terrace, Alice Springs, and from major AUSLIG sales centres in interstate capitals.

Radio Frequencies

For most of the way you're within reach of the Alice Springs RFDS base (callsign VJD Victor Juliet Delta), which can be contacted on

Broken Down

I was about 50 km past Ammaroo en route to Lake Nash when the engine of my Nissan 4WD suddenly cut out. I noticed a smell of burning, and a glance at the gauges showed the temperature in the red. With a sinking heart I opened the bonnet. My worst fears were realised: the radiator cap had come off and the radiator had boiled dry. I was carrying a spare cap, but my major concern was that the engine might have overheated to the point where it was seriously damaged.

It took the engine over an hour to cool down sufficiently for me to refill the radiator. In the meantime I looked around at the stunted scrub, which offered neither shade nor hope of water. The day was very hot and utterly still, the only sound the incessant buzzing of flies. I hadn't seen another vehicle since the Arlparra Store, over 100 km back, and no-one came along while I was stopped. The Sandover Highway is a very lonely road in summer, and despite the fact that I had plenty of water, the silence and emptiness of the landscape caused my imagination to work overtime. You can appreciate my immense relief when I finally turned the ignition key and the engine, after coughing a bit, ran as sweetly as before.

Denis O'Byrne

5410 and 6950 kHz between 7.30 am and 5 pm Monday to Friday (public holidays excepted). Use 2020 and 5410 kHz for after-hours emergency calls. For further information on services, contact the base (☎ (089) 52 1033).

Nearer Lake Nash you enter the zone serviced by the Mount Isa base (callsign VJI – Victor Juliet India), which can be reached on 2020 amd 5110 kHz between 8 am and 5 pm Monday to Friday. For after-hours emergency calls, use 5110 kHz. Ring the base (☎ (077) 43 7887) for an update on services.

THE ROUTE
Plenty Highway to Ammaroo (217 km)
Turning off the Plenty Highway 26 km from the Stuart Highway, the Sandover crosses a vast, semiarid plain virtually all the way to the Ammaroo turn-off. Indeed, the landscape is so flat that some low granite outcrops about 10 km past the Atartinga turn-off become objects of great interest – the highest offers quite a nice view, so it's worth stopping to stretch the legs. You pass occasional attractive patches of shady white-barked gums, but mainly the vegetation consists of mulga woodland on clay soils and low gums and spinifex on sandy areas. This is marginal cattle country – the average station en route has only about 25% useful grazing land. For example, Atartinga covers 2240 sq km but its 1200-head herd is concentrated on about 600 sq km. The spinifex areas along the highway carry billions of termites but only one cow to every 10 sq km.

At 127 km from the Plenty Highway you cross the western boundary of **Utopia station**. Purchased by the federal government in 1976 for local Aborigines, the station is home to about 700 Alyawarra people, who live in 20 small outstations scattered over an area of 2500 sq km. These communities are governed by a council based at Arlparra, which you pass 27 km further on. The fence 23 km past Arlparra marks the boundary between Utopia and Ammaroo stations. Almost all the minor roads that turn off the highway between the two fences lead in to Aboriginal communities and are off limits to the travelling public.

Ammaroo to Lake Nash (335 km)
Past Ammaroo, the country becomes gently undulating, with stony rises that give sweeping views over a vast sea of grey-green scrub. This is the southern end of the **Davenport Range**, which sweeps north-west for 200 km to the Devil's Marbles south of Tennant Creek. At this point the **Sandover River** is five km to the south. The river is extremely scenic, with colourful gums and a sandy bed, but as it parallels the road throughout, you'll see it only by taking the occasional tracks that lead off in that direction. Unfortunately you never see the river from the road, although you do enter the Sandover floodout later on – the river tends to alternate between defined channels and broad areas that are subject to flooding.

About 60 km past the hills you come to a red sandy plain covered mainly by low mallee and spinifex, a scene that with only minor interruptions takes you almost all the way to Lake Nash. The main variation in plant communities is a large, open grassy area that you cross 200 km from Ammaroo. An outlier of the vast natural grasslands of the Barkly Tableland to the north, this isolated patch of mitchell grass grows on black clay soil (more commonly known as blacksoil), which is as hard as a rock when dry and incredibly sloppy when wet. It takes only a light shower to turn this short section of road into a skating rink. Such areas occur in a great arc from southern Queensland through the Barkly and on to the Kimberley in Western Australia. Mitchell-grass habitats are the arid zone's most productive grazing lands – they cover only about 10% of the Northern Territory yet carry up to 50% of the total Territory cattle herd.

You see more blacksoil country 317 km past Ammaroo, then the glittering iron roofs of the **Alpurrurulam Aboriginal Community** come into view on the left and the end of the highway is just five minutes away, at **Lake Nash homestead**. The largest of the Sandover's stations, Lake Nash covers

THE CENTRAL DESERTS

13,000 sq km and carries, on average, a herd of 41,000 high-quality Santa Gertrudis beef cattle.

Everything about Lake Nash is big: it has the world's largest commercial herd of Santa Gertrudis, the property's bore runs are so long that the vehicles assigned to them travel a total of 96,000 km per year, and the average paddock covers several hundred sq km. The station's workforce of 28 is also huge by local standards.

ALTERNATIVE ROUTES

The Sandover Highway ends at Lake Nash homestead, where you have a choice of three routes: north to Camooweal, east to Mount Isa or south to Urandangi. All are minor dirt roads, and as they include blacksoil sections, they become impassable after rain. When dry, they are normally suitable for conventional vehicles in the hands of experienced outback motorists.

Caution must be exercised, as signposting is poor throughout and available maps seldom show the roads' true positions. If in doubt, the best approach is to fill up with fuel at Alpurrurulam and ask for directions and an update on road conditions – if the people at the store can't help, ask at the council office across the road.

Lake Nash to Camooweal (183 km)

The recommended option is to go via Austral Downs homestead, this being a much better road than the alternative route further east via Barkly Downs homestead. The Austral Downs Road turns off the Sandover Highway 13 km before Lake Nash. From here the road heads mainly due north over flat terrain, crossing the **Ranken River** and passing Austral Downs at the halfway mark, before meeting the Barkly Highway 43 km west of Camooweal. There is good shade for a lunch stop or a camp at the Ranken crossing, but most of the way you're on the vast grassy plains of the **Barkly Tableland**, a region notable for its lack of trees.

Although a very small town, **Camooweal** offers a wide range of services, including fuel sales, mechanical repairs, hotel accommodation and meals. For details, ring the *Post Office Hotel* (☎ (077) 48 2124).

Lake Nash to Mount Isa (205 km)

From Lake Nash, cross the Georgina River and head north-east for 65 km to meet the Camooweal-Urandangi Road. Here you veer left towards Barkly Downs and Camooweal. After about 10 km you come to a series of three rough creek crossings, where you turn right onto the Old May Downs Road – the turn-off is on a rise just past the third creek and, being unsignposted, is easy to miss. (If you keep going straight on you'll end up at the Barkly Downs homestead.) From here it's a straightforward run of about 70 km, past large windmills and the **Old May Downs homestead ruins**, to meet the Barkly Highway about 60 km out from Mount Isa. This latter section is relatively scenic, thanks to the stark red ridges that typify the Mount Isa area.

A major regional centre, **Mount Isa** is home to one of Australia's largest mining companies and has a population exceeding 20,000. Contact the Mount Isa Civic Centre (☎ (077) 44 4244) for information on services, amenities and points of interest in the town and surrounding area.

Lake Nash to Urandangi (172 km)

The main route heads north-east from Lake Nash, meeting the Camooweal-Urandangi Road at the 65-km mark. Turn right here and drive south for 69 km to **Headingly homestead**, where you go around the southern end of the airstrip, keeping the buildings on your right, and head through the gate.

The road is wide and dusty through low gidgee scrub for the final 38 km from Headingly to **Urandangi**. This sleepy little outpost began to die at the end of the droving era but still lingers on. It has an interesting old pub (☎ (077) 48 4988), where fuel, meals, basic accommodation and camping facilities are available. Large yellowbelly live in the nearby **Georgina River**, though getting them to bite is a challenge most of the time. There are plenty of shady camp sites down by the river crossing on the road leading to the Plenty Highway.

FACILITIES

Arlparra Store

The Arlparra Store on Utopia station mainly serves the Aboriginal communities of that area. It sells diesel, super and unleaded petrol and has a well-stocked minisupermarket with all basic food requirements – you can also buy hardware items, tools and vehicle parts. The ladies of Utopia are famous for their batik work, and you may be able to pick some up here, although the outlets in Alice Springs are a safer bet. The store is open from 9 am to 5 pm Monday to Friday and from 9 am to noon on Saturday.

Alpurrurulam

The community store sells diesel, super and unleaded petrol, all basic food requirements, minor hardware items and vehicle parts (including tyres). It's open from 8 to 11 am and 3 to 5 pm Monday to Friday and from 8

to 11 am on Saturday. There is also a mechanical workshop (open from 8 am to 5 pm), where minor repairs can be attended to. Although visitors are welcome to use the commercial facilities, which are right at the entrance to Alpurrurulam, you should not proceed further into the community.

Bush Camping

Good camp sites near the road are few and far between along the Sandover Highway, particularly past Ammaroo. One good option near Ammaroo is about 10 km up the Elkedra Road, which turns off opposite the homestead; a small creek offers pleasant camping with shade and firewood. The spot is just past the big windmill at Honeymoon Bore, where you can refill your water containers.

There are roadside stops with small shade shelters, barbecues and water tanks at the Ammaroo turn-off and about 30 km before Lake Nash. Night traffic is virtually nonexistent most of the time, so you're unlikely to be disturbed. Camping is only permitted

Time out while hiking (MacDonnell Ranges) (DO)

within 50 metres of the line where the highway crosses Aboriginal land on either side of Arlparra.

Six km past Alpurrurulam and within sight of the Lake Nash homestead, you come to a track heading off to the left immediately before a grid. The track leads you down to a large waterhole (Lake Nash), where there are some good camp sites among scrubby coolabahs near the water's edge. The station manager doesn't mind people camping here, provided they take their rubbish with them. However, there is no firewood whatsoever, and because of its clay soil, this is definitely not the place to be in wet weather. Yellowbelly live in the waterhole but, sadly, tend to be rather small.

Finke & Old Andado Tracks

This area, south-east of Alice Springs, is full of interest. The countryside is varied, with the red sand-dune country of the western Simpson Desert predominating. However, it's far from boring, and in spring, after rains, the whole area is ablaze with wildflowers.

A number of tracks offer various options: you can do the two main tracks as a loop from Alice Springs, but it's well worth dipping down into South Australia to visit Mount Dare and the Dalhousie Hot Springs in the Witjira National Park.

Old Andado station, on the edge of the Simpson Desert, is a fascinating spot; a visit with the homestead's owner, Molly Clark, is a step back into the 1920s. The Finke Track follows the route of the old Ghan railway line between Alice Springs and the small Aboriginal settlement of Finke, the main highlight along the way being a rough detour to the spectacular outcrop known as Chambers Pillar.

The Old Andado Track can successfully be negotiated with care by 2WD, but if you want to head along the old Ghan line or down

to Dalhousie and on to Oodnadatta, then a well-prepared 4WD is called for.

HISTORY

Archaeological evidence suggests that Aboriginal occupation of this area dates back at least 40,000 years. These days there are communities at Santa Teresa and Finke.

European exploration into the area started in the 1860s with the indefatigable explorer John McDouall Stuart, who was determined to cross Australia from south to north. His party of three men and 13 horses set out from Adelaide in March 1860 and reached as far as what is now Attack Creek, north of Tennant Creek, where they were forced to turn back on 26 June, after a skirmish with the local Aborigines. It seems, however, that Stuart exaggerated the severity of the attack and it was probably just the last straw. The fact that he did make it so far north meant that he was able to get the backing from the South Australian government for a second expedition the following year. It too was unsuccessful and Stuart only advanced 160 km on his previous effort, being forced to turn back around Newcastle Waters due to lack of a reliable water supply and dwindling provisions. Finally, in 1862, Stuart succeeded in crossing from south to north, and then returned to Adelaide.

Many of the geographical features of the Centre were named by Stuart: the Finke River, Chambers Pillar, the MacDonnell Ranges and Central Mt Sturt (later renamed Central Mt Stuart) to name a few – and the route he took on all three trips was to become the route of the Overland Telegraph Line. This line, when it was completed in 1872, linked southern Australia with Darwin and, via a submarine cable, Java; this was Australia's first international telegraph link.

The next major developmental stage in this area was the construction of the railway line between Port Augusta and Alice Springs. The line made it as far as Oodnadatta in 1890, and for the next 30 years supplies were carted by camel from the railhead there to outlying districts and Alice prings. The line eventually reached Alice Springs in 1929, and it remained in use until 1982 when a new line was constructed some distance to the west. The route of the old line was never far from permanent water, and for this reason it was often washed out during periods of heavy rain.

Pastoral activity followed the opening up of the area which the Overland Telegraph Line brought. By the turn of the century most of the workable land was taken up with pastoral leases.

INFORMATION

Permits are not required to travel on any of the tracks listed below. If, however, you are travelling on to the Witjira National Park, permits must be obtained for this. The best place to buy one is at Mount Dare homestead, but they are also available from the Pink Roadhouse in Oodnadatta if you are coming from the south.

The RFDS base in Alice Springs (☎ (089) 52 1033) covers this area, and the frequencies monitored are 2020, 5410 and 6950 kHz from 7.30 am to 5 pm weekdays.

The best map of the area is once again the excellent Westprint series, this time the Alice Springs-Oodnadatta sheet. It is available from the AANT office (☎ (089) 53 1322) on Gregory Terrace in Alice Springs.

THE ROUTE

Alice Springs to Finke

The first 10 km of this route, along the bitumen Stuart Highway, is a breeze. From the airport turn-off a sign points south to Ewaninga and Chambers Pillar. The Old South Rd is well-formed dirt and has quite a bit of traffic as far as Maryvale station, 110 km south along the old railway line.

After 30 km you come to **Ewaninga Rail Siding** west of the Ooraminna Ranges, and the line from here to Alice Springs is still intact and maintained by the Ghan Preservation Society. The old Ghan train makes regular trips out this far from MacDonnell Siding, five km south of Alice Springs.

Just south of Ewaninga is the **Ewaninga Rock Carvings Conservation Reserve**, a small reserve which protects a number of images carved into the smooth sandstone rocks. The images – of snakes, spirals, animal tracks and other designs – are believed to have been carved between 5000 and 1000 years ago. There's a walking trail with interpretive signs, barbecue facilities and pit toilets. Bring your own firewood.

From Ewaninga the track continues south, past the **Ooraminna Siding**, until after another 37 km there's the **Deep Well station** turn-off, and 10 km more to the **Hugh River Stock Route**, which heads west for 60 km to join the Stuart Highway, and the boundary of the 3200-sq-km Maryvale station. This rough track is an alternative access point to the old Ghan line, or you can use it to make a good day-trip loop from Alice Springs, visiting **Rainbow Valley** and Ewaninga (see Alternative Routes, later in this section).

Maryvale homestead is 33 km south of the boundary fence. Limited tourist facilities are available (see Facilities below). At Maryvale you have to make the decision of whether to continue south or to head south-west for the rough 44-km detour to **Chambers Pillar**. The latter trip is highly recommended and well worth the effort (see Detours, later in this section).

The old railway line and increasingly rough and sandy track continues 35 km south-east from Maryvale via sand-dune country known as the Depot Sandhills to **Alice Well**, just off the track on the bank of the Hugh River. This was once an important supply depot during the construction of the Overland Telegraph Line, and up until 1928 had its own police station.

It's another 44 km to the **Horseshoe Bend station** turn-off, and soon after the very distinctive **Colson Pinnacle** comes into view east of the road. From here the sand dunes continue and the small Aboriginal community of **Finke** is reached after 40 km.

Finke

This is another town which owes its existence to the railway line. It started life as a railway siding and gradually grew to have a

European population of about 60. With the opening of the new Ghan line further west, administration of the town was taken over by the Aputula Aboriginal community. The community store here is also an outlet for the local artists, who make crafts such as carved wooden animals, bowls, traditional weapons and seed necklaces. Be aware that this is Aboriginal land – alcohol and taking of pictures are prohibited.

Finke is linked to the Stuart Highway, 150 km to the west, by the well-maintained dirt road sometimes known as the Goyder Stock Route. It's a fairly uninteresting stretch of road, although the **Lambert Centre**, just of the road, is an interesting curiosity (se Alternative Routes).

Finke to Old Andado

The road heads off from Finke to the eas basically following the line of the Fink River. The river was named by Stuart in 186 after his friend William Finke, who helpe fund some of his peregrinations into th outback.

After 30 km you pass right by the **Ne Crown homestead** (fuel available), an from here there are two choices: south t

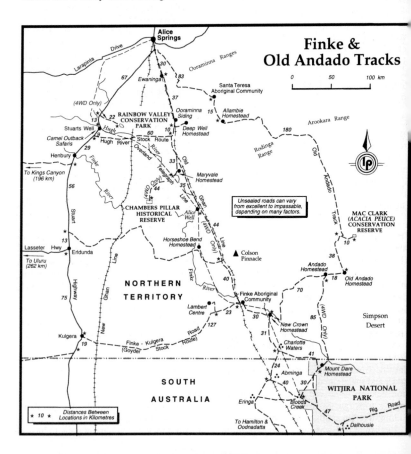

Charlotte Waters, Abminga and eventually Oodnadatta (with a possible detour to Dalhousie Springs; see Alternative Routes), or north and west to Andado and Old Andado. If you're coming down from the north, this is the first place you'll come across one of Adam and Linnie Plate's distinctive signs. The Plates run the Pink Roadhouse in Oodnadatta and have worked tirelessly at putting up signs at strategic spots right throughout the western Simpson region, and largely thanks to them, navigation in the area is relatively straightforward.

Shortly after leaving New Crown, the track once again crosses the Finke River and then swings to the north for the 70-km run to Andado station. This stretch passes through some beautiful sand-dune country, which is ablaze with wildflowers after good rains. For much of the way the track runs along the valleys between the sand dunes, but every now and then swings up and over a dune to the next valley. The road is in good condition with a firm gravel base; it's no problem at all to roll along at 90 km/h, but just keep well to the left when crossing the dune crests.

At **Andado station** you are confronted with yet another choice: south along a sandy but very pretty and well-defined 4WD track to Mount Dare (85 km; see Alternative Routes below), or east along a *very* corrugated bladed track to Old Andado. Andado station has no tourist facilities and visitors passing through should respect the privacy of the owners. At over 10,000 sq km, Andado is the third-largest station in the Territory.

Old Andado Homestead

The 18-km track to Old Andado is in a bad way – it's a private road which is not often graded. It's quite sandy in places and it requires a good deal of concentration if you want to maintain enough speed to get over the corrugations without your fillings coming loose. Mercifully, it's only a short distance.

The homestead, the easternmost on the western side of the Simpson Desert, is situated in a pretty valley between two huge lines of dunes. The homestead is run as a tourist

Gate and sign announcing Old Andado Station (HF)

facility by the no-nonsense Molly Clark, one of the great battlers of the Centre.

The Andado pastoral lease was first taken up by Robert McDill in 1909, and he built the bush timber and corrugated-iron homestead in 1922. In 1955 Molly and her husband, Mac, took up the management of Andado station from the 'new homestead', 18 km to the west. Pastoral activity on the edge of the desert is an even more marginal activity than elsewhere, and when Mac was killed in a plane crash on the property, and Molly Clark was forced to clear the land entirely of stock for three years as part of the government brucellosis-eradication programme, there was little future in Andado station.

Despite these enormous setbacks, Molly Clark struggled on and eventually sold the property, while keeping the old homestead to run as a small-scale tourist operation. Today, visitors can camp or stay in dongas, and eat meals cooked in the old homestead kitchen on a vintage combustion wood stove. Molly Clark, now in her 80s but still going strong, does all the work around the place herself, and so needs advance warning of guests – don't expect much of a welcome if you just rock up unannounced.

Old Andado to Alice Springs

At Old Andado the track swings north for the 326-km trip to the Alice. It takes around five hours to do in one hit, but it's well worth stopping at the Mac Clark Conservation Reserve along the way. The majority of the track, pioneered by the Clarks and now generally known as the Old Andado Track, runs along a valley between two lines of dunes, and, although sandy in places, is not difficult to negotiate.

Thirty-eight km north of Old Andado a track heads east for a distance of 10 km to the 3042-hectare **Mac Clark *(Acacia peuce)* Conservation Reserve**. The *Acacia peuce* tree is found in only three places in Australia: near Boulia and Birdsville in Queensland, and, the smallest stand (around 1000 trees), here on the western edge of the Simpson Desert. It is a rare arid-zone tree which can survive in a climate where very little else can – the average annual rainfall is a meagre 150 mm and summer daytime temperatures of 40°C are the norm rather than the exception.

The *Acacia peuce* trees grow very slowly to a height of up to 17 metres, and are very long-lived – up to 500 years. The trees, also known as waddis after the Aboriginal fighting clubs which were carved from its wood, have a very spiky foliage which offers little shade. It's these leaves which are the key to the tree's survival: the moisture loss from such needle-like leaves is very low. The adult trees have a spreading form similar to casuarinas, or she-oaks (but classified as acacias, or wattles, due to the occurrence of seed pods rather than cones), while young trees are far more columnar.

The wood of the *Acacia peuce* is extremely dense and hard (it's impossible to drive a nail into), and so was highly prized. Many trees were felled and used for fence and stockyard posts early this century. Fortunately, the rarity of the tree has been recognised, and this reserve, named after pastoralist Mac Clark who had a great interest in the *Acacia peuce*, is one of a number of measures aimed at ensuring the tree's survival.

From the Mac Clark Conservation Reserve turn-off, the track continues north and slightly west through sand-dune country, looping away to the west around the edges of the Arookara and Rodinga ranges, before arriving at **Allambie station** after 180 km. From here the track improves markedly, and it's a further 15 km to the **Santa Teresa Aboriginal Community**. This community is on the site of the old Catholic mission station, which was moved here in the 1950s, having functioned at a site north of Alice Springs for a number of years prior to that. There are no tourist facilities, and a permit is not required to transit straight through. However, visits to the community itself must be arranged in advance (☎ (089) 56 0999).

From Santa Teresa it's just a short hop (83 km) to the Stuart Highway 10 km south of Alice Springs along an interesting road which skirts the western edge of the Ooraminna Ranges.

DETOURS
Chambers Pillar Historical Reserve

Chambers Pillar is a huge finger of sandstone which towers nearly 60 metres above the surrounding plain. The sandstone beds which form the pillar were formed over 350 million years ago, and subsequent erosion of the softer surrounding material has left the pillar in its present form.

In the past it was an important landmark, first for European explorers and, later, for travellers heading north to Alice Springs from the head of the railway line before it was pushed all the way through to the Alice. In 1860, on his first attempt to cross the continent, Stuart was the first of these explorers to find the pillar, and he named it after James Chambers, who, like Finke, was one of Stuart's Adelaide backers. Subsequent visitors included John Ross in 1870, who was on an expedition to determine the future route of the Overland Telegraph Line, and Ernest Giles, who, in 1872, passed the pillar while on his attempt to cross to the west coast of Australia.

Many of these early visitors carved their names into the rock, leaving a permanent reminder of their visit, and this has given the pillar an interesting historical aspect. Unfortunately, many less worthy graffiti artists in recent times have added to the gallery, at the same time defacing much of historical significance. (Just in case you feel like immortalising yourself in stone, be warned that it will cost you a fine of up to $5000 if you're caught.)

To the Aborigines, Chambers Pillar also has great significance. It is said that the powerful gecko ancestor, Itirkawara, killed some of his ancestors and took a girl of a different kin group. They were banished to the desert where both turned to stone – Itirkawara became the pillar and the girl became **Castle Rock**, about 500 metres away.

The 4WD track to the pillar is signposted from the store at Maryvale station. From the station store to where the track turns left near the boundary fence (12 km), there are patches of bulldust, but from here for the next 22 km it is less of a problem. After the track does the left turn it climbs a rocky rise and you come to a fork in the track; veer right. The very rocky track continues along the top of the rise, and from here there are excellent views of Chambers Pillar. The track descends and the last 10 km are over sand dunes. This track is unsuitable for trailers or caravans.

Note that despite the existence of other station tracks in the area, the route described is the only public access route to the pillar. Do not try to exit the reserve to the new Ghan line or Stuart Highway to the west.

Facilities at the reserve consist of a visitor information board, barbecues, picnic tables and long-drop dunnies. Firewood should be brought in from outside the reserve. Camping is permitted but there is little shade and no water.

ALTERNATIVE ROUTES
Alice Springs to Maryvale via Rainbow Valley
The alternative to heading straight for Maryvale station along the Old South Road is to travel south along the Stuart Highway and then cut across to the east along the Hugh River Stock Route. The main advantage of taking this route is that it allows you to visit the excellent **Rainbow Valley Conservation Park**.

The turn-off to the park is 77 km south of Alice Springs, and from here it's 22 km along a 4WD track which has many sandy patches. Close to the campsite in the park there are a number of claypans, which should be skirted if there is even a hint of moisture in them.

Although colourfully named, the crumbling sandstone cliffs at Rainbow Valley are various shades of cream and red, and late in the day the setting sun can cast some wonderful effects. The red colours are caused by leached iron-oxide staining, while in the lighter parts iron oxide is not present and these areas have been bleached by the sun. If you're lucky enough to visit when there's water in the claypans, you can get some stunning photos.

The park is not as instantly attractive as some of the more spectacular sights in central Australia, but it has a charm which certainly repays any time spent here. Because it doesn't get overrun with visitors, it's a great place to spend a couple of days – wander and scramble in the **James Range**, admire the views and soak up the timeless atmosphere of the Centre.

Facilities at the park are basic. There's a campsite with nothing more than barbecue places, so you'll need to bring all your own supplies, including firewood. Remember to bury all toilet wastes and take other rubbish away when you leave.

Once back on the Stuart Highway, head south for 13 km to Noel Fullerton's **Camel Outback Safaris** (☎ (089) 56 0925) on the highway at Orange Creek station. As well as using the fuel and roadhouse services, you can take a short ride on a camel for a few dollars, or for the more adventurous there are

Chambers Pillar (TW)

For those of you who like precision, the centre is at latitude 25°36'36.4"S and longitude 134°21'17.3"E.

The Lambert Centre is in a shallow gully west of Finke. The unmarked turn-off heads north off the Finke-Kulgera Road 23 km west of Finke. From the road, you head 6.5 km north, passing Mulga Bore on the left and an airstrip on the right. A track to the left through a gate heads west for eight km to the spot, which is marked by a replica of the flagpole atop parliament house in Canberra!

The centre was named the Lambert Centre after Bruce Lambert, a surveyor and first head of the National Mapping Council.

Charlotte Waters & Mount Dare Loop

While it is possible to travel direct between Finke and Old Andado, it is much more interesting to head south from New Crown and loop around through Charlotte Waters, Abminga, Bloods Creek and Mount Dare to Andado station. This loop also gives you access to the Dalhousie Mound Springs (94 km round trip from Bloods Creek) and the trans-Simpson Rig Road (see the Simpson Desert section for details on Dalhousie and on across the Simpson).

From New Crown station, a good track heads due south to historic **Charlotte Waters**, 31 km away and just shy of the South Australian border. This once important repeater station and supply depot on the Overland Telegraph Line has all but disappeared.

At Charlotte Waters you can either head east the 41 km direct to Mount Dare, or continue south and cross into South Australia (border marked by a Pink Roadhouse sign) and head for the ruin of **Abminga**, 24 km south from Charlotte Waters. This siding was once the railhead for Mount Dare and Bloods Creek to the east. The track forks here again, the right taking you south to Oodnadatta via Eringa and Hamilton. The left fork, however, is the one we want as it heads direct to the ruins of **Bloods Creek station**, 40 km to the south-east. Today, a windmill is all that marks the site of what was an important camping spot for workers on the Overland Telegraph Line. The strategic location meant

extended trips into the desert; Rainbow Valley is a popular destination.

From the camel farm it's a further nine km south along the highway to the **Hugh River Stock Route** turn-off. This is quite a reasonable track which heads east to the Old South Road (61 km). Care is required at the Hugh River crossing about halfway.

Finke to the Stuart Highway

The other option from Finke is to head due west along the Finke-Kulgera Road (sometimes referred to as the Goyder Stock Route) to Kulgera, 150 km away on the Stuart Highway. It is a well-maintained but basically uninteresting road.

The only highlight along the route is the **Lambert Centre**. If you can imagine picking Australia up by the one point where it would balance (ie the centre of gravity), this is it. Yippee! A team from the Queensland University spent two years doing computer calculations to come up with the exact spot. Exactly why they would want to is unclear.

that the site continued to be used after the line was finished; eventually a pub and store opened up. It was from Bloods Creek that the drover and bushcraft expert Ted Colson set off with six camels and an Aborigine and made the first return European crossing of the Simpson, going to Birdsville and back in 1936.

At the Bloods Creek windmill you can either continue south-east for the 47-km run to **Dalhousie Mound Springs**, or head north-east to Mount Dare homestead, 30 km away in the **Witjira National Park**. In the late 1960s Mount Dare station became part of the Witjira National Park, but the homestead was leased privately to provide tourist services to the increasing numbers of visitors who were coming through this way.

At **Mount Dare** (☎ (086) 707 7835), Phil and Ronda Hellyer look after travellers' needs. The store sells basic supplies (including ice, frozen meat and bread), and there's a bar with deliciously cold beer. Excellent meals are available if you're staying there. Fuel supplies (super, diesel, unleaded) and basic mechanical repairs are also available.

Accommodation costs $62/114 a single/double in the old homestead building, including dinner and breakfast, or you can camp for $4 per person. Facilities for campers include hot showers and long-drop dunnies. The camping area is not all that attractive and if you're heading north there's good bush camping just over the Northern Territory border by the Finke River bed.

At the homestead there is a track heading north and then west to Charlotte Waters (41 km), or you can take the much more interesting route direct to Andado. This route crosses into the Northern Territory after 14 km, and for the next 17 km follows the course of the Finke River. This section is quite heavily treed, and although the track is good, it winds increasingly through the surprisingly dense scrub, is horrendously dusty, and, at times, is a metre below ground level!

Sign announcing Mount Dare Homestead (TW)

After crossing the Finke River, the track heads on to Andado station, 54 km away, passing through a wonderfully varied landscape – high sand dunes and wide-open plains dotted with cattle and crossed by meandering, tree-lined watercourses.

ORGANISED TOURS

There are a number of outfits in Alice Springs that run organised tours to various parts of the routes already described.

Oak Valley Day Tours (☎ (089) 56 0959) is an Aboriginal-owned and run organisation that makes day trips to Ewaninga and Rainbow Valley. These trips also go to Mpwellare and Oak Valley, both on the Hugh River Stock Route and both of cultural significance to the Aboriginal people. The cost is $90 ($70 children) and this includes lunch, and morning and afternoon tea.

Outback Flavour Tours (☎ (089) 55 0444) has evening tours to Rainbow Valley. These leave Alice Springs at 3.30 pm in winter and 4 pm in summer, and you are taken to Rainbow Valley for sunset and an evening meal. The cost is $49 per person.

Another operator is Outback Experience Tours (☎ (089) 53 2666), which has day trips from Alice Springs to Chambers Pillar and Rainbow Valley for $95 per person. It also has 2½-day trips which go all the way to Mount Dare and Dalhousie Springs for $295, although this is an awful lot to cram into a very short time. Another of its 2½-day trips goes only as far as Old Andado ($275), giving you more time to take in the surroundings and less time in the 4WD.

Austour (☎ toll-free 1800 335 009) does a good five-day loop from Alice Springs which heads off west to Mt Conner, Ipolera and Uluru, and then crosses the Stuart Highway returning to Alice Springs via Mount Dare and Old Andado. It's possible to tag along in your own vehicle, and the cost for this is $750 if you have your own camping gear, or $950 if you want accommodation. This is an excellent trip because

it takes in areas (such as a loop around Mt Conner) which are closed to the individual traveller.

FACILITIES

Maryvale Station

At Maryvale station (☎ (089) 56 0989) there's a shop selling basic provisions and fuel (diesel and super). It is open daily (except Sunday afternoon) from 10 am to 5 pm. Credit cards are not accepted.

Finke

At the Finke community store (☎ (089) 56 0976) you can buy groceries as well as craft items made by the local artists. The store is open weekdays from 9 to 11 am and from 3 to 4.30 pm, and on Saturday from 8.30 to 11 am. Fuel (super, unleaded, diesel) and basic mechanical repairs are undertaken by the garage, but the opening hours seem to be infinitely flexible.

There's an unofficial camping ground on the outskirts of town, which you can get directed to from the store. Unless you really want power, it's probably better to head out of town a bit further and bush-camp.

New Crown Station

The track from Finke to Andado passes right by the New Crown homestead (☎ (089) 56 0969), so even if you don't need to stop, slow down sufficiently so you don't shower the place in dust.

Fuel supply (diesel, unleaded, super) is the only service offered to travellers. This is sold during daylight hours; credit cards are not accepted.

Old Andado Station

At Old Andado station (☎ (089) 56 0812) there's twin accommodation available in dongas at $17 per person. This is good value as it includes dinner and breakfast. You can also camp nearby for $4, but there's little shade. Booking in advance is essential; credit cards are not accepted.

There is no fuel or vehicle service here. There's an airstrip but no aviation fuel.

Simpson Desert

Recognised as one of the world's outstanding sand-ridge deserts, the Simpson Desert sprawls across more than 150,000 sq km at the junction of the Northern Territory, Queensland and South Australian borders. The desert's most obvious characteristic is its remarkable system of parallel dunes, which rise to 40 metres and stretch without a break for up to 200 km. Their direction maintained by the prevailing winds, the dunes run from south-south-east to north-north-west and are made up of sand blown in from the flood plains and lakes that border the desert's eastern and southern margins. There are 11 major dune systems and nine minor ones, each with its own physical characteristics – such as dune height, length and width, crest shape, vegetation and the nature of the valleys between the dunes.

Although it receives an extremely unreliable average rainfall of only 130 mm per year, the Simpson Desert is by no means biologically boring. Sand ridges aside, it has a number of major habitat types, including spinifex grasslands, gidgee woodlands and coolabah floodouts, and collectively these are home to 800 plant species, over 180 birds, 24 native mammals and probably 90 or more reptiles. In a good season the desert is an exciting place to be for wildlife enthusiasts.

One of Australia's last great wilderness areas, the desert was occupied by Aborigines until 1900 and was not crossed by a White person until 1936. It is only recently that tourists have arrived, using the vehicle tracks that oil explorers carved through the desert during the 1960s. Several of these have since become 4WD routes, popular with increasing numbers of adventurous travellers who come seeking both a challenge and spiritual refreshment in the endless horizons and awesome sense of solitude.

The recreation boom and a new awareness of the desert's fragility and unique values have led to the declaration of several conservation areas over most of South Australia's portion of the desert: Witjira National Park (7770 sq km) centres on Dalhousie Springs in the west, while the combined Simpson Desert Regional Reserve (29,640 sq km) and Simpson Desert Conservation Park (6930 sq km) stretch from Witjira to the Diamantina River on the desert's eastern flank. The Simpson Desert National Park (5550 sq km) occupies the south-west corner of Queensland. All these areas are crossed by one or more of the routes described below.

Before setting out on a Simpson Desert crossing, it's wise to reflect that in recent times several foolhardy travellers have paid the ultimate penalty for failing to prepare for its dangers. The hazards include great heat, lack of water and extreme isolation from human habitation and all facilities. Desert travel is not recommended from October to April, when temperatures nearing 40°C are frequently experienced.

TRACK SUMMARY
The Rig Road

Built during the 1960s to a standard suitable for laden semi-trailers, the Rig Road takes you right across the desert, from Mount Dare homestead to the Birdsville Track. It generally avoids the areas of higher dunes and has been sheeted with clay throughout. However, it is no longer being maintained and so is subject to guttering and drift sand – conditions which make a 4WD essential. It is by far the easiest route across the desert, and the changing colours of its sand dunes (from tomato-red in the west to white in the south-east) and varied topography and vegetation also make it the most interesting. The Rig Road is lined by borrow pits where clay was extracted during its construction. These can hold water for a considerable period after heavy rain and at such times become a focus for desert wildlife.

The French Line & QAA Line

Bulldozed across the desert by the French Petroleum Company in 1963, the so-called French Line runs at right angles to the sand ridges and was never intended to do more than provide temporary access for geological survey work. Kept open by 4WD traffic, its driving conditions are extremely difficult, as it crosses literally hundreds of soft dunes – these are steepest on the eastern side, so travel in a west to east direction is recommended. The QAA Line was constructed in like manner and also presents difficult conditions, although it is a little easier than the French Line.

ROUTE OPTIONS

There are three major route options between Mount Dare homestead (the last resupply point on the desert's western side) and Birdsville. All tracks include clay surfaces which are closed when wet.

Via The French Line & QAA Line

This route involves a total distance of 507 km, of which 275 km includes soft dune crossings. The French Line is not recommended to inexperienced desert motorists, who are advised to choose one of the other two options.

Via The Rig Road, K1 Line & QAA Line

Covering a total distance of 701 km, this route is mainly firm when dry, though 100 km of it includes soft dune crossings.

Via The Rig Road & Birdsville Track

This route is firm when dry and covers a total distance of 773 km.

HISTORY

In 1845 Charles Sturt was attempting to prove the existence of an inland sea near the centre of the continent when he became the first White person to visit the Simpson Desert. Crossing Sturt's Stony Desert with a small party on horseback, he followed Eyre Creek, which he named, and struck westwards into the desert. On 14 August, at latitude 24.7°, near the present border between Queensland and the Northern Territory, he was forced back by the waterless red ocean of sand ridges that stretched before him. Sturt wrote in his journal:

Grass had entirely disappeared and the horses wound about working their way through the pointed spinifex with which the ground was universally covered. Ascending one of the sand ridges I saw a numberless succession of these terrific objects rising above each other to the east and west of me. Northwards they ran away from me for more than fifteen miles, with the most undeviating straightness, as if those masses had been thrown up with the plumb and rule.

Several expeditions nibbled at the desert's fringes in later years, but the first to penetrate it to any extent was led by David Lindsay in 1886. Accompanied by a White station owner and a desert Aborigine, he took camels from Dalhousie Springs via Approdinna Attora Knolls to about latitude 25.5° on the Queensland and Northern Territory border, where he turned around and returned to Dalhousie. He could easily have continued but didn't bother, as the area to the east was already well known.

Assisted by Aboriginal informants, Lindsay had found water at several of the native wells that were scattered through the desert's southern and eastern parts. The wells, sunk to depths of seven metres, were located in depressions between the sandhills and gave access to freshwater soaks. They were the focus of life for the Aboriginal groups who then lived in the desert, providing them with security in drought. After good rains had filled the claypans, Aborigines were able to leave the wells for extended periods and thus exploit the land's resources over a much wider area.

The first White person to cross the desert's full width was pastoralist Ted Colson. In 1936, he took camels from Bloods Creek (near Mount Dare homestead) to Birdsville. Colson and his Aboriginal companion travelled close to the Northern Territory border throughout their journey, visiting Approdinna Attora Knolls en route. Having reached Birdsville, the two men turned around and rode back across the desert to Bloods Creek. Colson received no support for this outstanding feat, which was accomplished without fanfare; it seems that he undertook the trek purely in the spirit of adventure.

Wind-sculpted sand in the Simpson (DO)

The first scientific expedition into the Simpson was mounted in 1939 under the leadership of Dr C T Madigan. With eight men and 19 camels, he travelled northwards from Old Andado homestead to the junction of the Hale and Todd rivers, then east to the Queensland border, where he turned southeast to Birdsville. Between the Hale River and Eyre Creek – a distance of 326 km – the party crossed 626 sand ridges, many 30 metres high, and gathered much valuable data. Ten years previously Madigan had made several reconnaissance flights over the desert and recommended that it be named after Allen Simpson, the then president of the South Australian Branch of the Royal Geographical Society of Australasia.

Interest in the desert lapsed until its potential for oil exploration was recognised in the early 1960s, when Dr Reg Sprigg and his company, Geosurveys of Australia, were contracted to carry out gravity surveys in the region. As part of this work, Sprigg and his family completed the first motorised cross-

ing of the desert, travelling from Mount Dare to Birdsville along the Northern Territory border and using fuel and supplies carried in by light aircraft. Two years later, by which time the French Line had been bulldozed, the Spriggs made the first south-north motorised crossing, their route taking them from Cowarie homestead to the Plenty River, on the desert's northern fringe. These feats signalled the beginning of the current recreation boom.

INFORMATION
Tourist Offices

For tourist information of a general nature, contact the Pink Roadhouse in Oodnadatta (☎ (086) 70 7822), the Mount Dare homestead (☎ (086) 70 7835) and Birdsville Auto (☎ (076) 56 3226). Road reports for the desert's eastern side – in particular conditions at the crossings of Eyre Creek and Warburton Creek – should be obtained from the Birdsville police (☎ (076) 56 3220). Mount Dare homestead and the Oodnadatta

THE CENTRAL DESERTS

police (☎ (086) 70 7805) are the best sources of road information for the western half of the desert.

Emergency

Birdsville has a well-equipped hospital staffed by registered nurses. Mount Dare homestead has a comprehensive RFDS medical kit, and in the event of an emergency its staff can administer drugs and perform other procedures by acting on directions they receive over their HF radio.

Registration & Permits

All travellers intending to cross the Simpson Desert should register their intentions with the police at either Birdsville or Oodnadatta, depending on their starting point. The police will be pleased to check your preparedness – if you don't wish to take their advice, they will ask you to sign a waiver. Having registered, don't forget to report in at the other end – otherwise you may trigger an unnecessary

search, the cost of which will have to be met by yourself.

Travel in the Simpson Desert within South Australia requires a permit in the form of the Desert Parks Pass, which covers entry to most of the conservation areas in that state's outback. The accompanying booklet contains useful information on Witjira National Park, the Simpson Desert Regional Reserve and the Simpson Desert Conservation Reserve. The package includes several small-scale touring maps, one of which takes you across the desert from Oodnadatta to Birdsville. The Pass costs $50 per vehicle and is available from the Pink Roadhouse in Oodnadatta, Mount Dare homestead, Birdsville Fuel Services and Birdsville Auto in Birdsville, and the Ghan Store in Marree. For information, contact the Department of Environment & Natural Resources regional office, PO Box 102, Hawker, SA 5434, or the Desert Parks Information Line (☎ (086) 48 4244).

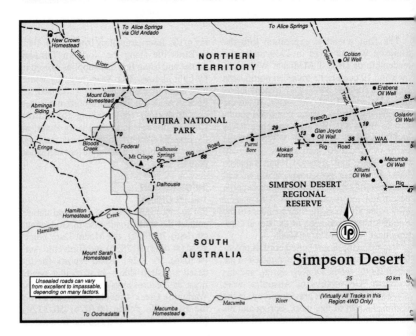

A permit from the Department of Environment & Conservation ranger in Birdsville ☎ (076) 56 3247) is required to travel within the Simpson Desert National Park. This will mainly affect travellers intending to take the QAA Line from near Poeppel Corner east to the old rabbit-proof fence. For information, contact the department's regional office ☎ (076) 58 1761), PO Box 202, Longreach 4730.

Books

The only worthwhile reference on the desert as a whole is *The Simpson Desert* by Mark Shephard (The Royal Geographical Society of Australasia & Giles Publications, Adelaide, 1992). It covers natural history, Aboriginal life, exploration and conservation issues, as well as giving sound advice on preparing for a crossing.

The *Natural History of Dalhousie Springs*, edited by W Zeidler & W F Ponder (South Australian Museum, Adelaide, 1989),

is a fascinating explanation of the ecology and cultural history of the artesian springs on the edge of the Simpson.

Maps

The small-scale map-cum-guide entitled *Dalhousie and Simpson Desert*, published by Westprint Heritage Maps, covers the various tracks between Mount Dare and Birdsville and is contained in the Desert Parks Pass package. For a more detailed coverage, you'll need the Dalhousie, Poolowanna and Pandie Pandie 1:250,000 topographic maps from AUSLIG. The QAA Line appears on the Birdsville sheet, while a small portion of the Rig Road's western end lies on the Gason sheet. These maps are available through AUSLIG sales outlets in all capital cities.

Radio Frequencies

An average of about 12 vehicles per day cross the desert in winter, with a dramatic

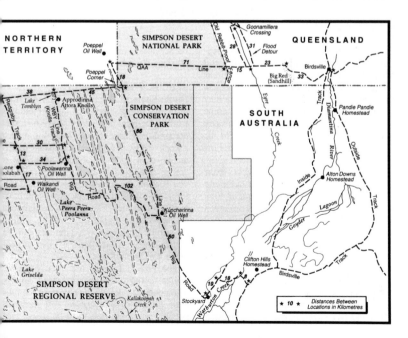

Steaming Purni Bore (TW)

increase to around 50 over the July and September school holiday periods. Having said that, averages are not a reliable indicator, as in the event of a breakdown the next vehicle may be days away. In hot weather you may have to wait weeks for someone to come along. For this reason it's advisable to carry an HF radio fitted with frequencies for the RFDS bases at Alice Springs and Port Augusta.

To speak to Port Augusta RFDS base (callsign VNZ – Victor November Zulu), use 8165 kHz between 7 am and 5 pm, or 4010 and 6890 kHz between 7 am and 9 pm seven days. After-hours alarm frequencies are 2020 and 4010 kHz. Contact the base (☎ (086) 42 2044) for more details of its services.

The Alice Springs RFDS base (callsign VJD – Victor Juliet Delta) can be reached on 5410 and 6950 kHz between 7.30 am and 5 pm Monday to Friday, excluding public holidays. For after-hours emergency calls, use 2020 and 5410 kHz. For more information on services, contact the base (☎ (089) 52 1033).

SPECIAL PREPARATIONS

For the Simpson Desert driver, lack of traffic, difficult driving conditions and remoteness from all facilities put new emphasis on travel preparation. Carry enough water for at least a week – those in a hurry can cross the desert in two days under ideal conditions, but if you're interested in taking a better look, you'll want to spend longer. Also, don't forget that you might break down and have to wait for rescue. Calculate fuel needs based on the distance of your chosen route, adding at least 30% for unexpected detours and the higher fuel consumption you can expect under 4WD conditions.

The French Line is particularly rough, thanks to the many inexperienced drivers who neglect to deflate their tyres to the recommended 15 psi or less on soft surfaces. For this reason, trailers must be robust and all items should be packed to avoid breakages. Always place heavy items (such as full jerry cans and spare wheels) so that they won't raise the vehicle's centre of gravity to a dangerous level – roof racks are not the place!

Owing to the blind crests met with throughout, the lead vehicle in each party should carry a flag (bright orange is ideal) on a long pole fixed to the bullbar. This will warn oncoming vehicles of your approach.

For obvious reasons it's essential to carry ample drinking water at all times in the Simpson Desert. As a rule of thumb, allow a minimum of five litres per person per day in warm weather, plus extra water for washing. Always carry a good reserve for emergencies. You can fill up your jerry cans at Mount Dare homestead and Birdsville, as their water supplies are quite acceptable to all but the most sensitive stomachs. The water from Dalhousie Springs and Purni Bore is drinkable at a pinch.

THE ROUTE
Mount Dare Homestead to Dalhousie Springs (70 km)

Leaving Mount Dare, the generally rough track to Dalhousie Springs crosses a mix of gibber uplands and sand ridges for the 44 km to **Opossum Creek**, where ancient coolabahs and shady gidgees make a pleasant spot to boil the billy. The creek was named after the brush-tailed possums that lived along its banks in earlier times. Sadly, this species has all but vanished from arid Australia over the past 50 years.

Eleven km later and still in gibber country, you cross **Christmas Creek** with its depressing graveyard of dead trees. These died after losing their water supply when nearby **Crispe Bore**, which flowed into the creek, was capped in 1987. The artesian bore is one of many to be capped in recent years following official awareness that the outback's major source of groundwater – the Great Artesian Basin – is being needlessly depleted. This is the place to collect firewood for a camp at Dalhousie Springs, as there is none further on.

Past Christmas Creek the track climbs up onto a barren gibber tableland, from where, 64 km past Mount Dare, you look out over an eroded, salt-encrusted basin dotted with dense patches of tall, lush reeds and dark scrub. These are the Dalhousie springs, the only natural source of permanent surface water in an arid area as large as many European countries. One km further on, you come to a T-intersection, with the lonely stone ruins of Dalhousie homestead lying nine km to your right and the Dalhousie Springs hot pool and camping area four km to the left.

Dalhousie Springs Spread over an area of about 70 sq km, this group of 80 artesian springs is recognised as being of world significance because of its unique geological and biological value. The springs are so isolated from other permanent surface waters

Simpson Desert signpost (TW)

that they contain many species of aquatic fauna found nowhere else. This was one of the major reasons the surrounding 776,900-hectare Witjira National Park was declared, in 1985.

The main spring is a steaming oasis of deep, dark-blue water measuring about 150 metres by 50 metres and fringed by low paperbarks and reeds. A fantastic sight in its desolate setting, the pool attracts a large variety of wildlife, including goannas, water birds and dingoes. The camping area on its banks is bare and uninviting, but a swim in the pool on a cold winter's morning more than makes up for this. From here you can explore other springs in the area, including several – such as the one beside the old Dalhousie ruins – where the native vegetation has been choked out by tall date palms. The original palms probably grew from seed brought in by the Afghani camel drivers who serviced this area at the turn of the century.

The Rig Road – Dalhousie Springs to the French Line (97 km)

Leaving the camping area, you cross the aptly named Gluepot (a terror when wet) and pass extinct mound springs perforated with rabbit burrows, before climbing onto a gibber tableland at the nine-km mark. These are the last gibbers you see until Big Red (near Birdsville), so make the most of them. At 20 km you enter a large seasonal swamp, where long, deep ruts tell a graphic story of what it's like to drive on when wet.

Ten km after entering the swamp you pass some low mesas and notice the track becoming sandier, with tall saltbush on either side. However, you don't enter the Simpson Desert proper until 52 km from the Dalhousie Springs camping ground, when you see low sand ridges topped with cane grass beside the track. The dunes gradually become higher, and spinifex begins to appear on the flanks and in the swales, setting the scene for much of what follows. The distinctive large hoofprints of camels soon become apparent along the track – it's an unlucky traveller who doesn't see at least one of these animals during the crossing.

Purni Bore Cresting a sand ridge 68 km from the spring, you arrive without warning at a large pool surrounded by luxuriant beds of reeds and bushy wattles. Clouds of steam and sulphurous smells billow from the near-boiling water that gushes from a pipe beside the track, and native hens scurry into the reeds as you approach. The tracks of camels, dingoes, donkeys, rabbits, hopping mice and many birds cover the nearby sand ridges. This is the little world of Purni Bore, an isolated wetland fed by a flowing artesian bore originally drilled in search of oil and gas. It's a beaut spot for wildlife enthusiasts – 35 species of birds, including several water birds, have been sighted here, and with time and patience you'll see most of them for yourself. Unfortunately the dingoes haven't learned to fear man, so it's not a good idea to leave food or clothing lying around where they can get it.

The Rig Road – The French Line to the WBY Line (181 km)

Twenty-nine km past Purni Bore, the Rig Road turns sharp right (south) at the beginning of the French Line, which spears straight ahead, over a high sand ridge. After 13 km of easy travel between the dunes you arrive at **Mokari airstrip**, which was used to service this area during the oil-exploration days. The grave of Jaroslav Pecanek, an Oodnadatta identity who fell in love with the desert and asked to be buried here, lies under a low tree near the airstrip's southern end.

From Mokari you head eastwards once more across the sand ridges, with deep washouts running both along and across the road, just to make it interesting. Here the dunes are well vegetated with cane grass, spinifex and bushes, but shade is at a premium. Thirty-six km from Mokari the Rig Road turns southwards at the beginning of the **WAA Line**, which continues due east across the dunes, meeting the Colson Track to Alice Springs about two km from the intersection.

Heading south, the Rig Road passes the turn-offs to the Macumba and Killumi oil wells, travelling mainly in open swales, before turning sharply east at 34 km from the

WAA Line. For the next 47 km you cross low, orange dunes whose bare, scalloped crests resemble waves on a choppy sea. There is less vegetation than previously to hold the sand ridges together, and drift sand has begun to cover the clay sheeting on the dune crossings. These soft patches invariably drop sharply on their eastern side, so a careful approach is warranted. Drift sand worsens the further east you go on the Rig Road.

Lone Gum & Eagles' Nests Eighty-one km from the WAA Line, you turn north up a broad valley with scattered mulga trees, a number of which support the stick nests of wedge-tailed eagles. Some of these nests are an unbelievable size, the result of many generations of use. In winter and spring in a good season, this area seems alive with eagles, breeding and rearing their young while rabbits and shingle-back lizards, which seem to be their main prey, remain plentiful.

Continuing on, you pass a **lone coolabah** tree growing on an area of gravel beside the road. Stunted by the harshness of its environment, the tree makes a fantastic sight in its barren setting. Coolabahs are invariably confined to areas that are subject to flooding, so its presence here is a mystery. Then, after 17 km heading north, the road swings east again. At the bend, a huge eagle's nest almost covers the crown of a gnarled corkbark, making a fitting climax to this fascinating section.

From the nest, the road heads east across flatter country for 34 km to the WBY Line, which makes an ideal detour of about 40 km each way to the Approdinna Attora Knolls. The final five km on this section winds around small salt lakes, where suspension-busting gutters wait to trap the unwary motorist. At the T-intersection with the WBY Line, you turn left (north) to the knolls or right (south) towards the K1 Line and the Birdsville Track.

The Rig Road – The WBY Line to the Birdsville Track (207 km)

About five km from the WBY Line, you pass the **Poolawanna oil well**, which is conve-niently located beside the road. It is one of six (including Purni Bore) to have been drilled in the southern Simpson Desert since the early 1960s, and no doubt more will be drilled in the future. So far, though, no-one has struck oil here.

Past Poolawanna the road wanders among low sand ridges and broad valleys for about 40 km before entering a silent, almost coastal world of large, dazzling salt lakes and yellow dunes averaging 25 metres high. The bigger dunes offer extensive panoramas with Sahara-like foregrounds of bare, wind-sculpted sand, and so are excellent vantage points for scenic photography. The dunes' paler colour indicates that their sand particles are relatively close to their source – as a grain of sand is blown further away, the clay within it weathers, releasing iron oxide (rust) that covers the grain with a red skin.

Here the road skirts the shores of several **lakes**, a feature of which are eroded banks that show how the sand has been deposited in layers over thousands of years. They are a perfect illustration of an environment devastated by rabbits. Large areas of the Simpson have been almost denuded by rabbits, but it's difficult to imagine a better example of their destructiveness than this one.

About 90 km from the WBY Line, you leave the lakes and cross high dunes, where the road is covered by deep drift sand. This can be a problem, although tyre deflation will normally get you over without too much effort. Then, at 102 km, you arrive at another T-intersection: the K1 Line to Poeppel Corner (see Alternative Routes) and the QAA Line are on your left (north); the Birdsville Track lies to the right.

Warburton Creek Turning south at the intersection, you almost immediately pass the turn-off to Kuncherinna oil well, then commence travelling down broad valleys between low dunes. At about 20 km, start watching for patches of bivalves and other shells, indicators of a long-gone wetter age over the desert.

Shortly after leaving these unusual deposits, the road enters a huge area of dead coolabahs and bare white sand. Probably killed by drought, these stark skeletons mark the northern edge of the Warburton Creek flood plain. Some trees have managed to survive, and provide the best shade since Dalhousie Springs. Drift sand now covers much of the road, making it necessary to deflate your tyres for easy progress.

At 60 km from Kuncherinna oil well, the road turns abruptly north-east to parallel the main channel of Warburton Creek, which is about eight km to the east. Travelling now over blacksoil flats interspersed with coolabah channels, you reach the main creek crossing 37 km further on. From here it is only eight km to the Birdsville Track, where you turn left to Birdsville or right to Marree. For more details on the Birdsville Track, see the Birdsville Track section later in this chapter.

ALTERNATIVE ROUTES
The French & QAA Lines: Purni Bore to Birdsville (364 km)

Leaving the Rig Road 29 km past Purni Bore, the French Line runs eastwards for 175 km to meet the K1 Line just past Poeppel Corner. Unlike the Rig Road, the French Line has a natural surface, and cuts at right angles across literally hundreds of soft dunes averaging 10 to 15 metres high. Although the crossings are straightforward when coming from the west (the usual direction of travel), the track's sandy sections have been deeply corrugated, making for slow, rough travelling.

The first 39 km from the Rig Road is difficult, thanks to very soft sand and high, steep ridges. Most travellers bypass this section by taking the Rig Road to the Colson Track, then heading north for 19 km to the French Line. This option adds 35 km to the total distance. Remember to deflate your tyres to at least 15 psi cold pressure before entering the sand.

For anyone in a hurry, the French Line is a monotonous experience: as you crest each rise (and on average there are about four of these to the km), the view in front is of the track spearing endlessly away across an arid ocean of lesser ridges to reach the horizon at the next highest point. However, the enthusiast with time to spare will find countless opportunities to soak up the desert atmosphere and to discover such small attractions as wildflowers, bird life and innumerable animal tracks in the sand. Many of the valleys contain clumps of shady gidgee trees that provide good shelter for an overnight camp or a meal break.

Approdinna Attora Knolls About 89 km past the Colson Track, you cross the northern end of **Lake Tamblyn**, a typical salt lake fringed by gidgees and crowded by red dunes. Reg Sprigg, the first person to cross the desert by motor vehicle, once used the lake as a landing strip, flying tourists in to camp among the gidgees and to experience desert solitude.

Just past Lake Tamblyn, a turn-off on the right (the WBY Line) takes you about eight km to the Approdinna Attora Knolls. Named by explorer Ted Colson, these two low, flat-topped hills of white gypseous rock are an important landmark in this world of sand ridges and saltpans. They also offer some of the best views in the Simpson Desert. An information sign explains that the knolls were once dunes formed of flour gypsum which later hardened to their present form.

To the south of the knolls lies **Wolporican soak**, one of the rare permanent sources of fresh water that allowed the desert's original inhabitants to survive in this hostile environment. In 1886 David Lindsay found the soak, accessed by a well about four metres deep; on being cleaned out, it yielded 140 litres in an hour. Wolporican was a major habitation site for the Wangkangurru people, who inhabited the desert's central and southern sections prior to 1900. Searching around the edge of claypans throughout the Simpson will often reveal evidence of Aboriginal occupation, in the form of stone tools and grinding stones, all of which were carried in from far away.

Poeppel Corner For a change in scenery, the track cuts across the northern end of several

Crossing a soft dune along the French Line (DO)

Crested pigeons come in to drink at Purni Bore (DO)

long, narrow salt lakes in the 45 km from the WBY Line to Poeppel Corner. After enduring the corrugations on the dunes, some people can't resist the temptation to go for a drive on the lakes' smooth surfaces, but this is definitely not recommended: the bed may not be as hard as it looks, in which case your vehicle will become deeply bogged in saline mud.

A major objective simply because of its remoteness, the steel marker at Poeppel Corner shows the exact intersection point of the Northern Territory, Queensland and South Australia state borders. Nearby is a replica of the original wooden marker that was installed in 1880 by surveyor Augustus Poeppel – he had just completed the daunting task of marking the border between South Australia and Queensland from Haddons Corner, about 300 km to the east. Poeppel's corner post was a 2.1-metre-long piece of coolabah that he'd cut 90 km away in the Mulligan River and dragged by camel to the intersection point.

Poeppel Corner to the Old Rabbit-Proof Fence Shortly after leaving Poeppel Corner, you meet the K1 Line, which runs north-south to link the QAA Line with the Rig Road. Turning north, the track now skirts a salt lake between the dunes, offering much easier going than the chopped-up sandy sections of the French Line. These conditions last for the 18 km to the QAA Line, where once again you head eastwards over the dunes towards Birdsville. Don't forget that your tyres should be deflated to at least 15 psi for the coming sand-ridge crossings.

Surveyed in 1979, the QAA Line crosses several salt lakes before entering the ancient flood plain of Eyre Creek. You notice an obvious improvement in the country – soft grasses begin to dominate between the sand ridges, which are higher and further apart than those on the French Line. As a result, driving conditions are somewhat less severe, although the dune crossings are still rough.

The 66-km section between the Northern Territory border, which you cross about five km east of the K1 Line, and the old rabbit-proof fence lies within the southern part of the 550,000-hectare Simpson Desert National Park. For permits and information on this area, contact the ranger in Birdsville (☎ (076) 56 3220) or the Department of Environment & Conservation's regional office in Longreach (☎ (076) 58 1761).

Rabbit-Proof Fence Seventy-one km from the K1 Line, you pass through the remains of the great Queensland rabbit-proof fence and enter cattle country. The fence, which once stretched for 800 km, was built in the 1890s in an attempt to keep rabbits out of western Queensland; a census taken in 1890 showed 130 men working on its construction near Birdsville. It was maintained by boundary riders stationed roughly 80 km apart until 1932, when they were paid off. Within 20 years much of the fence had either been buried by drifting sand, washed away in floods or corroded by salt, but is still plainly visible where it crosses the QAA Line. Here it forms the present boundary between Adria Downs station and the Simpson Desert National Park.

Eyre Creek Continuing past the rabbit-proof fence, you crest an orange-red sand ridge and suddenly find yourself looking out over a broad valley dotted with large coolabahs. This is part of Eyre Creek's present flood plain. Then, after more high dunes that separate blacksoil flats covered with trees and cane grass, you come to the creek's main channel, 15 km from the fence. If the creek is flooded, you must head north on stony ground for 28 km to Goonamillera Crossing at Dickery Waterhole, then back down along the creek to rejoin the main track. In good seasons the flood plain supports abundant bird life, of which emus, bustards, brolgas, crested pigeons and galahs are the most obvious.

Big Red The country opens out past Eyre Creek, but then 23 km later the Simpson Desert's last gasp rises in front of you as a towering wall of pale red sand: the Nappanerica Sand Dune, one of Birdsville's major tourist attractions. More commonly known as Big Red, this 40-metre-high monster is said to be the desert's highest. It's definitely the most difficult to drive over, although a detour to the north of the main track provides a reasonably easy crossing point. Take the time to climb up to the summit for inspiring views over dry lakes, gibber plains and lesser dunes to distant, shimmering horizons. The final 33 km to town is generally suitable for conventional vehicles.

The WAA Line (85 km)

There is no good reason to drive the WAA Line, which parallels the French Line, unless you want a somewhat more difficult run than that offered by the French Line. The track is little used and there are numerous steep ridges along the way. For this reason it is only recommended to travellers with plenty of experience in desert motoring.

The K1 Line (104 km)

Forming a scenically attractive link between the Rig Road and Poeppel Corner, this generally firm track runs up broad valleys between orange dunes averaging 13 metres high. For about 25 km at its southern end, you hug the edge of a narrow salt lake; while small compared to others, it makes an impressive sight as you hurtle along at 60 km/h. Extensive woodlands of gidgee, where you'll often see dingoes and camels, are another major feature of this route.

FACILITIES

Mount Dare Homestead

Situated in the middle of nowhere in Witjira National Park, Mount Dare homestead (☎ (086) 70 7835) boasts a landing strip, public telephone, ice, liquor licence, minor mechanical and tyre repairs, and fuel sales diesel, super and unleaded petrol and Avgas). There is also a small shop selling basic grocery lines, including milk, bread and frozen meat, but no fresh fruit or vegetables. Mount Dare is open every day, from early until late.

Accommodation with share facilities on a dinner, bed and breakfast basis only is offered in the old homestead ($62/114 a single/double – rates for children are available on application). The menu is limited (of necessity) but the meals are hearty and the atmosphere is country. Bookings are recommended for casual meals and also for accommodation. Camping in a bush setting, with shower and toilet facilities, is available at $4 per adult and $2 per child.

Birdsville

Being a regional centre, if one of only minor importance, Birdsville has a good range of facilities and services, including police, hospital, hotel, general store, post office, landing ground and mechanical repairs.

The *Birdsville Hotel* (☎ (076) 56 3244) serves excellent restaurant meals, with a three-course set menu every night. Its air-conditioned, self-contained, motel-style units cost $42/64/75/84 a single/double/triple/quad. The licensee also looks after the airstrip and is the local agent for Avgas – advance orders are not required.

The historic *Brooklands Store* sells limited general goods and all basic food needs, including bread and frozen lines. However, the availability of fresh fruit and vegetables depends on the supply truck, which comes in only once every two or three weeks. The store is one of the few buildings remaining from the town's brief heyday of the 1880s and '90s.

Birdsville Auto (☎ (076) 56 3226) sells diesel, super and unleaded petrol, as well as fast food, ice, vehicle parts, tyres and maps. Vehicle repairs are also available. Opening hours are 8 am to 6 pm seven days a week, and Bankcard, MasterCard and Visa are accepted. Diesel and petrol are also sold by *Birdsville Fuel Services* (☎ (086) 56 3263), which is open from 7.30 am to 7 pm seven days a week.

Shade and lawns are unknown at the dusty *Birdsville Caravan Park*, but it does have modern ablution and laundry facilities, electric barbecues, and powered sites with overhead lights and water. Powered sites cost $5 per person (to a maximum of $20), while

Big Red (TW)

unpowered sites cost $5 for up to three people and $10 for four or more. The park overlooks a lagoon, which is a great spot for bird-watchers.

Banking facilities are limited to a Commonwealth Bank agency in the post office. You can get cash with your Commonwealth Bank Keycard during local banking hours (for a surcharge of $2) and there is also an Express Money Order facility. Business hours are restricted because the manager is often away at the airstrip collecting mail.

Airstrips

Public use of the Dalhousie Springs airstrip (in Witjira National Park) and the Mokari airstrip (in the Simpson Desert Regional Reserve) is permitted only in an emergency. For an update, contact the ranger at Hawker on the Desert Parks Information Line (☎ (086) 48 4244).

Bush Camping

The only designated camping area in the desert is found at Dalhousie Springs, where facilities are limited to a toilet, showers and an information shelter. It is dusty and exposed but offers ready access to the main hot pool. There is very little shade and no firewood – you can legally collect dead timber from Christmas Creek, 15 km away on the road to Mount Dare homestead.

Past Dalhousie Springs you'll find countless good bush camp sites beside the various tracks described, though firewood and shade are often in short supply, if not absent altogether. For this reason it's a good idea to carry a gas stove, and a tarpaulin or two that you can use to rig up a shelter. A mosquito net over your bed will keep the flies out of your face first thing in the morning; you'll need a net as protection from mosquitoes around wetland areas such as Dalhousie Springs and Purni Bore. The best camp sites of all are to be found in the desert's gidgee woodlands, and among the coolabahs on the flood plains of Eyre and Warburton creeks.

Oodnadatta Track

One of Australia's most interesting outback routes, the 645-km Oodnadatta Track links Marree to Marla via Oodnadatta in northern South Australia. Here, as you cross generally flat to undulating terrain consisting mainly of desert sand ridges and vast plains covered with gibbers and stunted saltbush, the sense of space is profound. There is little grand scenery, but in terms of fascinating heritage sites – both natural and cultural – it is well in front of other, more famous routes. Its many attractions include artesian mound springs, Lake Eyre National Park and numerous relics of the Overland Telegraph Line (OTL) and Great Northern Railway. If you're an enthusiast for such things, allow at least four days for the 429-km section between Marree and Oodnadatta, as this contains all the notable highlights.

Despite its name, the Oodnadatta Track is actually a fairly good road by outback standards. However, you can still expect plenty of corrugations, potholes, dust and other hazards, while boggy sections and flooded creeks can close the road for days following a big rain. Conditions are usually suitable for robust conventional vehicles with strong suspensions and good ground clearance, but a 4WD is best for the detours. Travelling at speeds in excess of 80 km/h is not recommended, as loose surfaces, rough creek crossings, blind crests and sharp corners combined with inexperience and excessive speed cause a number of accidents each year. Diesel, super and unleaded petrol are available at Marree (0 km), William Creek (220 km), Oodnadatta (429 km) and Marla (645 km). LPG is sold only at Marla.

HISTORY

The track between Marree and Oodnadatta more or less follows the mound springs that occur in an arc from Lake Frome north through Marree and on to Dalhousie Springs, near the Northern Territory border. This region is Australia's driest and the springs are its major natural source of fresh water. For Aborigines, explorers and settlers, they were like stepping stones into the interior. Prior to White settlement the Aboriginal people used them as part of a major trade route that linked the Kimberley and Cape York to the south coast via central Australia. This was the original Oodnadatta Track. For White settlers the springs became the focus of their earliest attempts to develop the arid heart.

In 1858 South Australia's frontier was stalled at Glen's Station, about 80 km east of

Camping out in the desert (TW)

the northern tip of Lake Torrens. The country beyond was unknown to White people. Then, in the space of two years, it leapt 300 km to reach the Davenport Range, 90 km west of Lake Eyre. This was almost entirely due to the explorations of Major Peter Edgerton Warburton (the South Australian police commissioner) and Scottish surveyor John McDouall Stuart.

Warburton penetrated as far as Mt Margaret in the Davenports and became the first to report the springs' existence. Stuart added substantially to these discoveries when he led two expeditions into the country west and north-west of Lake Eyre between April 1859 and January 1860. His efforts reduced the unknown by a further 150 km – almost to the Macumba River, about 50 km north of Oodnadatta.

Stuart was particularly impressed by the height of some of the mound springs and the amount of water flowing from them. He judged that the plentiful good water and grass on the new pastoral leases that he'd surveyed would carry double if not treble the stock that the stations further south were carrying. What he didn't realise was that he'd seen the country after a succession of good rainfall years. Sadly for the settlers who followed in his footsteps, the grim reality was an average annual rainfall of 120 to 150 mm and an evaporation rate of 3600 mm, and this had reasserted itself by 1865. The grass withered, the sheep and cattle died in their thousands, and the newcomers went bankrupt.

Stuart also saw many well-used native pads, but seldom the people themselves. Those he did get close to were usually last seen heading at top speed in the opposite direction. To them, the combination of a horse and rider must have seemed like some fearful monster straight from the very worst of nightmares. On one occasion the explorers suddenly came upon an Aborigine hunting in the sandhills. Stuart described the encounter thus:

What he imagined I was I do not know; but when he turned round and saw me, I never beheld a finer picture of astonishment and fear. He was a fine muscular fellow, about six feet in height, and stood as i rivetted to the spot, with his mouth wide open and hi eyes staring.

Stuart sent his Aboriginal guide forward to speak with the man, but omitted to tell him to dismount. The terrified native remained motionless until the awful apparition was within a few metres, whereupon he threw down his waddies and jumped up into a mulga bush. There, trembling violently on his precarious perch and with one foot only a metre from the ground, he awaited his fate. Imagine his relief when all the creature did was utter a few unintelligible questions before walking away.

The reports of Stuart's explorations were received with great interest by the South Australian government. This was partly because the colony was keen for Adelaide to be the ultimate destination for a proposed telegraphic link between Australia and Europe via India. For this to happen however, a practicable route had to be found across the unknown centre of the continent to the north coast; Stuart had fuelled hopes that such a route might exist. Accordingly the government offered a substantial reward for its discovery.

In March 1860 Stuart departed on what proved to be the first of three epic attempts to win the prize. He passed through the Alice Springs area, but hostile Aborigines and an acute shortage of rations forced his retreat near Tennant Creek. In January 1861 he set out again, only to be turned back by dense waterless scrub further north, past Newcastle Waters. A final attempt brought success when, on 25 July 1862, he reached the Arafura Sea east of Darwin. Stuart returned in triumph, but the privations he'd suffered on his expeditions had reduced him to a living skeleton. He died a broken man just four years later.

The Overland Telegraph Line (OTL)

Stuart's explorations gave impetus to South Australia's lobbying for the telegraph line to be built entirely within its borders – it had gained control of the Northern Territory from

New South Wales in 1863. Eventually, after much heated opposition from Queensland, it won the battle, and signed a contract with the British-Australian Telegraph Company in April 1870.

Under the terms of this agreement, the South Australian government had until 1 January 1872 to construct 3000 km of telegraph line to link Port Augusta and Darwin. This would be built and maintained at the government's own cost, and for every day in default it would pay a penalty to the company, which had guaranteed to land the overseas cable in Darwin by that date. The fledgling colony, which then had a White population of only 185,000, had no time to contemplate the enormity of its task. In 1870 the frontier had not progressed past Mount Margaret station; nothing had been done either to explore or settle the route Stuart had travelled eight years previously. Thus, for about 2000 km the wire would be routed through country known only from Stuart's journals.

But with inspired optimism, the government raised a loan to cover the estimated cost

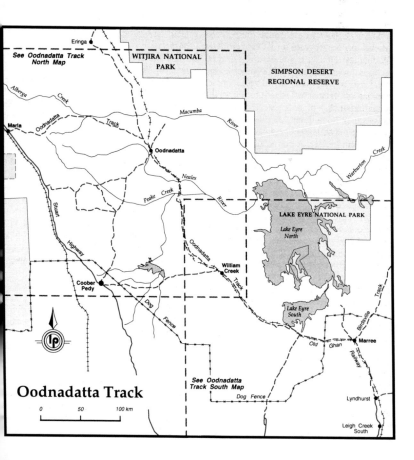

Oodnadatta Track

0   50   100 km

and set to work. For the sake of speed, the OTL was divided into three equal parts, to be built concurrently: the southern, central and northern sections. The former was to go north from Port Augusta to Marree, then follow the mound springs around the western side of Lake Eyre to meet the central section at the Macumba River near Oodnadatta. This was by far the easiest to construct, as the country through which it passed was well known and had been more or less settled. In fact, the only real difficulty proved to be a lack of suitable trees for use as poles, which had to be seven metres long and placed 12 to the km. Most of the 10,000 poles required were carted from the Flinders Ranges.

The first pole in the entire project was erected at Port Augusta on 1 October 1870. By January 1872, the southern and central sections – a total distance of 1890 km – were open for traffic, allowing direct contact between Adelaide and Tennant Creek. In the north, however, monsoonal flooding had caused such huge delays that there was still a gap of over 600 km between Tennant Creek and the King River. A pony express carried international messages between the operators at either end as 300 men laboured mightily to complete the line. The Telegraph Company made demands for compensation, but these ceased when their cable broke down in June. By the time it was repaired four months later, the two ends had been joined. The governor declared a public holiday to celebrate.

By now the route between Marree and Oodnadatta had become a well-established dray road along the seemingly endless line of white-capped telegraph poles. It was still very lonely country, however. Between the Macumba and Glen's Station – a distance of over 500 km – there were only four or five rough homesteads, and the new OTL repeater stations at Strangways Springs and The Peake.

Great Northern Railway

After their remarkable success with the OTL, it seemed to South Australians that nothing could prevent the development of their north. This belief was strengthened when, in the early 1870s, a run of good seasons created a wheat boom on the semiarid plains north of Port Augusta. This coincided with a spectacular gold rush near Darwin.

With the bit between their teeth, the optimists now demanded a rail link across the continent. Would-be farmers were convinced that wheat could be grown all the way to the Centre; the plough, they said, would transform the outback into 'a wheat-growers' golden glory'. This emotive nonsense caught the public's imagination, and dissenting voices were drowned out by the ensuing clamour. This reached such a height that at last the government capitulated, and so the Great Northern Railway was born.

By late 1883, when the narrow-gauge line reached Marree from Port Augusta, normal seasons had returned and the erstwhile wheat farmers were in full retreat to safer ground. It was now recognised that there was little prospect of wheat fields ever stretching to the Territory border. Not only that, the colonies were in the grip of a general depression. In Adelaide alone, there were thousands out of work.

Nevertheless, the South Australian government decided to press on with the railway as a means of relieving unemployment. Trainloads of jobless men were sent north to the railhead, which crept out along the OTL from newly established Marree in July 1884. The immediate destination was Strangways Springs, although a transcontinental link was still the ultimate goal.

In those days, at least in South Australia, railways were built manually, with picks, shovels and wheelbarrows, assisted by dynamite and horse-drawn scoops. But these new navvies, many of whom were no longer young, were mostly soft-muscled clerks and shop assistants. With the flies swarming about their faces, they must have stared aghast at the shimmering gravel wastes and quailed at the thought of what confronted them. Not surprisingly, the no-hoper element deserted in droves.

Yet many remained and became useful

labourers. For some, however, the only reward was a violent death. Gruesome accidents, thirst and murders claimed many lives. In the worst accident, five navvies were killed when a ballast train collided with a mob of cattle. Typhoid epidemics raged, and soon the Oodnadatta Track was dotted with graves.

The Great Northern Railway was built on the cheap, with light rails and minimum ballast. Although hundreds of men were employed on the project, the work progressed at a snail's pace. In 1889 the line eventually reached Oodnadatta, which was then just a place name on the OTL. It was hardly an epic in the annals of railroad construction.

Oodnadatta remained the railhead until January 1927, when once again the construction crews moved northwards. This time – to the relief of South Australian taxpayers – the federal government was putting up the money. By now the service was known as 'the Ghan', after the so-called Afghani camel

drivers it had replaced. It had also become legendary for its inefficiency and for the leisurely way in which it operated. After all, which other major train service would stop so that its passengers could pick wildflowers? This situation was unchanged after the line reached Alice Springs in 1929.

In more recent times the Ghan's faltering progress, laid-back style and olde-worlde charm made it an anachronism in a modern age of transport. It also offered adventure, because passengers never knew how long their journey was going to take. The line had been built through flood-prone areas, and heavy rains often resulted in washouts that closed the line for weeks. On at least one such occasion, the engineer had to shoot some goats to feed his hungry passengers. The Old Ghan may have provided an unforgettable experience for the tourists who travelled on it, but it was a financial nightmare for the treasury bureaucrats in Canberra.

The line closed for good in 1982, when the

Desert oak (DO)

present rail service to Alice Springs was opened. It has since been dismantled – much of the track went to Queensland to be relaid in the sugar-cane fields – but there are still many fascinating relics left to explore along the line. These, along with the remains of the OTL, had been left to deteriorate until recently, when various restoration projects were launched to save the best examples for posterity.

INFORMATION
Tourist Offices

For up-to-date advice on all touring aspects of the Oodnadatta Track, contact the Outback Tourist Park (☎ (086) 75 8371) in Marree, the William Creek Hotel (☎ (086) 70 7880), the Pink Roadhouse (☎ (086) 70 7822) in Oodnadatta, and the Marla Travellers Rest (☎ (086) 70 7001).

Lake Eyre National Park is managed by Department of Environment & Natural Resources rangers based at Hawker in the northern Flinders Ranges. For the latest information on public access and other park matters, call in to their office at Hawker, write to them at PO Box 102, Hawker, SA 5434, or ring the Desert Parks Information Hotline (☎ (086) 48 4244).

Emergency

There are well-equipped hospitals, staffed by registered nurses, at Marree, Oodnadatta and Marla. The William Creek Hotel has a very comprehensive RFDS kit, so the staff can administer drugs and perform other medical functions by acting on directions they receive over their HF radio. If an emergency evacuation is required, it only takes the RFDS 1½ hours to reach William Creek from Port Augusta.

Permits & Registration

There is no requirement to register your intentions with the police. However, it is a sensible precaution to leave a detailed plan of your movements with a responsible person who can give the alarm if you fail to check in.

The entry requirement for Lake Eyre National Park is possession of a current Desert Parks Pass, which covers entry to most of the conservation areas in South Australia's outback. It includes a booklet that gives details on the 4WD access routes into ABC Bay (on Lake Eyre North) and the Goyder Channel via Muloorina homestead. It also provides a few brief facts on the lake and its environs. You can purchase your Pass for $50 per vehicle per year from park rangers and selected commercial outlets (including the Ghan Store in Marree, the William Creek Hotel and the Pink Roadhouse in Oodnadatta).

Books

If the dynamics of flooding in the Lake Eyre basin are of interest, you can't go past the lavishly illustrated, large-format *Floods of Lake Eyre* by Victor Kotwicki (Engineering & Water Supply Department, Adelaide, 1986). The text is dry and technical but the photographs are superb. Of particular interest is the series of full-colour satellite shots of Lake Eyre as it dries up after the 1984 flood.

Explorations in Australia – The Journals of John McDouall Stuart, by John McDouall Stuart (Saunders, Otley & Co, London, 1865; facsimile edition by Hesperian Press, Perth, 1984), gives a fascinating day-by-day account of the great explorer's expeditions around Lake Eyre and on to the north coast. It's a must for history enthusiasts.

Basil Fuller's *The Ghan – The Story of the Alice Springs Railway* (Rigby, Adelaide, 1975) is out of print. If you find one, buy it: it makes interesting background reading.

Maps

The small-scale map-cum-guide entitled *Oodnadatta Track* published by Westprint Heritage Maps is a very useful basic reference for this trip. It covers the entire route from Lyndhurst (79 km south of Marree) to Marla and includes brief details on its various highlights. The guide – a single, large, folded sheet – is available from various outlets in Alice Springs, Port

Augusta, Leigh Creek, Marree, Oodnadatta and Marla.

For a more detailed map coverage of the Marree to Oodnadatta section, you'll need the Marree, Curdimurka, Billakalina, Warrina and Oodnadatta 1:250,000 topographic maps from AUSLIG. (The Marree sheet covers only the first six km and can be dispensed with.) The Wintinna sheet covers the Oodnadatta-Marla section. These maps are available from AUSLIG sales outlets in any capital city.

The RAA's *Northern Areas* map is also quite useful.

Radio Frequencies
The track is well used in the winter months, when you may only have to wait 15 to 20 minutes for another vehicle to come along. In summer it's an entirely different story: vehicles can be hours apart, so an HF radio could come in handy. The Port Augusta RFDS base (callsign VNZ – Victor November Zulu) covers this part of the world. It can be reached on 8165 kHz between 7 am and 5 pm, 4010 and 6890 kHz between 7 am and 9 pm, and 2020 and 4010 kHz between 9 pm and 7 am. For details, call the station (☎ (080) 88 0777).

SPECIAL PREPARATIONS
Water
It's essential to carry ample drinking water at all times on the Oodnadatta Track, as most local springs and bores yield unpleasant-tasting water which has a laxative effect. It's pointless attempting to beg or buy rainwater from the locals – not surprisingly, they regard their scant supplies as being more precious than gold. Marree's water supply is undrinkable, as is William Creek's, but the Oodnadatta supply is palatable if served either chilled or in hot drinks. Marla's water is quite acceptable.

Flies & Mosquitoes
Bushfly plagues are the track's down side in warm weather. Fly veils for your face and an insect-screened gazebo for meals are essential at such times; make sure to pack a net to cover any toddlers while they're having their daytime nap. Unfortunately, any areas with shallow permanent water (such as around springs and flowing bores) are usually swarming with mosquitoes at night.

THE ROUTE
Marree to William Creek (203 km)
In recent years, much of the Oodnadatta Track between Marree and William Creek has been realigned and sheeted with crushed rock in an attempt to eliminate the worst hazards of the old road. However, some would argue that there has been no real improvement in motoring conditions. There is some nice scenery on this section, but the major attractions are old railway sidings, artesian mound springs and the world's sixth-largest lake: Lake Eyre. (See the later Birdsville Track section for details on Marree.)

The Dog Fence Leaving Marree, the track spears westward over rolling gibber downs, passing through a rather ordinary-looking fence 42 km from town. In fact this is the world's longest man-made barrier, the Dog-Proof Fence. It extends 5490 km, from near Ceduna (in western South Australia) to Jimbour (about 200 km north-west of Brisbane in southern Queensland). Patrolled by government inspectors, the fence's sole purpose is to protect the sheep flocks of south-eastern Australia from attack by dingoes. A pair of dingoes acting together can kill dozens of sheep in a night, so any that make their way through the fence are vigorously pursued with bullets, traps and poison baits. Although dingoes do prey on calves, their depredations aren't considered a serious threat to the beef-cattle industry, which becomes dominant outside the fence.

The Inland Sea Continuing on for a further 26 km you pass a high hump-backed range on the right with a cairn on its highest point. This is **Hermit Hill**, climbed in 1858 by Benjamin Babbage, who thus became the first White person to cross the gap between Lake Torrens and Lake Eyre. These two great lakes were previously thought to be joined in a great barrier that would block progress to the north.

Sixteen km past Hermit Hill you come to a rough detour that leads to a nearby **lookout** point above the barren shore of Lake Eyre South. There's another lookout 10 km further on, where for a short distance the road runs right beside the lake with the old railway line in between.

Lake Eyre is actually two lakes – Lake Eyre North and Lake Eyre South – joined by a narrow channel. Covering a total area of 9700 sq km, the entire lakebed is included within the 13,560-sq-km Lake Eyre National Park. Although the lake has filled to near capacity only three times in the past 150 years (most recently in 1974), it does receive significant flooding once every eight years on average, thanks usually to heavy rains over central and western Queensland.

Lake Eyre is so shallow that even a major flood like that of 1974 takes only two years or so to evaporate. In the meantime the lake becomes a vast breeding ground for swarms of pelicans, seagulls, terns and many other water birds, and such a rare celebration of life in the desert is well worth a special trip. Most times, however, the lake is little more than a flat, blinding white expanse of dry salt crust: in 1964 Britain's Donald Campbell set a world land-speed record of 648.6 km/h on Lake Eyre North in his jet-powered car Blue-bird II. It's not a good idea to drive on the lakebed yourself, as your vehicle will soon break through the hard surface and sink into black saline slop.

Curdimurka Eight km past Lake Eyre you arrive at Curdimurka Siding, which com-memorates the fearsome kadimakara of Aboriginal belief – the kadimakara were thought to live under Lake Eyre and prey on anyone foolish enough to walk on it. This tiny abandoned outpost consists of a nine-roomed stone cottage, an elevated railway tank and a **tower-like water softener**. (The latter was designed to remove harmful salts from bore water that otherwise caused heavy scaling in locomotive boilers.) Prior to 1980

it was the base for a crew of railway fettlers who were responsible for maintaining a 30-km stretch of line noted for deep washouts after rain and drifting sand in drought times

In its day, Curdimurka was little different to most other sidings along the railway, but what makes it remarkable now is the fact that it is still in one piece. This is entirely due to the unflagging enthusiasm of the Ghan Railway Preservation Society, based in Adelaide, which has restored the entire complex including four km of railway and an adjacent section of the OTL. The cottage is of the standard design used for fettlers' quarters along the line. Its bedrooms are quite small, almost like cells, and have whitewashed walls and high ceilings to combat the hellish summers. Looking outside at the empty sur-roundings, you can easily picture a red dust storm rolling in to bury the place in a shriek-ing fury. All in all, Curdimurka is a powerful reminder of a lifestyle better imagined than experienced.

Mound Springs The road continues west-wards for 29 km from Curdimurka, at which point you come to a rough, ill-defined detour that heads south for five km to flat-topped **Hamilton Hill**. At the foot of this low but prominent feature you find **Blanches Cup**, one of the most remarkable of all the mound springs that line the track between Marree and William Creek.

Mound springs are the natural outlets of the Great Artesian Basin, a vast sandstone aquifer that can be likened to a saucer with one side slightly raised. Rainfall is soaked up where the basin's main water-bearing rocks outcrop, in the eastern ranges of Queensland and New South Wales. From here the water moves towards South Australia, taking an estimated 2.5 million years to reach the Oodnadatta Track.

Mound springs occur wherever the pres-sure in the aquifer is able to force water to the surface through cracks in the overlying impermeable rocks. The dramatic fall in pressure at the surface causes chemical changes in the water; magnesium, sodium and calcium carbonates are precipated at the

Railway tank and water softener at Curdimurka (DO)

outlet and slowly build up to form hillocks usually several metres high. In this flat, brown land, the white carbonate rock is visible for considerable distances.

Blanches Cup is a classic mound spring, owing to its symmetry and the large circular pool on top. Like all the other springs in this region, it has suffered greatly from introduced grazing animals as well as from the reduced flow rates resulting from the many bores that have been drilled into the aquifer. Nevertheless, the reed-fringed waterhole remains a beautiful paradox in the inhospitable surroundings of sun-baked salt flats and shrubby plants. You can easily appreciate why the early explorers went into raptures when they first laid their eyes on it.

A few hundred metres to the north lies **the Bubbler**, so named because of the frequent eruptions of gas that disturb the tranquil pool over its outlet. In reality the pool is more like quicksand, but the pressure from underneath allows you to wallow about in safety while enjoying a stimulating massage from the upwelling bubbles of sand and gas. You'd

pay big dollars to do this in a resort, but here the experience is free. Afterwards, however, comes the tedious task of removing the fine sand that makes its way into every nook and cranny.

A word of warning here: the surface of the Bubbler appears to be firm, an illusion that encourages many people to walk on it. What happens is that you take a couple of steps towards the bubbles and then suddenly you're in it up to your chest. However, there's probably no danger (other than from a heart attack), as the pressure almost immediately forces your legs back to the surface.

Coward Springs Leaving the Bubbler, you head north-west along the access track to where it meets the main road just before the Coward Springs turn-off. This old siding was an exception to the rule, as it once boasted an important little settlement with a hospital, hotel and store as well as several railway houses. The South Australian government established a plantation of date palms, but

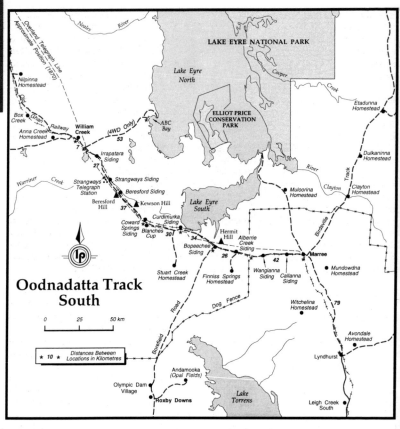

Oodnadatta Track
South

the bore water proved unsuitable and they failed to thrive.

Today, only the ruins of the station master's and engineer's cottages remain among the saltbush and scrub beside the flowing bore, which feeds a pool where you can enjoy a warm bath. The site of the pub is marked by a concrete cellar surrounded by tall date palms and shady athel trees.

Extinct Springs Six km from Coward Springs, by which time you're at last heading northwards, the track passes between a tan-coloured mound on the left and a high white hill on the right. The former is an extinct spring; the latter, **Kewson Hill**, is the largest active mound spring along the track. During his 1859 expedition, Stuart bogged his horse on top and had great difficulty getting it out again. An indication of what the flow from these springs must have been like way back in geological time is provided by huge extinct mounds such as flat-topped **Beresford Hill**, which is off on your left 22 km past Coward Springs, and Hamilton Hill (behind Blanches Cup).

About 2.5 km past Beresford Hill you'll see a rare sight on the Oodnadatta Track: a large clump of shady trees around a **dam**. Built to supply water for steam locomotives, it is now used mainly by cattle and wildlife, most obvious of which are the screeching hordes of corellas that frequently cover the trees.

Strangways Telegraph Station The roadside, reed-fringed pool of water 37 km from Coward Springs bore marks the old Strangways Siding bore. There is no longer any sign of this little settlement (it once had a pub and police station), but if you look to the west you may be able to spot a ruin on the low ridge about two km away. This was the Strangways Telegraph Station, one of 11 repeater stations constructed between Port Augusta and Darwin in 1871 to boost the morse signals that travelled along the OTL. Unfortunately, vandals have been busy here: only a large stone tank and some stone-walled sheep pens remain in good condition.

William Creek

Two km past Strangways Siding you cross salty Warriner Creek just downstream from a rusty railway bridge, where debris heaped against the piles gives you a good idea what these streams are like in a big flood. The track now leaves the gibber plains behind, and for the next 15 km or so passes through large crimson sand ridges covered with low scrub and separated by claypans and gravel flats. Like other sandy areas in the region, this is a great spot for winter wildflowers. The dunes, which cut out 17 km before William Creek, are outliers of the Simpson Desert dunefield 100 km to the north-east.

The thriving metropolis of William Creek (population 10) is South Australia's smallest town. It consists of the William Creek Hotel and three equally unpretentious houses set on a shimmering saltbush flat between two red dunes. As the rainfall is measured in drops here, there isn't much in the way of lawns and gardens. As well, the local bore water is fit only for sheep and cattle. This means that if you've got a thirst (and who wouldn't in a place like this?), you may be forced to make do with a cold ale.

The attraction of bush pubs lies in the fact that what they lack in frills they more than make up for in character and atmosphere, and in this regard the **William Creek Hotel** leaves most modern establishments for dead. Built in 1887 (it was a support station for camel drivers working on the OTL), the pub's external appearance is undistinguished, its ancient corrugated-iron cladding having been warped by the heat of too many summers and battered by the force of too many dust storms. Inside, however, is a friendly haven away from the glare and flies. During daylight hours the bar is lit by the golden rays that stream in through holes in the walls. You look up to see a ceiling of sagging planks that threaten to collapse on your head at any moment. Stuck there are strange things, including a pair of sand-filled underpants (a legacy of someone's dip in the Bubbler). Out the front, a parking meter collects donations for the RFDS.

While the pub offers a fascinating return to another era, it does boast a few concessions to modern technology. A colour TV sits beside an old pendulum clock, glossy stools of the very latest style line the counter and a new telephone resides in a corner. Yet despite the scorching summers, there is no air-conditioning – just ceiling fans to keep the super-heated air moving. This isn't a ploy to guarantee that customers retain a powerful thirst; rather it's a reflection of the huge cost of power-generation in remote areas. Fortunately the drinks are always served cold, regardless of the air temperature, which can reach 48°C in the bar.

The other tourist highlight is the annual William Creek Cup, held on the weekend before Easter.

William Creek to Oodnadatta (210 km)

On this section the track wanders generally northwards over much the same terrain as before. Careful driving is essential, as the greater part of it has been constructed simply by scraping the gibbers off to either side – always slow right down at creek crossings and grids in particular, as these can be quite dangerous. Although there are no mound

The Bubbler (TW)

Ruins of the Peake Telegraph Station (DO)

springs beside the road past William Creek, abandoned railway sidings and other relics provide plenty of interest.

Anna Creek Having torn yourself away from William Creek, you pass the turn-off to Anna Creek homestead and Coober Pedy. Anna Creek station covers 30,114 sq km and is the world's largest pastoral lease – most years it runs around 20,000 head of cattle (which, at an average value of $500 per head, is a huge investment in stock). The station also runs nearly 500 working horses, as most of the cattle work is still carried out in the traditional way. The average carrying capacity of this country is less than one beast per sq km and most years you'll wonder how it supports even that many.

Anna Creek is leased by the Kidman Pastoral Company, which was established by the legendary cattle king, Sir Sidney Kidman. The company's holdings have been much reduced since its heyday but it still operates a string of stations around the southern fringe of the Simpson Desert.

The Peake Telegraph Station You cross a number of mainly small creeks in the 112 km between William Creek and the **Ernest Giles Memorial**, a simple cairn commemorating Giles' arrival here in 1876 after his epic crossing from the west coast. Most of these streams are lined either by coolabahs, river red gums or gidgees, and several offer good shade and camping in welcome contrast to the gibbers that crowd in on either side. The ruins and water-softening plant at **Edward Creek Siding** (91 km from William Creek) are well worth investigating, while the nearby creek is an excellent spot to boil the billy.

Heading east from the Giles Memorial, a rough 4WD track takes you 16 km to **The Peake** ruins at Freeling Springs. The Peake homestead was South Australia's northernmost outpost of settlement in 1870, when construction of the OTL began. A year later a telegraph station was built beside the homestead, and in 1873 a police station was added. This made The Peake a sizeable community for both its time and place, but it was abandoned 18 years later when operations were moved to newly established Oodnadatta.

In recent years, restoration works have been carried out at this fascinating site, which is situated on a rocky terrace overlooking a broad, flat-bottomed valley covered in gidgee. There are a total of nine stone ruins, of which the seven-roomed telegraph station is the largest and most sophisticated.

In the hills behind are several deep shafts dating from 1898, when mineral lodes assaying 70% copper and several ounces of gold per ton were discovered. Two years later a number of mines were being developed and there was talk of employment for 3000 men, but in the end it came to nothing, and activity ceased in 1904. By that time, the smelter erected at great cost 300 metres south-west of the telegraph station had treated just 250 tons of ore, averaging 4% copper.

Algebuckina Thirty-two km from the Giles Memorial you arrive at the **Neales River**, where channels studded with coolabahs are spread over about a km. This is by far the largest watercourse on the Oodnadatta Track, but what really grabs your attention is the 578-metre-long **Algebuckina railway bridge**, with its soaring steel arches. A common fallacy is that the bridge – the longest in South Australia – was prefabricated for a crossing of the Murray River but was found to be too short. While this is easy to believe as it's so out of character with the rest of the railway, the truth is that it was specifically designed for the Neales crossing. The **graves** of three railway workers who died in this lonely spot lie beside the line at the bridge's northern end.

Excitement came to Algebuckina in October 1886 when gold was found on the Neales' northern bank, close to the bridge. A small rush took place, and five months later, by which time about 60 ounces had been won, 25 men were on the field. Sadly the rush proved a dud, as did the town site surveyed on the opposite bank at about the same time.

Also of interest here is a large salt waterhole on the downstream side (a good spot for bird-watchers). The easy climb up to the cairn above the old Algebuckina Siding, which is about one km south of the bridge, gives a good view over the Neales and surrounding country.

Leaving the river behind, the final 56-km stage into Oodnadatta takes you through a mix of gibber plains, ochre-coloured hills and an area of yellow dunes inexplicably called the **Plantation Sandhills**. Some of this country is breathtakingly harsh, and you

get a fine view of it from **Cadnaowie Lookout**, 17 km from the Neales. With only 20 km to go, you pass through **Duttons Gap**, where the sweating navvies toiled with picks and shovels to maintain a suitable gradient. The thought of it gives you a powerful thirst that will last all the way to Oodnadatta.

Oodnadatta

Oodnadatta's heyday lasted from 1889 to 1927, during which period the town was the terminus for the Great Northern Railway. From here, camel trains made round trips of

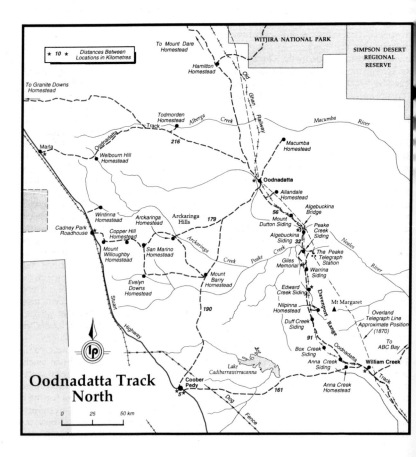

Oodnadatta Track North

up to 3000 km to resupply communities as far away as Newcastle Waters in the Northern Territory. However, the only obvious remaining sign of this relatively prosperous era is an impressive **old railway station**, which houses interesting displays of historic photographs. To gain entry, ask at either the general store or hotel for a key.

After the railway closed in 1980, most government functions were moved to Marla, on the new line, and the town was expected to die. However, it has managed to hang on and, despite its moribund appearance, remains an oasis of unexpected comforts in a hostile sea of gibbers. Today, half the town, including its hotel and general store, is owned by a council made up of local Aboriginal people, who comprise the bulk of the population of about 200.

The council welcomes visitors, and a few drinks in the hotel on pension day is a cross-cultural experience that shouldn't be missed. And if you're in town on Adelaide Cup Day (in May), you can attend the Oodnadatta Cup.

Oodnadatta to Marla (216 km)

Being of much more recent vintage, this final section is lacking in historic appeal. However, there's compensation in the fact that you've a much better chance than previously of seeing interesting wildlife such as emus, bustards, perenties, dingoes and red kangaroos. Most winters you'll see the bright crimson blooms of Sturt Desert Pea, which form large mats in rare good seasons. The Oodnadatta Track's best displays of wildflowers are seen on this section, particularly in the east, where the soils are generally sandy.

As before, you don't see much variation in the topography, which remains basically flat throughout, with numerous tree-lined creeks in the eastern half and gibber plains thereafter. The first 120 km or so makes an interesting drive as the road winds about in the headwaters of **Alberga Creek** and the Neales River. Here you'll find plenty of shady camp sites near the road, as well as occasional temporary waterholes after rain. This section is regularly graded, but like the

rest of the track is impassable in wet conditions.

The final 50 km past Welbourne Hill homestead takes you along the old Stuart Highway, which was realigned to the west in the early 1980s.

Marla

The little township of Marla (the name is a corruption of the Pitjantjatjara word for red kangaroo) came into existence in 1980 as a regional centre to replace Oodnadatta. Being new and somewhat prefabricated, it has little outback character – it's basically a government town populated by public servants on short-term postings from the city.

DETOURS
ABC Bay (53 km one-way)

Thirty-seven km past the Strangways Siding bore (or seven km before William Creek) you come to a 4WD track that leads to the western shore of Lake Eyre North. This straightforward route terminates at ABC Bay, where the desolation literally takes your breath away. Approaching the shore, you cross a wasteland of low breakaways entirely covered by small black stones. It's so ugly and lifeless that at first glance it seems as if some ghastly environmental disaster has befallen the place. On a satellite photograph, the area appears to have been scorched by a bushfire. But on the ground on a hot day, with the stillness and deathly silence working on your imagination, you can tell that in reality it's been seared by the furnaces of hell. For information, contact the rangers in Hawker (☎ (086) 48 4244).

Coober Pedy (166 km one-way)

The detour from William Creek to Coober Pedy, Australia's opal-mining capital, is worth taking if this is the only chance you'll have to visit the place. Coober Pedy (population about 5000) is a major regional centre and international tourist attraction, so it has an excellent range of commercial facilities. About 70 km from the Oodnadatta Track, you pass a track that turns off to **Lake Cadibarrawirracanna**, Australia's longest place name. The road is remote, rarely maintained, sees little traffic and has no reliable fresh water, so it definitely isn't recommended to either inexperienced or ill-prepared travellers. Before setting out, get an update on road conditions from the William Creek Hotel. For more information on Coober Pedy, see the Stuart Highway section earlier in this chapter.

ALTERNATIVE ROUTES

At Oodnadatta you're faced with a number of options which will take you to the Stuart Highway or further north to Mount Dare and ultimately either to Alice Springs or Birdsville. The roads to Mount Dare, Cadney Park and Coober Pedy are normally suitable for conventional vehicles with good ground clearance. None of them is busy, particularly in summer, so it's essential to be prepared for breakdowns and other problems that may arise. Check road conditions at the Pink Roadhouse.

Oodnadatta to Coober Pedy (190 km)

The main reason you'd take this road is for an alternative route to Coober Pedy. The country is flat, with gibbers almost all the way, and there are no facilities en route.

Oodnadatta to Cadney Park Roadhouse (179 km)

The **Arckaringa Hills**, about 80 km from Oodnadatta, make this by far the most interesting alternative to the Stuart Highway. Numerous colourful mesas provide some of the grandest scenery in outback South Australia, making fantastic subjects for photography in early morning and late afternoon. You're welcome to go for a walk in this area but camping is not permitted.

Also of interest is the *Copper Hill homestead*, 145 km from Oodnadatta, where basic tourist accommodation is available – you can drive around on the station tracks and see wildlife and nice scenery. Ring either the Pink Roadhouse or Copper Hill (☎ (086) 70 7995) for road conditions.

The famous Pink Roadhouse (DO)

Cadney Park (☎ (086) 70 7994) offers a range of services, including fuel (diesel, super and unleaded), restaurant and takeaway meals, motel rooms, cabins, camping and mechanical repairs.

Oodnadatta to Mount Dare Homestead via Eringa (250 km)

You'd take this slow but interesting road if you wanted to visit Dalhousie Springs (in Witjira National Park) or head off to either Alice Springs or Birdsville via the Simpson Desert. As an option, you can take the 4WD short cut from Hamilton homestead to Dalhousie Springs, but this can be extremely rough in places – the turn-off is one km north of the homestead and about 108 km from Oodnadatta.

FACILITIES
Marree

Despite its decline in fortunes in recent years, Marree still has a good range of facilities and services, including a hotel, caravan parks, a landing strip, small supermarkets, mechanical repairs, a post office agency, police and a hospital.

The old *Great Northern Hotel* (☎ (086) 75 8344) offers a selection of hearty counter and restaurant meals as well as old-style hotel accommodation. Tariffs range from \$35 for a single room to \$70 for four people sharing. You can get cash here from your Bankcard, MasterCard, Visa or American Express.

Marree has two quite reasonable caravan parks: the new *Oasis Caravan Park* (☎ (086) 75 8352) and the *Marree Tourist Park* (☎ (086) 75 8371). Both have six-berth on-site caravans (\$30 per van), as well as powered caravan and camping sites (\$5 per adult, \$2.50 per child and \$2 for power). The Marree Tourist Park is right at the junction of the Oodnadatta and Birdsville tracks, so it's a good place to get the latest information on both. It also sells diesel, super and unleaded fuel and offers mechanical repairs.

There are two minisupermarkets: the *Oasis Cafe* (attached to the Oasis Caravan Park) and the *Ghan Store*, both of which also sell takeaway meals and diesel, super and

unleaded fuel. The Ghan Store has the post office and Commonwealth Bank agencies, and there is an EFTPOS facility at the Oasis Cafe. Both establishments are open seven days.

William Creek

The lonely *William Creek Hotel* (☎ (086) 70 7880) dispenses ice, limited food lines, takeaway liquor, meals, basic motel-style accommodation, a camping ground, minor mechanical repairs and fuel (diesel, super and unleaded). The choice of meals is surprisingly varied – you can even get quiche and vegetarian fare, as well as crumbed local rabbit. Motel rates are \$25 per person in winter and \$20 in summer – the rooms aren't air-conditioned, which is a problem in summer. Alongside is a dusty camping area, with some shade and basic facilities, including showers, toilets, overhead lights and barbecues (firewood provided), but no powered sites. You pay \$4 per person or \$9 per family to camp; two on-site caravans are available (\$8/22 per person/family). Normal trading hours for fuel are 7.30 am to midnight seven days.

Oodnadatta

Owing to its location in the middle of nowhere, Oodnadatta's range of facilities is better than you'd expect in a much larger place. The town has a hospital, post office agency, general store, garages, roadhouse, hotel, museum, police station and landing ground. What is lacking are facilities to get cash from your plastic card.

The *Pink Roadhouse* (☎ (086) 70 7822) is the obvious tourism focus for this region, as all routes leading to Oodnadatta are dotted with the distinctive information signs erected by proprietors Adam and Linnie Plate. They've lived here for years and can give sound advice on all aspects of travel in the outback, so drop in for a coffee and a chat. You're welcome to browse through their private library of books, newspaper clippings and maps, all of which will add to your knowledge of the area. It's easy to find because it's painted bright pink.

Adam and Linnie offer fuel (diesel, super and unleaded), takeaway meals, a minisupermarket, minor mechanical repairs, a post office agency and a Commonwealth Bank agency (passbook only). The roadhouse's tourist accommodation comprises backpacker beds in a self-contained eight-bed shack ($9 per person), a six-berth on-site caravan ($25 for the first person plus $5 for each additional person), basic motel-style accommodation ($40 per twin room) and powered sites ($8.50 for the first person, $4 for each additional person and $4 for power). All accommodation units are air-conditioned. The Pink Roadhouse is open seven days.

The *Transcontinental Hotel* (☎ (086) 70 7804) is renowned for its good cooking (breakfast and dinner only); its air-conditioned but otherwise very basic rooms cost $30/55/70 a single/double/triple.

The *Oodnadatta General Store*, a reasonably priced minisupermarket, offers takeaway meals as well as diesel, super and unleaded fuel. Check the fuel prices here and at the Pink Roadhouse, as the store's are usually more competitive.

Marla

Now the major regional centre in northern South Australia, Marla boasts an excellent range of essential facilities, including a supermarket, hotel-motel, caravan park, garage, police station, medical centre and landing ground.

The commercial hub of this little town is the *Marla Travellers Rest* (☎ (086) 70 7001), a combination of hotel, motel, roadhouse, supermarket, garage and caravan park, which literally has everything most people would require. The garage has a qualified mechanic, and fuel (diesel, super, unleaded and LPG) is available 24 hours. After normal hours (6.30 am to 11.30 pm seven days), you can gain entry to the well-stocked supermarket by contacting the night watchman. The Commonwealth Bank agency in the supermarket has an EFTPOS facility.

Tourist accommodation at the Travellers Rest includes air-conditioned motel rooms ($69 a double with colour TV and telephone or $59 a double without), backpacker beds in air-conditioned four-berth cabins ($12 per person, no bed linen supplied) and powered caravan and tent sites ($2 per person and $4 for power). All guests have access to a swimming pool, and there are shady trees and lawns in the caravan park. If you're tired of your own cooking, the hotel section offers an excellent choice of takeaway, à la carte and restaurant meals.

Bush Camping

A small camping area at *Coward Springs* has toilets and warm-water showers, as well as shady trees and a hot pool to swim in. Cost is $8 per vehicle (paid into the honesty box when the manager isn't there, which is most of the time between October and April). The place is renowned for its mosquitoes, so if you don't have protection from these pests, go somewhere else.

The old workers' cottage at *Curdimurka* isn't staffed and has no facilities whatsoever, but it provides great shelter when it's raining (unlikely) or windy (very likely). A small fee is payable (in the honesty box) – and please clean up before moving out. Sadly, this unique place is beginning to suffer from the actions of the thoughtless minority.

Isolated bush camp sites offering good shelter from both sun and wind aren't all that common, owing to the fact that over vast areas, the tallest vegetation is stunted saltbush. Popular spots such as Beresford Siding and the Neales River have generally been degraded by people-pressure, and you should avoid them if for no other reason than to protect your health. The best places to look for private sheltered sites are along creeks and in sandhill areas, but don't leave it too late in the day.

Firewood There's a general lack of trees between Marree and Oodnadatta, but the millions of sleepers along the railway are a great source of firewood. Most are old, easily splintered and make excellent coals for cooking. If you have the space, carry at least one with you, as the country away from creeklines is virtually devoid of dead timber. You'll also find that popular camping areas have long been stripped of firewood.

Birdsville Track

Seared by the relentless sun and scoured by countless raging dust storms, the 517-km Birdsville Track between Birdsville and Marree earned notoriety as one of Australia's most hazardous stock routes. The track's grim reputation was built on death, as the lives of many people and entire mobs of cattle have been lost to its dangers – thirst, heat and dust storms. Linking a series of unreliable waterholes and artesian bores across one of Australia's harshest regions, it was a droving highway along which up to 50,000 head of cattle a year walked from Queensland to the railway at Marree. Until relatively recent times it was little more than an ill-defined pad that wound among dry river channels and across barren gibber plains, with the bones of dead stock pointing the way to the next water.

But progress has come to the Birdsville Track, and it's now a much tamer version of earlier times. The drovers were replaced by road trains in the 1960s, and as a result the track has been upgraded to the point where it is now mostly a good dirt road. Catering mainly to tourist traffic, the air-conditioned Mungeranie Hotel, near the halfway mark, dispenses fuel and creature comforts such as cold drinks, soft beds and hot showers. Purists might lament that the spirit of the track is dead, but those who live along it are unlikely to share that sentiment.

For the casual tourist there is little spectacular scenery in this desolate landscape of polished stones, sand ridges and occasional scrubby creeks. Many find the experience crushingly monotonous, but for others the loneliness, impenetrable silence and vast empty spaces provide the opportunity for a unique and fascinating adventure in outback touring. If you take the time – and an enthusiast could easily spend a week or more exploring the track's various attractions – it offers an opportunity to vividly appreciate the courage of those who lived and worked here in the days when the drover was king. Those who aren't interested can drive its full length in one day and never know what they've missed.

HISTORY

The Diamantina River system between Lake Eyre and Birdsville was explored by the surveyor John Lewis in 1874, but the credit for pioneering the actual Birdsville Track was earned about six years later by E A Burt, the first Birdsville storekeeper. Burt's route quickly came to prominence because it gave the stations of south-west Queensland's channel country a link to Adelaide, their closest major market and supply point. In good seasons, mobs of up to 2000 cattle streamed south, taking an average five weeks to travel from Birdsville to Marree. The drovers' spartan needs were provided for by isolated stores at Mirra Mitta, Tidnacoordooninna, Cannuwaukaninna and Mulka, but these, like the old homesteads at Lake Harry, Mount Gason, Apatoonganie and Oorawillanie, have long since been abandoned. Today their scant remains and parched surroundings evoke images of hard, lonely living and eventual failure in the face of overwhelming odds.

Apart from cattle, the main traffic until the 1930s comprised camel trains from Marree. In the care of Afghani cameleers, strings of up to 75 animals carried virtually everything that Birdsville and the surrounding stations required in the way of stores, building materials and general cargo. The trek from Marree to Birdsville took about 24 days, with each beast carrying between 250 and 450 kg. Camels are superbly adapted to the track's dry conditions, but by the late 1930s they'd been replaced by road transport and most had been set free to wander in the desert.

In a land where water has sacred significance, only the foolhardy tempted fate by walking between the far-flung homesteads

One of Adam & Linnie Plate's distinctive signs, this one at Marla (RvD)

scattered along the way. Many were fatally ignorant of local conditions, and their epitaphs, if they were ever recorded, can be found among the terse entries in early police journals. On 22 December 1885 the Birdsville policeman wrote:

Traveller found a dead body. Three or four days old. Ten miles over the border in South Australia. Three men perished 10 miles from Clifton Hills station, ten or twelve days ago. No water.

More recently, the publicity surrounding the Page family's tragic demise only served to enhance the track's fearsome reputation. In late December 1963 the Pages were driving from Marree to Queensland when their vehicle broke down at Dead Man's Sandhill, about 90 km from Birdsville. Their water supplies were extremely limited, and in the great heat they waited with increasing desperation for help to arrive. However, in those days travellers were a rarity on the Birdsville Track in summer and the Pages had neglected to advise people of their movements. Tormented by thirst, they finally left their car in a despairing quest for water.

The abandoned vehicle was found several days later by a rabbit-shooter, who raised the alarm. A search party was quickly organised but it was too late for the Pages, whose bodies were located shortly afterwards. The parents and two of their three children had perished in a dried-up waterhole, no doubt lured there by the coolabah trees and their false promise of salvation. The eldest son's body was found on a sand ridge about one km away. Their lonely grave beside the waterhole is marked by a small metal cross bearing the stark inscription: 'The Pages Perished Dec 63.'

INFORMATION
Tourist Offices
For up-to-date advice of a general nature, contact the Outback Tourist Park in Marree (☎ (086) 75 8371), the Mungeranie Hotel (☎ (086) 75 8317) and Birdsville Auto (☎ (076) 56 3226). Road reports are best obtained from the Marree police (☎ (086) 75 8346) and the Birdsville police (☎ (076) 56 3220). Just to be on the safe side, you can also check road conditions by ringing the Mungeranie Hotel.

Registration
Despite the popular belief that all travellers on the Birdsville Track should register with the police at one end and sign off at the other, the police no longer wish to be involved in these matters. They suggest that you keep friends or relatives informed of your movements so that they can notify the authorities should you fail to report in on time. However, the police are happy to provide advice, and travellers can leave messages with them for others to collect.

Emergency
Marree and Birdsville both have well-equipped hospitals staffed by registered nurses. The Mungeranie Hotel has a comprehensive RFDS medical kit, and in the event of an emergency its staff can administer drugs and perform other procedures by acting on directions they receive over their HF radio.

Books
Mail for the Back of Beyond, by John Maddock (Kangaroo Press, Kenthurst, 1986), tells the fascinating story of the motor mail officers of the Birdsville Track. It gives you an appreciation of how easy the motorists have it today. The Marree-Birdsville mail was carried by camels until 1936, when it was taken over by a truck service which lasted until 1975. Since then the mail has been carried by aeroplane.

Eric Bonython's *Where the Seasons Come and Go* (Illawong Pty Ltd, Yankalilla, 1985) is an absorbing read covering history, life-

styles and adventure in the Coopers Creek country up to the 1950s. The Bethesda Mission on Lake Killalpaninna features prominently.

Land of Mirage, by George Farwell (Seal Books, 1972), is a story of cattle-droving and station life along the track in the late 1940s, with plenty of history thrown in. It's definitely worth reading, although hard to get, as it's now out of print.

Several chapters of *Outback on your Doorstep*, by Brian Sheedy (Roadwrite Publishing, Fitzroy, 1993), are devoted to the Birdsville Track, including history, route descriptions and information on its various highlights. It's recommended as a touring reference.

Maps
The small-scale map-cum-guide entitled *Birdsville and Strzelecki Tracks* published by Westprint Heritage Maps is a comprehensive if limited reference covering the major and minor tourist routes of South Australia's north-eastern corner. The guide – a single large folded sheet – is available from outlets in Birdsville, Marree, Innamincka and Leigh Creek.

For a more detailed coverage, you'll need the Marree, Kopperamanna, Gason and Pandie Pandie 1:250,000 topographic maps from AUSLIG. (A small section of the track also falls on the Cordillo sheet.) These maps are available through AUSLIG sales outlets in all capital cities.

Radio Frequencies
An average of about 25 vehicles use the Birdsville Track each day in winter, so if you require assistance, you shouldn't have to wait too long. In summer, however, the next vehicle can be anywhere from four hours to a week away. For this reason, anyone travelling the track outside the busy season should carry an HF radio fitted with frequencies for the RFDS bases at Port Augusta and Broken Hill; Port Augusta is the usual base for this region, but it doesn't hurt to have Broken Hill as a backup.

To speak to Port Augusta (callsign VNZ –

THE CENTRAL DESERTS

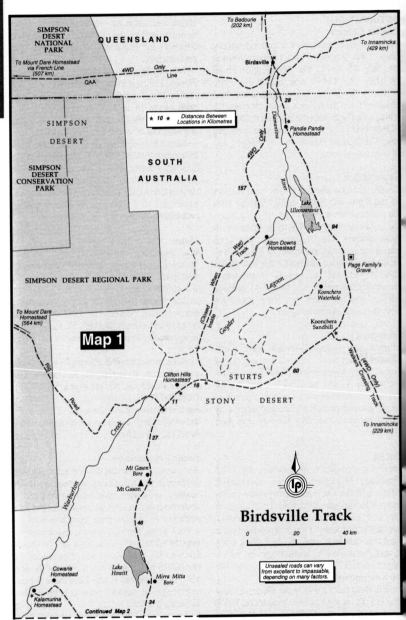

Birdsville Track

0   20   40 km

Unsealed roads can vary
from excellent to impassable,
depending on many factors.

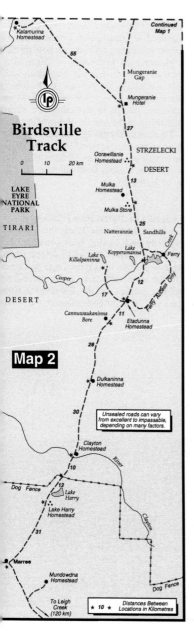

Victor November Zulu), use 8165 kHz between 7 am and 5 pm and 4010 and 6890 kHz between 7 am and 9 pm seven days. The station offers a 24-hour emergency service: use 4010 and 6890 kHz as daytime alarm frequencies and 2020 and 4010 kHz between 9 pm and 7 am. For more details, call the operator (☎ (086) 42 2044).

The Broken Hill RFDS base (callsign VJC – Victor Juliet Charlie) can be reached on 4055 and 6920 kHz between 7 am and 7 pm Monday to Friday. Alarm calls are received on 4055 and 6920 kHz during business hours and on 2020 kHz after hours. Call them (☎ (080) 88 0777) for further information.

SPECIAL PREPARATIONS
Water
It's essential to carry ample drinking water at all times on the Birdsville Track, as you never know when you may strike trouble. As well, local bores yield water that smells and has a laxative effect when you're not used to it. Marree's water supply is undrinkable, while Mungeranie's is best when chilled or drunk with tea and coffee. The Birdsville supply is quite acceptable and is regarded as the best bore water on the track. Always be careful collecting water from flowing arte-sian bores, as it usually comes out of the ground at scalding temperatures.

Flies & Mosquitoes
Bushfly plagues are the track's down side in warm weather. Fly veils for your face and an insect-screened gazebo for meals are essen-tial at such times; make sure to pack a net to cover any toddlers while they're having their daytime nap. Unfortunately, areas near wet-lands or shallow waterholes are usually swarming with mosquitoes, except on cold nights.

THE ROUTE
Birdsville
Queensland's most isolated town sprawls on a barren stony rise overlooking the Diaman-tina River, with the great silence of the Simpson Desert waiting just beyond its western edge. So remote that it wasn't visited

by a politician until 60 years after its birth, Birdsville is best known for its tremendous heat waves (temperatures of 50°C are common in summer), its annual race meeting and, of course, its association with the famous Birdsville Track. With a population of about 80, it presents a mere shadow of a more glorious past, which is still evident in several old stone buildings (such as its police station and the sole surviving pub).

Within 10 years of its establishment in the late 1870s, Birdsville had a population of 90 Whites and 180 Aborigines, as well as three pubs, a cordial factory and a border customs post. Prior to federation in 1901, a duty was levied on all cattle leaving Queensland and on all goods that came up from Marree; smuggling, particularly of whiskey, was apparently a thriving enterprise.

Federation removed the town's status, and the terrible drought that followed saw the population drift away. The final straw was the 1905 hurricane that levelled most of the town's less substantial buildings. After that

disaster, Birdsville almost expired, but i managed to hang on as a minor regiona centre. Increasing tourism has now restore a glimmer of prosperity – Birdsville' caravan park was recently improved, and new roadhouse has brought such dubiou conveniences of city life as fast food an self-serve pumps to this otherwise sleepy dusty town in the middle of nowhere.

The famous **Birdsville Races**, which tak place on the first weekend in September, se the town's population swell from 80 to 500 or more, as visitors from all over Australi fly in for the fun.

Birdsville to Clifton Hills (198 km)

Known as the Outside Track, this section i relatively new, having been constructed i the 1960s to allow trucks to detour aroun the swamplands of Goyder Lagoon. Gener ally the road surface is good, apart from bulldust patches on the Diamantina floo plain and, in Sturts Stony Desert, the rough

Sturts Stony Desert (DO)

Birdsville Races – a flying survival kit

Birdsville's big event each year is the two-day race meeting held in early September. Country races are often low-key occasions when the locals get together to bet on the horses and have a few beers, but Birdsville attracts thousands of people from all over the country. And they drink more than just a few beers.

The weekend is also notable for the hundreds of light aircraft that fly in. Normally one of the remotest runways in Australia, Birdsville aerodrome gets so busy that the Civil Aviation Authority has to issue special flight rules to help control the traffic. So being a city-based private pilot, I decided that this was an experience we ought to try.

Things to Do Getting drunk is the favourite activity, ahead of falling over and wearing tasteless T-shirts. Brawls used to be popular but these days the crowds are fairly good-natured.

Evening entertainment is provided by Fred Brophy's boxing troupe who set up their tent in the centre of town, right across from the pub. This must be one of the last traditional travelling boxing troupes left in Australia, if not the world, and their days may be numbered as such acts are now outlawed in several states – but not Queensland. The bass drum booms out across the desert as the spruiker works the crowd ('Here's Mad Dingo. Who reckons he could fight Mad Dingo?'). There's always a few blokes drunk enough to try a few rounds against the professionals, and no shortage of others who will pay to see them try.

Oh yes, there are horse races too, on Friday and Saturday. The bookmakers work with speed and efficiency to take your money, though you may find they move a bit slower if your horse wins.

Places to Stay & Eat Put your tent up right beside the plane, or just hang a plastic sheet over the wing. It can get cold at night and the ground is hard and stony so bring a good sleeping bag and mat.

The Diamantina Shire Council provides temporary toilets and showers, complete with hot running water straight from the bore. Your nose will remind you that the sewerage treatment pump runs 24 hours a day.

Don't count on eating at the pub, they're too busy selling beer. Hot dogs and steak sandwiches from the roadside stalls are as good as it gets, so bring your own.

Getting There & Away From Melbourne's Moorabbin Airport to Birdsville is about 1900 km as the crow flies, and even further on the route we took in a single-engine Piper Arrow. We had planned a loop through central Queensland, but then rain arrived over most of eastern Australia so we headed for Arkaroola in the Flinders Ranges instead. Amended flight plans are a fact of life for small aircraft.

The manager at Arkaroola who refuelled the Arrow was surprised that we were going to the Birdsville Races. He said we seemed too intelligent.

Undeterred, we continued on the last leg, a two-hour flight that took us into a 'designated remote area'. The flat brown uniformity of the desert offers very few recognisable landmarks so we had to trust the instruments and were quite glad when a town finally appeared ahead of us.

This had to be Birdsville – if only because no other town would have so many planes at the aerodrome.

Even if you're not a pilot or the friend of one, consider getting a few people together to charter a plane; check the Yellow Pages under 'Aircraft Charter' or 'Flying Clubs'. If you prefer a commercial carrier, Flight West (an Ansett-related airline) flies from Brisbane four times a week, but you will need to book months ahead.

You can of course go by road, and several outback tour operators offer camping trips to the races. Buses will also take your camping gear if it's too heavy or bulky for the plane.

On Sunday morning the first engines start before dawn, waking everyone except the terminally inebriated, and from first light there is a steady stream of planes taking off. For some, an early start is essential if they are to get home in daylight, even though the passengers might prefer to be sleeping off their hangovers. By midday Birdsville is just about empty again except for the council workers who are already cleaning up.

Getting Around The pub is right beside the aerodrome and you can walk to anywhere in the town in a few minutes. Shuttle buses will take you to the racecourse about 5 km south of town for a $2 donation to the local hospital.

Jim Hart

stony conditions often experienced in gibber country.

On leaving Birdsville, the track drops down onto the Diamantina River's coolabah-studded flood plain and almost immediately crosses the main channel. Rising in western Queensland, where it is fed by monsoonal rains, the river runs mainly as a braided channel for 800 km before flooding out in Goyders Lagoon, an extensive seasonal swamp about 80 km downstream from Birdsville. When full, the lagoon overflows into Warburton Creek, which meanders around the Simpson Desert's southern fringe before reaching Lake Eyre.

Minor floods are fairly common in the Diamantina but cause little inconvenience. However, major events (above eight metres) inundate large areas and can close the track for weeks at a time. The biggest flood in living memory occurred in 1974, when the river level reached 9.5 metres at Birdsville and completely swept away the Alton Downs homestead, causing a dramatic helicopter rescue of its occupants. While there have been 13 floods above six metres at Birdsville since 1970, there were no events of that magnitude in the 15 years prior to 1970.

Past the Diamantina bridge, the track spears southwards for nearly 100 km across broad blacksoil flats hemmed by long, yellow sand ridges. Clumps of coolabahs indicate that you're still on the flood plain, while lines of stunted coolabahs growing on some of the sandhills show how high the water can reach. Generally, however, there is no shade for anything much larger than a rabbit, of which there are thousands in the sandy areas. You may spot a flock of brolgas stalking purposefully among the lignum bushes, but more likely the only moving thing (apart from the flies) will be a dense whirling column of grey dust as a willy-willy dances across the plain.

Dead Man's Sandhill At 85 km from Birdsville you're opposite the grave of the Page family, about three km to the east and on the opposite side of Dead Man's Sandhill. There is no track in to the site, but you can walk or drive across the plain and climb the sandhill for a view over the waterhole where they met their appalling deaths. The dune, which parallels the road at this point, was named after an earlier tragedy in which five stockmen from Innamincka perished of thirst on their way to the Birdsville Races in the summer of 1912.

Sturts Stony Desert Approaching the 100 km mark the track suddenly leaves the flood plain and enters the armour-plated desolation of Sturts Stony Desert. Lying squeezed between the sand ridges of the Simpson Desert and the Strzelecki Desert, this enormous wasteland of polished, iron-stained stones was crossed on horseback by the explorer Charles Sturt on his search for the inland sea in 1845. He decided that it had 'no parallel on the earth's surface', and most people would agree with him. Sturt's description is as valid today as it was then:

...the whole expanse appeared to be as level as the ocean, nor had it as far as we could see a single shrub or a blade of vegetation upon it. The stones indeed lay so thick on the ground, that it was impossible for any herb to have forced its way between them.

Sturt's north-easterly route into the Simpson Desert, where lack of water and a wilderness of high sand ridges forced him to turn back, would have taken him across the Birdsville Track about 40 km past the Kooncher Sandhill.

Koonchera Soon after entering Sturts Stony Desert, you cross the southern end of the mighty Koonchera Sandhill. Although no monster at this end, it grows to become one of the largest dunes on the Diamantina flood plain. A waterhole near its northern end was the scene of a tremendous massacre of Aborigines in the early years of settlement, when a state of open warfare existed in the region. Later, a mob of over 1000 cattle heading towards Marree perished near the sandhill in a ferocious duststorm.

Looking south-eastwards from the crossing point, you can see what appears to be mighty range of fiery hills shimmering in the heat-shrouded distance. The mirage magnifies and deceives, but that red, Sahara-like sand ridge is still a spectacular sight close up. You drive close to it on the 4WD Walkers Crossing Track to Innamincka, which turns off five km past the Koonchera Sandhill.

Clifton Hills

Leaving Koonchera, you cross more sandhills and two or three coolabah creeks in the 33 km to **Melon Creek**, where you find good sheltered camp sites among shady trees. Soon after, the track heads out onto a vast stony plain dotted with distant trees. This is the inhospitable setting for **Clifton Hills homestead**, 43 km past Melon Creek, which was built here in the 1940s after an earlier site was buried by shifting sand. Perhaps this is the main reason why the station owners chose a stark moonscape of brown rocks on which to build their new home. Clifton Hills covers about 12,600 sq km – the largest station on the Birdsville Track.

Clifton Hills to Cooper Creek (183 km)

A few km past the homestead the track crosses several low rises that offer views of much kinder country down on Warburton Creek's broad flood plain. Although it's difficult to picture in drought times, a good rain or a flood transforms the blacksoil flood plains of this region into the Outback's finest cattle-fattening pastures. Between these rare events, the cattle survive on the hardy but nutritious saltbush that dominates much of the local vegetation.

This section is the track's most interesting, thanks to its varied scenery and poignant evidence of human endeavour. Its major highlights are the Mt Gason and Mirra Mitta bores, the Mulka ruins, Mungeranie Gap, Cooper Creek and camping at the Mungeranie Hotel. However, this section of road is also the roughest, with numerous bulldust holes and stony sections; heavy rain can render it impassable for days at a time. Past Mt Gason, the track follows almost exactly in the hoofprints of the mobs that once walked from Birdsville to Marree.

Mt Gason Eleven km past Clifton Hills, you arrive at the turn-off to the so-called Rig Road, which crosses the southern edge of the Simpson Desert to Mount Dare homestead. Some shady trees in a nearby creek make a good spot to boil the billy before starting out on this remote, 564-km, 4WD trek.

For the next 15 km the track winds over stony, undulating country on the edge of higher ground before arriving at a rare stand of the endangered **Mt Gason wattle** (*Acacia pickardii*). These low, tough-looking trees are known only from the Mt Gason area and another site near Old Andado homestead in the Northern Territory. This stand has been fenced, in an attempt to determine whether or not cattle and rabbits have any effect on regeneration.

Twelve km further on, you come to the turn-off to **Mt Gason Bore**, located on a stony rise two km to the west. This is the first in a string of artesian bores spaced roughly 40 km apart that took the mobs from Warburton Creek across the gibbers to Marree. Drilled in 1900, the bore reached a depth of 1350 metres and is the deepest between Clifton Hills and Marree. As at Mirra Mitta Bore and Cannuwaukaninna Bore, which you pass further south, scalding-hot water smelling of sulphur gushes from a pipe into an open drain that takes it away to cool sufficiently for cattle to drink. In winter the steam billows up like bushfire smoke and is visible for considerable distances. You'll find the stone remains of the old Mt Gason homestead on a rise a few hundred metres west of the bore.

Mt Gason itself is about five km south of the bore. Rising a mere 35 metres above the plain, this little mesa is the most prominent feature between Birdsville and Lake Harry – it only looks mountainous when you see it towering high in the shimmering mirage. It was named after Samuel Gason, the first police officer on the Birdsville Track. Later he supervised a massacre of Aborigines north of Alice Springs after an attack on the Barrow Creek Telegraph Station in 1874.

Mirra Mitta Bore Leaving Mt Gason Bore, you continue south across Sturts Stony Desert until, at 45 km, your eye is caught by an emerald-green patch of reeds sprouting among the gibbers. This is watered by a drain fed by Mirra Mitta Bore, which you pass a km further on. Although its setting is almost unbelievably hostile, the bore once boasted a drovers' store and eating-house as well as a thriving vegetable garden. The store was little more than an iron shed, which meant that its occupants froze on winter nights and thought they were roasting in hell during the blinding dust storms that lashed it in summer. Modern softies will find it amazing that, of their own free will, people actually spent years living in this unpromising spot.

Mungeranie Twenty-eight km past Mirra Mitta Bore you come to picturesque **Mungeranie Gap**, a major scenic highlight of the Birdsville Track. If you're here in the early morning or late afternoon, it's worth going for a walk among these colourful low hills to capture their stark beauty on film. The country changes to patchy bare gibbers and low sand ridges in the next eight km to **Mungeranie Roadhouse**, where a cold beer does wonders for the dust in your throat.

Among its services, the roadhouse offers sheltered camping sites beside the Derwent River. This perfect oasis of shady trees has permanent water from a flowing bore and, like other wetland areas on the track, is a beaut spot for bird-watchers. Half-dead coolabahs on the nearby sandhill are roosting places for the screeching flocks of corellas that come in daily to drink. When they land, it seems as if the bleached limbs have miraculously burst into great masses of white flowers, although flowers were never so noisy. Water birds such as ducks, herons and native hens are also common here.

Mulka The gibber plain continues to soften past Mungeranie, with grass and shrubby patches becoming more common. At 27 km

from the roadhouse you pass the old **Oorawillanie homestead**, now just a pile of rubble and scattered rubbish on a gravel rise beside the road. Drought put the station out of business many years ago, and it now forms part of the Mulka lease.

Low sand ridges begin to dominate over the next 13 km, which takes you to the crumbling stone ruins of the **Mulka homestead** and general store off on your right. Once a substantial building for these parts, it was the home of Mr and Mrs George Aiston for 20 years, until George died in 1944. The Aistons obviously loved this harsh country, as they'd previously lived at the Mungeranie police station, where George had been a mounted constable from 1912 to 1924; he'd resigned, bought Mulka station and established the store rather than be posted to Adelaide. A remarkable man, Aiston had co-authored the academic book *Savage Life in Central Australia* and became an honorary consulting anthropologist to the Australian Institute of Anatomy. After his death, Mrs Aiston stayed on and ran the store, before finally abandoning it in the mid 1950s.

Natterannie Sandhills Eight km past Mulka, you say goodbye to the gibbers of Sturts Stony Desert and enter a world of high yellow sand ridges that roll away on either side like jumbled waves on an ocean. Known as the Natterannie Sandhills, this area marks the convergence of the Strzelecki Desert to the east and the Tirari Desert to the west. Parts of the Tirari, which runs onto the eastern shore of Lake Eyre, are the closest thing Australia has to true desert.

These days the sandhills hold no terrors, as the road is firm and wide, but in the droving era they were a nightmare for anyone travelling in a motor vehicle. Even the famous Birdsville mail officer Tom Kruse, who was an expert in taking heavy vehicles through difficult country, found them tough going, as it was impossible to escape the boggy patches. Each time the truck became stuck, he had to unload it, get it back onto firm ground, then load up again.

It usually took him eight hours to get through the worst section of about 12 km. Unfortunately, the tyre-deflation method couldn't be used because the effort involved in hand-pumping the big tyres up again put the driver at risk of heat exhaustion or worse.

Kruse was forced to employ various strategies in his attempts to defeat the Natterannie Sandhills. Trucks fitted with dual rear wheels carried six-metre lengths of 75-mm bore casing which were laid on the sand such that the dual tyres could grip them and so find traction. Otherwise the slopes had to be laid with heavy iron sheets, which were liable to fly up and damage the vehicle's underparts if tackled at speed. He even tried using conveyor belts to create a half-track vehicle, but with limited success. This was a fearful journey in hot weather (which means most of the time here), yet the mail officers were forced to endure it every fortnight for many years until the road was finally upgraded.

Cooper Creek

After 17 km of harsh, scrubby sand ridges, the timbered Cooper Creek flood plain is a welcome sight, to say the least. Five km wide at the crossing, its outstanding feature is an abundance of spreading coolabahs, which invite you to stop and boil the billy. Coolabahs are exceptionally hardy trees, but even they can be killed by drought, as you'll see at the crossing's northern end. On the positive side, this area of standing dead timber does make a good source of firewood.

The Cooper rises in the central highlands of Queensland, and by the time its floodwaters flow into Lake Eyre they will have travelled about 1520 km. Floods seldom cut the Birdsville Track, but when they do the only way across for vehicles is via a ferry 10 km upstream from the road crossing. There are two things you must do on the ferry: get

Corellas come in to drink at the Derwent River at Mungeranie (DO)

out of the vehicle, and wear a life-jacket. These rules are in response to an accident many years ago when a crosswind blowing against the side of a truck caused the ferry to capsize. The truck driver, who was still sitting in his cabin, was drowned.

If a crossing on today's modest ferry is an adventure, you can imagine what its predecessor, the MV *Tom Brennan*, must have been like. This tiny steel craft was used to transport supplies across the Cooper after the 1949 flood, which was the first to reach the track in 30 years. After many years of occasional service, it's now permanently grounded on the southern bank as a memorial to the motor mail officers.

Cooper Creek to Marree (134 km)

This section's major highlights are Cannuwaukaninna Bore, and a lookout and ruins at Lake Harry. Although sandhills and gibbers still dominate, the country is generally kinder south of Etadunna. The road surface is good throughout, if stony in parts.

The Missionaries Leaving the Cooper behind, the track spears across a rolling gibber plain until, at 12.5 km from the *Tom Brennan* memorial, it passes a tall metal cross on the roadside at **Etadunna homestead**. This was placed in memory of the dedicated missionaries who came to this area in the 1860s with the intention of converting the local Aboriginal people to Christianity.

In 1866 a Moravian mission station was established at Lake Kopperamanna, three km north-west of the Birdsville Track crossing of Cooper Creek. However, faced with a searing drought and an unfriendly reception from the Aborigines, the Moravians departed for good the following year. Just months after the Moravians arrived, Lutheran missionaries from Germany built their Bethesda Mission beside nearby **Lake Killalpaninna**. It, too, was abandoned, but after this false start the Lutherans returned and established a permanent presence.

In its heyday in the 1880s, Bethesda had a population of several hundred Aborigines and a dozen Whites. It was laid out like a small town, with over 20 mud-brick buildings, including a church with a 12 metre-high tower complete with steeple, and survived largely on the income derived from its flocks of sheep. Despite extraordinary hardships, the missionaries persevered until they were forced to leave forever in 1917; their sheep flocks were devastated by drought and rabbit plagues. Today there is virtually nothing to indicate they were ever there, apart from a sad little cemetery and a few timber uprights. Nevertheless, the lake when full is a magnificent jewel among the sand ridges – you could easily spend several days there birdwatching, bushwalking and dining on yellowbelly, bream and rabbits.

Lake Killalpaninna is about 17 km northwest of Etadunna and is accessible by a 4WD track that turns off opposite the cross. Directions and permission to enter must be obtained from the homestead (☎ (086) 75 8308) – there is an entry fee of $5 per vehicle and a key deposit of $5. For information, ring the homestead.

Cannuwaukaninna Past Etadunna the track crosses a vast saltbush plain for most of the 11 km to Cannuwaukaninna Bore, where another small wetland attracts numerous birds. It also attracts swarms of mosquitoes, which makes a good reason not to camp nearby in warm weather. At one time there was a drover's store here, much like the one at Mirra Mitta, but it, too, has long since been demolished and carted away for use elsewhere. In this isolated country very little recyclable material goes to waste, particularly sheets of corrugated iron.

Leaving Cannuwaukaninna, you pass **Dulkaninna homestead**, at 28 km; the power line stretching across the gibbers to the house carries electricity generated by a water-driven turbine installed at the flowing bore. Thirty km further on, **Clayton homestead** is situated on the banks of a sandy creek which boasts the largest coolabahs between Marree and the Cooper Creek.

Lake Harry Ten km past Clayton you come to a grid in a rather ordinary-looking fence

This is, in fact, the world's longest artificial barrier. This is the famous **Dog Fence**, which protects the sheep flocks of south-eastern Australia from attack by dingoes. Once stretching for 9600 km, it is now reduced to 5490 km, between Ceduna (in the west of South Australia) and Jimbour (about 200 km north-west of Brisbane). The large brown claypan on your left at the grid is Lake Harry.

Soon after, the track passes close to a low mesa with twin wheel ruts climbing to its summit. Although only 40 metres above Lake Harry, the hill is arguably the most prominent feature seen along the track – it's worth climbing for the view. Those who make the effort will be rewarded with a timeless panorama over a vast patchwork carpet of brown, yellow and dark green, with the road a narrow white ribbon stretching from horizon to horizon. The final part of the climb is steep and loose and is not recommended to those who are inexperienced with 4WDs. Most people would be better advised to walk the last bit.

Continuing on for another eight km, you'll see the stone remains of the **old Lake Harry homestead** off on the left. Set amid a scatter of low, ochre-coloured hills, with the mirage giving an illusion of water in the nearby lake, this forlorn ruin dates from 1870, when it was built as an outstation of Mundowdna. Thirty years later Lake Harry became a camel depot for the bore-sinking gangs then working along the stock route between Marree and Mt Gason. Around the same time, the South Australian government established a trial plantation of over 2000 date palms, but although it looked promising at first, the experiment failed, largely because of poor water quality and a high labour requirement. Today not even a stump remains, but it's said you can still find Lake Harry palms lining the streets of Renmark and Mildura (on the Murray River).

Twenty-two km past Lake Harry, you cross a grid and enter sheep country, which is readily identifiable by the way the vegetation has been eaten out. Then the glittering iron roofs of Marree come into view across the plain and the end of the journey is just minutes away.

Marree

Established in 1883 on a gibber plain three km from Hergott Springs, Marree was a thriving railway town of 600 residents just two years later when the present Great Northern Hotel was under construction. The Great Northern Railway to Port Augusta and on to Adelaide immediately made Marree the focus for a vast area of the outback. In 1885 alone, between 40,000 and 50,000 head of cattle from Queensland and the Northern Territory were entrained for Adelaide, while camel trains carried supplies and general cargo to places as far away as the Gulf of Carpentaria. At one time Marree was home to 60 Afghani cameleers and their families, who lived in their own 'Ghantown', complete with mosque. In 1910, around 1500 camels were operating out of Marree.

However, progress sounded the death knell to Marree's role as a major regional centre when first the cameleers and then the droving teams were replaced by motor vehicles. Most people thought the end had come when, in 1980, the narrow-gauge railway to Alice Springs was replaced by the present service, which bypasses the town. Today, with a population of about 100, Marree clings to life as a minor regional centre and survives mainly on welfare cheques and tourism. Several fine old residences, the abandoned railway station and its grand old hotel are all that remain of its more prosperous past.

The Marree Picnic Races, held on the Queen's Birthday Weekend in June, attract a good crowd. The Marree Australian Camel Cup will take place every second year (on a day to be fixed), in July – the inaugural race was held in 1993.

DETOURS
Kalamurina (55 km one-way)
Camping is permitted at the Kalamurina (pronounced Kalla-murna) homestead (☎ (086) 75 8310), on the banks of Warburton Creek 52 km north-west of the

Mungeranie Hotel. Here you have a choice of a camping ground with toilets and hot showers ($10 per night per vehicle) or bush sites with no facilities among the coolabahs along the creek ($5). The area will appeal to nature-lovers, as the creekbank environment offers interesting bushwalking and plenty of bird life, particularly when the big waterhole near the homestead is full – it usually lasts 12 months after a flood and contains many fat yellowbelly and bream. At such times the contrast with the nearby sandhills and gibber flats is nothing short of fantastic.

The Kalamurina Road turns off the Birdsville Track 1.5 km north of Mungeranie. It is narrow and often rough, with plenty of bulldust patches, but is usually suitable for conventional vehicles in dry conditions. For information on access and camping, ring the homestead. Overcrowding is unlikely to be a problem, owing to the station's remoteness from tourist traffic.

Innamincka (229 km one-way)

The Walkers Crossing Track to Innamincka turns off the Birdsville Track 122 km south of Birdsville. Winding across the Cooper Creek flood plain and through the big sandhills of the Strzelecki Desert, it offers a different experience in remote touring. En route you pass producing wells of the **Moomba oil and gas field**, which is linked by pipelines to both Sydney and Adelaide. The track surface is generally good in dry conditions, but there are numerous soft sandy sections which restrict its use to 4WD vehicles only. It is definitely not recommended in summer, when the heat and lack of both water and other traffic create potentially dangerous conditions. Good camp sites are common almost right along the track.

Innamincka is a popular outback tourist destination, thanks to Burke and Wills, the **Coongie Lakes** and a series of large waterholes on Cooper Creek. As such, it offers an excellent range of facilities and services, including a hotel, general store, landing strip, fuel sales (diesel, super and unleaded petrol and Avgas) and camping facilities. Information on the town and sur-

rounding area, including conditions on the Walkers Crossing Track, can be obtained either from the Innamincka Trading Post (☎ (086) 75 9900) or the ranger (☎ (086) 75 9909).

As the track crosses the Innamincka Regional Reserve, you must hold a Desert Parks Pass, which costs $50 per vehicle and can be purchased from outlets in Birdsville, Marree and Innamincka. The Pass is your entry ticket to most conservation areas in South Australia's outback, so it's a good investment for those travelling further afield.

ALTERNATIVE ROUTES
The Inside Track

Until the 1960s the Birdsville Track south to Clifton Hills wound among the channels of Goyder Lagoon, which is filled by flooding of the Diamantina River. (When wet, this 1300-sq-km blacksoil swamp is a disaster for any sort of vehicle, so the present Outside Track was constructed to avoid it.) Known as the Inside Track, this original part of the old stock route covers about 157 km, which makes it 25 km shorter than the new road. It is the more scenic of the two, as well as being slower, rougher and relatively little used – in short, it's an attractive alternative for the more adventurous 4WD traveller. The Inside Track joins the Outside Track 60 km west of the Koonchera Sandhill and 16 km east of Clifton Hills homestead.

FACILITIES
Birdsville

See the Simpson Desert section earlier in this chapter for information on Birdsville's facilities.

Mungeranie

The isolated *Mungeranie Hotel* (☎ (086) 75 8317) offers a wide range of services and amenities, including a landing strip, public telephone, ice, shop (grocery lines and limited hardware items), takeaway liquor, takeaway and restaurant meals, basic motel-style accommodation, camping ground, minor mechanical and tyre repairs, and fuel (diesel, super and unleaded). The normal

Turn-off to Innamincka via the Walkers Crossing Track (DO)

trading hours for fuel are 8 am to 8 pm Monday to Saturday and 10 am to 4 pm on Sunday. A surcharge of $10 applies to fuel sales after 10 pm. Avgas should be ordered at least one month in advance.

Beds in the pub's small, air-conditioned motel units (two beds to a unit) cost $25 each. A little camping area down by the permanent waterhole has good shade and plenty of native birds, but no powered sites or firewood. The charge is $4 per adult.

Marree

See the Oodnadatta Track section earier in this chapter for information on Marree's facilities.

Bush Camping

Isolated bush camp sites offering good shelter from both sun and wind aren't all that common, owing to the fact that over vast areas the tallest vegetation is shrubby salt-bush. The best places to look for private sheltered spots are along creeks and in sandhill areas, but don't leave it too late in the day. Excellent camp sites are available on the Cooper Creek flood plain, with its many shady coolabahs. However, the clay sticks like glue when moist, so camping here is definitely not recommended in wet weather – at such times the sandhills offer the best option. You can camp at Lake Killalpaninna for a fee of $10 per vehicle per night, payable at the *Etadunna homestead* (☎ (086) 75 8308).

Strzelecki Track

What does a Polish-born, sometime eccentric explorer who called himself a 'count' have to do with inland Australia? Not very much really, but his name is immortalised in the name of the track and the creek it follows through the arid expanse of north-eastern South Australia.

For most modern-day travellers the Strzelecki Track (pronounced 'stres-LEK-ky'), which was originally a stock route, runs from Lyndhurst, a small hamlet on the northern edge of the Flinders Ranges, 560 km north of Adelaide, to Innamincka on historic Cooper Creek, a total distance of 460 km. In days of old this stock route continued north from Innamincka to Arrabury Station and on to the meeting of the Windorah-Birdsville road, 60 km west of Beetoota.

There is a choice of routes south of Innamincka, but the route described here is the original and best one, heading up Strzelecki Creek. Popular alternatives are included in the Alternative Routes entry later in this section, but none touch the old one for character or adventure.

The Strzelecki traverses extremely arid country. For the most part the track is well defined, graded and passable to a normal passenger car, when dry. Some sandy sections do occur in the northern areas, but these are normally fairly short.

HISTORY

Long before the arrival of Europeans, Aboriginal people lived along the permanent waters of Cooper Creek. Little remains of their passing in this harsh desert country, but not far from Innamincka a spectacular array of rock engravings testify to the rich culture that was once here.

It was Charles Sturt, one of Australia's greatest explorers, who discovered and named Strzelecki Creek on 18 August 1845, after Paul Edmund de Strzelecki, a self-taught geologist who, among a few other claims to fame, was the first European to discover, climb and name Australia's highest mountain, Mt Kosciusko, in 1840. Obviously Sturt was impressed by his reputation!

Sturt was on the last legs of his great central Australian trip, trying to find his elusive 'inland sea', when he stumbled across the life-saving waters of this ephemeral creek. Later he followed it north and discovered the more permanent waters of Cooper Creek, which, when in flood, feed Strzelecki Creek. The creek itself flows into Lake Blanche, but water rarely reaches this far south to flood the salt-encrusted bed.

The area around the junction of Cooper and Strzelecki creeks was to become etched into the Australian psyche, not by the successful exploits of Sturt and his men but by the death of the explorers Burke and Wills in 1860.

The route that was to become, for the most part, the Strzelecki Track, runs between the northern extremity of the Flinders Ranges and Cooper Creek, and was blazed by a top bushman who happened also to be a cattle thief.

Cattle-duffing (rustling) and the branding of cleanskins (unbranded cattle) was for many during the early days of settlement an easy way of stocking a station. But Harry Redford had bigger and better plans. With 1000 head of cattle stolen from Bowen Downs, north-east of Longreach in central Queensland, he set out on an ambitious and highly dangerous drive south over untracked country to Adelaide in South Australia. If it wasn't for a distinctive white bull amongst the cattle he stole, he would have got away with it, but he was finally caught and brought back to face justice at the Roma court in Queensland in 1873. However, his exploits in blazing a new track south was such that the jury declared him not guilty! While public outrage followed, Harry went on to freedom and to carve a name for himself as one of the greatest drovers in Australian history, with escapades in the Northern Territory and Far North Queensland.

Relying on waterholes and the very infrequent floods, the Strzelecki was always a much tougher route than the Birdsville Track, and at times the track was not used for years. Travellers also had to cross the infamous Cobbler Desert at the southern end of the track – a sea of deeply furrowed and convoluted sandhills.

Before the discovery of gas and oil in the Cooper Creek basin in the early 1960s, the track was largely unused. But the discovery and the development of the fields throughout this region has transformed the area. While the main roads have been upgraded, a network of lesser roads crisscross the deserts, some heading to wells and camps, while others just peter out in the sea of sand

INFORMATION

Tourist Information

Lyndhurst The small township of Lyndhurst doesn't have an information centre, but the Lyndhurst Hotel (☎ (086) 75 7781) can certainly let you know what the track is like.

The nearest medical facilities and police station are at Leigh Creek South, 38 km south of Lyndhurst. The Leigh Creek hospital (☎ (086) 75 2100) and the Leigh Creek South police station (☎ (086) 75 2004) are in Black Oak Drive.

Innamincka The Innamincka Hotel (☎ (086) 75 9901) and the Innamincka Trading Post (☎ (086) 75 9900) can help travellers with information about the surrounding area.

There are no medical facilities or police station in this remote region, the nearest being Leigh Creek South. However, Innamincka is covered by the RFDS, and in an emergency RFDS paramedics based at Moomba can be called in.

Other Information

Much of the horror of travelling the Strzelecki has been nullified since the Moomba gas fields came into operation in the 1960s. The track has been upgraded and rerouted to service these fields and those surrounding the main camp and processing plant at Moomba itself.

For the most part the track is a good dirt road where it is quite easy to travel at 80 km/h or faster. Keep out of the way of the road trains thundering either north or south loaded with all the paraphernalia that a vast oil and gas field requires.

Keep to the main track. While some of the oil rig roads may look to be a better route, they are private roads and are not for use by the public. Some lead long distances into the desert and just stop, and you can easily run out of fuel chasing dead ends. Contact the Northern Roads Condition Hotline (☎ (08) 11633) to check on current road conditions.

While there is no need to register with police, you should be aware that there are no supplies between Lyndhurst at the southern end of the track and Innamincka at the northern end. Moomba has no facilities for tourists and does not supply anything to passing travellers; only emergency assistance is given. However, there is a public telephone at the security gate at the entrance to Moomba.

As for most of the routes in this book, you need to be self-sufficient to travel this track. Summer can be hot, you will meet few other travellers, and a breakdown can be life-threatening.

Books & Maps

The best single map for the track is *Birdsville and Strzelecki Tracks* published by Westprint.

There is no guidebook covering this area and no dedicated book on the track itself. There are a number that cover the history of the surrounding area, including *Drought or Deluge: Man in the Cooper's Creek Region* by H M Tolcher; a small book called *Innamincka – the Town with Two Lives* (Innamincka Progress Association) by the same author is a little beauty containing many historic photographs.

For a comprehensive insight into the natural history of the area, the best book is *Natural History of the North East Deserts*, edited by M Tyler, C Twidale, M Davies & C Wells (Royal Society of South Australia).

Radio Frequencies

If you have an HF radio with you, the important frequencies to have are the RFDS bases at Broken Hill, Port Augusta and Mount Isa, and the Telstra (OTC) base in Sydney. While it is not imperative you have all of them, it's certainly the best position to be in.

For Broken Hill (callsign VJC), the primary frequency is 4055 with a secondary frequency of 6920. Port Augusta (callsign VNZ) has a primary frequency of 4010 and secondary frequencies of 6890 and 8165. Mount Isa (callsign VJI) has a primary frequency of 5110 and secondary frequencies of 4935, 6965 and 7392.

Sydney's Telstra base (callsign VIS) has the best land mobile operation set-up out of all the Telstra bases. You should have no problem getting them during the day. The Selcall for the beacon is 0899 and the operator is 0108. The main radphone OTC channels are 405, 607, 802, 1203 and 1602.

THE ROUTE
Lyndhurst
Lyndhurst, at the start of the Strzelecki Track, is 560 km north of Adelaide and is reached by a good bitumen road. It is considered by many to be the stepping-off point for the real outback. Here the bitumen ends, and the dirt road heading north leads to Marree

and the Birdsville and Oodnadatta tracks, while the Strzelecki Track heads off to the east.

Turning east just opposite the general store, the bitumen continues a short distance past the pub and over the disused railway line that once took the famous Ghan train all the way to Alice Springs. The track leads away in front of you.

This small outback town caters for passing travellers with fuel, food and accommodation.

One of the characters of the north is Talc Alf, a local artist whose abode and gallery is

just north of the pub. He carves sculptures out of the soft talc stone that is mined at nearby Mount Freeling. Give him a chance and he'll let you know his fairly strong views on politics, conservation, tourism, tourists and life in general.

Five km north of the town, close to the Marree road, are the **ochre cliffs and quarries** that were once worked by Aboriginal people. The ochre from these cliffs was traded as far north as the Gulf of Carpentaria and south all the way to the coast. Listed on the Register of the National Estate, these quarries, unlike many others, have never been mined by Europeans.

Lyndhurst to Strzelecki Crossing (275 km)

As you head north along the Strzelecki, the Flinders Ranges are a blue smudge on the south-eastern horizon. The track passes through arid pastoral country made famous by Sir Thomas Elder who, in the 1860s, had taken up the expansive Murnpeowie Station,

where he bred horses for the Indian Army and ran more than 100,000 sheep.

About 76 km from Lyndhurst a track heads east off the Strzelecki Track towards the **Mount Freeling talc mine**. Less than 30 km further north, the route passes through the **Dog Fence**. Sheep get more scarce as you head north, and once through the fence, you'll see only cattle.

Creek crossings are numerous across these vast plains, but most are kept in good condition and the creeks only flow after rare, heavy rain in the distant ranges. MacDonnell Creek is 50 km north of the fence, just north of the road; on the western bank of this occasional waterway are the ruins of **Blanchewater Station**.

In 1860, when the Burke and Wills saga was being played out, Blanchewater, then more commonly known as Mount Hopeless, was the northernmost station in South Australia. It was this property that the explorers were trying to reach when they perished. Blanchewater was also where Harry Redford

Ochre quarries north of Lyndhurst (TW)

sold his ill-gotten stock, rather than chance the sale at the Adelaide stockyards.

Forty km further on, a track from the south joins the Strzelecki. This track heads down past the eastern flank of the Flinders Ranges to Arkaroola and the Gammon Ranges National Park.

The **Montecollina Bore**, the only bore drilled on the Strzelecki Track for the use of drovers, is just over 20 km further north. This is a popular spot to camp. There are no facilities, and you should even bring your own wood if you want the enjoyment of a fire.

Pushing ever north, the Strzelecki Track passes through the **Cobbler Desert**, its eroded forms being blamed on the rabbit plagues and heavy stocking rates of last century.

The creek that the track takes its name from is now just a few km to the west, but the first time you see it will be some 50 km further north, and you know then that you are close to the **Strzelecki Crossing**.

About three km south of the crossing a track heads west off the main road, leading in a short distance to the creek and **Yaningurie Waterhole**. This is a popular spot to camp, and with its water and trees it is hard to beat. Bring your wood in from some distance away and *don't* cut trees down.

The main road, often called the Strzelecki Track but really the **Moomba Road**, swings across the river. See the later Alternative Routes entry for details on this route.

At the crossing itself, just past the track junction, the wide bed of the creek, dotted with its box trees, is a good place to stop and have a brew or even camp. On the northern bank, beside the Moomba Road, a wayside stop and picnic area has been established, but the creekbed is better.

Just before the main road crossing of Strzelecki Creek, a major track heads off to the right. Take this track, which puts you on the original Strzelecki Track heading up the creek to Merty Merty Station. This is by far the more enjoyable of the runs north and a little more of an adventure. For the most part,

the track winds up the wide bed of the creek and the run through the box trees can often flush some sample of wildlife, whether that be a solitary kangaroo, a lazy, well-fed wedge-tailed eagle or a scavenging dingo.

Along this route, be prepared for more of a track instead of a road, with some rough sections and some soft, sandy stretches.

Another track heads east from Strzelecki Crossing, this one to Bollards Lagoon station and the meeting point of three states at **Cameron Corner**, 95 km away. The *Border Store* (☎ (080) 91 3972) at the Corner has limited supplies and fuel (diesel, super and unleaded).

Strzelecki Crossing to Innamincka (157 km)

From the crossing, the track begins to follow the normally wide dry creekbed north. It makes a pleasant change from the harsh gibber and sand country you passed through further south. This first section of the track between here and Merty Merty Station is probably the most unused part of the Strzelecki, and the track is sandy in places.

As you head north, the sand ridges become more pronounced, but because you are heading in the direction in which the dunes are running, they are really no problem.

About 43 km north of the crossing, **Merty Merty Station** will be seen close to your left-hand side, while a large reddish sandhill is prominent stretching away to the south on your right. Another track, looking a bit better than the one you are on, joins the Strzelecki from the right, close to the homestead. This leads to Cameron Corner, 134 km away, via Bollards Lagoon homestead.

Just north of Merty Merty Station is a signposted track junction. The track coming in from the west is from the Moomba Road, while the Strzelecki Track veers north. This is a popular spot for a photograph as the sign is unique – a bush-made, welded type rarely seen elsewhere.

A few km north you will begin to see the first signs of a gas field: large, robotic arms wave to their computer master's beat, pumping the liquid gold across the sand ridges to Moomba. A couple of these pumps can easily be seen just off to the east. Strictly speaking you shouldn't approach them, but most travellers are interested enough to do the short diversion. Please don't interfere with this equipment – the producers are near-paranoid about vandalism, and access would definitely suffer if any damage was done.

Less than 70 km north of Merty Merty is a major T-junction and a better class of road. Turn right at the junction and then turn left after a couple of km at another signposted junction. From here it is another 45 km of easy running north to Innamincka and the end of the Strzelecki Track.

Innamincka

On the banks of Cooper Creek is the small town of Innamincka. Here you can buy a cold beer, have a meal and fuel up. There's plenty to do in the surrounding area, so allow a bit of time to soak up the atmosphere and enjoy the waters of the historic, picturesque creek.

Close to the Queensland border, Innamincka owes its beginnings to the government's customs post which taxed all the stock travelling from one colony to another. Such a hold-up of stock and thirsty drovers meant that a pub soon followed to help quench the thirst of the hard-working men who pushed the stock south to markets. With their revelry came a need for a police station and lock-up, and by the turn of the century, Innamincka was a town of four or five buildings.

With the advent of free trade between the states as a result of Federation, the customs post went in 1901. But the years that followed were the years that saw Sidney Kidman, the 'Cattle King', build his empire, and the Cooper fairly hummed with the clash of branding irons and the rattle of stirrup and spur. The pub and the police post were still required.

In 1928 the **Australian Inland Mission** (AIM) built a hostel there, and a few years later it and the Strzelecki Track played a part in John Flynn's establishment of the Royal Flying Doctor Service.

Until the beginning of WW II, a mail truck

ploughed its way up the track to Innamincka from Farina, now just a few old stone ruins south of Lyndhurst. The war saw an end to that, and afterwards the mail came up every two weeks from Broken Hill via Tibooburra in New South Wales.

In 1951 the AIM closed down the hostel and within a year the police post and the pub had gone as well. The town was dead, and a couple of the stations around the area claimed the remains – the pub becoming stockmen's quarters for nearby Innamincka Station, while the hostel was partly demolished and anything worth salvaging transported to Arrabury Station, 160 km north. About the only thing of substance left was the monster bottle heap that stretched for over 200 metres and was over a metre high. It was obvious why Innamincka needed a police post.

With the 1960s came the search for oil and gas and big strikes of both in the surrounding dune country. In 1974, Mike Steel, a tour operator, traveller and part-time author, saw the potential in the area and started what you see today.

Nowadays there are around 12 permanent residents of Innamincka, which is about as big as it's ever been. Mind you, there is a good chance you'll arrive when the place is seemingly overflowing with stockmen from the nearby stations, oil workers from Moomba, road workers from up and down the track, and a few other travellers.

A picnic **race meeting** is held each year, generally towards the end of August, and that really makes the place bounce. Then there may be a few hundred to over a thousand people in town! Needless to say, accommodation is stretched at these times and even camping close to town can be crowded.

Take the opportunity to visit **Coongie Lakes**, a short distance to the north-west. It is a spectacular wetland alive with birds. The lakes form one of the great freshwater lake systems in central Australia and rely on the occasional flooding of the Cooper for their ephemeral waters. Coongie Lake itself is the southernmost lake of this complex and the only one travellers are allowed to visit. It is

THE CENTRAL DESERTS

Ruins of Blanchewater Station (R & VM)

also the one with the most water. The whole region is a haven for bird life; in the years of plenty when the lakes are full, the area is bursting at the seams with all forms of animal life.

ALTERNATIVE ROUTES

North of the Strzelecki Crossing there are a number of alternative routes north.

The **Moomba Road** heads north from the Strzelecki Crossing for 95 km to Moomba, the high-tech heart of these spread-out oil and gas fields. Some 44 km up this main road from the crossing, and 50 km south of Moomba, a track heads east, meeting up with the real Strzelecki Track just north of Merty Merty Station.

From Moomba you can also head east for 40 km and join up with the Strzelecki proper, or head north for 24 km before swinging east for the last 60-odd km to Innamincka. All these routes are good dirt roads and are well maintained.

The road north from Moomba is handy for those who want to travel to the **Walker Crossing Track** that gives access, when opened, across the Cooper Creek flood plain to the Birdsville Track, 185 km north of Moomba. Further along the Moomba-Innamincka road, access to a number of historical sites along the Cooper is easy, but as they are also within an easy drive of Innamincka, don't bother heading for them from the old Strzelecki Track.

ACTIVITIES
Canoeing

Canoeing is excellent along the Cooper and at Coongie Lakes. These are both exceptional wildlife experiences, with a host of waterbirds to regale you with their variety and beauty.

One of the best canoe trips starts at the far end of Cullyamurra Waterhole, where the vehicle access ends. From there you can take an easy paddle upstream as far as the Innamincka Choke and check the Aboriginal engravings nearby, or head off downstream all the way to the causeway at Innamincka itself. It makes for a very pleasant day.

The other waterholes in the area also offer some interesting paddling.

If you want to rent a canoe, contact Jeff Mueller (☎ (086) 75 9591); his house is 350 metres behind the hotel at Innamincka. A two-person Canadian canoe costs $30 for a 24-hour hire.

Fishing

Anywhere there is a decent stretch of water there is the chance of catching a feed of fish.

These days the amateur with a rod and line has a good chance of catching a feed, as nets have been banned for a few years now – and more importantly, the ban is policed. The yellowbelly is the prize catch of these waters, and it tastes delicious.

ORGANISED TOURS

Local tours can be arranged at the hotel or general store in Innamincka. Given enough warning, they can take you out to Coongie Lakes or along the Cooper to the Dig Tree and the other historic places scattered along the waterway.

A number of tour operators include the Strzelecki Track and the area around Innamincka on their tours. Few include it as the total package, but rather as a route to do and a place to see while on their way to somewhere else. That's a pity really, but their loss is the independent traveller's gain. If that is what you want to do, the best spot to start is Tourism South Australia (☎ (08) 212 1505), 1 King William St (PO Box 1972), Adelaide, SA 5000.

There are a couple of companies that include the Cooper and Coongie Lakes in guided bushwalking trips. EcoTrek (☎ (08) 383 7198), PO Box 4, Kangarilla, SA 5157, and Exploranges (☎ (08) 294 6530), 37 Walker St, Somerton Park, SA 5044, have irregular departures.

FACILITIES
Lyndhurst

The *Lyndhurst Roadhouse* (☎ (086) 75 7782), in the centre of town, is the last chance to buy fuel (diesel, super and unleaded), a hamburger, cool drinks and an ice cream. It also stocks more traditional bushie supplies, such as Akubra hats and tins of baked beans, and general food items.

The *Lyndhurst Hotel* (☎ (086) 75 7781), just a few hundred metres away, is the newest building in town because a fire totally destroyed the original a few years back. The pub offers travellers cold beer, meals and friendly banter. Accommodation is also available in single or triple rooms, ranging from $25 a day for a single to $60 for a triple. The costs are reduced the longer you stay. A cooked breakfast is available and meals are also served for lunch and dinner. On Sunday there is a barbecue, and on Friday there's a special fish dinner for just $5. The bar and dining areas are air-conditioned and they are

Strzelecki Track (R&VM)

also good spots to find out what the track is like.

If you need a spare tyre, a battery or limited repairs, the Strzelecki Tyre Service (☎ (086) 75 7783), close to the roadhouse, can provide all you need.

Lyndhurst has no bank or post office, and EFTPOS is not available. The nearest banks and post office, with full facilities, are at Leigh Creek, 38 km south.

For travellers, toilets and showers are situated close to the main road junction. People heading east may think nothing of them, but those coming west may revel in the luxury.

As far as camping is concerned, there is nothing at Lyndhurst that comes even close to a camping ground. If you are desperate,

the closest, best spot to erect a tent is about five km north of the town, where the main road crosses a grid. Off to the east, a line of low scrub marks a low depression and a spot to camp. It's not brilliant.

Innamincka

The *Innamincka Hotel* (☎ (086) 75 9901) offers cold beer, meals and accommodation, and it's a good place to obtain information about the surrounding area. If you are there on Sunday evening during the tourist season, don't miss the banquet of roasts at the pub. For $10 there is a great feed, a roaring log fire and plenty of friendly company, including most of the locals. The accommodation

---

Historic Sites of the Cooper

Aboriginal Sites Aboriginal rock engravings can be found at the far end of Cullyamurra Waterhole, close to the bottleneck on the Cooper known as the Innamincka Choke. To find this spot, follow the vehicle track out along Cullyamurra Waterhole to its end and then walk along the foot track to the rock area that can be seen on both sides of the creek.

This is a good spot to explore, with a couple of nice swimming holes and some good fishing. If you are camped on the waterhole, there is no better way to get to the site than by canoe.

Explorers Signs of the earliest White explorers can also be seen in this region. While the township has a monument to both Charles Sturt, who discovered and named the creeks in this area during his 1845 expedition, and to Burke and Wills, who perished near here in 1860, it is the latter whose monuments and camps evoke the most poignant memories (see History in the Facts about the Outback chapter for more about Burke and Wills).

Their camp, near a tree now known as the Dig Tree, can easily be visited from Innamincka. Sitting under the shady trees that surrounded the camp and that still exist today, watching a turbid river flow past, you cannot help but be struck by the irony of it all. Here was an area that supported hundreds of Aborigines and yet Burke and his men starved to death.

The blazed Dig Tree that played such an important role in the saga still stands at the site and is probably the most important reminder of early European exploration in Australia. Nearby are a couple of other blazes and carved trees which, although dating back a few years, are not part of the original saga. A memorial to Wills can be found at the western end of Tilcha Waterhole; Burke's memorial is on the edge of Burke Waterhole. The place where Charles Grey died, south-west of Coongie Lakes at a place called Lake Massacre, is not open to travellers.

About seven km west of Innamincka is a marker indicating the place where John King was found alive by Alfred Howitt's party. Howitt's depot camp on the Cooper is marked by a monument on the north side of the river. This spot can be found by following the road from the Innamincka township towards and then past Innamincka Station. A track heads down to the river 11 km past the station to the site of the camp.

Other Sites Finally, there are the ruins of the Australian Inland Mission hostel at Innamincka itself. These ruins are among the most important in outback Australia, and efforts are under way to bring this building back to its former glory. ■

is in motel-style, air-conditioned units costing $30/50 for singles/doubles.

Right next door is the *Innamincka Trading Post* (☎ (086) 75 9900). Here you can buy most of your daily requirements such as milk and bread, plus souvenirs, maps and books and the like. They also supply fuel – diesel, super and unleaded, camping gas and Avgas. The Trading Post also has accommodation available for an overnight stop or longer in the *Burke Lodge Cabins*, with three two-bedroom cabins available for $25 per person. Kids are charged $15, while there is no extra cost for toddlers. Each cabin has four beds, and there is an outside barbecue area for your use. Tea or coffee-making facilities can be provided if required, along with a continental-type breakfast for $5.

Innamincka has no banking or post office facilities, and EFTPOS is not available. However, major credit cards are readily accepted at the hotel and trading store.

Just a stone's throw away are some excellent toilets and showers which are a boon to travellers and campers. A donation to help in the upkeep is greatly appreciated. A solar-powered telephone nearby is your link with the outside world.

At Innamincka you can also hire a canoe, get some welding done and even get a few things repaired. Contact the Trading Post for details.

Camping is allowed down near the creek on the town common. If you want to camp elsewhere in the area (and there are plenty of magical spots to camp), you will need a Desert Parks Pass, which is available from the ranger at Innamincka if you haven't picked one up beforehand.

Camping along the Cooper

There are numerous camp sites spread along the river both up and downstream from Innamincka, but you'll need a Desert Parks Pass.

One of the most popular sites is *Cullyamurra Waterhole*, about 13 km east of Innamincka. It is a spectacular waterhole, stretching upriver for at least six km to a natural rock bar called the Innamincka Choke. This waterhole is reputedly the deepest waterhole in central Australia and has been measured at 28 metres. It has never been known to dry up. One of the best ways to enjoy this waterhole and any others in the area is by canoe.

Tall, gnarled gums line the creek and offer shade for camp sites, but wood for fires is scarce. Much damage has been done in recent years to the magnificent trees along this section of river by unthinking people chopping down branches and even whole trees to feed their fires. If you must have a wood fire, bring in the firewood from elsewhere. In such a popular spot, gas fires are better.

West of Innamincka, along the 15-Mile Track that is also the route to Moomba, is *Queerbidie Waterhole* (or Queerbidie WH), 2.5 km west of Innamincka. A further 1.5 km on, a turn-off towards the river leads to a number of sites spread along a short section of waterway. Some of these sites are a little back from the water, while at others you will need to carry your gear a short distance to get close to the creek.

Less than 5.5 km west from the township on the Innamincka-Moomba road, another track heads off to the river and to *Ski Beach*. Camping is also possible further west along this main road at Kings Marker (seven km west of Innamincka), Minkie WH (12 km) and Tilcha WH (14 km).

While most of the abovementioned sites have rubbish bins, it's a much better idea to take your rubbish to the rubbish pit at Innamincka.

Camping at Coongie Lakes

The trip out to Coongie Lakes, north-west of Innamincka, is 106 km each way, and in dry weather a normal car can get there. You need a Desert Parks Pass to travel this road and to camp. You'll pass through a number of different vegetation types on your drive out to the lake. While the return trip can be done in one day, it is better to spend a little longer.

Along the track there are some pleasant camping spots: Bulyeroo WH (37 km from Innamincka), Scrubby Camp WH (45 km) and Kudriemitchie WH (85 km). Up to Kudriemitchie you are allowed wood fires and even generators and dogs; further north they are all banned.

Don't forget that this area is part of a working cattle station and cattle may be seen along the way. Take care.

Just before the track ends at Coongie, a couple of turn-offs to the east lead to some camp sites along the lake shore. Remember that only gas fires are allowed out here. Rubbish can be dumped only at the rubbish disposal pits at Kudriemitchie and Scrubby Camp.

Airstrips

Every homestead along the Strzelecki has an airstrip close by. These are meant for light aircraft and can be dotted with anthills, potholes and animals.

Innamincka has a well-used airstrip that sees many people flying in for a weekend or longer. The airstrip is on the highest ground around and only a short distance from the pub. At times, when the Cooper is running a banker, this is the only way supplies and people can move in and out of the tiny outpost. Avgas is usually available – contact the Trading Post for more details. If you are flying in and will need fuel, it's best to check beforehand.

ALTERNATIVE TRANSPORT
Bus

The Stateliner bus company (☎ (08) 233 2777), 21 Mackay St, Port Augusta, SA 5700, services Lyndhurst once a week, with a bus departing from Port Augusta for Lyndhurst each Thursday. The return fare is $102.60. Check with them for a current timetable.

Air

Innamincka is serviced by plane each Saturday by the Augusta Airways mail run. A single one-way fare costs $165. Contact them at Port Augusta Airport (☎ (086) 42 3100) for flight details; the mailing address is Port Augusta Airport, Port Augusta, SA 5700.

Ruins of the Australian Inland Mission at Innamincka (R & VM)

Cooper Creek (R & VM)

Gunbarrel Highway

The Gunbarrel Highway was the first link between central Australia and Western Australia. Built to service the Woomera Rocket Range and the Giles weather station, it was completed in 1958.

Today much of the 'real' Gunbarrel is out of bounds to normal travellers and there is a little confusion as to which of the useable roads is really the Gunbarrel. Some call the Laverton-Warburton road the Gunbarrel, but

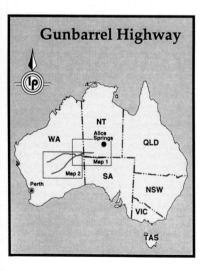

Gunbarrel Highway

NT
WA   Alice Springs
      QLD
      Map 1
Map 2 SA
Perth
      NSW
      VIC
      TAS

it is definitely not. The road east from Carnegie Station to Docker River is the real Gunbarrel – well, a lot of it is. Some of the original Gunbarrel now passes through an Aboriginal area that to most of us is a 'no go' area. The diversion via Warburton Aboriginal Community which some call the Gunbarrel, isn't.

Likewise, the stretch of road between Docker River and Ayers Rock is called the Gunbarrel, but in fact it's not. The real Gunbarrel heads south from Giles weather station, crossing into South Australia just south of the Northern Territory border. It then parallels the border before passing back into the Territory and finishing at Victory Downs Station. Much of this route is also a 'no go' area for travellers. Confused? Well, aren't we all?

This text looks at the Gunbarrel in today's accepted terms, keeping as much as possible to the original route but obviously staying away from the areas that demand very special permission to enter. In that light, the trip starts at Yulara, the resort servicing visitors to Uluru (Ayers Rock), and heads west to Docker River Aboriginal Community before crossing the border to Giles weather station and then striking south-west in a gunbarrel-straight line to Warburton – it's not really all that straight, but that's the general idea. From this point the route swings north, joining with the ridgy-didge Gunbarrel west of Jackie Junction. From there we are on the original Highway all the way to Carnegie Station.

HISTORY

There was a flurry of activity in this region back in 1873 when three explorers were vying for the honours of discovering what lay between the Overland Telegraph Line, which stretched across central Australia from north to south, and the Western Australian coast. Major Peter Warburton pushed north from Alice Springs, finally making the coast near De Grey, north of present-day Port Hedland, but almost dying in the attempt.

William Gosse left Alice eight days after Warburton had set out, but Gosse and his men, although initially heading in much the same direction as Warburton, swung south. They eventually became the first Whites to see Uluru, which Gosse named Ayers Rock. In his journeys south and west from Ayers Rock, Gosse also named the Mann and Tomkinson ranges, before giving up his quest to cross the continent near Mt Squires in the Cavenagh Ranges of Western Australia.

Ernest Giles had already been in the region west of Alice in 1872. Later he tried to cross a vast salt lake he called Lake Amadeus. To the south he could see a cluster of rounded peaks, the highest of which he called Mt Olga. However, it was Gosse who actually got to the Olgas before him – by a month, a year later.

A year later, from the Olgas, Giles and his men, who included William Tietkins as his second-in-command, pushed south-west into the desert, establishing a depot at Fort Mueller, west of the Tomkinson Ranges. Retreating back to more permanent waters, at a place he called Circus Water in the Rawlinson Ranges, he tried to push west for the next three months. Time and again he was repulsed.

During March 1874 Giles explored and named the Petermann Ranges and in April, from a depot he called Fort McKellar in the Petermanns, he gave his westward push one last effort. He took with him a young stockman by the name of Alf Gibson, and so one of the great stories of the exploration of Australia began. One hundred and forty km west of Circus Water, Gibson's horse knocked up. Giles gave him his horse and, knowing that it was impossible to continue, sent Gibson back to bring help from their base camp. Gibson never made it. Giles, alone and on foot, with hardly a skerrick of water, did! Arriving at Circus Water, he

---

Len Beadell – the Last Explorer

Len Beadell was born in 1923 in the Sydney suburb of West Pennant Hills. He was just 12 when he started his career as an unpaid assistant surveyor for the Sydney Water Board. He started working full-time with the board after finishing high school, but was conscripted in 1942. After serving in New Guinea, he rejoined the water board at the end of the war to help map remote Arnhem Land. A little later he was asked to do a job for the Defence Department: lay out a rocket range!

It was the beginning of the town of Woomera and the Woomera Rocket Range, which were later to lead to the A-bomb tests at Emu and Maralinga.

It was also the beginning of the last phase of Australian exploration. Len and his men, whom he later christened 'the Gunbarrel Road Construction Party', carved out a series of roads through 2.5 million sq km of wilderness west of Alice Springs.

He started to survey the Woomera range in 1947; it was not until 1952 that he was called on to find the site for Emu. The next year was taken up with building the road from Mabel Creek (then on the Stuart Highway) to Emu, preparing for the A-bomb tests at Emu, and then picking a new site which was to be called Maralinga. Surveying around Maralinga took up all of 1954 and much of the next year, and the remainder of 1955 was spent making the road between Emu and Maralinga. Late that year the first 160 km of the Gunbarrel Highway was completed, from Victory Downs to Mulga Park. This was Len Beadell's first major road, and also his most well known.

In 1956 the site for the Giles weather station was chosen and the Gunbarrel was continued out to this new site. Building an airstrip at Giles was next on the agenda, and the rest of the year was taken up with a new road south from Giles to Emu via Mt Davies, although that road wasn't finished until 1957.

The last section of the Gunbarrel, west to Carnegie Station, a little east of Wiluna in Western Australia, was pushed through during 1958. It was the first road link across central Australia and, as the name suggests, it was as straight as Len could make it – 'to keep the country looking tidy,' as he says during his lecture tours.

That same year he was awarded the British Empire Medal for his surveying work and his opening up of this part of the country.

drank his fill and came upon a dying wallaby. 'I pounced upon it and ate it, living, raw, dying – fur, skin, bones, skull, and all,' he was to write later; his only regret was that he couldn't find its mother!

Two days later, Giles staggered back into the depot at Fort McKellar and, finding Gibson missing, immediately turned back to look for him, taking Tietkins with him. Both nearly died in the effort. Giles named the desert the Gibson Desert. Retreating back to civilisation, Giles arrived back at Charlotte Waters in July 1874, and a couple of months later learnt that both Warburton and Alexander Forrest had crossed the western half of the continent.

Giles was still determined to write his name in the history books. His third expedition, eight months later, was the relatively short trek from Fowlers Bay, on the southern coast, to Finnis Springs south of Lake Eyre.

Again he nearly died of thirst, but it proved to him that camels, of which he had two on that trip, were the best animals to use.

His fourth and most successful expedition left a month after his third had finished, in May 1875. Striking north and west from Port Augusta, Giles used the waterholes he had discovered on the previous trip, passing the northern end of Lake Gairdner. Finally, after much hardship, he and his men, Tietkins included, crossed the Great Victoria Desert, discovering a life-saving spring that Giles called Queen Victoria Springs. In November the expeditioners were welcomed into Perth, and the parties followed. Giles, though, was still fired with the thought of exploring and finding rich pastoral land.

Leaving the party scene in January 1876, he and his men, with camels, pushed north along the Western Australian coast and then inland to the Ashburton River, about 480 km

---

Other roads and sites followed. In 1960 the Sandy Blight Junction Road was built, while the following year a road was pushed from Sandy Blight Junction east to the existing Northern Territory road system near Mt Liebig, 290 km west of Alice Springs. In 1962 the road between Sandy Blight Junction and the Gary Junction via Jupiter Well was completed, as was the Anne Beadell in the south and the Connie Sue Highway between Rawlinna and Warburton. In 1963 the Gary Highway was pushed north and then west, via Well 35 on the Canning Stock Route, to Callawa, a little north-east of Marble Bar.

The last road graded by the Gunbarrel Road Construction Party was the Windy Corner-Talawana track, via Well 23 and Well 24 on the Canning. It was, as the title on Len's last book suggests, the end of an era.

Many of the roads bear the names of his wife and children. There's the Anne Beadell Highway, after his wife, the Connie Sue Highway, after their oldest daughter, the Gary Highway after their son, and Jackie Junction after their youngest daughter.

A noted author, his seven books recount his times and adventures. Those books, *Blast the Bush*, *Bush Bashers*, *Beating about in the Bush*, *Too long in the Bush*, *Still in the Bush*, *End of an Era* and *Outback Highways*, have been reprinted many times. Illustrated with his own cartoon-like drawings and photos he took at the time, they capture an innocence long gone in Australia. But they also capture the excitement and the adventure of what these pioneers were doing.

In the lecture tours he still does regularly around Australia he speaks to packed houses. His wit, style and modesty are charming, and the stories are so real, so close to our age, that they are uniquely inspiring.

Len retired in 1988 and now has more time to spend in the bush that he loves. That year saw him awarded an Order of Australia Medal, and the Mount Palomar Astronomical Observatory in California named an asteroid after him in recognition of the work he had done in opening up central Australia, enabling them to undertake their studies of meteorite impact craters. In 1989 the governor of South Australia presented him with an Advance Australia Award. Since then he has been involved in three documentaries, including one on Woomera and one titled *Beadell Country*.

Generally, he joins a 4WD tour at least once a year as a special guest taking people on 'his' tracks. For their own holidays, he and his family still head out along the roads he built. ∎

Mt Beadell (R & VM)

from the coast. From a depot at this point in May, he turned his eyes and thoughts east – almost 800 km away was where he and Gibson had parted.

Striking east, he almost lost the camels when they ate a poisonous plant, but once they had recovered, Giles pushed on, finally reaching the Alfred & Marie Range, the furthest point west he had sighted on his 1874 expedition. By late August the group were back on the Overland Telegraph Line at Peake, after passing along their old route through the Rawlinson, Petermann and Musgrave ranges.

While Giles was the first to do a double crossing of the western deserts, he is probably Australia's least known successful explorer. He died penniless and unknown in 1897. His book *Australia Twice Traversed*, originally published in 1889, occasionally appears as a facsimile. It is one of the most readable of all the books written by Australia's explorers.

In 1891 the Elder Scientific Exploring Expedition set forth from northern South Australia, heading west to the Everard Ranges, Fort Mueller and Mt Squires, then south to Queen Victoria Springs and Esperance on the coast before striking north to Lake Wells. Led by David Lindsay, with Lawrence Wells as his lieutenant, it was the first of the 'scientific' expeditions that were to fill in the gaps left by the earlier explorers.

Over the next 40 years, the country along the Overland Telegraph Line and around Alice Springs was taken up as pastoral country. By 1900 gold had been discovered in a couple of isolated regions north-west and east of Alice, and with the discovery of the untold riches at Kalgoorlie and Coolgardie in Western Australia, prospectors looked at the region along the Petermanns. One was Harold Lasseter, who in 1930 led an expedition to find a 'golden reef' he had supposedly discovered 33 years previously.

The legend of the reef and the Lasseter story has been told again and again. While the expedition had struck west from Alice

Springs, Lasseter was later to head south, eventually on his own, to Ayers Rock and then west through the Petermann and Rawinson ranges to a point somewhere around Lake Christopher.

Lasseter states in his diary that he found and pegged the reef on 23 December. Retracing his steps, his camels bolted when he was about 50 km east of present-day Docker River Aboriginal Community. Realising he couldn't make it back to Ayers Rock and safety, he stayed in a cave on the edge of a creek for a few weeks, waiting for a rescue party that he was sure would be sent to look for him. Despairing, he finally set out on the impossible task, eventually collapsing and dying beside Irving Creek. His body and diary were later recovered, and while other search parties and gold-prospecting parties went out, and still do, no sign of his fabled reef has ever been found. If it was a hoax, Lasseter paid the supreme price!

Apart from the occasional prospector, the next person on the scene was Len Beadell, building the odd road or two for the Woomera Rocket Range.

The Gunbarrel Highway, which he constructed, ran between Victory Downs, west of Kulgera on the Stuart Highway, headed west, and then south along the northern edge of the Musgrave Ranges. From there the Highway followed the Mann and Tomkinson ranges before swinging north to a spot in the Rawlinson Ranges where Len Beadell established Giles as a weather station. Today the station is used for helping amass the information for weather forecasts and for aircraft flying 13,000 metres overhead, but its original purpose was to ensure that the day chosen for the big bangs at Emu or Maralinga were perfect and that the wind was in the right direction.

Passing along the southern edge of the Rawlinsons, Beadell's route swung south to Warburton Mission. North of the mission he established a road junction for the last push, which ran west and then slightly north to Mt Everard before swinging south, passing the Mungilli Claypan and Mt Nossiter, and finally reaching the easternmost outpost of civilisation in Western Australia, Carnegie Station.

This road, the first across central Australia, took from 1955 to 1958 to survey and build and ushered in the modern world to this ancient landscape. It was Len who called it the Gunbarrel Highway.

INFORMATION
Tourist Information
The best places for tourist information are at Alice Springs or Ayers Rock, or from the Western Australian Tourism Commission.

The Central Australian Tourism Industry Association (CATIA, ☎ (089) 52 5199) can be contacted by writing to PO Box 2227, Alice Springs, NT 0871.

The Ayers Rock Resort (☎ (089) 546 2144) can be contacted at PO Box 46, Yulara, NT 0872.

The Western Australian Tourism Commission (☎ (09) 220 1700) is best contacted by writing to 16 St George Terrace, Perth, WA 6000.

Police
Contact the police in Wiluna and Yulara before you go and let them know your intended route and time of arrival. They are also a good source of information on the latest conditions of the route. Don't forget to tell the police at the other end that you have made it safely. The Wiluna police station (☎ (099) 81 7024) is in Thompson St. The Yulara police station (☎ (089) 56 2166) is on the Lasseter Highway at Yulara.

Permits
Permits are required to travel the enormous area of Aboriginal land in this region of Australia. For the Gunbarrel route described here, there are few hassles; permits take about three weeks to be issued. Areas that require special permission and permits are much harder, and unless you have good reason, a permit will not be issued.

To travel the full length of the Gunbarrel demands two permits, one from Western Australia and the other from the Northern

Territory. For the area in the Territory, apply to the Central Land Council (☎ (089) 51 6320, fax 53 4345), 31-33 Stuart Highway, Alice Springs, NT 0871. For those areas on the Western Australian side of the border, apply to the Aboriginal Affairs Planning Authority (☎ (09) 483 1333, fax 321 0990), 35 Havelock St, West Perth, WA 6005.

The permits lay down certain conditions for travel which should be adhered to. These conditions include no photography on Aboriginal land and that the trip be done as quickly as possible.

Books & Maps

Apart from Len Beadell's books on the area (see the boxed story on this last Australian explorer), there are few others.

Westprint publishes a map on the Gunbarrel Highway. To do the whole route you'll also need their Ayers Rock map. Also good is the Royal Automobile Club of Western Australia's map *Perth to Alice Springs – via Gunbarrel Highway or Warburton Road*. This map is available through the state automobile associations or good map shops Australia-wide.

Radio Frequencies

The need to carry an HF radio may be argued, especially if you are on the well-used Warburton-Laverton road, but for the remote tracks such as the Anne Beadell or the route west of Papunya, the argument for carrying one is greatly reinforced. Certainly it's a good idea for anywhere off the bitumen.

Across the vastness of the Gunbarrel and the 'Bomb Roads' there are a number of RFDS bases. The base at Alice Springs (callsign VJD) has a primary frequency of 5410 and a secondary frequency of 6950. If you are further south, the Port Augusta base (callsign VNZ) has a primary frequency of 4010; secondary frequencies are 6890 and 8165.

Along the Gunbarrel and Gary highways, the base at Meekatharra is hard to beat. Its callsign is VKJ and its primary frequency is 4010; secondary frequencies include 2280 and 6880. This base may be closed soon;

check with the base at Alice Springs. Up towards the Canning Stock Route, the Port Hedland base may be worth a try. Its callsign is VKL and it has a primary frequency of 4030; secondary frequencies are 2280 and 6960.

For those working through the Telstra (OTC) bases, the best ones to go for are, once again, dependent on where you are. Sydney (callsign VIS) is good if you are anywhere in the eastern portion of this trip. OTC 24-hour channels include 405, 607, 802, 1203, and 1602. Other frequencies for Selcall and Tonecall are also available. The Selcall for the beacon is 0899, while for the operator it is 0108.

In the western portion of these roads, the best station to use is Perth (callsign VIP). Its main OTC 24-hour frequencies include 427, 806, and 1226. Other frequencies are available. The Selcall for the beacon in Perth is 0799, while for the operator the Selcall is 0107.

THE ROUTE

This route takes you from the flash resort at Yulara west along the Docker River road to Giles, then south-west to the Warburton Aboriginal Community. Soon after, veer off the Warburton-Laverton road and head for Carnegie Station and Wiluna along the original track of the Gunbarrel Highway. The total distance is 1400 km.

Until you are west of Warburton, the track is generally passable to normal cars. Once on the real Gunbarrel, the route deteriorates and a 4WD is advisable.

Travelling times between Yulara and places further west depend on how quickly you like to drive on sandy dirt and corrugated roads. Between Yulara and Warburton, allow 10 to 11 hours; between Warburton and Carnegie Station, allow 12 to 13; from Carnegie to Wiluna, allow four to five hours. Obviously these figures are for driving times only.

Yulara

The modern Ayers Rock Resort is in the township of Yulara, which is in the desert on the edge of Uluru National Park. While the township caters mainly for the resort, the resort caters mainly for well-heeled tourists who flock to **Ayers Rock** to see it change colour, to photograph it, or video it. Like anything in nature, it doesn't always perform. Even so, the Rock and the nearby Olgas are worth seeing and spending a couple of days enjoying.

The resort, which includes a camping ground, has hotels that are like any luxury international hotel anywhere. The camping ground, the Emu Walk Apartments, the Outback Pioneer Hotel, the Desert Gardens Hotel and the Sails in the Desert Hotel can accommodate 5000 people a day, at varying levels of luxury.

Fuel, limited repairs and supplies are available at Yulara, and you can really go overboard on the souvenirs.

Yulara to Warburton (564 km)
Pulling out of Yulara, turn left as if heading to visit the Rock, but eight km down the road, take the turn-off to the Olgas and Docker River.

Heading west, **the Olgas** (Kata Tjuta) dominate the skyline and as you get closer they take on more and more character. You really should have spent a day exploring them before striking west, but if not, try to make time to stop for an hour before continuing on. With the bulk of Mt Olga off to the right, turn left onto the dirt road at the junction 49 km from Yulara.

Irving Creek, where Lasseter died, is crossed 83 km further west, and 100 metres past the crossing a track on the right leads 750 metres to a hand-operated water pump. Shaw Creek is crossed 26 km further on, while just nine km past Shaw Creek the Churnside Creek is crossed. Neither are any problem.

As you come up to the eastern bank of the **Hull River**, 191 km from Yulara, there is a track junction and parking area on your left. You are allowed to camp here. A walking track leads a short distance along the creek to a cave. This is **Lasseter's Cave**, where Lasseter waited vainly for rescue. A monument nearby tells the story. You might be lucky enough to see this area when there is water in the Hull. With all the comforts of modern travel and a brew cooking over a small wood fire, it's a pleasant spot. Lasseter probably thought otherwise.

Fourteen km further west, the road begins to pass through an area clothed in desert oaks, and the scenery, with the Petermanns in the background, is spectacular.

The road enters **Docker River Aboriginal Community** 26 km further on, and a short distance later the service station and store are off to your left. Fuel and limited supplies are available here.

The **Sandy Blight Junction Road** leaves the main road 26 km west of Docker River and heads north. Our route veers to the left, keeping to the main road. After a couple of creek crossings, a signpost on the left, 13 km past the junction, indicates you are at Giles's **Schwerin Mural Crescent**. The panorama of range country around you is magnificent.

At the T-junction 36 km past the Schwerin Mural Crescent sign, turn right onto the original Gunbarrel Highway, now heading west towards Giles. Left is also along the original Gunbarrel back into South Australia, but you need special permission to travel that route.

Twenty-nine km further on, you come to the **Warakurna Roadhouse** where you can camp, have a meal, refuel and top up with water.

The turn-off to **Giles weather station** is less than 500 metres west of the roadhouse. This station plays an important part in the forecasting of Australia's weather and is hooked up to the world meteorological network, but was originally established to check on wind conditions before and during the big atomic bangs at Emu and Maralinga. You can visit the station, but advance permission is required.

Continuing west along the Gunbarrel for another 16 km brings you to where the original Gunbarrel veers off to the right. This is a definite 4WD route and you need a special permit to travel it.

The original Gunbarrel Highway swings along the southern ramparts of the Rawlinson Range and comes to a Len Beadell marked tree, 84 km from the junction. Off to the north is Lake Christopher, which is the closest known point to the gold reef that Lasseter talked about.

Another 13 km along this route sees you at another marked tree. For the next 163 km the road alternates from chopped-up to quite sandy, as it swings further and further south. At Jackie Junction, 276 km from the Warakurna Roadhouse, you need to turn right (west). Continuing south will take you to the Warburton Aboriginal Community, 66 km away.

Heading west from Jackie Junction, cross the Todd Range, passing just to the south of Mt Charles.There is a lookout and a cairn on the top of Mt Samuel, which is on the left 76 km from Jackie Junction. After another six km you will meet the Heather Highway coming in from your left. This route heads north from the Warburton-Laverton Road to join the Gunbarrel at this point.

From the junction with the old Gunbarrel, head south-west along the Warburton road; the going is relatively easy, although the corrugations can be wicked. You will enter the **Warburton Aboriginal Community** 214 km from the junction, or 230 km from the Warakurna Roadhouse.

The store and the place to get fuel is on the left as you pass through the centre of the town. There is accommodation and a camping area.

Warburton to Carnegie Station (486 km)

The Heather Highway turns off the Warburton-Laverton road 41 km south-west of the community and here you need to turn right. At a T-junction 47 km past this major turn-off, turn right, and 37 km later the rough old Gunbarrel comes in on the right at a junction, where you turn left to head for Carnegie and Wiluna.

A large gum tree, marked by Len Beadell in 1958 and sporting a plaque, is on the right, 11 km west of the junction. Less than 300 metres past the tree, a track off to the left leads 800 metres to a hand pump and water. It might not be brilliant, but if you were dying of thirst you'd love it.

Camp Beadell, 49 km west of Beadell's tree, is a couple of hundred metres off to the left of the road. If you want a large, cleared area for a group camp, this could be it. A hill on the left and a track to it, six km after the

turn-off to Camp Beadell, brings you to **Mt Beadell**, with good views of the surrounding country.

Twenty-five km later you pass into the **Gibson Desert Nature Reserve**. Passing through the Browne Range, another 25 km on, the red bluff of **Mt Everard** will be on the left. Just six km further along the road is a major road junction – Everard Junction. At this point you are on a flat plain that is covered in spinifex all round, with scrub in the distance. The Browne Range rises to the east and the Young Range can be seen to the north-east. The Gunbarrel stretches away to the west.

The road north is the **Gary Highway**, which leads to the Canning Stock Route. A Len Beadell plaque can be found on the left. See the section on the 'Bomb Roads' later in this chapter for more details on this route.

You will pass out of the Gibson Desert Nature Reserve 31 km from the junction with the Gary Highway. One km later is the Geraldton Historical Society Bore on your left, 150 metres off the road. The water isn't nice, but it's drinkable.

The sign denoting the boundary of the **Mungali Claypan Nature Reserve** is passed 48 km further on, while the claypan itself is crossed just a little over four km later. Seven km from the eastern boundary of the Mungali Reserve, you cross the western boundary, and just before that, you will have passed through a junction with **Eagle Road**.

For the next 75 km or so the Gunbarrel continues westward and is rough and chopped-up. In places, much of it has been washed away and there are a number of small diversions. Where the road passes through breakaway country, there are a number of minor creek crossings, all of which can be rough.

Sandhill country is met once again 85 km from the western boundary sign of the Mungali Reserve; the road is sandy but it is no problem to a 4WD.

Just before you get to the turn-off to **Carnegie Station**, you can see the station on your left, with the track junction a short distance later, 67 km from first striking the

Mt Olga (PS)

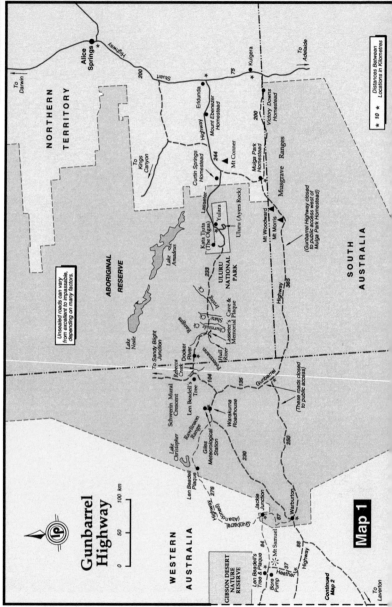

Gunbarrel Highway

Map 1

0   50   100 km

WESTERN AUSTRALIA

GIBSON DESERT NATURE RESERVE

Len Beadell's Tree & Plaque

Bore Pump

Heather

Mt Samuel

Jackie Junction

Gunbarrel (Abandoned)

Highway (Gunbarrel)

64

57

88

67

Warburton

To Laverton

Continued Map 2

Len Beadell Plaque

276

Highway (Gunbarrel)

Lake Christopher

Giles Meteorological Station

Rawlinson Range

230

Len Beadell's Tree

Schwerin Mural Crescent

104

250

Warakurna Roadhouse

135

Gunbarrel

(These roads closed to public access)

Rebecca Creek

To Sandy Blight Junction

Docker River

Hull River

Ranges

Bowden

Lasseter's Cave & Memorial Plaque

Shaw

233

Mulga

ABORIGINAL RESERVE

Lake Neale

Lake Amadeus

Kata Tjuta (The Olgas)

Yulara

Uluru (Ayers Rock)

ULURU NATIONAL PARK

Mt Woodward

Mt Morris

Highway

365

Musgrave Ranges

SOUTH AUSTRALIA

(Gunbarrel Highway closed to public access west of Mulga Park Homestead)

Mulga Park Homestead

Victory Downs Homestead

200

Curtin Springs Homestead

Lasseter

244

Mt Conner

Highway

Mount Ebenezer Homestead

Erldunda

NORTHERN TERRITORY

To Kings Canyon

Stuart

Highway

200

Alice Springs

To Darwin

75

Kulgera

To Adelaide

Unsealed roads can vary from excellent to impassable, depending on many factors.

Distances Between Locations in Kilometres

10

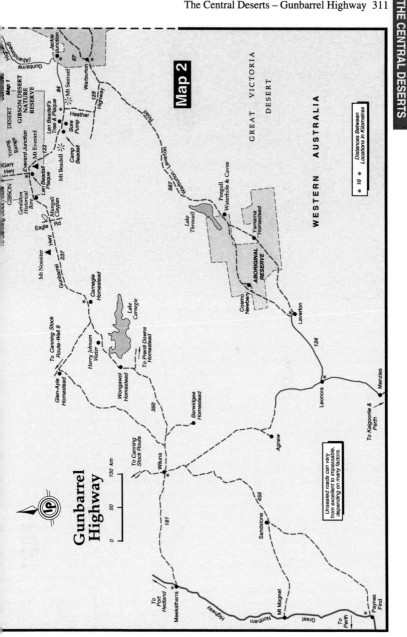

Gunbarrel Highway

Map 2

Lasseter's Cave (R & VM)

sand ridge country and 486 km from Warburton. At Carnegie you can buy fuel and limited supplies, camp, and even stay in the shearers' quarters. This is the end of the 'real' Gunbarrel, where Len and his men finished making their road across central Australia. For most travellers the trip continues westward for another 350 km to Wiluna.

Carnegie to Wiluna (350 km)

Heading west from Carnegie, the road is formed dirt and generally in better condition than the Gunbarrel. A Y-junction 30 km from the station is where those travellers who want to join the Canning Stock Route at Well 9 must veer right. The track north goes via Glen-Ayle Station for 145 km to the stock route. Our route westward to Wiluna is via the left fork.

Continuing towards Wiluna, the road swings more in a southerly direction. At **Harry Johnson Water**, on your right 69 km from Carnegie, there is a good campsite near

water. A picnic table, shelter and barbecu are at this spot.

The road continues to swing south, at on stage skirting the north-western extremity the salt lake known as **Lake Carnegie**. Th turn-off to Wongawol Station homestead on your left, 97 km west of the Glen-Ayl turn-off, and the station, which has no faci ities for travellers, is also on your left.

Heading almost due south, the road passe the turn-off to Prenti Downs on the left, 2 km south of Wongawol. The road begins t swing more westerly, and 164 km fro Wongawol the turn-off to Barwidgee Statio is on the left. Another 16 km further on is track off to the right which leads north t Glen-Ayle Station.

The small community of **Wiluna** i entered another 43 km west, 350 km west o Carnegie Station. For all intents and pu poses this town is the end of the road. Fo travellers, there is the choice of headin north up the Canning Stock Route; continu ing westwards 181 km to Meekatharra on th

Great Northern Highway; or swinging south or 455 km through Sandstone to Paynes Find, itself 424 km north of Perth on the Great Northern Highway

Wiluna can supply fuel, limited repairs and groceries. For more details on this outback community, see the Canning Stock Route section in the North-West chapter.

ALTERNATIVE ROUTES
Warburton-Laverton Road
Instead of taking the real Gunbarrel west, the shortest distance to Perth and the south-west of Western Australia from central Australia is via the Warburton-Laverton road. The distance between these two communities is 570 km and it is all dirt. Allow seven to eight hours as an average driving time.

How long it's been since the graders were last out will determine how bad this run is. It can be badly corrugated and a bit sandy in places, but is still generally passable in a normal car with sufficient ground clearance – driven with care, and if it hasn't rained.

The Route From Warburton, head out on the road west, but at the road junction 41 km from the community, veer left towards Laverton, leaving the real Gunbarrel to 4WDs.

The run south is uneventful, through typical desert country. As you approach a large salt lake called Lake Throssell, visible on your right, the **Peegull Waterhole and Caves** are on your left, 295 km from the road junction.

The turn-off to **Yamarna Station** is 36 km further south. If you take this option, you will reach the station 43 km from the turn-off. It has fuel and limited supplies. From Yamarna you can travel to Laverton, another 146 km away.

If you continue on the main road south instead of taking the Yamarna road, the first turn-off to **Cosmo Newbery** is struck 102 km further on, and a second road leads the same way a few km later. This Aboriginal community has no facilities for the traveller. Some 87 km past the first junction into the community, you come to the bitumen. Turning left will take you to the mining

community of Laverton, just six km away; turning right will take you to Leonora, 118 km further south-west.

ORGANISED TOURS
Nobody really runs tours of the Gunbarrel as a stand-alone destination. The highway is included in a number of operators' itineraries, including AAT King's Tour (☎ (03) 274 7422 or toll-free ☎ 008 334 009), 29 Palmerston Crescent, South Melbourne, Vic 3205; Amesz Tours (☎ (09) 250 2577), 4 Elmsfield Rd, Midvale, WA 6056; Austrek Safaris (☎ (09) 370 5209); and Russell Guest's 4WD Safaris (☎ (03) 481 5877), 38 Station St, Fairfield, Vic 3078. While all carry passengers, Amesz and Russell Guest's take people who drive their own vehicle as tag-alongs.

For a complete list of tour operators, contact the Western Australian Tourism Commission (☎ (09) 220 1700), 16 St George Terrace, Perth, WA 6000.

FACILITIES
Don't expect fancy all-night supplies of fuel along the Gunbarrel – even at Yulara the service station closes around 7 pm. While most places have unleaded and super, at times some of them run out of unleaded, super, or both. Diesel seems to be more readily available.

Yulara, Warakurna, Carnegie and Wiluna are the most consistent suppliers of fuel and supplies along the route described.

Yulara
If you are camping and you want to stay and see Uluru (Ayers Rock), you have no option but to stay in the well set-up and expensive *camping ground* (☎ (089) 56 2055) at the Ayers Rock Resort in Yulara. Prices range from $9 a night per person for a campsite up to $60 for an on-site van. If you want to stay somewhere with a roof over your head, you have the choice of various levels of luxury. The *Outback Pioneer Lodge* (☎ (089) 56 2170) has beds in 20-bed dorms for $18 for the first night, dropping to $10 on subsequent nights. In the same complex, the

Outback Pioneer Hotel has expensive units with bathroom for $185. The *Emu Walk Apartments* (☎ (089) 56 2100) offer the best deal. There are one- and two-bedroom flats which accommodate four and six people respectively. The cost is $130 for the small apartments and $150 for the larger ones. Rooms at the *Desert Gardens Hotel* (☎ (089) 56 2100) cost $200 a double, while at *Sails in the Desert* (☎ (089) 56 2200), doubles are $245.

In the Town Square of Yulara you will find a small supermarket, takeaway outlets, a newsagency and a tavern.

The service station (☎ (089) 56 2229) at the resort is next to the camping ground and has unleaded, super, diesel and LPG. Ice is also available, as are spare parts, tyre and mechanical repairs. It's the cheapest fuel you'll see until Wiluna.

Vehicles can be hired from Avis (☎ (089) 56 2266), Budget (☎ (089) 56 2121) and Territory Rent-a-Car (☎ (089) 56 2030); although you can go anywhere, the vehicle must be returned to a company agent in the Northern Territory. That makes it a little difficult to head west to Wiluna, unless you want to come back as well.

For more information on the facilities, tours and nightlife offered by the resort, contact the Ayers Rock Resort (☎ (089) 56 2144), PO Box 46, Yulara, NT 0872.

Docker River

This community has a service station that can supply petrol and diesel to passing travellers.

Warakurna Roadhouse

This roadhouse (☎ (089) 56 7344) is just a short distance from the Giles weather station. Unleaded, super and diesel are available, as are a range of limited supplies. A caravan park means you have a few more luxuries than camping in the bush and you can fill up with water.

Warburton

This large Aboriginal community has the *Warburton Roadhouse* (☎ (089) 56 7656), with super, unleaded and diesel. Limited accommodation is also available.

Carnegie Station

Carnegie Station (☎ (099) 81 2991) can supply unleaded, super and diesel. It's a good place to camp – green lawns fed by the near unlimited water, hot showers, and hospitality. Camping costs $8 per person per night while the cabins cost $15, and there are cooking facilities provided. Souvenirs, general food supplies, cool drinks and the like are all you can expect. Emergency repairs are also available.

Wiluna

This is the biggest and best-equipped supply centre you would have seen since leaving Yulara. It has everything you need to keep you going, including food, fuel, general supplies, accommodation and camping.

For details on Wiluna, see the section on the Canning Stock Route in the North-West chapter.

ALTERNATIVE TRANSPORT

Getting to Ayers Rock and the Yulara Resort is relatively easy. It is serviced by air and by bus from Alice Springs with connections to anywhere in Australia from there. Air services include both Ansett and Qantas from all over Australia, with charter flights from Alice Springs as well. The bus service is Greyhound Pioneer Australia.

Beyond the resort, any form of travel, unless it's on an organised tour, is much more difficult. While once there was a bus service that ran between Perth and Ayers Rock using the Laverton-Warburton road, this is not running at present. For the latest information, contact the Western Australian Tourism Commission (☎ (09) 220 1700).

'Bomb Roads'

The 'Bomb Roads' cover the desert country of western South Australia and adjoining Western Australia, north of the Indian-

Pacific Railway line. They were constructed by Len Beadell in the 1950s to provide an infrastructure for the Woomera rocket tests and Emu A-bomb tests. In all, there are over 5000 km of desert tracks, the most important being the east-west Gunbarrel Highway. While the Gunbarrel was the first link across central Australia from east to west, others followed, and with an interconnecting grid of north-south roads, this region is a favoured one for desert-lovers and 4WD adventurers.

ANNE BEADELL HIGHWAY

This highway runs from Coober Pedy west via the atomic bomb test site of Emu, through Vokes Hill Junction, across the WA/SA border into Western Australia, crossing the north-south Connie Sue Highway at Neale Junction. Continuing westward, the Anne Beadell passes through the Yeo Lakes region before reaching Yamarna station, the first habitation and fuel since leaving Coober Pedy. From here it is station tracks to the mining community of Laverton.

For nearly the entire way, the track is sandy and often very narrow. Staking a tyre in the scrub country is a definite possibility. The route is easier than the Canning or the Simpson, as it rarely crosses any sand ridges. However, it is extremely remote – even over the cooler winter months, travellers are few and far between.

It's 1196 km from Coober Pedy to Yamarna station, so you will need to carry a fair amount of fuel. From Yamarna to Laverton, it's 146 km.

Permits

Doing this trip on your own, you will need a couple of permits, as the track traverses Aboriginal land, and Department of Defence land around Emu. Permission to cross Mabel Downs station is also required from the property owners, and as the privilege of crossing this land has been abused in the past, it might not be easy. The track runs past the homestead's front door, so you do need permission.

Permission to enter the area around Emu can be obtained from the Area Administration, Defence Support Centre (☎ (086) 74 3370), PO Box 157, Woomera, SA 5720. To traverse Aboriginal land, you need to contact the Maralinga-Tjarutja Council (☎ (086) 25 2946), Alice Springs, NT 0870, or the Maralinga Land Council, PO Box 435, Ceduna, SA 5690.

The Route

From Coober Pedy, head west towards Mabel Creek on what is a good station track. The 50 km will take just over an hour.

The track to Emu passes a shearing shed 66 km from **Mabel Downs homestead** and soon becomes a track, first across gibber country, then in between sand ridges. The Dog Fence is passed at the 102-km mark, with the not-to-be-relied-upon Tallaringa Well just off to the left of the road at the 157-km point. The 235-km drive to Emu from the station will take between five and six hours.

At **Emu** there is little left from the atomic-test days. The sites where the bombs were let off, known as Totem I and Totem II, are 15 km east of the actual township and landing ground that was Emu. A crossroads marks the spot. Turning to the left will take you to the low rise where the official 'viewing area' was for the blasts; turning to the right will take you to the actual bomb sites. A few bits of twisted steel and a small depression in the landscape, along with a concrete monument, mark the two spots where the bombs, on tall steel towers, were detonated. Take heed of the radioactivity warning signs around the area.

The airstrip at Emu is occasionally used by mining companies, and there are a few tracks around the old town site, so make sure you are on the right one. Basically, when coming from Mabel Downs, the airstrip is off to the right; you do a dogleg to the left then to the right, to get onto the main track west.

The 153 km from Emu to Vokes Hill Junction takes between five and six hours on what is a much less used track. About 50 km from Emu a track veers off to the right. This leads into prohibited Aboriginal land – definitely no entry. Keep on the main track west, passing between a long line of dunes covered in spinifex and mulga or low acacia scrub with the occasional stand of mallee.

From **Vokes Hill Junction** it is 175 km (five hours) to the WA/SA border. The road south from the junction leads 250 km through Aboriginal land to the small railway siding of Cook, on the Indian-Pacific Railway line. Heading westward, the track remains much the same as before, and you know you are getting close to the state border when you begin to cross the long, thin expanse of the salt-encrusted **Serpentine Lakes**.

West from the border the track begins to swing north-west and, in the process, begins to cross a few sand ridges, before again swinging west and once again running between the east-west dunes. From the border to **Neale Junction**, at the crossroads with the Connie Sue Highway, it is 348 km, which should take you between nine and 10 hours. The area from 45 km east to 23 km west of the Connie Sue Highway junction is proclaimed as the **Neale Junction Nature Reserve**.

From Neale Junction to Yamarna station, it is 235 km (about six hours). Around **Lake Yeo** you pass into another nature reserve. There are a few tracks through this region – stick to the main one, which tends to swing north of west, passing through the Pitcher Range and then the rugged mesa country of the Morton Craig Range. The ruins of Yeo station are passed 165 km from the junction. You'll start to see cattle as you get closer to **Yamarna station**, 70 km further on. Here you can get fuel and very limited supplies.

From the station, the road condition improves, and the last 146 km to Laverton takes just 1½ hours.

At **Laverton** there's fuel, accommodation, a camping ground, and a couple of stores supplying most requirements. From here you can head south on bitumen to Kalgoorlie (360 km away), or north to Wiluna (a distance of about 400 km, depending on which route you take).

CONNIE SUE HIGHWAY

The Connie Sue runs from the railway siding of Rawlinna north to Neale Junction (the intersection with the Anne Beadell Highway), then continues north to meet up with the main Laverton-Warburton Road just a few km west of the Aboriginal community at Warburton. In all it is 581 km from Rawlinna to Warburton, and another 70 km to the junction with the Gunbarrel Highway.

Permits

To enter Warburton Aboriginal Community you will need a permit from the Aboriginal Affairs Planning Authority in Perth (see Permits in the earlier Gunbarrel Highway section for details). No permit, no fuel!

The Route

Rawlinna, on the Indian-Pacific Railway line, is 140 km north-west of Cocklebiddy which is 1240 km from Perth along the Eyre Highway. While a number of people live at Rawlinna, there is no store to speak of, so don't expect to get fuel or supplies here.

You may need a little help to actually get onto the Connie Sue Highway – there are tracks in all directions north of the line. Some go to Seemore Downs, 30 km north (deserted), while others head to Premier Downs, 50 km north and a little further east, slightly closer to the actual route. It's all a bit of a guessing game, but once you get onto the right road you will know it: it's straight as an arrow, like many of Len Beadell's roads.

Once north of the treeless plain that is the Nullarbor, the country turns into arid grasslands dotted with trees, bordering the fringe of the Great Victoria Desert. It's a relatively easy drive for the 300 km to **Neale Junction**, but allow six hours for the trip. There is a nice cleared area at the junction for camping, with plenty of room if your group consists of more than a couple of vehicles.

North of the intersection with the Anne Beadell Highway, the track becomes a little sandier and rougher, but is still generally no problem. A few sand ridges make the track twist and turn and will also make you shuffle a few gears, or even lower your tyre pressures, but generally there is nothing too difficult.

About 140 km from the Neale Junction you pass into the **Barker Lake Nature Reserve**, named after a salt lake far off to the north-west of the track. The country is a little rockier through this next section, the road skirting such high points as Hanns Tabletop Hill, Skipper Knob and Point Brophy before entering sandier country again north of Manton Knob, 210 km north of the Anne Beadell Highway.

You leave the reserve 30 km north of Manton Knob, passing through stands of majestic desert oak, and 35 km later meet the main Laverton-Warburton Road. Turning right here will take you into the **Warburton Aboriginal Community**, just six km along the main road; you can get fuel and limited supplies here.

From Warburton, the Connie Sue Highway continues north 68 km to Jackie Junction, where the Connie Sue ends at the Gunbarrel Highway, but this stretch of the road is through an area of very restricted access and driving it requires special permission. Most travellers head north-east to Giles, Docker River and Uluru (Ayers Rock) on a major dirt road, or from Warburton turn south-west towards Laverton, where 40 km down the road they can head northwards and follow the Gunbarrel Highway through to Carnegie station.

GARY HIGHWAY

The Gary heads north from the Gunbarrel Highway to join up with the Canning Stock Route at Well 35, before pushing west, as the Callawa Road, to a point north-east of Marble Bar. Since the Kidson Track was graded in 1963, Len's road west of the Canning has fallen into disuse. From the Gunbarrel to the Canning along the Gary Highway, it's 364 km.

Permits

No permits are required to use this road.

Lake Cohen (R & VM)

The Route

The junction of the Gunbarrel and Gary highways, known as **Everard Junction**, is 10 km west of the low mountain of the same name, 236 km east of Carnegie station and 220 km west of Jackie Junction, or 251 km from Warburton Aboriginal Community via the Heather Highway.

The area surrounding the junction and a vast area to the east is protected in the **Gibson Desert Nature Reserve**. As you head north from the Gunbarrel Highway, the Browne and Young ranges are to the east. Fourteen km north of the junction you pass Charlies Knob. The track is washed away in parts through this range country but, while slow going, is generally no problem.

After you leave the ranges, for the most part the track traverses a flat to slightly undulating plain covered in spinifex and dotted with small trees. It's a very easy run, with nary a sandhill in sight.

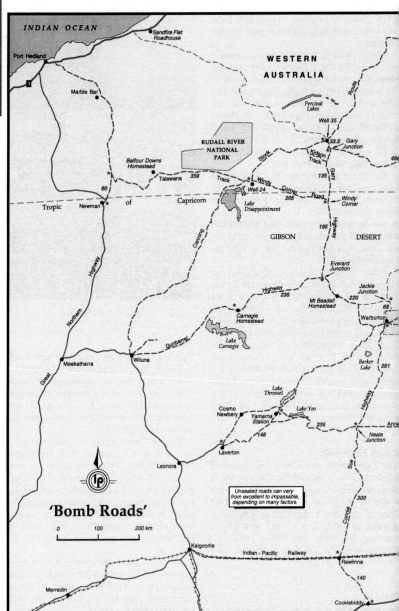

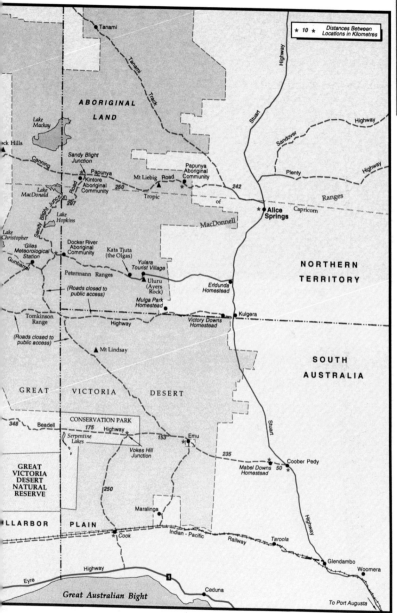

★ 10 ★ Distances Between
Locations in Kilometres

Tanami

Tanami Track

ABORIGINAL
LAND

Lake
Mackay

ck Hills

Canning

Sandy Blight
Junction

Papunya Road

Kintore
Aboriginal
Community

Lake
MacDonald

Sandy Blight Junction

257

Lake
Hopkins

Lake
Christopher

'Giles
Meteorological
Station

Gunbarrel

Docker River
Aboriginal
Community

Petermann Ranges

(Roads closed to
public access)

Tomkinson
Range

(Roads closed to
public access)

Mt Lindsay

GREAT   VICTORIA   DESERT

348 Beadell

Serpentine
Lakes

GREAT
VICTORIA
DESERT
NATURAL
RESERVE

CONSERVATION PARK

175   Highway

Vokes Hill
Junction

250

Maralinga

LLARBOR   PLAIN

Cook

Indian - Pacific

Highway

Eyre

Great Australian Bight

Mt Liebig
250

Tropic

of

MacDonnell

Papunya
Aboriginal
Community

242

Kata Tjuta
(the Olgas)

Yulara
Tourist Village

Uluru
(Ayers
Rock)

Mulga Park
Homestead

Highway

Erldunda
Homestead

Victory Downs
Homestead

Kulgera

153   Emu

235

Mabel Downs
Homestead

Railway

Ceduna

Highway

Stuart

Sandover   Highway

Plenty   Highway

Ranges

Capricorn

Alice
Springs

NORTHERN

TERRITORY

SOUTH

AUSTRALIA

Stuart

50   Coober Pedy

Tarpola

Glendambo

Woomera

To Port Augusta

THE CENTRAL DESERTS

Everard Junction, looking north along the Gary Highway (R & VM)

The NT/WA border west of Sandy Blight Junction (R & VM)

Lake Cohen, 84 km north of Everard Junction and just to the west of the road, is normally a shallow dry lakebed, but occasionally it does fill with water. Then it is worthy of a camp, and a mecca for bird life. Ducks of a few species, along with red-necked avocets and banded stilts, vie with white-faced herons, white-necked herons, native hens and coots for food in the shallow waters of the lake.

The road junction of **Windy Corner** is 195 km north of Everard Junction, a drive of between four and five hours. There's a book to sign at the junction; it's not there for any particular safety reason but everybody seems to fill it in, telling all and sundry how their particular trip is going.

While the Gary Highway continues north, the Windy Corner road strikes west to the Canning Stock Route. For more details, see The Talawana Track-Windy Corner Road, later in this section.

The Gary Highway heads across lightly rolling gibber plains for 73 km, where a faint track to the east leads to **Veevers Crater**. This crater, 20 km off the main track, is another meteorite impact crater. It is only 80 metres in diameter but is a nearly perfect circle, seven to eight metres deep.

A short distance later the Gary Highway passes through a 10-km-wide swath of sand-ridge country that has the road twisting and turning a little. Soon, however, it's back into more open country. Twelve km further on, 105 km west of Windy Corner, the Kidson Track joins the Gary Highway from the west. This track heads west 65 km to join the Canning Stock Route just south of Well 33.

Gary Junction, 30 km further north, is 135 km (nearly three hours) north of Windy Corner and 330 km north of the Gunbarrel Highway. This is where the Gary Highway turns hard left and strikes out for the Canning Stock Route. At Gary Junction you'll find a Beadell plaque on top of a fuel drum: turn right for Alice Springs or left to the Canning.

After passing through another strip of sand-ridge country, and 33.5 km beyond Gary Junction, another junction on the right is met. You are now on the main Canning

Tietkens Tree with Mt Tietkens in the background (R & VM)

Stock Route. Going straight ahead leads to Well 35, 14 km away, while turning right will lead to Well 36 and on to Halls Creek. The drive from Gary Junction to Well 35 will take nearly three hours.

SANDY BLIGHT JUNCTION ROAD

This road through the desert country of central Australia strikes north from the Gunbarrel Highway at a point 27 km west of Docker River Aboriginal Community and finishes at Sandy Blight Junction, nearly 300 km north and close to Kintore Aboriginal Community. The drive will take you between six and seven hours. From here you are just 500 km west of Alice Springs.

Built by Len Beadell, and named after a particularly bad bout of this desert scourge, the Sandy Blight Road is a relatively easy run north. For most of the way it crosses sandy country, and where it does traverse sand ridges they are generally pretty small and no problem.

For much of the way the road passes through quite dense stands of desert oak, and these make this drive magnificent.

Permits

You require permits from the Central Lands Council in Alice Springs to traverse this road.

The Route

Docker River Aboriginal Community, 215 km west of Yulara along the Gunbarrel Highway, can supply fuel and limited supplies.

The Gunbarrel Highway around Docker River passes through some of the most spectacular country in central Australia. Travel down this road in the early morning or late afternoon and you will be impressed with the colours, the surrounding ranges, the vegetation and the general aura of the place.

The junction of the Sandy Blight Road is 26.5 km west of Docker River. Veering right off the highway, the road parallels Rebecca Creek and passes the western end of the Anne Range, 13 km north of the junction. Fourteen km further on, with the Walter James Range off to the west, there is a track that leads to **Bungabiddy Rockhole**, deep within the range. It's a nice spot and popular with the locals.

The road continues north, and while it can be a little washed out, it is generally fairly easy (but slow) travelling.

Past the track junction to the Aboriginal community at Tjukurla, 66 km north of the junction, the track swings around the western end of the salty, strung-out Lake Hopkins. The road is now heading almost due north, and the first of the sand ridges are crossed 83 km north of the Gunbarrel Highway.

A large desert oak 143 km from Docker River has an original Len Beadell plaque on it. The road north of here is a little more chopped-up than normal but is not difficult. A further 53 km north, another large oak on the right bears one of Len's plaques.

From here the road crosses sand-ridge country and passes through the Sir Frederick Range and the Mu Hills. The NT/WA border, with a log blazed by Len on the left, is 203

km north of the junction and 230 km from Docker River.

From the border the road heads almost due east for 25 km, deeper into the Northern Territory, before heading north again and crossing the **Tropic of Capricorn**, 251 km north of the Gunbarrel. You'll find yet another Len Beadell plaque and marker where the road crosses the Tropic.

Heading north, the horizon is dominated by the bulk of the **Kintore Range**; Mt Leisler (901 metres) is the highest point around for quite some way. At the far north of the range is Mt Strickland. It's a magnificent scene, one to which your eyes are drawn time and again.

Tietkens Tree, an old, dead tree, which was blazed by the explorer William Tietkens in 1889, stands below the bluff of Mt Leisler beside the road, 18 km north of the Tropic.

With the Kintore Range rearing up to your left, it is a pleasant 28 km to the end of the road at Sandy Blight Junction. Turning right here will lead finally to Alice Springs; turning left takes you back into Western Australia and to the Canning Stock Route (see the following section for more details).

CANNING-PAPUNYA ROAD

This road is one of the few that wasn't named by Len, although the section west from Gary Junction to the Canning Stock Route is really part of the Gary Highway. Between Sandy Blight Junction and Gary Junction, Len called the road the Gary Junction Highway but it is one of the few names that has neither stuck nor been officially recognised. The route east to Mt Liebig was just a minor connecting road.

Built between 1960 and 1962, this road gives access west from Alice Springs to Well 35 on the Canning Stock Route, via Papunya, Sandy Blight Junction, Jupiter Well and Gary Junction.

All up, the distance between the Canning and Alice is 1028 km. Like most of Len's roads, this one traverses the easiest country possible. In only a couple of places does it cross sandhills, the rest of the time running down the valleys between the dunes.

Permits

Permits from the Central Land Council in Alice Springs are required for travel west of Papunya to the border.

The Route

From Alice Springs the route heads north along the Stuart Highway for 20 km, then turns west along the Tanami Track to the Papunya turn-off, 137 km from Alice. This is where the bitumen ends; the next 105 km, to **Papunya**, is good dirt. The total travelling time from Alice is two to three hours.

Between Papunya and Kintore Aboriginal communities the road deteriorates slightly, but is still relatively good, well-maintained dirt. Fifty km west of Papunya, off to your left, you will see **Mt Liebig**, the highest peak at the western end of the Amunurungara Range. At this point the road begins to follow Len's route west.

As you begin to approach the Henty Hills and the Ehrenberg Ranges, around the 100-km mark, the first of the sandhills begin to appear. The road continues to be sandy but good.

Sandy Blight Junction is 250 km west of Papunya, and nearby is the Aboriginal community of **Kintore**. The main access to this community, where you can get fuel and limited supplies, is 17 km west of the junction. The drive from Papunya to Kintore takes about three hours.

The road continues to be graded and in fair condition. The WA/NT border is crossed 42 km further west, and 170 km from Sandy Blight you see the remains of **Len's burnt-out ration truck** on the right side of the road. The story is told in Len's book *Beating About the Bush*.

Just 10 km further on you come to a track junction. Veering right, it's six km to **Kiwirrkurra Aboriginal Community**, probably the most remote community in Australia. The last 180 km will take between two and three hours. Fuel and limited supplies are available here, but only if you have been in contact with the Kiwirrkurra community first.

To continue west to the Canning Stock Route, you need to veer left (instead of right) back at the track junction, and from this point the road quickly becomes a sandy track, showing a definite lack of maintenance. In places it has been washed away and a new track skirts the original. In other spots the sand along the road can be deep, forcing you to crawl along in second gear for km after km. It chews the fuel! Occasionally the track crosses a sandhill, but this shouldn't cause you any problems.

Jupiter Well is found in a magnificent stand of desert oak 327 km west of Sandy Blight and about five hours' drive west of Kiwirrkurra. An Aboriginal community outstation has been established here in recent years; whether you'll find anyone there will depend on the time of year. No fuel or supplies are available, and don't rely on getting water here either.

Gary Junction and the highway running south are found 161 km (about four hours) further west, where you will find a Len Beadell plaque. Continuing westward, you reach Well 35 on the Canning Stock Route. See the earlier section on the Gary Highway for more details.

TALAWANA TRACK-WINDY CORNER ROAD

The last road built by Len and his men, this track heads west from Windy Corner on the Gary Highway to Western Australia's Pilbara region. Travelling via Well 24 and Well 23 on the Canning Stock Route, it is today the main route by which the centre of the Canning is accessed from the west.

Permits

No permits are required to travel this road.

The Route

The Windy Corner Road takes 205 km to reach the Canning Stock Route just a couple of km north of Well 24. The drive takes about five hours.

For the first 70 km the track passes across undulating, gravelly country covered with spinifex. After that, the road begins to pass between low sandhills, but the going is pretty easy. Just over 40 km from Windy Corner the road skirts the **Connolly Basin**, an ancient, eroded meteorite-impact crater some nine km in diameter.

The track continues west, and 96 km from Windy Corner a drum on the right marks the approximate position of the **Tropic of Capricorn**. Early in the season, when the area has received good rainfall and the spinifex is seeding, the seed stems can be over a metre tall, with seeds so thick in the air that it's like driving through a light snowfall. The seeds block up radiators in minutes and make it very difficult to keep engines cool. In fact, at one spot the track passes the burnt-out shell of an old Land Rover – obviously one that didn't survive.

The track joins with the Canning Stock Route 205 km west of Windy Corner and just north of Well 24. The route west from here will take you along the Canning to a point 22 km south of Well 23. **Well 23** is where most Canning travellers pick up the fuel that has been prearranged and dumped there for their

use. Please don't use any that is not yours – a life could easily be lost for such thievery.

The 39 km from where the Windy Corner Road meets the Canning Stock Route to the point where you leave the Canning and head west on the Talawana Track is a pretty easy run, taking less than two hours.

West of the Canning, the Talawana Track skirts the southern boundary of the **Rudall River National Park**, a vast area of desert country surrounding the ephemeral Rudall River and the salt lakes of Lake Dora and Lake Blanche. The country changes between sand dunes and spinifex-covered plains.

Talawana, 200 km west of the Canning, is a rarely used outstation of Balfour Downs, so don't expect anything to be available. While the route is generally easy, some sections of the road can be washed away and others can be sandy. Allow five to six hours for this 200-km stretch.

From Talawana, station tracks head 40 km north-west to **Balfour Downs**, a remote cattle station that has no facilities for travel

Len Beadell's burnt-out truck (R & VM)

ers. Heading south and then west on station tracks for 120 km will bring you to the old Northern Highway. The run from Talawana to the here takes two to three hours.

You are about 60 km (40 minutes) north of the mining community of **Newman**, (where you'll find all the fuel and other supplies you could need) and the bitumen of the Northern Highway.

West of Jupiter Well, heading towards Sandy Blight Junction (R & VM)

The South

Eyre Highway

Ask most Australians what they think the ultimate road trip is and they will answer 'crossing the Nullarbor'. It's more than 2700 km from Perth to Adelaide – not much less than the distance from London to Moscow.

The long and sometimes lonely Eyre Highway crosses the southern edge of the vast Nullarbor Plain. Nullarbor is bad Latin for 'no tree', but though there is a small stretch where you indeed see no trees at all, the road is actually flanked by trees for most of the way, as this coastal fringe receives regular rain, especially in winter.

The surfaced road runs close to the coast on the South Australian side. The Nullarbor region ends dramatically on the coast of the Great Australian Bight, at cliffs that drop

The South

0   250   500 km

steeply into the ocean. It's easy to see why this was a seafarer's nightmare, for a ship driven onto the coast would quickly be pounded to pieces against the cliffs, and climbing them would be a near impossibility.

The Indian-Pacific Railway runs on the actual Nullarbor Plain, unlike the main road, which only fringes the great plain. One stretch of the railway runs dead straight for 478 km – the longest piece of straight (though not flat) railway line in the world.

HISTORY

The highway across the Nullarbor takes its name from John Eyre, the explorer who made the first east-west crossing in 1841. In 1877, a telegraph line was laid across the Nullarbor, roughly delineating the route the first road would take.

Later in the century, miners en route to the gold fields followed the telegraph line across. In 1896, the first bicycle crossing was made, and in 1912 the first car was driven across, but in the next 12 years only three more cars managed to complete the route.

In 1941, the war inspired the building of a transcontinental highway, just as it had the Alice Springs-Darwin route. It was a rough-and-ready track when completed, and in the 1950s only a few vehicles a day made the crossing. In the 1960s, the traffic flow increased to more than 30 vehicles a day, and in 1969 the Western Australian government surfaced the road as far as the South Australian border. Finally, in 1976, the last stretch from the South Australian border was surfaced, making the Nullarbor crossing a much easier drive, though still a long one.

INFORMATION
Tourist Offices

There's a tourist bureau (☎ (090) 39 0171) in Norseman at the western end of the highway, at 68 Roberts St, open daily from 9 am to 5 pm. At the eastern end of the highway, the first tourist office is at Ceduna (☎ (086) 25 2972), in the main street. There is a much larger facility in Port Augusta – the Wadlata Outback Centre (☎ (086) 42 4511),

41 Flinders Terrace, is also the tourist information centre.

All of the roadhouses have stacks of pamphlets relating to tourist sights in the area and to the towns nearby.

Permits

No permits are required to cross the Nullarbor, even though the Yalata Aboriginal Land is crossed at one stage. If you go off road, you will need a permit; contact the Yalata Roadhouse (☎ (086) 25 6990). A permit is also needed to bush camp in the Nullarbor National Park and Nullarbor Regional Reserve; contact the South Australia National Parks & Wildlife Service in Ceduna (☎ (086) 25 3144).

Books & Maps

There are a number of helpful publications which cover the Nullarbor. One of the most comprehensive is the free *Across Australia*, available in Perth and Adelaide from Leisure Time Publications. The accommodation information in the Western Australia Tourist Commission's *Golden Heartlands* is also useful.

The South Australia National Parks & Wildlife Service issues an interesting pamphlet called *Parks of the Far West*, which helps to break the monotony of the journey by giving interesting detail about the landforms you pass. There are details about off-road options on either side of the sealed highway in Peter & Kim Wherrett's *Explore Australia by Four-Wheel Drive*.

If you stick to the highway, no special maps are required – just follow the road.

Radio Frequencies

If you should strike mechanical trouble, you're unlikely to have to wait long for another vehicle to pass by. For those with HF radios, the RFDS base at Port Augusta (callsign VNZ) monitors the following frequencies from 6 am to 9 pm daily: 2020, 4010, 6890 and 8165 kHz. Kalgoorlie RFDS base (callsign VJO) monitors 2020 kHz from 7.15 am to 5 pm Monday to Friday and from 9 to 10 am on Saturday and Sunday.

SPECIAL PREPARATIONS

Although the Nullarbor is no longer a torture trail where cars get shaken to bits by potholes and corrugations, and where travellers stranded by breakdowns die of thirst waiting for another vehicle, it's still wise to avoid difficulties whenever possible.

The longest distance between fuel stops is about 200 km, so if you're foolish enough to run out of petrol midway, you'll have a long trip to get more. Finding help in the event of a mechanical breakdown can be equally time-consuming and very expensive, so make sure your vehicle is in good shape and that you've got plenty of petrol, decent tyres at the right pressure and at least a basic kit of simple spare parts. Savvy motorcyclists fit a cheap rear tyre for the trip, as the centre of the tread will wear quite markedly.

Carry some drinking water (four litres per person), just in case you do have to sit it out by the roadside on a hot summer day. Remember, there are limited supplies of fresh water between Norseman and Ceduna.

There are no banking facilities between Norseman and Ceduna, so take plenty of cash. Some roadhouses have EFTPOS facilities and accept major credit cards.

Take it easy on the Nullarbor. Many people try to set speed records, and plenty have made a real mess of their cars when they've run into big kangaroos, particularly at night. The police also pull out their radar guns every now and then, especially near the WA/SA border.

THE ROUTE

From Norseman, where the Eyre Highway begins, it's 725 km to the WA/SA border, near Eucla, and a further 490 km to Ceduna (from an Aboriginal word meaning 'a place to sit down and rest') in South Australia. From Ceduna, it's still another 793 km to Adelaide via Port Augusta. It is, in the immortal words of a trans-Australian truckie, 'a bloody long way!'

Norseman

To most people, Norseman is just a cross-roads where you turn east for the trans-Nullarbor journey, south to Esperance along the Leeuwin Way or north to Coolgardie and Perth. The town, however, also has gold mines, some still in operation. The **Historical & Geological Collection** in the old School of Mines has items from the gold-rush days; it's open on weekdays from 10 am to 4 pm and admission is $2.

An interesting gold-mining tour is conducted by the Central Norseman Gold mining operations every weekday at 10 am and 1 pm; the 2½-hour tour costs $5 and bookings can be made at the tourist bureau. You can get an excellent view of the town and the surrounding salt lakes from the **Beacon Hill Mararoa Lookout**, down past the mountainous tailings.

Norseman to Cocklebiddy (441 km)

From Norseman, the first settlement you reach is **Balladonia**, 193 km to the east. After Balladonia, near the old station, you may see the remains of old stone fences built to enclose stock. Clay saltpans are also visible in the area. **Newmann's Rocks**, 50 km west of Balladonia, are also worth seeing. The Crocker family have a fine art gallery (☎ (090) 39 3456), with paintings of the Eyre Highway. Phone between 9 am and 4.30 pm to arrange a visit.

The road from Balladonia to Cocklebiddy is a lonely section. To Caiguna, it includes one of the longest stretches of straight road in the world – 145 km, the so-called 90-Mile Straight.

Caiguna, over 370 km from Norseman, is a good place to stop. Some 10 km south of Caiguna is the memorial to John Baxter, Eyre's companion, who was killed on 29 April 1841 by hostile Aborigines.

At Cocklebiddy are the stone ruins of an Aboriginal mission. **Cocklebiddy Cave** is the largest of the Nullarbor caves. In 1983 a team of French explorers set a record here for the deepest cave dive in the world.

With a 4WD, you can travel south of Cocklebiddy to **Twilight Cove**, where there are 75-metre-high limestone cliffs, or to the

The most-photographed road sign along the Eyre Highway (RN)

Eyre Bird Observatory (see the later Detours section).

Cocklebiddy to Eucla (271 km)
Ninety-one km east of Cocklebiddy is **Madura**, close to the hills of the Hampton Tablelands. At one time, horses were bred here for the Indian Army. You get good views over the plains from the road.

The ruins of the **Old Madura Homestead**, several km west of the new homestead by a dirt track, have some old machinery and other equipment. Caves in the area include the large **Mullamullang Caves**, north-west of Madura, with three lakes and many side passages.

The **Mundrabilla Roadhouse** is on the lower coastal plain, with the Hampton Tablelands as a backdrop. From Mundrabilla it is 66 km to Eucla.

Eucla & the WA/SA Border
Just before the South Australian border is Eucla, which has picturesque ruins (just the chimneys stick out now) of an old **telegraph repeater & weather station**, first opened in 1877. The telegraph line now runs along the railway line, far to the north. The station, five km from the roadhouse, is gradually being engulfed by the sand dunes. You can also inspect the historic jetty, which is visible from the top of the dunes. The dunes around Eucla are a truly spectacular sight.

The 3340-hectare **Eucla National Park** is only a 10-minute drive from the town. It features the Delisser Sandhills and the high limestone Wilson Bluff. The mallee scrub and heath of the park is typical of the coastal vegetation in this region.

At Eucla, many people have their photo taken with the international sign pinpointing distances to many parts of the world; it's near a ferro-concrete sperm whale, seldom seen in these parts.

At **Border Village**, 13 km from Eucla, connoisseurs of kitsch will appreciate a five-metre-high fibreglass kangaroo. Remember to set your watch forward 1½ hours – or 2½ hours when daylight-saving time operates in South Australia.

Border Village to Nullarbor Roadhouse (188 km)

Between the WA/SA border and Nullarbor Roadhouse, the Eyre Highway runs close to the coast, and there are six spectacular **look-outs** over the Great Australian Bight – be sure to stop at one or two.

After about 90 km, you reach a turn-off (4WD only) to the well-known **Koonalda Cave**. It has a 45-metre-high chamber, entered by ladder. Like other Nullarbor caves, it's really for experienced cave explorers only.

Around **Nullarbor Roadhouse** are many caves, which should be explored only with extreme care (again, they are recommended to experienced cave explorers only). Watch out for wombat holes and poisonous snakes

in the area. A dirt road leads to a beach, 30 km away – ask directions at the roadhouse.

Nullarbor National Park (593,000 hectares) and **Nullarbor Regional Reserve** (2.28 million hectares) contain part of the largest arid limestone landscape in the world. The treeless terrain is better appreciated travelling north of the Eyre Highway along the Cook Road.

Nullarbor to Nundroo (144 km)

The road passes through the Yalata Aboriginal Reserve (600,000 hectares), and Aborigines often sell boomerangs and other souvenirs by the roadside. You can also buy these in the **Yalata Community Roadhouse**.

Winter and early spring is a good time to whale-watch (southern right whales); the best viewing point is **Twin Rocks**, at the Head of the Bight, and for seven km west of the rocks. The turn-off to Twin Rocks is about 20 km east of the Nullarbor Road-

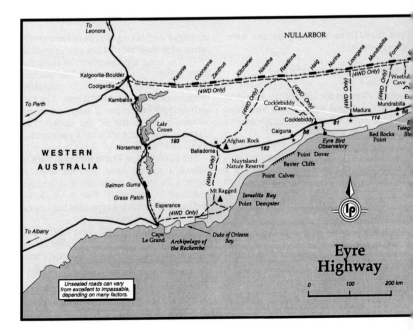

Eyre Highway

Unsealed roads can vary from excellent to impassable, depending on many factors.

0   100   200 km

house. Get a $2 permit from the Nullarbor or Yalata roadhouses. The edge of the Nullarbor is at **Nundroo**, 51 km from Yalata.

Nundroo to Ceduna (161 km)

Between Nundroo and Penong is the ghost town of **Fowlers Bay**. There is good fishing here, and nearby is **Mexican Hat Beach**.

You can make a short detour south of Penong to see the Pink Lake, Point Sinclair and **Cactus Beach**, a surf beach with left and right breaks that is a 'must' for any serious surfer making the east-west journey.

Eastbound from Penong to Ceduna, there are several places with petrol and other facilities. **Ceduna**, effectively the end of the solitary stretch from Norseman, is equipped with supermarkets, banks and all the comforts.

DETOURS

Look at any map of the central Nullarbor and you will see that very few roads head south. There are, however, a number leading north to the transcontinental railway line. Two detours from the normal route are described here. One leads south to the Great Australian Bight; the other takes you north to the railway, east along it and back south to the Eyre Highway.

Eyre Bird Observatory

Established in 1977, the observatory is housed in the Eyre Telegraph Station. This 1897 stone building in the Nuytsland Nature Reserve is surrounded by mallee scrubland and looks up to spectacular roving sand dunes which separate buildings from the sea. A small museum at the rear of the station has exhibits from the days of the telegraph line and of the legendary stationmaster William Graham.

Full board is the usual arrangement: $45 per person per day (with discounts for YHA and Royal Australian Ornithological Union members).

The observatory is about 50 km south-east

THE SOUTH

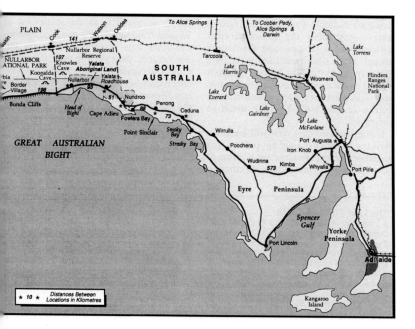

of Cocklebiddy, and if you are travelling independently, you will need a 4WD to get there. The turn-off from the Eyre Highway is 16 km from Cocklebiddy, and from there it is 14.5 km to the microwave tower. Turn right at the tower and drive to the lookout carpark. Down below you see the sandhills near the station and the road snaking out towards it. From here the road gets rough; keep an eye out for a small arrow that indicates the track down the escarpment. At the base of the escarpment the drive is through about 12 km of sand to the observatory, so tyres may sometimes need to be deflated.

Return transport to the bird observatory from Cocklebiddy or the microwave tower can be arranged for about $25.

From the buildings, there is a one-km walk, via the dunes, to the beach and the lonely Great Australian Bight. You can also drive out here and along the sand.

Into the Nullarbor

Possibly the best detour into the Nullarbor is in South Australia: drive north through the Nullarbor National Park and the regional reserve, east along the transcontinental railway line to Ooldea, and then south through Yalata Aboriginal Land to the Eyre Highway. From Eucla or Border Village, it is a full day of driving, best broken into two days. Take plenty of water. Because of rough sections of road a 4WD vehicle would be preferable.

If you take two days, you will need two permits: a bush-camping permit for Nullarbor Regional Reserve and a permit to cross Yalata Aboriginal Land (see Permits in the Information section earlier). There is a fuel outlet at Cook (☎ (086) 41 8506), but it is not always open when you need it – phone ahead to find out its hours.

From Border Village, it is 146 km to the Cook turn-off. If you go to a few (or all) of the Nullarbor lookouts, this stretch of sealed road will take some time. It is 107 km north to Cook.

Turn right and follow the rough road which parallels the transcontinental railway on its south side to Watson, passing by Fisher and O'Malley stations. Cross to the north side of the line at Watson, follow the improved road to Ooldea and then cross to the south again (the Telecom repeater station should be to your left) – it is about 141 km from Cook to Ooldea. Proceed south to the Eyre Highway, crossing Ifould Lake, a large saltpan, on the way. Leave the gates in this section as you found them, and make sure you close the dog-barrier gate.

ALTERNATIVE ROUTES
Esperance to Balladonia

For those travelling in the south-west of Western Australia, there is one good alternative route from Esperance. You can cut north-east to the Eyre Highway from near Cape Arid National Park utilising the 4WD-only Balladonia Road. To get there, head out from Esperance on Fisheries Rd, and when Grewer Rd comes in on the right, turn left. This becomes Balladonia Road and allows you to traverse part of Cape Arid National Park.

On this route you will pass Mt Ragged, the highest point in the Russell Range, where there is a tough walk to the top (three km

---

The Last Place on Earth

A latter-day visitor to the Eyre Bird Observatory was eccentric US millionaire Harold Anderson. Convinced that some form of nuclear Armageddon was nigh, and that Eyre's isolation made it just the place to sit out the firestorms and nuclear winters that would wrack the rest of the world, he decided to donate to the observatory all the books he thought would form the perfect account of the earth and its history.

Anderson returned to the USA, collated the books and despatched them to Australia. Not long afterwards he was mugged and died, in his early forties, never to see the books on the shelves at the observatory. They are still there, alongside all the written paraphernalia any avid bird-watcher could need. ■

return, three hours). Good topographic coverage is found in the 1:250,000 AUSLIG series *Balladonia* and *Malcolm*. Good information on the national park is in the CALM pamphlet *Cape Arid & Eucla*.

You have to be self-sufficient with both fuel and water, and after Duke of Orleans Bay (to the south of the route), there are no facilities until Balladonia.

ACTIVITIES
Bird-watching
The Eyre Bird Observatory is one of the best places in the country to go bird-watching (see the earlier Detours section).

A wide range of desert flora and fauna is studied. Twitchers can expect to see many pink cockatoos, brush bronzewings and the odd furtive mallee fowl. There are many birds of prey along all sections of the highway, dispensing with road kills. By far the most spectacular is the wedge-tailed eagle.

Cycling
The Eyre Highway is a real challenge to cyclists, who are attracted by the barrenness and distance, certainly not by the interesting scenery. As you drive across, you see many of them, at all times of the year, lifting water bottles to parched mouths or sheltering under the lone large tree that punctuates stretches of the highway.

Obviously, excellent equipment is needed and adequate water supplies must be carried. The cyclist should also know where all the water tanks are located. And as for the sun, adequate protection should be applied even in cloudy weather. Realise that the prevailing wind for most of the journey will be west to east, the preferable direction to be pedalling.

Spare a thought for the first cyclist to cross the Nullarbor. Arthur Richardson set off from Coolgardie on 24 November 1896 with a small kit and water bag. Thirty-one days later he arrived in Adelaide, having followed the telegraph line. Problems he encountered

THE SOUTH

Dune near the Eyre Bird Observatory (JW)

were the hot winds, '1000 in the shade' and 40 km of sandhills west of Madura station.

FACILITIES
Norseman

The *Gateway Caravan Park* (☎ (090) 39 1500) has tent sites ($11), vans ($26) and on-site cabins ($35). The backpackers' hostel in Norseman closed down and still hasn't reopened. The *Norseman Hotel* (☎ (090) 39 1023) charges $25/40 for singles/doubles, the *Railway Hotel Motel* (☎ (090) 39 1115) has rooms for $20/30 and the *Norseman Eyre Motel* (☎ (090) 39 1130) charges $62/69.

Bits & Pizzas has a wide range of eat-in or takeaway meals, and also cooked breakfasts with the works for $7.50. The *BP Roadhouse* at the start of the Eyre Highway has a wide range of food, including tasty fish & chips.

All types of fuel, including LPG, are available. There are banking facilities in town.

Balladonia to Cocklebiddy

The *Balladonia Hotel/Motel* (☎ (090) 39 3453) has rooms from $58/66 a single/double, and its dusty caravan park has tent/caravan sites for an exhorbitant $8/14. At Caiguna, the *John Eyre Motel* (☎ (090) 39 3459) has rooms for $50/65 and a caravan park with tent/caravan sites from $5/12.

The *Wedgetail Inn* (☎ (090) 39 3462) at Cocklebiddy has a marauding and contrary goat, extremely expensive fuel, overpriced rooms (from $58/66), and tent/caravan sites for $6/12. Hey, it does have wedge-tailed eagles overhead!

Balladonia, Caiguna and Cocklebiddy have all types of fuel (including LPG), and telephones.

Cocklebiddy to Eucla

The *Madura Hospitality Inn* (☎ (090) 39 3464) has rooms from $60/70 and tent/caravan sites from $5/12.

At Mundrabilla, 114 km to the east, the *Mundrabilla Motor Hotel* (☎ (090) 39 3465) has singles/doubles from $45/55, and a caravan park with tent/caravan sites from $5/10 and cabins for $20.

Madura and Mundrabilla have all types of fuel (including LPG).

Eucla & the WA/SA Border

The *Eucla Motor Hotel* (☎ (090) 39 3468) has single/double rooms for $58/68; its Eucla Pass section has rooms for $18/30 and the tent/caravan sites are $4/10 (showers are $1). The *WA-SA Border Village* (☎ (090) 39 3474) has tent/caravan sites from $6/12, cabins from $35 a double and motel units from $60/68.

All types of fuel (including LPG) are available in both Eucla and at Border Village.

Eucla to Ceduna

The *Nullarbor Hotel-Motel* (☎ (086) 25 6271) has tent sites from $8, backpackers' singles/twins for $15/25, units from $55/65 and a restaurant. Just look for the fibreglass southern right whale.

The *Yalata Aboriginal Community Roadhouse* (☎ (086) 25 6990) has tent sites from $3.50 and singles/doubles from $30/35; there's also a restaurant and a takeaway.

The *Nundroo Inn* (☎ (086) 25 6120) has singles/doubles for $58/63 and a caravan park with tent sites. There is a licensed restaurant, takeaway and a pool.

The *Penong Hotel* (☎ (086) 25 1050) has basic singles/doubles from $20/30, and serves counter meals. The service station across the road has a restaurant and takeaway.

All types of fuel, including LPG, can be obtained from Nullarbor, Nundroo and Penong, but not Yalata.

Eastbound from Penong to Ceduna, there are several places with all types of fuel and other facilities. Ceduna is effectively the end of the solitary stretch from Norseman, and is equipped with supermarkets, banks and all the comforts.

ALTERNATIVE TRANSPORT

As the Eyre is the most important transcontinental route, there are daily scheduled bus services all the way from Perth to Adelaide with Greyhound Pioneer Australia. There is also a rail option, one of the great railway journeys of the world (see the Indian-Pacific entry in the Getting Around chapter at the start of this book).

Flinders Ranges

For many seasoned travellers the Flinders Ranges in South Australia are the epitome of the outback. Certainly they are, for the vast majority of Australians, the easiest outback destination to get to. One other thing is certain: of all the regions in Australia's outback, the Flinders has had more glossy coffee-table books produced about it than any other. That does say something about its grandeur and attraction.

While the Flinders officially begin near Crystal Brook, just 195 km north of Adelaide, it is further north where they take on their distinguishing outback characteristics. It's also further north where they reach their highest point and are at their grandest.

On these pages we describe the loop route from Hawker north via Wilpena, Blinman and Arkaroola to Lyndhurst, which is one of many that can be done in the Flinders. While it could be done as a stand-alone trip, it is also an enjoyable route north to Lyndhurst or Marree and the start of the Strzelecki, Oodnadatta and Birdsville tracks.

Much of the route could be travelled, generally, in a normal car, as the conditions vary from good bitumen to slow but reasonable dirt. Only in the far north, beyond Arkaroola, do the tracks become real 4WD.

All told, this trip covers around 450 km of rugged outback range country. You could travel this route in a longish day, but you wouldn't see much and you'd enjoy it even less. There are a number of places to stock up with supplies, and you could stay in a motel or hotel every evening you are away.

HISTORY

The Adnyamathanha, or 'hill people', as they are now called, have inhabited the Flinders Ranges for many thousands of years. The ranges and the people who lived there were an integral part of the long-distance trade routes that crossed the continent. Ochre and pituri, a mildly narcotic drug, were traded over long distances, as were stones for axes and tools, and shell for decoration.

Dotted amongst the hills and valleys are a number of important archaeological sites that include ochre quarries (the ochre being used as a paint decoration in ceremonies), rock quarries (sources of tools) and art sites. The latter are the most vivid reminders of the richness of this ancient culture. The sites in the Flinders are rich in rock engravings, or petroglyphs, a form of art that probably predates the painted art work which, in the Flinders, lacks the richness and variety found at art sites in northern Australia.

The last full-blood Adnyamathanha died in 1973, but all the descendants of the tribal groups that inhabited the ranges and the surrounding country have strong ties to the land. Most live in the towns of the region; Nepabunna, east of Copley, is a small community.

The first White person to see these ranges was Matthew Flinders, from the deck of his ship *Investigator* in March 1802 as it sailed up the large gulf now called Spencer Gulf. From his anchorage south of present-day Port Augusta he sent a group to climb the highest peak in the vicinity, naming it Mt Brown after his intrepid botanist.

Edward John Eyre was next on the scene in 1839. Over the next two years, on a number of separate trips from Adelaide, he explored along the western edge of the range, striking west and north, but ran into a series of salt lakes that he thought was one giant ring of salt blocking his way north. His last expedition saw him push east, from north of Mt Deception, past Mt Aroona and deep into the ranges near Mt Serle, before following the Frome River north out of the labyrinth of gorges and rugged ridges surrounding him. Following the edge of the range north-east, he climbed a low hill that he named, supposedly before he even climbed it, Mt Hopeless, and once again spied a barrier of salt.

Just four years later the pastoral expansion

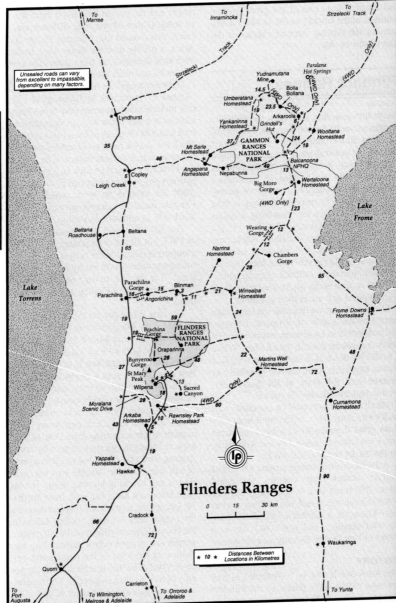

Flinders Ranges

had reached the southern edge of the Flinders Ranges near Gladstone, and slowly but surely pushed north. Wilpena Pound, one of the natural wonders of the Flinders, was discovered soon afterwards by William Chace, who had been sent out by the Browne brothers (both doctors). By 1851 these two influential doctors had taken up the Wilpena, Aroona and Arkaba runs. The runs incorporated some of the best-watered and most scenic country in the ranges, and today Wilpena and Aroona make up the picturesque Flinders Ranges National Park, while Arkaba is still privately owned but operated in part as a tourist lease.

Other pioneer pastoralists pushed further. Big John McKinlay claimed much of the area south of Mt Serle but sold off most of his holdings to others who followed. By the early 1860s all of the range country was held under pastoral lease.

Earlier, in 1846, copper had been found near Mt Remarkable and in 1859 it was also discovered at what became known as Blinman. Other discoveries followed, but while some were fantastically rich they were generally only small, and the mines, plagued by long distances from markets, little water, poor or nonexistent roads, never made a profit. Today the ruins of those mining ventures are some of the best-preserved and poignant reminders of our recent past, scattered throughout the ranges in narrow, forgotten valleys.

From the 1870s the area south of Hawker was opened up to more intensive farming. This was in conflict with the view of the surveyor-general, G W Goyder, whose name is immortalised in Goyder's Line. That line, Goyder said, indicated where the rainfall and the country changed from prospective farming land to pastoral country. A run of good seasons pushed the wheat farmers well north, towards and even into Wilpena Pound, but in the end, normal seasons returned and Goyder was proven right. The scattered stone ruins of old farm houses around Hawker, and the occasional abandoned old wheat harvester, are all that remains of their dreams and aspirations.

In the far north, among the convoluted ridges and gorges of the area we know as the Gammon Ranges, W B Greenwood found a wealth of different minerals, triggering a gem rush that had prospectors combing the hills looking for sapphires and rubies.

His discovery of the uranium-rich ore torbernite in the area around Mt Painter is what he is most remembered for, but it was years before the new mineral could be identified. Working with Douglas Mawson, later of Antarctica fame, the two pegged many claims in the region. With the ore being used to produce radium, which in 1924 was worth, supposedly, the modern equivalent of $2 million an ounce, other prospectors rushed to secure leases in the rugged range country of the northern Flinders. Bigger, more easily worked discoveries of the ore overseas saw the Flinders mines wane, only to be revived again when the USA was developing the atomic bomb in the 1940s.

Like most of the minerals found in the

Grass trees in the Flinders (R & VM)

Flinders, however, these finds were small deposits, far from markets. Other minerals were found throughout the ranges, but it is only the Leigh Creek coal fields, the barytes mine just east of the Flinders Ranges National Park, and the talc mine in the far north at Mt Fitton, that have been the most enduring.

Since the end of the WW II the area has become a major tourist drawcard, and while it's not in the same league as the Great Barrier Reef or Uluru (Ayers Rock), tourism is an important part of the local economy.

INFORMATION
Tourist Offices
The best way to obtain tourist information is to write or phone Flinders Outback Tourism (☎ (086) 42 2469, fax 41 0781), PO Box 41, Port Augusta, SA 5700.

For information on the national parks, contact the Department of Environment & Land Management, Far North Region, Hawker office (☎ (086) 48 4244).

Police & Hospitals
Hawker has a police station (☎ (086) 48 4028) in Eighth St; the Great Northern War Memorial Hospital (☎ (086) 48 4007) is in Fifth St.

Leigh Creek is the only other town in the region with a police station and hospital. The police station (☎ (086) 75 2004) and hospital (☎ (086) 75 2100) are both in Black Oak Drive.

Permits
No permits are required to travel the region and it is not necessary to notify the police of your travels.

Permits, however, are required if you want to camp in the national parks in the area. They can be obtained at the ranger headquarters at Wilpena or Balcanoona. The regional base for all the parks in the far north of South Australia is in Hawker (☎ (086) 48 4244), on the corner of Wilpena Rd and Elder Terrace.

Books & Maps
There is a good range of books available that cover all aspects of the Flinders Ranges. Hawker Motors in Hawker has a good selection of Flinders books for sale.

The Story of the Flinders Ranges by Hans Mincham (Rigby) is the best book on the history of the area. Most of the towns, including Hawker, Quorn and Port Augusta, have local history books published about them, while a couple of small paperbacks have been published on local mysteries such as the murder in the Gammon Ranges detailed in the book *Cloud over the Gammon Ranges* by Alan Bailey (Endage Print).

Flinders Ranges – an Australian Aura by David Berndstoecker (South Australian Government Printer) and *The Flinders Ranges – a Portrait* with text by Hans Mincham and photography by Eduard Domin (Little Hills Press) are just two of the glossy coffee-table books on the region. The latest glossy book, *Flinders Ranges, South Australia: the Art of the Photographer* by Stavros Pippos (Endeavour Publishing), is arguably the best.

If you are into the natural delights of the area, *The Story of the Flinders Ranges Mammals* by Dorothy Turnbridge (Kangaroo Press) is a good insight into the animals of the ranges. *Fossils of the Flinders and Mt Lofty Ranges* by Neville S Pledge (South Australian Museum) covers the fossils found in the region, while a book and a small brochure that share the same name, *Corridors Through Time – the Geology of the Flinders Ranges*, covers the geology.

The best guidebook on the area for those wanting to camp and 4WD is *The Flinders Ranges – an Adventurer's Guide* by Ron & Viv Moon (Kakirra Adventure Publications). A couple of good walking guides are also available, including *A Walking guide to the Flinders Ranges* by Adrian Heard (State Publishing South Australia) and *Flinders Ranges Walks* by Peter Beer (Conservation Council of South Australia). Probably the best walking guide to the Flinders, though, is *Grant's Guide to the Flinders Ranges* by Grant Da Costa (Acacia Vines). For rock climbers, *A Climber's Guide to Moonarie*

(South Australian Climbing Club) is available from good outdoor shops in Adelaide.

The *Official Visitor's Guide – Flinders Ranges and Outback* covers all of the Flinders and much of the outback and gives good detail on the facilities, places to stay, commercial tours etc of the region. It has one big advantage: its free! It is available in many stores in the local area.

The Department of Recreation & Sport publishes maps which cover the length of the Heysen Walking Trail. These are available from the Department's shop in Adelaide (see the boxed story on the Heysen Trail for details). However, the best single map of the area for general touring is *Flinders Ranges, South Australia* produced by the Flinders Ranges & Outback of South Australia Regional Tourist Association. This map is readily available locally or from the automobile associations in each state.

Radio Frequencies

There is really no need for an HF radio in this region. If you have one fitted to your vehicle, the frequencies to have are the RFDS base at Port Augusta (callsign VNZ; primary frequency 4010; secondary frequencies 6890 and 8165) and the OTC base in Sydney (callsign VIS). OTC 24-hour channels include 405, 607, 802, 1203, and 1602. Other frequencies for Selcall and Tonecall are also available. The Selcall for the beacon is 0899, while for the operator it is 0108.

Other Information

This trip is relatively easy. Distances between facilities are not great, the roads are generally pretty good, certainly for outback standards, and they are used regularly. A bitumen road is not far away, and if anything does go wrong it is fairly easy to get help. Travellers can contact the Department of Road Transport's Far Northern Roads Condition Report (☎ (08) 11633) for current details on road conditions.

THE ROUTE

The route described here is one of a number that can be used to traverse the ranges from south to north, but it offers a good insight into the delights of the ranges, the variety of landforms and the mix of history that lies within these rocky ramparts.

Hawker

For many travellers the adventure begins at the small township of Hawker, 375 km north of Adelaide. You can reach this outback town by travelling the blacktop via Port Augusta and Quorn or via Melrose, Wilmington and Quorn. Or you can take in a short section of excellent dirt road by travelling via Jamestown and Orroroo. The latter route is the shortest from Adelaide, while the route via Melrose is the most picturesque.

Established in 1880, Hawker originally serviced the many wheat farms that were established in the area and now caters for the sheep properties that took their place. Tourism is also an important industry, ever since the railway stopped passing through the town in 1970.

Hawker is a good place to use as your major resupply point. It has everything a traveller needs, including a choice of stores, fuel outlets, vehicle repair places and accommodation, but only one pub.

Although there is a choice, **Hawker Motors** in the centre of town is where most tourists go for fuel, minor repairs, souvenirs and information. The business was established by Fred Teague, who is something of a legend in the Flinders, and he and his family are a good source of information on the history of the area and what is going on now. Inside the store is a good little museum and a wide range of books for sale.

Many travellers use the town as a base to explore the area, but Quorn is better if you are travelling around the area south of Hawker, and Wilpena is more central if you are exploring to the north.

Hawker to Blinman (154 km)

Heading north-east on the bitumen to Wilpena Pound, the road initially traverses gently undulating country, with the main range away to the left. Dominating the distant vista to the north are the bluffs of the

THE SOUTH

The southern wall of Wilpena Pound (R & VM)

of the best drought-protected properties in the Flinders. Surprisingly, much of the property was completely inaccessible to vehicles up until a few years ago. Then the new owners, members of the well-known Rasheed family who own and manage Wilpena Pound, pushed a couple of tracks into the country bordering the Elder Range and began to control the rabbits and goats that had run unchecked for generations. The results have been spectacular, and the family were recognised for their work by winning a major state conservation award in 1992.

Those tracks also make much of the range country accessible for keen 4WD travellers who can join an organised self-drive trip through the property. Trips vary in duration from one to three days, and travellers camp in idyllic secluded isolation on gum-tree-lined flats beside the ranges. A few goats still exist in the rugged back country, but the native wildlife has flourished. Red kangaroos and the more stockily built hill wallaroo, or euro, are often seen at close quarters, while the natural water points that dot the property are a magnet for animals, including a wide variety of birds.

southern wall of Wilpena Pound. As you progress, the Elder Range off to the west begins to draw the eyes more and more.

Arkaba Station The turn-off to Arkaba Station Woolshed is 19 km north of Hawker. This historic working woolshed is just a few hundred metres off the main road and caters to passing travellers with coffee, scones and cool drinks, as well as a good range of local art, craft and souvenirs. Arkaba runs the best 4WD tag-along trips in the area, with trips that offer some of the best country in the Flinders along the Elder Range and the southern ramparts of the Wilpena Range. For those without a 4WD, tours can be arranged through the Wilpena Pound Resort.

A cottage is available here for rent and a tented camp is also located on this renowned and strikingly spectacular property.

Arkaba Station was one of the first properties taken up in the area, and with its good supplies of spring-fed water it remains one

Arkaba Station to Wilpena Pound Less than five km further along the bitumen, the **Moralana Scenic Drive** veers off to the left. This road is actually a private road that cuts across Arkaba Station; public access is allowed, but straying from the road or camping is not! The 28 km (one way) drive gives splendid views of both the Elder Range and the southern wall of Wilpena Pound.

Rawnsley Park, a small sheep property of just over 3000 hectares, on the left of the road 10 km further north, offers a large caravan and camping ground, as well as self-contained cabins and bunkhouse-style accommodation. It is popular during school holidays but is quiet the rest of the time. Worthy of note is that pets are allowed, provided they are kept under control.

As you continue northwards along the bitumen, the southern rampart of the Wilpena Pound Range, Rawnsley Bluff, crowds in from the west. Soon after, seven km from the turn-off to Rawnsley Park, there is a minor signposted track on the left to **Arkaroo Rock**, an Aboriginal art site within the national park. A short walk from the carpark brings you to this small but important site. It's an enjoyable walk through open forest alive with birds. Keen rock climbers can reach the 100-metre sandstone walls of Moonarie via a longer walk from the carpark, and there are many routes up the cliffs to challenge the most dedicated climber.

Back on the bitumen, you will enter the **Flinders Ranges National Park** three km further along the road, with the main road now running parallel to the main range of the Pound. The drive is very enjoyable, with a red-gum-lined rocky creek beside the road and a dense forest of smallish native pines crowding the road and the creek.

Wilpena Pound The turn-off to Wilpena Pound Resort, and the only entrance into Wilpena Pound, is 18 km north of Rawnsley Park, or 52 km north of Hawker. Turning left here will lead you four km to the main parking area, the ranger's office and the entrance to the resort and the camping ground. Fuel and limited supplies are available. If you can't stop here for a day or two, it is definitely worth a visit for a day. The walking is superb and there are a number of walking trails you can take, depending on your fitness and keenness. The Heysen Trail passes through the national park.

Wilpena Pound is one of the most sensational visual features of the Flinders, and it's also a spectacular geological structure – a natural amphitheatre 11 km long and five km wide. 'Wilpena' is an Aboriginal word that is taken to mean 'the place of the bent fingers' or 'a cupped hand', both of which are very appropriate.

The range that forms its perimeter slopes gently up from the inside to a line of bluffs and high peaks, which drop steeply on the outside to the surrounding hills and plains. **St Mary Peak** (1190 metres), the highest peak in South Australia, is on the north-western extremity of the Pound. The summit gives fine views of the encircling ranges, as well as occasionally attracting snow!

Only two creeks flow out of the Pound. One is **Wilpena Creek**, which gives the only practical access; where it leaves the Pound is where you will find the caravan park and all the facilities of the resort. The gums that line the creek here are magnificent and it is no wonder that the area is popular with travellers. The second creek is Edeowie Creek, which leaves the Pound by a series of waterfalls and a tortuous course through **Edeowie Gorge**, in the far north-west of the Pound's surrounding ramparts.

The flat, well-watered floor of Wilpena Pound was used by the early pioneers as a grazing lease for sheep and cattle, and for many years much of it was ploughed and wheat was grown, the tall peaks attracting more than their fair share of rainfall. In 1914 a flood down Wilpena Creek washed away the only track access into the Pound, and wheat-growing was abandoned. In 1920, on the expiration of the lease, the area was declared a forest reserve. Over the next few years the Pound and its surrounds were leased by a number of people.

In 1945 tourism had reached the stage where Wilpena Pound was proclaimed a National Pleasure Resort. A couple of years later a resort was built at the entrance to the Pound, and this was taken over in the 1950s by Kevin Rasheed, whose family still run this popular operation.

In 1970 the state government purchased Oraparinna Station, proclaiming Oraparinna National Park. In 1972 Wilpena Pound was

THE SOUTH

Aerial view of Wilpena Pound (R & VM)

THE SOUTH

The Heysen Trail
The Heysen Trail is one of Australia's premier long-distance walking tracks. It starts far to the south at Cape Jervis, 110 km south of Adelaide, and travels through the Mt Lofty Ranges and much of the Flinders. The trail will eventually cover the whole length of the Flinders, but at present there are a couple of gaps – one around Quorn and the other in the far north up to Mt Hopeless. Luckily the sections that are covered in the Flinders are the most picturesque.

In 1967, long before a recognised trail was established, C W Bonython became the first to walk the complete length of the range, a story told eloquently in his book *Walking the Flinders Ranges* (Rigby). Since then, others have followed and completed the long walk.

The trail is named after one of Australia's greatest painters, the late Sir Hans Heysen, who painted extensively in the areas around Aroona and Arkaba. He first visited the ranges in 1926, returning again and again to paint and capture the mood of the ranges that he described later as 'the bones of Nature laid bare'. While other painters followed, and many still paint in these hills, it was probably Heysen more than any other who really opened people's eyes to the grandeur and the majestic beauty of the Flinders.

The Heysen Trail is mapped and marked from Crystal Brook to Quorn in the south and central section of the range, and from Hawker to Parachilna further north. Good access via dedicated access tracks, and where the trail crosses a road, means you can walk the route for a day or longer.

A book and a series of maps produced by the South Australian Department of Recreation, Sport & Racing give you all the required information. The 1:50,000 topographic strip maps not only provide the normal geographical information, but also mark the route clearly and give good descriptions of the route, places to see, and some timely reminders about walking in this essentially arid country.

To walk the Heysen Trail you must be fit, have the right equipment, and know how to use it. A good knowledge of map-reading and route-finding is essential. It is surprising how many people get lost following the well-marked trail. And getting lost in this country can be one very short step away from dying.

Remember that the trail traverses private land for much of the way. Treat the privilege of crossing it with the consideration it deserves. Be extremely careful with fire, obey all the regulations, leave gates as you find them, don't disturb stock and don't camp right beside water so stock can't come and drink.

All of the Heysen Trail is closed to walkers from 1 November to 30 March, the only exceptions being a couple of short walks within the Flinders Ranges National Park. Contact the South Australian National Parks Service for details.

The books and maps on the Heysen Trail are available from good map shops throughout Australia and from a number of stores in the Flinders. The Department of Recreation, Sport & Racing also produces 15 maps covering the length of the trail, each costing $5.50. These maps can be purchased from the Department's shop outlet (☎ (08) 226 7374), Shop 20, Ground Floor, City Centre Arcade, Adelaide, or write to the Department of Recreation, Sport & Racing, GPO Box 1865, Adelaide, SA 5001. ■

added to the national park to form the Flinders Ranges National Park. Since then, extra additions have taken the park to its present size of 92,746 hectares, but the Pound is still the major drawcard. Since 1988 the government has been trying to get a five-star international resort built here, with a well-watered golf course and the like, catering for the expected hordes of well-heeled tourists. It seems this plan has been wrecked on the rocks of recession, much to the delight of the people who love the Flinders and the Pound as a natural wonder belonging to everyone.

Wilpena Pound to Blinman Back on the main road north, the bitumen quickly ends. Just before you cross Wilpena Creek, one km north of the turn-off to Wilpena, a track heads off to the right to **Sacred Canyon**. This small gorge contains some of the best of the easily accessible Aboriginal rock engravings in the Flinders.

Nearly five km north of the turn-off to

Wilpena, at a major road junction, take the road to the left. This is the start of one of the best drives in the Flinders; early morning, when the sun lights up the walls of the distant Heysen Range, is the time to go. The road is reasonably good dirt with the odd rough patch, so a normal car should have no problems.

For the first 12 km to **Yanyanna Hut** the road traverses rolling hills cut by charming, tree-lined creeks. In the early morning, kangaroos and emus are commonly seen, as are flocks of raucous pink and grey galahs and snow-white corellas. Yanyanna Hut and its nearby yards testify to the days when this area was a working property.

From here the road swings in a big arc, the vegetation changes to native pine, and the scenery gets better. The **Bunyeroo Valley Lookout** two km from the hut is worth a stop to admire the view and get the camera out. The Heysen Range dominates the background to the west, while a lower range of more rounded peaks between the lookout and the main wall of rock is the ABC Range. To the south are the battlements of the eastern wall of Wilpena, dominated by St Mary Peak.

For the next two km the road traverses a ridge with spectacular views, before descending steeply to run beside **Bunyeroo Creek**. The next two km is through a winding gorge with the road running, in typical Flinders fashion, along the creekbed. Normally the creek does have water through it, and after heavy rain it is closed to normal traffic. Heed the 'Road Closed' signs if they have been erected. There are a couple of good campsites along this section, although none have any facilities.

As you leave the gorge, the road swings up out of the creek and heads north. A carpark on the left is a good spot to stop and take a walk down into Bunyeroo Gorge proper. For the next 10 km the road heads north, with the rugged Heysen Range off to the left and the ABC Range directly off to the right.

Turn left at the T-junction 10 km north of the carpark. (Turning right at this junction will lead east to a number of good campsites in the Aroona Valley or along Brachina Creek and its tributaries, and from there you can head either north to Blinman or south to Wilpena.) Heading west, the road quickly becomes confined by the surrounding bluffs and cliffs of the Heysen Range into **Brachina Gorge**. The road seems to spend more time in the creekbed than out of it. After heavy rain this road is also closed to normal traffic, so take heed of the warning signs.

There is some excellent camping through here; although it is popular during school holidays, especially in spring, it is one of the best places in the Flinders. The creek is fed by natural springs and it is rare for there to be no water in the gorge. From any of the campsites, there are walks to be enjoyed down along the creek or up the steep hills for an eagle's-eye view of the surrounds.

Seven km west of the T-junction, the road crosses the creek for the last time and climbs a low rise and leaves the park. A lookout on the right gives an enjoyable view of the western battlements of the range, while to the west the flat plains of the desert country begin and sweep away to the shores of Lake Torrens and beyond.

The road improves as it leaves the range country and strikes west for another 12 km before reaching the bitumen at a T-junction. Here you turn right (north) towards Parachilna. Hawker is 70 km south along the bitumen. In the evening, as you head north, the ranges look superb, rearing up from the plain you are now travelling on.

The small railway siding of **Parachilna** is 19 km north of where you joined the bitumen road; you need to turn off to the left to get to the Prairie Hotel or the public showers and toilets that are available. The historic pub can supply accommodation, fuel and a top meal that would do a city restaurant proud.

About 100 metres past the turn-off to the hotel, take the road that strikes east towards the range and the township of Blinman. Nine km later you enter **Parachilna Gorge**, and two km further on a road junction is met. Keep right at the junction, although the left-hand route makes a pleasant scenic drive through Glass's Gorge to Blinman. Good camp sites beside the creek become available just before the road junction off to the left and continue for the next few km.

Parachilna Gorge is not within the national park: it's a recognised camping area maintained by the local shire. A camping permit is not required, and you can take the family pet. Because of that, the spectacular nature of the area, and the almost constant water supply in the spring-fed creek, the gorge is very popular with campers. Even so, you could have a camp site to yourself. The experience of camping here amongst these red-raw ranges, with a trickle of water running past and a lazy wind sighing through the gum trees, is hard to beat.

Camping spots are numerous for the first few km after they appear, but once you arrive at the **Angorichina Tourist Village**, 16 km east of the bitumen, you are really out of the best of the camping areas. Angorichina caters for campers, caravanners and those wanting self-contained cabins, units, on-site vans and bunkhouse-style accommodation. The small general store has fuel, groceries, souvenirs and limited repair facilities.

There is some excellent walking around the gorge, with the Heysen Walking Trail heading south from an obvious picnic site close to the road, about three km before Angorichina. This part of the long-distance walking trail leads south along the Heysen Range all the way to Wilpena and, while you don't need to go that far, you can enjoy a day walk along this marked trail. Another walk is along Oratunga Gorge (on the north side of the road, less than one km before the picnic area), but the best one is along Parachilna and Blinman creeks up to the Blinman Pools and waterfalls.

Blinman

The small township of Blinman is 15 km east of Angorichina. At the T-junction on the edge of town, turn left for the hotel, general store, post office and the **old mine**. In reality the main centre of the town is Blinman North. Blinman, a few km south, is deserted and offers no facilities.

Copper was discovered here in 1859 by Robert 'Pegleg' Blinman, and the original town of Blinman was surveyed in 1864. It was too far for the miners to walk from the mine, so in 1867 a new town was established a little closer to the mine, and Blinman North took over as the main centre of the community. In those years the population was around 1000 – about 985 more than at present. The mine closed in 1874 but was worked spasmodically over the next 30 years. About the only person who ever really made any money out of it was Pegleg, when he sold the mine to the Yudnamutana Copper Mining Company for £70,000 – a lot of money in 1862!

Fuel, a choice of accommodation and meals are available in Blinman and if it's a hot day the kids will probably enjoy a swim in the pub's swimming pool. If you have taken the route described, you are 154 km north of Hawker, but by the shortest route, directly north from Wilpena, the distance is only 111 km.

Bunyeroo Valley with the Heysen Range in the background (R & VM)

Brachina Creek (R & VM)

Blinman to Copley (297 km)

To continue on the loop through the Flinders, head south past the road junction you came in on to another road junction three km south. This is the original township of Blinman. Turn left here, and six km further east, keep right at the junction. A few km further on, the road begins to wind through a small gorge, and 14 km from the Blinman hotel, you pass the turn-off on your left to Narrina Station.

The road passes through The Bunkers range before levelling out across lightly undulating country as Wirrealpa homestead is approached, 35 km from Blinman. Just past the homestead, which is on your right, you meet with a major dirt road coming from the south, which is another route, shorter but nowhere near as scenic, to Wilpena and Hawker.

Turn north and follow the road as it traverses a relatively flat plain with the ranges off to the left. Numerous creeks are crossed but these are nearly always dry, except after heavy local rain when they run for a few hours or maybe a day before being soaked up by the dry sands. The turn-off to Chambers Gorge is 28 km north of Wirrealpa.

Chambers Gorge Chambers Gorge offers some enjoyable camping in an area vastly different to the gorges further south. Here the country is harsher, the vegetation thinner, and the majestic red gums and the native pine no longer dominant. The gorge itself starts about nine km from the turn-off, and within about 400 metres there is a prominent bluff on the left with a small, normally dry creek coming in from the same direction. Access past this point is 4WD. On the southern rim of the gorge is the cube-capped dome of Mt Chambers, resplendent with scree slopes down its flanks.

While the gorge often has water in it, it should not be counted on, especially as a source of drinking water. Don't camp where there are signs indicating no camping near permanent water, as this is the only water source for wildlife and stock in the vicinity. Most of the camps are close to the creek, before the bluff, while the one at the bluff is the most popular and has the most spectacular setting.

Walking in the gorge is worthy of a few hours, especially so in the cool of the morning. Within a few km the gorge opens out and finally, at the edge of the expansive Frome Plains, ends at an impressive rock column known as **Windsor Pillar**.

Back near the first prominent bluff, a short walk up the creek will bring you to one of the best Aboriginal rock engraving sites you will find anywhere. It's worth spending an hour or so here, resting in the shade and pondering on what this country must have been like when these people chipped their designs thousands of years ago. Certainly it was more temperate and water was more abundant than it is now.

Chambers Gorge to Arkaroola On the main route north, 12 km beyond the turn-off to Chambers Gorge, the road begins to pass through **Wearing Gorge**. About two km long, the gorge is a pleasant respite from the sun and heat of the flat plains. Once out of the gorge, the road runs east for 10 km, meeting the main access road north from the small township of Yunta at a T-junction. This route south is the shortest to Adelaide from this point, as Yunta is on the main road between Broken Hill and Adelaide.

Turn left at the T-junction and head north with the immense salt expanse of Lake Frome, occasionally visible, off to the right. Wertaloona homestead, 23 km north of the road junction, is off to the right, while almost directly opposite is the track to **Big Moro Gorge**. The track west to the gorge is 4WD and the 15-km trip takes around 40 minutes. There are some good camp sites along the creek. While the gorge isn't as spectacular as those further south, it's still worth exploring and enjoying.

Heading ever northwards, you come to a major T-junction 13 km north of the Big Moro Gorge turn-off. This is the main Copley-Balcanoona road. Turning left (west) at this junction will lead you on a good dirt road 95 km back to the bitumen at Copley, five km north of Leigh Creek and

159 km north of Hawker. Turning right will take you across a creek, and on your right is **Balcanoona**, now the main ranger station for the Gammon Ranges National Park. If you want to camp in the park, this is the place to go for information and for a camping permit.

The **Gammon Ranges National Park** covers an area of over 128,000 hectares and takes in a strip of land from the edge of Lake Frome, past and including Balcanoona homestead, mushrooming out to protect all the country from Arkaroola, Bolla Bollana and Umberatana in the north, to Arcoona Bluff, Mt McKinlay and Italowie Gorge in the south.

The park encompasses some of the most rugged and least explored country in the Flinders. John McKinlay explored much of the region on his travels looking for pastoral land in 1850, but so rugged and dry was the country that much of it wasn't taken up until later. In 1909 John Grindell secured most of the area in the east and south of what was later to become the national park. The Gammon Ranges themselves were not crossed until Warren Bonython and a friend walked across them in 1947. Today the ranges are a magnet for bushwalkers sufficiently experienced and well equipped to tackle the convoluted gorges and sheer ridges that make up the range country.

There is some excellent camping within the park, and for those with a 4WD an enjoyable selection can be had at places such as Grindell's Hut, Lochness Well or Mainwater Well. Walkers have a much wider choice of campsites. Water is often very scarce in the park so travellers need to be self-sufficient.

Back at the creek crossing just before Balcanoona, a main dirt road heading off to the left, just north of the creek, is the main road to Arkaroola and the one to take.

Nine km from the junction the main access road into the Gammon Ranges National Park heads off to the left. From this junction it is about 10 km to **Grindell's Hut**, about the only spot in the park a normal car has a chance of getting to, driven with care.

Continuing north, the Arkaroola road

skirts the main bulk of the range off to the west, running parallel to the national park boundary. Less than nine km further on, you enter the **Arkaroola Sanctuary**, and 24 km from the Balcanoona road junction you come to another road junction where you need to keep left. Heading right at this point takes you via a scenic drive to **Paralana Hot Springs**, 26 km along the range.

Arkaroola Less than two km up the Arkaroola road from the junction, you pass the original Arkaroola Station, and six km from the junction, you come to a T-junction in the heart of Arkaroola village. You are 307 km north of Hawker by the way you have come, or 248 km by the shortest route (via Wilpena, past the barytes mine, and Wirrealpa to Balcanoona and Arkaroola).

Here you can camp, stay in the caravan park or choose from the wide range of other accommodation available. There is a store, service station, licensed restaurant and swimming pool, and a museum, art gallery and an astronomical observatory. You could easily spend a couple of days here.

The **Arkaroola Sanctuary & Resort** was established by Reg Spriggs in 1968 when he took over the 61,000-hectare station lease. He immediately got rid of the sheep, and over the years that followed brought the rampant feral goat and rabbit populations under control. Now the Arkaroola Sanctuary probably has a better example of the area's flora and fauna than the adjoining national park, all due to the eradication of the vermin on the place.

There are many geological features in this privately owned reserve, many of which, such as **Mt Painter** and the **Armchair**, are registered by the Geological Society as Rock Monuments, while a significant percentage of the area is listed on the Register of the National Estate.

There are many attractions worth visiting, and if you have a 4WD there are some enjoyable drives through the ranges to places of interest. These include Echo Camp Waterhole, Paralana Hot Springs, Bolla Bollana copper mine and smelter in the far north-west of the property, and the Yudnamutana mine and smelter, which is a real highlight. The resort also runs tours to these places for those without a 4WD.

One trip that you can only take in the resort's vehicles is the Ridgetop Tour. This highly recommended tour takes visitors through some of the most rugged country in the ranges to **Sillers Lookout**, where you can get fabulous views of the surrounding peaks and valleys, out across the plain to Lake Frome.

Even if you are only slightly interested in the stars, you should not miss the **astronomical observatory**. With the clear desert air and no artificial light to impinge on the scene, the views of our galaxy and beyond are unbelievable.

There are many good day-long walks in the reserve. One of the most enjoyable is the 2.5 km walk into **Bararranna Waterhole**, and many longer walks are available for those fit and well equipped.

Camping is only allowed in the camping area near the resort, and fires are only allowed in the fireplaces in the camping area.

Arkaroola to Copley The route beyond Arkaroola is really only suitable for 4WDs as it traces a path around the Gammon Ranges National Park. Normal cars will have to retrace their steps to Balcanoona and head to Copley on the main dirt road.

For those wanting to push on, turn left at the T-junction you met as you entered the village and head past the shops, down along Wywhyana Creek, keeping right at the next two track junctions that lead to the caravan and camping areas.

After the second junction, the road continues along Copper Creek and less than seven km from the resort a track heads off to the right to **Bolla Bollana Spring**. A short distance later the road crosses Bolla Bollana Creek and then, on the left, is the turn-off to the parking area for the short walk to the **Bolla Bollana smelter**.

Just a little over nine km from the resort, a turn-off to the right leads to **Nooldoonildoona Waterhole**. This is a pleasant spot, ideal for a lunch break and a bit of exploring.

The road divides 12.4 km from the resort, both branches leading to the same place; the right-hand (northern) route is a little rougher, but it's more enjoyable than the left-hand (southern) route. The right-hand route passes along Wild Dog Creek to a track junction 23.5 km from Arkaroola. From here, the right branch leads north six km to the **Yudnamutana mines** and smelter site which are well worth visiting. The left (south) branch is your route to Umberatana homestead.

You are very much on station tracks now, so leave gates as you find them. Keep right at the next couple of track junctions, and 14.5 km after you turned south, with **Umberatana homestead** on your right, pass through the gate and keep left. If you look up to the left along the ridge line once you are past the windmill, you'll see the remains of a stone fence – imagine building it! The fence finishes a couple of km later.

Nearly 19 km south of Umberatana homestead you come to **Yankaninna Station**. The track passes close to the homestead and outbuildings; keep the house on your left. Less than one km past the homestead you will pass a track junction on your left, signposted 'Yadnina'. This leads into the Gammon Ranges National Park and eventually back to Balcanoona.

Nine km east of Yankaninna, with the track skirting the ramparts of the **Yankaninna Range**, cross Gammon Creek and then begin to swing more and more south as you pass **Arcoona Bluff**, which at 953 metres is one of the highest peaks in this part of the range. Just over five km from the Gammon Creek crossing, a track heads off to the left, entering the national park and leading to a small camping area on Arcoona Creek.

Less than 500 metres south of this junction the main track you are on crosses the same creek and two km later passes through an outstation. The numerous small creeks that are crossed as you head south are all spawned in the rugged mountains to your left. Twenty km from the outstation you pass **Mt Serle**

Remains of Sliding Rock copper mine north of Blinman (R & VM)

Station homestead on your right, and four km later meet the main Copley-Balcanoona road, 46 km east of the bitumen at Copley. The total distance from Arkaroola is 98 km.

Turn right at this main dirt road and head west an easy 46 km to **Copley**. At Copley you can head north 35 km to Lyndhurst, or south five km to Leigh Creek or 159 km to Hawker. By the way you have come, the total distance is about 450 km, but you have seen and experienced much more of these magnificent outback ranges than you would have if you had travelled up the bitumen.

Copley has a hotel and roadhouse and can offer accommodation, fuel, repairs, food and meals. Leigh Creek offers a more modern extensive shopping facility, and the meals from the licensed canteen are excellent.

ALTERNATIVE ROUTES

There are a number of alternative routes through the ranges, depending whether you want a quick trip or one that's a little different.

Paralana Hot Springs (R & VM)

Some of the shorter alternatives between such places as Wilpena and Blinman, or Wilpena and Balcanoona via the barytes mine road and Wirrealpa, have already been mentioned, but none are as scenic as the route described.

Certainly if you are in a hurry, the 159 km run up the bitumen from Hawker is the way to go, but the Flinders Ranges will be just a line of blue mountains off to your right.

If you're coming from Adelaide and you want the shortest way to the northern Flinders, the quickest route is to head up the Barrier Highway (the Broken Hill road) from Adelaide 313 km to Yunta. Here you turn north onto a good dirt road and, travelling via Frome Downs, reach Balcanoona in another 271 km.

ACTIVITIES
Walks
Walking is the main activity in the Flinders.

There are a host of day walks and marked walking trails, or you can wander the Heysen Walking Trail for a day or more.

Don't forget that this is an arid region and water can be scarce – be prepared!

Some of the walks that can be done in the gorges along the way have been mentioned already. At Arkaroola, in the far north, there are also many walks ranging from an hour to days. It's best to contact the visitor information centre at Arkaroola (☎ (086) 48 4848) for more details. In the nearby Gammon Ranges National Park there are no marked trails; the area is really only for experienced, well-equipped walkers. Contact the ranger at Balcanoona (☎ (086) 48 4829) for more information, and provide details of your walk, route and expected time of return.

Wilpena and the surrounding national park is the best set-up area for walking, and there are a number of marked trails and short walks up to a day for those wanting to better experience the Flinders.

In Wilpena itself, some of the walks to do include the old homestead and Wangarra Lookout, which take between one and two hours. The popular walk to St Mary Peak is a highlight, but it is a fairly strenuous one, taking eight to nine hours. The walk across the Pound to Edeowie Gorge takes about the same amount of time and leads north-west to Edeowie Creek and its waterfalls.

There are other walks in and around the Pound, while a little further afield, but still in the park, there are a couple of marked trails from the Aroona Ruins. From the ruins, you can follow the Heysen Trail north to Parachilna Gorge, a six-hour, one-way trip. In the east of the park there is Wilkawillana Gorge to enjoy for four to five hours.

At Yanyanna Hut, north of Wilpena and on the route described, there is an enjoyable six to seven-hour walk across undulating country to Elatina Hut. A little further along the route is a two-hour walk, which includes a little rock-hopping into Bunyeroo Gorge.

ORGANISED TOURS
There is a good choice of organised tours

along this route. From Hawker, Flinders Ranges Safaris (☎ (086) 48 4031), PO Box 36, Hawker, SA 5434, operates 4WD tours through the Flinders and beyond. Other 4WD tour operators include Butler's Outback Safaris (☎ (086) 42 2188), 3 Prosser St (PO Box 671), Port Augusta, SA 5700, and Sambell's Scenic Tours (☎ (085) 22 2871) in Gawler, just north of Adelaide. Intrepid Tours (☎ (086) 48 6277), 29 First St, Quorn, SA 5433, has a wide choice of half-day to four-day trips.

Arkaba Station (☎ (086) 48 4217 or ☎ & fax 48 4195), via Hawker, SA 5434, runs 4WD tag-along tours along the spectacular, picturesque Elder and Wilpena ranges. These can be for a day or longer. All meals, cooked in a camp oven, are provided, and the campsites are exclusive and idyllic. The guide can tell you the history of the place and much about the flora and fauna.

Graham Dunn's Bush Retreat (☎ (08) 339 1989) is also on Arkaba Station. Graham conducts nature walks and tours based at a tented camp in a secluded spot on the property.

Rawnsley Park (☎ (086) 48 0030), Hawker-Wilpena Rd, Hawker, SA 5434, operates local 4WD tours to surrounding points of interest, and horse-riding excursions of two hours, half a day or a full day.

Overnight horse-riding trips of up to seven days are operated by Wilpena Pound Saddle & Pack Horse Treks (☎ (086) 48 6075). These trips operate out of Rawnsley Park, but also include such places as the Chace Range, The Bunkers and Willow Springs Station.

The Wilpena Pound Motel (☎ (086) 48 0004), c/o Wilpena Pound Holiday Resort Office, Suite 6, 219 East Terrace, Adelaide, SA 5000, operates 4WD tours and coach tours to local points of interest, as well as a half-day and a full-day 4WD trip across parts of Arkaba Station.

Scenic flights over the Pound are readily available for 15 or 30 minutes. Longer flights to Lake Torrens, Arkaroola, Lake Eyre, Andamooka and other outback destinations can also be arranged. Contact the Wilpena Pound Motel for information.

The Flinders Ranges Camel Farm (☎ (086) 48 4874), McLaren Flat, SA 5171, based in Blinman, operates one to seven-day camel trips in the Blinman and Wilpena areas between April and October. Other trips are also available through the outback of South Australia. Contact Rex Ellis, the operator, on the above number or at his base at McLaren Flat (☎ (085) 56 7236).

The Arkaroola Tourist Village (☎ (086) 48 4848) has its famous Ridge Top Tour, along with 4WD tours to local points of interest. Scenic flights over the rugged ranges and further afield are also available from Arkaroola.

Motorcycle trips through the Flinders are available with Flinders Ranges Bike Tours (☎ (086) 42 4878) based in Port Augusta.

Ecotrek (☎ (08) 383 7198), PO Box 4, Kangarilla, SA 5157, and Exploranges (☎ (08) 294 6530), 37 Walker St, Somerton Park, SA 5044, have extensive tours and walking trips through the Flinders, while Flinders Rides (☎ (085) 28 2132), PO Box 19, Stockport, SA 5410, has a good selection of horse-riding trips throughout the region.

FACILITIES
Roadhouses

While roadhouses may be a little thin on the ground in the Flinders Ranges, there are a couple of establishments that come close.

Hawker Motors (☎ (086) 48 4014), on the corner of Wilpena and Cradock Rds, is not the only place in Hawker for fuel, but it is the biggest and the best known. It is also the service depot for automobile club members and can supply all fuels (including LPG), parts and accessories, batteries and tyres, camping gas refills, souvenirs, books and maps, along with ice and cool drinks.

The *Beltana Roadhouse* (☎ (086) 75 2744) is just off the main bitumen highway, north of Parachilna and south of Leigh Creek. It offers all fuels, ice and groceries along with dining and takeaway foods, and is licensed. Public toilets and showers are also located here.

In Leigh Creek, *Leigh Creek South Motors* (☎ (086) 75 2016) in Black Oak Drive (the main street into the town centre off the highway) is the only place to get fuel. It can also supply tyres as well as LPG and repair facilities, along with a range of food, cool drinks and the like.

The *Copley Roadhouse & Caravan Park* (☎ (086) 75 2288) offers very limited supplies and fuel, as well as a basic camping ground.

Fuel Outlets

There are a number of other outlets for fuel in the area that are not associated with roadhouses, as follows:

Hawker
> Range View Motors in Wilpena Rd (☎ (086) 48 4049) has fuel and repair facilities; it is also the Toyota agent.

Rawnsley Park
> On the way north to Wilpena; has fuel (see below for more details).

Wilpena Pound
> The general store has all fuels and camping gas.

Parachilna
> Fuel is available at the hotel – see below.

Angorichina Tourist Village
> In Parachilna Gorge; has a store (☎ (086) 48 4842) which sells all fuels as well as camping gas.

Blinman
> The Blinman Hotel (see below for details) and the Blinman Post Office & Agency (☎ (086) 48 4874) sell fuel, but LPG is not available.

Arkaroola
> The Arkaroola Resort (☎ (086) 48 4848) has a wide range of supplies, including all fuels, limited spares and repairs.

Copley
> The Packsaddle General Store (☎ (086) 75 2268) has your three main types of fuel. See below for details.

Camping

Throughout the Flinders there is a choice of bush camping, with few if any facilities, and camping in commercial-type camping grounds. During the school holidays, especially the spring and autumn holidays, and on long weekends, it pays to book in advance at the commercial camping areas.

At Hawker you can stay at the *Hawker Caravan Park* (☎ (086) 48 4006), where there are on-site vans and self-contained

cabins, as well as the normal caravan park facilities. Dogs are allowed by prior arrangement. Across from the Railway Station Restaurant on the edge of town is the *Flinders Ranges Caravan Park* (☎ (086) 48 4266), where there are on-site vans and the normal facilities, including en suites for vans, and free barbecues. Dogs are also allowed. Prices are around $9 for an unpowered site, $12 for a powered site and $28 for an on-site van for two people, while the cabins at the Hawker Caravan Park cost $48 for two people.

There is a large, pleasant camping ground at *Rawnsley Park* (☎ & fax (086) 48 0030) with powered sites and on-site vans. Unpowered sites cost $8.50 for two, while powered sites cost $14.50.

At *Wilpena Resort* (☎ (086) 48 0004) there is a large, idyllic camping area that can be popular and crowded during the school holidays. A small number of powered sites have just become available. Powered/unpowered sites are $18/10 for two people.

Throughout the national park, there is a wide choice of camping spots. Many people prefer the gorges or the area around Aroona. You need a permit, and camping fees vary. Self-registration, using the 'iron rangers' near the camping areas within the park, costs $3 per vehicle per night, while permits issued by a ranger from the national parks office cost $2 per adult for each night. Contact the national parks office at Wilpena (☎ (086) 48 0048) or Hawker (☎ (086) 48 4244) for further details.

At Parachilna, campers and caravanners can stay behind the *Prairie Hotel* for a very moderate fee. It's a good opportunity to sample some excellent food from the dining room, but space out the back is limited. See below for more details.

In Parachilna Gorge you can camp for nothing. There are no facilities and nobody to pick your rubbish up, so please look after this area – it is popular.

The *Angorichina Tourist Village* in Parachilna Gorge Rd has on-site vans ($30), camping sites ($7) and caravan sites ($10). Pets are allowed only at the manager's discretion.

THE SOUTH

The old smelter site at Yudnamutana (R & VM)

At Blinman, the *Blinman Hotel* (☎ (086) 48 4867) allows campers and caravanners to pull up under the peppercorn trees. Price is a nominal $5 per person but space is limited.

The *Arkaroola Tourist Resort* (☎ (086) 48 4848) has a large camping area suitable for tents and vans. Prices are $10 per night for a site, with another $5 per night for power.

You can camp in the Gammon Ranges National Park if you have a permit issued by the ranger at Balcanoona (☎ (086) 48 4829). The same camping fees apply as for the Flinders Ranges National Park. The area around Grindell's Hut is the most popular but there are others. Grindell's Hut can also be rented – contact the ranger for details.

The *Copley Roadhouse & Caravan Park* (☎ (086) 75 2288) has basic facilities, and dogs are allowed. An unpowered site is $5 and a powered site is $8.50.

The *Leigh Creek Caravan Park* (☎ (086) 75 4214) has powered and unpowered sites, but no pets are allowed.

Hotels, Motels, Cottages & Bunkhouses

In Hawker you can stay at the *Hawker Hotel-Motel* (☎ (086) 48 4102) or the *Outback Motel* (☎ (086) 48 4100). Prices range from $25 a single in the hotel to $60 a double in the motels, for a room only.

Just out of Hawker there are a number of properties to stay on. *Yappala Station* (☎ (086) 48 4164), nine km from Hawker on the main road north to Leigh Creek, has self-contained units from $40 per couple per night. Two km south of town are the *Windana Cottages* (☎ (086) 48 4136), which

cost from $50 a double per night, but it's cheaper the longer you stay. As is the case with most self-contained flats, you need to bring your own linen, toiletries and food.

Arkaba Station (☎ (086) 48 4195) has a lovely, fully self-contained cottage that sleeps six. Costs range from $90 per night for two people to $100 for four, with a minimum stay of two nights.

The *Wilpena Motel* (☎ (086) 48 0004) has accommodation costing $76/82 single/double, room only. Meals are available in the restaurant. There is a wide choice of activities on offer from the resort and there is a large pool and barbecue area.

The *Prairie Hotel* (☎ (086) 48 4895) in Parachilna offers cold beer, the best food in the north, and accommodation. There is backpacker accommodation with no cooking facilities for $10 a night, and single/double rooms with breakfast for $30/50. Family rooms are available.

The *Angorichina Tourist Village* (☎ (086) 48 4842) has bunkhouse accommodation for $12 per night, plus self-contained cabins with five, six or eight beds from $42 a night.

The *Blinman Hotel* (☎ (086) 48 4867) has a variety of rooms for $20 to $30 a person per night. Up the road a little and close to the old mine is *The Captain's Cottage* (☎ (086) 48 4894). This historic 1860 cottage offers self-contained accommodation in two separate sections. The study sleeps two people and costs $70 a double, while the main part of the cottage, which can sleep two to nine people, costs $100 for the first two people and $15 extra per person. Breakfast provisions can be arranged at $5 extra per person.

Arkaroola Tourist Resort (☎ (086) 48 4848) has bunkhouse accommodation for $10 per person per night, while rooms in the motels range up to $99 for two people. There is a licensed restaurant with excellent meals and a bar. There is often a very pleasant barbecue around the pool which goes down well with guests and camping ground visitors.

A few of the sheep stations throughout the Flinders offer shearers'-quarters-style accommodation. These include *Nilpinna Station* (☎ (086) 48 4894), 35 km north-east of Parachilna, *Oratunga* and *Angorichina* stations (☎ (089) 48 4863), just out of Blinman, and *Gum Creek Station* (☎ (086) 48 4883), south of Blinman. Prices are in the vicinity of $10 a head, children may be cheaper, and there is generally a minimum charge per night. You will need to bring your own bedding and food at these places.

Shopping
Hawker This is the place to go for supplies as there are a number of stores, including *Gloede's General Store* (☎ (086) 48 4005), the *Hawker Shopping Centre* (☎ (086) 48 4064) and the *Sightseer's Cafe & General Store* (☎ (086) 48 4101). All are close to the centre of town and an easy walk from one another.

Other Places Apart from the roadhouses and resorts mentioned, there is very little else when it comes to buying supplies. After Hawker, the best place to buy anything is Leigh Creek. The shopping centre, found

just off the main road north, has a couple of well-stocked supermarkets, a newsagency, butcher and post office.

The *Packsaddle General Store* (☎ (086) 75 2268) in Copley, just a few km north of Leigh Creek, supplies fuel and camping gas refills, along with a full range of meat, groceries and smallgoods.

Airstrips
Hawker has a good private airstrip capable of taking good size aircraft. The strip is run by the Hawker District Council. No fees are payable and no aviation fuel is available. The strip is unusable after rain. For further information, contact the overseer (☎ (086) 48 4114) or the district council (☎ (086) 48 4011).

The Arkapena airstrip at Wilpena is pretty short, so it is recommended that light aircraft land at nearby Oraparinna airstrip. Both strips are under the control of the National Parks Service; contact the office in Hawker (☎ (086) 48 4244) for further details. The

THE SOUTH

Arkaroola (TW)

Wilpena Motel can arrange to pick you up from the strip, and you can ring the motel for information on the serviceability of the strip and how to find it.

At Arkaroola there is a private, 2200-foot (700-metre), good bush strip capable of taking most sorts of light aircraft. Avgas is available and there is a collection fee payable to Arkaroola. Contact the Arkaroola Resort (☎ (086) 48 4848) for more details.

Leigh Creek has a public aerodrome which is a major field capable of taking quite large aircraft. Contact Doug Austin at Leigh Creek (☎ (086) 75 2006) for further information.

ALTERNATIVE TRANSPORT
If you don't have your own vehicle, there are a few ways of getting to and around the Flinders. Some of the tour operators listed in the earlier Organised Tours section have trips running from Adelaide, Port Augusta or elsewhere, but they are 'organised tours' and you go where they want you to go.

Car Rental
There are a couple of places where you can hire vehicles, but neither are very handy to the centre of the Flinders. The closest are Budget (☎ (086) 42 6040), 16 Young St, Port Augusta, and the Handy Ute & Car Hire (☎ (086) 42 4255) at the Mobil Davenport Service Station, 46 Stirling Rd, Port Augusta.

Bus
Stateliner Express (☎ (08) 233 2777), 21 Mackay St, Port Augusta, SA 5700, has a bus network throughout South Australia and regularly services the main towns in the Flinders, including Hawker, Parachilna, Arkaroola, Lyndhurst and Leigh Creek. You can contact them on the above phone number or at their Port Augusta bus terminal office in Mackay St (☎ (086) 42 5055).

Greyhound (☎ 13 2030), at the same address as Stateliner, has a service on Friday from Port Augusta to Hawker and on to Leigh Creek. A return fare to Hawker costs $30.60, and to Leigh Creek $78.80. Contact

the office at the Port Augusta bus terminal in Mackay St (☎ (086) 42 5055).

Train
The railway network, whether coming from Adelaide or from the eastern states, can only get you to Port Augusta, and that's it. From there you can hire a vehicle, catch a bus, or hoof it. For more details on timetables, call ☎ 008 88 8417.

Air
Augusta Airways (☎ (086) 42 3100), Port Augusta Airport, Port Augusta, SA 5700, operates scheduled services between Adelaide, Port Augusta and Leigh Creek. It also has scenic flights and charter flights to anywhere in the outback.

Silver City Highway

For those travelling northwards from the southern capital of Melbourne, the Silver City Highway is one of the best introductions to the vastness and uniqueness of the Australian outback. If you are journeying west from Sydney or east from Adelaide, the Silver City Highway cuts across your course – you would probably meet it at the outback mining community of Broken Hill, from where the highway gains its name. From this town, travellers can head south to Wentworth (the southernmost town on the highway, at the junction of the mighty Darling and Murray rivers), or north through Tibooburra into south-east Queensland, and to Cooper Creek, the Channel Country, Windorah, Birdsville and places beyond.

Broken Hill, the largest town in western New South Wales, is a long way from anywhere: Sydney is nearly 1200 km to the east, while Melbourne is 900 km to the south. Adelaide, over 500 km to the south-west, is the closest capital, the major source of supplies and the place where most Broken Hill residents go for holidays.

Officially, the Silver City Highway starts on the New South Wales side of the Murray

River, opposite Mildura, the 'capital' of the Sunraysia district, as this section of the Murray is called. There are a number of ways of travelling the 30 or so km from Mildura to Wentworth, the real start of this route north into the outback. From Wentworth to 'the Hill', it's 261 km, all of it good bitumen. North of the Silver City, the bitumen peters out 32 km from the centre of town and a well-maintained dirt road continues to the NSW/Qld border, 393 km away at Warri Gate.

This is officially the end of the Silver City Highway, and it shows. The road deteriorates as it heads north-west to Cooper Creek or north-east to Noccundra and Thargomindah, but in normal conditions it is still passable to ordinary vehicles, driven with care. Although this road is slowly being upgraded, it will be a long time before it is sealed.

HISTORY

For millennia, the region west of the Darling River has been inhabited by Aboriginal people. While communities were concentrated on the reliable water resources of the rivers in the good seasons, their wanderings took them across the rocky broken ground of the Barrier Range, where Broken Hill now stands, to the dunes of the sand-ridge country around Cameron Corner.

Charles Sturt was the first European to penetrate this country, in 1845. He named the Barrier Range but missed the wealth underneath, before pushing north to his Depot Glen near present-day Milparinka. Plagued by hot weather and a lack of water, he and his men continued northwards to a point north of present-day Birdsville, but their effort was in vain. The inland sea that Sturt had set out to find had vanished a few thousand years before, and he and his men retreated the way they came. It was one of the great survival feats of Australian exploration, and in stark contrast to the next expedition that passed this way.

In 1860 Burke and Wills led their well-prepared expedition north from Menindee (on the Darling River) to a depot they established on Cooper Creek. From this point,

Burke, Wills and two others left the majority of the expedition at the depot and rushed to cross the continent. However, on their return, they discovered that the main party had left the depot just hours before their arrival. The Burke and Wills team were left with just a few stores, and all but one perished on the banks of the Cooper near present-day Innamincka. King was the only survivor. And, while this doomed expedition had seen the country in much better condition than Sturt, it was the search parties who went out looking for them who really had the pioneer pastoralists flocking to this vast semidesert country cut by rivers such as the Darling, Barcoo and Diamantina.

Wentworth became an important river port for the steamer trade plying the Darling and Murray rivers from 1850 onwards, and Broken Hill came to prominence when Charles Rasp discovered the silver-lead-zinc deposit there in 1883. It was the richest deposit of its type ever discovered, and by the 1890s a town of 20,000 had been established, working the vast reef. Since then, minerals worth nearly $2 billion have been extracted from the ground. The mine has been the foundation for Broken Hill Proprietary (BHP), the biggest company in Australia, and for the town of Port Pirie, on the coast of South Australia, where the ore is smelted. Broken Hill is past its peak, the vast ore body stripped of its richest deposits. Within 10 or 20 years the ore will disappear, but the town will remain a tourist destination and an important service town for this part of the country.

Both Tibooburra and Milparinka, a little further south, owe their existence to gold and to the rushes that occurred during the 1870s and '80s. While gold was found, it was never in huge quantities, and the lack of water was always a problem.

Today Tibooburra is a minor service town offering basic facilities for the surrounding stations and the ever-increasing numbers of tourists who travel to this 'Corner Country' for the outback experience and to visit nearby Sturt National Park. Milparinka is, but for the hotel, deserted.

Galahs (R & VM)

INFORMATION
Tourist Offices
The following tourist centres can supply you with information on the Silver City Highway and the towns and centres through which it passes. The national parks offices listed can help you with details on Mootwingee and Sturt national parks.

Wentworth Tourist Information Centre, 58 Wentworth St, Wentworth, NSW 2648 (☎ (050) 27 3624); open seven days a week

Broken Hill Tourist & Travellers Information Centre, corner Blende and Bromide Sts, Broken Hill, NSW 2880 (☎ (080) 87 6077, fax 88 5209); open from 8.30 am to 5 pm daily (except Christmas Day)

National Parks & Wildlife Service, Broken Hill District Office, 5 Oxide St (PO Box 459), Broken Hill, NSW 2880 (☎ (080) 88 5933)

National Parks & Wildlife Service, Mootwingee Visitors Centre (☎ (080) 91 2587)

National Parks & Wildlife Service, Tibooburra District Office, Briscoe St, Tibooburra, NSW 2880 (☎ (080) 91 3308)

Emergency
You will find police stations and hospitals in the following towns:

Wentworth
    Police (☎ (050) 27 3102)
    Hospital (☎ (050) 27 3201)
Broken Hill
    Police (☎ (080) 87 0299)
    Hospital (☎ (080) 88 0333)
Tibooburra
    Police (☎ (080) 91 3303)
    Hospital (☎ (080) 91 3302)

THE ROUTE
Officially the Silver City Highway starts on the New South Wales side of the border, near Mildura, but it is at Wentworth, 30-odd km further west, that it takes on its distinctive character and leaves behind the more settled areas of Victoria, and the Murray River with its citrus groves. From Mildura you can travel either south of the river through Merbein, crossing the Murray nine km east of Wentworth, or cross the Murray just north

of the centre of Mildura, head a short distance north and turn left onto the Silver City Highway at the small hamlet of Buronga. From there it is 24 km to Wentworth.

Wentworth to Broken Hill (261 km)

The township of **Wentworth** straddles the Darling River just upriver from its confluence with the Murray, but the main part of town is on the western bank of the Darling. Here is a wide choice of accommodation and a good selection of places to handle all your supply requirements.

Just a few hundred metres past the Darling River bridge, turn right and follow the highway north. The manicured farmlands of the orchards and vineyards quickly give way to open grazing country, setting the scene for the drier, more expansive country further north.

The **Anabranch**, a major channel of the Darling River, is crossed 66 km north of Wentworth. There is a spot to stop and enjoy the slowly flowing waters close to the road bridge, and at a pinch you could stop here for the night.

Another 50 km brings you to a high point overlooking the low lake country to the east and **Popiltah Lake**, 121 km north of Wentworth. It is a popular spot to stop and enjoy the view. It also makes the best overnight stop on the run north to Broken Hill.

Coombah Roadhouse (☎ (080) 91 1502), 16 km north of Popiltah Lake, can supply all fuels, takeaway foods and snacks. From the roadhouse it is a steady run north, through country that gets progressively drier, to Broken Hill, 124 km further on.

Broken Hill

With a population of over 22,000, Broken Hill has much to offer the first-time visitor. Founded on the richest deposits of silver, lead and zinc ever found, 'the Hill' has a rich mining heritage, which is well recorded in the **Railway & Mineral Museum**, and the mines that are open to the public. These include the **Day Dream Mine** (33km north-west of the Hill on the way to Silverton) and

the **original BHP mine** (almost in the middle of town).

Broken Hill also offers travellers some of the finest art collections in Australia. For some years the town has been the centre for a number of well-known **Australian artists**, including Pro Hart, Jack Absalom and Eric Minchin. Their galleries, amongst others, are well worth visiting, especially Pro Hart's, which has one of the biggest private collections in Australia.

The Heritage Trail, which starts and ends at the tourist centre, can be completed in a couple of hours. This easy and enjoyable drive gives you a good idea of the history and development of the Hill, while the Heritage Walk covers about two km and takes the visitor around many of the original buildings of the central commercial area.

The town is also a major centre for the **Royal Flying Doctor Service**, and at their base at the airport they have an information shop and museum.

There are far fewer hotels and clubs in the Hill than there used to be, but there's still a very good choice of places to eat and drink. Being a major service town, it has all the supplies you require, and you can get anything repaired here.

Broken Hill is also an excellent base from which to explore the local area. One place not to miss is the old ghost town of **Silverton**, 21 km north-west. Once a rich mining centre, Silverton has been the operational centre for a number of movies, and the **Silverton Hotel** (☎ (080) 88 5313) and **Goal Museum** are beauties. Penrose Park, just a stone's throw from the Silverton Hotel, is a pleasant spot for a picnic, and its bushlike camping area is a quiet spot to put the tent up for a night or more. Though there are limited amenities, it only costs $2.50 per adult per night and children are free. Contact the caretaker of the park (☎ (080) 88 5307) for details.

South-east of the Hill are the **Menindee Lakes**, Broken Hill's watery playground, and nearby **Kinchega National Park**. To the north-east of Broken Hill is Mootwingee National Park, with its rugged country and

THE SOUTH

THE SOUTH

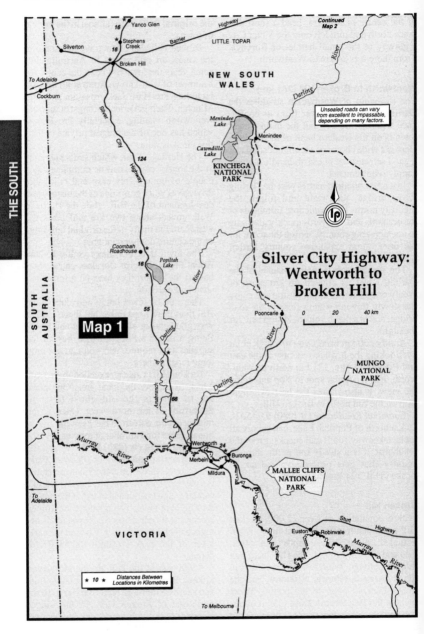

Silver City Highway: Wentworth to Broken Hill

Map 1

Unsealed roads can vary from excellent to impassable, depending on many factors.

★ 10 ★ Distances Between Locations in Kilometres

THE SOUTH

QUEENSLAND

Cameron Corner

Warri Warri Gate

STURT NATIONAL PARK

Fort Grey Homestead

56

140

★ 10 ★ Distances Between Locations in Kilometres

Gum Vale Homestead

Tibooburra

Mount Wood Homestead

Mt Poole

42

Mount Poole Homestead

To Bourke

Depot Glen

Milparinka

Hawker Gate House

Mt Brown

57

Salt Lake

Green Lake

Cobham Lake

16

Unsealed roads can vary from excellent to impassable, depending on many factors.

Silver City Highway: Broken Hill to Warri Warri Gate

47

Highway

60

0   20   40 km

Packsaddle Roadhouse

NEW SOUTH WALES

65

City

65

White Cliffs

90

MOOTWINGEE NATIONAL PARK

Silver

Fowlers Gap Research Station

55

15

Mootwingee Historic Site

Map 2

60

SOUTH AUSTRALIA

23

Highway

Wilcannia

16

Yanco Glen

River

Stephens Creek

16

Barrier

LITTLE TOPAR

To Sydney

Silverton

21

Broken Hill

To Adelaide

Darling

Cockburn

To Wentworth

To Menindee

Continued Map 1

The Silverton Hotel attracts all sorts (TW)

The old courthouse at Milparinka (R & VM)

Aboriginal heritage, while a little further east is the opal town of White Cliffs.

Broken Hill to Warri Warri Gate (393 km)

Wend your way out of town leaving the stark silhouettes of the mining headgear to the south. The Silver City Highway twists and turns through the streets of the Hill before finally heading towards Stephens Creek and places further north, about two km from the centre of the city.

Stephens Creek was once important to the townsfolk of Broken Hill. At one stage in the not-so-distant past, hotels within 10 miles (16 km) of the town were not allowed to serve alcohol on a Sunday. Needless to say, hotels popped up just outside the city limits to help quench a miner's thirst – Stephens Creek was one of them. As in most such places, the licence has long gone, and with a fire taking away the rest, Stephens Creek is now just a name on the map.

Yanco Glen, another 16 km up the road, is nothing more than a hotel. It offers a cool beer and that's about all.

A road junction 23 km north (55 km from Broken Hill) marks the turn-off for those who want to head east to the Mootwingee National Park, 75 km away. This road also leads to the opal-mining community of White Cliffs, 215 km from the junction.

Mootwingee National Park

This park protects 68,900 hectares of harsh sandstone country of the Byngnano Range and the surrounding sand and gibber plains that are so characteristic of this part of New South Wales. It is approximately 135 km from Broken Hill.

Near-permanent waters tucked into the narrow, rugged gorges that cut through the range made the area a welcome place for Aboriginal people in days gone by, while the 1860 Burke and Wills expedition passed this way as well. There are many Aboriginal sites in the ranges, and the **Mootwingee Historic Site**, surrounded by the park and the most-visited area within it, gives visitors a fine chance to discover this heritage. A Cultural Resource Centre, along with a network of trails and the guided walks led by Aboriginal rangers, help people discover the art and imagine what life must once have been like in this region.

A camping area at *Homestead Creek* offers basic camping facilities and nothing else. A camping fee applies. For further details, contact the ranger at the Mootwingee National Park Visitors Centre (☎ (080) 91 2587), or the Broken Hill District Office (☎ (080) 88 5933).

White Cliffs

This small outback community is a little different from most: many of the inhabitants live underground. Their homes are extensive, multi-room affairs, some even sporting underground swimming pool areas and the like. Think about it: if you are an opal miner and your house becomes too small, what do you do? Well, you bring home the mining equipment you work with each day and add a room to your underground home – it's as easy as that.

A few houses and buildings aren't underground, and these include the hotel and the general store. The *general store* (☎ (080) 91 6611) can supply fuel and a good range of foods; it is also the tourist centre. The *White Cliffs Hotel* (☎ (080) 91 6606) can supply a cold beer or three. There is a *caravan park* in town, as well as the *White Cliffs Dug-out Motel* (☎ (080) 91 6677).

Mootwingee Turn-off to Milparinka

Continuing north along the Silver City Highway, the road heads almost due north, dipping through the occasional wide, low creekbed and skirting the infrequent rocky hill or low range.

Fowlers Gap, a research station, lies close to the creek of the same name, 55 km north of the Mootwingee road junction, and here you'll find a pleasant wayside stop – if the weather isn't too hot.

Packsaddle, 65 km further north, offers a cold beer, very limited supplies and fuel to the passing traveller. Located close to Packsaddle Creek, there is a wayside stop beside the gum-lined creekbed (like most in this part of the world, it rarely has water in it).

A reasonable dirt road joins with the Silver City Highway 47 km north of Packsaddle. This road, from the south-east, is the northern access to White Cliffs and Mootwingee National Park.

The road passes through a wide sweep of low sand-ridge country north of Packsaddle, and 63 km from this small outpost of civilisation the road winds between a series of lakes. Off to the right is the normally dry Salt Lake, while to the left are the freshwater swamps of Green Lake, Lake Patterson and Cobham Lake, the latter being the closest thing to a permanent lake.

Milparinka Milparinka is just a couple of km off the main road, 57 km further on. While the main road continues north, you need to turn left at the signposted junction. Cross the gum-lined creek, turn left again at the T-junction, and a few hundred metres on you are at the pub – the life centre and the only inhabited building in Milparinka.

The *Milparinka Albert Hotel* (☎ (080) 91 3963) is a favourite watering hole. The cool, solid stone building offers a welcome respite from the heat, and the open square, with its water fountain and surrounded by the rooms that make up the accommodation available here, is very welcome. The pub can also supply meals and fuel.

This town once was the centre for a brief, relatively rich gold rush that took miners into the surrounding hills searching for the elusive metal. During those heady days, the pub and the nearby courthouse and police station were built. While the pub survived intact, the other two fine buildings were destined to become a pile of rubble, until the locals got to work a couple of years ago and saved these monuments.

Just a short distance from Milparinka is Sturt's **Depot Glen**, where this veteran explorer, along with his men, was trapped for months during his 1845 expedition to find an 'inland sea'. So certain were they of finding a vast body of water that they had taken a boat with them – local legend has it that the boat was abandoned near here when the explorers retreated to the Darling River.

Depot Glen today is much the same as when Sturt and his men were there. Gums still line the creek, and corellas and galahs, two common birds of the Australian inland, wheel in noisy profusion at the slightest disturbance. Near the creek and where the explorers camped is a blazed tree and a monument to James Poole, Sturt's second-in-command, who died while the party was trapped here. Just a short distance away, deeper in the hills, the waters of the creek, confined by the rocky range, are deeper and more permanent.

A few km north of the creek, past the homestead, is **Mt Poole**. A rocky monument crowns its low but lofty prominence; to keep the men in his party occupied during their enforced stay, Sturt had them build a marker on top of this hill, stating in his journal:

I little thought when I engaged in that work, that I was erecting Mr Poole's monument, but so it was, that rude structure looks over his lonely grave and will stand for ages as a record of all we suffered in the dreary region to which we were so long confined.

Although both sites are easy to find, it's best to stop at the pub and get directions.

Tibooburra Back on the main road heading north, it's an easy run to Tibooburra, 42 km away. For all intents and purposes, Tibooburra is a single street, which happens to be the main road north, with a few houses, offices and pubs along the way. Even so, it's the biggest town since Broken Hill and can supply all the general daily requirements for the traveller, such as food, fuel, basic repairs and a range of accommodation, including a number of hotels, a motel and a caravan park.

The town also acts as the main service centre for the outlying sheep stations and for the nearby Sturt National Park. The Tibooburra District office of the National Parks & Wildlife Service (☎ (080) 91 3308), Briscoe St, is a good place to start if you want to find out a bit about the history and the fauna of the area. Just a km north of the town, at Dead Horse Gully, a small camping area is run by the National Parks & Wildlife

Service; a display of old gold-mining equipment is worth seeing.

Each year over the New South Wales Labour Day long weekend, the town puts on its rodeo and gymkhana.

Sturt National Park This park takes up 344,000 hectares of the very north-west corner of New South Wales, having as its northern and western boundary the Queensland and South Australian borders, marked in this part of Australia by the famous Dog Fence.

The protection the fence offers to sheep also seems to be of benefit to kangaroos, which abound in the park. With their major predator kept under control and the water points put in for sheep and cattle, the roo numbers have increased since the coming of Europeans, and that makes the park and its inhabitants one of the major attractions of western New South Wales.

Here you will generally see the western grey kangaroo and the red kangaroo. The male of the latter species is easy to identify, but to the uninitiated, the female (or blue flier) looks similar to the grey roo, a species where the male and female are less easy to tell apart. In the range country that cuts across parts of the park, the heavier-built euro, or hill wallaroo, may be seen.

Wedge-tailed eagles and emus are also common in the park, but many other species of birds, not as big or as majestic, also call this stark country home.

For most travellers who come this way, a visit to **Cameron Corner**, where the three states of New South Wales, South Australia and Queensland meet, is on the agenda. The Corner lies 140 km north-west of Tibooburra and is reached by a good, well-signposted, dirt road. On the way, you will pass through Fort Grey, where Sturt set up a base camp during his 1845 expedition. A camping area near the station of the same name is an ideal spot to enjoy this section of the park.

At Cameron Corner a gate through the Dog Fence leads to a small camping area in South Australia, while just a drive of a few hundred metres will lead you past the Corner

post to the Corner Store. Here you can get snacks, a cool drink and fuel. From the Corner, you can head west to the Strzelecki Track and Cooper Creek, covered in the Central Deserts chapter.

There are other places to visit in the park, and other spots to camp, including the old Mount Wood homestead. The **museum** here is well worth a look. To the north of the homestead there is another camping area, at The Gorge.

Continuing north from Tibooburra, the road continues to be good dirt all the way to the border at **Warri Warri Gate**, 56 km from Tibooburra. Here you need to open the large gate through the Dog Fence; be sure to close it after you. You're now in Queensland and at the end of the Silver City Highway, but as this is a hell of a place to stop, we'll push a little further north to take you to some form of habitation and a choice of places to go next.

North of Warri Warri Gate

Travelling through Queensland, the country remains much the same as before. A road junction 34 km north of the border gives you your first choice of where to go. Turning left here will take you via Santos and Orientos stations north to Nappa Merrie on Cooper Creek, a total distance of 224 km. Not so long ago, this was a sandy track, but recent years have seen it steadily upgraded north to Nappa Merrie, with a new bridge across Cooper Creek five km east of Nappa Merrie.

Nappa Merrie is where the famous Burke and Wills 'Dig Tree' is located, about 50 km east of Innamincka (covered in the Strzelecki Track section in the Central Deserts chapter). From Innamincka you can head north to Birdsville or Betoota, and from there to places further north.

Continuing along the main road north of Warri Warri Gate, Naryilco homestead is passed 18 km further on, and another track to Santos comes in from the left just north of here. Yet another track to Santos meets the road 45 km north from Naryilco. A few km further on, just before the crossing of the

THE SOUTH

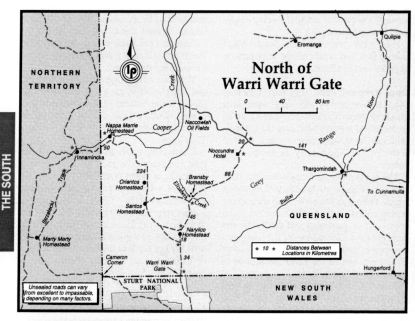

North of Warri Warri Gate

NORTHERN TERRITORY

Eromanga

Quilpie

0   40   80 km

Nappa Merrie Homestead

Cooper

Naccowlah Oil Fields

Creek

20

141

Range

Innamincka

50

Noccundra Hotel

Thargomindah

224

Bransby Homestead

88

Grey

To Cunnamulla

Orientos Homestead

Elizabeth Creek

Santos Homestead

45

Bulloo

QUEENSLAND

Strzelecki Track

Merty Merty Homestead

Naryilco Homestead

18

★ 10 ★   Distances Between Locations in Kilometres

Cameron Corner

Warri Warri Gate

34

Hungerford

Unsealed roads can vary from excellent to impassable, depending on many factors.

STURT NATIONAL PARK

NEW SOUTH WALES

Blazed tree honouring James Poole at Depot Glen (R & VM)

normally dry Elizabeth Creek, is the abandoned Bransby homestead on the left.

Noccundra and its famous pub is 88 km north of the road junction, 186 km north of the border. Here you can get a beer, meals and accommodation. Fuel and emergency repairs are also available, as well as up-to-date information on all the roads in the region.

From Noccundra you can head east on bitumen to Thargomindah, and from there to Cunnamulla and the Matilda Highway (covered in the Tropics chapter). Alternatively, if you want to stay on dirt roads and tracks, you can continue north to Eromanga, Windorah and beyond.

ORGANISED TOURS

Contact the various tourism bodies and regional tourist information centres for details of local tour operators, including Broken Hill's Outback Tours (☎ (080) 87 7800), which offers 4WD tours to the surrounding national parks, or Lindon Aviation

Grey kangaroos in Sturt National Park (R & VM)

(☎ (080) 88 5257), based in Broken Hill, which operates mail flights.

FACILITIES
Wentworth

Wentworth is a major town and, as such, offers all facilities, including branches of most banks.

There is plenty of accommodation – travellers can choose from a wide range of hotels, motels, holiday units and caravan parks. The *Cod River Lodge* (☎ (050) 27 3071) has motel rooms for $30 a double, while the *Willow Bend Caravan Park* (☎ (050) 27 3213) offers en-suite cabins ($36 a double), on-site vans ($23 a double) and powered/unpowered sites ($11/9 a double). For a complete listing and prices, contact the Wentworth Tourist Information Centre (☎ (050) 27 3624), 58 Wentworth St.

Broken Hill

This major centre can supply all requirements. All major banks are represented, including New South Wales credit unions.

A 24-hour towing service is operated by O'Connor Motor Wreckers (☎ (080) 87 5943, after hours ☎ 87 8635), 107 Rakow St, while the district office of the Royal Automobile Association of South Australia (☎ (080) 88 4999) also handles emergency road services.

There are over 20 hotels and nearly 20 motels, along with self-contained cottages, hostels and three caravan parks, at varying prices. The budget-conscious can choose from two hostels: the YHA *Tourist Lodge* (☎ (080) 88 2086), 100 Argent St, and *Astra House* (☎ (080) 87 7788), 393 Argent St. The Tourist Lodge offers shared kitchen facilities, meals by arrangement and single rooms for $18; YHA members can bunk down for $12 a night. At Astra House, backpackers can find accommodation with kitchen facilities from $10 per night.

The three caravan parks, *Broken Hill* (☎ (080) 87 3841), *Lake View* (☎ (080) 88 2250) and *Silverland Roadhouse* (☎ (080) 88 7389), offer accommodation in cabins (with or without en suites) and on-site vans, while powered and unpowered sites are also available. Prices are around $28 a double for a cabin, $23 for an on-site van and $10/8 for powered/unpowered sites, with small additional charges for extra people. Both Lake View and Silverland Roadhouse caravan parks allow dogs, under control.

Tibooburra

This small outback community offers supplies, fuel and accommodation, not to mention a cold beer.

The *Tibooburra Supply Store* (☎ (080) 91 3343) has food and all fuels, but not LPG. The post office (☎ (080) 91 3340) is also the agency for the Commonwealth Bank, but only passbooks are accepted.

There's a National Parks & Wildlife Service district office (☎ (080) 91 3308) in Briscoe St.

Accommodation is available at both the hotels. The *Family Hotel* (☎ (080) 91 3314) in Briscoe St is famous for its walls painted by Clifton Pugh. It has dining-room and counter meals, and laundry facilities are available for guests. Singles/doubles cost $20/30 and breakfast can be arranged. The *Tibooburra Hotel* (☎ (080) 91 3310), also in Briscoe St, has rooms available from $21 a double.

The *Granites Motel-Caravan Park* (☎ (080) 91 3305), Brown St, offers motel accommodation from $36/46 a single/double, with use of a communal kitchen. The caravan park has all facilities, including on-site cabins ($34 a double) on-site vans ($24) and powered/unpowered sites ($12/10 a double). Dogs are also allowed, under control.

ALTERNATIVE TRANSPORT

Air

Southern Australian Airlines (☎ 13 1313, Broken Hill booking agent ☎ (080) 87 7843) and Kendell Airlines (☎ 13 1300, Broken Hill booking agent ☎ (080) 87 1969) both operate flights between Mildura and Broken Hill. Hazelton Airlines (Broken Hill agent ☎ (080) 87 1969) also has flights to the area.

Bus & Train

There are regular bus services, run by private companies as well as by public state transport authorities, from the eastern capital cities to Broken Hill and Mildura.

At the bus terminal in Broken Hill, 23-25 Bromide St, you'll also find the booking office of Greyhound Pioneer Australia (☎ (080) 88 4040).

Country Link, run by Australian National Rail in New South Wales, operates a rail service to Broken Hill. Contact Country Link (☎ 008 028 354) or the Broken Hill Railway Station (☎ (080) 87 0441), Crystal St, for current timetable details and costs of rail and coach transport.

For details on bus services to Mildura (for connection to Wentworth), contact V-Line (☎ 13 2232), which is run by the Victorian Public Transport Corporation.

Car Rental

If you were hoping to hire a vehicle around Wentworth, you will need to check the hire-car companies based in Mildura.

In Broken Hill, however, all the major car-hire companies are represented, along with Broken Hill 4WD Hire (☎ (080) 88 4265), 2 Williams St, and Silver City Vehicle Hire (☎ (080) 87 3266, fax 88 5775), 320 Beryl St, both of which have 4WD vehicles.

The North-West

Gibb River Road

The Kimberley, that vast hunk of Australia that takes up the far north-west corner of Western Australia, is much bigger than the UK or Japan, nearly half the size of Texas and, for those who relate to Australia, bigger than Victoria and Tasmania combined.

It's closer to Asia than to the rest of Australia: Indonesia is less than 500 km away, and Wyndham, Western Australia's northernmost port, is nearer to Jakarta than it is to Perth and closer to Singapore than to Melbourne. By road it is 3400 km from Melbourne to Halls Creek, in the far southeast of the Kimberley, while from Perth to Broome, on the other side of the Kimberley, it is a mere 2300 km.

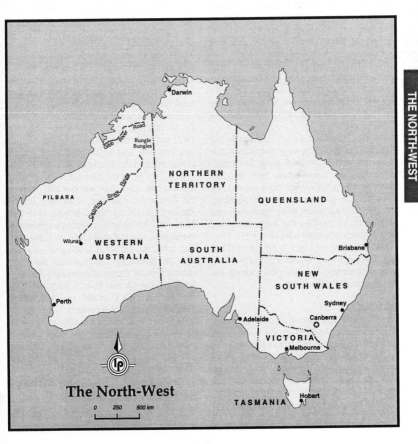

The North-West

0   250   500 km

Population-wise, there are less than 30,000 people in the Kimberley, mainly in towns such as Broome, Derby and Kununurra.

To the north and west, the area is bordered by a torn and twisted coastline, and one of the most spectacular and dangerous stretches of water in the world. To the south and east, sweeping lines of rugged sandstone ranges delineate the Kimberley from the sameness of the desert country that encroaches on the southern boundary.

The main around-Australia highway swings north from Broome to Derby and then heads east, inland to Fitzroy Crossing and Halls Creek, before heading north to Wyndham and Kununurra, but it misses out on the 'real' Kimberley. To see that, you need to travel the Gibb River Road.

This rough road cuts through the very heart of the Kimberley. At 710 km, it represents the shortest distance between Derby in the west and Kununurra and Wyndham in the east, but it is also the slowest route, and one not to be rushed.

The road has been slowly improved over the years, but one good wet season sees much of the past effort washed away. In 'good' years, after the graders have been out, the road is nearly good enough for a normal car, if you don't mind it losing a few things along the way. In 'bad' years, after heavy rain and no graders for months, the route is a terror for even well-prepared 4WDs.

For the most part, the Gibb River Road passes through pastoral country, but there are some interesting national parks along the way that are worth visiting.

HISTORY

Long before the Europeans came here, Aboriginal people lived in the country we now call the Kimberley. It was probably the first place on the Australian mainland where Aborigines landed when they arrived from Asia. A number of sites have been found that date back at least 18,000 years, but because the sea level has changed greatly, both before and since that time, many of the sites inhabited by ancient peoples would now be under water.

The richness of Aboriginal culture is vividly portrayed in the art that can still be found in the area – the Kimberley contains some of Australia's greatest collections of prehistoric art. If you are lucky enough to see a rock gallery of the distinctive, vividly painted 'Wandjina figures', then you, like many before you, will be impressed.

For hundreds of years, and perhaps longer, Macassan bêche-de-mer (trepang, or sea cucumber) fishermen from islands far to the north were sailing to the Kimberley coast and establishing fishing camps there.

The first European known to have sailed this coast was the Dutch navigator Abel Tasman, in 1644. He went on to explore Australia's southern coast, where his name is immortalised in the island of Tasmania. The English buccaneer William Dampier was next on the scene, making two visits, in 1688 and 1699. His reports were less than favourable, curtailing English interest in the region until the early 1800s.

Nicolas Baudin's expedition in the ships *Le Geographe* and *Naturaliste* between 1800 and 1804 mapped much of the Australian coastline and scattered French names along much of the Kimberley coast.

Matthew Flinders circumnavigated Australia at the same time without even spying the Kimberley coastline. That was left to Phillip Parker King, who between 1818 and 1821 led four coastal mapping expeditions to this area, naming such places as Careening Bay (after the enforced landing of his ship) and the Buccaneer Archipelago (in commemoration of Dampier's voyage). He also travelled far up the Prince Regent River, sketching King's Cascade, still a favoured spot for remote boat travellers.

In 1837 the famed ship of Charles Darwin, the HMS *Beagle*, under the command of John Wickham and John Stokes, mapped much of the coast, including the area around Derby and Brecknock Harbour.

The first overland trip in the Kimberley was undertaken by George Grey. He landed on 2 December 1837 at Hanover Bay, a spot that is just as remote today as it was back in Grey's time. Although the expedition didn't

Lookout, Kununurra (TW)

discover anything of note, Grey waxed so lyrical about the place that a pastoral company was formed some years later to establish a settlement near the Glenelg River. Like the expedition, this venture failed. Grey was, however, the first European to discover samples of the Wandjina art that dots many of the caves and overhangs of the Kimberley.

By the 1860s pearlers were plying the coast, and the first tentative steps at a pastoral industry were being taken. In 1879 Alexander Forrest left Beagle Bay and followed the Fitzroy River upstream as far as Geikie Gorge before heading towards the coast along the ramparts of the King Leopold Ranges. Failing to reach the coast, he retraced his steps along the range, continuing east and discovering the Ord River. His reports of good grazing land along the Fitzroy and the Ord rivers had settlers scrambling for a slice of the action. These included such pioneers as Nat Buchanan, the Durack

family, and the MacDonald family who still own and operate Fossil Downs, just outside Fitzroy Crossing.

In the early 1930s there were less than 10,000 people in the Kimberley, with Broome the cosmopolitan 'capital' of the area. Hundreds of boats worked out of Broome, searching for pearl shell and occasionally finding pearls as well. In the late 1930s a plan was developed for the formation of a Jewish home state centred around Argyle station in the eastern Kimberley, and it was not until the birth of modern Israel in 1948 that the idea died a lost cause.

WW II brought raids by Japanese bombers, not only on Broome, Wyndham and Derby but also on a couple of Aboriginal missions. Secret landfalls by Japanese troops occurred during these years, but the rugged terrain that had repulsed Grey and his followers served Australia well.

The population of Broome plummeted

THE NORTH-WEST

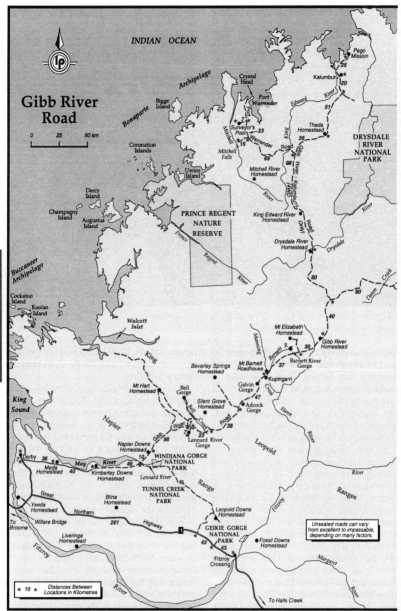

Gibb River Road

INDIAN OCEAN

Bonaparte Archipelago

Bigge Island

Crystal Head

Port Warrender

Pago Mission

Kalumburu

0   25   50 km

Coronation Islands

Surveyor's Pool

Warrender

Mitchell Falls

Mitchell River Homestead

Edward River

Theda Homestead

DRYSDALE RIVER NATIONAL PARK

Uwins Island

Darcy Island

Champagny Island

Augustus Island

PRINCE REGENT NATURE RESERVE

Gibb River – Kalumburu Road (4WD)

King Edward River Homestead

Drysdale River Homestead

Buccaneer Archipelago

Cockatoo Island

Koolan Island

Walcott Inlet

Prince Regent River

Drysdale River

King River

Mt Elizabeth Homestead

Gibb River Homestead

King Sound

Beverley Springs Homestead

Mt Barnett Roadhouse

Barnett River Gorge

Mt Hart Homestead

Bell Gorge

Galvin Gorge

Kupingarri

Silent Grove Homestead

Adcock Gorge

Napier

Lennard River Gorge

Leopold

Hann River

Derby

Meda Homestead

Napier Downs Homestead

WINDJANA GORGE NATIONAL PARK

Kimberley Downs Homestead

Lennard River

Range

TUNNEL CREEK NATIONAL PARK

Ranges

Great

Blina Homestead

Northern

Yeeda Homestead

Willare Bridge

Highway

Leopold Downs Homestead

GEIKIE GORGE NATIONAL PARK

Fitzroy

Unsealed roads can vary from excellent to impassable, depending on many factors.

To Broome

Liveringa Homestead

Fossil Downs Homestead

Fitzroy Crossing

Margaret River

★ 10 ★ Distances Between Locations in Kilometres

To Halls Creek

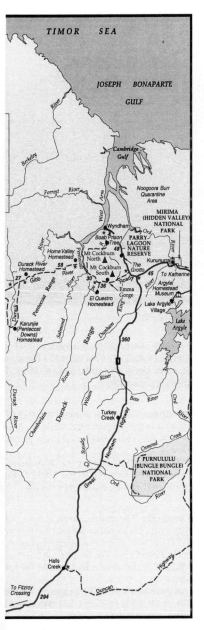

after the war and the introduction of plastics for buttons saw the demise of the pearling industry. In the 1950s the main road north of Broome was improved from a horse track to a wide horse track, but it was not fully bitumenised until 1987. The road network was so poor that until the late 1950s, all police patrols were by horseback.

In 1963 the Ord Dam wall was completed and Lake Argyle, the largest lake in Australia, began to form. It took over two years to fill, even though the river, in full wet-season flood, would be capable of filling every dam that supplies Perth with water, from empty to full, in 20 minutes! The dam, and the irrigation area that was set up for it to serve, has never reached its full potential.

Mineral finds resulted in rushes back at the turn of the century, but it was the discoveries of oil at Blina, east of Derby, diamonds near Lake Argyle in the late 1970s, bauxite on the Mitchell Plateau around the same time, and oil and gas offshore that really opened up the Kimberley.

While cattle have waned in importance over recent years, much of the land still remains under grazing. Over 30% of the Kimberley is Aboriginal land of one form or another, and this percentage is growing. More than 10% of the land is protected in national parks or conservation reserves, but sadly, much of this is basically inaccessible to travellers. Even so, the area represents one of the great outdoor travel destinations in Australia, rich in Aboriginal culture, European history and spectacular natural beauty.

INFORMATION
Tourist Offices
The Derby Tourist Bureau (☎ (091) 91 1426, fax 91 1609), 2 Clarendon St, PO Box 48, Derby, is a good source of up-to-the-minute information. Likewise, at the opposite end of the Gibb River Road, Kununurra has its Visitor Centre (☎ (091) 68 1177, fax 68 2598), close to the heart of town, at 75 Coolibah Drive. Wyndham's Information Centre (☎ (091) 61 1054) is in the old port area, at the Old Port Post Office, O'Donnell St.

Hidden Valley, Kimberley (RI)

The Western Australian Tourist Centre (☎ (09) 483 1111), Forrest Place, Perth, can also provide information on the Kimberley.

The Department of Conservation & Land Management (CALM) has regional headquarters (☎ (091) 68 0200) at Kununurra, in Konkerberry Drive. You can contact them for any information on the national parks and conservation reserves in the Kimberley.

Permits

There is no requirement for permits if you stick to the main road and the route described.

Emergency

Derby The police station (☎ (091) 91 1444) is at the corner of Villiers and Loch Sts, while the hospital (☎ (091) 93 3333) is further west along Loch St.

If you are unfortunate enough to need towing, the Derby RACWA agency is the BP Colac Service Station & Roadhouse (☎ (091)

91 1256), 84 Loch St. Kimberley Towing Service (☎ (091) 91 1311) is at 717 Brearley St, while Derby Motorplus WA (☎ (091) 91 1844) is in Loch St.

Wyndham The police station (☎ (091) 61 1055) is in the old port area, while the hospital (☎ (091) 61 1104) is in the new part of town.

The RACWA agency in Wyndham, Branko BP Motors (☎ (091) 61 1305), Great Northern Highway, can arrange towing.

Kununurra The more modern town of Kununurra has its police station (☎ (091) 69 1122) just west of the main shopping centre, in Coolibah Drive. The hospital (☎ (091) 68 1522) is in the same street, a little further west.

Kununurra's RACWA agency, Elgee Toyota (☎ (091) 68 2236), 231 Bloodwood Drive, can help with towing.

Books & Maps

There are a number of good maps of this area. The Hema map *The Kimberleys*, Australian Geographic's *The Kimberley*, and the Western Australian Department of Land Administration StreetSmart Touring maps *East Kimberley* and *West Kimberley* are by far the best for the general tourer.

The best guidebooks to the area are *The Kimberley – an Adventurer's Guide*, by Ron & Viv Moon, published by Kakirra Adventure Publications, and *The Australian Geographic's Book of the Kimberley*.

There are a host of other books that cover different aspects of the Kimberley, its people, history and its natural wonders. Many of these are available in bookshops in the towns of the region.

Radio Frequencies

For those who have an HF radio, the important frequencies to have are the RFDS bases at Derby, Port Hedland and Alice Springs, and if possible the frequencies for the Telstra (OTC) base in Darwin and Perth.

For the RFDS base at Derby (callsign VJB), the primary frequency is 5300 with secondary frequencies of 6925 and 6945. Port Hedland's callsign is VKL and its primary frequency is 4030; secondary frequencies are 2280 and 6960. Alice Springs callsign VJD) is a good base to call from the eastern Kimberley if you can't get through to Derby. Its primary frequency is 5410 and its secondary frequency is 6950.

The Perth Telstra base (callsign VIP) has OTC channels 427, 806 and 1226. Other frequencies for Tonecall and Selcall include 507, 834, 1229 and 1610. The Selcall for the beacon in Perth is 0799 and for the operator, 0107.

The Darwin Telstra base (callsign VID) has OTC channels 415, 811, 1227 and 1622. These are only available between 8 am and 8 pm as voice call, but 24 hours as Tonecall and Selcall. Other Tonecall and Selcall channels are 607, 834, 1229 and 1610. The Selcall for the beacon at Darwin is 0599 and the operator, 0105.

There are generally better communications through the RFDS base in Derby, so when it is working (business hours only), it is the one to go for.

SPECIAL PREPARATIONS

Even in the good times, the road is remote and travellers can be thin on the ground. Have a breakdown and you can be there for a while waiting for help. Be prepared.

To check on road conditions throughout the Kimberley, contact the Main Roads Department (☎ 008 01 3314 all hours), or the departmental offices at Kununurra (☎ (091) 68 1755) or Derby (☎ (091) 91 1133). Alternatively, you could check with the police stations at Derby, Kununurra or Wyndham (see Emergency) or the tourist bureaus (see Tourist Offices).

The country dries out very quickly after the wet-season rains stop, and water can be scarce along the way. Those contemplating walking or riding the route, please take note!

The road is very rough, and tyre damage is common. Carry at least two spares.

THE ROUTE

While you can travel just as easily both ways along the Gibb River Road, the best way to take in the expansive views is from the north-east, and this is the way the trip is described here.

Kununurra

The modern township of Kununurra is 45 km from the WA/NT border and owes its existence to the construction of the Ord Dam in the 1950s and '60s. It is the Kimberley's verdant town, being literally awash with green for most of the year. The sea of water close to the town assures Kununurra of a never-ending supply, and this year-round bounty of liquid gold makes Kununurra different to the other towns in the region.

Today, Kununurra's population owes its living not only to the irrigation area along the river but also to the wealth of minerals in the area, both on land and out to sea.

Kununurra is 825 km south-west of Darwin, 360 km north of Halls Creek and

THE NORTH-WEST

1062 km north-east of Broome via Highway 1. There are good facilities here – everything the traveller needs, from camping and caravan parks to hotels and motels.

The town makes a good base for exploring the surrounding area, and you could join in the fun at the many local festivals such as the Ord River Festival or the Bushman's Rodeo. Paddle a canoe on the Ord or go fishing for the elusive barra, either on your own or with the help of a guide. A couple of national parks and nature reserves in the area are also worth checking.

Mirima (Hidden Valley) National Park This small park is just on the edge of town. Called Hidden Valley by Europeans, the park protects some Bungle Bungle-style rock formations amongst a maze of cul-de-sacs, amphitheatres and twisting, sheer-sided valleys. There are examples of Aboriginal art in some of the overhangs, but these are not as spectacular as other galleries deeper in the Kimberley.

Animal life includes dingoes, agile wallabies, echidnas and a number of bats. Birds are the most obvious and include numerous birds of prey, finches, pigeons and parrots.

The best way to see the park is by walking, and a number of walks of up to one km have been established to points of interest and good lookouts.

Ord River There are two dams on the Ord River. The first, just out of town, where Highway 1 crosses this mighty river, is the Diversion Dam, holding back the waters of Lake Kununurra. The main dam is 74 km away via a good bitumen road, and its wall holds back the waters of **Lake Argyle**. This makes a very enjoyable day trip, but if you have a boat or a canoe, or like a spot of fishing, you can make it into something more than that.

Kununurra to the Kalumburu Road (293 km)

Heading west along the bitumen on Highway 1 makes an easy start to this trip. A major road junction 45 km west of Kununurra has you heading towards Wyndham and leaving Highway 1 and the road to Halls Creek, Derby and Broome.

Seven km north of this junction, a signposted dirt road turns off to the left (west). This is the start of the Gibb River Road.

If, instead of turning left onto the Gibb River Road, you continue straight ahead, you reach **Wyndham**, 48 km up the road. Despite the size and importance of Kununurra, Wyndham is still the official centre for the huge shire of East Kimberley, and you may want to visit this historic port while you are in the area (see the later Detours section).

Initially the Gibb River Road is well maintained, and this is as good as it gets. The **King River** is crossed 17 km from the highway. This river crossing is normally dry, except early in the dry season. The impressive rampparts of Mt Cockburn South can be seen to the north. In fact, for the next 50 km there are wide and expansive views of the **Cockburn Range** and its towering cliffs of red raw rock. In the evening light it is dramatically impressive.

The turn-off to **Emma Gorge** is another seven km along the road. This is part of El Questro station, and at the Emma Gorge Resort you can pamper yourself in luxury. You can also drive the one km off the Gibb River Road to the carpark, walk into the gorge proper and have a swim, but it will cost you $5. Situated near the gorge is the resort with a range of bush cabins, a bar and a shop.

The main access track into **El Questro station** is 12 km further along the Gibb River Road. This cattle station, which has opened its doors to tourism in a big way, takes in over 400,000 hectares of typically rough, broken Kimberley cattle country. Camping is available along the Pentecost River, or you can stay in more luxurious accommodation – in fact, fancier accommodation in the Kimberley would be hard to find. Fishing, camel rides and helicopter trips are all on the agenda.

The **Pentecost River** is crossed 58 km from the main highway. Once again there is water across the causeway only early in the dry season. The river is tidal to the downstream side of the crossing and there are some camps along the edge of the river on the eastern bank. These are really only good for an overnight stop or if you are a keen fisher. In fact the rough track that gives you access to these camps leaves the Gibb River Road just before the causeway, and eventually leads across the salt plains to Wyndham.

For the next km or so the road parallels the Pentecost River, and on a sweeping corner just eight km from the crossing, a track leads off to the right to **Home Valley station**. Owned by the Sinnamon family, it is one of three they control in the nearby area – the stations cover a total of one million hectares (over two million acres). Visitors are welcome at Home Valley; you can camp, or stay in the basic but clean accommodation close to the main homestead. There's a wide range of activities here, from barra fishing to horse riding, scenic flights to 4WD trips.

One of the most interesting 4WD trips you can take in the area is only available if you join a tour run by the Sinnamon family. The tracks traversed are on their property and are closed to the public, due more to the fragile nature of the tracks than anything else. The route followed is the original Wyndham-Karunjie station road, and where it climbs the near sheer-faced escarpment of the New York Jump-up, you can see where the original pioneers built the road to get their wagons up and down this natural barrier. Along the way, the tour can also take you into some top barra-fishing spots.

Back on the road again, the route climbs the range. Near the top, 1.5 km from the junction, a **lookout** gives an expansive view of the entire Cockburn Range. This is a top spot to sit on a cooling Kimberley evening, having a cold beer and enjoying the changing hues that colour the cliffs of the range. From here you can also see, to the north, the twin rivers of the Pentecost and the Durack, as well as the West Arm of Cambridge Gulf.

A camping spot is found 11.5 km further on. A track on the right leads down to a small camp beside a watercourse that generally has some water in it. There is only a little shade, but for an overnight camp it is fine.

Bindoola Creek is crossed for the first time just over five km further on, and again 18 km beyond that. Both crossings are generally dry and present no problems.

After climbing Gregory's Jump-up at the 121-km mark, it is just three km to the **Durack River homestead** turn-off. This station is owned by the Sinnamon family. The homestead and the camping area are less than one km off the main road. Camping along the river is superb, and you can fish, swim or canoe. Overnight accommodation and meals are also available, as are fuel and limited supplies.

Just over three km from the turn-off to Durack River is the track to **Karunjie station**, the third of the Sinnamon properties. It is open to travellers by prior arrangement at Home Valley or Durack River. The homestead is 45 km from the main road.

From this junction the road continues to be rough and stony. Spare your tyres by taking it easy. For most of the time the road winds across flat ground, occasionally climbing a jump-up, or escarpment, where the going gets rockier and rougher. After a time on this plateau country, the road descends, via another jump-up, to a flat or creekbed. This country is extremely harsh and unforgiving. Water is scarce between the rivers at any time, except during and straight after the Wet.

The **Durack River** is crossed 151 km from the bitumen and just 27 km past the Durack River homestead turn-off. This is a wide crossing between quite high banks but is generally no problem. A number of tracks on both banks lead to camping spots up and downstream and there are some nice waterholes in either direction.

Dawn Creek is crossed 24 km further on, and here you will find a reasonable campsite and permanent water down to the right. After another 24 km of rock and dirt road, a track heads off to the right. Just 100 metres along this track is a good camp on the Campbell River that comes with its own shade and water. Walkers and cyclists will appreciate both!

Just before the crossing of Russ Creek, 20 km from the Campbell River camp, a track leads off to the right from the Gibb River Road to a fair camp.

At the 241-km mark from the highway (293 km from Kununurra), 21.5 km from the Russ Creek crossing, you come to a major road junction. To continue on the Gibb River Road, turn left. If you want to take a diversion to the Mitchell Plateau or the Aboriginal community at Kalumburu, turn right (see the later Detours section). Both places are worthwhile, but, while the Gibb River Road is passable to a normal car during good times, the road to the Mitchell Plateau is definitely 4WD and the road to Kalumburu is not much better.

Kalumburu Road to Derby (417 km)

Veering left and continuing along the Gibb River Road, there is no appreciable change in the road conditions. They rarely get better,

and in fact, with the increased traffic that this section carries, heading towards the Mitchell Plateau and Kalumburu, the road may be more chopped up. By this time, if you have been crazy enough to tow a van along this road – and some people do – you'll be wishing you hadn't.

Just 16.5 km from the junction you will come to a creek crossing. A track leads off to the left, just before the creek, to a campsite along the creek. This has water in it early in the Dry, but is not to be relied upon at other times.

The track into **Gibb River station** is 46 km from the Kalumburu junction, and it's obvious from the sign on the front fence that they don't have fuel or supplies and want nothing to do with travellers.

Three km further on, Bryce Creek is crossed, and another 1.5 km brings you to Mistake Creek. Generally both these waterways are as dry as a badger. Nine km past the Mistake Creek crossing is the **Hann River** crossing. This is one of the major rivers in

Boating on the Pentecost River at El Questro Station (R & VM)

the central Kimberley and you are up near its headwaters. The river often has water in it at the crossing. A couple of minor creek crossings follow.

Sixteen km south of the Hann River you come to the turn-off to **Mt Elizabeth station**, run by the Lacey family. Their father pioneered this area of the Kimberley back in the 1920s, and the family are keenly aware of the heritage, both Aboriginal and European, of this wild place.

The homestead is 30 km from the main road, and accommodation and camping are available. Booking is essential for accommodation and a phone call would be appreciated if you want to camp (see the later Facilities section).

From the homestead it is possible to travel to the remote western coast around the Walcott Inlet area. This is a private road and you pay a fee to use it. It is extremely rough, and unless you are experienced, or with others who are, we would not recommend it. The Laceys offer trips out to Walcott Inlet as part of their Bushtrack Safaris operation, and as they know the art sites and the best fishing spots, it pays to go with them.

Just a little less than 10 km down the main road from the turn-off to Mt Elizabeth is the track to **Barnett River Gorge**. This track heads west, off the road, and winds around a little before you get to the river. The furthest point is about four km from the road, but this is not the best camping spot, although the walking and the river are excellent here. A couple of tracks which veered off this track earlier give access to some exceptional camping. Across the river from the camping area, under an overhang, observant walkers will find some reasonable, but old and faint, Aboriginal art.

The Barnett River is crossed 26 km further along the Gibb River Road. This normally has water in it but is generally no problem to a 4WD.

On the right, a km past the river crossing, is the turn-off to the **Mt Barnett Roadhouse** and camping area. The roadhouse dispenses

Manning Gorge (R & VM)

Pedalling through the Kimberley in the 1950s

Alex and Jacky Sklenica bicycled through the Kimberley back in 1954. Here's what they had to say about it in 1990, after they had just completed a similar return trip in their trusty 4WD:

Repacking our push bikes, we were considering possible routes from Wyndham to Derby. A shorter but very rough 700 km on the Durack and Gibb River track, confusingly crossed by stock routes petering out in the bush and no supply points along the way. Or the 1000 km via Turkey Creek, Halls Creek, Fitzroy Crossing. This longer way, still rather a bush track than road in 1954, was used mainly by drovers and station vehicles. A decisive advantage was that food supplies would be available from shops at Halls Creek and Fitzroy Crossing.

The Wyndham Police and locals in the pub offered advice, wished us luck and one grinned: 'You know what I am thinking.'

We had to travel light and live mostly off the land. A limited amount of basic food supplies were bought in Wyndham. Water, still remaining after the previous 'rainy' and some edible plants would have to be found on the way. Not a beginner in the Australian bush, I carried also a few fishing hooks and a line and a single shot .22 rifle. We hoped to catch fish, but knew that our main food source would consist of pigeon, ibis meat, ducks, galahs and wallabies.

We were unable to ride our bikes over the frequently sandy or rock-strewn stretches, but had to walk, pushing the bikes or sometimes ride on firmer surfaces parallel to the road.

There were no camping grounds, National Parks or tourists there. During four months, we met only one car with two Melbourne tourists and one Frenchman riding a motorcycle around Australia. When, on rare occasions, we met with station people, we stopped to boil a billy and to exchange news.

Once a passing stockman from Bohemia Downs stopped his truck near our little camp fire for a bit of a talk, sharing with us a billy of tea. Looking our scanty outfit over, he said: 'On bikes...but how...what do you eat?'

Pointing to our saddle bags I replied: 'We have some flour, tea, sugar and such here and there is plenty of game around waterholes.'

When leaving our camp, he dropped an apparently empty plywood tea-chest: 'Perhaps you can use this as a table.'

Inside the tea-chest was his present: a loaf of bread and a pound of butter wrapped in sheets of newspaper. Fresh bread and real butter! Immediately, we boiled another billy, spread slices of buttered bread on the tea-chest and read every scrap of newspaper, adverts including. This was indeed a happy camp, still vivid in our memory.

There were no marked tracks through spear grass and spinifex leading to Geikie or Windjana gorges. Near Tunnel Creek, overhanging rock shelters were still periodically inhabited by nomadic natives. We found and left undisturbed spears, stone knives and scrapers.

We met a mounted police patrol and sat till midnight smoking and talking, listening to natives singing around a camp fire near the billabong.

A period in our life when we were not tied to conventions and restrictions of crowded civilisation. A time when we were free to walk over the horizon. A slice of damper and roasted wallaby washed down with Bushell's was a repast. A shady tree, the warmth of a small fire on cool nights, bright stars our roof. Unforgettable memories of an unfenced land, of outback people and times past.

Alex Sklenica

Just such a short time ago, and much has changed. Yet so much remains the same. ■

fuel and all those things that hot, thirsty travellers love, and the camping down on the Barnett River must be experienced to be fully appreciated – it's magic, though it can be crowded at times. Pay at the store.

Spend some time lazing around the river – the sandy beaches, scattered rocks, cool water, sheer cliffs 100 metres upriver, shady trees and lily-covered backwaters make this an idyllic spot. There may be the odd freshwater croc or two, but they will stay out of your way. If you have a canoe, the waters of the river also make a pleasurable, gentle paddle. It is even possible to snorkel in the **Lower Manning Gorge**.

There are some Aboriginal art sites around the area. These can be found on the opposite bank of the river, at the end of the walking track.

A longer walk (about an hour each way) takes you to the **Upper Manning Gorge**. This track starts on the opposite bank from the camping ground and cuts across country, following a marked trail of old drink cans hanging in trees, and the odd stone cairn.

While the upper gorge has a small, sandy beach, it's the waterfall and huge pool surrounded by cliffs that are the real attractions. Take lunch and spend the whole day up in the gorge – it's great.

Back on the Gibb River Road and heading south, you pass, on your left, the Aboriginal community that owns Mt Barnett. Generally the road improves from here; while it is still stony dirt, the ridges of sharp rock jutting above the road surface that were so common north of Gibb River station have almost disappeared.

The turn-off to **Galvin Gorge** is 14 km south of the roadhouse, and a reasonable camping area can be found at the end of the track which leads about one km west from the road. A walk of a couple of hundred metres takes you to the main pool and waterfall. It is a top spot to swim and will be appreciated by those pedalling a bike or doing the trip on foot. Beside the pool, in the shadiest part of the cliff face, is a small sample of the local Aboriginal art, in this case a Wandjina head.

As soon as the road passes the turn-off to Galvin Gorge, it begins to climb the Phillips Range. Over the next 10 km there are good views of the surrounding country.

The Adcock River is crossed 12 km from the Galvin Gorge road, and five km further on, a track leads off to the left to **Adcock Gorge**. The track into the gorge and the small camping area is five km long and, apart for the last few hundred metres, is pretty good. At the end of the track is a small, idyllic camping area, and the refreshing waters of the gorge.

Continuing along the main road, you cross a couple of minor creeks before coming to the turn-off to Beverley Springs station on your right. Just four km past here, and 158 km from the Kalumburu junction, you will find the short access track to **Mount House station** on your left. This large, well-known Kimberley property has limited supplies and fuel for travellers, and accommodation is possible if you book beforehand.

The turn-off to the little-known **Surprise Falls** is 15.4 km south of Mount House. Less then eight km along a flat, faint track is a small camping area, just two minutes' walk from the falls. At the base of the falls is a large pool, ideal for a swim, and for those energetic enough to climb the low cliff, a number of small pools can be found which are perfect for a swim with a view.

The first permanent water across the road is crossed 24 km south of the turn-off into Mount House. This is **Saddlers Spring**, and tracks on both sides of the road lead a short distance to reasonable overnight camping spots beside the creek. On the left just one km past the creek crossing is the **Iminji Aboriginal Community**. There are no facilities here for travellers.

Some nine km south is the turn-off to **Bell Gorge**, probably the most scenic relatively accessible gorge in the heart of the Kimberley. The 30-km run into the gorge can be extremely slow, taking up to two hours.

The track into Bell Gorge parallels the northern face of the rugged **King Leopold Ranges** before swinging slightly north and running beside Bell Creek. There is some excellent camping along here. Shady trees

THE NORTH-WEST

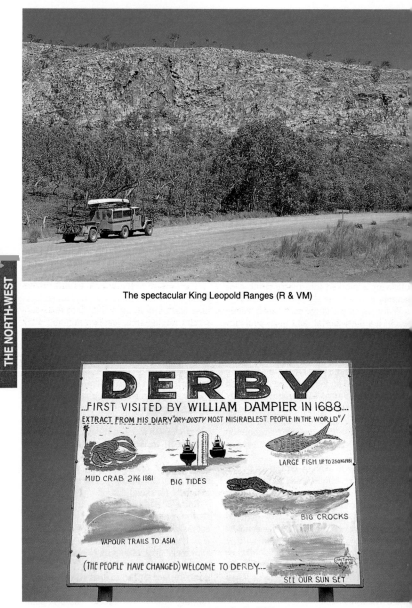

The spectacular King Leopold Ranges (R & VM)

Sign announcing Derby (TW)

and pandanus palms make a verdant, sylvan scene, the canoeing and swimming are very enjoyable, and you can wet a line for some sooty grunters, which make a great meal. Less than four km on, the track ends beside a large boab tree that has a bell carved into its trunk.

From this spot, a walking trail heads north a few hundred metres to the lip of one of the most spectacular waterfalls and gorges in the Kimberley, formed as the river slashes its way through the Isdell Range. Spend a bit of time enjoying the scenery and exploring the falls and the surrounding area.

This area is now managed by the Department of Conservation & Land Management (CALM), which should see some facilities, such as pit toilets, placed at the camping ground to cater for the large number of travellers who stay here. Once a part of Mount Hart station, the area is destined to be a national park.

At the junction back on the main road, almost due south, is a distinctive bluff called Rifle Point. About four km from the junction, the road begins the long climb of the King Leopold Ranges. As the route winds its way up the battlements of the range, you'll have some good views of the surrounding area. As well, the clatter of gravel will give way to the hum of bitumen for a short stretch over the steepest part of the range country.

Over the next 10 km the road crosses a number of small creeks before coming to Dog Chain Creek, 21 km south of the Bell Gorge turn-off. Some of the previous creeks have small campsites beside them, but the one here at Dog Chain is definitely the best, with water and plenty of shade. If it wasn't so close to the main road, it would be good for a week's stay.

The road continues to wind its way through the range country, and just over two km from Dog Chain Creek there is a major road junction with a good dirt road heading off to the left. This is the Millie Windie Road. Two hundred metres along this road, a lesser track heads south into **Lennard River Gorge**.

It is about a seven-km drive into the carpark from where you can access the Lennard River Gorge, and the road is often very rough, passable only to serious 4WDs. The drive and the walk down the hill to the gorge rim are worth it, though.

A trail marked by some small rock cairns leads down to the water at one end of the gorge. Here in the heat of the Dry, it is cool, the deep, dark water always refreshing.

Seven km south from the Lennard turn-off, a track heads off to the right to Mount Hart homestead, some 50 km from the Gibb River Road. A few hundred metres past this junction, the road crosses Apex Creek, which has a small camping area on its banks, just after the crossing. Less than 1.5 km later you pass through **Inglis Gap**; a small parking area on the left gives extensive views of the surrounding plains and ranges. From here you descend the final ramparts of the King Leopolds and head across rocky, undulating country towards the Napier Range, the final barrier before reaching the flat plains that border the great rivers of the western Kimberley.

The road gets better all the time, and while there are a few minor creek crossings in the next 40 km, a number of them are bridged and the rest are well maintained. The turn-off to Napier Downs station is 278 km from the Kalumburu junction and 55 km south of Inglis Gap.

You begin to pass through Yammera Gap just 500 metres from the turn-off to Napier Downs. This short pass leads through the **Napier Range** – a sheer-sided limestone range that was once, millions of years ago, a coral reef. Observant, imaginative individuals would have seen a rock formation on the right just before entering the pass that in silhouette looks like, and has been called, Queen Victoria's Head.

The Lennard River is crossed nine km south of the pass, and 400 metres further on is the turn-off to **Windjana Gorge** and **Tunnel Creek**. This road also leads further east, and joins the main highway 43 km west of Fitzroy Crossing. Windjana Gorge and Tunnel Creek are national parks, and only the former allows camping. Neither should be missed.

THE NORTH-WEST

Once south of the Napier Range, the road passes through flat, lightly treed, pastoral country. The turn-off to Kimberley Downs station is 46 km from the road junction to Windjana Gorge, and the bitumen begins just a short distance beyond the Kimberley Downs turn-off. You'll appreciate it!

The turn-off to Meda station and the **May River** is 40 km further on. Six km along, this access track comes close to the May River.

The Napier Range

This prehistoric barrier reef that grew in a Devonian sea has a magnetic appeal to travellers. The adjoining Oscar Range and Geikie Range are also part of this ancient reef system, and while you can see and experience one aspect of it at Geikie Gorge National Park, just north of Fitzroy Crossing, it is the Napier Range that holds the greater (and less developed) attractions.

Windjana Gorge is 25 km east of the Gibb River Road, 127 km east of Derby. Geologists consider it of major importance: here, exposed for all to see, are the remains of an ancient reef complex, with all its intricate relationships locked into the rocks.

The Lennard River has cut its way through the range, forming a narrow, picturesque canyon about 3.5 km long, up to 200 metres wide and in places nearly 100 metres deep. The near-vertical walls of the gorge are an impressive backdrop to the line of green along the sandy bed of the dry-season stream. Late in the dry season, when the river does not flow, it forms a chain of pools, home to fish and a few freshwater crocodiles.

In the sediment and ancient river gravels, scientists have found the remains of extinct crocodiles and turtles, as well as ancient mammals, such as the large marsupial wombat diprotodont.

A ranger is based at the gorge during the dry season and there is a pleasant camping area close to the mouth of the gorge. Walking and canoeing are enjoyable ways of seeing the splendour of the gorge, and if you are quiet there is always the chance of seeing a shy croc or agile wallaby. Bird-watching is also rewarding, with a number of species, such as sandstone shrike thrushes and great bower birds, being common.

There are some Aboriginal art sites around the area, but they are a little difficult to find without prior knowledge. Ask the ranger for directions to the red Wandjina figure on the southern wall of the gorge.

Once again, this place has a part in the Pigeon story. Here, he and his men attacked a group of settlers who were about to drive their wagons and cattle through the gorge to open a new endeavour north of the range. Further east along the Napier Range towards Tunnel Creek are the ruins of Lillimooloora, where Pigeon started his uprising by killing a policeman and releasing the prisoners he had with him.

Tunnel Creek is 30 km east of Windjana Gorge, and, while camping is not allowed, this is a place not to be missed by anyone travelling through the Kimberley. As its name indicates, Tunnel Creek has carved a tunnel through the Napier Range, and it is so big that you can walk through it with no problems during the Dry.

There is always water in the stream, even if there is none (or very little) on the north side, where the carpark is – how much water depends on the previous wet season and how much water there is in the tunnel. Sometimes you can walk through the 750-metre-long tunnel and only get wet up to your knees. At other times you may need to swim.

Although the roof has collapsed about halfway along the tunnel, you still need a good torch to thoroughly enjoy the walk through the range. Other chasms and offshoots from the main tunnel can also be explored, but the highlight is the far end. Here Tunnel Creek flows out into the open air under a large rent in the cliff face. It's a peaceful place, worthy of an hour or two before you venture back the way you have come, to the far side of the range and the carpark.

Some samples of Aboriginal art can be found near the northern entrance, while the southern end of the tunnel was a site for stone axes and the like.

Tunnel Creek was Pigeon's hideout during his days as an outlaw or freedom fighter, and it was no doubt a very effective one.

For information on either of these small parks, see the ranger at Windjana or the ranger at Geikie Gorge National Park (☎ (091) 91 5121), or the district ranger at the Department of Conservation & Land Management regional office in Kununurra (☎ (091) 68 0200). ■

Camping is allowed here. It is a popular spot with the locals, and a good fishing area, but be careful where you swim – big estuarine crocs have been seen. This is one of the better spots to camp near Derby.

Back on the main road, a major T-junction is reached 36 km beyond the May River turn-off; to the right is Derby, and you'll hit the outskirts in less than four km (it's about seven km to the centre of town). You're 417 km from the Kalumburu junction and 710 km from the green town of Kununurra.

Derby

Derby lies just above the high-tide mark on a low tongue of land in King Sound, just north of the mouth of the Fitzroy River. Mud flats surround the town on three sides. While Derby may lack the all-season green of Kununurra and the razzmatazz of trendy Broome, it's an honest, friendly place.

Derby was officially proclaimed in 1883, a couple of years after Yeeda station had been founded on the banks of the Fitzroy River, 50 km south, by George Patterson. By 1890 the town boasted a jetty (used for the shipping of wool), a resident magistrate and a police force.

While European settlement in the eastern Kimberley had been based on cattle brought overland from Queensland, the western Kimberley was opened up by sheep graziers bringing their flocks from the south. By the mid-1890s, sheep swarmed over the flat plains right up to the sheer rock walls of the Napier Range.

The local Aboriginal people resisted the White invasion, and took to spearing the Europeans' stock as a way of supplementing their food supply. During this time an Aborigine called Jandamarra, but known to the Whites as 'Pigeon', led a revolt that lasted for three years before he was killed near Tunnel Creek. The **Pigeon Heritage Trail** starts in Derby and takes in the cemetery where Pigeon's first victim is buried, plus the gaol and the **Prison Tree**. From here it leads out to Windjana Gorge, the ruins of Lillimooloora (once a police post, and where Pigeon claimed his first victims),

then on to Tunnel Creek, where the final chapter was played out.

Apart from the heritage trail, there is **Myall's Bore** (reputedly the longest cattle trough in the southern hemisphere) and **Wharfingers House** (which houses the local museum). Derby is a good base for exploring the local area, and as it promotes itself as the 'Gateway to the Gorges', it is an ideal spot to explore these. The **RFDS base** opens its radio section to the public most mornings for those interested in seeing how the RFDS supports the people in the bush.

The town can provide all a traveller requires. Accommodation ranges from a caravan park to motels. There are supermarkets, butchers, a good range of shops, and repair facilities for vehicles, your outboard motors and boats.

From Derby you can take a scenic flight over the coast and islands or inland across the range country. Other tours include one around town on an 18-seat wagon, or down to Yeeda station, or out to a pearl farm. Longer tours in 4WD vehicles are also available, or you can hire vehicles that come complete with camping gear from the local Avis dealer.

There is some excellent fishing from river, shore, jetty or boat. Boat-fishers will have more luck than the others because they will be able to access more places, including the offshore islands. Barra is the prize fish that most people chase, but many other species fight just as hard and are equally tasty: threadfin salmon, sawfish, tarpon, catfish, and black bream, or sooty grunters, are just some you can catch off the shore, while boaties may get into queenfish or Spanish mackerel.

The jetty is a good spot to cast a line or a net for mud crabs; it's also where you will find the best fish & chips in Australia. A small restaurant beside the jetty caters for takeaways and for sit-down meals. Note, though, that it is closed on Monday.

Offshore are the 'Iron Islands': Cockatoo and Koolan. **Cockatoo Island** has now opened its doors to tourism, with overnight accommodation. The island is something

THE NORTH-WEST

entirely different from what you have been seeing, but typical of the wild Kimberley coast.

Then there is, of course, the **Fitzroy River**. There are five areas where you can camp on the banks. Access is possible at a number of spots, but elsewhere the river banks are off limits to travellers because most of the river downstream from Fitzroy Crossing is within the Noogoora burr quarantine area.

The most accessible area takes up the western bank of the Fitzroy River downstream from the **Willare Bridge**, which is where Highway 1 crosses the Fitzroy River, 58 km south of Derby. Camping is popular in amongst the trees within the first few hundred metres of the bridge, but there are spots all the way downstream to the old highway route at Langley Crossing.

Other places to camp by the river are downstream from Fitzroy Crossing to a point (adjacent to Alligator Hill) about 10 km south of the Fitzroy Bridge; east of Liveringa station, along the Camballin-Noonkanbah Road, at the Fitzroy Weir, 155 km south-east of Derby; at Myroodah Crossing just south of Liveringa, 120 km from Derby; and near Udialla, west of Liveringa.

Finally there are the festivals that add so much to anyone's trip through the bush. These are the times that locals from near and far come to town to socialise and have some fun. There is a country music festival in July, horse-race meetings in June, and on 26 December the annual Boxing Day Sports, which is just a little different to your normal sports day. The big event of the year, though, is the Boab Festival. Held each July, it includes a rodeo, mardi gras and more.

From Derby it is just 222 km to the lights, golden beaches and trendy boutiques of Broome. Or if you want to head further south, you are a mere 2520 km from Perth!

DETOURS
Gibb River Road to Wyndham
It's worth making a short detour to visit the historic town of Wyndham, an easy run on bitumen from the turn-off where the Gibb

River Road starts. Fifteen km north from here, or 22 km from Highway 1, you come to **The Grotto**. This secluded spot, just to the left of the road, offers a chance for a swim. Early in the dry season the falls may still be running, adding more charm to this rocky defile immersed in the green of trees, fern and palms.

The **Old Road** to Wyndham veers off to the right just metres north of here and heads across the flood plains to Alligator Hole, Marlgu Billabong and Parry Lagoon. Alligator Hole is a fine swimming spot, and the latter two areas are ideal for bird-watching. This dirt road rejoins the bitumen 12 km north of The Grotto. Wyndham is 14 km further north.

Wyndham
Wyndham, on the shores of Cambridge Gulf, was founded in 1886 to supply the cattle stations that were being established in the region, and to give easier access to the newly found gold fields at Halls Creek.

In 1919 the meatworks opened, and this enterprise kept the town going over the next 60 years. The factory closed its doors for the final time in the late 1980s, and soon afterwards a fire gutted much of the building.

Wyndham's proximity to South-East Asia meant that many great aviators, setting world air endurance records, passed through the town during the 1920s and '30s. The Ord River Dam revitalised the area in the 1960s, while in the late '70s, offshore gas and oil and mineral finds further south, maintained the impetus.

Much of the original character of the town has been retained, no doubt due to the fact that the old port area is five km away from the newer hub of the town.

The selection of accommodation in the town includes a hotel and club, and a caravan park. There is also a supermarket, a bakery, a couple of general stores and a few places to buy fuel or get your vehicle repaired. A hospital and police station are also here.

In August, Wyndham stages its Top of the West festival, with 10 days of revelry, as well as a music festival, a gymkhana and the Wyndham Cup race meeting, which is a lot of fun for locals and visitors alike.

Check the local **old port area**, which still reeks of the old days when horses and carts rattled down the street, and pioneers such as 'Patsy' Durack came in from his Argyle station. The three **old cemeteries** in town are also poignant reminders of days gone by, as is the **Boab Prison Tree** found along the Karunjie Road, just after it turns off the Moochalabra Dam Road, 30 km from Wyndham.

One place that should not be missed is **Five Rivers Lookout**. From this spot above the old port area, you have a grand spectacle of the old town, and of Cambridge Gulf and the rivers that feed it. The view is better in the morning. To the north is the mouth of the mighty Ord River, to the south are the King, Pentecost and Durack rivers, while to the west is the Forrest River.

The **Moochalabra Dam** is Wyndham's water supply and is a pleasant spot for a picnic. There is also some Aboriginal art in the overhangs along the tall cliffs that are on your right, just before the picnic area.

The fishing is brilliant around Wyndham, and those with a boat will find it a mecca. Land-based fishers can try the wharf at the old port, or any of the rivers in the area. The road out to the dam gives good access to the King River, which is a fine spot for barra. Otherwise, you can charter a boat for some fishing further afield.

If you enjoy bird-watching, the place to go is the **Parry Lagoon Nature Reserve**. To get there, head south along the bitumen for 14 km before turning left onto the Old Halls Creek Road, which heads east across the flood plains of the Ord River. Parry Lagoon, along with Marlgu Billabong and Police Hole, holds water long after the dry season bleaches the rest of the plain a dusty gold. The bird life is fantastic.

Gibb River-Kalumburu Road

The road to the Mitchell Plateau and Kalumburu leaves the Gibb River Road 40

THE NORTH-WEST

Prison Tree at Derby (TW)

km north of the turn-off into Gibb River station. There is an immediate decrease in the standard of the road, and it certainly doesn't get any better – this is 4WD territory. The route north is nearly always closed for a few months of the wet season, and even after the rains have stopped, no vehicles move across the blacksoil plains for another month or so.

Drysdale River station (☎ (091) 61 4326), 60 km north of the road junction, can supply fuel and limited supplies. River bank camping is also available close by.

Beyond here, the road continues to be rough, and can be really chopped up at times. At the 98-km mark north of Drysdale River, the turn-off to the Mitchell Plateau is reached, and for most people this is an interesting and enjoyable side trip.

The Mitchell Plateau The Mitchell Plateau offers excellent scenery, good camping, a chance to get to the coast, and a good opportunity to see some fine Aboriginal art.

About 6.5 km from the junction you come to the **King Edward River**, and once across the stream there are some excellent camping spots close to the river. The swimming is very pleasant here, and if you walk upstream, the observant will find some exceptional art sites – some of the best in the Kimberley.

As the track continues, it can become even rougher – it really depends on the previous wet season. About 15 km from the river crossing, you climb up onto the plateau and begin to see the palms that are so distinctive in this area. Forty-five km further on, the track crosses **Camp Creek**, and this, if it is vacant of mining camps or whatever, is probably the best spot to camp, unless you really want to spend your time on the coast.

Just over three km from this spot is the turn-off to **Mitchell Falls**. This track terminates at Mertens Creek, 15 km from the turn-off, and from here it is a half-hour walk to **Little Mertens Falls**. Ten minutes on are the spectacular **Big Mertens Falls**, while another 10 minutes will bring you to Mitchell Falls. You'll find some good Aboriginal art and spectacular scenery along the way,

and the water is delightful – take your bathers.

Back on the main track heading north from Camp Creek, it's 23 km to the turn-off to **Surveyor's Pool**. The side track will take you nearly seven km west, and then you need to walk another four km to the pools. It's a top spot, but lacks the dramatic scenery of the Mitchell Falls walk.

Continuing north, the track leads to Crystal Creek and the nearby mangrove-lined bay, or into Port Warrender, a total of around 45 km from Camp Creek. The tracks to either spot can be extremely bad – the track to Port Warrender can have three to six-metre washaways in it, at which times it is, of course, impassable.

Kalumburu

Heading north to Kalumburu from where the Mitchell Plateau road turns off, the road continues as before. Theda River station is passed 35 km north (196 km from the Gibb River Road), and another 51 km brings you to the **Carson River** crossing, which is another good spot to camp. Twenty km up the road, you enter the particularly friendly Kalumburu Aboriginal Community.

You need a permit before you enter the Aboriginal reserve. You also need a camping permit to take advantage of the excellent camping on the coast. It is worth it for the fishing alone. All enquiries and arrangements for permits should be directed to the Kalumburu Aboriginal Corporation (☎ (091) 61 4300, fax 61 4331), PMB 10, via Wyndham, WA 6740.

Visitors to the Aboriginal community are most welcome, but you are asked to respect the community's privacy, and to follow the rules and guidelines, the most important being no entry to the reserve without a permit (which must be arranged in advance), and no alcohol of any kind to be brought onto the reserve. Entry to the reserve is only allowed during working hours (Monday to Thursday from 7 to 11 am and 1.30 to 4 pm, and Friday from 7 to 11 am).

You can purchase limited food supplies at the general store, and fuel (unleaded, super and diesel) is available from the service station (open from 7 to 11 am and 2 to 4.30 pm). Travellers should also note that repair facilities are very limited and virtually no spare parts are available. Cash only is accepted as payment for fuel and supplies. Camping within the reserve costs $5 per person per night.

There is some great fishing around Kalumburu. If you don't have your own boat, it is possible to hire one through the Corporation, but you really need to give them a bit of advance notice.

Kalumburu also has its own airstrip, and while there are no landing fees payable, you are required to pay the normal visitor's fees. If you give the Corporation a couple of weeks' notice, they may be able to organise a hire vehicle, as well as tours and scenic flights. Those wanting aviation fuel can arrange it through the Kalumburu Mission (☎ (091) 61 4333). Again, you will need to let them know well in advance so that the fuel can be freighted in by barge if necessary.

Access to Kalumburu is only advisable by 4WD in the Dry (normally from June to October), and only well-built, off-road trailers should be taken on the trip.

ALTERNATIVE ROUTES
If you've been visiting Wyndham (see the earlier Detours section), you can pick up the Gibb River Road where it crosses the Pentecost River. Head back out of town for six km the way you came, to the airport and the signposted road to Moochalabra Dam. This turns right, off the bitumen (when coming from town).

The turn-off to **Moochalabra Dam** is 19 km further on. Turning left here will take you to the dam and some Aboriginal art. Continuing straight ahead, there are some campsites off to your right as you parallel the King River. Five km past the dam turn-off, you will come to the **Boab Prison Tree**, once used by police patrols to hold their prisoners; it's a better example than the famed one at Derby.

Over the next few km the road twists and turns through a few junctions, with few (if any) being signposted. Nine hundred metres from the Prison Tree, turn right, then 2.1 km further on, turn left. Turn left 1.7 km past this junction and pass through a gate. You are just 35 km from Wyndham.

You are now on the **Old Karunjie Track** and the route is fairly plain to follow. Stick to the main track, which swings in a large arc around the great red massif of the Cockburn Range. Minor tracks spear off the main one, heading across the salt plains to the West Arm of Cambridge Gulf and some fishing spots. Be careful – get bogged out here and you are in the diabolicals!

You come close to the **Pentecost River** 39 km after you pass through the gate. There are a number of campsites on your right but they are for dedicated fishers. There are numerous tracks in this area, but just keep heading south and you'll end up in the right place. Less than eight km after first seeing the river, you will pass through another gate. Another two km will see you at the Gibb River Road, just before the crossing of the Pentecost River.

The distance from Wyndham via this rough route is 83 km and you are just 58 km from the main highway via the Gibb River Road. From here on it is the Gibb River Road all the way to Derby.

ACTIVITIES
There is a wide choice of activities in this area. Walking, canoeing (and boating), fishing and bird-watching would have to be at the top of the list of things you can do on your own. Good fishing and bird-watching spots have already been mentioned in the earlier route descriptions.

Walking
There are some excellent walks beginning just out of Kununurra. Mirima National Park, on the outskirts of town, has three short marked trails, but you can spend hours wandering through here.

If you camp on El Questro station, there are ample opportunities for walks into some of the magnificent gorges in the area. Once you have a mud map from the store, you can enjoy walks to El Questro Gorge, Moonshine Gorge or Zebidee Springs. The latter is not to be missed: the springs run with hot water, and the small thermal pools and waterfalls they form as they run down the escarpment are divine. Shaded by lush tropical growth, there is no better place to spend a hot Kimberley day. Take a picnic lunch.

At Durack River station, hike around Jack's Waterhole and enjoy the bird life.

At the Barnett River Gorge, take the walk up or downstream along the river. The shallow cascades, the deep pools lined with pandanus palms and the bird life are very enjoyable.

If you stop at Mount Barnett Roadhouse and camp down on the river, you will be on Manning Creek. The Lower Manning Gorge, just a stone's throw from the camping area, is worth exploring. There is some Aboriginal art on the north bank, below the gorge. A longer walk (about an hour each way) is to the Upper Manning Gorge. Once there, you can explore the falls and gorge. This walk is across rocky ground that blasts the heat back into your face at any time, apart from early morning and evening. Spend the day at the top end of the gorge – you won't be disappointed.

In 1992 an expedition led by Peter Treseder, and supported in part by Australian Geographic, walked from Mount Barnett down the Isdell River, through all its gorges to the sea at Walcott Inlet. They used rubber rafts (carried in their backpacks) to get over large sections of water, before heading back up the Charnley River to Mount Elizabeth station. From there it was down the Barnett River to where they had started.

Galvin, Adcock and Bell gorges, further south along the Gibb River Road, all warrant a little exploration.

At Windjana Gorge, take a walk up the gorge below its towering, shady cliffs. A wander through the range at Tunnel Creek will probably mean getting wet, and you may even have to swim. Carry a torch, preferably one that is going to keep working if it gets wet. The 750-metre walk through the range can take as little as one hour return but is

Big Mertens Falls (R & VM)

much more enjoyable if you take longer. The far end is worth more than an hour on its own.

Canoeing & Boating

Taking a canoe or a small boat to the Kimberley adds another dimension to the adventure.

Chamberlain Gorge on El Questro station is ideal for both a canoe or a small outboard-powered boat, but the waters of the Lower Manning Gorge and Windjana Gorge are really only suitable for a canoe. On waters such as Jack's Waterhole at Durack River station, only non-motorised craft are allowed.

The best canoeing and boating, though, is around Kununurra. The waters of the Diversion Dam, just outside town, can handle quite large craft, as the ski jumps testify, while Lake Argyle is so big that it is like an inland sea and can be dangerous to canoes.

The shallow waterways that adjoin the open waters of the Diversion Dam are locally called 'The Everglades', and the area is ideal for canoeing and bird-watching. There are a couple of places to launch a small boat or canoe adjacent to the highway or the caravan parks that abut the waterway. An evening paddle is great, but take notice of where you paddle: after a couple of hours out here paddling between reeds and trees, you might have trouble finding your exact launching spot.

One of the best trips is down the Ord River, from just below the wall at Lake Argyle to Kununurra at the Diversion Dam. This trip is suitable for a small outboard-powered boat, or it's a good two-day paddle in a canoe.

All up, the trip is 55 km long. For much of the way, the river is lined with dense stands of paperbarks, coolabahs and pandanus palms. Carlton Gorge is about 15 km downriver from the launching spot, and there are a couple of reasonable campsites in the gorge on the left. At the 23-km mark, a creek joins the Ord, and here is another good camp. For the next 10 km there are a couple of good sites to stop overnight, but then the river runs into the top end of the Diversion Dam and access to the bank is limited. The water also slows, so it's a paddle without a current to help for the last 20 km to the dam wall near the highway.

The Western Australian Department of Youth, Sport & Recreation's *Canoeing Guide (No 10)* to this stretch of water is sometimes available in Kununurra.

ORGANISED TOURS

Numerous tour operators around Australia include the Kimberley as a major destination. However, there are also quite a few local tour operators based in Kununurra, Wyndham and Derby who specialise in their surrounding area, as well as offering more extensive trips exploring the whole of the Kimberley region. For a comprehensive list of all operators, contact the Western Australian Travel Centre.

Local Tour Operators

Kununurra

Bungle Bungle Experience Safaris, PO Box 833, Kununurra 6743 (☎ (091) 61 4322, fax 61 4340)

Desert Inn Backpackers Oasis, PO Box 819, Kununurra 6743 (☎ (091) 68 2702)

East Kimberley Tours, PO Box 537, Kununurra 6743 (☎ (091) 68 2213, fax 68 2544)

Kimberley Wilderness Adventures, PO Box 564, Kununurra 6743 (☎ (091) 68 1711, fax 68 1253)

Kununurra Backpackers Adventure, PO Box 564, Kununurra 6743 (☎ (091) 68 1711, fax 68 1253)

Swagabout Safaris & Cruises, PO Box 588, Kununurra 6743 (☎ (091) 69 1257, fax 69 1233)

Wyndham

I J & S A Thorley, 907 Koolinda St, Wyndham (☎ (091) 61 1201, fax 61 1106)

Derby

Bush Track Safaris, PO Box 7, Derby 6725 (☎ (091) 91 4644, fax 91 1162)

Kimwest Tours, PO Box 68, Derby 6728 (☎ (091) 91 1426, fax 91 1609)

General Tour Operators

AAT King's, 29-33 Palmerston Crescent, South Melbourne 3205 (☎ (03) 274 7422, fax 274 7400)

Australian Pacific Tours, PO Box 118, Hampton 3188 (☎ (03) 277 8555, fax 597 0687)

Amesz Tours, 4 Elmsfield Rd, Midvale, Perth (☎ (09) 250 2577)

Pathfinder, 3/16 Irwin St, Perth (☎ (09) 221 5411)

Vehicle Guide Services

Bush Track Safaris, Mt Elizabeth station (☎ (091) 91 4644)

Peter Murray Kimberley Safaris, PO Box 207, Broome 6725 (☎ (091) 92 1223)

Russell Guest's 4WD Adventure Safaris, 38 Station St, Fairfield 3078 (☎ (03) 481 5877, fax 482 4713)

Portman's Australian Adventures, 29B Mount Slide Rd, Kinglake 3763 (☎ (057) 86 1780, fax 86 1818)

Abseiling

Kimberley Ropeworks (☎ (091) 68 2600), Lot 707 Pindan Ave, Kununurra, has experienced guides for abseiling excursions on Kimberley rock.

Boat Tours & Fishing

The Kimberley has the most spectacular and rugged coastline in Australia. The scenery is awe-inspiring and the fishing is fantastic, not only along the coast but also in the inland rivers. A number of boat charters and fishing safaris operate locally. These include:

Alligator Airways, Hangar No 5, Kununurra Airport (☎ (091) 68 1333, fax 68 2704) for float-plane fishing safaris
Buccaneer Safaris, PO Box 532, Derby (☎ (091) 91 1991, fax 91 1609)
Kimberley Charter Company, PO Box 192, Wyndham (☎ (091) 61 1310, fax 61 1053)
Kimberley Sportfishing, 1878a Lemonwood Way, Kununurra (☎ (091) 68 2752)
Ultimate Adventures, PO Box 442, Kununurra (☎ (091) 68 1610, fax 69 1041)

Canoeing

Canoe tours down the Ord River can be organised through a number of operators based in Kununurra. All camping and cooking gear is normally provided and you can camp at permanent campsites along the way. Take your own sleeping bag, food etc. Contact Desert Inn Backpackers Oasis, Swagabout Safaris & Cruises or Kununurra Backpackers Adventure for more details (see Local Tour Operators above).

Scenic Flights

There are a host of tour and scenic flight operators throughout the Kimberley, such as Aerial Enterprises (☎ (091) 91 1132), Alligator Airways (☎ (091) 68 1575), Kingfisher Aviation (☎ (091) 68 1626) and Ord Air Charter (☎ (091) 61 1335). Contact the Kununurra or Derby tourist bureaus for a comprehensive listing.

FACILITIES
Kununurra

Kununurra is a major centre. The town boasts a large supermarket complex, general stores, chemists, a laundry, a bakery, butchers, fishing-tackle shops, service stations and fuel supplies, as well as LPG and major repair facilities. Elgee Toyota (☎ (091) 68 2236), 231 Bloodwood Drive, is the local agency for the RACWA, and also does towing.

A number of banks are represented in Kununurra. Both the Commonwealth and Rural & Industry banks have ATM facilities, and there are also National and Westpac bank agencies.

There's a wide choice of accommodation, from hotels to hostels, as well as numerous caravan parks. The *Quality Inn* (☎ (091) 68 1455) has singles/doubles from $67/102. The *Country Club Private Hotel* (☎ (091) 61 1042) charges $50/60, and the *Lakeside Resort* (☎ (091) 69 1092) $80/87. At the *Hotel Kununurra* (☎ (091) 68 1344), prices range from $69 to $89.

For the budget-conscious there is the *Kununurra Backpackers* (☎ (091) 68 1711), which costs $12 a single in the dormitory section. Twin rooms are $14 per person. Facilities include a swimming pool and spa, fully equipped kitchens and a laundry. Bike hire and 4WD tours can also be organised. The *Raintree Lodge Youth Hostel* (☎ (091) 68 1372) has dorm beds at $10 for members ($12 for nonmembers), while the *Desert Inn* (☎ (091) 68 2702) charges $11.

There are four caravan parks within Kununurra, as well as a park just out of town. The *Kona Caravan Park* (☎ (091) 68 1031), on the edge of Lake Kununurra, and the *Town Caravan Park* (☎ (091) 68 1763), in the centre of town, have powered/unpowered sites ($14/12 for two people), as well as on-site vans ($50) and villa units ($85 a double). At the *Kimberleyland Holiday Park* (☎ (091) 68 1280), also on the shores of Lake Kununurra, powered/unpowered sites cost $15/10 a double.

Dogs are not allowed in any of these parks; however, they are permitted at *Young's Coolibah Caravan Park* (☎ (091) 68 1653). Unpowered camping sites cost $10 a double, with power obtainable. Chalets ($40 a double) are also available. The *Hidden Valley Caravan Park* (☎ (091) 68 1790) is on the Weaber Plains Road, and is another park where dogs are allowed (at the owners' discretion). Powered/unpowered sites cost $14/12 a double.

Wyndham

The northernmost town and harbour in

Western Australia, Wyndham has been developed into two main areas: the old town and the new. While Wyndham lacks the variety and number of services available at Kununurra, the town certainly has a wide range of facilities, including a supermarket, general stores, a hardware store, a bakery, service stations and fuel supplies. The RACWA agency in Wyndham is Branko Motors (☎ (091) 61 1305).

The Rural & Industry Bank has an ATM facility here, and there are Commonwealth and National Australia bank agencies.

Accommodation is varied. The *Wyndham Community Club* (☎ (091) 61 1130) has units costing $45/55 a single/double, while at the *Wyndham Town Hotel* (☎ (091) 61 1003) prices are $65/75 in fully self-contained units. For more budget-priced accommodation, you can stay at the *Wyndham Roadhouse* (☎ (091) 61 1290) for $15/25. Campers and caravanners can stop at the *Three Mile Caravan Park* (☎ (091) 61 1064), which is close to the shops. Powered/unpowered sites cost $14/11, while on-site vans are available for $25 a night. Pets are allowed, on a leash.

Emma Gorge Resort
Part of El Questro station, the Emma Gorge Resort is only one km off the Gibb River Road. An airstrip is near the resort. The facilities of the resort include tented cabins, a restaurant and bar, a comprehensively stocked shop, laundry facilities and a large swimming pool. Emma Gorge itself is just a short walk away. The tented cabin accommodation costs $48/80 a single/double, with a family cabin (one double and two singles) available for $136. For further details, contact El Questro station (see below).

Travellers who would like to explore Emma Gorge but are not planning to stay overnight, pay a fee of $5 per adult.

El Questro Station
El Questro station is a working cattle station, but it also welcomes visitors and offers a range of accommodation, from the most luxurious to secluded riverside camping. It has

its own private airstrip for those wishing to fly in.

For the tourist with heaps of money, there is the homestead, with luxury, fully inclusive accommodation at $540 per adult twin share or single. At a more realistic level, self-contained bungalows cost $60 per adult twin share ($90 for a single room). Meals can be provided.

The self-sufficient camper has a choice of two types of sites: some sites are close to shower/toilet facilities and the store, while those who want to get away and have a bit more privacy can choose from a selection of riverside camping sites. Cost per adult is $7.50 a day.

Travellers who would like to explore El Questro but are not planning to stay overnight, are charged a fee of $7.50 per adult.

For more details you can contact the station; ☎ & fax (091) 61 4320, PO Box 909, Kununurra, WA 6743.

Home Valley, Durack River & Karunjie Stations
The Sinnamon family run three stations, all working cattle stations that have also opened their doors to tourists. Travellers will find a visit to any of their stations a worthwhile experience, as the Sinnamon family knows the Kimberley region extremely well.

Home Valley station (☎ (091) 61 4322, fax 61 4340) is on the Cambridge Gulf surrounded by some spectacular scenery. Accommodation is available at the homestead, with dinner, breakfast and shared facilities included, for just $65 per person. Pleasant camping is also possible for $5 per adult. The Sinnamons also have a wide range of 4WD tours available throughout the Kimberley region.

Durack River station (☎ (091) 61 4324) is one of the largest cattle stations in Australia, and it is also one of the best places to camp along the Gibb River Road. The homestead and camping area are less than one km from the Gibb River Road beside a large waterhole. A store provides limited supplies, and fuel is also available, as well as minor emergency vehicle repairs. Accommodation

Newman gums (RI)

costs $50 per person; camping, with toilets and shower facilities, is $5. The camping is very pleasant along the waterhole, which provides the opportunity to swim, canoe or fish. Again, 4WD tours of the area are available.

At *Karunjie station* (☎ (091) 61 4322), the main hub of the Sinnamons' pastoral operation, travellers can camp for $5 per adult. You are welcome to become involved in station activities or join one of the 4WD tours of the rugged and still untamed surrounding country. Camping is possible only by prior arrangement.

Mount Elizabeth Station
The Lacey family runs Mount Elizabeth station (☎ (091) 91 4644). Travellers can stay here, enjoy the Laceys' hospitality, and join a scenic flight or one of the organised 4WD tours. On either you'll see some of the wildest, most remote country in the Kimber-

ley and some fine examples of Aboriginal art.

The homestead has eight beds available for guests, plus a cottage with six beds. Bed, breakfast and dinner costs $60 a single on a shared basis, while the cottage offers self-catering accommodation for $20 per person (shared facilities). Camping is also available, with hot showers and toilets, for $5 a single. A small store provides limited supplies.

Mount Barnett Roadhouse & Manning Gorge
The beautiful Manning Gorge and Mount Barnett Roadhouse (☎ (091) 91 7007, fax 91 4692) are both on Mount Barnett station on the Gibb River Road.

The roadhouse has limited food supplies, snacks and cool drinks, and all fuels, but no LPG. The workshop can also carry out mechanical repairs. The store normally closes from noon to 1 pm for lunch.

The roadhouse is also the place to get your permit to camp at Manning Gorge. The pleasant camping area is beside Lower Manning Gorge, a delightful swimming spot. Toilets and barbecues are provided. The cost is $4 per person per night.

Mount House Station

At the homestead (☎ (091) 91 4649), visitors can stay in self-contained accommodation with shared facilities. A single room is $20; the hire of linen costs an extra $5 per person. Prior bookings are essential.

A store offers a limited range of food supplies (including bread, meat and some fresh produce). All fuels are available, as well as tyres and batteries.

Derby

Derby is one of the original towns of the Kimberley region and can supply all a traveller's requirements. There are a couple of supermarkets that operate seven days a week, along with a chemist, butchers, a bakery, and hardware and fishing stores, to name just a few of the facilities. There's also a choice of service stations supplying all fuels and LPG, the *Colac Roadhouse & Service Station* (☎ (091) 91 1256) being the RACWA agent. If you need any repairs, there are a number of automotive repair facilities available.

The ANZ Bank has full banking facilities, and the post office has both passbook and keycard facilities for the Commonwealth Bank. The Challenge and Rural & Industry banks have agencies here.

Accommodation ranges in price: a unit at the *King Sound Tourist Resort Hotel* (☎ (091) 93 1044) costs $85/96 a single/double, while rooms at the *Derby Boab Inn* (☎ (091) 91 1044) are $55/75, and the *West Kimberley Lodge* (☎ (091) 91 1031) charges $30/45. The *Spinifex Hotel* (☎ (091) 91 1233) offers backpacker accommodation ($10 a single) and self-contained rooms ($35 to $45 a single, and $45 to $60 a double).

Campers can stay at the *Kimberley Entrance Caravan Park* (☎ (091) 93 1055); dogs are allowed, on a leash. A powered site costs $14 a single/double; a tent site is $5 a single. On-site vans are also available ($30 a single/double).

Airstrips

There are public aerodromes at Derby and Kununurra, while Wyndham's airstrip (☎ (091) 61 1002) is owned and maintained by the Wyndham-East Kimberley Shire. Aviation fuel is readily available.

Throughout the Kimberley there are also small, privately owned and maintained airstrips on station properties. Aviation fuel can often be organised, but you need to give them prior notice of your requirements.

ALTERNATIVE TRANSPORT
Air

A wide choice of aircraft charters operate all over the Kimberley – see the earlier Organised Tours section or contact the Derby or Kununurra tourist bureaus.

Both major towns are also regularly serviced with commercial flights by Ansett Australia from Perth, while local air charter services link Wyndham and Kununurra. Ansett Australia has offices in Derby (☎ (091) 91 1266) and Kununurra (☎ (091) 68 1444). For flight details you can also contact Ansett Australia on ☎ 13 1300.

Bus

Being important centres in the Kimberley region, the towns of Kununurra and Derby are serviced daily by a number of commercial bus and coach companies. These include Deluxe Coachlines (☎ (091) 92 2425) and Greyhound Pioneer Australia (☎ 13 2030). Bookings for the latter can be made in Kununurra at the Visitor Centre (☎ (091) 68 1177), Coolibah Drive, and in Broome at Broome Travel (☎ (091) 92 1561), Hammersley St.

I J & S A Thorley (☎ (091) 61 1201), in Wyndham, operate a regular bus service from Kununurra to Wyndham ($20 one way). The service connects with all flights at the airport.

Car Rental

There are a number of companies in the Kimberley that hire 4WDs to travellers. Drivers usually need to be over 25 years of age. Some companies also offer camping-equipment packages along with the hire of the vehicle. Avis has offices in Derby (☎ (091) 91 1357) and Kununurra (☎ (091) 68 1258), as does Hertz (☎ (091) 91 1348 in Derby, (091) 68 1257 in Kununurra).

Motorcycle Rental

It is difficult to hire a motorcycle to tour around the Kimberley, but Road Runner Motor Cycle Hire (☎ (091) 92 1971), 7 Farrell St, Broome, has a range of motorcycles available. Bikes up to 250 cc can be hired by any person who has held a car licence for at least 12 months. Unfortunately these smaller bikes can only be taken from Broome (and environs) to Derby. To travel further afield, you will need to hire a 500 cc bike, for which you need to hold a full motorcycle licence. These larger bikes can be ridden into the more remote areas of the Kimberley and up the Gibb River Road.

For those riders who would prefer to go on an organised tour, Road Runner is currently coordinating with a local 4WD tour operator to travel with a guide and back-up vehicle carrying food, camping equipment etc. Contact Road Runner for more details.

The Bungle Bungles

In the short time since the Bungle Bungle massif was 'discovered', it has become one of the Kimberley's major attractions. Rated by many as one of the scenic wonders of Western Australia, the Bungles are more often than not viewed from the air, with visitors taking one of the scenic flights out of Kununurra, Turkey Creek or Halls Creek. For the traveller with a 4WD, the diversion off the main highway around Australia is short, rough, interesting and well worthwhile.

Secluded by distance and by the surrounding ranges, the Bungles remained hidden from prying eyes until 1982. Known to a few drovers, helicopter pilots and local Aboriginal people, the area became an instant hit when it was featured in a TV documentary on the scenic wonders of Western Australia.

In March 1987 the Purnululu (Bungle Bungle) National Park was gazetted (the Kija word 'purnululu' means sandstone). The 210,000-hectare park abuts a 110,000-hectare conservation reserve, and while the park takes in much more, the Bungle Bungle massif is really the only place that is readily accessible to the public. The surrounding country along the Ord River is prone to severe erosion – the reason that this area and much of the country in the headwaters of the Ord River and surrounding Lake Argyle were proclaimed water catchment reserves as far back as 1967.

Since the park's formation, basic camping facilities have been established at a couple of places close to the range, and a ranger station has been erected as well.

INFORMATION
Tourist Offices

The Halls Creek Tourist Information Centre (☎ (091) 68 6262), Great Northern Highway, is open from May to September. The Shire of Halls Creek (☎ (091) 68 6007) may also have useful information.

In Kununurra, the Visitor Centre (☎ (091) 68 1177, fax 68 2598) is at 75 Coolibah Drive, while the regional headquarters of CALM (☎ (091) 68 0200) is in Konkerberry Drive.

Another source of information about the route is the Western Australian Tourist Centre (☎ (09) 483 1111), Forrest Place, Perth.

Emergency

There are hospitals at Halls Creek (☎ (091) 68 6002) and Kununurra (☎ (091) 68 1522). Police stations can also be found at Halls Creek (☎ (091) 68 6000) and Kununurra (☎ (091) 69 1122). There are other emergency services in Wyndham (see the earlier Gibb River Road section).

Other Information

The track off the main highway into the national park has been rerouted and upgraded in recent times but still remains a rough, dusty 4WD track.

No permits are required to enter the park (other than an entrance fee, payable at the information bay adjacent to the ranger station). There are a couple of camping areas, and these have been set up with basic facilities.

The best maps and books for the area (those covering the Kimberley) are listed in the earlier section on the Gibb River Road.

It is not essential to have an HF radio for a trip into the Bungles. If you do have one, the frequencies required are the same as for the Gibb River Road.

THE ROUTE

From Kununurra, head west across the Ord River Diversion Dam wall to the intersection of Highway 1 and the road to Wyndham, 44 km from the town centre.

Turn left here and head down the bitumen of Highway 1, admiring the scenery of rolling hills and rugged mountain ranges. Initially the Carr Boyd Range is off to the left (east), with the Durack Range far off to the west.

The **Durham River** crossing, approximately 35 km south of the main road junction, offers a reasonable spot to camp, as does the Bow River rest area 95 km further south.

Turkey Creek and its roadhouse (☎ (091) 68 7882) are 152 km south of the junction (196 km from Kununurra). Fuel and limited supplies are available, and there is also a camping/caravan park (dogs allowed) and accommodation.

Continuing south along the highway, the turn-off to the Purnululu National Park is well signposted, 56 km south of the roadhouse. Turn left here onto a dirt road, which soon deteriorates into a dirt track. The information sign just past the track junction is worth a read: it will let you know what the latest situation is with the track, camping in the park, or whatever.

The first 40 km of the track east is across

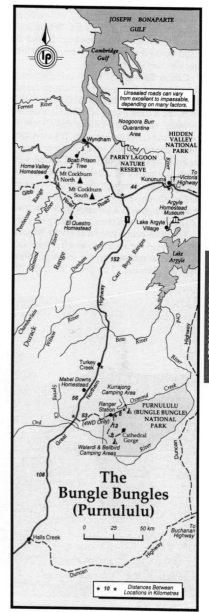

Mabel Downs station property, and no diversions are allowed off the track. Where there are private station tracks leading off from the main track, it is obvious (or marked) which track to stay on.

Calico Springs, 31 km from the bitumen, is a popular camping and rest stop on the run in and out of the Bungles. While permission from the station owner is officially required to camp here, many people don't seem to bother, and camp here anyway. It's a top spot, with a couple of tall, rocky bluffs crowding in on a small area of flat land dotted with trees and palms. A small creek fed by the spring trickles through the gap in the range, and with the shade and permanent cool water, this spot is a pleasant interlude from the dust and heat of the surrounding country.

The intersection known as **Three-Ways** is 53 km from the bitumen, and it is here that the **ranger station** and the self-registration bay are located. The drive in from the highway will have taken you between two and three hours. Fill in your visitor's form, and from here you have a choice of places to go.

The **Kurrajong camping area**, seven km north, gives access to the western side of the Bungle Bungle range. This camping area has toilets, water, and separate areas for those camping with generators and those without.

This side of the range has a couple of gorges worth exploring, including Echidna Chasm and Froghole/Mini Palms. Both walks are pleasant and each is less than two km in length. If you are short of time, don't miss out on **Echidna Chasm**. As you progress further up this gorge, it becomes narrower and narrower and the walls get sheerer. Finally it is just an arm span wide and towers upwards well over 100 metres. It is a spectacular place.

The **Walardi camping area** is 13 km south of the ranger station, just a little north

The Bungle Bungles (Rl)

of the **Bellbird camping area**, which is the tour operators' camping area. Walardi is set up similarly to Kurrajong, with toilets and water as well as separate areas for groups and those with generators.

The Walardi and Bellbird camping areas give the easiest access to the southern section of the Bungle Bungle massif, and from a track junction just north of the camping sites it is only a short drive (16 km) to the end of the vehicle track.

A two-km return walk to **Cathedral Gorge**, arguably one of Australia's most sensational and awe-inspiring natural wonders, takes you past spectacular domes and along an ever-narrowing ravine. Suddenly, around a corner, it opens up into a large amphitheatre. The walls crowd in on all sides, the smallish patch of sky adding to the grandeur of a magical place. This sight makes the trek, and all the dust, worthwhile. A much longer walk (30 km return) leads to **Piccaninny Gorge**, further east along the southern ramparts of the range.

To return to the bitumen and the highway, it is a case of retracing your steps back the way you have come.

About five km from the Walardi camping area is the airstrip and helipad. Scenic helicopter flights operate from here in the peak of the tourist season.

ORGANISED TOURS

There are quite a number of tour operators, both around Australia and locally (working out of Halls Creek and Kununurra), who include the Bungle Bungles as a major destination in their trips around the Kimberley. For more information, see the earlier Gibb River Road section, or contact the appropriate tourist information office or the Western Australian Tourist Centre.

Scenic Flights

There are quite a few scenic-flight operators based in Halls Creek and Kununurra. See the earlier Gibb River Road section, or contact the Halls Creek or Kununurra tourist bureaus.

Cathedral Gorge (R & VM)

FACILITIES

For full details on facilities at Halls Creek or Kununurra, see the earlier Gibb River Road section (for Kununurra) or the later Canning Stock Route section (for Halls Creek).

Airstrips

Halls Creek has an airstrip, which is run by the Halls Creek Shire Council (☎ (091) 68 6007) and which is well used by charter and scenic-flight operators. Aviation fuel is readily available.

The Pilbara

The Pilbara region encompasses some of the hottest country on earth. It also contains the iron ore that accounts for much of Western Australia's prosperity. Gigantic machines are used to tear apart the dusty red ranges of this isolated, harsh and fabulously wealthy

THE NORTH-WEST

area. The Pilbara towns are almost all company towns: either mining centres where the ore is wrenched from the earth or ports from which it's shipped abroad.

It is possible to get a feel for the majesty and contrast of this ancient, raw frontier by driving through it. There are no 'classical' outback routes that traverse it, but you can get deep into the arid areas and the fascinating Hamersley Range.

There is no doubt that the ancient Hamersley Range contains some of Australia's most stunning scenery. The landscape is dotted with spectacular red-rimmed gorges, occasional waterfalls and palm-fringed waterholes. It is a land synonymous with the Dreamtime, and abounds in Aboriginal artefacts. The eroded forms of prehistory are overlaid with the machinery and impedimenta of modern explorers in search of the abundant raw materials and minerals.

South of Karratha and the Pilbara coastline are two magnificent interior national parks, one based on the Chichester Range and the other on the Hamersley Range. These contribute to part of an excellent loop journey from the coastal highway.

The description that follows assumes that the loop starts in Karratha or Roebourne, passes through Millstream-Chichester and then Karijini national parks, returning to Karratha via the western gorges, Tom Price and the Hamersley Iron private Dampier-Tom Price road. Thus the only backtracking is in the national parks. It is a contrived route – there are many other possible points of entry and exit.

INFORMATION
Tourist Offices

In Karratha, the new Karratha & Districts information centre (☎ (091) 44 4600), on Karratha Rd just before you reach the T-intersection of Dampier and Millstream Rds, has heaps of information on what to see and do in the Pilbara. For information on the Pilbara's national parks, contact the Department of Conservation & Land Management's Karratha regional office (☎ (091) 86 8288) in the SGIO Building,

Welcome Rd, PO Box 835, Karratha, WA 6714.

In Roebourne, information is available at the Roebourne District tourist bureau (☎ (091) 82 1060), Old Gaol complex, Queen St.

The Wittenoom tourist centre is in the Ashburton shire offices, on Third Ave (☎ (091) 89 7011). There is an unofficial tourist bureau (☎ (091) 89 7096) in the Gem Shop on Sixth Ave.

It is good that these quasi-visitor services are there, as the Department of Conservation & Land Management's national park offices are more often than not unattended; the Millstream visitor centre is much better than the isolated Karijini ranger station on Juna Downs Rd.

The Tom Price tourist information centre (☎ (091) 89 2375) is on Central Ave, and the Newman tourist information centre (☎ (091) 75 2888) is at the corner of Fortescue Ave and Newman Drive.

Port Hedland is also a popular starting point for a tour of the Pilbara. The sleepy tourist bureau (☎ (091) 73 1711) is at 13 Wedge St, across from the post office.

Permits

A permit is required to travel on private Hamersley Iron roads. You will need one to travel on the Dampier-Tom Price Rd (used for the homeward part of the described loop). This is obtained easily from the security gate (☎ (091) 43 5364) at Hamersley Iron's workshop between Karratha and Dampier.

There is a speed limit of 80 km/h on this road. A map on the back of the permit shows turn-offs and restricted access roads.

Books & Maps

There are a number of good publications which cover this route. Useful ones include: the Western Australia Tourist Commission's booklet *Western Australia's Unique North*; the Department of Conservation & Land Management pamphlets *Hamersley Range National Park*, *Millstream-Chichester National Park* and *Geology of the Gorges*; and the department's booklet *North-west Bound: From Shark Bay to Wyndham*.

The StreetSmart map of the *Pilbara* is also indispensable for this trip.

Radio Frequencies

Should you strike mechanical trouble, it's unlikely that you'd have to wait long for another vehicle to pass by. For those with HF radios, the RFDS base at Port Hedland (callsign VKL) monitors 4030 kHz from 7 am to 5 pm Monday to Friday and 8.30 to 9.30 am on Saturday, but not on Sunday.

SPECIAL PREPARATIONS

If you are travelling away from the main coastal highway in this area, always carry sufficient water and check that you have enough fuel to get to the next petrol station. If travelling into remote areas, make sure you tell someone your travel plans, and don't leave your vehicle if you are stranded.

Occasionally the roads are closed after heavy rain. Check road conditions with the Main Roads Department (☎ 008 13 316).

Fuel is available in a number of locations but is considerably more expensive than in the coastal towns. In Wittenoom, for instance, it is 10 cents a litre dearer than in Karratha and 15 cents more expensive than in Port Hedland. Fill up those long-range fuel tanks – the closest fuel to Millstream is in Roebourne or Wittenoom. Around Karijini, fuel is available at Wittenoom, Tom Price, and the Auski Roadhouse at the junction of the Great Northern Highway and Wittenoom Rd. Newman is a little further away.

The only banking facilities in the area are at Tom Price, Newman, Karratha and Port Hedland, so bring plenty of cash to pay for supplies, accommodation and fuel while travelling in the parks.

THE NORTH-WEST

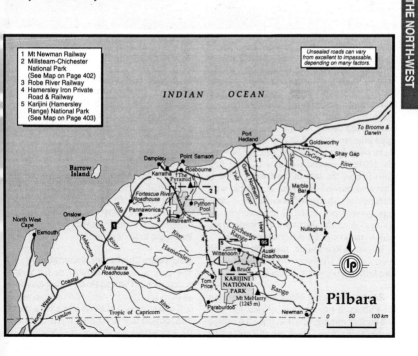

1 Mt Newman Railway
2 Millsteam-Chichester National Park (See Map on Page 402)
3 Robe River Railway
4 Hamersley Iron Private Road & Railway
5 Karijini (Hamersley Range) National Park (See Map on Page 403)

Unsealed roads can vary from excellent to impassable, depending on many factors.

Pilbara

Near Newman (RI)

THE ROUTE
Karratha/Roebourne to Millstream-Chichester (190/150 km)

The town of **Karratha** ('good country'), the commercial centre for the area, was developed due to the rapid expansion of the Hamersley Iron operations and the Woodside offshore natural-gas project. The rich town is now the hub of the coastal Pilbara. The area around Karratha is replete with evidence of Aboriginal occupation – carvings, grindstones, etchings and middens are all located on the **Jaburara Heritage Trail**, which starts near the information centre.

To get to Roebourne, head for the North West-Coastal Highway from Karratha and turn left; Roebourne is 33 km from this turn-off.

Roebourne is the oldest existing town in the Pilbara. It has a history of grazing, gold and copper mining, and was once the capital of the North-West. There are still some fine old buildings to be seen, including an **old gaol**, an 1894 **church** and the **Victoria Hotel**, the last of the five original pubs. Roebourne is close to the fascinating historic port of Cossack and the nearby fishing village of Point Samson.

From Roebourne you follow the North-West Coastal Highway for 27 km to the turn-off for Millstream, then take the signposted gravel road. It passes through grazing land, with the occasional dry creek crossing. The most spectacular natural feature here is **The Pyramid**, dominating the landscape to your right.

Millstream-Chichester National Park

The park includes a number of freshwater pools, such as **Python Pool**, which was once an oasis for Afghani camel drivers and which still makes a good place to pause for a swim. The turn-off to Python Pool is reached some 61 km after you leave the North-West

Coastal Highway. The road is now bitumen and climbs up from Python Pool close to the summit of **Mt Herbert**, where there are great views of the Chichester Range.

Once down the hill, the road reverts to gravel and you pass through undulating sandstone country. Ten km from the end of the bitumen, the road crosses the Hamersley Iron railway line. At this T-intersection, turn left onto the Wittenoom-Roebourne Road (it's near Camp Curlewis) and follow it for about 20 km until you reach the Millstream-Pannawonica Road turn-off. Turn right, and follow the road for 11.5 km to the 30-km loop road through the park (Snappy Gum Drive).

The **visitor centre** in the impressive 200,000-hectare Millstream-Chichester National Park is at Millstream Homestead, 150 km south of Roebourne, 21 km off the road to Wittenoom. The old homestead has been converted into an information centre with a wealth of detail on the Millstream ecosystems and the lifestyle of the Yinjibarndi people.

The **Chinderwarriner Pool**, near the visitor centre, is another pleasant oasis, with pools, palms (including the unique Millstream palm) and lilies; it is well worth a visit. Take time to do the six-km **Cliff Lookout Drive** for great views of the palm-fringed Crossing Pool and the Fortescue River. The lush environment is a haven for birds and other fauna such as flying foxes and kangaroos. Over 20 species of dragonfly and damselfly have been recorded around the pool.

The park also has a number of walking and driving trails, including the half-hour Homestead Walk, the 6.8-km Murlunmunyjurna trail (which links the homestead with Crossing Pool) and the eight-km Chichester Range Camel Track.

Millstream-Chichester to Wittenoom (188 km)

To get to Wittenoom, your base for exploring the Karijini (Hamersley Range) National Park, return the way you came to the Wittenoom-Roebourne Road. Turn right here, and in 28.5 km you will cross the

Hamersley Iron railway line – keep a lookout for those one to two-km-long iron-ore trains.

The next 100 km of driving takes you through relatively featureless country, occupied by stations such as Tambrey, Mount Florance and Mulga Downs; the latter was the home of mining tycoon Lang Hancock. The spectacular Hamersleys loom straight ahead across the Fortescue basin.

Wittenoom

Wittenoom, the Pilbara's tourist centre, is at the northern end of the Karijini (Hamersley Range) National Park. It had an earlier history as an asbestos-mining town, but mining finally halted in 1966; it is the magnificent gorges of Karijini that now draw people to the area.

Warning Even after 25 years, there is a health risk from airborne asbestos fibres. Avoid disturbing asbestos tailings in the area, and keep your car windows closed on

Python Pool (JW)

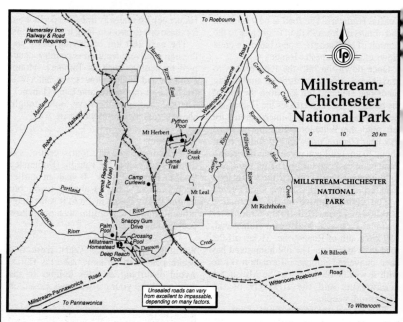

Millstream-Chichester National Park

windy days. If you are concerned, seek expert medical advice before going to Wittenoom.

Karijini (Hamersley Range) National Park

Like the gorges in central Australia, those of Karijini are spectacular, both in their sheer rocky faces and in their varied colours. In early spring, the park is often carpeted with colourful wildflowers.

The famous **Wittenoom Gorge** is immediately south of the town. A surfaced road runs the 13 km to this gorge, passing old asbestos mines and a number of smaller gorges and pretty pools.

Travel down the Newman road for 24 km and there's a turn-off to **Yampire Gorge**, where blue veins of asbestos can be seen in the rock. Fig Tree Well, in the gorge, was once used by Afghani camel drivers as a watering point. Look carefully at the bird life around the fig tree – if you're lucky, you'll

see a spotted bowerbird feeding on the ripe figs. About five km further along are two old buses, temporary homes to geologists in the 1960s.

The road continues through Yampire Gorge to **Dales Gorge**. On the left-hand side of the road, just before the turn-off to Dales Gorge, there is a freshwater tank; it is 10 metres from the information board. A few km along the Dales Gorge track is a turn-off to the right; it takes you to the **giant termite mound**, popular with 'I've been there' snapshooters.

At the end of this road you can get to **Circular Pool** and a nearby lookout, and by a footpath to the bottom of **Fortescue Falls**. The walk from Circular Pool along Dales Gorge to the falls is recommended; you will be surprised by how much permanent water is in the gorge.

The Joffre Falls road leads to **Knox Gorge**; nearby is a 1.5-km return walk to Red Gorge lookout. From the Joffre Falls

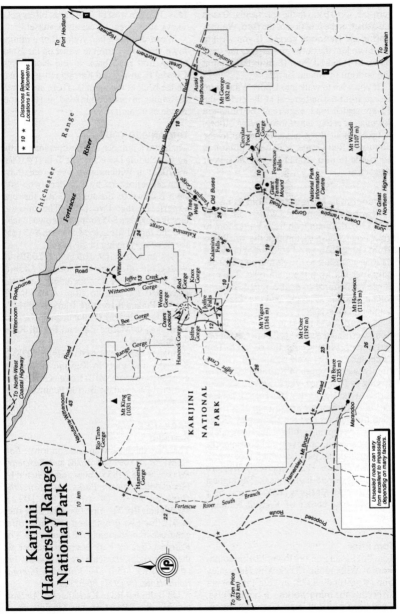

Karijini (Hamersley Range) National Park

turn-off, it is 16 km to the spectacular **Oxers Lookout**, at the junction of the **Red**, **Weano**, **Joffre** and **Hancock** gorges. If you wish to get down into the gorge proper, take the steps down to Handrail Pool (turn to the right at the bottom) in Weano Gorge.

If you wish to walk into Upper Wittenoom Gorge from the settlement at the end of the 12-km sealed road, enquire at the Bungarra Bivouac or at the tourist information offices. It takes about three hours to get up to the bottom of Red Gorge, and at this point it is advisable to turn around for the three-hour return trip.

Wittenoom to Karratha via Tom Price
Following the Nanutarra-Wittenoom Road (SH 136), the main road from Wittenoom to Tom Price, you pass through the small **Rio Tinto Gorge**. About 43 km from Wittenoom there is a turn-off to the **Hamersley Gorge**, only four km from the main road. The evidence of the force of nature, reflected in the folded ribbons of rock, adds to the awe-inspiring landscape.

The turn-off to the Hamersley-Mt Bruce Road (restricted access) is 22 km further on, and from this intersection it is 63 km to Tom Price; the route is well signposted. (If you simply want to return to Karratha instead of driving to Tom Price, you can take a shortcut across to the Hamersley Iron road; it is clear on the StreetSmart *Pilbara* map as a right-hand turn not far past the Hamersley Gorge Road.) You can also follow the Hamersley-Mt Bruce Road, however, and continue the loop through the park, in which case you'll pass **Mt Bruce** (1235 metres), Western Australia's second-highest peak. The highest mountain is **Mt MeHarry** (1245 metres), near the south-east border of Karijini National Park.

Tom Price
Tom Price is an iron-ore town, 128 km southwest of Wittenoom. Check with Hamersley Iron (☎ (091) 89 2375) in Tom Price about inspecting the **mine works** – if nothing else, the scale of it all will impress you. **Mt Name-**less, four km west of Tom Price, offers good views of the area, especially at sunset.

When you have had your fill of a mining town, use your permit to travel on the Hamersley Iron road back to the North-West Coastal Highway and Karratha (use the map on the back of the permit). There are no real highlights on this 270-km road, just the experience of using it.

ORGANISED TOURS
There are a number of tour operators in the area, including Dave's Gorge Tours (☎ (091) 89 7026) in Wittenoom. Dave's tours have been recommended by travellers, who give rave reviews to the tune of 'it's the best experience that I've had'. The one-day circuit tour costs $45 (bring your own lunch), and the famed Miracle Mile costs $45 ($50 for those not staying in the hostel).

Design-a-Tour (☎ (091) 89 7059) in Wittenoom offers one-day tours of Karijini and the gorges for $55, including lunch (an extra $10 for pick-up from Auski Roadhouse). Pilbara Adventure Tours (☎ (091) 73 2544), based in Port Hedland, go to Karijini, as well as to Marble Bar and Rudall River National Park.

Snappy Gum Safaris (☎ (091) 85 1278) in Karratha runs tours to Karijini, but mainly concentrates on Millstream-Chichester National Park and the Burrup Peninsula near Dampier.

FACILITIES
Karratha
There are three caravan parks in town: *Balmoral Rd* (☎ (091) 85 3628) and *Rosemary Rd* (☎ (091) 85 1855), both administered by Fleetwood Caravan Parks, and *Karratha Caravan Park* (☎ (091) 85 1012), Mooligunn Rd. The first two have tent sites at $12 for two people and will also offer cabin accommodation in the near future. The Karratha Caravan Park is a little cheaper. At the other end of the scale are the *Quality Inn* (☎ (091) 85 1155) and *Karratha International Hotel* (☎ (091) 85 3111).

On Balmoral Rd in Karratha, *Los Amigos*, opposite the BP station, has Mexican food.

The Pyramid (JW)

Dales Gorge (JW)

The *Universal*, on the same road, does good Chinese food. For a snack, there are a number of cafes and takeaway places in the Karratha shopping centre, including *Adriennes Cafe*. A little out of town, the *Tambrey Centre* has a tavern and serves good counter meals; visitors are welcome to use the pool.

Roebourne

The *Harding River Caravan Park* (☎ (091) 82 1063), with tent sites at $8 for two, is one km down a road on the north side of the bridge, just off the North-West Coastal Highway. The *Mt Welcome Motel* in Roe St is the main accommodation, with singles/doubles for $40/60.

Both the *Roebourne Diner*, good for eat-in and takeaway meals, and the *Poinciana Room* are in the Victoria Hotel-Mt Welcome Motel. Also on Roe St is a *snack bar*, open seven days.

Millstream-Chichester National Park

There are basic *campsites* (☎ (091) 84 5144) at Snake Creek (near Python Pool), Crossing Pool and Deep Reach; tent sites cost $5 for two people, plus $3 for an extra adult. The southern site at Crossing Pool does not allow generators.

Karijini National Park

There are several basic *campsites* within the park, including Dales Gorge, Weano Gorge and the Joffre intersection ($5 for a tent site for two) – contact the rangers (☎ (091) 89 8157) for more information.

Wittenoom

The *Gorges Caravan Park* (☎ (091) 89 7075), Second Ave, has tent sites from $9 and on-site vans from $25 for two people.

Wittenoom Bungarra Bivouac Hostel (☎ (091) 89 7026), 71 Fifth Ave, has beds at $7 per night. Another budget place is the *Old Convent* (☎ (091) 89 7060), Gregory St, which has an elongated dormitory in the front verandah ($8 per person) and double rooms ($30). Spare a thought for the pious who suffered this. *Nomad Heights* (☎ (091) 89 7068) on First Ave is a small arid/tropical

permaculture farm where you can book trips into the gorges; the cost is $6 per night.

Wittenoom Holiday Homes (☎ (091) 89 7096) on Fifth Ave has cottages from $25 per person. The *Fortescue Hotel* (☎ (091) 89 7055) on Gregory St is the classic 'pub with no beer' – it's closed until further notice.

At present you have to bring your own food with you, as there are no restaurants in town. You can get basic supplies at the caravan park or at the local store.

Auski Roadhouse

Some 40 km from Wittenoom, on the Great Northern Highway, is the *Auski Tourist Village Roadhouse* (☎ (091) 76 6988); shady, grassed tent/caravan sites are $8/13. Why Auski? Because it was set up by Aussies and Kiwis.

Tom Price

The *Tom Price Caravan Park* (☎ (091) 89 1515) has powered caravan sites ($13 a double) and on-site vans ($35 a double). *Hillview Lodge* (☎ (091) 89 1625) has overpriced singles/doubles ($85/95).

The *Red Emperor* cafe in the shopping mall provides reasonable food, and the *Tom Price Hotel* has standard counter meals.

Port Hedland

You can camp by the airport at *Dixon's Caravan Park* (☎ (091) 72 2525). Tent sites cost $12 for two people ($14 with power), backpackers' rooms are $12 per person, and on-site cabins with en suite are $55 a double. The park has a pool, and a great recreation room with all cooking facilities, tape deck and TV. More convenient is the *Cooke Point Caravan Park* (☎ (091) 73 1271) on Athol St, which is also adjacent to Pretty Pool. Dusty, powered sites cost $15 for two people, and on-site vans are $35. *South Hedland Caravan Park* (☎ (091) 72 1197) on Hamilton Rd is the third park in the area.

On the corner of Anderson St, there's the *Esplanade Hotel* (☎ (091) 73 1798), with rooms from $40 per person. The *Pier Hotel* has singles/doubles for $55/60. The *South Hedland Motel* (☎ (091) 72 2222), 13-17

Court Place, has rooms for $72/82. More expensive places are the *Quality* and *Hospitality* inns.

The *Pier*, the *Esplanade* and the air-conditioned *Hedland* hotels serve counter meals. There are plenty of supermarkets, if you want to prepare your own food. *Marg's Kitchen*, opposite the tourist bureau, is open till late.

Maureen's Bakehouse on Richardson St has been heartily recommended for its home-made salad rolls. Nearby is the *Coral Trout*, where you can get fish & chips – the mackerel here is superb.

The *Oriental Gallery*, on the corner of Edgar and Anderson Sts, offers a good-value weekday lunch. There are three other Asian restaurants in town: *Bangkok Rose*, *Dynasty Gardens* and *Golden Crown*.

Canning Stock Route

The Canning Stock Route stretches for over 1700 km across the seemingly desolate heart of Western Australia, between Wiluna in the south and Halls Creek in the north. It is the longest stock route in the world, eclipsing the great cattle drives of America, and for most of its length passes through completely uninhabited country.

Just think: here you can drive for the same distance as the complete length of Great Britain and half-way back again, or from Nagasaki in the south of Japan to the island of Hokkaido in the north, or from Los Angeles across California and Oregon to Seattle in Washington state – and hardly see a soul. It's a long haul in anybody's language.

It is the hardest and longest 4WD trip in Australia. The number of sandhills that need to be crossed vary, depending on who you believe and if they counted every hill or just the big ones. There are at least 800, but most people stop counting after day two or three.

The route passes through the Gibson Desert, the Great Sandy Desert and, in its northern part, the western section of the Tanami Desert. Because of that, one may

think the country, or the scenery, never changes. Nothing could be further from the truth. The variety of desert landforms and the subtle changes of vegetation weave their magic on all who travel this vast landscape.

Nobody travels the Canning in summer. It usually begins to see the first adventurers in late April or early May, and by the middle of October the season is coming to a close. June to August are probably the best months. If you are the first of the season, you may be plagued by faint or nonexistent tracks and by tall spinifex that can block your vehicle's radiator in less than 10 minutes.

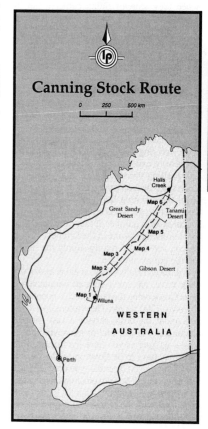

THE NORTH-WEST

Needless to say, you need to be very well set up to travel the Canning. Most would consider the route to be out of the realm of the small 4WD. The ability to carry the huge amount of fuel, water and supplies for the minimum two-week trip means that anything smaller than a four-cylinder Jackaroo or Pajero is completely out of the question. While the four-cylinder utes, such as the Hilux and Rodeo, do well out here, the real kings of the Canning are the six-cylinder diesel Landcruisers and Patrols.

Mind you, some people have walked the Canning. Of course Alfred Canning, after whom the route is named, and his men did (when they weren't riding camels), but in more recent times some adventurers looking for a challenge have walked or run the route. The handful who have done it have either pushed a specially designed cart to carry their supplies or have had vehicle backup. Either way, it's a hard slog!

Bicycle and motorcycle riders are just as rare. The deep, soft sand and the distances between water tends to turn most off. As the only place you can get fuel dropped is approximately halfway along the stock route, carrying fuel and water is a problem that is only overcome by a backup vehicle.

Travelling the stock route in company is much safer than on your own. If you want to travel the Canning but don't know anyone who wants to go, 4WD clubs often have trips and there are a number of tour operators who take tag-alongs. Some of the latter even cook for you and they certainly supply the safety and the companionship.

Wiluna and Halls Creek, at either end of the stock route, are small outback communities, Halls Creek being the larger with a population of around 1200 people. These towns, like those throughout the bush, service a vast pastoral region and you can find or get anything you want – as long as you have the time to wait. Parts may have to be flown in on the weekly mail plane. Forget the cost – you need the parts to keep rolling! The only other option is to sell your truck as it stands, hitch a lift to the more settled parts of the country and give up on exploring the real Australia.

HISTORY

One of the great attractions of travelling the stock route is the sense of history that pervades most of the 54 wells that dot its course. You cannot help being touched by the freshness or the closeness of this saga in Australia's history.

Major Peter Warburton crossed from central Australia to the north-western coast in 1873, passing over some of the country the northern section of the stock route would later cross. In 1874 John Forrest and his party travelled from the Western Australian coast to the Overland Telegraph Line, finding and naming a few points on the southern end of what was to become the stock route.

On 2 June of that year he found what he described as 'one of the best springs in the colony', naming it Weld Springs. When they were attacked by Aborigines here, Forrest and his men built a small stone fort to protect themselves from further attacks. That fort still remains today at what became Canning's Well 9.

In 1876 Ernest Giles passed just to the north of Forrest's tracks on his return from the west coast. But it was to be another 20 years before another White person travelled this region.

In 1896 two expeditions set out for south-to-north crossings. The Calvert Expedition was led by Lawrence Wells, but tragedy struck when two members, including his cousin, became lost and died of thirst. David Carnegie's party had better fortunes in that all but one survived a double crossing of the desert (Charlie Stansmore died after a shooting accident), but they failed to find any gold or a cattle route – the main reasons for the trip. Both expeditions advised the government that a cattle route was impossible and the search for one should be stopped.

Now the stage was set for Alfred Canning.

By the early 1900s, Kimberley cattlemen were in dire straits and were clamouring for a stock route to be made between their meat-producing area in the north-west and the populated gold fields of the south. Earlier, in 1898, the movement of cattle from the East Kimberley to the coast around Derby had

Near Oxers lookout (R & VM)

been banned to stop the spread of cattle tick. An overland, desert route was seen as a natural barrier to the spread of this cattle-borne problem.

In April 1906, Canning, already a surveyor with a good reputation, was chosen to lead a group of men to survey a route between Wiluna and Halls Creek.

In April of that year the party of eight men, 23 camels and two ponies left Perth, heading via Day Dawn to Wiluna. Pushing north across the untracked wilderness of the desert country, they arrived in Halls Creek at the end of October, spending Christmas there before heading south back into the desert at the end of February 1907.

Searching for water all the way, they found and used many rockholes that were regular sources of water for the Aboriginal people. In April, at a rockhole called Waddawalla (later known as Canning's Well 40), party member Michael Tobin was speared to death.

In July the group returned to Perth and Canning's report that a route could be made

through the desert was met with a standing ovation in parliament. And, Canning was the obvious choice to lead a well-sinking party.

By the end of March 1908 the well-sinking party of 30-odd men congregated at Wiluna, ready to head into the harshness of the desert. By the time they reached Flora Valley station at the northern end of the stock route in July 1909, they had sunk, lined and set up 31 wells. They retraced their route a month later, reaching Wiluna around the end of April 1910 after establishing another 21 watering points.

For many of the wells, timber had to be cut and carted for long distances so the wells could be lined. The deepest well on the stock route is Well 5, dug out to a depth of 32 metres, while the shallowest is Well 42 at just 1.5 metres.

Canning, on his arrival at Wiluna, sent a three-word telegram back to Perth: 'Work completed – Canning.'

The first stock weren't far behind Canning and his men. In April 1911 a couple of drovers, George Shoesmith and James

Thompson, along with one of their three Aboriginal stockmen, were attacked and fatally speared near Well 37.

But over the next 30 years the route was never used to anywhere near its full potential. Cattle were brought down it only occasionally, so in 1929, after much lobbying, the government sent out William Snell to refurbish the route. He only got as far north as Well 35, and Canning was called out of retirement at the age of 70 to finish the job!

From then until just after WW II, use of the stock route increased a little, with the last mob of cattle being taken down in 1958.

The first vehicle to travel part of the stock route was part of Michael Terry's 1925 expedition. Other sections of the stock route succumbed to the motor vehicle, but it was not until 1968 that a group of surveyors drove the complete length of the route. During the 1970s a handful of travellers challenged the route, and by the end of the 1980s some 10 to 20 groups a year were travelling its length. Today, a couple of hundred adventurous souls travel the stock route each year.

INFORMATION
Tourist Information, Hospitals & Police
Wiluna The Wiluna Shire Council (☎ (099) 81 7010) in Scotia St is a good place to seek information on the surrounding area and the stock route.

Medical facilities are available from the Wiluna Medical Centre (☎ (099) 81 7063) in Lennon St. It also has support from the RFDS in emergencies.

The police station (☎ (099) 81 7024) is in Thompson St, and travellers are asked to inform the police of their departure/arrival if travelling the Canning.

Halls Creek For information on the surrounding area, visit the Halls Creek Tourist Information Centre (☎ (091) 68 6262), on the Great Northern Highway; it's open from May to September. The Shire of Halls Creek (☎ (091) 68 6007) in Thomas St can also supply information, as can the Poinciana

Roadhouse (☎ (091) 68 6164) on the Great Northern Highway.

The hospital (☎ (091) 68 6002) is in Roberta Ave. The police station (☎ (091) 68 6000) is on the Great Northern Highway.

Other Information
At either end of the stock route there is private pastoral land, and the normal restrictions apply. Do the right thing for the other travellers who are following you.

Some important phone numbers include:

Glen-Ayle Station (☎ (099) 81 2990)
Bill Shepard's Roadhouse (☎ (091) 75 1535)
Carranya Homestead (☎ (091) 68 8927)
Carnegie Homestead (☎ (099) 81 2991)

Permits
No permits are required if you travel the stock route as detailed.

If you take the track via Glen-Ayle Station (☎ (099) 81 2990), you will need permission from the station owners to use their station tracks. It's best to contact them before you leave and then see them as you pass through – the house is close to the track you use, so it is no trouble to do the right thing.

Registration
It is advisable to register with the police at either Wiluna (☎ (099) 81 7024) or Halls Creek (☎ (091) 68 6000) before you set out. At either of these police stations, complete a Notification of Travel in Remote Areas.

Don't forget when you get to the other end to check into the relevant police station and report your safe arrival. Nobody will be happy if they start a search for you and you are already back in civilisation taking it easy. In fact, you could even be sent the bill for the cost of the search!

Books & Maps
The best maps of the Canning are produced by the Royal Automobile Club of Western Australia and by Australian Geographic. A full range of 1:250,000 topographic maps are also available, but these are hardly required

unless you are doing something off the beaten track.

Far and away the best books for travellers are the *Canning Stock Route – a Traveller's Guide for a Journey Through History* by Ronele & Eric Gard, published by Western Desert Guides (80 Glenelg Ave, Wembley Downs, WA 6019), and *The Canning Stock Route*, published by Australian Geographic PO Box 321, Terry Hills, NSW 2084). There's an interesting insight into Canning and his travels on the stock route in a book by E Smith, *The Beckoning West*, published by St George Books. It's hard to get but well worthwhile for history buffs.

Radio Frequencies

The RFDS bases at Meekatharra and Derby are the best radio bases to work through. Don't forget that the RFDS bases are only open during normal business hours.

The primary frequency for the RFDS base at Meekatharra (callsign VKJ) is 4010, while its secondary frequencies are 2280 and 6880. Derby base (callsign VJB) has a primary frequency of 5300 and secondary frequencies of 6925 and 6945.

If you are working through Telstra, still more commonly called OTC, then the best bases are Perth (callsign VIP) and Darwin (callsign VID). For Perth the main OTC

Flora of the Canning

With luck, your trip up the Canning will coincide with rain somewhere along its course. The chances of that happening are, in fact, pretty good as the stock route traverses such a vast segment of land, from the more temperate south to the subtropical north.

The occasional southern winter storm or tropical thunderstorm brings with it an unexpected bounty as the country bursts into new and colourful life. For those who love wildflowers, the desert can be a wondrous place.

Acacias, or wattles, are one of Australia's most common plants. On the Canning there are a number of species that colour the scenery. Prickly acacia, with its pale-yellow flower, is common along the complete length of the stock route, while gidgee is found along creeks in the southern section of the route. Pindan wattle, which is found in the north, stands out with its yellow flowers. Another colourful wattle with bright-yellow flowers is locally called elephant-ear wattle; a good stand of these can be seen on the way to Well 38.

Grevilleas are one of the really magnificent flowers of Australia. There are about 200 species in Australia, and you'll see a few different ones on the Canning. The holly grevillea or Wickham's grevillea has yellow flowers, while the similar prickly grevillea, found in the northern section of the stock route, has spectacular red-orange flowers. These plants can be found on rocky hills or on sandy plains and dunes, but the desert grevillea and the honey grevillea are found only on the dunes and sandy plains. These two plants have bright yellow-orange flowers and are loaded with nectar. If there are not too many ants on them, the flowers are lovely to suck or to drop into a cup of water for a pleasant, refreshing drink.

Hakeas are closely related to the grevilleas, and more than 90 of the 110 or so species found in Australia can be seen in Western Australia. The most common hakea on the Canning is the easily identifiable corkwood hakea, named for its distinctive bark. The flowers are a creamy yellow.

About 25 species of **cassia** can be found in the Australian inland, including several along the stock route. These shrubs are usually less than two metres high and all have yellow, buttercup-shaped flowers. The green cassia, desert cassia, blunt-leaf cassia and the cockroach bush are just some you might see.

Found throughout the length of the Canning, and elsewhere in inland Australia, is the fluffy **mulla mulla**, sometimes called pussy tails. These low-growing plants have pink, purplish or white flowers that are commonly seen because they persist for a long time after rain.

Vivid displays of the delicate, star-shaped, pink flower of the **desert-fringe myrtle** can be seen on the dunes, and the yellow-green, bird-shaped flower of the **parrot-pea bush** is found north of Well 36.

Daisies of many sorts can also be seen, as well as bright-purple **parakelia,** and if you are lucky, vivid displays of the magnificent **Sturt's desert pea**. ■

Killagurra Springs, or Well 17 (R & VM)

radphone channels are 607, 806 and 1226, and these are available 24-hours a day. Selcall for the beacon at Perth is 0799, while the operator's Selcall is 0107. For Darwin the main voice call channels are open only between 8 am and 8 pm and include channels 415, 811, 1227 and 1622. Darwin can be extremely hard to get, especially in the morning. Selcall for the beacon at Darwin is 0599, while the operator's Selcall is 0105.

The Sydney OTC base is too far away for good communications, even though it is the best equipped.

Warning

This is not an easy trip, and you need to be thoroughly prepared and have your vehicle in first-class shape before you set foot on the Canning. People still die in this extremely remote region of Australia when their vehicle breaks down. In the last 10 years the number has reached double figures. Those who have been rescued, just in the nick of time, survived because they did everything right, luck was on their side, and they didn't

panic. If your vehicle fails out here, you are in real trouble!

SPECIAL PREPARATIONS

Let's consider that you have a first-class vehicle and it is well maintained. For the Canning you will need to carry, in addition to what you carry for the normal remote outback tracks, a good supply of water – a minimum of 40 litres for each vehicle – and a huge amount of fuel.

Fuel

To travel the route and see a few of the sites along the way (some are 50 or more km of the main track), a six-cylinder diesel Cruiser will need to carry 280 to 300 litres of fuel, while a petrol Cruiser will need 350 to 370 litres. A big V8 Ford may need 500 or more litres, while a small four-cylinder diesel may get away with 200 to 220 litres. Basically, that is what you require to travel from Well 23 to Halls Creek or vice versa. From Wiluna to the resupply point at Well

Camping area at Durba Springs (R & VM)

23, a six-cylinder diesel will need about 160 to 180 litres of fuel.

Now, that is a lot of fuel, but you'll only get away with that amount if you organise a fuel drop at Well 23. Bill Shepard at the Capricorn Roadhouse (☎ (091) 75 1535) in Newman is the man to get in touch with, but do it well in advance: he only drops fuel two or three times a year. As well, it only comes in 200-litre drums, so work out your fuel consumption before going, so that when you leave Well 23 you are fully fuelled for the run north. What doesn't fit in, leave behind! Considering the remoteness of Well 23, $220 for a 200-litre drum is pretty good.

Tyres

Carry at least two spares, complete, and a couple of extra tubes. A good tyre repair kit and pump are essential. Tyre pressures will play a very important part in successfully tackling the Canning. Too high and you won't get up the hills, too low and you will take tyres. Because of the loads being carried, it's not necessary to drop pressure as low as you would for a day's run along the beach: 170 to 180 kPa (25 to 26 psi) should do nicely out in this region.

In places, you will be travelling over very rocky and broken ground so extreme care is needed. Take it slowly and you should be OK. Travel too quickly, or with tyre pressures too low, and tyres will start blowing.

Trailers

The Canning is no place for a trailer. It is possible to take a well-constructed trailer over the stock route, but those who have done it once will never do it again.

THE ROUTE
Wiluna

Once considered the wildest town in Australia, Wiluna sits on the edge of the desert country and was gazetted as a town in 1898. During its boom years in the 1930s the population peaked at around 9000 and the town had four hotels. While its population waned after WW II, recent mining activities have seen the town gain a few more people. Today the population is around 300.

Facilities at this small outback community include fuel, food supplies, limited repairs and accommodation.

The town is well known for its emu farm run by the Ngangganawili Community, about 20 km east of the town. The community produces fine leather and meat from their animals, with the leather finding a ready market overseas. Sadly, the farm is not open to visitors.

If you want some fresh fruit, the **Desert Gold Orange Orchard**, just out of town, is worth a visit. You can buy not only oranges but also grapefruit, tangelos, lemons and some stone fruits.

Wiluna to Well 9 (295 km)

This track lies across pastoral land, and during times of heavy rain can be officially closed to all traffic. As with travelling across any pastoral land, leave gates as you find them and leave stock completely alone. Do not camp close to any stock-watering points. While it is remote, the track is easy to negotiate with few problems in the Dry.

Well 1 is just seven km north from Wiluna and has good water. **Well 1A** is called North Pool; it's on the Negara River and is a popular swimming hole with locals.

Well 2, 41 km north of Wiluna, lies close to the track on the east side and supplies good water. **Well 2A** lies another 37 km north and was the last one built by Canning and his men. It once held good quantities of water, but do not rely on it now.

Sections of the track between **Well 3** and **Well 4** can become boggy after even quite light falls of rain. Water from Well 3, which is 31 km north of Well 2A, is unreliable, and the water from Well 4, another 32 km north, is salty.

The crossing of **Lake Nabberu**, which is really a series of lakes, can be a problem and even Canning's men built a corduroy road across it from logs. The remains of this crossing can be seen 4.5 km west of Well 4.

Well 4A lies two km off the main route, 35 km north-east of Well 4 and just a short distance from **Little Windich** and **Windich springs**. Found and named by Forrest, these springs are used today by numerous mobs of cattle; it is not the best place to camp, as the water is polluted.

Well 5 is 215 km north of Wiluna and 38 km from the turn-off to Well 4A. It was the deepest well constructed by Canning and his men, more than 100 tonnes of rock being blasted and removed by hand during the well's construction. Because of its depth the water is hard to get.

Well 6, or Pierre Springs as Forrest called it, is 19 km further on, and was reconditioned by the Geraldton 4WD club in 1991. It now provides good, reliable water and the surrounds also make a nice spot to camp.

Mt Davis, four km north of Well 6, is worth a climb. Once you have panted your way to the top, you'll have a great view of the surrounding country. Observant travellers may even find some Aboriginal art.

Set in a dense stand of mulga, 100 metres off the track and 23 km from Well 6, **Well 7** is in a dilapidated state but still provides good water. Willy Willy Bore, **Well 8**, with its good water, Scorpion Bore and Canning Bore are all passed on the way to Well 9, a further 39 km north. Cattle are often seen in this area; please do not disturb them or camp close to water.

Well 9 is Forrest's famous Weld Springs and is now contained in a Historic Reserve. Here, Forrest and his men built a fort to protect them from attack by Aborigines and the remains of this fort can still be seen today. While the spring is now almost dry, the well, fitted with a windmill, still produces a good supply of water. Pigeons and finches abound.

At this point the track from Carnegie homestead via Glen-Ayle homestead joins the stock route; this track is often used by those coming from the east along the Gunbarrel Highway. It is also a wet-weather alternative when the track between Wiluna and Well 9 is closed. Permission is required from Glen Ayle Station to use this track and you may have to pay a small fee of around $10 per vehicle. It is about 200 km from Carnegie homestead (where you can get fuel) to Well 9 via Glen-Ayle.

Well 9 to Durba Springs (211 km)

Once you leave Well 9, you are approaching the end of the pastoral country. Soon it changes and you enter sandhill country, where the real adventure begins. The Durba Hills, at the very north of this section, are one of the gems of the trip and time should be allowed to enjoy them.

Well 10 was called the Lucky Well by the drovers of old, as they considered themselves lucky to have escaped the sandhill country and reached this far south. It is still in good condition, 20 km north of Well 9, and supplies decent water.

Heading for **Well 11**, you cross the first of the sandhills, but they really shouldn't be a problem. At the well on the edge of the salt expanse of **White Lake**, 15 km north of Well 10, a sign to travellers has been erected by Australian Geographic. Water from this well is too salty to drink.

Nearly 21 km north of Well 11, the first big sandhill will test your skill. If you haven't dropped your tyre pressures, now is the time to do so. Here you'll also see the southernmost patch of desert oaks on the stock route. These trees are magnificent and are a highlight of the trip. As you head north the sandhills get bigger, and north of Lake Aerodrome, named by Snell, you will find **Well 12**, surrounded by desert oaks. It usually has reasonable water. The distance between Well 11 and Well 12 is 33 km.

There is little remaining of **Well 13**, another 27 km north, but it is a good place to camp as there is a lot of mulga and other trees to provide shelter and firewood. The well has collapsed and is dry.

While **Well 14**, 16 km north, has caved in and is dry, there are still the remains of the timber fence and stock trough amongst the tea-trees. From here to Well 15, the track is prone to flooding, and at least one group in the past (who left a sign) has been stranded in this area for a few days.

Well 15, which is 25 km north of Well 14 and 136 km north of Well 9, is collapsed and

dry. About halfway to Well 16, a collapsed trolley can be seen beside the track. This was abandoned by Murray Rankin on his first attempt to walk the Canning in 1974. He succeeded in 1976.

A few hundred metres west off the track, and 38 km north of the previous well, **Well 16** is set amongst picturesque white gums. This well normally has water, but it is unfit for human consumption.

As the track heads north, it begins to skirt the western edge of the **Durba Hills**. Approaching the hills from the south in the evening is an unforgettable experience, as the rugged escarpment glows fiery red in the rays of the setting sun.

Sunday Well lies 14 km north-east from the main track, the turn-off being nearly nine km north of Well 16. Now no more than a hole in the ground and surrounded by tea-tree, it can be easily missed.

About 18 km north of Well 16, a track leads north-east into the base of the escarpment, below the prominent **Canning's Cairn**. The climb to the top is relatively easy and the view excellent. Aboriginal petroglyphs can be found on the southern wall.

The turn-off north-east to **Biella Spring** is about seven km north of Canning's Cairn. Once you have travelled the two km from the junction, it is a pleasant half-hour walk into the gorge to the spring, where you will generally find water. There are a number of Aboriginal rock paintings to be found here.

At the northernmost point of the range a major track junction is found, 32 km from Well 16. Turning north will keep you on the main stock route, while turning hard right will take you into **Well 17**, also known as Killagurra Springs, named by Canning. Continuing straight ahead, the track leads to Durba Springs, five km from the main track junction. Killagurra Springs is a registered sacred site and is indeed a very special place. Treat it with the respect it deserves. The Aboriginal art is the best you will see on the trip. There is permanent water here.

Durba Springs is a place not to miss; you should spend, at the very minimum, two nights here. The camping area now boasts a

THE NORTH-WEST

pit toilet courtesy of the Land Rover Owners Club of Western Australia. Do not chop any timber down in the gorge – it is too precious a place for that. Bring in any firewood from some distance away. Do not use soap in the water and do not bury any rubbish here. By taking these few simple steps, Durba Gorge and its surrounds will remain the attractive, magical place that it is.

From the camping spot, you can explore the head of the gorge and the surrounding country. There are many art sites within the nearby hills and gorges, and the area is a haven for birds. If nothing else, just relax and soak in the atmosphere of this tranquil place.

Durba Springs to Well 23 (205 km)

Once you head north from the Durba Hills, you enter some of the toughest country on the Canning. Further on, you skirt the

Cheap real estate at Lake Disappointment
(R & VM)

western margin of the vast salt expanse of Lake Disappointment. North of Well 22 you meet the Talawana Track, a major escape route to the west, and just a little further on is Well 23, which is the site of Bill Shepard's fuel dump.

Well 18 lies only 33 km north of the Durbas, but it will take you up to four hours to cover that distance. The well lies about one km east off the track and is dry and in disrepair.

Three km further on, a track heads east from the main track to **Onegunyah Rockhole**, found at the base of a small normally dry waterfall. A few km south of **Well 19**, which is 26 km north of Well 18, you will cross the **Tropic of Capricorn**, marked by a survey peg, FX15. Well 19 is on the edge of a claypan and is completely silted up.

Savory Creek is often a major obstacle to get across, 23 km north of Well 19. While it often has water, it is very salty, as can be readily guessed once you see the banks of the creek. If the main crossing is too daunting, there is another one three km west which should be drier and easier.

Once across, the track turns in towards **Lake Disappointment**, but swings north a short distance from the lakeshore. A faint track continues to the lake and is worth a detour, but beware of the boggy patches.

This lake is a vast sea of salt and only has water in it after unseasonable heavy rain. The stock route travels along its western edge for over 70 km, but this is about the only place you have a chance to see and touch it.

The turn-off to **Well 20** is 15 km north of Savory Creek and the well is 10 km west from the main track. All that remains is a hole in the ground.

Well 21, with its poor water, is 32 km north of the turn-off to Well 20 and eight km east of the main track, along a major diversion track that leads east and joins the main route just south of **Well 22**. Well 22, which is 40-odd km north-east of Well 21 along the diversion, is on a white-gum flat between the dunes and is very picturesque. However, the well is dry.

The **Talawana Track**, graded by Len Beadell in 1963, is met some nine km north of Well 22. By heading west here, you can reach the main township of Newman within 450 km.

Well 23, and the **fuel dump** that most people use, is another 22 km north. While most people stop here for fuel, the water from the well is undrinkable.

A 125-km diversion route, known as the **Airstrip Track**, leaves the stock route at this point and heads north, then west and finally east, bypassing many of the big dunes that the main route crosses north-east of Well 23, and finally meets with the main track just north of Well 26. While the Airstrip Track is a little easier, the main route is the more interesting, so you should stick to that.

Well 23 to Well 33 (269 km)

This section of the Canning brings you variety and enjoyment as you revel in the waters of Well 26, the splendour of stands of bloodwood and desert oak, and the secrets of underground, water-filled caves.

Situated just off the track, **Well 24** is dry. Three km further north, the **Windy Corner Track**, another that was put in by Len Beadell, joins with the Canning. North of here a vast sea of waving spinifex leads to **Well 25**, once again dry with just a few surface timbers laying around. Just north of this well, a series of three big dunes will test your technique and your tyre pressures. By the time you have covered the 59 km to Well 26 from the refuelling point, you'll be looking forward to stopping and enjoying this oasis. You are 765 km from Wiluna, barring detours and side trips.

Well 26 was fully restored by a large group of people led by David Hewitt in 1983, to commemorate the route's 75th anniversary. It provides plenty of good drinking water and a chance to freshen up. There is no firewood available here, so you should start collecting some five or more km back along the track. A visitor's book is also at the well and most travellers use it to record their thoughts and their adventures so far.

A steady drive north for 31 km leads to

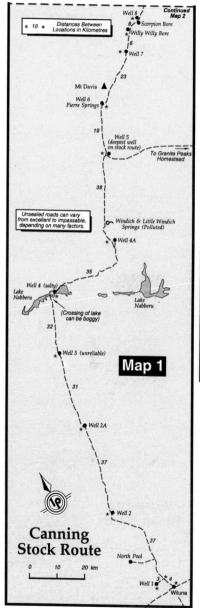

Map 1

Canning Stock Route

Continued Map 2

THE NORTH-WEST

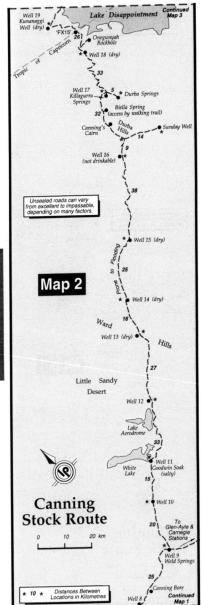

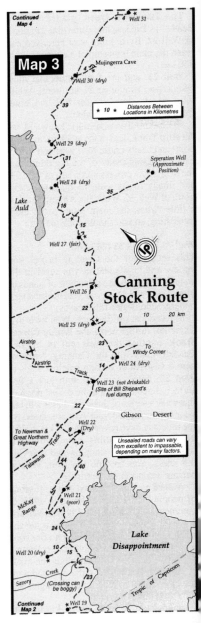

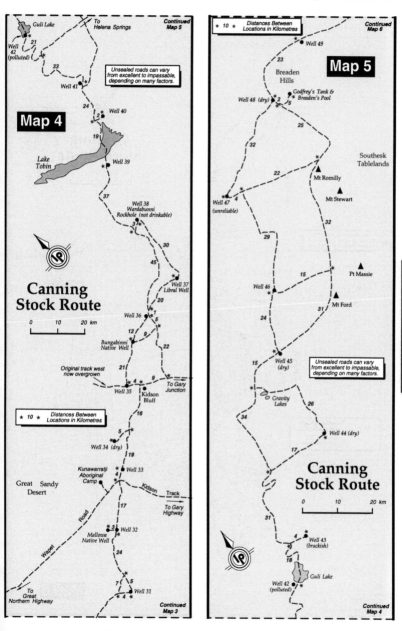

Continued Map 5
Continued Map 6

Map 4

Guli Lake

Well 42 (polluted)

To Helena Springs

Unsealed roads can vary from excellent to impassable, depending on many factors.

Well 41

Well 40

Lake Tobin

Well 39

Well 38
Wardabunni Rockhole (not drinkable)

Canning Stock Route

0   10   20 km

Well 37
Libral Well

Well 36

Bungabinni Native Well

Original track west now overgrown

Well 35

Kidson Bluff

To Gary Junction

★ 10 ★ Distances Between Locations in Kilometres

Well 34 (dry)

Kunawarratji Aboriginal Camp

Well 33

Great Sandy Desert

Kidson Track

To Gary Highway

Wapet Road

Mallowa Native Well

Well 32

To Great Northern Highway

Well 31

Continued Map 3

★ 10 ★ Distances Between Locations in Kilometres

Map 5

Well 49

Breaden Hills

Godfrey's Tank & Breaden's Pool

Well 48 (dry)

Southesk Tablelands

Mt Romilly

Mt Stewart

Well 47 (unreliable)

Pt Massie

Well 46

Mt Ford

Well 45 (dry)

Unsealed roads can vary from excellent to impassable, depending on many factors.

Gravity Lakes

Well 44 (dry)

Canning Stock Route

0   10   20 km

Well 43 (brackish)

Guli Lake

Well 42 (polluted)

Continued Map 4

THE NORTH-WEST

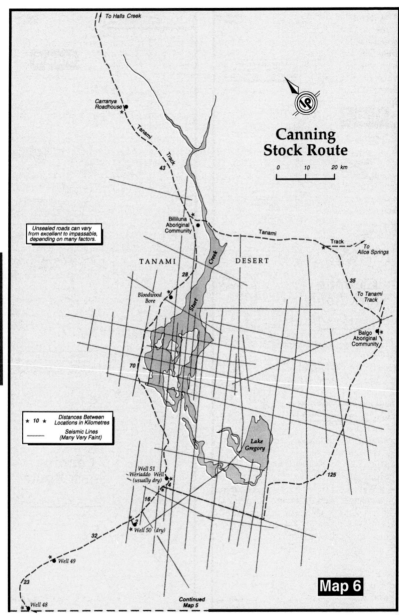

THE NORTH-WEST

Well 27, which has fair water in an emergency. A further 15 km brings you to a track which heads east for 35 km to **Separation Well**. The trip to Separation Well is a slow drive and leads to a shallow depression where members of the 1896 Calvert Expedition split up to head for Warburton's Joanna Spring.

Warburton had plotted the position of Joanna Spring incorrectly and neither Calvert group found the spring. Charles Wells and his companion died, while Lawrence Wells, the leader of the expedition and leading the second group, made it through to the Fitzroy River. Over the following few months, six expeditions, all with Lawrence Wells as leader or member, pushed into the desert, finally finding the bodies of Charles Wells and his partner at a place Lawrence Wells called Discovery Well.

Little remains of **Well 28** and **Well 29**, which are both dry, but there is some good camping just before and just after Well 29, which is a total of 152 km north of Well 23.

What remains of **Well 30** lies 39 km north of the previous well and in amongst a glorious stand of bloodwood trees. It is an ideal campsite, although there is no water.

Just four km east is **Mujingerra Cave**, a limestone cave with crystal-clear water. Reached through a narrow tunnel, it is not for the faint-hearted. Be careful when approaching the entrance, and park your vehicle some distance away. Please don't pollute this fragile environment with soap.

Well 31 is four km east off the main route and is dominated by a good specimen of a cabbage-tree gum. The turn-off is 26 km north of Well 30. The 31-km run north to **Well 32** is easy and you may even hit top gear for a change. Well 31 is dry, but Well 32, which is alongside the main track on the east side, normally supplies reasonable water. About three km west of Well 32, along a distinct track, is **Mallowa Native Well**, set amongst green acacias. Like many of these soaks, you may have to dig for water here if none is visible on the surface.

The Kidson Track crosses the Canning 17 km north of Well 32. Just three km west

along this relatively good road is the Kunawarratji Aboriginal Community and another 575 km further on is the Great Northern Highway. East will lead to Len Beadell's Gary Highway, Windy Corner and Sandy Blight Junction, all just as remote as the junction you are already at.

Well 33 is just four km north of the Kidson/Canning track junction on the east side of the main track. Although it is a pleasant camp, there is no firewood. The dingoes are also friendly and will flog anything left lying around – smelly shoes seem to be a real favourite. The flat surrounding the well and the well itself can be completely flooded, presenting a vastly different picture to normal. The water from the well is generally drinkable.

Well 33 to Well 39 (163 km)

Some of the most historic and poignant places lie along this section of the stock

Climbing a sand ridge north of Well 24
(R & VM)

route. Take your time and make the effort to see it all.

Another good spot to camp is at **Well 34**, which is five km west of the main track, the turn-off being found 19 km north of Well 33. Little remains at this spot and there is no water.

Once you pass Kidson Bluff to the east, a track junction is met, 16 km north of the turn-off to Well 34. Here you can turn left and travel four km to **Well 35**. This well was burnt out (like many on the Canning – a timely reminder to be careful with your own fire), but a bore casing does provide a limited supply of water if you need it. You're now just over 1000 km north of Wiluna.

From Well 35 you can proceed north on an alternative route through a magnificent stand of desert oaks, to **Bungabinni Native Well**, which has a plentiful supply of fresh water and a visitor's book. From there you pass **Well 36**, with its fair water and nice camping spot amongst the desert oaks, before rejoining the main stock route just a few km further on, a total distance of 37 km from Well 35.

At the junction before Well 35, you can also turn right, following the **Gary Highway** for nine km before turning north again back onto the main stock route. About 27 km north of here the alternative route previously described joins with the main route.

One km past this junction a track veers off to the east, heading 20 km to **Well 37**, or Libral Well. This well produced good water in Canning's day and still does. The surrounding area makes for a pleasant camping spot, and the history and the graves in the close vicinity make for an interesting few hours of exploration.

Well 37 is often called the Haunted Well, although that seems to be a relatively recent name. It no doubt received its name from the number of people who were killed here.

The first stockmen to take cattle down the Canning were attacked and killed by Aborigines at this point. The two drovers, Shoesmith and Thompson, along with their Aboriginal helper, are buried at a spot about 50 to 60 metres almost due north of the well.

The grave of an oil prospector, John McLernon, clubbed to death by Aborigines in 1922, can also be found here. He was killed some km east of the well and was buried at the base of a desert oak about 250 metres north-east of the well. The tree is blazed but only the most observant will see the original blaze.

Other plaques and headstones also exist around the well, although the Aboriginal helper of Shoesmith and Thompson lies unmarked close to their grave.

From Libral Well, you can backtrack to the main stock route or continue north on a diversion track for 30 km to **Well 38**. This diversion track will no doubt become the main track. It passes beside Well 38, also known as **Wardabunni Rockhole**, which is often dry or, more often than not, green and stagnant. The walls of the rockhole reveal the initials of some of the early explorers.

Just three km further on from Well 38, you meet up with the old stock route track, and the route swings north. Travelling another 37 km north, you reach **Well 39**, the water of which is reasonable in an emergency.

Well 39 to the Breaden Hills (288 km)

Here, history and a variety of desert land-scapes vie with one another for attention, and it's easy to spend days soaking up the atmosphere.

A few km north of Well 39, a stand of desert oaks makes a good camp, although firewood is a little scarce.

The crossing of **Lake Tobin** is generally easy, and speed across the salt flat is something to enjoy! At the northern extremity of the lake, 19 km north of Well 39, is the turn-off to **Well 40**. Two km east from the main track, this well is the site where Michael Tobin, a member of Canning's 1907 survey party, was killed by an Aborigine. This is a good spot to camp; the well supplies reasonable water, but there is no firewood.

The turn-off to **Well 41** is 24 km north of Well 40 and the well itself is another two km west of the main stock route. Its tannin-stained water is quite good for drinking.

Just a short distance south of the turn-off

to Well 41, a seismic line heads north-east and is a possible route to David Carnegie's **Helena Springs**. However, a scraped track 33 km north of Well 41 is the most direct route. This track leads 88 km east to the historic site, but the trip is slow and bumpy and there is no water at the end. The track was put in by a group led by Peter Vernon, who has blazed a number of trails out here and who in July 1988 ran the complete length of the Canning from Wiluna to Halls Creek in 35 days.

On the south-western end of Guli Lake, **Well 42** is 54 km north of Well 41 and is the shallowest well constructed on the stock route. The well's timber and the nearby bush have suffered from unthinking passing travellers looking for firewood. The water is generally polluted.

Well 43 is four km north-east off the main route. Just a few metres away from the original is a new well dug by a group of travellers. This new well can supply brackish water in an emergency. The old well once supplied thousands of litres per hour of good water but is now dry.

The distance between the turn-off to Well 43 and the turn-off to **Well 44** on the main stock route is 31 km. Well 44 is some 17 km north-east off the main vehicle route. It is nothing much more than a hole in the ground and is completely dry. You can also travel from Well 43 via scraped tracks and seismic lines to Well 44, a total distance of around 40 km.

To continue to Well 45 from Well 44, you can either backtrack to the main vehicle route or continue on a scraped track to join up with the stock route 26 km north of Well 44, near the Gravity Lakes and about 15 km south of **Well 45**. On the main route the distance from the Well 44 turn-off to Well 45, located on the main stock route track, is 49 km. Well 45 is caved in and is generally dry.

From Well 45 you have the option of following the main vehicle route north-east, a distance of 88 km, to a major track junction just south of Well 48. Here you can turn off to the Breaden Hills. This route from Well 45 bypasses Wells 46 and

47 by up to 22 km, but access tracks do make each well accessible.

A better choice is to head north along a scraped track that follows the original route of the Canning Stock Route directly to **Well 46**, a distance of 24 km. This well provides excellent water and is a great spot to camp.

You can head directly east from here, 15 km to the main vehicle route, meeting it 31 km north of Well 45.

However, by heading north from Well 46 along another bumpy, scraped track for 29 km, you will join up with the main access track to **Well 47**. Well 47 lies four km further to the west and is a very unreliable source of water.

From here you can head back north-east, past the scraped track you came north along, a total of 26 km to join up with the main stock route track 63 km north of Well 45 and 27 km south of Well 48. This way the total distance between Well 45 and Well 48 is 106 km, compared to 88 km via the main route, but you have seen all the wells along the way.

Alternatively you can head 32 km from Well 47 in a more northerly direction across faint, scraped tracks directly to Well 48, a total distance from Well 45 of around 89 km. Whichever way you get to Well 48, it is worth visiting the Breadon Hills nearby.

From the track junction just south of Well 48, a track leads five km north-east into the heart of the **Breaden Hills**. Breaden's Pool is a five-minute walk from the parking area, while the walk to Godfrey's Tank takes a little longer. Both are named after members of David Carnegie's 1896 expedition, and in the rock walls above Godfrey's Tank there are the initials of members of both the Carnegie and Canning parties. Aboriginal carvings can also be found.

Breaden Hills to Tanami Track (180 km)

The end of the stock route looms, and once north of the Breaden Hills, you are into pastoral country – remote pastoral country, but still pastoral country. Care needs to be taken here because of the large number of seismic survey lines that lead nowhere. In recent years some people have died in this area!

The turn-off to **Well 48** is just two km north of the track junction that takes you into the Breaden Hills. The well lies a short distance to the west, just off the main route north. It once supplied small amounts of good water but is now dry.

From the carpark at the Breaden Hills to **Well 49** it is 30 km, 23 km east of the turn-off to Well 48. At the well you'll find the grave of Jack Smith, a stockman, who died here after a fall from a horse. This well also has some of the best water on the Canning, but to get a drink, you'll need a long rope and plenty of energy.

As you head north, you pass the Australian Geographic's **notice to travellers** and then the last lot of desert oaks on the Canning. You are fast approaching civilisation; this spot is a good one for a last camp on the stock route proper. **Well 50** lies two km south off the main track, 32 km north of the previous well. It is caved in and dry.

The turn-off to **Balgo Aboriginal Community** can be found 16 km further on, and just four km past here is **Well 51**, or Weriaddo, the last well on the stock route. The well has caved in and the bore next to it is also usually dry.

You are now on **Billiluna Station**, a property run by Aborigines, and there are many tracks and seismic lines throughout the area.

Stick to the main route north. About 70 km north of Well 51 you will pass **Bloodwood Bore**, and after a further 28 km you will join up with the **Tanami Track**.

While modern travellers head up or down the Tanami Track, the original stock route, now unused, continues northwards along Sturt Creek and its occasional shady waterholes. North of present-day Sturt Creek station the original route leaves the Sturt Creek, following Cow Creek, crossing the Elvire River near the Old Flora Valley station before ending at Old Halls Creek, 16 km south of present-day Halls Creek.

Turning west at the Tanami Track junction will lead you to **Halls Creek**, 175 km away. The nearest fuel, with luck, is at the **Carranya**

The flat country at Well 33 is prone to flooding (R & VM)

Roadhouse, 43 km north up the Tanami Track.

At this stage you'll feel elated that you have driven and experienced the Canning. If you are like most, you will be a little sad that this great adventure is over.

ALTERNATIVE ROUTES

We've included a number of minor alternative routes between wells in the main description of the track but there are a number of ways onto and off the stock route.

The very southern section of the stock route is liable to be cut and closed to traffic due to flooding around Lake Nabberu (Well 4). The alternative route for travellers during those times, or for travellers approaching from the east along the Gunbarrel Highway via Carnegie Station, is to travel to Well 9 via Glen-Ayle Station. You will need permission from Glen-Ayle to travel these private roads and you may have to pay a small usage fee of around $10 per vehicle.

Granite Peaks Station, almost due west of Glen-Ayle, is reached via the Granite Peaks road from near Wiluna. This route will bring you out at Well 5, or from near Granite Peaks you may head to Glen-Ayle and join up with the stock route further north. You need permission from Granite Peaks to use the track between the homestead and the stock route.

The Talawana Track joins the stock route nine km north of Well 22 and heads west 450 km to the mining town of Newman. It is a relatively good dirt road that traverses remote desert country all the way to civilisation.

North of Well 24 the Windy Corner track, graded by Len Beadell in 1963, joins the stock route. This track leads east 210 km to the Gary Highway. See the 'Bomb Roads' section in the Central Deserts chapter for more details.

Just south of Well 33 is a crossroad. West is the Wapet Road that runs over 900 km to Broome or Port Hedland on the west coast. East takes you along the Kidson Track 75 km to the Gary Highway.

Approaching the Breaden Hills (R & VM)

426 The North-West – Canning Stock Route

At the T-junction before Well 35, you can turn west to the well or swing east and then north to Well 36. At the point where the Canning swings north, another track continues east 34 km to Gary Junction at the northern end of the Gary Highway. From this point you can either head south to the Gunbarrel Highway (300 km) or continue east to Alice Springs (900 km).

Both routes are through remote desert country but the going is easier than the Canning. The latter route passes through Aboriginal land and a permit is required. See the section on the 'Bomb Roads' in the Central Deserts chapter for more details.

South of Well 51, the last section of the Canning heads north to Billiluna and the Tanami Track. This area can be flooded due to Lake Gregory, to the east, overflowing. A track heads south-east and then north-east 125 km to the Balgo Aboriginal Community, which is 35 km south of the Tanami Track. Fuel, accommodation and limited supplies are available here. Once again you should have a permit, but if the Canning is flooded you should receive a sympathetic hearing. Travellers intending to visit the community should contact the Chairman, Balgo Hills Community Aboriginal Corporation, via Halls Creek, WA 6770.

ORGANISED TOURS

Amesz Tours (☎ (09) 250 2577) was one of the first commercial operators taking travellers along the Canning. Trips are run once or twice a year, carrying passengers as well as taking tag-alongs.

Geoff and Lisa Portman, who operate Portman's Australian Adventures (☎ (057) 86 1780), generally have at least one trip along the Canning each year. Most begin in Alice Springs. These are tag-alongs only and no passengers are carried.

Russell Guest's 4WD Safaris (☎ (03) 481 5877) has been operating very successful escorted convoys all over outback Australia for quite a few years. You can join one of his trips to the Canning, either driving your own vehicle or travelling along as a passenger in the escort vehicle.

Western Desert Guides (☎ (09) 341 2524), 80 Glenelg Ave, Wembley Downs, WA 6019, is run by Eric and Ronele Gard, two people who know the Canning better than most. They run tag-along trips and also carry passengers on their regular jaunts along the Canning.

Wildlife Walkabout Safaris (☎ (097) 52 4262), PO Box 6, Busselton, WA 6280, is run by Rob Breedon. Trips are run once or twice a year, depending on demand, and you can join him in your own 4WD or travel along as a passenger in the safari bus.

FACILITIES
Wiluna

Located 950 km north-east of Perth and 1890 km west of Alice Springs, the town of Wiluna, you have to say, is remote. Most supplies are available and it is your last chance to stock up before tackling the Canning.

Canning Trading (☎ (099) 81 7020) in Wotton St is open seven days a week and you'll be able to find just about all your general requirements in the store. Along with food, it also supplies fuel, aircraft refuelling, vehicle hire, ice, camping gas refills and mechanical and tyre repairs. It is also the post office and agency for the Commonwealth Bank, but don't expect Keycard facilities!

Fuel, general supplies, hardware, clothing and ice are available from the Ngangganawili Community Store (☎ (099) 81 7034), also in Wotton St. The store is only open Monday to Friday from 9 am to noon and 1.30 to 4 pm.

The Club Hotel/Motel (☎ (099) 81 7012), on the corner of Wotton and Wall Sts, offers cold beers and a range of meals for breakfast, lunch and dinner, while snacks are obtainable throughout the day. On Sunday, weather permitting, there is a barbecue costing just $7 per head. Accommodation is also available in the hotel, plus fully air-conditioned motel rooms. Costs for the hotel range from $20 to $45 for a single/twin share, while twin share in the motel is $45 to $80 per room.

Travellers can also stop over at the Wiluna Shire Caravan Park (☎ (099) 81 7021) in

Lennon St. Facilities include powered, grassed caravan and camping sites, laundry, ablutions, hot showers and a barbecue area. Dogs are also allowed, on a leash. An unpowered tent site is $3 per person; a powered site is $4.50.

Halls Creek

Halls Creek is a major rural centre, and the needs of the outback traveller are well catered for.

The *Kimberley Super Value Store* (☎ (091) 68 6186) on the Great Northern Highway has general food supplies, fruits, vegetables and hardware items. It is open seven days a week, with limited trading hours on the weekend and public holidays – Saturday the store is open from 8 am to noon, and on Sunday and public holidays from 9 am to noon.

There are also a number of other general stores in Halls Creek along with a bakery, butcher and liquor store.

Service stations and roadhouses have fuel supplies, and any repairs necessary can be carried out in one of the mechanical workshops in town. Aviation fuel is also available from the Halls Creek Trading Post (☎ (091) 68 6107). The cheapest spot for fuel, and the service centre that can supply the biggest range of spares (especially Toyota parts), is Baz Industries (☎ (091) 68 6150), 137 Duncan Rd.

There is a variety of accommodation available in Halls Creek. You can choose to stay in the *Halls Creek Caravan Park* (☎ (091) 68 6169), Roberta Ave, which has all facilities. A powered caravan site costs $12 for two people per night, while an unpowered tent site is $5 per person, with power costing an additional $2 per site. Travellers not staying in the park are able to use the shower facilities for just $1.50. Dogs are allowed, on a leash.

Alternatively, there are two motels, both of which also have meals available. The *Halls Creek Kimberley Hotel/Motel* (☎ (091) 68 6101), Roberta Ave, has accommodation from $60/95 a single/double, with a family room costing $125. Breakfast is an additional $12 per person. Prices at the *Halls Creek Motel* (☎ (091) 68 6001), 194 Great Northern Highway, start from $45/75, room only.

For the budget-conscious, accommodation at $15 a single is available at the *Halls Creek Backpackers* (☎ (091) 68 6101), part of the Kimberley Hotel/Motel. The dormitory has shower and toilet facilities, but no kitchen.

Airstrips

Wiluna has a private airstrip. Contact the Wiluna Shire (☎ (099) 81 7010) for details.

Halls Creek also has an airstrip which is run by the Halls Creek Shire Council and which is well used by charter and scenic-flight operators. Contact the council (☎ (091) 68 6007) for information. Avgas is readily available.

The Tropics

Darwin

Population 67,900

The 'capital' of northern Australia comes as a surprise to many people. Instead of the hard-bitten, rough-and-ready town you might expect, Darwin is a lively, modern place with a young population, easy-going lifestyle and cosmopolitan atmosphere. It is still a frontier town, and is also ethnically diverse with anywhere between 45 and 60 ethnic groups represented.

Darwin is an obvious base for trips to Kakadu and other Top End natural attractions such as Litchfield Park. It's a bit of an oasis too – whether you're travelling south

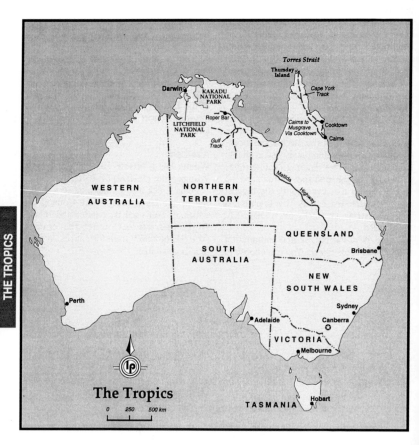

THE TROPICS

to Alice Springs, west to Western Australia or east to Queensland, there are a lot of km to be covered before you get anywhere, and having reached Darwin, many people rest a bit before leaving.

Information

The Darwin Region Tourism Association Information Centre (☎ (089) 81 4300) is at 33 Smith St, in the mall. It's open from 8 am to 6 pm Monday to Friday, from 9 am to 2 pm on Saturday, and 10 am to 5 pm Sunday. It has free maps of the city and several decent booklets.

The main post office (☎ (089) 80 8200) is at 48 Cavenagh St, on the corner of Cavenagh and Edmunds Sts. Darwin's telephone area code is 089.

The Australian Nature Conservation Agency (ANCA, ☎ 81 5299) is in the Commercial Union building on Smith St between Lindsay and Whitefield Sts.

The Conservation Commission (☎ 89 5511) has its office way out in Palmerston, some 20 km from the city centre, which is a real nuisance.

The Department of Mines & Energy (☎ 81 4806) is in the Centrepoint Tower, Smith St Mall. For fishing information, the Department of Primary Industry & Fisheries (☎ 89 4821) has its office in the Harbour View Plaza, Bennett St. The Northern Land Council (☎ 20 5100) is at 9 Rowling St, Casaurina, Darwin (PO Box 42921, NT 0820).

Other useful addresses include:

Motoring Organisation
  Automobile Association of the Northern
  Territory, 79-81 Smith St (☎ 81 3837)
Police
  West Lane (☎ 27 8888)
Medical Facilities
  Royal Darwin Hospital, Rocklands Drive,
  Casaurina (☎ 22 8125)
Royal Flying Doctor Service
  Aerial Medical Services, 99 Smith St
  (☎ 45 2455)

Drying billabong carpeted with water lilies (NTTC)

THE TROPICS

Bookshops Bookworld on Smith St Mall is a good bookshop. For maps, the NT General Store on Cavenagh St has a good range. Other places to try include the NT Government Publications office or the Ministry of Lands, Housing & Local Government (☎ 89 6830) on the corner of Cavenagh and Bennett Sts.

Warning Don't swim in Darwin waters from October to May, when 'stingers' (box jellyfish) are prevalent. There are crocodiles along the coast and rivers; any crocs found in the harbour are removed, and other beaches near the city are patrolled to minimise the risk.

Things to See
There are a number of old buildings in the town centre, including the **Victoria Hotel** on Smith St Mall, the stone **Commercial Bank**, the **old town hall**, **Brown's Mart**, the 1884 **police station** and **old courthouse** at the corner of Smith St and the Esplanade, and **Government House**, built in stages from 1870.

At **Aquascene**, Doctor's Gully, near the corner of Daly St and the Esplanade, fish come in for a feed every day at high tide. Feeding times depend on the tides (☎ 81 7837 for tide times).

The excellent **Indo-Pacific Marine & Australian Pearling Exhibition** are housed in the former Port Authority garage at the Wharf Precinct. The former is a successful attempt to display living coral and its associated life, and the living coral-reef display is especially impressive. The Pearling Exhibition deals with the history of the pearling industry in this area.

The excellent **Museum of Arts & Sciences** is on Conacher St, Fannie Bay, about four km north of the city centre. It's bright, spacious, well laid out, not too big and full of interesting displays. A highlight is the Northern Territory Aboriginal art collection. The **Fannie Bay Gaol** museum is another interesting museum a little further out of town at the corner of East Point Rd and Ross Smith Ave.

Popular beaches include **Mindil** and **Vestey's** on Fannie Bay, and **Mandorah**, across the bay from the city centre.

Places to Stay
Darwin has hostels, guesthouses, motels, holiday flats and a clutch of up-market hotels. The city's many caravan parks are all several km out of the city centre.

Camping The closest place to the city is the *Leprechaun Lodge Motel* (☎ 84 3400), which has a limited number of camping/caravan sites at the rear – enquire at the reception desk. Other camping areas include:

Shady Glen Caravan Park (☎ 84 3330), 10 km east of the city centre, at the corner of Stuart Highway and Farrell Crescent, Winnellie, has camp sites at $12 for two ($15 with power) and on-site vans at $35 for two.
Overlander Caravan Park (☎ 84 3025), 13 km east of the city centre at 1064 McMillans Rd, Berrimah, has camp sites at $10 for two ($12 powered) and on-site vans for $29 to $31.
Palms Caravan Park (☎ 32 2891), 17 km south-east of town on the Stuart Highway at Berrimah, has camp sites at $12 for two ($14.50 powered).

Also consider camping at Howard Springs, 26 km south-east along the Stuart Highway, where there are two caravan parks.

Hostels There's a host of backpacker-type hostels, with several of the cheapest places on or near Mitchell St, conveniently close to the transit centre. Most places have guest kitchens, and the showers and toilets are almost always communal. Dorm beds are typically $12.50, while double rooms range from around $30 to $40.

The most popular places include: *Ivan's Backpackers Hostel* (☎ 81 5385) at 97 Mitchell St; the purpose-built and very popular *Frogshollow Backpackers* (☎ 41 2600) at 27 Lindsay St; the small and informal *Fawlty Towers* (☎ 81 8363) at 88 Mitchell St; the 180-bed *Darwin City Youth*

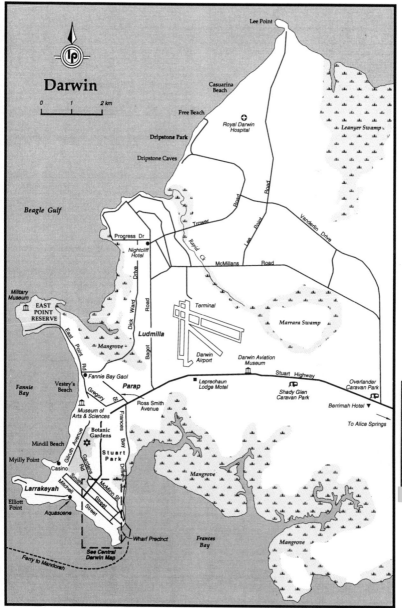

Hostel (☎ 81 3995) at 69A Mitchell St; and *Elke's Inner City Backpackers* (☎ 81 8399) at 112 Mitchell St, just north of Daly St.

Guesthouses Darwin has several small guesthouses which are good for long or short stays. Among those close to the centre is the friendly *Park Lodge* (☎ 81 5692) at 42 Coronation Drive, Stuart Park. All rooms have fan, air-con and fridge; bathrooms, kitchen, sitting/TV room and laundry are communal. Air-conditioned doubles cost $45 daily; weekly rates are cheaper. Numerous city buses, including Nos 5 and 8, run to this part of Darwin along the highway; ask the driver where to get off.

Motels, Hotels & Holiday Flats The *Larrakeyah Lodge* (☎ 81 2933) at 50 Mitchell St, right opposite the transit centre, offers air-con rooms with fridge and shared facilities at $35/49 for singles/doubles. There is a TV lounge, laundry and coffee shop.

The pleasantly tropical *Hotel Darwin* (☎ 81 9211) on the Esplanade offers very good value for money in the heart of the city centre. It has air-conditioned twin rooms from $30, and there's a communal kitchen.

In the city centre at 35 Cavenagh St, the *Air Raid City Lodge* (☎ 81 9214) has air-con rooms – all with shower and toilet, fridge and tea/coffee-making facilities – for $46/56. At 53 Cavenagh St, on the corner of Whitefield St, the *Tiwi Lodge* (☎ 81 6471) is a motel with air-con rooms at $60, with the usual facilities.

The *Tops Boulevard Motel* (☎ 81 1544) at 38 Gardens Rd, the continuation of Cavenagh St beyond Daly St, is a comfortable modern motel. Double rooms cost $70, or studio rooms with cooking facilities are $80, and these sleep three people. All rooms have private bathroom, fridge and TV. There's also a pool, tennis court and restaurant.

THE TROPICS

You don't often get the chance... (NTTC)

There are also places worth considering in the suburbs. The *Parap Village Apartments* (☎ 43 0500) at 39 Parap Rd, Fannie Bay, has fully equipped and furnished three-bedroom flats for $175 and two-bedroom flats for $145. The *Seabreeze Motel* (☎ 81 8433) at 60 East Point Rd, Fannie Bay, has singles/twins for $65/75.

Places to Eat
City Centre – cafes, pubs & takeaways
Next to the transit centre on Mitchell St there's a small food centre with a couple of reasonably priced stalls and open-air tables. *Graham's*, at the far end, is popular with travellers and serves roast dinners in the evenings for $5, or full-on cooked breakfasts for $4. A couple of other places here offer a range of Asian dishes, and charge $5 for a heaped plateful – good value.

There's a good collection of fast-food counters in Darwin Plaza towards the Knuckey St end of the Smith St Mall. Further up the mall, the fancy new Galleria shopping centre has a few good places. Also on the mall is Anthony Plaza where the *French Bakehouse* is one of the few places you can get coffee and a snack every day.

Opposite Anthony Plaza is the Victoria Arcade, where the Victoria Hotel has lunch or dinner for around $6 in its upstairs *Settlers Bar*. The barramundi burgers ($7 including chips and salad) are excellent, as are the steaks. In the arcade the *Sate House* has good cheap Indonesian fare.

In the *Green Room* at the Hotel Darwin you can have a barbecue lunch by the pool for $10, or there are à la carte dishes too. *El Toro's* is a popular Mexican restaurant in The Saloon hotel at 21 Cavenagh St.

City Centre – restaurants
The *Maharajah Indian Restaurant* at 37 Knuckey St has a good, reasonably priced takeaway selection. The menu is extensive with dishes from $9 to $13. The *Pancake Palace* on Cavenagh St near Knuckey St is open daily for lunch and in the evening until 1 am. Also on Cavenagh St is *Guiseppe's*, one of the few pasta places

in Darwin. Main dishes are in the $9 to $12 range, or there's pizza from $11.

The numerous Chinese places are generally rather up-market. The *Jade Garden* on the Smith St Mall (upstairs, roughly opposite the Victoria Arcade) offers a nine-course meal for $12 a head.

The *Sizzler* restaurant on Mitchell St is one of the chain found around Australia. It's amazingly popular, with queues out onto the footpath every night. The reason is that it's very good value: for around $12 you can fill your plate from a wide range of dishes, and have a dessert too.

Probably the best restaurant in the city centre area is *Peppi's* at 84 Mitchell St. It's fully licensed, and a two-course meal for two will set you back around $80 with drinks.

On Smith St, just beyond Daly St, the *Thai Garden Restaurant* serves not only delicious and reasonably priced Thai food but pizzas too! There are a few outdoor tables. There's a takeaway 'Aussie-Chinese' place across the road, and a 24-hour Chinese fast-food joint next door.

Out of the City Centre
The *Parap Hotel* on Parap Rd between Gregory and Hingston Sts does counter meals. It also has *Jessie's Bistro*, where buffalo and beef steaks cost around $12. There are two other Jessie's Bistro locations – one in the *Casuarina Tavern* and the other in the *Berrimah Hotel* on the Stuart Highway at Berrimah.

In the Botanic Gardens, the *Holtze Cottage* restaurant is a carnivore's delight. It's fully licensed and specialises in buffalo, kangaroo, crocodile and camel meats. It is open daily for lunch and dinner.

At the end of the jetty, the *Arcade* is a small, Asian-style food centre, with a number of different shops selling Chinese food, pizza or excellent fish & chips. *Christo's on the Wharf* here is a more up-market place, open for lunch and dinner Tuesday to Friday.

Markets
Easily the best all-round eating

THE TROPICS

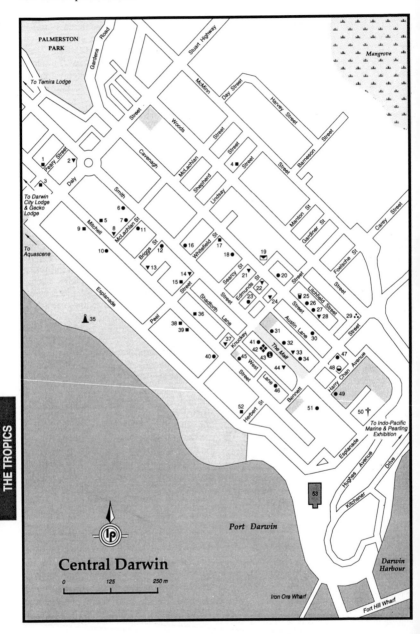

Central Darwin

Port Darwin

Darwin Harbour

Iron Ore Wharf

Fort Hill Wharf

PALMERSTON PARK

To Temira Lodge

To Darwin City Lodge & Gecko Lodge

To Aquascene

To Indo-Pacific Marine & Pearling Exhibition

Mangrove

0   125   250 m

PLACES TO STAY

1	Elke's Inner City Backpackers
3	YWCA
4	Frogshollow Backpackers
5	Fawlty Towers
9	Ivan's Backpackers Hostel
15	Sherwood Lodge
17	Tiwi Lodge
36	Larrakeyah Lodge
38	Darwin Transit Inn & Transit Centre
39	Darwin City Youth Hostel
52	Hotel Darwin

PLACES TO EAT

2	Thai Garden Restaurant
8	Peppi's Restaurant
13	Sizzler Restaurant
14	Toots Eatery
21	Guiseppe's
22	Inshore Water Gardens Restaurant
24	Maharajah Indian Restaurant
25	Roma Bar
28	Night Tokyo Japanese Restaurant
33	Hog's Breath Cafe
37	Golden Oldies Cafe
44	Victoria Hotel

OTHER

6	Thrifty Rent-a-Car
7	Rent-a-Rocket
10	Performing Arts Centre
11	Rent-a-Dent
12	Automobile Association of the Northern Territory
16	Australian National Parks & Wildlife Service
18	International Vaccination Clinic
19	General Post Office
20	NT General Store
23	Squire's Tavern & Rockitz Niteclub
26	Green Turtle Environment Centre Shop
27	Royal Brunei Airlines
29	Chinese Temple
30	Garuda
31	Paspalis Centrepoint & Singapore Airlines
32	Ansett Airlines
34	Bookworld
35	Leichhardt Memorial
40	Indigenous Creations
41	Darwin Plaza
42	Galleria Shopping Centre
43	Darwin Region Tourism Association Office
45	Malaysian Airlines
46	Police
47	Qantas Airlines
48	City Bus Depot
49	Brown's Mart
50	Christ Church Cathedral
51	Old Town Hall
53	Government House

experience in Darwin is the bustling Asian-style market at Mindil Beach on Thursday nights during the dry season. People begin arriving from 5.30 pm, bringing tables, chairs, rugs, grog and kids to settle under the coconut palms for sunset and decide which of the tantalising food smells has the greatest allure. There are cake stalls, fruit-salad bars, arts & crafts stalls – and sometimes entertainment in the form of a band or street theatre.

Similar food stalls can be found at the Parap market on Saturday morning, the market at Rapid Creek on Sunday morning and in the Smith St Mall in the evenings (except Thursday), but Mindil Beach is the best for atmosphere and closeness to town. During the Wet, it transfers to Rapid Creek.

Entertainment

Live bands play upstairs at the *Victoria Hotel* from 9 pm Wednesday to Saturday nights. The *Billabong Bar* in the Atrium Hotel, on the corner of the Esplanade and Peel St, has live bands on Friday and Saturday nights until 1 am.

The *Darwin Hotel* is pleasant in the evening for a quiet drink. There's a patio section by the pool. It's livelier on Friday nights when there's a band in the Green Room, or on Wednesday to Saturday nights in the Pickled Parrot Piano Bar.

The *Brewery Bar* in the Frontier Hotel on the corner of Mitchell and Daly Sts is another good venue. The *Beachcomber* bar at the rear is a popular disco and nightclub.

Popular clubs and discos, often with live

THE TROPICS

bands, include *Rockitz*, *Dix*, *Sweethearts* and *Circles*. They're open nightly, with cover charges only on Saturday. Very popular on Sunday is the *Beachfront Hotel* at Rapid Creek.

The *Nightcliff Hotel* at the corner of Bagot and Trower Rds, about 10 km north of the city centre, has live music every night except Monday and Tuesday. More laid-back is the *Top End Folk Club* which meets every second Sunday of the month at the Gun Turret at East Point Reserve.

The *Performing Arts Centre* (☎ 81 1222) on Mitchell St, opposite McLachlan St, hosts a variety of events from fashion award nights to plays, rock operas, pantomimes and concerts.

Finally, there's the *Diamond Beach Casino* on Mindil Beach off Gilruth Ave – as long as you're 'properly dressed'.

Things to Buy

Aboriginal art is generally cheaper in Alice Springs, but Darwin has a greater variety. The Raintree Gallery at 29 Knuckey St is one of a number of places offering a range of art work; Shades of Ochre at 78 The Esplanade is another.

T-shirts printed with Aboriginal designs are popular but quality and prices vary. Riji Dij at 11 Knuckey St has a large range. Another place worth trying is Indigenous Creations at 55 Mitchell St.

Getting Around

To/From the Airport Darwin's busy airport, about six km from the centre of town, handles international flights as well as domestic ones. The taxi fare into the city centre is about $12.

There is an airport shuttle bus (☎ 41 1656) for $6, which will pick up or drop off almost anywhere in the centre. When leaving Darwin, book a day before departure.

Car Rental Darwin has a couple of cheap local car-rental operators, as well as several of the national companies.

Rent-a-Rocket (☎ 81 6977) and Rent-a-Dent (☎ 81 1411), both on McLachlan St, offer very similar deals on their mostly 1970s and early 1980s cars. Costs depend on whether you're staying near Darwin or going further afield to Kakadu, Katherine, Litchfield Park and so on. For local trips, with Rent-a-Dent you pay $35 a day, depending on the vehicle, and must stay within 70 km of Darwin. This includes 150 free km, with a charge of 20c per km beyond that distance. With these deals you can't go beyond Humpty Doo (45 km south-east of Darwin along the Arnhem Highway) or Acacia Store (about 70 km south of Darwin on the Stuart Highway). The prices drop for longer rentals.

Territory Rent-a-Car (☎ 81 8400) at 64 Stuart Highway, Parap, is probably the best value. Discount deals to look for include cheaper rates for four or more days' hire, weekend specials (three days for roughly the price of two) and one-way hires (to Jabiru, Katherine or Alice Springs).

There are also 4WD vehicles in Darwin. The best place to start looking is probably Territory Rent-a-Car, which has several different models – the cheapest, a Suzuki four-seater, costs around $75 a day including insurance, plus 35c a km over 100 km.

Most rental companies are open every day and have agents in the city centre to save you trekking out to the Stuart Highway. Budget (☎ 81 9800), Hertz (☎ 41 0944), Thrifty (☎ 81 8555) and Territory also have offices at the airport.

Bicycle Darwin has a fairly extensive network of bike tracks. It's a pleasant ride out from the city to the Botanic Gardens, Fannie Bay, East Point or even, if you're feeling fit, all the way to Nightcliff and Casuarina.

Darwin Bike Rentals in Top End Travel (☎ 41 0070) at 57 Mitchell St has bikes from $8 a day (8 am to 5 pm), or $10 for 24 hours. They also have tandems and mountain bikes, and hourly, weekly and monthly rates. Many of the backpacker hostels have bicycles, and these are often free for guests to use.

Litchfield National Park

This 650-sq-km national park, 140 km south of Darwin, encloses much of the Tabletop Range, a rugged sandstone plateau with eroded cliffs dropping away to blacksoil plains. It is only a couple of hours' drive from Darwin and so is a very popular weekend getaway with the locals – in fact the local saying is 'Kaka-don't, Litchfield do'.

The main attraction of the park is its superb waterfalls, which tumble down from the plateau, and swimming holes, but the beautiful country, excellent campsites, and the 4WD, bushwalking and photography opportunities are also highlights. It's well worth a few days, although weekends can get crowded.

HISTORY

The Wagait Aboriginal people lived in this area, and the many pools, waterfalls and other prominent geographical features had great significance.

In 1864 the Finniss Expedition explored the Northern Territory of South Australia, as it was then called. Frederick Litchfield was a member of the party, and some of the features in the park still bear the names he gave them.

In the late 1860s copper and tin were discovered, and this led to a flurry of activity with several mines operating in the area. The ruins of two of these are still visible today – at Bamboo Creek (which operated from 1906 to 1955) and Blyth Homestead.

The area was then opened up as pastoral leases, and these were in existence right up to the proclamation of the national park in 1986.

FLORA & FAUNA

The dominant trees of the open forest are the Darwin woollybutt (Eucalyptus miniata) and the stringybark (Eucalyptus cinerea), while below these, sand palms, banksias, cycads, acacias and grevilleas form the lower

THE TROPICS

Magnetic termite mounds (NTTC)

level. Around the waterfalls and permanent springs are pockets of surprisingly thick monsoon rainforest.

The more open plains are covered with the high spear grass *(Sorghum intrans)* which is so common throughout much of the Top End.

The wildlife of the park is another of its attractions, with the bird life being especially prolific. Two of the most commonly sighted birds are the distinctive red-tailed black cockatoo and the sulphur-crested cockatoo. Smaller parrots such as the beautiful rainbow lorikeet, northern rosella and the red-winged parrot are also often seen.

The jabiru, or black-necked stork *(Xenorhynchus asiaticus)*, is found in the flooded areas of the park during the Wet, and predatory birds such as black kites *(Milvus migrans)*, whistling kites *(Haliastur indus)* and wedge-tailed eagles *(Aquila audax)* are often seen soaring in the thermals above the plateau.

The antilopine wallaroo is the largest mammal in the park, but dingoes are also sighted from time to time. Most of the smaller mammals are nocturnal, and so are not often seen. These include the northern quoll (rare), the northern brown bandicoot and the northern brushtail possum.

One unusual feature of the park are the so-called magnetic termite mounds found on the blacksoil plains. These mounds are up to two metres high and gain their name from the north-south orientation. It is believed they are aligned this way as a means of controlling temperature – during the hottest part of the day, only the narrow northern edge is exposed to the full sun.

INFORMATION

Permits are not required to enter the park, unless you plan to walk and camp in remote areas. There is a ranger station at Batchelor (☎ (089) 76 0282), about 10 km from the eastern edge of the park. If you have an FM radio, information about the park and its attractions is broadcast on 88 MHz.

The Conservation Commission (☎ (089) 89 5511) in Darwin publishes a very good map of the park. If more detail is required,

the topographic sheet maps which cover the park are the 1:100,000 *Reynolds River (5071)* and the 1:50,000 *Sheets No 5071 (I-IV)*. These are available from the Department of Lands, Housing & Local Government (☎ (089) 89 6830) at the corner of Cavenagh and Bennett Sts in Darwin.

Pets and firearms and prohibited.

THE PARK

There are two routes to Litchfield Park, both about a two-hour drive from Darwin. One, from the north, involves turning south off the Berry Springs-Cox Peninsula road onto the well-maintained Litchfield Park Rd, which is dirt but suitable for conventional vehicles except in the wet season. A second approach, also called the Litchfield Park Rd, is along a bitumen road from Batchelor into the east of the park. The two access roads join up so it's possible to do a loop from the Stuart Highway.

If you enter the park from Batchelor, it is about 15 km to the first major batch of **magnetic termite mounds,** signposted just off to the right of the road.

Another four km brings you to the **Florence Falls** turn-off on the eastern edge of the plateau. The falls lie in a pocket of monsoon forest five km off the road along a good track. This is an excellent swimming hole in the dry season, as is **Buley Rockhole,** a few km away, where you can also camp.

From Florence Falls a 4WD track takes you north across the Florence Creek to a T-junction, from where you can turn right (east) and head back to the Litchfield Park Rd near the park's eastern boundary.

Back on the main road it's another four km from the Florence Falls turn-off to the turn-off to the **Lost City,** 10.5 km south of the road along a 4WD track. The feature here is the large sandstone block and pillar formations which, with a little imagination, resemble ruined buildings. This track continues another four km along a very rough section as it comes down off the range, to the **Blyth Homestead Ruins.** This homestead was built in 1929 by the Sargent family, and remained in use until the area was declared

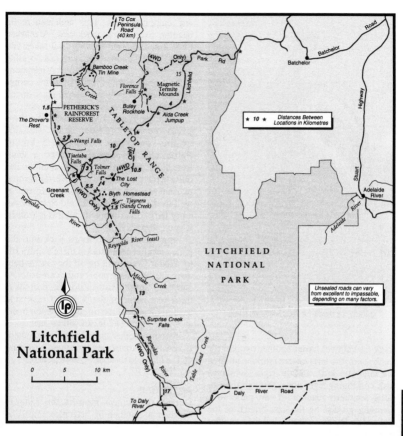

Litchfield National Park

0   5   10 km

a national park in 1986. The track then continues another 1.5 km, where it joins the Tjaynera Falls track (see below).

Fourteen km beyond the turning to Florence Falls is the turn-off to **Tolmer Falls**, which are a 400-metre walk off the road. Caves around the gorge here are home to various bats; ancient rock formations take spectacular forms, and the rock pools above the falls are well worth a look. There's a 1.5-km loop walking track here which gives you some excellent views of the area.

It's another three km along the main road to **Greenant Creek**, where there's a day-use area and a 1.8-km walking trail to **Tjaetaba Falls**, on the north side of the road. Just beyond Greenant Creek is the turn-off to **Tjaynera (Sandy Creek) Falls**, which lie nine km off the road along an incredibly corrugated 4WD track. From the end of the track it's a 1.7-km walk to the falls from the carpark and campsite along a track lined with lofty paperbark trees. The pool here is deep and cool, and is far less crowded than Wangi Falls (see below).

On the way to the falls from the main road, there's a turn-off to the north after 5.4 km, and this is the southern end of the Lost City

Jabiru, or black-necked stork (NTTC)

and camping areas. This area can really become overrun on weekends. A marked three km, 1½-hour walking trail takes you up and over the top of the falls, but it's quite a steep walk. There's an emergency telephone at the carpark here – every year a few people get into difficulty while swimming in the pool, although it's not dangerous if care is taken.

From the Wangi Falls turn-off it's three km to **The Drover's Rest**, on the west side of the road, and another 1.5 km to **Petherick's Rainforest Reserve**, a small freehold forest reserve which actually lies outside the park. There are waterfalls, some thermal springs and monsoon rainforest, as well as the wreckage of an old Spitfire! An entry fee of $3 is charged, but this is waived if you camp here.

From here the road loops back into the park, and after about six km there's a turn-off to **Walker Creek**, not far off the road, where there are more rock pools and a campsite. At **Bamboo Creek**, reached along a short 4WD track just north of the Walker Creek side road, remnants of the tin mines which operated here in the 1870s can still be seen.

It's only another three km to the northern boundary of the park, and from there it's around 40 km of dirt to the Cox Peninsula road.

ACTIVITIES

During the winter months the rangers conduct a number of activities aimed at increasing your enjoyment and knowledge of the park. On Tuesday at 10 am there's a guided walk to Tolmer Falls, on Wednesday at 8 pm a slide show at the Wangi picnic area, and on Thursday at 10 am the magnetic termite mounds are the feature of a talk.

Helicopter rides over the park are available from The Drover's Rest on the western edge of the park. The cost is $55 ($45 for children) for a 15-minute ride.

ORGANISED TOURS

There are plenty of companies offering day trips to Litchfield from Darwin. Woolly Butt (☎ (089) 41 2600), operating out of Frogshollow Backpackers in Darwin, is

track (see above). After another two km the track forks, the left (eastern) fork heading to the falls (1.5 km), and the right (southern) fork continuing right down through the isolated southern reaches of the park, to a camping ground on the east branch of the **Reynolds River** (six km), and then another at **Surprise Creek Falls** (13 km). Don't be tempted to swim here as saltwater crocodiles may be lurking. The track crosses the Reynolds River and eventually links up with the Daly River Rd, 17 km beyond Surprise Creek. From this intersection you can head east to the Stuart Highway or south-west to Daly River. This track through the south of the park is impassable during the Wet.

The main road continues from the Tjaynera turn-off another seven km to the turn-off to the most popular attraction in Litchfield, **Wangi Falls** (pronounced 'wong-gye'), two km along a side road. The falls here flow year-round and fill a beautiful plunge pool. There are also extensive picnic popular. The price is $65 including morning tea and lunch.

FACILITIES
Camping
The Conservation Commission (☎ (089) 89 5511) in Darwin maintains a number of campsites within the park. Those at *Florence Falls* (separate 2WD and 4WD areas), *Buley Rockhole* and *Tjaynera Falls* have facilities such as toilets, showers and fireplaces, while the bush camps in the south of the park are very basic. The cost is $4 per person at *Wangi*, $2 at Florence Falls 2WD, and $1 at all the rest.

It's also possible to camp at *Petherick's Rainforest Reserve*, on the western edge of the park, for $5 per person, and at *The Drover's Rest* for a similar fee.

Fuel & Supplies
Fuel is available at Batchelor, or the Finniss River Store, which is on the northern access road into the park.

Batchelor has a supermarket, otherwise there's the Finniss River Store and The Drover's Rest, both with provisions and takeaway food.

Kakadu National Park

Kakadu National Park is one of Australia's natural marvels. The longer you stay, the more rewarding it is. It's a very popular destination, and there are limited 4WD opportunities, although even these are gradually disappearing as the tracks within the park are upgraded.

Kakadu stretches more than 200 km south from the coast and 100 km from east to west, with the main entrance 153 km by bitumen road east of Darwin. It encompasses a great variety of superb landscapes, swarms with wildlife and has some of Australia's best Aboriginal rock art.

The name Kakadu comes from Gagadju,

Kakadu National Park (RS)

one of the local Aboriginal languages, and part of Kakadu is Aboriginal land, leased to the government for use as a national park. There are several Aboriginal settlements in the park, and about half the park rangers are Aborigines. Enclosed by the park, but not part of it, are a few tracts of land designated for other purposes – principally three uranium-mining leases in the east.

GEOGRAPHY

A straight line on the map separates Kakadu from the Arnhem Land Aboriginal land to its east, which you can't enter without a permit. The Arnhem Land escarpment, a dramatic 100 to 200-metre-high sandstone cliffline, which provides the natural boundary of the very rugged Arnhem Land plateau, winds circuitously some 500 km through east and south-east Kakadu.

Creeks cut across the rocky plateau and tumble off the escarpment as thundering waterfalls in the wet season. They then flow across the lowlands to swamp the vast flood plains of Kakadu's four north-flowing rivers, turning the north of the park into a kind of huge vegetated lake. From west to east the rivers are the Wildman, the West Alligator, the South Alligator and the East Alligator. Such is the difference between dry and wet seasons that areas on river flood plains which are perfectly dry underfoot in September will be under three metres of water a few months later. As the waters recede in the Dry, some loops of wet-season watercourses become cut off, but don't dry up. These billabongs are often carpeted with water lilies and are enticing for waterbirds.

The coastline has long stretches of mangrove swamp which are important for halting erosion and as a breeding ground for marine and bird species. The southern part of the park is drier, lowland hill country with open grassland and eucalypt woodland. Pockets of monsoon rainforest crop up here as well as in most of the park's other landscapes.

In all, Kakadu has over 1000 plant species, and a number of them are still used by the local Aborigines for food, bush medicine and other practical purposes.

SEASONS

The great change between the Dry and the November-March Wet makes a big difference to Kakadu visitors. Not only is the landscape transformed as the wetlands and waterfalls grow, but Kakadu's lesser roads become impassable in the Wet, cutting off some highlights like Jim Jim Falls. The local Aboriginal people recognise six seasons in the annual cycle.

The 'build-up' to the Wet, known as *Gunumeleng*, starts in October. Humidity and the temperatures rise (to 35°C or more) – and the number of mosquitoes, always high near water, rises to near plague proportions. By November, the thunderstorms have started, billabongs start to be replenished and the waterbirds disperse.

The Wet proper, *Gudjuek*, continues through January, February and March, with violent thunderstorms and an abundance of plant and animal life thriving in the hot, moist conditions. Around 1300 mm of rain falls in Kakadu, most of it during this period.

April is *Banggereng*, the season when storms (known as 'knock 'em down' storms) flatten the spear grass, which during the course of the Wet has shot up to two metres in height.

Yekke, which lasts from May to mid-June, is the season of mists, and the air starts to dry out. It is quite a good time to visit: there aren't too many other visitors, the wetlands and waterfalls still have a lot of water and most of the tracks are open.

The most comfortable time is the late Dry, July and August – *Wurrgeng* and *Gurrung*. This is when wildlife, especially birds, congregates in large numbers around the shrinking billabongs and watercourses, but it's also when most tourists come to the park.

FAUNA

Kakadu has about 25 species of frog, 50 types of mammal, 77 fish species, 75 types of reptile, 280 bird species (one-third of all Australian bird species) and 4500 kinds of insect. There are frequent additions to the list, and a few of the rarer species are unique to the park. Kakadu's wetlands are on the

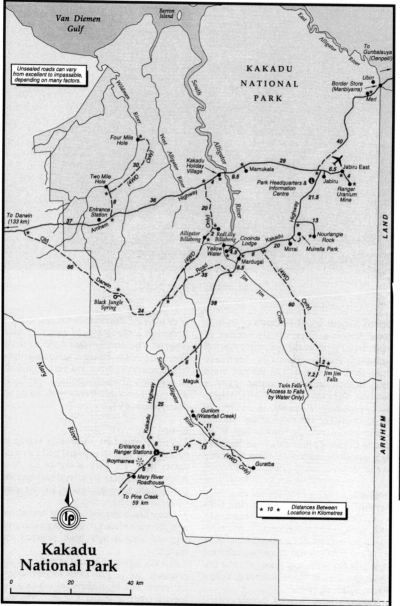

Kakadu
National Park

Cormorant drying its wings (RS)

United Nations list of Wetlands of International Importance, principally because of their crucial significance to so many types of waterbird. You'll only see a tiny fraction of these creatures in a visit to the park since many of them are shy, nocturnal or few in numbers. Take advantage of talks and walks led by park rangers – mainly in the Dry – to get to know and see more of the wildlife; obtain details from the Kakadu Park Information Centre. Cruises are run on the South Alligator River and Yellow Water Billabong to enable you to see the water life.

Reptiles
The park has both types of Australian crocodile. Twin and Jim Jim falls, for example, both have resident freshwater crocodiles, which are considered harmless, while there are about 3500 of the dangerous saltwater variety in the park. You're sure to see a few if you take a South Alligator River or Yellow Water Billabong cruise.

Kakadu's other reptiles include several types of lizard, like the frilled lizard, and five freshwater turtle species of which the most common is the northern snake-necked turtle. There are many snakes, including three highly poisonous types, but you're unlikely to see any. Oenpelli pythons, probably unique to the Kakadu escarpment, were only discovered in 1977.

Birds
Kakadu's abundant waterbirds reside in beautiful wetland settings and make a memorable sight. The park is one of the chief refuges in Australia for several bird species, among them the magpie goose, green pygmy goose and Burdekin duck.

Other fine waterbirds include the jabiru, or black-necked stork, with its distinctive red legs and long straight beak, pelicans and darters.

Herons, egrets, ibis and cormorants are common. You're quite likely to see rainbow bee-eaters and kingfishers (of which there are six types in inland Kakadu). Majestic

Arnhem Land escarpment (NTTC)

white-breasted sea eagles are often seen near inland waterways too, and wedge-tailed eagles, whistling kites and black kites are common. At night you may hear barking owls calling – they sound just like dogs. Also spectacular is the red-tailed black cockatoo, and there are brolgas and bustards.

Mammals

Several types of kangaroo and wallaby inhabit the park, and the shy black wallaroo is more or less unique to Kakadu. You might be lucky enough to see a sugar glider in wooded areas in the daytime. Kakadu is home to 25 species of bat, and a key refuge for four endangered varieties.

Water buffalo, which ran wild after being introduced to the Top End from Timor by European settlers in the first half of the 19th century, have been virtually eradicated because they were potential carriers of cattle disease and did much damage to the natural environment.

Fish

You can't miss the silver barramundi, which creates a distinctive swirl near the water surface. It can grow well over a metre long and changes sex from male to female at the age of five or six years.

ROCK ART

Kakadu has about 5000 Aboriginal rock-painting sites dating from 20,000 or more years ago up to the 1960s. They range from hand prints to paintings of animals, people, mythological beings and European ships, constituting one of the world's most important and fascinating rock-art collections. They provide a record of changing environments and Aboriginal lifestyles over time.

In some places they are concentrated in large galleries, with paintings from different eras sometimes superimposed on one another. Some sites are kept secret – not only to protect them from damage, but also because they are private or sacred to the

Aborigines. Some are even believed to be the residences of dangerous beings, who must not be approached by the ignorant. Two of the finest sites, however, have been opened up to visitors, with access roads, walkways and explanatory signs. These are Ubirr and Nourlangie Rock. Park rangers conduct free art-site tours once or twice a day from May to October.

The dominant colours of all the art are yellow, red and white, obtained by grinding natural minerals to powder and mixing them with water.

In the last few decades the rock-painting tradition has all but died out following the traumas that European settlement caused in Aboriginal society. Aborigines today devote artistic energy instead to painting on eucalyptus bark, often in traditional styles and usually for sale. But they still regard much of the rock art as important and take care to protect it.

INFORMATION

The excellent Kakadu Park Information Centre (☎ (089) 79 2101), on the Kakadu Highway a couple of km south of the Arnhem Highway, is open daily from 8 am to 5 pm. Here you'll find informative displays, including a special building devoted to birds, and a video room with several interesting films available. There are details of guided art-site and wildlife walks, and it's also where you pay the $10 entry fee (children under 16 free). This entitles you to stay in the park for 14 days, and there are random checks at various places throughout the park to check tickets.

There's also an information centre at Jabiru Airport. In Darwin you can get information on Kakadu from the ANCA (☎ (089) 81 5299). Top End tourist offices usually have copies of the *Kakadu Visitor Guide* leaflet, which includes a good map.

THE PARK
Arnhem Highway

From where the Arnhem Highway to Kakadu turns east off the Stuart Highway, it's 120 km to the park entrance, and another 103 km east across the park to Jabiru, sealed all the way. The Kakadu Highway to Nourlangie Rock, Cooinda and Pine Creek (also sealed but for 40 km) turns south off the Arnhem Highway shortly before Jabiru.

A turn-off to the north, 18 km into the park along the Arnhem Highway, leads to camp sites at **Two Mile Hole** (eight km) and **Four Mile Hole** (38 km) on the Wildman River, which is popular for fishing. The track is not suitable for conventional vehicles except in the Dry, and then only as far as Two Mile Hole.

About 35 km further east along the Arnhem Highway, a turn-off to the south, again impassable to conventional vehicles in the Wet, leads to campsites at **Alligator** and **Red Lilly** billabongs, and on to the Kakadu Highway.

The **South Alligator River Crossing** is on the highway 60 km into the park, about two km past Kakadu Holiday Village. The cruises on the tidal river here are a good opportunity for crocodile-spotting. During the Dry there are daily two-hour tours at 10 am and 4 pm for $24.50. The schedule seems to vary through the season, so call ☎ (089) 41 0800 for details.

Seven km east of South Alligator, a short side road to the south leads to **Mamukala**, with views over the South Alligator flood plain, an observation building, a three-km walking trail and bird-watching hides.

Ubirr

This spectacular rock-art site, also called Obiri Rock, lies 43 km north of the Arnhem Highway. The turn-off is 95 km from the park entrance and the road to Ubirr is sealed most of the way, but there are several creek crossings which make it impassable for a conventional vehicle for most of the wet season – sometimes for 4WD vehicles too. The rock-art site is open daily from 8.30 am to sunset between June and November.

Shortly before Ubirr you pass the Border Store, near which are a couple of walking trails close to the East Alligator River, which forms the eastern boundary of the park here. There is a backpackers' hostel and campsite nearby.

An easily followed path from the Ubirr carpark takes you through the main galleries and up to a lookout with superb views – a 1.5-km round trip. There are paintings on numerous rocks along the path, but the highlight is the main gallery with a large array of well-executed and preserved X-ray-style wallabies, possums, goannas, tortoises and fish, plus a couple of *balanda* (White men) with hands on hips.

The Ubirr paintings are in many different styles. They were painted at times ranging from probably 20,000 or more years ago up to the 20th century. Allow plenty of time to seek out and study them.

Jabiru

The township of Jabiru (population 1730), built to accommodate the Ranger Uranium Mine workers, has a supermarket, Westpac Bank, chemist, shops and a public swimming pool. Six km east is Jabiru Airport, and nearby the **Ranger Uranium Mine**. Minibus tours of the mine ($10) are available three times a day through Kakadu Air (☎ (089) 79 2411).

Nourlangie Rock

The sight of this looming, mysterious, isolated outlier of the Arnhem Land escarpment makes it easy to understand why it has been important to Aborigines for so long. Its long, red, sandstone bulk – striped in places with orange, white and even black – slopes up from surrounding woodland to fall away finally at one end in sheer, stepped cliffs, at the foot of which is Kakadu's best known collection of rock art.

The name Nourlangie is a corruption of *nawulandja*, an Aboriginal word which referred to an area bigger than the rock itself. The Aboriginal name of the rock is Burrunggui. You reach it at the end of a 13-km sealed road, which turns east off the Kakadu Highway, 21.5 km south of the Arnhem Highway. Other interesting spots nearby make it worth spending a whole day in this corner of Kakadu. The last few km of the road are closed from around 5 pm daily.

From the main carpark, a round-trip walk

of about two km takes you first to the **Anbangbang shelter**, which was used for 20,000 years as a refuge from heat, rain and the area's frequent wet-season thunderstorms. From the gallery you can walk onto a lookout where you can see the distant Arnhem Land cliff line, including Lightning Dreaming (Namarrgon Djadjam), which is the home of Namarrgon. There's a 12-km marked walk all the way round the rock, for which the park office has a leaflet.

Heading back towards the highway, you can take three turn-offs to further places of interest. The first, on the left about one km from the main carpark, takes you to **Anbangbang Billabong**, with a dense carpet of lilies and a picnic site. The second, also on the left, leads to a short walk up to **Nawulandja Lookout**, with good views back over Nourlangie Rock.

The third turn-off, a dirt track on the right, takes you to another outstanding – but little visited – rock-art gallery, **Nangaloar**, or Nangaluwurr. A further six km along this road, followed by a three-km walk, brings you to **Gubara Pools**, an area of shaded pools set in monsoon forest.

Jim Jim & Twin Falls

These two spectacular waterfalls are along a 4WD dry-season track that turns south-east off the Kakadu Highway between the Nourlangie Rock and Cooinda Lodge turn-offs. It's about 60 km to Jim Jim Falls, with the last km on foot, and about 67 km to Twin Falls, where the last few hundred metres are through the water up a snaking, forested gorge – great fun on an inflatable air-bed. Jim Jim – a sheer 215-metre drop – is awesome after the rains, but its waters can shrink to nothing at the end of the Dry. Twin Falls doesn't dry up.

Yellow Water & Cooinda

The turn-off to the Cooinda accommodation complex and the superb Yellow Water wetlands, with their big waterbird population, is around 48 km down the Kakadu Highway from its junction with the Arnhem Highway. It's then 4.5 km to Cooinda, and a couple

Jim Jim Falls (RI)

more to the starting point for the boat trips on Yellow Water Billabong. These go three times daily year-round and cost $22.50 ($11.50 for children) for two hours. There are also twice-daily tours of 1½ hours for $19.50 ($10.50). This trip is one of the highlights of most people's visit to Kakadu. Early morning is the best time to go as the bird life is most active. You're likely to see a saltwater crocodile or two. It's usually advisable to book your cruise the day before at Cooinda – particularly for the early departure.

Yellow Water is also an excellent place to watch the sunset from, particularly in the dry season when the smoke from the many bushfires which burn in the Top End at this time of year turns bright red in the setting sun. Bring plenty of insect repellent as the mosquitoes are voracious.

Cooinda Turn-off to Pine Creek

Just south of the Yellow Water and Cooinda turn-off, the Kakadu Highway heads south-west out of the park to Pine Creek on the Stuart Highway, about 160 km from Cooinda. On the way there is a turn-off to the very scenic falls and plunge pool at **Waterfall Creek** (also called Gunlom) which featured in the film *Crocodile Dundee*. It's 37 km along a good dirt road.

ACTIVITIES
Walking

Kakadu is excellent but tough bushwalking country. Many people will be satisfied with the marked trails, which range from one to 12 km. For the more adventurous there are infinite possibilities especially in the drier south and east of the park, but take great care and prepare well; tell people where you're going and don't go alone. You need a permit from the park information centre to camp outside the established campsites. The Darwin Bushwalking Club (☎ (089) 85 1484) welcomes visitors and may be able to help with information too. It has walks most weekends, often in Kakadu. Or you could join a Willis's Walkabout guided bushwalk (see the following Organised Tours section).

Kakadu by Foot is a helpful guide to the marked walking trails in Kakadu. It is published by the ANCA (☎ (089) 81 5299) but seems to be in short supply; it costs $1.95.

Fishing
Fishing is permitted in most areas, but there are some restricted areas so check at the information centre to be sure. Fishing with anything other than hand lines and rods with lures is not permitted, and the usual Northern Territory bag limits apply.

Crocodiles of course pose a threat to the unwary, so give them a wide berth if you're boating. Boating on the East Alligator River is permitted, but as the river forms the boundary between the park and Arnhem Land, landing on the Aboriginal land on the east bank is not permitted.

There are boat ramps at Yellow Water, South Alligator River, Mardugal, Jim Jim Billabong and Manbiyarra.

ORGANISED TOURS
There are hosts of tours to Kakadu from Darwin and a few that start inside the park. Two-day tours typically take in Jim Jim Falls, Nourlangie Rock and the Yellow Water cruise, and cost from $170. Companies which seem to be popular include: Hunter Safaris (☎ (089) 81 2720), $190 for two days; All Terrain (☎ (089) 41 0070); and Saratoga (☎ (089) 81 3521).

A one-day tour to Kakadu from Darwin is really too quick, but if you're short of time it's better than nothing. You could try Australian Kakadu Tours (☎ (089) 81 5144), who will whiz you to Yellow Water and Nourlangie Rock and back to Darwin for $88.

Longer tours usually cover most of the main sights plus a couple of extras. Some combine Kakadu with the Katherine Gorge. One of the popular ones are Katherine Adventure Tours (☎ (089) 71 0246), which charge $270 for three days (including

Litchfield), or $450 for a five-day trip, both from Katherine.

You can take 10-hour 4WD tours to Jim Jim and Twin falls from Jabiru or Cooinda ($115, dry season) with Kakadu Gorge & Waterfall Tours (☎ (089) 79 2025).

Willis's Walkabouts (☎ (089) 85 2134) are bushwalks guided by knowledgeable Top End walkers, following your own or pre-set routes of two days or more. Many of the walks are in Kakadu. Prices vary, but $750 for a two-week trip, including evening meals and return transport from Darwin, is fairly typical.

Magela Tours (☎ (089) 79 2227) is an Aboriginal-owned and run operation, and it offers day tours around Kakadu, concentrating on the less visited sites. The cost is $250 per person with pick-ups in Jabiru.

Into Arnhem Land
A couple of outfits offer trips into Arnhem Land from Kakadu. Kakadu Parklink (☎ (089) 79 2411) has weekday tours from Jabiru or Cooinda into the Mikinj Valley for $135 ($108 children). The trips are usually accompanied by a local Aboriginal guide.

Scenic Flights
Kakadu Air (☎ (089) 79 2411) does a number of flights over Kakadu. A half-hour flight from Jabiru costs $50, or it's $90 for an hour.

FACILITIES
There are a number of fuel stations within the park, and there's a wide variety of accommodation. Note that accommodation prices in Kakadu can vary tremendously depending on the season – dry-season prices (given here) are often as much as 50% above wet-season prices.

Fuel & Repairs
Fuel (super, unleaded and diesel) is available at South Alligator River (Kakadu Holiday Village), Jabiru, Cooinda and at the Mary River Roadhouse (☎ (089) 75 4564), just outside the park's southern boundary on the Kakadu Highway to Pine Creek. The Border

THE TROPICS

Store at Manbiyarra sells diesel and unleaded fuel only (no super).

Mechanical repairs can only be undertaken at Jabiru, although emergency repairs and towing can also be arranged at Cooinda.

Camping

There are sites run by the national parks, and also some (with power) attached to the resorts: *Kakadu Holiday Village*, South Alligator, $20 for two with power, $16 without; *Gagadju Lodge Cooinda*, $13/7; and *Kakadu Frontier Lodge*, Jabiru, $20 with power.

The three main national park campsites, with hot showers, flushing toilets and drinking water, are: *Meri*, near the Border Store; *Muirella Park*, six km off the Kakadu Highway a few km south of the Nourlangie Rock turn-off; and *Mardugal*, just off the Kakadu Highway, 1.5 km south of the Cooinda turn-off. Only the Mardugal site is open during the Wet. The fee for use of these camping sites is $7 per person, payable at the Kakadu Park Information Centre.

The national parks provide about 15 more basic campsites around the park, and at these there is no fee. To camp away from these you need a permit from the park information centre.

Accommodation

There are a number of accommodation centres around the park.

South Alligator Just a couple of km west of the South Alligator River on the Arnhem Highway is the *Kakadu Holiday Village* (☎ (089) 79 0166), which has four-bed rooms for $28 per person, or singles/doubles for $110. The hotel has a restaurant and a basic shop.

Ubirr The basic *Hostel Kakadu* (☎ (089) 79 2333) has accommodation at $12 per person, and the national park rangers put on a slide show each Thursday evening.

The *Border Store* has snack food and is open daily until 5 pm.

Jabiru The *Gagadju Crocodile Hotel* (☎ (089) 79 2800) is probably most famous for its design – it's set out in the shape of a crocodile, although this is only apparent from the air. There's nothing very exotic about the hotel itself, although it is comfortable enough. Room prices start at $90/100.

The *Kakadu Frontier Lodge* (☎ (089) 79 2422) has four-bed rooms at $22 per person, or $80 for a whole room. The only cooking facilities are a few barbecues.

Apart from the restaurants at the two resorts, the licensed *Miners Hut* restaurant in the town has takeaway burgers and a more expensive eat-in section with meals from $10. There's also a bakery across the road.

Cooinda This is by far the most popular place to stay, mainly because of the proximity of the Yellow Water wetlands and the early morning boat cruises. It gets mighty crowded at times, mainly with camping tours. The *Gagadju Lodge Cooinda* (☎ (089) 79 0145) has some comfortable units for $110 a single or double, and much cheaper and more basic air-con 'budget rooms', which are just transportable huts of the type found on many building sites and more commonly known in the Northern Territory as 'demountables', or 'dongas'. For $12 per person they are quite adequate, if a little cramped (two beds per room), although there are no cooking facilities.

The restaurant in the bar here serves unexciting but good-value meals, or there's the expensive *Mimi Restaurant*, with main courses at around $15.

ALTERNATIVE TRANSPORT

Greyhound Pioneer Australia runs daily buses from Darwin to Cooinda via Jabiru and back, with connections from Jabiru to Ubirr. They leave Darwin at 7 am, and stop at Humpty Doo, the Bark Hut, Kakadu Holiday Village, Jabiru ($48, 3¼ hours), Nourlangie Rock and Cooinda ($52, five hours). The return service leaves Cooinda at 3 pm.

Cobourg (Gurig) Peninsula

This remote wilderness, 200 km north-east of Darwin, includes the **Cobourg Marine Park** and the Aboriginal-owned **Gurig National Park**. It is much more remote than Kakadu and requires a 4WD to access it.

Both parks are on the UN register of Wetlands of International Importance as they are the habitat of a variety of waterfowl and other migratory birds. The coastline here is beautiful and there are some excellent beaches. It's not really possible to explore the inland parts of the park as there are virtually no tracks within the park apart from the main access track.

Gurig is also home to a wide variety of introduced animals – Balinese banteng cattle, buffalo, Indian sambar deer and pig – all imported by the British when they attempted to settle the Top End last century.

The park is jointly managed by the Conservation Commission (☎ (089) 89 5511) and the local Aboriginal inhabitants.

HISTORY

Although European navigators had explored along this coastline, it was the British who tried to make a permanent settlement. After two unsuccessful attempts (at Melville Island and then Raffles Bay on the Cobourg Peninsula), a third attempt was made at Port Essington in 1838. The garrison town was named Victoria Settlement, and at its peak was home to over 300 people. The British intention was that it would become the base for major trade between Australia and Asia, but by 1849, after the settlement had survived a cyclone and malaria outbreaks, the decision was made to abandon it.

INFORMATION

Entry to Gurig is by permit, which has to be obtained in advance from the Cobourg Peninsula Sanctuary Board, PO Box 496, Palmerston, NT 0831.

You pass through part of Arnhem Land on the way, and the Aboriginal owners here severely restrict the number of vehicles going through – only 15 are allowed in at any one time – so you're advised to apply up to a year ahead for the necessary permit (fee $10) from the Northern Territory Conservation Commission (☎ (089) 89 4411) at PO Box 38496, Palmerston, NT 0830.

At **Black Point** there is a ranger station and visitor centre (☎ (089) 79 0244), which has an interesting section dealing with the Aboriginal, European and Maccassan people, and also has a brochure detailing the history of Victoria Settlement and a map of the ruins. No trailers are allowed into the park.

THE PARK

The track to Cobourg starts at Oenpelli and is accessible by 4WD vehicle only – and it's closed in the wet season. The 288-km drive to Black Point from the East Alligator River takes about six hours and the track is in reasonable condition – the roughest part coming in the hour or so after the turn-off from Murgenella. The trip must be completed in one day as it's not possible to stop overnight on Aboriginal land.

Victoria Settlement at Port Essington is well worth a visit, but it is accessible by boat only. The ruins still visible include various chimneys and wells, the powder magazine and parts of the hospital. A charter boat service (☎ (089) 79 0263) is available from Black Point to Port Essington. It needs a minimum of six people and the cost is $60 per person for the round trip, which takes all day.

ORGANISED TOURS

Wimray (☎ (089) 45 2755) does day tours from Darwin for $230, which include a flight over Melville Island on the way, a cruise on Port Essington, visits to Aboriginal sacred sites, a tour of the Victoria ruins and game fishing.

Scenic flights are available locally through Watair (☎ (089) 79 0263), or enquire at the Black Point store.

THE TROPICS

Camping on the Little Bynoe River, along the Gulf Track (R & VM)

FACILITIES

There's a shady *campsite* with 15 sites about 100 metres from the shore at Smith Point. It's run by the Conservation Commission (☎ (089) 89 5511) and facilities include a shower, toilet and barbecue. There's no electricity, and generators are banned at night. The charge is $4 per site for three people, plus $1 for each extra person.

At Black Point there's a small store open daily from 3 to 5 pm only. It sells basic provisions, ice, camping gas and fuel (diesel, super, unleaded, outboard mix), and basic mechanical repairs can be undertaken. Be warned that credit cards are not accepted here.

There's an airstrip at Smith Point which is serviced by charter flights from Darwin.

The fully equipped, four-bed *Cobourg Cottages* (☎ (089) 79 0263) at Smith Point overlooking Port Essington cost $100 for the whole cottage, but you need to bring your own supplies. There's also a one-off $20 fee levied by the Aboriginal park owners on people staying at the cottages, and this goes to their funeral fund.

The only other accommodation option is the ultraluxury, award-winning *Seven Spirit Bay Resort* (☎ toll-free 1800 891 189), set in secluded wilderness at Vashon Head and accessible only by air or boat. It charges a mere $399/698 for single/double accommodation, but this includes three gourmet meals, a day trip to Victoria Settlement, guided bushwalks and fishing. Accommodation is in individual, open-sided, hexagonal 'habitats', each with semi-outdoor private bathroom! Return transfer by air from Darwin costs $270 per person.

Gulf Track

Steeped in history and lined by unmarked graves, the Gulf Track from Roper Bar in the Northern Territory's Top End to Normanton in north-west Queensland crosses some of tropical Australia's wildest and most remote country. Until recent times the Track was little more than a set of wheel ruts winding through the endless bush. Those days are gone, but there is still a powerful sense of adventure, thanks to the Gulf's vast untouched forests, the lack of facilities and population, and the saltwater crocodiles that lurk in its numerous untamed rivers. Its attractions include some great fishing opportunities, detours to scenic coastline, abundant wildlife and bush camping beside flowing rivers.

For the average traveller, excessive speed and complacency with road conditions are the Track's major motoring hazards. A 4WD vehicle isn't normally required during the dry season unless you plan to take the tracks that lead to the coast from Hell's Gate and Wollogorang. However, conventional vehicles should have good ground clearance and solid supensions – the river crossings are usually no problem by June, when water levels will have dropped to no more than 600 mm over the Track. Fuel (diesel, super and unleaded) is available at Roper Bar (0 km), Borroloola (373 km), Wollogorang (631 km), Hell's Gate (689 km), Doomadgee (769 km), Tirranna (831 km) and Burketown (864 km).

Traffic on the Gulf Track varies from none in summer to an average of about 30 vehicles per day at the height of the winter tourist season. Travel is not recommended between the beginning of December and the end of March, when extreme heat and humidity make conditions uncomfortable or even dangerous. Apart from that, heavy rain at this time can close the road for lengthy periods. The most pleasant time to visit the Gulf is during the winter months, when you will encounter cool mornings, warm days and balmy evenings.

HISTORY

The Gulf Track more or less follows in the footsteps of the eccentric German explorer

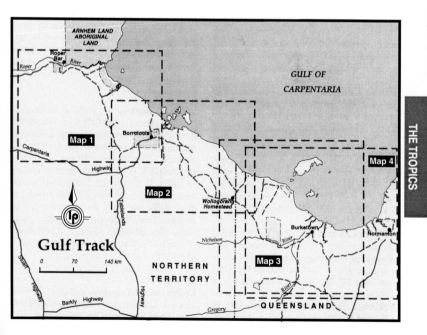

Ludwig Leichhardt, who skirted the Gulf of Carpentaria on his trek from Brisbane to newly settled Port Essington (near Darwin) in 1845. Leichhardt was attempting to find an overland trade route to India for the merchants and squatters of New South Wales; with the boundless enthusiasm of the times, these optimists could see the new port becoming the Singapore of Australia – 'a safe harbour where the wealth of Asia could be exchanged for grain and horses.' However, Port Essington was abandoned four years later, and the hardships of Leichhardt's route killed any hope that it could be used for trade.

After Leichhardt, the wilderness between Burketown, which was established in 1865, and the Roper lay undisturbed until 1872, when D'Arcy Uhr took 400 head of cattle through to the Top End gold fields. This was no mean feat as, apart from being virtually unknown to White people, the country en route was thickly timbered, poorly pastured and inhabited by thousands of hostile Aborigines. The first drover to follow Uhr starved to death near the Limmen Bight River after losing his entire mob to Aboriginal attacks, flooded rivers and stampedes.

No further use was made of the route until 1878, when the legendary Nat 'Bluey' Buchanan drove 1200 cattle from Aramac in central Queensland to a station near Darwin. At the Limmen Bight River the drovers returned to camp to find their cook dead with dough on his hands and his head in a dish; he'd been making bread when his assailant crept up and beheaded him with his own axe. For hours afterwards the hills echoed with gunfire as the dead man's mates carried out a terrible vengeance. It was a sound that was to be heard all too often along the Track for many years to come.

Three years later Buchanan was back, this time in command of 70 men charged with taking 20,000 head of cattle from St George in south-eastern Queensland to the Daly River near Darwin. To cross the vast sweep of Aboriginal-controlled territory west of Burketown, he separated the cattle into 10 mobs and sent them off a day or two apart.

The rigours of the trail claimed many cattle but only one drover, who died of an unknown sickness. It was an epic in Australian droving history and established Leichhardt's hazardous track around the Gulf as the major stock route from Queensland to the Top End.

In 1886 the drovers were joined by a stream of desperadoes and penniless adventurers on their way to the Halls Creek gold rush in Western Australia's Kimberley. The would-be diggers suffered unimaginable privations on their long tramp through the wilderness, and many succumbed to madness, starvation, thirst and Aboriginal spears. Two mounted constables riding down from Roper Bar to newly established Borroloola found a man who, demented by suffering, had dug his own grave and was walking round and round the hole. With no other choice they left him to his fate.

Yet 10 years later, by which time the gold rush and the great cattle drives were over, traffic on the Gulf Track had dwindled to a trickle. It is only in recent times, with the upgrading of the road and the resulting increase in tourism, that you could again describe it as well used. Even so, there are days in the middle of the winter tourist season when you can drive 200 km and not see another vehicle.

INFORMATION
Tourist Offices
Micabo Travel (☎ (089) 75 8844) in Borroloola is the best source of general information on Borroloola and the Gulf Track. You can also ring the Roper Bar Store (☎ (089) 75 4636), Wollogorang station (☎ (089) 75 9944) and Hell's Gate Roadhouse (☎ (077) 45 8258) for the facts on those particular areas. Road reports can be obtained from the police at Ngukurr, near Roper Bar (☎ (089) 75 4644), Borroloola (☎ (089) 75 8770) and Burketown (☎ (077) 45 5120).

Emergency
Unlike many other outback routes, the Gulf Track is fairly well served with medical facilities. There are clinics staffed by registered

---

Absalom's Yabbies

My introduction to Roper Bar was memorable: who should I meet there but the famous Australian bush artist and raconteur Jack Absalom. He and his wife, Mary, were on one of their regular pilgrimages to the Bar. Although it's a long way from their home in Broken Hill, most people who've camped by the Roper River will understand why they do it.

We were on the subject of fishing when Jack started waving his arms about to indicate the size of the local yabbies. I must have looked a bit sceptical because he went straight to his freezer and pulled out the biggest yabby I've ever seen. In fact, I didn't know they grew that big. He let me in on a little secret that he promised is much more effective than traps at catching yabbies: simply toss a handful of chook pellets into the water near the bank to attract them, wait a minute or two, then snaffle them with a throw net.

Denis O'Byrne

---

nurses at Ngukurr, Borroloola and Burketown, and a good-sized hospital at Doomadjee. Roper Bar, Hell's Gate and Wollogorang have comprehensive RFDS medical kits and adjoining airstrips.

Maps

The best road guide to use is the 1:750,000 *Gulf Savannah* map which is produced by Queensland's Department of Geographic Information and is available from Sunmap agencies throughout the state. Alternatively, write to the Sunmap Centre (☎ (07) 896 3203), on the corner of Main and Vulture Sts, Woolloongabba, Qld 4102.

The *Northern Territory Fishing Map* with accompanying guide, produced by the Northern Territory Department of Primary Industry & Fisheries, is a useful reference for the Gulf Track between Roper Bar and Wollogorang. It contains plenty of information on a variety of topics, such as boating and fishing regulations, popular angling species, fishing charters and the location of many fishing spots. You can buy one at newsagencies and tackle shops throughout the Territory, or write to the Department of Primary Industry & Fisheries (☎ (089) 89 2211), GPO Box 990, Darwin 0801.

Radio Frequencies

For the Track's western half you'll need 6840 and 7975 kHz to contact the St John Ambulance base in Darwin (callsign VJY – Victor Juliet Yankee); it operates between 8 am and 5 pm Monday to Friday. These are also after-hours emergency frequencies. You can telephone St John (☎ (089) 27 911) for service details.

The eastern half of the Track is serviced by the Mount Isa RFDS base (callsign VJI – Victor Juliet India), which can be contacted on 2020 and 5110 kHz during office hours (8 am to 5 pm Monday to Friday). For after-hours emergency calls, use 5110 kHz. Ring the base (☎ (077) 43 7887) for an update on services.

THE ROUTE
Roper Bar

The place where Leichhardt crossed the magnificent Roper River en route to Port Essington lies 174 km by road east of Mataranka on the Stuart Highway. Access from the highway (the turn-off is six km south of Mataranka) presents no difficulty, as all but the last 40 km is sealed.

Over 100 metres wide at the bar and lined by huge paperbarks, this popular fishing spot lies at the river's tidal limit and has a boat ramp, camping ground, store and landing strip. The road crosses the river here, then continues on for a further 30 km to the Aboriginal community at Ngukurr, which is off limits to visitors. In the early days, steam ships and large sailing vessels tied up at the bar to discharge cargo. The wreck of one of them, the *Young Australian*, lies about 25 km downstream.

Roper Bar to Borroloola (373 km)

Although this section often resembles the

THE TROPICS

twin wheel ruts of earlier times, it mainly presents good going across undulating country carpeted with a mosaic of scrub, tall forest and open parkland. Along the way you pass swamps and spectacular sandstone escarpments, wind through stony hills and ford several rivers. Although the latter are a magnificent feature of this region, their fording places tend to be disappointing: they're sited at constrictions in the main channels and so feel the full force of wet-season flooding. However, the atmosphere and scenery a short distance away on either side are invariably superb. Below the crossings the rivers generally open out into broad stretches of water that take you all the way to the Gulf.

St Vidgeon Ruins Seventy km from Roper Bar, during which there is little to delight the eye, you arrive at the old St Vidgeon homestead – a lonely ruin on a stony rise conjuring up stark images of battlers eking a scant living from the hostile bush. Bougainvilleas still bloom bravely in the overgrown front yard, providing a splash of vibrant colour in a sea of brown and green. The station is now owned by the Northern Territory government, which is considering a national park in the area. One of the park's gems will be **Lormaieum Lagoon**, a stone's throw from the homestead and only about a km from the Roper River. Fringed by paperbarks and covered by large water lilies, the lagoon has many birds and a peaceful atmosphere, making it a great spot for a picnic.

Past St Vidgeons, the Track mainly winds about through scrub and forest, with occasional vibrant patches of flowering wattles and grevilleas in late autumn to early winter. One of the best is about 30 km down the Track – it's worth stopping for a while to enjoy the birdsong and scented air. Large domed termite mounds and clumps of tall

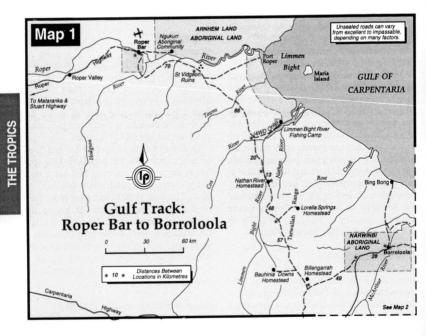

Map 1

Gulf Track:
Roper Bar to Borroloola

Lormaieum Lagoon (DO)

native pine are also of interest in this particular area.

The Limmen Bight The crossing of the Limmen Bight River, 178 km from Roper Bar, is certainly nothing to write home about. In fact, it's rather a dismal place, thanks to its grey rocks, flood-torn vegetation and a still, dark waterhole that brings lurking crocodiles to mind. The river is much prettier downstream, however, and this area is reached by a 4WD track that turns off on the left about 20 km before the crossing. The track takes you past a permanent **fishing camp**, where you must pay a small fee to continue on to pleasant shaded campsites and boat-launching points on the river's tidal section. The Gulf of Carpentaria's larger estuaries offer excellent boat fishing, and this one is no exception.

The Limmen Bight marks a change in the country, which to this point is mainly flat to undulating. For about 50 km southwards from here, the road runs up narrow valleys between rugged ridges, with some dramatic scenery along the way.

You pass the turn-off to **Nathan River homestead** 13 km from the Limmen Bight crossing. Nathan River, too, has been purchased by the Territory government, and potential uses such as fish farming and tourism are being investigated. In the meantime the property is off limits to visitors.

Sixteen km past the homestead you come to a striking grey-and-orange escarpment that crowds in on the left. About the same distance further on is one of the Track's most pleasing sights: a large and beautiful parkland dominated by big ghost gums. There are some nice camp sites close to the road here, although a nearby wet swamp means swarms of mosquitoes at night.

Leaving the gums behind, you pass the turn-off to **Lorella Springs homestead** and enter the harsh stony undulations of the Tarwallah Range. Twenty-four km further on is **Tarwallah Creek** and a delightful waterhole lined by pandanus palms and overhung by tall river gums and paperbarks. The pool looks ideal for a cooling dip, but up this way, sensible travellers do their swimming in a bucket until they know it's safe to do otherwise.

The next 83 km, which takes you to the bitumen Carpentaria Highway, is notable mainly for its suspension-busting washouts and gutters, as the Track winds through harsh, stony hills punctuated by alluvial flats. En route you pass the turn-off to Daly Waters and **Cape Crawford**, the latter being worth a visit if you're short of fuel or desperate for a cold drink (see the later Detours section). Of interest on this section are the metre-high termite mounds that rise like red fingers from the stones, showing that at least something other than flies can thrive in this hostile environment. Once you reach the highway, it's yellow speargrass and low open forest on flat terrain for the remaining 28 km to Borroloola.

Borroloola

Until 1885 there were no facilities at all between Burketown (then a busy little port) and the store at Roper Bar. It's true that there were a few widely scattered homesteads along the way, but these were little more than rough forts armed against Aboriginal attack. Then 'Black Jack' Reid brought a ketch loaded with alcohol and supplies up the McArthur River to the Burketown Crossing, where he built a rough store. So Borroloola was born.

A year later, by which time traffic on the Gulf Track had greatly increased, thanks to the Kimberley gold rush, the embryonic township had a population of 150 Whites – 'the scum of northern Australia', according to the Government Resident. It boasted four corrugated-iron stores (three of which doubled as pubs), a market garden and a dairy farm. A decade later, the gold rush and the great cattle drives were over and the White population had shrunk to six. Borroloola probably would have died altogether were it not for its location on one of the Gulf's largest rivers; it survives today as a minor administrative centre and supply point for the region's cattle stations. After a century of slumbering under the tropical sun, however, the town is set to boom again, with the planned development of a giant silver, lead and zinc mine and the creation of a deep-water port on the Gulf.

Sprawled along two km of wide main street, Borroloola was blown away by Cyclone Kathy in 1984 and much of its old character has been lost in the rebuilding. Its colourful past is preserved mainly in the many interesting displays housed in the **old police station**, which dates from 1886 and is open from noon to 3 pm Monday to Friday. Here you can learn about the Hermit of Borroloola and the Freshwater Admiral, two of the many colourful eccentrics spawned by the local lifestyle. The town is much quieter these days, although bloody re-enactments of what it was like a century ago sometimes take place when the booze is flowing freely, such as on pension days.

Borroloola is connected to the outside world by bitumen roads leading to the Stuart and Barkly highways, and by scheduled daily air services to Darwin and Katherine. The town's population is only about 800, but being an isolated tourism and regional centre, it offers a wide range of government and business services and facilities. These include a medical centre, post office, police station, aerodrome, mechanical repairs, car hire, tourist accommodation, supermarkets, butchery and marine suppliers. A number of businesses sell fishing tackle and bait, but there are no takeaway outlets for spirits and wine. An official passport to the Gulf Capital costs $10 and gives you the right to discounts on accommodation, fuel and meals at various outlets in Borroloola and elsewhere in the Top End.

The Commonwealth, Westpac and ANZ banks have agencies in town, and all three have EFTPOS facilities and take credit cards. The handiest is the Westpac agency at Gulf Mini Mart, which is open seven days a week.

Borroloola attracts around 10,000 visitors annually, most of them coming for the fishing – the Fishing Classic held at Easter each year draws a large number of enthusiasts.

THE TROPICS

The McArthur River is tidal as far as the Burketown Crossing near town, and can be accessed by boat from formed ramps at Borroloola and King Ash Bay, about 40 km downstream. Fishers with large enough craft can venture out into the Gulf around the Sir Edward Pellew Group. Don't despair if you don't have a boat: you can catch a wide variety of fish, including barramundi and threadfin salmon, from various spots along the river's tidal section, between Batten Point (near King Ash Bay) and the Burketown Crossing. Fishing safaris with a local guide are also available (see Organised Tours).

Borroloola to Wollogorang (258 km)

This section of the Track is generally in excellent condition, with long straight stretches that encourage drivers to increase speed until they're bowling along at 100 km/h or more. However, it's best to tread lightly on the accelerator pedal, as loose corners and occasional gutters cause numerous accidents each year. The forests are taller between Borroloola and Wollogorang and the Track's river crossings tend to be much more attractive than before. Several offer good camp sites near the road.

The Wearyan River Leaving Borroloola, the Track spears wide and smooth through a seemingly endless forest of slender stringybarks to the Wearyan River, 56 km out. Here there is a fine waterhole and a good camp site just upstream from the stony crossing, which in the dry season is about 40 cm deep. Large stones hidden under the water are a trap for low-slung vehicles, whose drivers should check on foot before continuing. Of interest are the unusual cycad palms that grow to heights of six metres on either side of the narrow valley.

The Gulf rivers are notable for their wildlife,

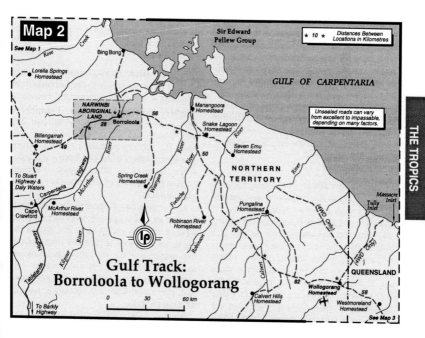

Gulf Track: Borroloola to Wollogorang

Timbered valley near Nathan River (DO)

and the Wearyan River is no exception. Although the atmosphere is magnificent, if you decide to camp here you're likely to lie awake most of the night listening to mosquitoes whine, dingoes howl, curlews scream, fish splash, flying foxes screech and squabble, and heavy things go thump in the bush. The exercise in insomnia reaches its climax at dawn, when an army of kookaburras cackles loudly in the paperbarks and river gums above your head.

The Robinson River The Track narrows past the Wearyan River crossing, and continues on through attractive stringybark forest and patches of tropical bush before dropping down into the Robinson River valley, 105 km from Borroloola. A km later you come to the crossing, where mussel shells, yabby claws and fish scales on the sand give some idea of the river's bounty. Travellers with 4WD vehicles can get access to nice camp sites beside shallow flowing water, but the rubbish that's normally strewn about shows that the crossing is also a popular spot for drinking parties.

Robinson River to Wollogorang Seventy km further on you come to the **Calvert River** crossing, where there is a beautiful waterhole bordered by pandanus and low paperbarks. This makes a startling contrast to the stony undulations and low woodland that dominates the scenery past the Robinson River. The pink blooms of turkey bush – a nondescript species at other times – are an outstanding feature of these harsher areas in early winter.

Continuing on, you pass through 40 km of low but attractive open forest before entering an area of high, rocky hills. For 20 km the Track winds about, a pleasant change from the previous long straights, and crosses spring-fed creeks lined by lush tropical vegetation. Care is needed, as savage washouts and narrow gutters are usually common through the hills.

Sixty km from the Calvert and four km

past the Redbank copper mine turn-off, you arrive on top of the range, to be greeted by the most dramatic scenery between Borroloola and Burketown.

From this lofty summit, a long, steep descent takes you down into a narrow, rugged valley, after which the Track straightens out again for the final 12 km to **Wollogorang**. Covering over 7000 sq km, this vast cattle property boasts a fully licensed roadhouse and an 80-km frontage of pristine sandy beaches on the Gulf of Carpentaria. The coast can only be reached by

4WD vehicle; a small fee is charged for access (see Detours).

Wollogorang to Burketown (232 km)

This section of road was one of the worst in Australia until 1993, when the horrendous bulldust holes on the Queensland side were covered with gravel. Now you can safely sit on 100 km/h most of the way – unless, of course, a big Wet has destroyed the government's good work. The country has little going for it in the way of scenery, being mainly flat and covered with scrubby vegetation. In

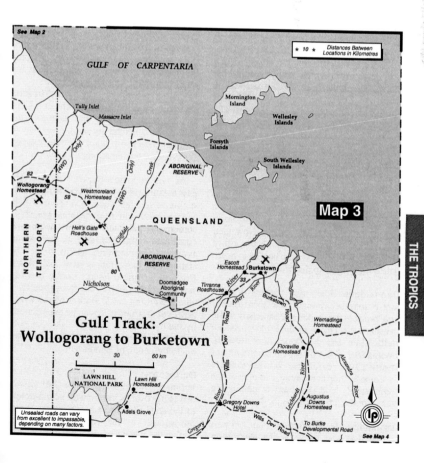

THE TROPICS

fact, apart from Hell's Gate and the Gregory River, there is little reason to linger on this section.

Hell's Gate Fifty-eight km from Wollogorang you arrive at the Hell's Gate Roadhouse, located among low outcrops of grey conglomerate that rise like fat dumplings from the surrounding bush. In the droving days the police from Turn-Off Lagoon, on the Nicholson River, escorted westbound travellers as far as these rocks, after which they were on their own. Prompted by visions of the spear-wielding warriors who awaited them, they named the place Hell's Gate.

The roadhouse was established by present owners Bill and Lee Olive in 1986, for a very simple reason: the federal government's disease-control programme had reduced the cattle herd on their nearby Cliffdale station from 7000 to 1000 and they needed to find another means of earning a living. The friendly little oasis they've created in the middle of nowhere is a credit to these two battlers.

Bill runs day and half-day tours of the area, and you should ask him about access to the coast, 120 km away. The coastal Aborigines lived traditional nomadic lifestyles into the 1930s, having managed to survive as a group thanks to good cover and the area's limited value for cattle-grazing. Now their descendants own the coastal strip north of Cliffdale, and the Olives are hoping to negotiate access rights to the beaches and inlets.

Doomadgee Other than patches of open forest along occasional creek lines, there is little break in the mallee and paperbark scrub that lines the Track for the 80 km between Hell's Gate and the Doomadgee turn-off. Doomadgee is an Aboriginal community of about 1300 residents. While you are welcome to shop at the store, camping on the community's land is subject to permission being obtained from the council.

Doomadgee to Burketown Four km past Doomadgee you arrive at the **Nicholson River** crossing, which is the longest and least attractive of all the Track's fords. The river is about 600 metres across, and in the dry season its bed of solid rock presents a desolate picture. Scattered small waterholes and low trees do little to gladden the eye – a swim would be nice but signs on the bank warn of saltwater crocodiles.

In remarkable contrast, the **Gregory River**, 57 km further on, presents a lush picture of running water crowded by tropical vegetation. Herons stalk the shallows, and the milky water holds promise of feasts of yabbies. However, motorists must exercise extreme care here, as the single-lane concrete crossing has a sharp bend in it and you can't see the other side. If you're towing a caravan, it would be wise to stop before the causeway and send someone across (it's only 200 metres from bank to bank) to warn any oncoming traffic of your approach.

On the other side, the little **Tirranna Roadhouse** dispenses creature comforts, and advice on camping and fishing in the area. At Tirranna the dry scrub gives way to an open blacksoil plain that keeps you company for the remaining 33 km to Burketown.

As you approach Burketown, you will pass the turn-off to **Escott Lodge** and cattle station on your left, about 4.5 km out of town and about 28 km from Doomadgee. This station caters for all travellers, with self-contained rooms available as well as an excellent camping area on the river. The station and the camping area are 13 km from the junction. Escott Lodge is a top spot to catch a barra, but the property is also a working cattle station where every aspect of this hardy life can be experienced by the traveller.

Back on the main track, it is less than five km to the centre of Burketown.

Burketown

For many, Burketown is 'on the Gulf', but in reality it is over 30 km from the actual waters of the Gulf of Carpentaria. Even so, it sits precariously on the very flat plains that border the waters of the Gulf, just a few metres above the high-tide mark. Just a stone's throw from the waters of the Albert River, Burketown operated as a port with ships coming up the muddy waters of the river to service the town and the hinterland.

The river was first sighted by Captain John Stokes on the 1841 survey by the HMS *Beagle*. He was enthusiastic about what he thought was a rich region to the south, imagining English villages and church towers dotting the land which he called the 'Plains of Promise'. While Burketown was named after the infamous Burke and Wills exploration party of 1860, Burke and his party were really a long way east; other, more successful explorers came closer to Burketown and the Albert River. Then again, they didn't die!

Founded in 1865, Burketown almost came to a premature end a year later when a fever wiped out most of the residents. Then, in 1887, an extremely big tidal surge almost carried the town away, and while nothing so dramatic has occurred since, the township is often cut off from the rest of Australia by floods.

Once (by all accounts) the wildest township in Australia, Burketown today is much more peaceful and friendly. Not only is it the administrative centre for a vast region dotted with huge cattle properties, it is also a major supply centre for travellers heading to, from, or along the Gulf. Being such an important centre, it can supply all your normal requirements and, while perhaps not pretty to look at, is a good base from which to explore the surrounding area, take in a little fishing or fly out to any of the islands in the Gulf.

As you enter the town, the Burketown & Gulf Regional Tourist Information Centre (☎ (077) 45 5177), Musgrave St, is on your right, opposite the camping ground. It is a good place to start your visit, and can help with information and with organising tours and flights. There is a Westpac Bank agency at Nowland Engineering (☎ (077) 45 5107), while the Commonwealth Bank agency is at the post office (☎ (077) 45 5109), in Beames St.

There are a few **historic sites** to see

around the place: the old wharves, the boiling-down works (where meat, hooves and hides were processed) and, not far away, the tree emblazoned by the explorer Landsborough. Landsborough had been sent out to try and find the Burke and Wills expedition and had set up a base on the Albert River before pushing south. Like many historic sites, this one is fast decaying under the onslaught of the weather and the white ants. Soon there will be nothing here but a fence around an old tree stump. The cemetery is also interesting. Those with a little more time can head 30 km further north, to as close as you can get to the waters of the Gulf.

Lawn Hill National Park and the **Gregory Downs Hotel**, both within a couple of hundred km south, are places worthy of a visit if you are staying in the area for a few days.

Burketown to Normanton (233 km)

From Burketown the Track improves as it sweeps across the flat plains of the Gulf to Normanton. The road, which follows the original coach route between Darwin and Port Douglas, was known as the Great Top Road.

Turning right at the pub and heading south, you'll pass the 100-year-old artesian bore on the right, just on the outskirts of town. At Harris Creek, 15 km from the centre of town, the dirt begins, and while the bitumen was pleasant, you should be used to the corrugations and the bulldust by now. If you're not, you have another few hundred km to relish the idea. Talking of bulldust, you'll find that on these vast, flat plains, it is finer, deeper and seemingly more enveloping than anywhere else in Australia. The dust hides suspension-wrenching potholes, and if you think it is bad in an air-conditioned 4WD, it is dynamite on a motorcycle!

As you head south on the Burketown Road, most of the creek crossings of any note have been upgraded to a bitumen causeway-type affair. How bad the road is depends on when the graders have been out and how bad the preceding wet season has been – sometimes it can be little better than a track, while

Cycad palms at the Wearyan River (DO)

at other times it is a wide, graded road interspersed with a few corrugations, potholes and stretches of bulldust.

Floraville Station The turn-off to Floraville Station is found at the 73-km mark, on the right. A 'Historic Site' sign indicates that this is more than a station track, and it is worth the 1.3-km diversion to check the plaque and monument to Frederick Walker, who died here in 1866. He was a wild lad in his time, but a fine explorer, who had been sent out to find Burke and Wills. While he didn't find them, he did discover their Camp 119, from which they made their final push to the Gulf.

Walker's monument is found through the gate, heading towards the station. Keep left at the first track junction, about 400 metres from the road, and turn left again a short time later. By now you should be able to see the monument, down the rise a little, across a narrow creek. The station people and the homestead just a short distance away should

be left alone – they are trying to run a business, and though they are friendly enough, being continually interrupted doesn't make for a productive day.

Leichhardt Falls Just one km after the turn-off to Floraville, the road drops down the sandy bank of the Leichhardt River and winds its way across the rock bar that makes up the wide bed of the river here. A narrow, short bridge crosses the stream in one spot.

The best place to pull up for a short wander, and probably the best camp on the run between Burketown and Normanton, is at the small, sandy, tree-covered island on the left, about halfway across the river's rocky bed, just past the narrow bridge. From here it is only a short walk downstream to the spectacular Leichhardt Falls. There are pools of water to cool off in (don't swim in the big stretch of water above the road crossing – there are crocs!), the trees offer plenty of shade and the bird life is rich and varied, although the noisy corellas number in the thousands and definitely dominate the scene.

History has it that the Falls was a spot where a number of the early explorers camped on their trips through this harsh land. Both McKinlay and Landsborough camped here in 1861 in their separate expeditions to find Burke and Wills, blazing trees in the vicinity of the falls.

In a big flood, there is so much water coming down the river that the falls are barely a ripple, as shown by some of the photos in the local tourist information office in Burketown. Those sorts of floods occur every 10 years or so, and looking down into the gorge below the falls, you realise that once-large trees are now just sticks jutting out of the sand. It would be spectacular to fly over the falls when the river was in flood.

The owners of Floraville, who found Walker's grave and erected the monument to him, are also responsible for the thought-provoking sign near the road crossing in the middle of the riverbed. 'God Is' is all that it says.

There are no facilities here, although at times the local shire puts in a couple of rubbish bins. Really it's better, if you are going into Burketown, to take your rubbish with you.

Leichhardt Falls to Normanton Once you have climbed the eastern bank of the Leichhardt River, the road winds a short distance and crosses a causeway before reaching a road junction, which can be easy to miss. You are less than four km from the Floraville Station turn-off, less than two km from the eastern bank of the Leichhardt and a total of 77 km from Burketown. You need to turn left here for Normanton. Heading south on the better-looking road will take you to the Burke & Wills Roadhouse, 146 km away on the Burke Developmental Road (described in the Matilda Highway section towards the end of this chapter).

Turn left at the junction, go through a gate (leave it as you found it – it could be closed), and 500 metres later you will begin crossing the rough – very rough – bed of the **Alexandra River**.

After the Alexandra, the road continues in a north-easterly direction, crossing the occasional creek (some have a causeway) and ploughing through bulldust and across corrugations. The turn-off to **Wernadinga station** is 16 km from the Alexandra River crossing, while the track into Inverleigh station is 84 km from the river (85 km from the road junction).

You cross the **Flinders River** 28 km past the Inverleigh turn-off, and then three km later the Big Bynoe River. The Little Bynoe River is crossed 2.5 km further east. Just up the top of the eastern bank, 500 metres from the river, is a track heading south (right); it leads less than two km to Burke and Wills' **Camp 119**. This is a good spot to have a brew, and if you want to camp, a track leads a short distance back to the edge of the **Little Bynoe**, where you can pitch a tent.

Camp 119 was the northernmost camp of the Burke and Wills expedition. Leaving their companions, Gray and King, to mind the camels and their equipment at Cooper

Sign announcing Hell's Gate Roadhouse (DO)

Creek (near present-day Innamincka in South Australia), Burke and Wills pushed north across the wet and flooded country to try and reach the waters of the Gulf. It was 11 February 1861. While the water was salty and they observed a rise and fall in the tide, they were disappointed that the barrier of mangroves and mud kept them from seeing waves lapping on the shore.

Returning to Camp 119, they planned their dash back to Cooper Creek. No longer was it an exploratory expedition with mapping and observing a prime consideration, but a

dash south for survival. In the end, only King survived.

Camp 119 is marked by a ring of trees and a centre one blazed by Burke and Wills. A couple of monuments also mark the spot.

All the rivers previously mentioned are home to estuarine crocodiles, so swimming is not advisable. A huge number of cattle use the places for drinking and cooling off, so unless the river is flowing, it's not recommended for drinking either.

Continuing eastwards you reach the bitumen at a road junction 32 km east of the

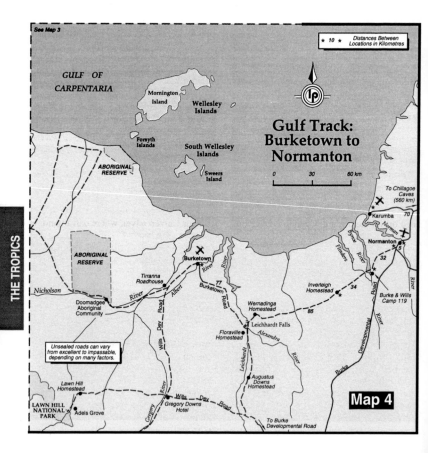

turn-off to Camp 119. Turn left here, and five km later you are in Normanton.

Normanton
On the banks of the Norman River, Normanton is a good base from which to explore and experience the surrounding area. It's a larger town than Burketown and can provide all your requirements, with four pubs and a number of food and fuel outlets. There are also a number of historical places to enjoy.

Don't forget to check some of the **historic buildings** in this once-important port, and if your timing is right, go for a ride on the **Gulflander**, a unique train that runs from the historic railway station to the once-rich gold-mining town of Croydon.

For more information on Normanton, see the section on the Matilda Highway towards the end of this chapter.

From here you can head south 380-odd km along the all-bitumen Burke Developmental Road to Cloncurry, Mount Isa and beyond, or you can head 300 km east to Georgetown and eventually Cairns via the Gulf Developmental Road, which is now (save for about 100 km) all bitumen.

Heading north out of town will take you to **Karumba**, on the coast, 70 km away (see the Matilda Highway section). North of Normanton, on the way to Karumba, you can head off on the dirt and the Burke Developmental Road to Dunbar station and then east to Chillagoe and the coast. This rough, dusty, 560-km trip takes you through remote country without any supply points.

DETOURS
Cape Crawford (43 km one-way)
Nine km past the Bauhinia Downs turn-off and 262 km from Roper Bar you arrive at a T-junction; turn right here for the *Heartbreak Hotel* (☎ (089) 75 9928) at Cape Crawford. The pub has fuel sales (diesel, super and unleaded), takeaway meals, a licensed dining room, air-conditioned, motel-style accommodation (starting at $50 for two) and a pleasant caravan park with lawns and shade.

Also available are 4WD tours of two to eight hours' duration that take you to a variety of outstanding attractions, such as strange rock formations, cool ferneries and tumbling waterfalls, none of which are open to the general public. Travellers with money to burn can take a scenic flight by helicopter over the spectacular **Lost City**, which rivals the Bungle Bungles and will one day no doubt become a major tourist attraction in the Gulf country. For details of tours and facilities, ring the hotel. Note that despite its name, Cape Crawford is a long way from the coast.

Wollogorang Fishing Excursions
With permission from the Wollogorang Roadhouse (☎ (089) 75 9944) you can take 4WD tracks to the **Calvert River** (115 km one-way) and **Massacre and Tully inlets** (90 km one-way) for great fishing and camping in isolated wilderness. It takes three hours to get to the river and over two hours to the inlets, each of which includes about seven km of sandy beach driving – there are plenty of marvellous camp sites under shady sheoak trees along the beach front. Massacre Inlet was the scene of a slaughter of Aborigines by settlers in the early 1880s – the Aborigines had made the mistake of attacking Westmoreland homestead and killing all the White people living there.

You really need a boat to get good results from the Calvert River, where barramundi is the main attraction. Casting out from the sandy beaches at both inlets yields species such as threadfin salmon, golden snapper, cobia, red bream, queenfish and mangrove jacks. The inlets are also good spots for mud crabs, so take a large metal bucket or drum for cooking your catch. Access to these areas is subject to a fee of $12 per vehicle per day.

Lawn Hill National Park
This magnificent oasis is an easy 220 km from Burketown via the **Gregory Downs Hotel** (☎ (077) 48 5566), an old Cobb & Co staging post, where fuel and basic (but comfortable) accommodation are available. The Gregory River flows all year past the pub, and there are many excellent camp sites

THE TROPICS

along its timbered banks. Just before Lawn Hill you pass **Adel's Grove** (☎ (077) 48 5502), where there is a small store and a caravan park. Here you can take a guided tour of a beautiful tropical garden planted by a French botanist in the 1930s. Canoe hire and safe swimming in Lawn Hill Creek are also on offer.

The main attraction at Lawn Hill itself is a rugged gorge where colourful walls tower 60 metres above deep waterholes fringed by monsoon rainforest. Spectacular range scenery, Aboriginal art and the famous **Riversleigh fossil field** are other major features.

The park's camping ground is extremely busy during the winter months, so you need to book at least six weeks in advance to be sure of securing a site. For details, contact the ranger (☎ (077) 47 5572).

ORGANISED TOURS
Borroloola
Peter Fittock of Croc Spot Tours (☎ (089) 75

8721), opposite the McArthur River Caravan Park, offers a choice of several boat tours, of which his nightly croc-spotting excursions are very popular – for $20 you cruise the river with a spotlight and discover why you should never go swimming there. Peter runs one-day river and reef fishing trips ($65 and $110 per person, respectively), as well as overnight safaris (by arrangement) out to the Sir Edward Pellew island group. Minimum numbers apply to all tours. Tackle and bait are provided if required.

Skyport (☎ (089) 75 8844) operates scenic flights (by arrangement) up the McArthur River and over the Sir Edward Pellew Group. The cost is $250 per hour for the plane, which carries a maximum of five passengers. Brolga Air (☎ (089) 75 8791) offers a similar service but is more expensive, at $92 per person per hour with a minimum of three passengers.

Wollogorang
Fishing, exploring and pig-shooting safaris

Noisy corellas at Leichhardt Falls (R & VM)

THE TROPICS

operate from the roadhouse (☎ (089) 75 9944), with costs for fishing and exploring tours starting at $80 per person per day for six people. Hunting expeditions are more expensive. Alternatively, for $40 and upwards per person per day, you use your own vehicle and equipment and just hire the guide. These costs do not include meals and accommodation (see Facilities).

Hell's Gate

Bill Olive (☎ (077) 45 8258) runs half-day and full-day 4WD tours for groups of five or more, taking in spectacular escarpment landscapes and lagoons rich in bird life – the coast will be included if negotiations over access rights are successful. Bookings are preferred and prices are available on application.

Burketown

The Burketown & Gulf Regional Tourist Information Centre (☎ (077) 45 5177), Musgrave St, Burketown, can supply tourist information and can also organise tours and scenic flights around the area or flights out to Sweers and Mornington islands in the Gulf, through operators such as Escott Barramundi Lodge or Savannah Aviation. For the fishers, the information centre can also arrange boat hire.

FACILITIES
Roper Bar

The *Roper Bar Store* (☎ (089) 75 4636) caters mainly to tourist traffic and nearby Aboriginal communities. Its services include fuel sales (Avgas is available, subject to a week's notice), a minisupermarket, clothing, fishing tackle, hardware items, motel-style accommodation and a caravan park. Overnight rates in the store's six air-conditioned demountable units, each of which has shower facilities and sleeps four adults, are $36 a single plus $12 for each additional person. Sites in the grassed camping area, which is only about 100 metres from the river, cost $3.50 per adult, $2 per child and $7 for power if required.

Borroloola

The *Borroloola Inn* (☎ (089) 75 8766) has a total of 16 air-conditioned rooms, starting at $40 for a twin room. Its bistro restaurant serves a range of sensibly priced and generous meals, including (of course) local barramundi. The pub's Sunday-night barbecue is excellent value ($12 for all you can eat), and the swimming pool, which is surrounded by large mango trees, is arguably the nicest place in Borroloola.

Just down from the pub, the *Borroloola Holiday Village* (☎ (089) 75 8742) has air-conditioned units with en suite, cooking facilities, colour TV and telephone (from $97 for a twin room). There are four economy rooms sleeping just one person each ($50), while budget beds in the bunkhouse cost $30. The bunkhouse contains four rooms each sleeping five people, with share kitchen and laundry. Excellent barbecue facilities with lawn and shade trees are scattered about the complex.

There is little shade at the *McArthur River Caravan Park* (☎ (089) 75 8734), also in the main street, where powered sites cost $13.50 per night (add $2.50 if you're using an air-conditioner). Unpowered sites cost $10 for two adults plus $2.50 per extra adult and $1.50 for each child aged under 12. Unfortunately, the park's on-site vans are rarely available because of the shortage of long-term accommodation in town.

There's good fishing from the river bank at King Ash Bay, where the *Borroloola Boat & Fishing Club* (☎ (089) 75 9861) has its headquarters. Bush camping is permitted nearby, and if you join the club – a life membership costs $50 and an annual membership $20 – you can make use of its toilet, shower and bar facilities. The bar is open from 5 to 8 pm daily. Caravanning members can hook up to the club's electricity supply, provided they're prepared to help pay for the diesel.

Wollogorang

Wollogorang Roadhouse (☎ (089) 75 994), open seven days a week, has a licensed restaurant offering good, wholesome country cooking at reasonable prices. There is also a snack menu (including steak sandwiches, which come highly recommended). The roadhouse has six air-conditioned units, each sleeping three, at $45 a single, $55 a double, $61 a twin and $67 a triple. Camping sites cost $3 per person. Fuel, including Avgas and jet-A1, is also available, as is takeaway beer.

Hell's Gate

Plates piled high with station-style meals are also a feature at the *Hell's Gate Roadhouse* (☎ (077) 45 8258), where a licensed restaurant serves breakfast, lunch and dinner – the Sunday-night barbecue shouldn't be missed if you're in the area. There are four air-conditioned, two-bed rooms, with B&B costing $25 per person for a tropical breakfast, $35 with a cooked meal. Avgas is available. The roadhouse is open seven days a week from 7 am to 10 pm (or later). Bookings are recommended for accommodation.

Doomadgee

The well-stocked *Doomadgee Retail Store* sells fuel, meat, groceries, limited hardware items, Aboriginal art and a good range of motoring accessories. It's open from 8.30 am to 5 pm Monday to Friday and from 8.30 to 11.30 am on Saturday.

Tirranna

Fuel, ice, limited food lines (including meat, milk and bread), minor mechanical repairs and generous sit-down and takeaway meals are available at the *Tirranna Roadhouse*, on the banks of the Gregory River. There's also a pleasant little camping area out the back with shade trees and lawn, where sites cost $5 per vehicle per night. Free bush camping is available along the river.

Burketown

Accommodation is available at the *Albert Hotel/Motel* (☎ (077) 45 5104, fax 45 5146), on the corner of Beam and Musgrave Sts, in the town centre. There are four motel units, with all amenities, as well as barbecue and laundry facilities. Singles/doubles cost $50/70. The hotel also has rooms with shared facilities ($12.50 to $25 a single, $25 to $40 a double). Major credit cards (Bankcard, MasterCard and Visa) are accepted.

The *Burketown Caravan Park* (☎ (077) 45 5010, fax 45 5145) has powered sites with all amenities, including washing machines and barbecues. Pets are allowed. A tent site costs $9.50 a double, while a powered site is $12.

The *Burketown General Store* (☎ (077) 45 5010) can supply most general needs, including fuel.

Escott Lodge (☎ (077) 45 5108) caters for all forms of travellers. There are self-contained rooms, a camping ground and a licensed dining room, and from here you can organise a safari, joy flights, boat hire or a trip out to Sweers or Mornington islands.

Normanton & Karumba

There is a good range of facilities in these towns. See the later Matilda Highway section for details.

Bush Camping

For almost its entire length, the Gulf Track passes through station country, and the lessees are not likely to be impressed if they find you driving about on their land without permission. However, access to camp sites at the various river crossings is generally unrestricted, except on Aboriginal-owned land surrounding Doomadgee, where a permit is required from the local community council. Other than at crossings, there are few good camp sites beside the Track, mainly because of the dense vegetation cover.

The reality of camping in the Gulf country is that you'll be eaten by mosquitoes at night if you don't have adequate protection. The insect-screening on caravans, campers and tents should be checked for holes before you leave home – you'll need plenty of ventilation if sleeping inside and it takes only one hole to let the mozzies in. Box-type nets are best if you want to spend your nights outside, as these can be hung so they don't touch your body. Protection from heavy fog and dew is also required, so you will find either a canvas tarpaulin or a gazebo a useful camping accessory for the Gulf Track.

Cairns

Population 64,500

The tourist capital of Far North Queensland and perhaps the best-known city on the Queensland coast, Cairns has become one of Australia's top travellers' destinations. It is also a staging post for journeys into the wilds of Cape York, or excursions to the tropical beauty of Cape Tribulation. On the debit side, Cairns' rapid tourist growth has destroyed much of its laid-back tropical atmosphere. It also lacks a beach, but there are some good ones not far north.

Cairns marks the end of the Bruce Highway and the railway line from Brisbane. The town came into existence in 1876 as a beachhead in the mangroves, intended as a port for the Hodgkinson River gold field 100 km inland. Initially, it struggled under rivalry from Smithfield and Port Douglas further north, but was saved by the Atherton Tableland 'tin rush' from 1880 and became the starting point of the railway to the tableland.

Information

The Far North Queensland Promotion Bureau (☎ (070) 51 3588) has an information centre on the corner of Grafton and Hartley Sts, open weekdays from 9 am to 5 pm, Saturday to 1 pm.

There are dozens of privately run information centres, such as the Cairns Tourist Information Centre (☎ (070) 31 1751) at 99 the Esplanade, which are basically booking offices for tours. Also good for information are the various backpackers' hostels, as most have a separate tour-booking service. The only problem here is that each booking agent and hostel will be selling different tours,

depending on the commission deal they have with the tour companies – shop around.

The GPO, on the corner of Grafton and Hartley Sts, has a poste restante service. For general business (stamps etc), there's also an Australia Post shop in the Orchid Plaza on Lake St. The telephone area code for Cairns is 070.

The RACQ office (☎ 51 4788) at 112 Sheridan St is a good place to get information on road conditions if you're driving up to Cooktown, into Cape York or across to the Gulf of Carpentaria.

The National Parks & Wildlife Service (☎ 52 3096) at 10 McLeod St is open weekdays from 8.30 am to 4.30 pm and deals with camping permits for Davies Creek, the Frankland Islands, Lizard Island and Jardine River.

For books, Proudmans in the Pier complex, and Walkers Bookshop at 96 Lake St, both have a good range. For maps, go to the RACQ or check Sunmap at 15 Lake St.

Things to See

A walk around the town centre turns up a few points of historical interest, although with the spate of recent development, the older buildings are now few and far between. The oldest part of town is the **Trinity Wharf** area, but even this has been redeveloped. There are still some imposing neoclassical buildings from the 1920s on Abbott St, and the frontages around the corner of Spence and Lake Sts date from 1909 to 1926. A walk along the **Esplanade**, with views over to rainforested mountains across the estuary and cool evening breezes, is very agreeable.

The **Pier** is an impressive up-market shopping plaza with expensive boutiques and souvenir shops downstairs, and some interesting eating possibilities upstairs. On Saturday morning there's a food market inside, and on Sunday there's a craft market. These are known as the Mud Markets.

Right in the centre of town, on the corner of Lake and Shields Sts, the **Cairns Museum** is housed in the 1907 School of Arts building, a fine example of early Cairns architecture. It has Aboriginal artefacts, a

Palm Cove (RI)

display on the construction of the Cairns-Kuranda railway, the contents of a now demolished Grafton St joss house, exhibits on the old Palmer River and Hodgkinson gold fields, and material on the early timber industry.

A colourful part of town on weekends is the **Rusty's Bazaar** area bounded by Grafton, Spence, Sheridan and Shields Sts. The bustling weekend markets held here are great for people-watching and for browsing among the dozens of stalls full of produce, arts & crafts, clothes and lots of food. The markets are held on Friday nights and Saturday and Sunday mornings – Saturdays are the busiest and best.

North-west of town, in Edge Hill, are the **Flecker Botanic Gardens** on Collins Ave. A boardwalk leads through a patch of rainforest to **Saltwater Creek** and the two small **Centenary Lakes**. Collins Ave turns west off Sheridan St (the Cook Highway) three km from the centre of Cairns, and the gardens are 700 metres from the turning. Just before the gardens is the entrance to the **Whitfield Range Environmental Park**, with walking tracks which give good views over the city and coast. You can get there with Cairns Trans Buses or the Red Explorer.

Also in Edge Hill, the **Royal Flying Doctor Service** regional office at 1 Junction St is open to visitors daily from 9 am to 4.30 pm; entry is $5.

Activities
Cairns offers an amazing amount of organised activities for the hordes of adventurous tourists. See the earlier information section for booking details, and shop around before you make a decision.

Diving Cairns is the scuba-diving capital of the Barrier Reef, which is closer to the coast here than it is further south. The competition is cutthroat, and the company offering the cheapest deal one week may be old news the next. A chat with people who have already done a course can tell you some of the pros and cons.

Prices differ quite a bit, but expect to pay around $350 to $400 for two days in the pool and classroom, one day travelling to the reef and back, and two more days on the reef with an overnight stay on board.

White-Water Rafting Three of the rivers flowing down from the Atherton Tableland make for some excellent white-water rafting. Most popular is a day in the rainforested gorges of the Tully River, 150 km south of Cairns. The Tully day trips leave daily from Cairns year-round, and cost about $120. There are cheaper half-day trips on the Barron River (about $65), not far inland from Cairns, or you can make two-day ($220 to $360) or five-day ($750) expeditions on the remote North Johnstone River which rises near Malanda and enters the sea at Innisfail. There are also sea-kayaking expeditions on offer.

Other Activities You can go bungee-jumping for $70 to $90 or tandem skydiving for about $270. For something a bit more sedate, try a chopper ride over the reef or a wide range of other aerial tours from $90 up, or go hot-air ballooning over the tablelands for $135 including champagne breakfast. Horse rides through the forests around Palm Cove, north of Cairns, cost $45. There are also various mountain-bike tours on offer, including a half-day ride to Port Douglas for $49.

Organised Tours
As you'd expect, there are hundreds of tours available from Cairns. Some are specially aimed at backpackers and many of these are pretty good value. Agencies include Tropical Paradise Travel (☎ 51 9533) at 25 Spence St, and Going Places (☎ 51 4055) at 26 Abbott St. Once again, shop around.

Daintree, Cape Trib & Cooktown Jungle Tours, KCT and Tropics Explorer all offer good-value and fun-oriented trips north from Cairns.

A day trip to Mossman Gorge and the Daintree River, including a cruise, will cost $48. There are day trips to Cape Tribulation,

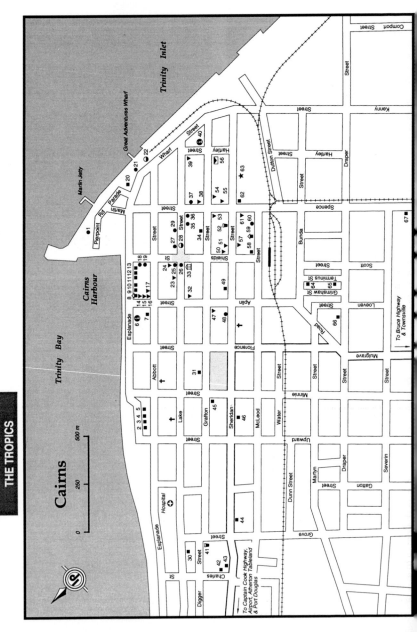

THE TROPICS

PLACES TO STAY

2	Bel-Air Backpackers
3	Rosie's Backpackers
4	Silver Palm Guesthouse
5	Caravella's 149 Hostel
7	Wintersun Apartments
8	YHA on the Esplanade
9	Hostel 89
10	Bellview
11	Jimmy's on the Esplanade
12	Caravella's Hostel 77
13	International Hostel
20	Hilton Hotel
30	Cairns Backpackers Inn
31	Parkview Backpackers
34	Aussie II Hostel
42	City Court Garden Apartments
43	Captain Cook Backpackers
44	Castaways
45	Tracks Hostel
46	Inn the Tropics
49	Pacific Coast Budget Accommodation
58	Grand Hotel
59	YHA McLeod St Hostel
62	Coconut Palms Hostel
64	Dreamtime Travellers Rest
65	Ryan's Rest Guesthouse
66	Gone Walkabout Hostel
67	Up Top Down Under

PLACES TO EAT

14	Greens
15	Meeting Place
16	End of the World Nightclub
17	Pumphouse Bar & Restaurant
23	Fiesta Cantina
24	Base Rock Cafe & Bar
32	Galloping Gourmet
38	Blue Moon Cafe
39	Samuel's Saloon & Playpen Nightclub
47	George's Greek Taverna
50	La Fettucine
51	Continental Shelf Deli
53	Mozart's Pastry
54	Tiny's Juice Bar
55	Taj Indian Restaurant
57	John & Diana's Breakfast & Burger House
61	Bangkok Room Thai Restaurant & Hog's Breath Cafe

OTHER

1	The Pier & Radisson Plaza Hotel
6	Cairns Tourist Information Centre
18	Johno's Blues Bar
19	Air Nuigini
21	Great Adventures Office
22	Trinity Wharf & Transit Centre
25	Qantas & Sunstate Airlines
26	City Place Amphitheatre
27	Ansett & Eastwest Airlines
28	Lake St Transit Bus Stop
29	Orchid Plaza & Australia Post Shop
33	Cairns Museum & Swagman's Restaurant
35	STA Travel
36	Central Arcade, Fox & Firkin Hotel & Tropo's Nightclub
37	Tropical Paradise Travel
40	Far North Queensland Promotion Bureau
41	Cock & Bull Hotel
48	RACQ
52	Rusty's Pub & Bazaar
56	Post Office
60	National Parks & Wildlife Service
63	Police Station

but you'd be better off taking one of the overnight or longer packages, which cost around $69 for two days, $79 for three days or $92 for five days, and include Mossman Gorge, the Daintree River and accommodation at Crocodylus Village and/or Jungle Lodge and/or PK's Jungle Village. Mountain Bike & Rainforest (☎ 55 3089) has day trips from around $80.

Barrier Reef There are dozens of options available for day trips to the reef. It's worth asking a few questions before you book, such as how many passengers the boat takes, what's included in the price (usually at least snorkelling gear and lunch) and how much the extras (such as wetsuit hire and introductory dives) cost, and exactly where the boat is going. Some companies have a dubious definition of outer reef; as a general rule, the further out you go, the better the diving.

Outback There are a number of companies that operate 4WD trips between Cairns,

Scarlet Banksia (JC)

Alice Springs and Darwin, via the Gulf Country and Kakadu. Frontier Safaris (☎ 31 6711) has a three-day camping trip from Cairns to Alice for $99, a six-day trip to Alice and Uluru (Ayers Rock) for $278 and a nine-day round trip for $350. Costs don't include meals.

K'Gari Expeditions (☎ (018) 18 4961) offers a 12-day expedition from Cairns to Darwin via Normanton, Lawn Hill National Park, Katherine Gorge and Kakadu for $828, including all meals and camping gear, or $944 for a 16-day round trip which puts you back in Cairns. It also has a 12-day (16-day round) trip to Uluru (Ayers Rock) via Lawn Hill, the MacDonnell Ranges and Kings Canyon for the same price.

Places to Stay

Cairns has hostels and cheap guesthouses galore, as well as plenty of reasonably priced motels and holiday flats. The accommodation business is extremely competitive and prices go up and down with the seasons. Lower weekly rates are the norm. Prices given here for the more expensive places can rise by 30% or 40% in the peak season, and some of the hostels will charge $1 or $2 less in the quiet times.

Camping There are about a dozen caravan parks in and around Cairns, though none of them are really central. Almost without exception they take campers as well as caravans. The closest one to the centre is the *City Caravan Park* (☎ 51 1467), about two km north-west on the corner of Little and James Sts, with tent sites for $12 and on-site vans for $28.

Out on the Bruce Highway, about eight km south of the centre, is the excellent *Cairns Coconut Caravan Village* (☎ 54 6644), with camp sites for $13.50, camp-o-tel units for $18 a double and cabin vans from $32.

Hostels The Cairns hostel scene is constantly changing as new places open up, old ones change hands and others rise and fall in quality and popularity. The type of accommodation is pretty standard – fan-cooled bunk rooms with shared kitchen and bathroom, usually also with sitting areas, laundry facilities and a swimming pool. Unfortunately, you have to beware of theft in some places – use lock-up rooms and safes if they're available.

The Esplanade has the greatest concentration of hostels, and is a lively part of town. The hostels here tend to pack them in, and have very little outside space – any outdoor area is usually cramped with a swimming pool. The hostels away from the city centre offer much more breathing space and are generally quieter, and there are courtesy buses that make regular runs into town.

On the Esplanade, *Caravella's Hostel 77* (☎ 51 2159), at No 77 is one of the longest established Cairns hostels and has old-fashioned but clean rooms, all with air-con ($10 per bed in four- to six-bunk dorms, $11 with a bathroom; doubles from $25 to $27, or $35 with private bathroom). *Bellview* (☎ 31 4377) at No 85 is a good, quiet hostel with

Take your pick... (PS)

clean and comfortable four-bed dorms at $14 per person, singles at $27 and twin rooms at $32. There are also motel-style units at $49 a double, and two smaller units at $42. *Hostel 89* (☎ 31 7477 or toll-free 1800 061 712) at No 89 is one of the best kept hostels on the Esplanade. It's a smallish and helpful place, with twin and double rooms and a few three- or four-bed dorms, all air-conditioned (from $15 per person, with singles/doubles at $25/30). At No 93 is *YHA on the Esplanade* (☎ 31 1919). There are two blocks, one with spacious, airy five-bed dorms with their own bathroom, the other with small twins and doubles. Some rooms have air-con. Dorm beds cost $14 and doubles $32; nonmembers pay an extra $1. *Rosie's Backpackers* (☎ 51 0235) at No 155 has several buildings with either spacious dorms or six-bed flats at $12 per person. This place is helpful and well run. It has a small pool and a popular Saturday-night barbecue.

Close to the city centre, *Parkview Back-packers* (☎ 51 3700) is at 174 Grafton St, three blocks back from the Esplanade. This is a very laid-back place where you can relax by the pool and listen to reggae music. It's in a rambling old timber building with a large tropical garden, and four- to eight-bed dorms ($12 per person). Over at 255 Lake St, *Cairns Backpackers Inn* (☎ 51 9166) occupies three houses. The dorms are big and roomy, and there are spacious gardens and living areas ($10 in a dorm, some of which have air-con, or twins/doubles for $24). The courtesy bus goes to the town centre 16 times a day. At 207 Sheridan St is *Castaways* (☎ 51 1238), a quiet and smallish place with mostly double and twin rooms ($24, or $28 with air-con). Rooms are fan-cooled and have a fridge, and there's a pool and courtesy bus.

Two blocks west of the train station at 274 Draper St, *Gone Walkabout Hostel* (☎ 51 6160) is one of the best in Cairns. It's small, simple and well run, with a friendly atmosphere. Rooms are mostly twins ($22) and doubles ($24), with a few four-bed dorms ($10 per bed), and there's a tiny pool. It's not a place for late partying, however. The YHA *McLeod St Youth Hostel* (☎ 51 0772) at 20-24 McLeod St has dorm beds for $12 and singles/doubles for $20/30; nonmembers pay $1 extra. The facilities are good and the hostel has parking spaces.

Guesthouses A couple of places in this bracket are in the hostel price range, the difference being that their emphasis is on rooms rather than dorms. *Dreamtime Travellers Rest* (☎ 31 6753) at 4 Terminus St is a small guesthouse run by a friendly and enthusiastic young Irish/English couple. It's in a brightly renovated timber Queenslander and has a good pool (double rooms from $28, or rooms with three or four real beds at $12 per person).

Another good guesthouse with a similar approach is *Ryan's Rest* (☎ 51 4734), down the road at 18 Terminus St. It's a cosy and quiet family-run place with three good double rooms upstairs at $30, and two self-contained flats downstairs with twins/doubles at $25, and a four-bed dorm at

$12.50 per person. At 153 the Esplanade, the *Silver Palm Guesthouse* (☎ 31 6099) is clean with singles/doubles from $27.50/32.50, including the use of a kitchen, laundry, pool and TV room. *No Worries* (☎ 31 6380) at 323 Draper St is a small B&B place with just eight beds (twins and doubles at $12 per person).

Motels & Holiday Flats Holiday flats are well worth considering, especially for a group of three or four people who are staying a few days or more. Expect pools, air-con and laundry facilities in this category. Holiday flats generally supply all bedding, cooking utensils etc.

Wintersun Motel Holiday Apartments (☎ 51 2933) at 84 Abbott St is quite a good place. Large, fully equipped, one-bedroom flats with immaculate 1960s decor and air-con cost $45/55. At 209 Lake St is *Castle Holiday Flats* (☎ 31 2229), one of the city's cheapest places. There's a small pool, and rooms with shared facilities for $25/30 single/double, one-bedroom flats for $45 and two-bedroom flats for $60.

There's a string of motels and holiday units along Sheridan St, including the *Pacific Cay* (☎ 51 0151) at No 193, with one-bedroom holiday units from $50 and two-bedroom units from $75, and the *Concord Holiday Units* (☎ 31 4522) at No 183, with one-bedroom units from $50.

Inn the Tropics (☎ 31 1088) at 141 Sheridan St is a relatively new place with a good pool, a small guests' kitchen and an open-air courtyard with tables. Clean and modern motel-style rooms with shared bathrooms cost $30/35, or $40/45 with an en suite.

The *Poinsietta Motel* (☎ 51 2144) at 169 Lake St is one of the cheapest central motels, with clean budget rooms for $42/46.

Places to Eat

For a town of its size, Cairns has quite an amazing number and variety of restaurants. Opening hours are long, and quite a few places take advantage of the climate by providing open-air dining.

Cafes & Takeaways The Esplanade has a large collection of fast-food joints and restaurants – the stretch between Shields and Aplin Sts is virtually wall-to-wall eateries, where you'll find Italian and Chinese food, burgers, kebabs, pizzas, seafood and ice cream – at all hours. The *Meeting Place* on Aplin St near the Esplanade is a good food hall with meals in the $7.50 to $12 range. *Greens*, also on Aplin St near the Esplanade corner, is a popular (though pricey) vegetarian and health-food takeaway.

The *Galloping Gourmet Takeaway* offers a full breakfast for $5, and has a lunch deal for $4 – both good value. *Mozart's Pastry* on the corner of Grafton and Spence Sts is good for a breakfast croissant and coffee, and also has a range of pastries, cakes and sandwiches. *John & Diana's Breakfast & Burger House*, at 35 Sheridan St, has virtually every combination of cooked breakfast imaginable, for $5 or less. Across the road is the *Continental Shelf*, an excellent eat-in deli.

Tiny's Juice Bar, on Grafton St near the Spence St corner, has a great range of fruit and vegetable juices as well as filled rolls and lentil and tofu burgers at good prices. The *Blue Moon Cafe*, nearby at 45 Spence St, is a friendly little place open for lunch and dinner, with Chinese and vegetarian dishes, sandwiches and soups at reasonable prices.

Central Arcade, on the Lake and Spence Sts corner, has several good eateries, including the hip and trendy *Glass Onion*, which has good coffee and a range of cakes, pastries and sandwiches.

Nightclubs & Bars Most of the hostels have giveaway vouchers for cheap meals at various nightclubs, pubs and bars around town, often with free or discounted drinks thrown in. *Samuel's Saloon*, near the corner of Hartley and Lake Sts, is one of the most popular places, with roasts, pastas and stews for $3.50. It even has a bus that collects hungry travellers from the hostels.

The *End of the World*, a nightclub on the corner of Abbott and Aplin Sts, has very basic food, but it's cheap and a lot of people seem to eat here, again with hostel meal vouchers. Next door on Abbott St is the *Pumphouse*, a lively bar with a good range of $3, $4 and $5 meals. The *Fox & Firkin Hotel*, an English-style tavern on the corner of Spence and Lake Sts, also has cheap meals; its $1 Sunday barbecue gets fairly hectic.

The *Base Rock Cafe & Bar* on Shields St is a bit more up-market than the other places, with both live music and DJs, and it has a wide range of meals priced from $4 to $16. It opens daily from midday until late.

Restaurants The *Bangkok Room Thai Restaurant* at 62 Spence St has a pleasant setting and friendly service, with tasty Thai dishes for around $12. Next door is the popular *Hog's Breath Cafe*, a saloon-style bar and grill. Further along Spence St, the *Taj* serves pretty good Indian food.

La Fettucine at 62 Spence St is a narrow and stylish little BYO place with excellent home-made pastas. *George's Greek Taverna*, on the corner of Grafton and Aplin Sts, is a fairly up-market place with Greek and seafood dishes at around $16. For Mexican food, try the *Fiesta Cantina*, in an arcade at 96-98 Lake St.

The Pier plaza has a couple of good eating options. The *Pier Tavern* is a popular pub with several bars and outdoor decking overlooking Trinity Bay and the Esplanade. Bistro meals in the Boat Bar are all $9.90, and there are live bands from Wednesday to Sunday. Up on the first level of the shopping plaza is *Donninis*, a smart but casual licensed restaurant with some of the best Italian food (and service) in town: gourmet pizzas from $9 to $15, pastas from $8 to $10 and Italian mains around $14.

Entertainment
Johno's Blues Bar, above McDonald's on the corner of Shields St and the Esplanade, is a big, lively place with blues, rock and R&B bands every night until late. There's a cover charge of $5 on Friday and Saturday nights. On Abbott St near the Aplin St corner, the *Pumphouse* is another backpackers' favour-ite, with a rowdy bar atmosphere and cheap meals.

The *Fox & Firkin Hotel*, on the corner of Spence and Lake Sts, and the *Cock & Bull*, on the corner of Grafton and Grove Sts, are both English-style taverns with good atmosphere and affordable meals. Quite a few pubs in Cairns have regular live bands, including the Fox & Firkin, the *Pier Tavern*, *Rusty's Pub* on the corner of Spence and Sheridan Sts, and the *Big O* on Wharf St opposite the Transit Centre.

Cairns' nightclub scene is notoriously wild, especially in the early hours of the morning. A huge complex on the corner of Lake and Hartley Sts houses three places: *Samuel's Saloon*, a backpacker bar and eatery; the *Playpen International*, a huge nightclub that often has big-name bands, stays open until sunrise and charges from $2 to $5 entry; and the more up-market *Court Jester* bar. The *End of the World* nightclub, on the corner of Abbott and Aplin Sts, is another popular place for a drink and a bop, with a huge video screen, low lighting, loud music and cheap drinks deals. *Tropo's*, next to the Fox & Firkin, has live bands, a disco and a $5 cover charge.

Free lunch-time concerts are held at the *City Place Amphitheatre*, in the mall on the corner of Lake and Shields Sts.

Things to Buy
Many artists live in the Cairns region, so there's a wide range of local handicrafts available – pottery, clothing, stained glass, jewellery, leather work and so on. Aboriginal art is also for sale in a few places, as are crafts from Papua New Guinea and places further afield in the Pacific. Apart from the many souvenir shops dotted around the town centre, the weekend markets at Rusty's Bazaar and the Pier are all worth a visit.

Getting Around
Local Flights Flights inland and up the Cape York Peninsula from Cairns are shared amongst a number of small feeder airlines. Sunstate flies to Bamaga ($261), Lizard Island ($143) and Thursday Island ($290).

Ansett flies to Weipa ($209) and Mount Isa ($254). Flight West (☎ 35 9511 or through Ansett) operates a service through the Gulf, Cape York Peninsula and to Bamaga and the Torres Strait Islands.

For a bit of airborne nostalgia, DC3 Australia has daily DC3 flights to Cooktown from $140 return, though these are tours rather than scheduled flights. For something completely different, Cape York Air Services (☎ 35 9399), the local mail contractor, does mail runs to remote outback stations on weekdays. Space permitting, you can go along on these runs for $140 to $275, depending on the length of the trip.

To/From the Airport The airport in Cairns has two sections, both off the Captain Cook Highway north of town. The main domestic and international airlines use the new section, officially called Cairns International Airport. This is reached by an approach road that turns off the highway about 3.5 km from central Cairns. The other part of the airport, which some people still call Cairns Airport, is reached from a second turning off the highway, 1.5 km north of the main one.

The Australia Coach shuttle bus (☎ 35 9555) from the main terminal costs $4 and will drop you almost anywhere in central Cairns; ring when you're leaving. A taxi is about $9.

Car Rental Avis, Budget, Hertz and Thrifty have desks at the international airport terminal. In town, the major firms are along Lake St, but local firms have mushroomed all over Cairns and some of them offer good deals, particularly for weekly rental. However, don't be taken in by cut-rates advertising: once you add in all the hidden costs, prices are fairly similar everywhere. Shop around and find the deal that suits. Generally, Mokes (ideal for relaxed, open-air sightseeing) are around $45 per day, VW convertibles $55, and regular cars from $50 up. Four-wheel drives start at around $110 – see the Cape York section for details.

Typical Far North Queensland architecture (PS)

The majority of Cairns' rental firms specifically prohibit you from taking most of their cars up the Cape Tribulation road, on the road to Cooktown, or on the Chillagoe Caves road. A sign in the car will usually announce this prohibition and the contract will threaten dire unhappiness if you do so. Of course, lots of people ignore these prohibitions, but if you get stuck in the mud halfway to Cape Tribulation, it could be a little embarrassing. Be warned that these roads are fairly rough and sometimes impassable in conventional vehicles.

Bicycle & Motorcycle Rental Most of the hostels and car-hire firms, plus quite a few other places, have bicycles for hire so you'll have no trouble tracking one down. Expect to pay around $10 a day. Jolly Frog (☎ 31 2379) at 101 the Esplanade has scooters from $25 and larger motorcycles from $55 per day.

THE TROPICS

Cairns to Musgrave via Cooktown

For those who don't have time to travel to the very top of Cape York, but still want to sample the delights of Far North Queensland away from the glitz and glamour of Cairns and Port Douglas, then an interesting loop to do is from Cairns to Cooktown and on to Musgrave via Battle Camp and Lakefield National Park, returning to Cairns via Laura and the Peninsula Developmental Road. For travellers who want to travel to the top of Cape York, but want something a little different to the main road, this route gives a more enjoyable alternative.

The route north from Cairns along the coast to Cape Tribulation and then through the ranges to Cooktown is very scenic and popular. The road north of Cape Tribulation was surrounded by controversy when it was built in the early 1980s because of environmental concerns about the effect it would have on the rainforest. Although the Green movement was out in force, the road was pushed through anyway. Indeed some damage was caused, but for many travellers it offers a chance to see and appreciate this wild part of Australia. The locals in Cooktown also appreciate this shorter access road from Cairns, rather than having to take the corrugated and much longer inland route.

North of Cooktown this route once again cuts across the Great Dividing Range before descending onto the vast flood plains that make up much of Lakefield National Park. During the Wet the rivers often coalesce to make a shallow inland sea, which in turn is replaced during the Dry by a sea of waving grass cut by tree-lined billabongs and lagoons.

At its northernmost point the route passes very close to the shores of Princess Charlotte Bay, before swinging westwards to the Peninsula Developmental Road at the small enclave of Musgrave.

Cooktown is just one of the highlights of this trip, and the natural delights of Lakefield National Park and the Aboriginal rock art in the Laura area are a couple of others. You could easily spend a couple of weeks just in this region of Far North Queensland.

HISTORY

Aborigines occupied much of this land long before the arrival of the Europeans. They inhabited the flood plains and the escarpment country as well as the rainforested mountains along the coast. They travelled the rivers by canoe and at times made forays out to the close offshore islands.

Captain James Cook almost came to grief near Cooktown during his voyage of discovery when he mapped the east coast of Australia. On the night of 11 June 1770 the *Endeavour* hit a reef and it was only after some heavy gear, including a few cannons, was dropped over the side that the ship was refloated. Eleven days later they pulled into the mouth of the Endeavour River and careened their ship for repairs. Cook stayed here until 6 August, his longest foray on the Australian mainland. In that time he managed to repair his ship while his botanist, Sir Joseph Banks, explored the river and collected specimens, including the first kangaroo to be described by a European.

Cook decided to escape the intricate maze of the inner reef. He landed on and named Lizard Island. He was later to come back inside the reef, preferring to navigate the inner reef to the constant danger of being pushed onto the outer reef. With his departure the Aborigines were left in peace for another 100 years.

In 1865 John Jardine, on his way back from Somerset on the tip of Cape York, sailed up the Endeavour River and later explored and named the Annan River, a little further south. For more information on the Jardine family, see the boxed story on Frank Jardine in the Cape York section.

When James Venture Mulligan discovered gold on the Palmer River in 1873, the area was changed forever. By 1874 over 15,000 men were on the Palmer River gold field, most of them coming via the newly founded port of Cooktown. The town quickly grew

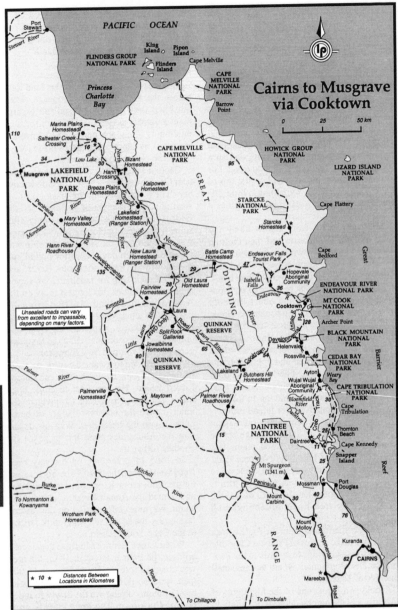

Cairns to Musgrave via Cooktown

and by the end of that year there was supposedly 36 shanties where you could buy grog!

The Aboriginal tribes of the area resisted the invasion of European and Chinese miners every step of the way. In fact the first group of miners (which included a warden and police) to travel to the gold field from Cooktown were attacked by a large group of Aborigines at a place they called Battle Camp. In that battle the Aborigines attacked in waves but were met by a vicious onslaught of gunfire from the Whites. Repulsed, the Aborigines resorted to hit-and-run tactics which over the years left dozens of miners dead. How many Aborigines were killed is impossible to say, but those who survived had to face the more deadly threat of new and potent diseases that the new invaders brought with them.

INFORMATION

The distances between fuel stops aren't great and the condition of the road is pretty fair at most times of the year. However, if you break down, you can still be in for a long wait. There is no LPG available beyond Cooktown.

There is no requirement for permits along this route and no need to register with police. However, in the Lakefield National Park you require a camping permit.

Tourist Information

Information sources along the way include:

Far North Queensland Promotion Bureau
  36-38 Aplin St, PO Box 865, Cairns, Qld 4870 (☎ (070) 51 3588, fax 51 0127)
Queensland National Parks & Wildlife Service
  Far North Regional Centre, 10-12 McLeod St, PO Box 2066, Cairns, Qld 4870 (☎ (070) 52 3096, fax 52 3080)
Cape Tribulation Tourist Information Centre
  Centre Rd, Cape Tribulation, Qld (☎ (070) 98 0070)
Cook Shire Council
  Charlotte St, PO Box 3, Cooktown, Qld 4871 (☎ (070) 69 5444, fax 69 5423)
Croc Shop
  8 Charlotte St, Cooktown (☎ (070) 69 5880). This company has spent years exploring and working

on Cape York. It also has a range of maps and books
Ang-Gnarra Aboriginal Corporation
  Post Office, Laura, Qld 4871 (☎ (070) 60 3214, fax 60 3231). Information on Aboriginal rock-art sites around Laura. Brochures and maps are available of the sites open to the public

Police

The police can often be a good source of information for travellers. The Cooktown police station (☎ (070) 69 5320) is on Charlotte St. The Hopevale Aboriginal Community police station (☎ (070) 60 9224) is at 4 Flierl St. Telephone the Laura police station on ☎ (070) 60 3244.

Hospitals, Clinics & Dentists

The Cooktown hospital (☎ (070) 69 5433) is on Hope St, and there is a dentist (☎ (070) 69 5679) on Helen St.

There is a clinic (☎ (070) 60 3320) in Laura.

Books & Maps

There are a number of good maps and guidebooks readily available, especially in the Cairns/Cooktown region. The Hema map *Cape York* and the RACQ maps *Cairns/Townsville* and *Cape York Peninsula* are the best. Ron & Viv Moon's *Cape York – an Adventurer's Guide* (Kakirra Adventure Publications) is the most comprehensive guidebook for the do-it-yourself camper and four-wheel driver.

The best book on Cooktown is the *Queen of the North* by Glenville Pike; *Cape York* by Hector Holthouse (Australian Geographic) also covers this area.

For the area around the Daintree River and Cape Tribulation, you can't go past the glossy coffee-table book produced by the Australian Conservation Foundation, *Daintree – Where the Rainforest Meets the Reef* (ACF and Kevin Weldon & Associates).

There are no modern books readily available that give a comprehensive look at the Aboriginal art of the area. Percy Trezise wrote *Quinkan Country* and *Last Days of a Wilderness*, as well as a report titled *Rock Art of South-East Cape York*, which was

THE TROPICS

Rainforest at Cape Tribulation (RI)

produced by the Australian Institute of Aboriginal Studies some years ago. They are difficult to get now.

THE ROUTE
Cairns to Cooktown via the Coast (254 km)

From Cairns you head north along the coast through Mossman towards the tropical village of Daintree. This is one of the most pleasant coastal drives in Australia and it is worth taking your time. For those cycling their way north, the pedalling is pretty easy and there are plenty of places to stop, enjoy the view and rest a while.

Turn off the Daintree Road 25 km north of Mossman, 101 km from Cairns, onto the Cape Tribulation Road. Five km later you cross the **Daintree River** by a small ferry. The ferry operates from 6 am to 6 pm. The road surface from the river crossing is constantly being worked on, and travellers will find sections of bitumen from here.

The road continues through rainforest and is generally good enough for the family car, driven with care. Some of the potholes can make it interesting for a heavily loaded cyclist, but there will be worse further north. Initially, much of the surrounding country is private land and there is little to do but drive, or ride, on.

At **Cow Bay**, 10 km north of the ferry, the Cow Bay Hotel provides accommodation and meals. **Thornton Beach** is 20 km north of the river crossing. You can launch a boat here and have a meal at the Thornton Beach Kiosk.

Cape Tribulation, 14 km further north, is a popular destination, with lush rainforest that tumbles down the hills right to the high-tide mark of a pleasant beach. There is accommodation of all styles and for all budgets. Food and fuel are available from the general store.

North from here the road deteriorates a little, and where it climbs the ranges becomes a challenge even for a 4WD after any rain. For walkers and those pedalling a mountain bike, the effort is rewarded with magnificent views over the offshore reefs and the surrounding rainforest.

The **Bloomfield River** is crossed 30 km north of Cape Tribulation. With a major new causeway just completed, the river crossing is now much simpler.

The **Wujal Wujal Aboriginal Community** is on the northern bank of the river. Stick to the main road heading north to Ayton and Cooktown and you won't need a permit. In the tiny hamlet of **Ayton**, accommodation and camping are available at the very pleasant Bloomfield Beach camping ground, or you can stay at the remote resort of the Bloomfield Wilderness Lodge. Food and fuel are available at the Bloomfield River Inn and the Ayton Store.

The road passes through **Cedar Bay National Park**, which stretches inland a short distance. There are no facilities here, and access into the park is either by boat or by walking along numerous small tracks through the bush.

Continue from Cedar Bay National Park to **Rossville**, another small hamlet, and then **Helenvale**, site of the famous **Lion's Den Hotel**, 42 km north of Wujal Wujal. There are a couple of lodges around Rossville and Helenvale which offer accommodation and camping.

From Helenvale, it is back onto the main Cooktown Road after four km for the last 28 km to Cooktown.

Cooktown

The 'Queen of the North', as it is often called, lies on the banks of the Endeavour River, close to where Captain James Cook careened his ship for repairs in 1770. Cooktown is a well-established town with a pervading sense of history. As well as fishing charters to the offshore reefs, it also has one of the best museums in Australia. There is a good range of accommodation with a number of camping/caravan parks, hotels, motels and lodges to pamper the jaded traveller, as well as all the usual facilities.

History With the discovery of gold on the Palmer River in 1873, Cooktown was founded and within a year had grown to a town of 15,000 people. By the turn of the century the population was over 35,000 and the place fairly hummed along with 65 registered hotels, 20 eating houses and 30-odd general stores. Other ports further south along the coast competed for the prize of being the port to feed the Palmer River gold field. But it was the demise of the gold field

---

The Lion's Den Hotel
Built in 1875, the pub has seen little maintenance since then. Its internal decorations have been left by generations of stockmen, tin miners and hippies (from the more recent Cedar Bay days), and the place just oozes character.

On our first trip to Cooktown, back in the 1970s, an army-boot-wearing, moustached, tin-mining lady told me that you haven't been to Cooktown if you haven't been to the Lion's Den. I wasn't game to argue!

Such is the fame of this outback watering hole that Bert Cummings wrote The Lion's Den – A Pub Yarn (Angus & Robertson) about it. While the book may not be the complete story of this wild place, it does give you some idea of what has, and does, go on in this hotel that has been on the edge of the frontier for over 100 years.

One thing that does set it apart from the norm is its licensees. The pub was in the same family from 1875 till 1964 and since then all the licensees have been women. Maybe they are the only ones who can hack the pace!

The pub offers accommodation, excellent camping down on the banks of the Annan River, limited supplies and fuel. For more information, see the Facilities section.

Viv Moon

due to its lack of rich reef gold that heralded the slow decline of Cooktown.

There was still no road communication to Cooktown in 1930, the town relying on small coastal freighters for its supplies and mail. Cooktown and Laura were connected by a light rail from 1885, but it never reached the Palmer River gold field, despite that being its major destination.

During WW II most of the town population was evacuated and the surrounding area became a forward base for US and Australian servicemen fighting in New Guinea and the Coral Sea.

In 1949 Cooktown suffered a major setback when it was devastated by a cyclone. Much of it was completely flattened and those buildings that remained were badly damaged.

Cooktown, however, refused to die, and in the 1950s the tourists began to arrive. At first it was just a straggle of keen adventurers, but by the 1970s it was a near flood, especially for the months of the dry season.

Today the future of the town is vested in tourism and the vast hinterland that it has served for over 100 years.

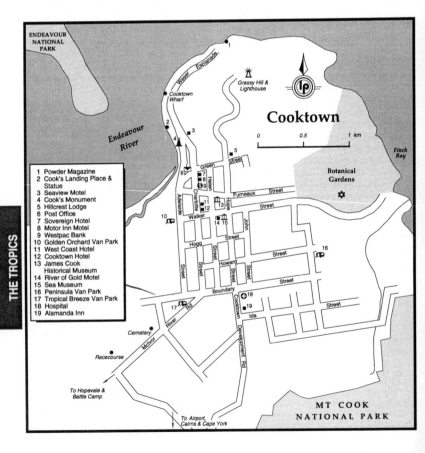

1 Powder Magazine
2 Cook's Landing Place & Statue
3 Seaview Motel
4 Cook's Monument
5 Hillcrest Lodge
6 Post Office
7 Sovereign Hotel
8 Motor Inn Motel
9 Westpac Bank
10 Golden Orchard Van Park
11 West Coast Hotel
12 Cooktown Hotel
13 James Cook Historical Museum
14 River of Gold Motel
15 Sea Museum
16 Peninsula Van Park
17 Tropical Breeze Van Park
18 Hospital
19 Alamanda Inn

Things to See & Do The **waterfront**, which in the past saw so much action, is a pleasant place to wander. At the north end you can check the **old powder magazine** from the days when there was a lot of mining going on, or cast a line from one of the best fishing spots on the coast. Further south you can look over the river to the north bank and the **Endeavour River National Park**, at a scene that has not changed since Cook repaired his stricken ship there.

A number of **monuments** dot the little park that borders the river, not only from Cook's day, but also from more recent times. In 1889, when Russia was considered a threat, one lone 1803 vintage cannon was installed to defend Cooktown.

The **James Cook Historical Museum** (☎ (070) 69 5386), on the corner of Helen and Furneaux Sts, should not be missed. It portrays much of the life and times of the early days and has some award-winning displays. The museum is open seven days a week from 10 am to 4 pm.

The **Cooktown Sea Museum** (☎ (070) 69 5209), Walker St, has interesting displays of the nautical history of Cooktown and Cape York.

The **Lighthouse** on Grassy Hill, named by Cook but no longer 'grassy', gives a good view of the surrounding area.

The **Cooktown Cemetery** has a unique Chinese shrine and many interesting gravestones, including that of Mrs Watson, the 'Heroine of Lizard Island'.

Many of the **historic buildings** along the main streets are still used commercially. The Westpac Bank building was built in 1878 and is typical of gold-rush buildings – some of the timber work inside is well worth seeing. The Cooktown Hotel, once called the Commercial, was opened in 1875, while the West Coast Hotel had been built a year earlier. The shire offices were erected in 1877 and the post office in 1897. There are many other buildings of historic significance, and just walking around this town is a worthwhile experience.

If you get sick of the historic trail, you can always head for one of the beaches. **Finch** Bay, less than two km east of the post office, is a popular spot for a dip or a barbecue. **Walker Bay** and **Archer Point**, further south, offer an unspoilt coastline.

The big month to be in Cooktown is June. The Cooktown Discovery Festival is held over the Queen's Birthday weekend, and highlights of the three-day event include a re-enactment of Cook's landing in 1770, along with a gala ball, various sporting events, horse races and rides and a fishing competition. Contact the Cooktown Discovery Festival (☎ (070) 69 5166), PO Box 630, Cooktown, Qld 4871 for further details. There is an art show in June as well.

The local Turf Club holds two, two-day race meetings a year – in June and August. These are popular events for the locals and the town is crowded with people from the stations as far away as Weipa for the sport and the socialising.

Cooktown to Musgrave (275 km)

Once you leave Cooktown you head into the most isolated part of the trip. It is 275 km to Musgrave without any fuel stops along the way. For those doing it the hard way – walking or pedalling – the distances between water, especially towards the end of the Dry, can be a fair way and other travellers few and far between. You must be prepared to carry enough water to get between the permanent water points.

Head out of town along the McIvor River Rd, past the cemetery, racecourse and airport before crossing the **Endeavour River**. The Endeavour Falls Tourist Park is 33 km from Cooktown and offers camping and a kiosk for basic supplies.

There is a junction at the 36-km mark. Right leads to the **Hopevale Aboriginal Community**. The Hopevale Show & Rodeo is staged in July or August each year. The community also has artefacts for sale. For full details, contact the Administration Clerk (☎ (070) 60 9185), Hopevale Aboriginal Community Council, Thiele St, Hopevale.

Back at the junction that took you to Hopevale, head west. About five km further

Lizard Island

Lizard Island is one of the better known islands of the Great Barrier Reef and it is readily accessible by air or boat from Cairns.

Named by Captain James Cook in 1770 after the big goannas that still roam the island, this speck of rock in a turquoise sea is home for a marine research centre and an up-market tourist lodge. All but 60 of the island's 1070 hectares is national park and as such is open to anyone who takes the time and effort to travel there. The waters around it are part of the Great Barrier Reef Marine Park.

Most people heading out to Lizard Island are day-trippers on organised tours, or guests staying at the lodge for longer. Don't expect any help from the lodge staff – campers don't rate too highly with them. They might be driving in a similar direction to you but you'll be walking, while the lodge guests get the seats.

Things to See & Do Don't go without taking some snorkelling gear. The waters off Mrs Watson's Beach are alive with coral and fish, as are all the bays and headlands of this island. Spear fishing is not allowed so the fish are friendly and the snorkelling is safe. Line fishing is allowed except for the area around the Blue Lagoon.

There are any number of walks to enjoy. Don't miss the walk up to Cook's Look, the highest point on the island. This is where James Cook spied his escape from the maze of reefs that surrounded the *Endeavour*.

The remains of Mrs Watson's cottage are at the opposite end of the beach to the camping ground. This remarkable woman lived here in 1881. When her husband was away fishing for bêche-de-mer, she was attacked by Aborigines and her Chinese servant was killed. Fearing more attacks, she collected some provisions and her diary, then alone with her young child and a wounded servant cast herself adrift in a large boiling-down pot. They drifted north-west at the whim of the currents, finally succumbing on one of the islands near Cape Melville. The last entry in her diary was dated 11 October 1881, a poignant '...nearly dead with thirst'. Her grave, and that of her child, is still well maintained in the Cooktown cemetery.

Accommodation If you have a pocket of money, you can book and stay in the Lizard Island Lodge (☎ (070) 60 3999). This up-market resort is one of the most exclusive and expensive on the reef. Dive trips, fishing, game fishing, sailing and boating are available.

Camping You can camp on the island at the very pleasant designated camping area just behind Mrs Watson's Beach. There are pit toilets, tables and water from a spring. Campers must be self-sufficient, and because fuel stoves are not allowed aboard the aircraft, you must rely on driftwood for a fire or eat everything cold. You require a permit from the QNP&WS, so you need to plan ahead before you go. Permits are available from the national park office (☎ (070) 52 3096), 10-12 McLeod St, PO Box 2066, Cairns, Qld 4871.

Getting There & Away Most people fly to the island, with the only scheduled flight at present being run by Sunstate Airlines (☎ (070) 13 13 13) from Cairns. A return air fare is $286. Charters can be organised through air charter services such as Hinterland Aviation (☎ (070) 35 9323) or Endeavour Air Service (☎ (070) 69 5860).

For those with a short amount of time, regular day trips are available from Cairns with Aussie Airways (☎ (070) 53 3980, fax 53 6315), PO Box 100, Manunda, Cairns, Qld 4871, or from the Bloomfield Beach camping ground (☎ (070) 60 8207, fax 60 8187). ∎

on is a stony river crossing and just downstream is **Isabella Falls**. This is a magic spot; it's worth a stop and even a swim!

Keep left at the next junction 2.5 km up the road. From here the road begins to climb the range and patches of rainforest begin.

The **Normanby River** is crossed 63 km from Cooktown. Early in the Dry this river will have water in it, but by the end of the season it is just a sandy bed. There are pools up and down stream. Keep on the main track heading west across flat country, and 20 km from the river crossing you will pass the turn-off to **Battle Camp Station**. The

One of the many beaches on Lizard Island (TW)

mountains to the south are the rugged Battle Camp Range. Less than three km further on you enter **Lakefield National Park**.

There is a large number of camping sites spread along the rivers and billabongs of the park. You will often see tracks leading to these as you travel along the main track. If you want to camp here, you'll need to get a permit. The ranger will let you know the best spot to camp. The ranger station is at New Laura Homestead, 51 km from the park boundary. For more information, see Camping in the boxed story on Lakefield National Park.

The **Laura River** is crossed 25 km from the park boundary (112 km from Cooktown). This crossing can be a little hairy early in the Dry, but by the end of the season it is generally no problem. The **Old Laura Homestead** on the far bank is worth a good look around. Pioneers lived here and in places like this right through the Cape, and after they had built such a place they thought they were on easy street. Most of us couldn't handle this

sort of luxury for too long before we'd be running back to modern civilisation!

Just past the homestead and within a km of the river crossing, you reach a T-junction. Turning left here will take you south to Laura, 28 km away. This is the nearest place for fuel and supplies if you have decided to stay in the park for longer.

Laura This is a good little town in which to enjoy a beer at the pub, or make a base to explore the surrounding area and visit the Aboriginal rock-art galleries. You can also visit the Jowalbinna Bush Camp, a wilderness reserve not far from Laura. For further information, see the Organised Tours section.

The Cape York Aboriginal Dance Festival is held near Laura, on the banks of the Laura River. It brings together Aborigines from all over Cape York for three excellent days. The festival is usually held every year during the Queensland September school holidays, although timing does vary from year to year.

Lakefield National Park

Lakefield National Park is the second-largest national park in Queensland and covers over 537,000 hectares. It encompasses a wide variety of country around the flood plains of the Normanby, Kennedy, Bizant, Morehead and Hann rivers.

During the wet season these rivers flood the plains, at times forming a mini inland sea. Access during this time is limited or nonexistent. As the dry season begins, the rivers gradually retreat to form a chain of deep waterholes and billabongs. Along these rivers, rainforest patches are in stark contrast to the surrounding grass plains and eucalypt woodland.

Flora & Fauna In the north of the park, around Princess Charlotte Bay, mud flats and mangroves line the coast and the estuaries of the rivers. It might be an area that is full of sandflies, mosquitoes and crocodiles, but this area is the nursery for the rich fish and marine life for which the area is so well known.

As the Dry progresses, the bird life begins to congregate around the permanent waters, and at times thousands of ducks and geese create an unholy noise but a spectacular sight. Groups of brolgas dance on the open plain, and tall stately jabirus stalk their way through the grass. Birds of prey soar on the thermals looking for a meal, while in the deepest, darkest patches of the rainforest, pheasant coucals and Torres Strait pigeons can be found. In all, over 180 species of birds have been identified in the park. At times like these, a small pair of binoculars come in handy.

Agile wallabies are probably the most commonly seen mammal in the park, but feral pigs are prevalent and a problem for the park staff. Bats make up the largest group of mammals found here. The large flying foxes are an impressive sight as they burst from their roosting spots in their thousands every evening search for nectar and fruit. You won't forget the sight, the smell, or the damage they can do to the trees in which they roost.

Crocodiles Both the freshwater and saltwater (estuarine) crocodile are found in this park. Lakefield National Park is one of five areas in the state designated as important for the ongoing conservation of the estuarine crocodile in Queensland, and for many people it offers the best chance of seeing one of these animals in the wild.

Fishing Lakefield National Park is one of the few parks in Queensland where you are allowed to fish, and the barramundi is the prize catch. A closed season applies between 1 November and 31 January, and at other times there's a bag limit of two fish per day, with no more than five fish to be taken out of the park. Line fishing is the only method allowed to catch these magnificent fish.

Canoeing & Boating Many of the big waterholes make for excellent canoeing or boating, and you can spend many enjoyable hours paddling a quiet stretch of water, watching birds or the animals as they come down to drink.

Camping Camping is allowed in a number of places, with a permit. A camping fee is payable for each night spent in the park, with a maximum of 21 nights allowed. Permits are available from the rangers at New Laura (☎ (070) 60 3260) or Lakefield (☎ (070) 60 3271). Bookings may be made six to 12 weeks in advance by writing to the ranger, Lakefield National Park, PMB 29, Cairns Mail Centre, Qld 4870. Say what you are interested in and the vehicle you have, and the ranger will let you know the best spots to camp. If you have the time, try a couple of different locations. ∎

Currently, festival times are irregular, but from 1995 it may be held every two years. Contact the Ang-Gnarra Aboriginal Corporation for up-to-date information on festival dates and activities (see the Information section).

The Laura horse races and rodeo are held from Friday to Sunday on the first weekend in July. It is a great weekend where the locals from the surrounding stations show their skills and let down their hair. It has become a tradition on the Cape with people coming from far afield.

Laura to Musgrave To continue to Musgrave and deeper into the Lakefield

National Park, turn right at the T-junction where you turned left to go to Laura. The **ranger station** at New Laura Homestead is 25 km north of the junction.

Heading north from here, you pass across vast grass plains, bordered by trees that line the rivers. Termite hills tower above the gold of drying grass and occasionally you'll see a shy wallaby skip across the road, or the occasional mob of wild pigs. The track can be deep in dust, and walkers and cyclists will find the sun unrelenting. After travelling 33 km, you pass the ranger station at **Lakefield Homestead**.

The turn-off to **Bizant**, occasionally a ranger station, is 15 km past the Lakefield ranger station, with yet another turn-off 10 km further on.

Just a few hundred metres past this track junction is the **Hann crossing** of the North Kennedy River. For travellers passing through the national park, this is by far the best place to stop.

Just downstream from the crossing there are a couple of waterfalls that drop into a large pool. The river is tidal to the base of the falls and we wouldn't advise swimming here. If you want to see how many crocodiles can inhabit a small stretch of water, take a spotlight down and check the pool one night. Count the eyes and divide by two!

There is some excellent camping upstream from the crossing. The sites are numbered and at times the place is booked out. It's safe to swim or paddle in the shallows here and the kids will love it. There are turtles in some of the pools that like a feed of bread.

The crossing itself demands a little care as it has potholes and is rough. Generally it doesn't cause any difficulty.

The **Morehead River** is crossed 13 km from the Hann crossing and is normally an easy crossing. The turn-off to **Low Lake**, a spectacular bird habitat, especially at the end of the Dry, is found 15 km further on. Continue straight ahead, and in less than two km you will come to the **Saltwater Creek** crossing. The crossing is sandy, but is generally no problem in a 4WD. You can camp around

here, but it isn't as good as the Hann crossing.

The road swings south-west as it begins to head towards Musgrave. Keep left at the next few track junctions, as the tracks on the right lead to Marina Plains Station. You leave the national park 16 km west of Saltwater Creek.

Stick to the main track heading westward and 34 km later you will hit the Peninsula Developmental Road, opposite **Musgrave**. Here you can get fuel, food and accommodation.

Musgrave Direct to Cairns (440 km)

This route along the Peninsula Developmental Road is covered in the later Cape York section. While the road is more highly maintained than the tracks you've been on, it is often very corrugated and stony – you'll even wish you were back on a dirt track at times!

ALTERNATIVE ROUTES

From Cairns there are a number of ways to get to historic Cooktown. The main route sweeps inland away from the coast and mountains, while the most scenic is the coast route. The Creb Track requires permission to cross private land at the southern end of the track.

Cairns to Cooktown via the Inland Route (322 km)

The route from Cairns to Lakeland is detailed in the Cape York section. Once you reach the small hamlet of **Lakeland**, you can either turn west towards the Cape, or you can continue onwards to Cooktown. From Lakeland, at the junction of the Peninsula Developmental Road and Cooktown Road, it is a corrugated and stony trip for most of the 82 km to Cooktown.

By the time you reach the **Annan River crossing** you are looking for a change and the river provides it. You can camp here, but it is close to the road. Walking downstream a short distance, you will come to an impressive narrow gorge and waterfall that really roars when it is in flood. It's worth a look at any time.

THE TROPICS

Quinkan Art

Quinkan art, as it is called, is one of the great art styles of northern Australia. Vastly different to the X-ray art of Arnhem Land in the Northern Territory, or the Wandjina art of the Kimberley in Western Australia, Quinkan art gets its name from the human-shaped, spirit figures with unusually shaped heads, called Quinkans.

Much study on the sites has been done since 1960 by Percy Trezise, an amateur archaeologist. Over 1200 galleries have been discovered. All of these are around the settlement of Laura, in the escarpment country that surrounds the lowlands along the great rivers of Lakefield National Park.

This great body of art is testimony to the Aborigines who once lived here. When the Palmer River gold rush began in 1873, the Aborigines fought to defend their land against the new invaders. Those who survived the bullets succumbed to disease, and the few remaining Aborigines became fringe dwellers on the outskirts of towns and missions.

The rock-art galleries contain many fine paintings of kangaroos, wallabies, emus, brolgas, jabirus, crocodiles, snakes and flying foxes – in fact, all the wildlife still seen along the rivers and plains.

Spiritual figures and ancestral beings also point to a lifestyle that was rich in culture and religious beliefs. Amongst the paintings there are 'good' and 'bad' spiritual figures, the 'good' being heroes of old and the figures depicting fertility and ritual increase, while the 'bad' were depicted by spirit figures such as Quinkans.

Other paintings depict tools such as boomerangs and axes, while in some galleries stencils of hands and implements can also be seen. Rock engravings are also found in small numbers, and in a couple of galleries there is evidence of the European invasion with images of horses.

Only the Split Rock and Guguyalangi galleries are open to the public. South of Laura and close to the main road, they are readily accessible, with a walking track joining the two.

There are a number of overhangs in the Split Rock group of galleries, and while Split Rock itself is the most visually stunning, within a hundred metres there are smaller galleries containing flying foxes, tall Quinkans and hand stencils.

The Guguyalangi group consists of over a dozen overhangs that are adorned with a vast array of figures, animals and implements and are possibly the best of the lot.

A walking trail leads from the carpark at Split Rock, past the galleries in this group and then up onto the plateau and to a lookout at Turtle Rock. The view from here is stunning. From this point the trail wanders through the open forest of the plateau for one km to the Guguyalangi group of galleries. The views here are, once again, spectacular. If you are going to do this walk, save it for the late afternoon or early morning as it can get quite warm wandering across the plateau at midday. Take some water and food and enjoy the art and solitude of this place.

The Giant Horse galleries, across the road from the Split Rock and Guguyalangi sites, are a little harder to see and consist of five shelters depicting many animals, including a number of horses. These galleries can only be visited with a guide from the local community, and pre-arrangement with the ranger is essential.

Percy Trezise and his sons, Steve and Matt, have established a wilderness reserve at Jowalbinna. The Jowalbinna Bush Camp is open to travellers and Steve runs the Trezise Bush Guide Service, specialising in guided walking trips to the many magnificent galleries in the nearby area.

The Magnificent Gallery, deep in the ranges behind Jowalbinna Bush Camp, stands out from the rest. Along a rock shelter, 50 metres or more in length, there is a profusion of colour, life and movement. Animals of all descriptions and sizes, along with spirit figures and Quinkans, adorn each and every available spot.

For more information on the Quinkan art around Laura, contact the Ang-Gnarra Aboriginal Corporation on ☎ (070) 60 3214 or fax 60 3231. Maps, brochures and information for self-guided walks around the art sites are obtainable from the ranger station, which is beside the caravan park.

It may also be possible to organise a tour of the art sites with a ranger, providing one is available. There is a ranger station, which is usually staffed, at the Split Rock Gallery carpark. Although there is no fee to visit the art sites, visitors are requested to make a donation of $3 per adult.

If you want to join Steve Trezise at Jowalbinna, ring ☎ (070) 60 3236. Alternatively, contact the Trezise Bush Guide Service (see the Organised Tours section). ∎

Hann Crossing, a popular camping spot (R & VM)

The turn-off to **Helenvale** and the famous Lion's Den Hotel is 55 km north of Lakeland, and this short detour is well worth the effort. It is just 32 km from Helenvale to Cooktown and the road is bumpy most of the way.

Cairns to Cooktown via the Creb Track (256 km)

The Creb Track is maintained by the state electricity authority and you require permission from the landowner at the southern end of the route to travel it. While it may be the shortest distance between Cairns and Cooktown, it is also the hardest and the slowest.

From the village of **Daintree**, 110 km north of Cairns, you follow the Upper Daintree Road for 17 km to near its end. Pass through a gate on your right and you will soon reach the headwaters of the **Daintree River**, which is easily forded in the Dry.

For the next 55 km the route is spectacular, taking you over high mountains and across many picturesque creeks. For most of the way, you pass through rich and varied rainforest before coming out on the north side of the **Wujal Wujal Aboriginal Community**. From here it is 74 km via Helenvale and the Lion's Den Hotel to Cooktown. The track is treacherous and impassable after rain.

ACTIVITIES

Along the coast, swimming and lazing on the beaches is the way to go. During the summer months, box jellyfish can be a danger. There are enclosures on some of the beaches for protection from these marine 'stingers'. Always seek local advice before plunging in for a cooling dip.

Snorkelling is also pleasant, but the water close to shore can be dirty from recent rain. The offshore reefs and islands are better if you have a boat or join an organised trip.

Many of the local resorts organise all sorts of activities, and you don't always have to be a guest. See the later Facilities section.

Cape Tribulation

At Cape Tribulation, beach walking and exploring the adjoining rainforest are enjoyable ways to spend a couple of days.

Cooktown

The Cooktown Sport & Gamefishing Club (☎ (070) 69 5415) runs a number of fishing tournaments between October and December each year. With barramundi and mangrove jack in the rivers and everything up to marlin in the offshore waters, the fishing and the catches can be pretty spectacular.

There is some excellent fishing in and around Cooktown and the nearby Great Barrier Reef. While there are numerous charter boats available in Cooktown, you can also hire yourself a boat from the Hire Shop (☎ (070) 69 5601), Charlotte St.

Visitors are welcome to join the Cooktown Bushwalkers (☎ (070) 69 5108, after hours ☎ 69 5131) on their walk on Sunday through Cooktown, taking in the flora, fauna, historical sites and unusual geological features. The group also conducts organised one to three-day walks further afield. For further information write to PO Box 195, Cooktown, Qld 4871.

Lakefield National Park

Lakefield National Park is magnificent for camping, fishing and bird-watching. See the boxed story on Lakefield National Park for further information.

Laura

The small township of Laura is a good base to explore the local area, including Lakefield National Park. There are a number of Aboriginal rock-art galleries in the area that can be visited. At the most popular, Split Rock Gallery, there is a walking trail up onto the escarpment and across the plateau to the Guguyalangi group of galleries. For more details, see the following section, as well as the boxed story on Quinkan Art.

ORGANISED TOURS

There are a host of tour operators who specialise in Cape Tribulation, Cooktown and Laura. Contact the Far North Queensland Coach & Off Road Association (FNQCORA, ☎ (070) 31 4565), or the Far North Queensland Promotion Bureau in Cairns, for full details.

Cape Tribulation

Land Companies that specialise in tours to Cape Tribulation include:

Deanes Country Tours
    PO Box 170, Smithfield, Cairns, Qld 4878 (☎ (070) 38 1404, fax 38 1556)
Bloomfield Track 4WD Safaris
    49 Macrossan St, Port Douglas, Qld 4871 (☎ (070) 99 5665)
Kangoala
    Coconut Beach Resort, PO Box 7457, Cairns, Qld 4870 (☎ (070) 52 1311, fax 51 6432)
Strikie's Safaris
    27 Macrossan St, Port Douglas, Qld 4871 (☎ (070) 99 5599, fax 99 5070)
Tropics Explorer
    PO Box 549, Cairns, Qld 4870 (☎ & fax (070) 31 2367)
Cape Tribulation Guided Rainforest Walks
    Cape Tribulation Rd, Cape Tribulation (☎ (070) 98 0070). Also offers a tourist information service
Jungle Tours
    71 Morehead St, Cairns, Qld 4870 (☎ (070) 35 4650, fax 35 4316). Specialises in walking treks, bushwalking, sea kayaking and mountain biking

Air You can visit Cape Tribulation by air as part of a tour. Hinterland Aviation (☎ (070) 35 9323, fax 35 9458), based at Cairns airport, runs a Cow Bay Reef & Rainforest trip.

Cooktown

Land Cairns-based operators include the following:

Kamp-Out Safaris
    PO Box 1894, Cairns, Qld 4870 (☎ (070) 31 4862, fax 31 1017). Safari tours to Cape Tribulation and Cooktown from December to May. During the Dry, extended wilderness adventures to the Cape
New Look Adventures
    PO Box 7505, Cairns, Qld 4870 (☎ (070) 51 7934, fax 51 2252)

Wild Track Adventure Safaris
    PO Box 2397, Cairns, Qld 4870 (☎ (070) 31 4565, fax 58 1930). One, two and three-day safaris to Daintree, Cooktown and Laura

You can also join one of the local operators in Cooktown:

Cooktown Tours
    Fisherman's Wharf, Cooktown
    (☎ (070) 69 5173). Local bus tours
Cooktown Lodge & Backpackers
    Cnr Charlotte & Boundary Sts, Cooktown
    (☎ (070) 69 5166). Tours around Cooktown, as well as 4WD tours to Laura, Cape Tribulation and Laura

Boat There are a number of boat trips out of Cooktown, some specialising in fishing, others in diving, some in both.

MV *Trudena* is a 45-foot charter boat operated by Jim Fairbairn (☎ (070) 69 5546). There are day cruises to the adjacent reefs for fishing and snorkelling, three-day charter trips to Lizard Island and the nearby reef, or six-day charters to Princess Charlotte Bay and surrounding coast and islands. Write to PO Box 464, Cooktown, Qld 4871.

MV *Reef Safari* (☎ (070) 69 5605 in Cooktown, ☎ (070) 55 1100 in Cairns, fax 55 1889) runs seven-day fishing safaris aboard the 54-foot boat. It departs from Cooktown or Lizard Island for Princess Charlotte Bay and the Great Barrier Reef. Write to PO Box 2086, Cairns, Qld 4870.

The *Coral Vista* (☎ (070) 69 5519) is available for half-day fishing charters from Fisherman's Wharf, Cooktown.

You can also explore and cruise the Endeavour River. For bookings with Cooktown River Cruises, contact Cook's Landing Kiosk (☎ (070) 69 5101), Webber Esplanade, Cooktown. Endeavour River Cruises also depart from Cook's Landing Kiosk. Contact Cooktown Cruises (☎ (070) 69 5712) for bookings and details.

Air Several companies operate in the Cooktown area:

Endeavour Air
    Charlotte St, Cooktown (☎ (070) 69 5860). Charter and scenic flights
Aussie Airways
    PO Box 100, Manunda, Qld 4870 (☎ (070) 53 3980, fax 53 6315). Operates a one-day Cooktown Heritage tour
Hinterland Aviation
    Cairns airport (☎ (070) 35 9323, fax 35 9458). Runs a one-day Cooktown Heritage tour

Hopevale Aboriginal Community
Munbah Cultural Tours (☎ (070) 60 9173), Post Office, Hopevale, Qld 4871, is operated by the local Aboriginal community. The programme costs $80 per person per day. Visitors are shown many aspects of traditional life and enjoy a river cruise or bushwalking. Accommodation is provided in bush-timber huts which are on the beach front, and all meals are included in the tour. Pick-up from Cooktown can be arranged. Photography is permitted on the tour.

Laura
The Ang-Gnarra Aboriginal Corporation (see the Information section) has a ranger service based beside the caravan park on the main north-south road. If the ranger is available, a guided tour of the rock-art galleries may be arranged.

Trezise Bush Guide Service (☎ (070) 60 3236) is based at Jowalbinna, just outside Laura, and specialises in one to four-day trips to some of the magnificent rock-art sites in the area, as well as Daintree, Lakefield National Park and the Deighton River Valley. You can even camp on the property at the bush camp beside the peaceful headwaters of the Little Laura River, but to do so you must use the guide service.

The guide service is $50 per adult per day, or $100 per family. A camping fee of $5 per adult per night applies, and accommodation and meals can also be organised. A 4WD is essential to reach Jowalbinna and maps are available in Laura. Visitors can also fly into Jowalbinna airstrip and stay for a day or overnight.

For more information, phone Jowalbinna

THE TROPICS

The Annan River Falls in flood (R & VM)

or the Cairns office (☎ (070) 55 1865, fax 31 2016), or write to PO Box 106, Freshwater, Cairns, Qld 4870.

FACILITIES
North of the Daintree River Ferry
Accommodation & Food From the crossing of the Daintree River to Cape Tribulation there are a number of places tucked away in the surrounding forest and/or close to the beach that make for a pleasant overnight stop.

At Cow Bay, the *Cow Bay Hotel* (☎ (070) 98 9011) has air-conditioned motel units and a licensed bistro. A single/double unit costs $55/60, including breakfast. *The Rainforest Retreat* (☎ (070) 98 9101) has a range of accommodation and barbecue areas. Self-contained units cost $40/60. Shared accommodation in four- and six-bed units with bathroom and linen costs $15 per person. The bunkhouse sleeps 20 with a shared bathroom and costs $13 per person, with linen provided. Although there are no cooking facilities in the dorm or bunkhouse, visitors are welcome to use the dining room kitchen.

Lync-Haven Rainforest Retreat (☎ (070) 98 9155) is 16 km north of the ferry in 16 hectares of rainforest. There are self-contained cabins which sleep eight for $60 a double, $10 for each extra adult and $7.50 per child. Accommodation in on-site caravans is $35 a double with linen, and if you have your own caravan, a powered site is $12 a double. There is also a camping area with unpowered/powered sites for $8.50/12 per person. There is a licensed restaurant as well as takeaway meals.

The Daintree Wilderness Lodge (☎ (070) 98 9105) has individual bungalows nestled in the rainforest with all amenities. Costs range from $75/98 a single/double to $148 for four people, and the price includes breakfast. A dining room is open for lunch or dinner.

Thornton Beach Kiosk (☎ (070) 98 9118) is on the beach at Thornton, 20 km north of the Daintree River ferry. Good budget-priced meals and refreshments are available from the beach-front bar and cafe.

Fuel Fuel is only available south of Thornton, at the Cow Bay service station (☎ (070) 98 9127), Buchanan Rd, Cape Tribulation.

Cape Tribulation
Accommodation & Food The wide choice of accommodation at Cape Tribulation suits all budgets.

Coconut Beach Rainforest Resort (☎ (070) 98 0033), with beach frontage, has up-market units, a store, restaurant and bar. Accommodation prices range from $180 to $250 for the luxury villas. Breakfast is included in the price. Activities include 4WD safaris, horse riding, mountain-bike hire, scenic flights, guided rainforest walks, fishing and tours to the reef.

Ferntree Rainforest Resort (☎ (070) 31 7793) and the *Jungle Lodge* (☎ (070) 98 0086)

THE TROPICS

are both just five minutes from Cape Tribulation and Myall beaches. Accommodation in the resort is available in suites at $80/95 or villas at $140/170 a single/double. The lodge offers a variety of accommodation. Cabins are $30/60, self-contained six-shares are $18 per person and a bed in a 10-bed dorm is $16 per person. There is a communal cooking hut, bar and restaurant at both the resort and lodge. Daily tours and activities include guided rainforest walks, horse riding, paddle trekking, sea kayaking and reef trips. There are also mountain bikes for hire.

PK's Jungle Village (☎ (070) 98 0040) is on the beach and has a bar and restaurant. Bungalows with shared amenities are $44 a double, while the dorm beds are $14 a single, which includes linen, shared amenities and a communal kitchen. Camping is $7 per person for an unpowered site. There are reef trips, diving, paddle treks, jungle walks and horse riding available.

Fuel & Supplies The *Masons Store* (☎ (070) 98 0070) at Cape Tribulation has the normal general store items, food supplies, takeaway meals and alcohol. Diesel, unleaded and super fuel is also available.

Bloomfield River to Helenvale
Accommodation & Food Once north of Cape Tribulation, there is no accommodation until the Bloomfield River.

The Bloomfield Wilderness Lodge (☎ (070) 35 9166, fax (070) 35 9180) is set back from the beach on Weary Bay and is surrounded by the Cape Tribulation National Park. This remote resort is only accessible from the sea, and the tariff includes scenic air transfer, all meals, and accommodation in luxury suites. The lodge offers river cruises, guided rainforest walks, local fishing, reef trips and 4WD safaris. Packages start at $885/1500 a single/double for three nights up to $1785/2860 for seven nights.

Cattle farm, outback Queensland (MA)

THE TROPICS

Bloomfield Beach Camping (☎ (070) 60 8207, fax 60 8187), 20 Bloomfield Rd, Ayton, is 11.2 km north of the Bloomfield River crossing, on the Cooktown side, with nine km of beach front. Grassed areas with plenty of trees make this a very pleasant park. There is a bar and restaurant and all meals, including morning and afternoon tea, are served. All the normal amenities are provided, and camping costs $6/8 a single for an unpowered/powered site. Pets are allowed, under control. Accommodation in on-site tents and newly completed cabins is also available. Reef trips, river cruises, scenic flights and bushwalks can be arranged; they offer day flights to Lizard Island and take campers to Hope Island, by boat.

Home Rule Rainforest Lodge (☎ (070) 60 3925, fax 60 3902) is just south of Helenvale at Rossville. The lodge has a dining room (dinners average $10), games room, licensed restaurant, general store and fuel (super, unleaded and diesel). Cabin-style accommodation costs $12 a single, including bed linen, and there is a communal kitchen and laundry facilities. Camping on the river bank, with all amenities, is $6 and children are $3. Activities include horse riding, bushwalking, a nine-hole golf course, river rafting, fishing and access to Cedar Bay National Park.

Mungumby Lodge (☎ & fax (070) 60 3972) is a short distance from Helenvale. Comfortable cabins with bathrooms are $119 a double per night; for five nights the cost is $99 per night. A child costs an extra $13 a night. All meals are available. Activities include swimming, horse riding and bushwalking. Day tours on foot and by 4WD, with an experienced nature guide, can also be arranged to surrounding areas, even as far as Laura.

The *Lion's Den Hotel* (☎ (070) 60 3911) at Helenvale has cold beer, heaps of character and characters, counter meals and accommodation at $15/20 a single/double. Breakfast, lunch and dinner are available. Camping is allowed behind the hotel beside the Annan River for just $2 per person per night, with use of the showers at the hotel.

It's a top spot to camp. For more information, see the boxed story on the Lion's Den Hotel.

Fuel & Supplies The *Bloomfield River Inn* (☎ (070) 60 8174), Bloomfield Rd, Bloomfield, has motor oils, unleaded, super and diesel fuel, as well as takeaway food, drinks and limited grocery supplies. The *Ayton Store* (☎ (070) 60 8125), West St, Ayton, also has supplies. The *Home Rule Rainforest Lodge* at Rossville has a general store for supplies and super, unleaded and diesel fuel. The *Lion's Den Hotel* sells basic food items such as meat, milk and bread, and has super fuel.

Cooktown

Accommodation Cooktown has a wide range of places to stay.

The *Golden Orchid Van Park* (☎ (070) 69 5641), at the corner of Charlotte and Walker Sts, has sites for $5 per person per night. The *Peninsula Van Park* (☎ (070) 69 5107), Howard St, is set amongst large shady trees and is a very pleasant place to stop. A range of accommodation with the usual facilities is available, plus barbecue areas. Pets are allowed, under supervision. Self-contained units, including linen, cost $40 a double; on-site vans cost $25 a double; the bunkhouse costs $25 a double, including linen; unpowered/powered camp sites cost $5/7 per person per night to $60 a double per week.

Tropical Breeze Caravan Park & Holiday Units (☎ (070) 69 5417), McIvor Rd, has all facilities as well as a fully stocked kiosk. Pets are not allowed. Accommodation in self-contained units ranges from $49 to $54 a double with reduced weekly rates; overnight vans cost $29 a double; while an unpowered/powered camp site is $10.50/13 a double. There are reduced prices for children aged from five to 15.

The *Cooktown Hotel* (☎ (070) 69 5308), the *Sovereign Hotel* (☎ (070) 69 5400) and the *West Coast Hotel* (☎ (070) 69 5350) are all on Charlotte St, the main street of Cooktown. All provide a wide choice of accommodation. Prices for the Cooktown are $15/25 a single/double, while the West

Coast has singles for $15. The Sovereign Hotel has a wider choice, from budget rooms to luxury apartments; prices range from $31 to $103 a single.

Motels include the *River of Gold Motel* (☎ (070) 69 5222), at the corner of Hope and Walker Sts, and the *Seaview Motel* (☎ (070) 69 5377) in Charlotte St. Prices vary from $45/65 a single/double. At the *Cooktown Motor Inn Motel* (☎ (070) 69 5357), Charlotte St, prices range from $20/35, breakfast included. It is also the agent for the Coral Coaches bus service from Cairns to Cooktown.

The Cooktown Lodge & Backpackers (☎ (070) 69 5166), at the corner of Charlotte and Boundary Sts, PO Box 501, offers a range of accommodation, with the best of shared facilities and linen included in the prices. A single room costs $20, while the dormitory is $13 for the first night and $12 thereafter. The lodge also runs organised trips.

The *Alamanda Inn* (☎ (070) 69 5203), Hope St, offers nice clean units for $30/38. Rooms are also available in the inn and the house for $30 a double and $22 a single respectively. The *Hillcrest Guest House* in the same street offers accommodation for $18/35.

The *Endeavour Falls Tourist Park* (☎ & fax (070) 69 5431), PO Box 242, Cooktown, Qld 4871, is 33 km north-west of Cooktown, on the McIvor Rd, towards Battle Camp and Lakefield. This picturesque park sits on the banks of the north branch of the Endeavour River and has all amenities, including fuel, a kiosk, takeaway food and barbecues, to name just a few. Pets are permitted on application. Unpowered/powered camp sites are $9/11 double, plus $2.50/3 per extra adult, with concessions for children. Self-contained holiday units cost $50 a double and $8 per extra person. Swimming and bushwalking are pleasant activities around here.

Fuel & Supplies In Cooktown you will find a butcher, bakery, chemist, dentist and a couple of supermarkets. Foodstore (☎ (070)

69 5569), Helen St, is open seven days a week and has EFTPOS and accepts major credit cards. There are also fruit shops, milk bars and takeaway shops. All are centred around Charlotte St.

Fuel is available from a number of outlets including Cape York Tyres (☎ (070) 69 5274), Charlotte St, and the Ampol Service Station (☎ (070) 69 5354), Hope St. The Ampol Service Station also has LPG, but remember, it is not available beyond Cooktown.

Post Office & Money The post office offers full postal services and keycard facilities are available at the Commonwealth Bank agency. There is also a Westpac Bank in Charlotte St with full banking facilities.

Airstrip There is a public aerodrome at Cooktown (☎ (070) 69 5360), which is used regularly by commercial airlines such as Flight West. Aviation fuel can be arranged.

Hopevale

The Hopevale Aboriginal Community has a number of shops including a hardware, butcher and a general store selling a variety of goods, including Aboriginal artefacts. Fuel (super, unleaded and diesel) is available at the service station. For further information, contact the Administration Clerk (☎ (070) 60 9185), Hopevale Community Council.

Laura

Accommodation & Food Apart from camping near the Laura River, you really only have a choice of staying at the pub or in the caravan park.

The *Quinkan Hotel* (☎ (070) 60 3255) is in the main street and has accommodation in twin rooms for $40 a single, including breakfast. You can also camp; an unpowered site is $5 a single, plus an extra $3 for power, with use of shower facilities. You can also have a meal and a cool beer under the mango trees.

The *Ang-Gnarra Aboriginal Corporation Caravan Park* (☎ (070) 60 3214, fax 60 3231), on the main north-south road, has most amenities including barbecues and campfire areas, hot showers and laundry facilities. Pets are allowed, under control. Only unpowered sites are available at present, costing $3 a single. The cafe across the street can supply meals and refreshments.

Fuel & Supplies All the supplies a traveller needs, including frozen and tinned food and all fuels, are available at the Laura Store (☎ (070) 60 3238) beside the pub. There is a post office at the store as well.

Airstrip There is a small airstrip just outside town. Aviation fuel can be organised through the Laura Store, but you'll need to give notice beforehand.

Musgrave
There is only one main building in Musgrave – the telegraph station built in 1887. It has very limited supplies, as well as souvenirs, fuel (super, unleaded and diesel), takeaway food, sit-down meals, cold beer and drinks.

Accommodation is available for $20/30 a single/double and breakfast can be arranged. You can also camp at Musgrave, and while there is no charge for camping, it costs $2 per person if you want to use the shower facilities.

Airstrip There is an airstrip beside the old telegraph station. If you give the people at Musgrave notice of at least one week, they can arrange a supply of aviation fuel.

ALTERNATIVE TRANSPORT
Air
Flight West Airlines (☎ (070) 35 9511, fax 35 9858) has regular scheduled flights from Cairns to Cooktown. Contact the Cairns office for bookings and flight details at PO Box 107, Cairns Mail Centre, Cairns, Qld 4870. The booking agent in Cooktown is at the Seaview Motel & Travel Centre (☎ (070) 69 5377), Charlotte St.

Saltwater crocodile (NTTC)

Cape York Air Services (☎ (070) 35 9399, fax 35 9108) calls into Laura on its Peninsula mail runs and, subject to space availability, takes passengers. For bookings and flight details, contact the office in Cairns at PMB 13, Cairns Mail Centre, Qld 4871.

Bus

Coral Coaches (☎ (070) 98 2600, fax 98 1064), 37 Front St, PO Box 367, Mossman, Qld 4873, runs a bus service six days a week (not on Monday) between Cairns and Cooktown, via Daintree and Cape Tribulation as well as via the inland route. The return fare for the inland route is $83, and the coast route is $92. For details and bookings, you can also contact the agent in Cooktown, the Cooktown Bus Service at the Cooktown Motor Inn (☎ (070) 69 5357), or the Cairns office (☎ (070) 31 7577).

Boat

Tropical Traders Pty Ltd (☎ (018) 77 2372) services the coast of Cape York carrying passengers as well as general cargo, 4WD vehicles and motorcycles. The vessel calls into Cooktown once a week. Phone for current departure times and for further information.

Vehicle Rental

There are a number of rental companies based in Cairns who have 4WD vehicles available for hire to drive to Cooktown; trying to get a vehicle any further up Cape York is definitely a problem. See the Cairns and Cape York sections for details. In Cooktown there are a couple of places where you can get a vehicle, but again you'll only be able to drive it in the surrounding area, and in some instances even as far as Laura.

Cooktown Motor Inn (☎ (070) 69 5357), and Endeavour Air (☎ (070) 69 5860), Charlotte St, Cooktown, have 4WDs available for hire, while the Hire Shop (☎ (070) 69 5601), Charlotte St, has normal vehicles for use in Cooktown.

The coastline of Cape York (R & VM)

THE TROPICS

Cape York

Cape York is one of the last great frontiers of Australia. It is a vast patchwork of tropical savannah cut by numerous rivers and streams, while along its eastern flank is the northern section of the Great Dividing Range. In amongst these ragged peaks and deep valleys are some of the best and most significant rainforests in Australia. Streams tumble down the rocky mountains to the sea, where just offshore the coral ramparts of the Great Barrier Reef stretch over thousands of sq km. The reef is protected in a marine park, and much of the land mass of the Cape is protected in a number of spectacular, rarely visited, wild, national parks.

Giving access to that vast natural wonderland is the route to the Cape. Initially the corrugated road you follow is known more officially as the Peninsula Developmental Road, but once that heads away to the mining town of Weipa, you follow the Telegraph Track to the 'Tip', and the real adventure begins.

North of the Weipa turn-off the track is definitely 4WD, and as you head further north, the creek crossings become more common and more challenging. By the time you get back from a trip to the Tip, you'll be an expert in water crossings!

From Cairns to the top of Cape York it is 952 km via the shortest and most challenging route, which is the one we'll describe in detail here. Most travellers will want to visit Cooktown, Weipa and a few other places off the main route, and those diversions will add considerably to the total distance covered.

There are a number of alternative routes. Down south you can choose between the inland route, or the coastal route via Daintree and Cape Tribulation. From Lakeland you can travel straight up the heart of the Cape or go via Cooktown and Battle Camp to Laura or Musgrave. See the earlier Cairns to Musgrave via Cooktown section for more details.

From the Archer River you can head north via Weipa and Stones Crossing, or via the Telegraph Track. Further north again you have the choice of continuing on the Telegraph Track or taking the newer bypass roads. See the later section on Alternative Routes for more details.

Vast areas of Cape York are also designated Aboriginal land, while the rest is mainly taken up with large pastoral holdings.

Covering an area totalling around 207,000 sq km, or about the same size as the state of Victoria, Cape York has a population of around 15,000 people.

The largest towns in the region are Cooktown, on the south-east coast, and Weipa, a large mining community on the central-west coast. A handful of smaller towns make up the remainder of the communities throughout the Cape.

HISTORY

Before the arrival of Europeans there were a large number of different Aboriginal tribal groups spread throughout the Cape. A unique group of people inhabited the islands dotted across the reef-strewn Torres Strait that separates mainland Australia from New Guinea. The Torres Strait Islanders came from Melanesia and Polynesia about 2000 years ago and are culturally distinct from the Aborigines. While they had a close affinity with the people further north, they influenced Aboriginal tribal groups near the top of Cape York and vice versa. The further south on the mainland, the less the influence from the north.

For the most part, the tribes of the Cape were aggressive, fighting between themselves and attacking the early European explorers. In fact, there are few accounts of early explorers that do not relate attacks by Aborigines or Islanders.

The rich Aboriginal and Torres Strait heritage is alive and well today and travellers will see much of it on their way through the Cape. Of special importance is one of the world's most significant collections of prehistoric art in the escarpment country surrounding Laura. For further information, see the boxed story on Quinkan Art in the

Frank Jardine & Somerset

John Jardine, Frank's father, was the government magistrate for the settlement of Somerset when it was established in 1863. Looking at the commercial aspects of the venture, he commissioned Frank and his younger brother Alick, both then aged in their early 20s, to overland a mob of cattle from Rockhampton to the new settlement.

That epic journey was the beginning of the Jardine legend on Cape York. It took them ten months to reach the Top, arriving at Somerset on 13 March 1865. Along the way they overcame lack of water, hostile Aborigines, flooded rivers and the maze of swamps and waterways around the headwaters of the Escape and Jardine rivers.

Later, Frank Jardine took over from his father as government magistrate. Before his arrival at Somerset and during the early part of his stay, attacks by Aborigines and Islanders on Europeans and shipwrecked crews were common. Within a few years of Jardine taking up his post, the attacks stopped. His uncompromising treatment of the Aborigines earned him the name of 'Debil Debil Jardine'.

Jardine established a couple of outstations at Bertiehaugh, Galloway and Lockerbie, where he ran cattle. From his base at Somerset he ran a fleet of pearling luggers throughout Torres Strait. Some say the family treasure came from a Spanish galleon he found wrecked on a remote reef south of New Guinea.

He married a Samoan princess called Sana, whom, the story goes, he kidnapped when she was being taken to New Guinea by missionaries.

When Jardine resigned as government magistrate, and the official government residence was moved to Thursday Island, he and Sana took over Somerset as their home. The grove of coconuts they planted, some of which are still standing today, is the most visible reminder of their time at this outpost. The family lived relatively well in this wild place, entertaining ship's captains and any visiting dignitaries, and the Jardine hospitality was legendary.

In 1886, during the building of the Overland Telegraph Line, Jardine was in charge of transporting supplies to the crew building the northernmost section of the line. During that time he explored and named the Ducie River, establishing Bertiehaugh Station on its banks some years later.

In 1890 the *Quetta* sank off the Cape, Queensland's worst shipping disaster. Jardine was responsible for saving many lives. From then on, ships passing through Albany Passage in front of Somerset would dip their flag in salute.

Frank died in 1919 and Sana in 1923. Both are buried on the foreshore at Somerset.

The Jardine story continued in this region until WW II when the family was evacuated from Somerset. Earlier, 'Chum' Jardine, the oldest son of Frank and Sana, had taken the family diaries to his new venture on the Aru Islands further west (now part of Indonesian New Guinea). In 1942 he was captured by the Japanese and beheaded for 'coast-watching'. The famous diaries and the family treasure, buried before the invasion, were lost.

During the 1920s, the Australian Museum had offered the family over £10,000 for the diaries – an incredible sum for those days. Although the journals are lost, a number of books were written from those historic pages. The most famous writer to have access to them was Ion Idriess, who wrote *The Great Trek*, *Drums of Mer* and *Head-hunters of the Coral Sea*.

What remained of the house at Somerset was burnt down in 1960, but there is still enough on the hill and down on the beach to remind people of this rich and exciting heritage. It is a great place to spend a few hours. ■

Clockwise from Frank Jardine, seated left: Archibald Richardson (the government surveyor), John Jardine Jr (too young to join the cattle drive), Alick and two of the Aboriginal team members, Barney & Eulah.

earlier Cairns to Musgrave via Cooktown section.

European history in Australia can trace its beginnings back to the early Dutch navigators who from 1606 explored much of the coastline. These included Janszoon and Tasman, and they were the first Europeans to report seeing the great south land. (It is unclear whether the Spanish navigator Torres, after whom the strait is named, actually sighted the land.) Their exploits are remembered in the names of bluffs and bays dotted down the Gulf side of the Cape.

James Cook mapped the east coast of Australia in 1770, and claimed the continent for England while on Possession Island, just off the northerly tip that he named York Cape. Over the next 100 years, other great English navigators, including Bligh, Flinders and King, mapped sections of the coast and bestowed their names upon it.

Ludwig Leichhardt was the first explorer to journey over a section of the Cape during his 1845 expedition from Brisbane to Port Essington on the Cobourg Peninsula in the Northern Territory. South of the Mitchell River they were attacked and John Gilbert, the great collector of animals and birds for the naturalist John Gould, was killed.

Edmund Kennedy and his party had a horrific time in 1848 heading up the east coast along the Great Dividing Range. Continually splitting his party, Kennedy was fatally speared by Aborigines while amongst the swamps and waterways of the Escape River, south-east of the Tip. Only Jacky Jacky, his faithful Aboriginal guide, reached their destination just a few km north at Albany Passage.

Frank Jardine and his brother led a group taking cattle from Rockhampton to the new government outpost at Somerset in 1863. This was to be the start of the Jardine legend on Cape York, with Frank Jardine dominating the top of the Cape until his death in 1917.

Other explorers followed, opening up the region. The discovery of gold on the Palmer River in 1873 was the great catalyst for the development of Cooktown, Laura and, later, Cairns.

In 1887 the Overland Telegraph Line from near Somerset to Palmerville and Cooktown was finally completed, linking the northernmost outpost with Brisbane. This is the route most travellers to Cape York follow today.

During WW II, Cape York was a major staging post for the battles going on in New Guinea and the Coral Sea. Some 10,000 troops were stationed on the Cape at such places as Iron Range and Portland Roads, on the mid-east coast; Horn Island, Mutee Heads and Jacky Jacky airfield (then called Higgins Field) at the northern tip of Cape York; as well as around Cooktown. Many relics of those days can still be seen, including wrecks of some of the 160-odd aircraft that were reported lost over the region.

During the 1950s bauxite was discovered along the coast near Weipa, and by the 1980s it had grown into the world's biggest bauxite mine. With reserves stockpiled well into the next century, Weipa will continue to be a major community and a place to visit for years to come.

During the late 1980s there was much talk about a space base being built on the Cape, either inland from Weipa or virtually opposite, on the east coast, but the plan has failed to be realised. It is not the first to come to grief on Cape York and it won't be the last.

INFORMATION

The wet season greatly restricts vehicle movement on Cape York. For that reason the best time to go is as early in the Dry as possible, generally from the beginning of June. The country is greener, there is more water around, there are less travellers and generally the roads are better than later in the season. The peak period is between August and September, with the last travellers being out of the Cape by the beginning of November.

If you plan to visit early or late in the season, it pays to check with the locals to see what is happening weather-wise and what the roads are like. Speaking to the police in Coen, Weipa or Cooktown wouldn't go astray, nor would a phone call to the friendly people at the Archer River

Zillia Falls, Atherton Tableland (RI)

Roadhouse. Alternatively, you can contact the Queensland Department of Transport (☎ 008 077 247) or the RACQ Road Reports (24 hours ☎ (07) 51 6711, or ☎ (07) 11655).

Occasionally people get caught out by the early rains of the Wet when they're at the very top of Cape York. They'll be looking at either an extended stay or an expensive barge trip with their vehicle back to Cairns.

Of course you need all the usual gear for travelling in a remote area, and you must carry water. Although you will cross a number of rivers south of the Archer River, water can be scarce along the main track north, especially late in the Dry.

It is possible to take a well-constructed off-road trailer all the way to the top, but be prepared to get bogged occasionally. Lesser built trailers will fall apart somewhere along the track. Caravans can make it to Cooktown, driven with care. They can even make it further north to Weipa, but the going is hard and we would not recommend it.

You are also entering crocodile country, so, while there are plenty of safe places to swim, be aware that any deep, dark, long stretch of water can hold a big hungry saltie.

The most common accident on the Cape is head-ons in the heath country south of the Jardine River. The track is narrow here with many blind corners, people travel too fast and sometimes they meet head-on. Nobody has been killed yet – more by good luck than good fortune. Drive slowly and keep your wits about you.

Tourist Information

There are no official tourist information centres along the route, although travellers will find information readily available from the many helpful locals in the roadhouses and towns along the way, such as Cooktown, Coen, Weipa and Bamaga.

The Seisia Camping Ground, at the very top of Australia, is a mine of information. For further details, see the Facilities section.

In Cairns there are a couple of places that can help you with information on travelling Cape York. See Information in the earlier Cairns to Musgrave via Cooktown section.

Police

The police can provide information to travellers on road conditions etc. Contact the following police stations: Coen (☎ (070) 60 1150); Weipa (☎ (070) 69 9119), Rocky Point; Lockhart River Aboriginal Community (☎ 070) 60 7120); and Bamaga (☎ 070) 69 3156), Sagauka St.

Hospitals & Dentists

There are three hospitals on Cape York: Coen (☎ (070) 60 1141), Weipa (☎ (070) 69 9155) at Rocky Point, and Bamaga (☎ (070) 69 3166). There is also a dentist (☎ (070) 69 9411) at Rocky Point, Weipa.

Permits

Permits are not required for travelling to Cape York via the main route described. This situation may change as the effects of Mabo and land rights become more advanced. This may affect camping in national parks as well, as these areas are liable to be claimed by Aboriginal groups.

Once you are north of the Jardine River, however, you will need a permit to camp on Aboriginal land, which in effect is nearly all the land north of the river. The Injinoo people are the traditional custodians of much of this land, along with other Aboriginal communities at Umagico and New Mapoon. Please respect the signs and by-laws of the community councils.

Designated camping grounds are provided in a number of areas, including Seisia, Pajinka and Punsand Bay. Camping elsewhere in the area requires a permit from the Injinoo Community Council (☎ (070) 69 3252) or Pajinka Wilderness Lodge. You can write to the Injinoo Community Council, PO Box 7757, Cairns, Qld 4870.

Alternatively, you can wait until you get to the Injinoo owned and operated ferry across the Jardine River. The $80 (return) fee includes the cost of camping at a number of pleasant, isolated sites, and the permit fees.

A plan of management is being developed for the area with a range of access fees, so things may change in the near future.

Travelling across Aboriginal land elsewhere

on the Cape may require a permit. Some are easy to obtain while others are difficult – it all depends on the community concerned. It is best to write to the relevant community council stating the reason for your visit, dates etc. Allow plenty of time for an answer.

Books & Maps
There are a wide range of books and maps on Cape York available in Cairns, Cooktown or Weipa and from good bookshops Australia-wide.

Hema and the RACQ both produce good maps of the region (see Books & Maps in the Cairns to Musgrave via Cooktown section). The Croc Shop map, *Cape York*, while a simple-looking map, has the latest information.

For guidebooks on Cape York, see Books & Maps in the Cairns to Musgrave via Cooktown section. *The Last Frontier: Cape York Wilderness*, written and published by Glenville Pike, really covers the history of the region well. For those interested in the Palmer River gold fields, the book *River of Gold* by Hector Holthouse (Angus & Robertson) is by far the best. If you want to know a little about the flowers of the region, a colourful, small book, *A Wilderness in Bloom*, written and published by B & B Hinton, is a good one to start with.

Radio Frequencies
Unless you are doing something way out of the ordinary, an HF radio, while nice to have, is not really necessary for the Cape.

The RFDS base in Cairns (callsign VJN) has a primary channel of 5145 and secondary channels of 2260, 4926, 6785 and 7465. The Mount Isa base (callsign VJI) has a primary channel frequency of 5110, with secondary frequencies of 4935, 6965, and 7392.

For those with a Telstra account, Sydney is the base to work through (callsign VIS). The OTC radphone channels available 24 hours a day at Sydney include 405, 607, 802, 1203 and 1602. All these channels are voice call, Selcall or Tonecall. Others are available for Tonecall and Selcall, while other frequencies are request only. Selcall for the beacon is 0899, while the operator is 0108.

Towing
Should you need a tow to the nearest town, the following towing services will be extremely useful:

Mount Molloy Service Centre & RACQ Service Depot, Brown St, Mount Molloy (24 hours ☎ (070) 94 1260)

Lakeland Cash Store & RACQ Service Depot (24 hours ☎ (070) 60 2133)

Cooktown Towing & Transport, McIvor Rd, Cooktown (☎ (070) 69 5545)

JBSI Transport, Lot 8 Iraci Ave, Evans Landing, Weipa (24 hours ☎ (070) 69 7795, fax 69 8112). Towing and salvage service anywhere on Cape York. Can also arrange to have your vehicle shipped back to Cairns

WRAFTEC Industries, 1 Iraci Ave, Weipa (☎ (070) 69 7877)

Camping Equipment Rental
Pickers Geo Camping & Canvas (☎ (070) 51 1944), 108 Mulgrave Rd, Parramatta Park, Cairns, Qld 4870, has a range of camping equipment and accessories for hire.

THE ROUTE
Cairns to Lakeland (248 km)
The route from Cairns heads out over the **Atherton Tableland** west of Cairns, and most people travel via Kuranda and Mareeba. This is a scenic drive up and over the Great Dividing Range.

The small township of **Mount Molloy** is 104 km north-west of Cairns, or 40 km south-west of the sugar port of Mossman. Bitumen roads wind through rainforest and rich farming land to get you to this point.

The bitumen continues along the Peninsula Developmental Road. At **Mount Carbine**, 30 km north-west of Mount Molloy, you can get fuel and limited supplies from the roadhouse.

The **McLeod River**, about 13 km west of the town, is one of the best spots to camp along this section of road and it is popular with travellers.

Further north the road climbs through the DeSailly Range and there are good views from **Bob's Lookout** that are worthy of a quick photo stop. The vegetation you see is pretty typical of what you will see for much of the trip. Forget deep, dark, impenetrable rainforest. Sure, you will see that, especially if you head off the main track, but jungle of this sort tends to be confined to narrow strips of riverine forest and to a few spots north of the mighty Jardine River. For the most part, the open forests are dominated by stringybarks, ironbarks and bloodwoods and other lesser species of eucalypt.

From Bob's Lookout the road continues to wind through range country skirting the headwaters of St George Creek before coming to the major turn-off west (left) to the **Palmer River gold fields** and **Maytown**, 51 km north-west of Mount Carbine and 185 km from Cairns.

For travellers with a little time, an excursion to the heart of the gold fields at Maytown is an interesting adjunct to a trip up the Cape. Contact the QNP&WS ranger at Chillagoe (☎ (070) 94 7163, fax 94 7213) for a camping permit, information, maps and current track. There are no facilities at Maytown.

The **Palmer River Roadhouse** is 33 km past the turn-off and by the time you get there you are almost out of bitumen, which ends approximately one km further north. The roadhouse overlooks the Palmer River and has fuel, accommodation, beer and limited supplies. There is a museum with a display of Palmer River gold field relics which is well worth a look.

Another 30 km sees you at **Lakeland** (248 km from Cairns), the small rural hamlet at the junction of the roads northeast to Cooktown and north-west to Weipa and the top of the Cape. Lakeland has fuel, food, accommodation, limited supplies and repairs.

The surrounding area is heavily farmed with many crops, including sorghum and peanuts. The entrance to **Butchers Hill Station** is just across the road from the Lakelands Hotel. This 400,000-hectare property, established in 1874, is not only a successful cattle station and peanut farm, but also provides accommodation and ranch-style holidays.

Lakeland to the Wenlock River (480 km)

A formed dirt road heads north to Laura and the Cape from Lakeland and this is about as good as the run north to the top gets. About 53 km north, and 12 km south of Laura, is the turn-off to the **Split Rock galleries**.

These Aboriginal rock-art galleries are well worth a look as they are the most accessible of the 1200 galleries found in this area. Together they represent one of the biggest and most important collections of prehistoric art in the world. See the earlier Cairns to Musgrave via Cooktown section for more on these galleries.

Just a few km further on, north of the Laura River crossing, **Laura** is a well spread-out town with the 'centre' being around the pub. See the Cairns to Musgrave via Cooktown section for more details on Laura and Lakefield National Park.

The road continues to be well-formed dirt as it heads north from Laura. Most of the creek crossings are dry, but early in the dry season some may have water in them. Some of these creek and river crossings provide a welcome spot to stop and camp. The Little Laura River, 12 km north of Laura, and the Kennedy River, 32 km north, are two such spots.

On the banks of the Hann River, 75 km north of Laura, is the **Hann River Roadhouse**. Food, fuel, minor repairs and a camping ground are available here.

From here to Musgrave it is 60 km of corrugated dirt road that in sections winds through some hilly country. A few bad creek crossings and nasty dips will keep your speed down. About the only spot worth camping at is the **Morehead River**, 28 km north of the Hann River.

Musgrave is one of the original fortress telegraph stations that were built along the Overland Telegraph Line and it is the only one you will see easily on the run north. You can get a meal here, as well as fuel and accommodation.

From near here, tracks run east to the

Rokeby National Park (R & VM)

Lakefield National Park or west to Edward River and the Pormpuraaw Aboriginal Community.

The road for the next 110 km to Coen is little different to what you have experienced before. There may be a few more bulldust patches which can play hell for a motorcycle rider or a low-slung conventional car, but if you've got this far you'll probably make it to Weipa.

About 65 km north of Musgrave you meet a road junction. The better, newer road leads left to Coen, while the older, rougher road swings right, crossing the **Stewart River** twice before reaching Coen. With little traffic, the first crossing of the Stewart River makes a fine camp site.

The old road also gives access to the road to **Port Stewart** on the east coast of the Cape (reasonable camping and good fishing) and Silver Plains Homestead where you can camp or be accommodated. Fishing and hunting trips to nearby rivers or to the close reefs of the Great Barrier Reef can also be organised.

Coen is the 'capital' of the Cape, and unless you take the turn-off into Weipa, it is the biggest town you'll see north of Cooktown. People have some funny times in this place, all of course in and around the pub, the social heart of any country town.

There is a choice of where to buy food and fuel and even a couple of places offering accommodation, and that doesn't include the police station with its lock-up, or even the hospital.

About three km north of Coen, the main road north parallels the **Coen River** for a short distance. There is some good camping along the river, and while it is a popular spot, there is generally no problem in finding a place to throw down the swag or erect a tent. Toilet facilities are provided.

For the first 23 km north of Coen the road is very well maintained, but once you have passed the Coen airfield the road quickly returns to its former standard. About two km past the airfield you reach the main access track to **Rokeby National Park**. This park straddles the Archer River and its tributaries,

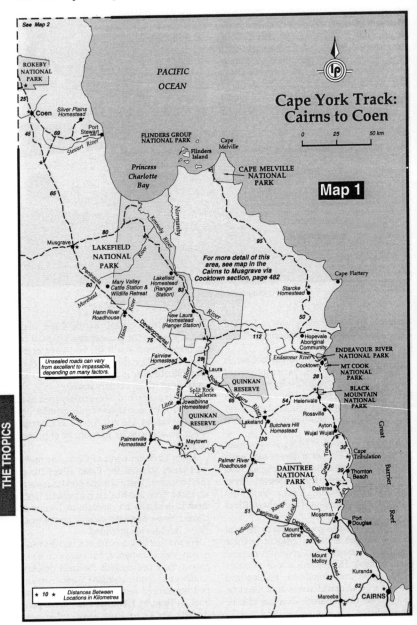

THE TROPICS

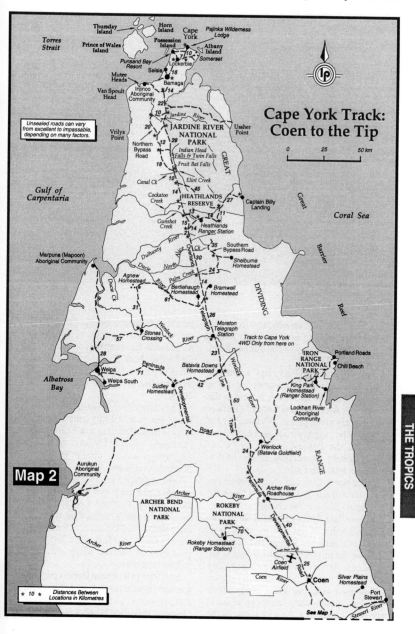

Cape York Track:
Coen to the Tip

Torres Strait

Gulf of Carpentaria

Coral Sea

Unsealed roads can vary from excellent to impassable, depending on many factors.

Map 2

★ 10 ★ Distances Between Locations in Kilometres

THE TROPICS

Twin Falls (R & VM)

taking in much of the country from the western edge of the Great Dividing Range almost to the boundary of the Archer Bend National Park.

Rokeby National Park has excellent camping on a number of lagoons and along the banks of the Archer River. Access to the more remote **Archer Bend National Park** is only by rarely given permit. No facilities are provided. The ranger station is about 70 km west from the Peninsula Developmental Road at Rokeby Homestead, or see the district ranger based in Coen.

Further north, the main road continues as before, until about 50 km north of Coen the road is more like a roller coaster.

The excellent **Archer River Roadhouse** is 65 km north of Coen and provides food, drinks, fuel, accommodation and camping. Just down the hill from the roadhouse is the magnificent **Archer River**. During the Dry this river is normally just a pleasant stream bordered by a wide, tree-lined, sandy bed. It is an ideal spot to camp, although at times space is at a premium. As with many of the

permanent streams on the Cape, the banks are lined with varieties of paperbarks, or melaleucas. Growing to more than 40 metres they offer shade for passing travellers and, when in flower, food for hordes of birds and fruit bats that love the heavy, sweet-smelling nectar.

The Archer River crossing used to be a real terror, but now, with its concrete causeway, is quite easy. However, any heavy rain in the catchment will quickly send the water over the bridge, cutting access to Weipa and places further north.

For the first 15 km past the Archer River crossing, the road can be corrugated. The main road to Portland Roads, Chili Beach and Iron Range National Park turns east off the main road, 20 km north of the Archer, and crosses the Wenlock River, close to the old gold field of Batavia. Many old relics can still be seen here.

Iron Range National Park is probably the greatest tropical rainforest park in Australia. Forget what you've heard about the Daintree; this place is better and wilder, with more unique animals and plants. There is a rich variety of vegetation, from heathland to dense rainforest.

The rare and vivid eclectus parrot, large palm cockatoo, shy fawn-breasted bower-bird, small red-bellied pitta and giant cassowary are some of the birds of the forest.

The spotted and the grey cuscus, both forms of tree kangaroos, and the spiny-haired bandicoot are three of the mammals in the park that are found virtually nowhere else. One animal that is commonly seen here is the northern native cat. This striking mammal, a small predator, sometimes wanders into camps and houses in the region looking for something to eat. If you're lucky enough to see one you won't forget the encounter – they are beautiful!

Some 10% of Australia's butterflies also reside in this park, including 25 species found no further south, with the park being their stronghold.

There are only a couple of camping areas in this park. Near the East Claudie River and Gordon Creek is the Rainforest camping ground. While the other is at Chili Beach, but this is hardly in the rainforest. Other small camp sites are dotted on or near streams along the road. The ranger is based at King Park Homestead.

Portland Roads is 135 km east of the Peninsula Developmental Road. It is a small fishing port with no facilities for the traveller, except a telephone. The fishing offshore, if you have a small boat, is excellent.

Chili Beach is just a few km south of Portland Roads and is where all the travellers camp. Pit toilets are provided. It is now part of the Iron Range National Park and a camping permit is required. You can get it from the ranger based at King Park Homestead or the QNP&WS headquarters in Cairns. While it is a pleasant spot, it would be even better if the wind would stop blowing – which it does occasionally late in the season. A small boat will give you access to the islands just offshore and to some good fishing.

Lockhart River Aboriginal Community is 40 km south of Portland Roads and has fuel and limited supplies, although repairs are not available. There is also a police station and a hospital. A permit is not required to enter the community.

Continuing north from the turn-off to Portland Roads, the main Peninsula Developmental Road swings westward to Weipa, 44 km north of the Archer River crossing. The road has been realigned and greatly improved. It is as good as a dirt road gets! See the Alternative Routes section for details. From this point the route north becomes more of a track, but is still reasonably well maintained.

Batavia Downs Station is on the left of the road and marks the second major turn-off to Weipa, 50 km north of the first, southern-most one. The final 23 km to the Wenlock River is along a road that is sandy and rough in places.

Wenlock River

The Wenlock River is the first major water challenge you meet on your way north to the Cape. It looks surprisingly easy, but it is astonishing how many people come to grief here. Early or late in the dry season, the river may be running high because of rains in the ranges to the east.

A base of rocks has been put down in the riverbed at the crossing point, and provided it hasn't been washed away in the last Wet, you shouldn't have too much trouble. If you do bog down, don't despair, you're not the first.

The north bank of the Wenlock River is a popular spot to camp and at times it does get crowded. Toilets are provided, as is a telephone. A small store is open sometimes and sells drinks, souvenirs and the like, and provides information and minor mechanical and welding repairs.

Wenlock River to the Jardine River (155 km)

The 155 km from the Wenlock River to the Jardine River is the best part of the trip, with some great creek crossings and excellent camp sites. Take your time and enjoy all the delights the Cape has to offer.

Walking to the Top

All the early explorers walked to the Top, as did most of the pioneers who followed, searching for gold and rich grazing land. In more recent times, those who 'humped the bluey' are few and far between.

In August 1930, John Carlyon began his walk down the eastern seaboard, a couple of years after Hector Macquarie had made history by being the first to drive a car – a small Austin – to the Top.

In the early 1950s Alex Sklenica and a couple of mates walked from Cairns to Cooktown and on to the Top where they joined the mail boat to travel around Torres Strait.

Sklenica was later to write about the trip:

Seeking gold in the '50s

...Cooktown, once a prosperous town with thousands of people and 60 pubs as we were told, was nearly a ghost town now.

A diesel, pulling two cars, maintained a once weekly rail service to Laura. Stockmen and prospectors using the train, added to this romantic outback setting. Camping a few days on the Laura River, we shot a few wallabies to prepare jerky and pemmican for the long walk still ahead of us.

Further on the track we met Norman Fisher who offered to take us on his 4WD truck for £5 to Coen. We shared the top of the load with four prospectors who hoped to find a 'pocket' of gold nuggets in creeks around the Wenlock area.

Our travel was reduced sometimes to two miles per hour. We helped to fill holes, cut fallen trees and made a log causeway to enable the 4WD truck to cross the 70 yard wide sandy bed of the Stewart River...

...Supplies diminishing. Walking, we chewed tips of Yakka tree blades, and sticks of dried wallaby meat.

The track along the telegraph line path worsened, the uncut vegetation reaching nearly the wires. Our mainly meat diet lacked sustenance. We craved for carbohydrates, fruit and the kind of vegetables we were used to.

On the 15 September, our remaining supplies consisted of half a pound of flour, three-quarters pound of tea, half a pound sugar, 1 spoon of cocoa and 4 spoons of salt.

Arriving at the Jardine River, we saw a small dinghy pulled up on the opposite shore. Nick, the best swimmer among us brought the dinghy to our side while with Lad, we stood guard with rifles. Gear loaded in the small dinghy, we swam across, holding onto the gunnels with one hand.

Later, Mr Cupitt from the Cape York telegraph station told us that he shot recently 14 crocodiles on the spot where we swam the river...

In May 1987 Ian Brown and a couple of friends walked from Coen along much of the Great Dividing Range and the east coast to arrive at the Top. Their trek took 56 days.

In September of that same year Barry Higgins and Steve Tremont began a trek in western Victoria that was to take them 15 months to get to the Top.

In June 1988 Peter Treseder walked and ran from the northernmost tip of Australia to Wilsons Promontory in Victoria. His time? An incredible 41 days – alone and unsupported. While those before him had taken to the coast and untracked wilderness of the range country, Peter had to average 134 km a day, and to do that he stayed on the Telegraph Track between the Top and Musgrave. From there he went through Lakefield National Park to Cooktown and south through the Daintree and 50 other odd national parks, before finishing at Australia's southernmost tip.

These recent trips have been sponsored in one way or another by Australian Geographic.

You don't have to join the short list of people who have walked to the Top, but it can be done. In fact, less people have walked to the Cape than have climbed Mt Everest! ■

THE TROPICS

The challenge of following the rough track along the historic Overland Telegraph Line means that the trip will take at least a very long day, even if all goes well. There are many small diversions from the original route, especially where there is a creek or river to cross. Most of the major creek crossings have water in them; however, it's not the water that is the problem but the banks on each side. Take care. Washaways elsewhere demand you keep your speed down.

Amongst the scattered timber and blanket of grass you can see zamia, or cycad palms. In places they form quite dense stands, and as they come in male and female forms they must be having quite a party! Aborigines once used the palm nuts as a food source. The nuts are poisonous when raw and need special preparation and cooking before they are safe to eat.

The track improves after 10 km and is reasonable until the first of the bypass roads leaves the old track.

The turn-offs to **Bramwell Station** and **Bertiehaugh Station** are 26 km north of the Wenlock River. Bramwell Station is on the east side of the road and offers very pleasant and reasonably priced accommodation and camping. The route westwards through Bertiehaugh leads to Stones Crossing and then onwards to Weipa.

Rocky Creek, 39 km north of the Wenlock River, can be a minor challenge to cross.

The first of the major bypass roads, the **Southern Bypass Road**, turns off the Telegraph Track 40 km north of the Wenlock. This route keeps to the high country, staying well away from the many creek crossings the Telegraph Track makes. See the section on Alternative Routes for more details.

Palm Creek, 43 km north of the Wenlock, is followed by Ducie Creek, South Alice Creek and North Alice Creek, before you reach the **Dulhunty River**, 70 km north of the Wenlock. This is a popular spot to camp. There are also some lovely places to swim, and the falls beside the road make a pleasant natural spa.

After crossing another major stream, a road leaves the Telegraph Track two km

north of the Dulhunty and heads for **Heathlands Station**, the base for the ranger for Jardine River National Park. This road also bypasses the **Gunshot Creek** crossing. This crossing, just 15 km past the track junction, is one of the hardest and most daunting on the route north and has a number of drops into the creek. The experience of other travellers and the nature of the previous wet season will determine the route you take. Many travellers backtrack to the road junction and take the safer, but longer, way around via Heathlands Station. You can rejoin the Telegraph Track just north of Gunshot Creek after a diversion of 27 km.

The vegetation changes again. No longer is it dominated by straggly eucalypts such as ironbarks and bloodwoods, but instead the country is covered in tall heathland. Take a close look and you'll be surprised at the flowers you can find. The open plains are dominated by grevilleas, hibbertias and small melaleucas, to name just a few, while the creek banks and wetter areas are clothed in banksias and baeckeas.

One of the plants that observant nature lovers will find is the pitcher plant. These are found along the banks of the narrow creeks, Gunshot Creek being a prime spot for them. These special plants trap insects in the liquid at the bottom of the 'pitcher', where their nutrients are absorbed by the plant. It's a unique adaptation to living in an area that is poor in plant food.

After the Gunshot Creek crossing the track is sandy until you come to the **Cockatoo Creek** crossing, 93 km north of the Wenlock River. Once again the actual riverbed is no drama; it's the banks that are the problem. In this case it is the north bank which often has a long haul of soft sand. A little speed makes a big difference here, as does lower tyre pressures. The Injinoo people have a permanent camp set up at Cockatoo Creek.

For the next 24 km the road improves slightly. A couple more creek crossings follow and 14 km past Cockatoo Creek the Southern Bypass Road joins up with the Telegraph Track. Just 10 km further on, the second major bypass, the **Northern Bypass Road**, heads west away from the Telegraph Track to the ferry that crosses the Jardine River. Stick to the Telegraph Track at this point and keep heading north, even though the track north does deteriorate a little. There are other tracks that lead back to the Northern Bypass Road and the ferry, if you don't want to drive across the Jardine River.

Within a few hundred metres a track heads off to the east, taking travellers to **Fruit Bat Falls**. Camping is not allowed here but it is a good spot to stop, have lunch and enjoy the waters of Eliot Creek. This is a good place for canoeing (see the Activities section for further information).

The turn-off to **Indian Head Falls** and **Twin Falls** is 6.5 km north of the previous track junction to Fruit Bat Falls. The track leads less than two km to an excellent camping area. On one side is Canal Creek and the delightful Twin Falls, while on the

The Telegraph Track can be pretty rough
(R & VM)

other is the wider Eliot Creek and Indian Head Falls which drop into a small, sheer-sided ravine.

Pit toilets and showers are set up within the camping area and the ranger from Heathlands keeps the place in good condition, with your help. This is the most popular camping spot on the trip north, and although it gets crowded, it is still very enjoyable. A camping permit is required and a small camping fee payable.

You can spend an enjoyable few days camped here, doing not much else but swimming and lazing in the creeks between lunch and dinner. If you have a mask and snorkel, the water is clear enough for a paddle and there are fish and turtles to watch; or walk around and enjoy some bird-watching.

Back on the Telegraph Track, over the next eight km there are Canal, Sam, Mistake, Cannibal and Cypress creeks to cross. All offer their own sweet challenge. Just south of **Mistake Creek** a track heads west to join up with the Northern Bypass Road, which leads to the ferry across the Jardine River. If you're having fun crossing the creeks, keep heading north at this point, but if you have had enough, it may pay to take the track out to the Northern Bypass Road and the ferry.

From Cypress Creek it is a 7.5 km run to **Logan Creek**. From here the road is badly chopped up and often flooded in places. You are now passing through the heart of an area the early pioneers called the 'Wet Desert' because of the abundance of water but lack of feed for their stock.

Bridge Creek, or Nolan's Brook, five km further on, once had a bridge, and when you get to it you'll know why. It is an interesting crossing, and though it is short it does demand a lot of care. Less than two km north of here the last track to the ferry heads west, while just 4.5 km past this junction the main track veers away from the original telegraph line route to the right and winds through tall open forest to the Jardine River.

Jardine River

The Jardine River has some magical camping spots along its southern bank, west

Wreck of a DC3, one of many on the Cape (R & VM)

of the ford. There are no facilities here, and because you are in a national park, a camping permit is required from the ranger at Heathlands Station.

The river is wide and sandy. If you want to swim, stick to the shallows where the sandbars are wide. Crocs don't like such open territory but may be lurking in the deep, dark, lily-covered holes that line sections of the river.

Fishing upstream of the crossing is not allowed as you are in a national park. Downstream from this point there is no problem and at times the fishing can be good, although closer to the mouth is better again.

The current makes paddling a canoe upstream a real chore, although in a boat you will be plagued with shallow water.

Jardine River Vehicle Ford The vehicle ford leads out across the wide, sandy bed of the fast-flowing Jardine River. Midway across the river is a steep-sided tongue of sand that constantly changes its position, up and down the river. This tongue of soft sand

often causes vehicles to bog in the middle of the stream. The water slowly gets deeper and is at its deepest, generally over a metre deep, within a few metres of the trees on the northern bank. The shallow exit point runs between a corridor of trees. There are some old timbers in this dark water between the trees which can easily stub a toe or hang up a vehicle, so be careful.

Never underestimate this crossing, even if it looks shallow. The 170 metres between entrance and exit is a long way – certainly most winch cables can't reach you if you stop mid-stream!

Remember, the Jardine River is inhabited by estuarine crocodiles, and although you might not be able to see them they are definitely there. In December 1993 a man was killed by a crocodile while he was swimming to the ferry at the ferry crossing, not far downstream from the vehicle ford.

In recent times the QNP&WS and the Injinoo Aboriginal Community have asked that all travellers use the ferry crossing and do not drive across the river at the vehicle

THE TROPICS

ford. For more information on the ferry, see the Northern Bypass section later on.

North of the Jardine (69 km)

From here to the Top it is less than 70 km and for most of the way the track is in good condition.

The track, once out of the trees bordering the Jardine River, swings to the west and finally joins up with the Telegraph Track. Turning right, or northwards, will lead to the main road north, while turning left will take you back to the river and the ferry point.

A number of minor tracks in this area lead back down to the river and some reasonable camp sites. The best camp site is on the northern bank where the telegraph line crosses the river; an old linesman's hut marks the spot. The sandy beach here is a pleasant swimming place – keep to the shallows – popular with travellers and locals alike.

Following the old line north brings you to a major crossroad, less than two km from the exit point on the Jardine. Ignore the Telegraph Track that leads away directly north – this is unused and leads into the heart of the swamp. The main road heading off to the west leads to the ferry crossing of the river. Turning right, or eastwards, will take you to Bamaga.

At the next T-junction, 22 km north of where you came onto this major dirt road, turn right. Left will lead to the coast at the old wartime port of **Mutee Heads**, just north of the Jardine River.

Just over seven km further on there is a small carpark beside a fenced area that encloses the remains of an **aeroplane wreck**. Dating back to WW II, these remains are of a DC-3 which ploughed in on its return from New Guinea. This is the easiest aeroplane wreck to see in the area but there are a few more scattered around the main airport, which is just a stone's throw away.

A couple of hundred metres past the carpark there is a second T-junction. Right will lead to the main airport, while left will lead to Bamaga.

Less than five km from the second T-junction, a signposted road heads off to the right leading to Cape York, Somerset and places close to the Tip. This is the road you will

require, but most travellers will need fuel and other supplies, and will continue straight ahead to Bamaga.

Bamaga is the largest community on the Northern Cape and is a spread-out town with all the facilities most travellers need. There is a hospital, police station, general store and service station. There is no camping ground at Bamaga, these being located at Seisia (Red Island Point) and Pajinka Wilderness Lodge at the Tip.

The Islander settlement of **Seisia**, five km north-west of Bamaga, is an idyllic spot for the weary traveller to relax after the long journey to the Top. There is an excellent foreshore camping ground, a kiosk and service station, and the nearby jetty is a great place for the family to fish.

The **Injinoo Aboriginal Community** is eight km south-west of Bamaga, at the mouth of Cowal Creek. The Injinoo camping area has basic facilities; camping here is at the discretion of the Injinoo Council.

The only other official camping areas north of the Jardine River are at the Punsand Bay Private Reserve and the Pajinka Lodge. Camping elsewhere north of the Jardine River is only possible with a permit from the Injinoo Community Council. For more details, see the Facilities section.

From Bamaga, turn north towards the Tip along a well-formed dirt road. The ruins of Jardine's outstation, **Lockerbie**, are 16 km north, close to the right-hand side of the road. While the galvanised iron and timber building is a more recent residence, built by the Holland family in 1946, nearby you will find mango trees and pathways established by Frank Jardine. There is usually a small store at the Lockerbie site and visitors are welcome to stop for refreshments, souvenirs and information.

Just north of Lockerbie a track heads west to **Punsand Bay**, about 11 bumpy, sandy km away. A few km later and the main track north begins to pass through an area of rainforest called the **Lockerbie Scrub**. This small patch of rainforest, only 25 km long and between one and five km wide, is the northernmost rainforest in Australia.

The Lockerbie Scrub

The Lockerbie Scrub is an important stretch of rainforest, despite being poorly named. It is regularly used as a stopover by migratory birds, and is home to some unique animals and insects. Surprisingly, it has been studied for some time, beginning with naturalists visiting the Jardine family at Somerset and their 'summer residence' at Lockerbie.

Vines and other climbing plants are common in this forest, while hickory ash, paperbark satin ash and cypress pines, which you can see here, were the trees that first attracted a small logging industry. Probably the most spectacular tree is the fig tree with its large, buttress-type roots. Palms and ferns of all sorts can be commonly found right through the forest, including some huge bird's-nest ferns.

Walking here is really enjoyable, and the thick canopy overhead keeps the area nice and cool. The road passes close to a stream at times and this can easily be followed. Keep an eye out for birds, and with luck you may even see the huge mounds, up to six or more metres high, of the orange-footed scrub fowl.

You'll no doubt see signs of much rooting around in the leaves and mulch that cover the forest floor. Sadly much of this is due to the wild pigs that infest the area. They are causing untold damage here, and to make matters worse, the cane toad is on its way – it is now already found north of the Jardine River.

Nature walks and night walks in the forest can be organised by the Pajinka Lodge or Punsand Bay Private Reserve. ■

Seven km from Lockerbie a Y-junction in the middle of the jungle gives you a choice of veering right for Somerset or left for the top of Australia. Less than three km from this point on the way to the Top, a track on the left will lead you seven km to the **Punsand Bay Private Reserve** with on-site tents, cabins and camping facilities.

Seven km further on will bring you to the **Pajinka Wilderness Lodge** and the camping area. Here is a small kiosk to service the camping area.

A walking track leads through the forest bordering the camping ground at Pajinka to the beach near the boat ramp. A scattering of mangroves line part of the beach as they do on most of the beaches on the Cape, and sometimes it is almost imperceptible where forest ends and mangroves begin. From the beach you can head overland on the marked trail, or, when the tide is low, you can head around the coast to the northern tip. Both routes are relatively easy walks of an hour or so, depending on how long you dabble your feet in the briny.

The islands of Torres Strait are just a stone's throw away and dot the turquoise blue sea all the way to New Guinea, just over

the horizon. Swimming is not recommended here as the tidal stream never seems to stop running one way or the other. The fishing, though, can be pretty good. Have your photo taken near the sign proudly proclaiming you have made it all the way to Australia's northernmost point.

ALTERNATIVE ROUTES
Weipa via the Southern Access Route

Once north of the Archer River, you can head to Weipa instead of heading directly to the Top. Weipa is one of the great mining communities in the country and here you can glimpse what life is like in a remote mining town and the west coast of the Cape.

The most direct route to Weipa is the continuation of the Peninsula Developmental Road, which stops following the route of the Overland Telegraph Line 44 km north of the Archer. The Peninsula Developmental Road continues to be a reasonably well-maintained dirt road for the 145 km to Weipa.

Just over halfway, at the 74-km mark, a track which left the Telegraph Track at Batavia Downs, south of the Wenlock River, joins up with the Peninsula Developmental

Sign at the top of Australia (R & VM)

Road at Sudley, 71 km east of Weipa. This track between Batavia Downs and Sudley is often chopped up and a couple of the creek crossings are muddy early in the Dry. This route gives people another option to leave or join the route to the Top.

As you get closer to Weipa, the mining activities increase and the road improves. Heed all the warning signs, especially where the road crosses the mine haulage ways.

Weipa via the Northern Access Route

The route via Stones Crossing, over the Wenlock River, to Agnew and eastwards to the Telegraph Track, south of Bertiehaugh, covers a total distance of 169 km.

This track crosses private land and, depending on the owner, access across Bertiehaugh is sometimes open, sometimes closed! This is a good run and well worth the effort, so ask other travellers at each end of the route for the latest advice.

Stones Crossing is 57 km north-east of

Weipa. First, take the Old Mapoon Road and at the 28-km mark veer right at the major Y-junction. The road swings east for 20 km before turning north for the last nine km to the crossing of the Wenlock River. This is a magic spot to camp, but remember that the river is tidal as far as the crossing itself and is inhabited by estuarine crocodiles.

From the river, the track deteriorates and heads north for 31 km before turning east. **Agnew** was once a wartime airstrip that is now dominated by tall termite mounds. You drive down the edge of the old airstrip before turning eastwards. From here you continue on a sandy, rough track for 50 km before coming to a track junction. Keep to the right and after 11 km you will meet the Telegraph Track, 26 km north of the Wenlock River.

Bypass Roads

The bypass roads avoid most of the creeks and rivers between the Wenlock and Jardine rivers. This route is also called the DCS Road or the 'main' Cairns Road.

Both sections of this road are corrugated and people travel too fast on them. In 1993, 21 head-on accidents occurred in the first two months of the Dry, most of those on the Southern Bypass Road. Be careful!

The Southern Bypass This road leaves the Telegraph Track 40 km north of the Wenlock River crossing and heads east and then north. The turn-off east to Shelburne Station is 24 km north of the junction, while another 35 km will find you at the junction to Heathlands ranger station, 14 km to the west.

When you reach a large patch of rainforest, 11 km north of the Heathlands turn-off, the bypass road swings north-west, while a track to Captain Billy Landing, on the east coast, continues straight ahead. Keep on the bypass road for the next 45 km to rejoin the Telegraph Track 14 km north of Cockatoo Creek.

The Northern Bypass This road leaves the Telegraph Track 10 km north of where the

The top of Australia (TW)

Southern Bypass Road rejoins the Telegraph Track, north of Cockatoo Creek.

This route heads west away from the Telegraph Track and for 50 km winds through tropical savannah woodland to the ferry across the Jardine River. At the 18-km and 30-km marks, tracks head east to the Telegraph Track.

The Jardine River ferry (☎ (070) 69 1369) normally operates seven days a week from 8 am to 5 pm, or contact the Injinoo Community Council (☎ (070) 69 3252) for ferry details. A fee is charged to use the ferry, which includes access and camping fees.

ACTIVITIES
Eliot Creek

If you have a canoe, this is a good place to put it in for an easy paddle downstream to the camping area at Indian Head Falls, one of the places not to miss on a trip to Cape York. The paddle between Fruit Bat Falls and Indian Head Falls is easy with a good, steady current pushing you all the way. The total distance is less than 10 km and is very enjoyable. At Indian Head Falls you will need to take your canoe out and portage, even if you are paddling further downstream.

Paddling further downstream leaves you with two options. One is to find the junctions of the Mistake Creek or, further north again, Cannibal Creek with the Eliot Creek and then paddle up these creeks to the Telegraph Track crossing of these relevant streams. The distance you need to paddle upstream is only about 500 metres to get you back to the road, which isn't all that far, even against a slight current.

Paddling the length of the Eliot Creek will bring you into the Jardine River about three km above the old ford or four km from where the telegraph line used to cross this stream. The total distance is less than 40 km and takes about a day. It is a really pleasant paddle, and for the first half the river is shallow and fast-flowing, dropping over the occasional small fall. It then begins to meander across the Jardine River flood plains and here it slows, becomes wider and deeper and is closed in by tall jungle.

The trip could be recommended wholeheartedly if it weren't for regular sightings of big, curious estuarine crocodiles, especially near the junction of the Jardine River.

Seisia

Red Island Point jetty is one of the top fishing spots in Australia, and Gebadi's Tackle Shop (☎ (070) 69 3279) can supply anything you need.

Weipa

Around Weipa itself and the areas north there are some excellent fishing places. Weipa River Safaris runs fishing safaris (see Organised Tours), but you can hire a boat yourself from the Weipa Snack Shack & Boat Hire Service (☎ (070) 69 7495) at the Evans Landing wharf. It has 13-foot aluminium boats, and it's best to ring and pre-book a boat during the tourist season. Cost is $60/40 per day/half day. The Shack also sells bait and fishing accessories and can give you information on the best spots to fish.

Bamaga

The Bamaga Festival is normally run in September each year.

ORGANISED TOURS

For most people travelling to the Cape, Cairns is the stepping-off point. It is a major city with everything you need to organise a trip north. Rental vehicles, camping equipment rental, guiding services, as well as a host of tour operators can organise part, or all, of your trip to the Cape.

A number of tour operators work from Seisia offering a wide range of tours, including bird-watching, nature tours, fishing and hunting safaris. Contact the Seisia Camping Ground (☎ (070) 69 3243) for details.

Guide Services

One of the most popular ways to see the Cape is in the company of a tag-along operator. Some companies supply a cook and all the food, while others only act as guides, supplying information, permits, HF radio facilities and recovery expertise. While they do not supply a vehicle, if you need to hire one they can organise it for you. Otherwise rental companies can supply vehicles. See the earlier Cairns section or the later 4WD Rentals section.

Most tag-along companies operate out of Cairns and include the following:

Cape York Connections
    PO Box 371, Port Douglas, Qld 4871 (☎ & fax (070) 98 4938, mobile (018) 770 569)
Guides to Adventure
    PO Box 908, Atherton, Qld 4883 (☎ (070) 91 1978, fax 91 2545)
Oz Tours
    PO Box 6464, Cairns, Qld 4870 (☎ (070) 55 9535, fax 55 9918)
Russell Guest 4X4 Safaris
    38 Station Street, Fairfield, Vic 3078 (☎ (03) 481 5440)

Motorcycle guide services include the following:

Cape York Motorcycle Adventures
    PO Box 525, Manunda, Cairns, Qld 4870 (☎ (070) 58 1148, mobile (018) 77 0399)
2 Wheel Adventures
    PO Box 397, Manunda, Cairns, Qld 4870 (☎ (070) 31 5707)

There are quite a number of operators running tours to Cape York in 4WD vehicles and coaches. For a comprehensive list of established and well-known tour operators, contact the Far North Queensland Coach & Off Road Association. See Information in the Cairns to Musgrave via Cooktown section.

Boat

With magnificent offshore reefs and islands, the coast of Cape York is a popular destination for fishing enthusiasts and divers. Many charters and safaris operate from Cairns. Contact the Far North Queensland Tourist Bureau for details (see Information in the Cairns to Musgrave via Cooktown section). The El-Torito departs from Thursday Island and cruises the Torres Strait. For cruise details and bookings, contact Jardine Shipping in Cairns (☎ (070) 35 1900, fax 35 1685), or the Jardine Hotel (☎ (070) 69 1555, fax 69 1470) on Thursday Island.

Jardine Adventures is based in Seisia.

Enquiries and bookings can be made at the Seisia Camping Ground (☎ (070) 69 3243).

Weipa River Safaris (☎ (070) 69 7597, fax 69 7562), PO Box 393, Weipa, Qld 4874, operates fishing safaris.

For information on fishing safaris on the *Reef Safari*, see Organised Tours in the Cairns to Musgrave via Cooktown section.

FACILITIES

Fuel

Diesel, unleaded and super are generally readily available along the route to the Cape, but there is no LPG after Cairns, except at Cooktown. Prices for fuel will vary between fuel stops and can be quite expensive in places. Weipa and Bamaga always seem to be cheaper.

Money

Probably the best option is to have a pass-book account with the Commonwealth Bank, which enables you to withdraw cash at any post office. Banking facilities are very limited on Cape York, and full banking facilities are only available in three banks: Weipa, Cooktown and Thursday Island.

Cheques are not normally accepted, but major credit cards, such as Bankcard, MasterCard and Visa, are accepted widely for most services. Australian travellers' cheques are also exchanged in some places along the way. However, in many places cash is still the only form of currency accepted.

Telephones

STD phones are located at most roadhouses and certainly in the towns.

Mount Carbine

The *Mt Carbine Roadhouse* (☎ (070) 94 3128) is virtually a one-stop shop for travellers, as are most of the roadhouses on the Cape. Open from 6 am to 10 pm, it dispenses fuel (diesel, unleaded and super), as well as limited repair facilities. It has a 24-hour emergency fuel supply service, and can organise towing. There are also general food items for sale, souvenirs, meals and takeaway food. It has EFTPOS and accepts major credit cards. Accommodation is available for $15 a single, or $21.50 for B&B. Camp sites, with showers, cost $5.

Palmer River

The *Palmer River Roadhouse* (☎ (070) 60 2152) has fuel and accepts only BP fuel cards or cash. It is also licensed, and refreshments, snacks and evening meals are available. On Friday evening there is a barbecue along with a live band and topless barmaids serving drinks. With miners from the local area, it can be a colourful night.

There is a caravan and camping park behind the roadhouse (no dogs allowed). Cost is $7 per person per night for a camp site and $11 for a caravan site ($40 weekly). Two-person on-site caravans are also available at $10 per person, but you need to supply your own linen.

Lakeland

The small township of Lakeland caters for surrounding properties and travellers, and most facilities are available. The *Lakeland Cash Store* (☎ (070) 60 2133) is a general store and service station. The store has a good range of food supplies, takeaway food etc, and the service station supplies fuel, mechanical repairs, welding and tyres and is the RACQ Service Depot. It is open seven days a week and accepts major credit cards.

The store also runs a caravan and camping park with on-site vans, powered and unpowered sites, hot showers and laundry facilities. Camping costs $4 per person for an unpowered site, or $10 nightly per couple for a powered site (children half price). It is also possible to store your caravan here. Dogs are allowed, under control.

The *Lakeland Hotel-Motel* (☎ (070) 60 2142) has refreshments, snacks, counter lunches and teas. Accommodation is available for $35/45 a single/double. Breakfast can also be arranged. Major credit cards are accepted.

The *Lakelands Roadhouse* (☎ (070) 60 2188, fax 60 2165), on the Peninsula Developmental Road, has all fuels, tyres, batteries, camping gas etc. It can make mechanical

Good catch of barramundi (R & VM)

Pandanus palms at the Tip (RvD)

repairs and provides emergency towing. The restaurant serves a range of meals and snacks. Shower facilities are also available. Open from 7 am to 10 pm, it has EFTPOS and accepts major credit cards.

Laura

See Facilities in the Cairns to Musgrave via Cooktown section.

Hann River

The *Hann River Roadhouse* (☎ (070) 60 3242) has fuel and does minor repairs, and has limited food supplies, snacks and a licensed restaurant. It even has its own air-strip. The combination of a camping ground with all amenities, including powered sites, and the nearby permanent water and fishing make it a pleasant spot to camp. Camp sites cost $4 a single. You can contact the road-house by writing to PMB 88, Cairns Mail Centre, Qld 4870.

Musgrave

The historic *Musgrave Telegraph Station* (☎ (070) 60 3229) sells fuel, refreshments, meals, takeaway food and cold beer. Accommodation is available for $20/30 a single/double and breakfast can be arranged. It is also possible to camp at Musgrave, and although there is no fee for this, it does cost $2 to use the showers.

An airstrip runs beside the station, and aviation fuel can be organised if you notify the station at least one week before you intend flying in.

Coen

Coen is a major town on the Cape and caters for most travellers' needs. The *Clark's General Store & Garage* (☎ (070) 60 1144) supplies groceries, fuel, gas refills for camping bottles, mechanical repairs and welding. The store is open seven days a week but the workshop is not usually open on Sunday.

Ambrust & Co General Store (☎ (070) 60 1134, fax 60 1128) has food supplies, and doubles as the post office with a Common-wealth Bank agency. There is also a fax

facility. Fuel and camping gas is available. It is also the agent for aviation fuel, although you will need to contact them beforehand to arrange supply and fuelling. The store runs a camping ground with most amenities for $5 a night per person for an unpowered site (power is $1 extra); there are special rates for children and families. Dogs are allowed, under control.

Counter or dining-room meals and accom-modation are available at the *Exchange Hotel* (☎ (070) 60 1133), with a choice of hotel rooms or motel units from $25/35 a single/double.

You can also stay at the very pleasant *Homestead Guest House* (☎ (070) 60 1157) for around $25 a single. It also serves snacks, takeaway meals and morning and afternoon teas, and is the Westpac Bank agency.

Archer River

The *Archer River Roadhouse* (☎ & fax (070) 60 3266) near the river is a great place to stop and enjoy a cold beer and friendly company, along with the famous Archer Burger. General food supplies, takeaway food, snacks, books and maps can be purchased, along with fuel. Limited repairs can also be carried out. It is open from 7 am to 10 pm.

Campers can pitch their tent in the camping ground with the use of all ameni-ties, for $5 per person per night, $2 for children. Accommodation is also available in units for $20 per bed or $45 a twin/double. Dogs are allowed, under control.

There is an airstrip near the roadhouse and aviation fuel can be supplied, but only if you give them plenty of warning to get fuel flown in. You can contact the roadhouse by writing to PMB 77, Cairns Mail Centre, Qld 4870.

Weipa

Weipa is the largest town on the Cape, and because it is a mining town, all facilities are available. These include a Commonwealth Bank (with full banking facilities), a chemist, large supermarket in the suburb of Nanum, and numerous mechanical service centres.

The *Pax Haven Caravan & Camping*

Ground (☎ (070) 69 7871, fax 69 8211) offers all amenities, including hot showers and green lawns. Dogs are allowed, on leash. Costs are around $5 per person per night for an unpowered site, plus $2 for a powered site. Tours of Comalco's mining operations are conducted daily during the tourist season and pickups and bookings can be made through the camping ground.

The *Albatross Hotel-Motel* (☎ (070) 69 7314, fax 69 7130), Trunding Point, has motel rooms and bungalows. Prices range from $85 for a single motel room, or bungalows from $50/80 for a double/family. Meals are served in the restaurant or the family bistro.

Lockhart River Aboriginal Community

Visitors to the Aboriginal community at Lockhart River are welcome to stop for fuel and supplies, but are asked to respect the community's privacy. Use of cameras and videos is not permitted. You can contact the Lockhart River Community Council on ☎ (070) 60 7144.

The *General Store* (☎ (070) 60 7192) can supply most food items, including meat, fruit and vegetables, as well as fuel (which is expensive). It also has a post office with a Commonwealth Bank agency (☎ (070) 60 7138).

There are no camping facilities, but accommodation is available at the *guesthouse* (☎ (070) 60 7139) and it is best to book ahead. The house is self-contained, but you need to supply your own linen. It costs $30 per person per day.

Jardine River

The new *Jardine River Roadhouse* is on the south bank of the river, at the ferry crossing. It supplies fuel and has a camping area as well. Contact the Injinoo Community Council (☎ (070) 69 3252) for further details.

Bamaga

A wide range of facilities are available in Bamaga, the largest community on the northern Cape. The *Bamaga Service Centre* (☎ (070) 69 3275, fax 69 3335) has fuel

available and can provide mechanical repairs, along with ice and camping-gas refills. It is open from Monday to Friday, and Saturday and Sunday mornings, and accepts major credit cards.

A reasonably well-stocked *supermarket* (☎ (070) 69 3186) is open seven days a week during the tourist season, with limited trading hours on the weekend. There is also a National Australia Bank agency within the store (passbook only accepted).

The post office (☎ (070) 69 3126) is also the Commonwealth Bank agency (again passbook only).

Beer and wine can be purchased from the *Bamaga Canteen*, fresh bread from the bakery, and ice from the ice works. There is also a snack bar and newsagency.

Seisia

The *Seisia Camping Ground* (☎ (070) 69 3243/3333, fax 69 3155) is definitely the place to go to learn about what is happening in and around the top end of Cape York. It is the booking agent for all tours, the ferry service, taxi service, and anything else that is available. You can get up-to-date fishing information and maps, along with general tourist information.

The camping ground overlooks the islands of Torres Strait and features palm-thatched picnic shelters, hot showers, washing machines and calm-water boating. Camping fees are $6 per person per night. Dogs are allowed. During the tourist season the Seisia Island Dancers give regular performances.

The new *Seisia Seaview Lodge* has units for $30 a single. Bookings are made through the camping ground.

The *Seisia Kiosk* (☎ (070) 69 3285) is open seven days a week. Hot food and meals are served in the restaurant, and snacks and takeaway food are available.

Fuel & Repairs Seisia Marine Engineering (☎ (070) 69 3321, fax 69 3278) provides general fabrication and engineering, gas refills for camping bottles, aluminium welding, boat repairs, trailer and suspension

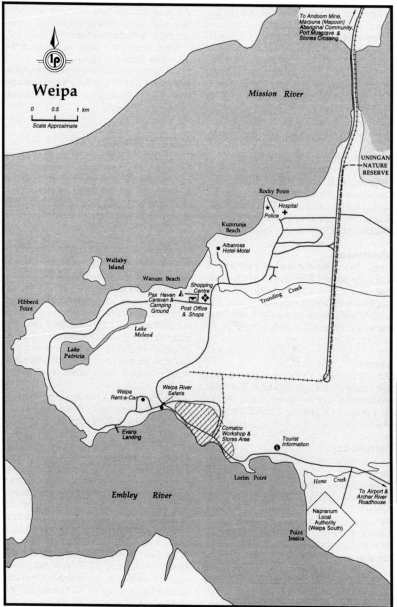

Weipa

0 0.5 1 km
Scale Approximate

Mission River

To Andoom Mine,
Marpuna (Mapoon)
Aboriginal Community,
Port Musgrave &
Stones Crossing

UNINGAN
NATURE
RESERVE

Rocky Point

★ Police + Hospital

Kumrunja Beach

■ Albatross Hotel-Motel

Wallaby Island

Wanum Beach

Shopping Centre

Pax Haven Caravan & Camping Ground

Post Office & Shops

Trunding Creek

Hibberd Point

Lake Mcleod

Lake Patricia

Weipa Rent-a-Car

Weipa River Safaris

Evans Landing

Comalco Workshop & Stores Area

ⓘ Tourist Information

Lorim Point

Home Creek

To Airport &
Archer River
Roadhouse

Embley River

Napranum Local Authority (Weipa South)

Point Jessica

THE TROPICS

repairs, and radiator clean-outs and repairs. Major credit cards are accepted.

Top End Motors (☎ (070) 69 3182), Tradesmans Way, is the place to go for all mechanical and welding repairs to your vehicle, along with batteries, tyres, oils and a range of spare parts.

The Seisia Palms Service Station (☎ (070) 69 3172) is Australia's northernmost service station and can supply super, unleaded and diesel fuel, outboard oils and marine products.

Injinoo Aboriginal Community
The small township of Injinoo is eight km south-west of Bamaga. It has a general store, Commonwealth Bank agency, fuel and mechanical repair facilities. For information, phone the Injinoo Community Council (☎ (070) 69 3252).

New Mapoon
Facilities are limited at this small settlement, with only general food items and ice available. However, a new camping ground is proposed in the area with beach frontage. For further information, contact the New Mapoon Community Council (☎ (070) 69 3277).

Umagico
Limited facilities, including a general food store and canteen, are available from this small community. For more details, contact the Umagico Community Council (☎ (070) 69 3251).

Punsand Bay
On a north-facing beach just a few km from the tip of Cape York is the *Punsand Bay Private Reserve* (☎ & fax (070) 69 1722, or ☎ (070) 55 9535). Facilities include hot showers, laundry, kiosk and basic food supplies, and a dining room serving meals for breakfast, lunch and dinner. Activities include night walks and tours to Cape York and the surrounding area. There is also a resident fishing guide.

Those with a tent can camp, an unpowered site costing $7 per person per night, or $5 extra per site will get you power. Accommo-dation is also available in on-site tents with beds, and cabins, for $65 and $95 per person per night, including all meals.

There is a regular ferry service from the reserve to Thursday Island.

For further information or bookings, write to Punsand Bay Private Reserve, Wilderness Base Camp, Punsand Bay, Via Bamaga, Cape York, Qld 4876.

Pajinka Wilderness Lodge
The Pajinka Wilderness Lodge (☎ (070) 31 3988) is run by the Injinoo Aboriginal Community and is only 400 metres from the northernmost tip of Australia. There is a resident naturalist and fishing guide, and 4WD tours with Aboriginal guides can be organised. The lodge is accessible all year round by air.

Cabin-style accommodation is available, and prices range from $170 to $240, depending on the number of people sharing a cabin. Camping costs $5 per person per night in the *camping ground*, with unpowered sites only available at present. A permit to camp is required and this can be obtained from the lodge or the Injinoo Community Council (☎ (070) 69 3252). Normal amenities are provided for campers, and a licensed kiosk supplies limited stores, takeaway food and ice.

For bookings or further information, contact the Cairns agent (☎ 008 802 968, fax 31 3966) PO Box 7757, Cairns, Qld 4870.

Station Properties
There are a number of properties that cater for the traveller, offering camping and accommodation, as well as organised tours.

These include: Bramwell Station (☎ (070) 60 3237), north of Wenlock River; Butchers Hill Station (☎ (070) 60 2155), near Lakelands; King Park Homestead (☎ (070) 60 7170); Mary Valley Cattle Station & Wildlife Retreat (☎ (070) 60 3254), near Musgrave, with its own airstrip; and Silver Plains Homestead (☎ (070) 60 3228), east of Coen on the coast.

Airstrips

There are four public aerodromes, at Cooktown, Coen, Iron Range and Laura, while throughout Cape York there are small, privately owned and maintained airstrips on station properties. Aviation fuel can be organised from most of the airstrips, but you need to give prior notice of your requirements.

Coen Aerodrome (☎ (070) 60 1136) is 24 km north of Coen on the Peninsula Developmental Road. Lockhart River Airfield (☎ (070) 60 7121) is approximately five km from the Lockhart River Aboriginal Community.

Weipa has a major airport with aviation fuel available. Jacky Jacky Airfield is nine km south-east of Bamaga and is the main airport for the Top.

ALTERNATIVE TRANSPORT
Air

A wide range of charter aircraft operate all over Cape York. Each company usually has its own scheduled scenic flights and safari tours. Contact the Far North Queensland Tourist Bureau for full details (see Information in the Cairns to Musgrave via Cooktown section).

Cape York Air Services operates the Peninsula mail run, the world's longest, dropping into remote cattle stations and towns. For more information, see Alternative Transport in the Cairns to Musgrave via Cooktown section.

Flight West Airlines has flights from Cairns to: Cooktown, Kowanyama, Edward River, Coen, Lockhart River, Bamaga, Horn Island and Thursday Island. For details on prices and current flight schedules, write to PO Box 107, Cairns Mail Centre, Cairns, Qld 4870.

Sunstate Airlines and Qantas (☎ 13 1313) have flights from Cairns to Lizard Island, Bamaga and Thursday Island. Ring for current flight details and reservations.

Ansett Australia (☎ 13 1300) has a daily flight from Cairns to Weipa.

Skytrans (☎ (070) 69 7248, fax 69 7193), based in Weipa, has flights twice weekly from Weipa to Bamaga and Thursday Island. For more information, see Alternative Transport in the Cairns to Musgrave via Cooktown section.

Air Cairns (☎ 008 816 117) operates flights six days a week from Thursday Island to all the islands around the top of Cape York. Contact the agent on Thursday Island (☎ (070) 69 1325) for flight details, costs and current flight times, or the main office in Cairns (☎ (070) 35 9003, fax 35 9125), PO Box 129, Stratford, Qld 4870.

Bus

No bus company actually runs a service all the way to the top of Cape York, but a number of companies run services from Cairns to Cooktown or Weipa.

Coral Coaches (☎ (070) 98 2600, fax 98 1064), 37 Front St, Mossman, Qld 4873, operates a daily bus service from Cairns to Cooktown. See Alternative Transport in the Cairns to Musgrave via Cooktown section for full details.

Cape York Coaches (☎ (070) 93 0176), 21 Vievers Drive, Kuranda, Qld 4891, operates a weekly service from Cairns to Weipa on Friday, and Weipa to Cairns on Saturday. The fare is $235 return. Bookings can also be made through Skytrans in Weipa (see Air).

Boat

A number of shipping companies cruise the coast of Cape York carrying a variety of cargo and stores. While many can transport vehicles, only a couple actually take passengers.

Jardine Shipping (☎ (070) 35 1299, fax 35 1685) operates a weekly service from Cairns to Thursday Island and Bamaga, taking vehicles, general cargo and passengers.

Gulf Freight Services (☎ (070) 69 8619) operates a regular service from Weipa to Cairns carrying freight, passengers, vehicles and pets. For details contact the Cairns office (☎ (070) 51 3411), 153 Lyons St.

Thursday Island Ferry Service Peddell's Ferry & Tourist Service (☎ (070) 69 1551, fax 69 1365), based on Thursday Island, operates a regular ferry service between Seisia and Thursday Island. During the peak tourist season, from June to October, the ferry runs from Monday to Saturday, leaving the jetty at Seisia at 8 am and stopping at Punsand Bay and the Pajinka Wilderness Lodge to pick up passengers. An adult return fare (same day) costs $55, one way costs $35. Bookings are essential and can be made through Peddell's direct or at the Seisia Camping Ground, Punsand Bay or Pajinka Lodge. Peddell's also operates a bus tour of Thursday Island in conjunction with the ferry service.

4WD Rental

There are a number of companies that hire 4WDs to travellers over 25 years of age, but the majority will only let you take them as far as Cooktown and Laura. Only a few companies, based in and around Cairns, will allow you to take the vehicle all the way to the Top; these include:

Brits Rentals
    230 Sheridan St, Cairns (☎ (070) 51 0871) – 4WDs and 4WD campervans available
Cairns Leisure Wheels
    16A Sheridan St, Cairns (☎ (070) 51 8988) – 4WDs available for hire from Cairns to Weipa, and the Top, to drivers over 26 years of age
Cairns OffRoad Accessories 4WD Hire
    55 Anderson St, Manunda, Cairns (☎ (070) 51 0088, fax 31 1804)
Crocodile Car Rentals
    50 Macrossan St, Port Douglas (☎ (070) 99 5555)

There are other car hire companies in Cooktown (see the Cairns to Musgrave via Cooktown section for details), Weipa and Seisia. However, you can only use the vehicles in the local area.

Seisia Hire Cars (☎ (070) 69 3368) operates from Seisia and has 4WDs available for daily or weekly hire. Visitors can use the vehicles to explore the surrounding area, including the Tip, Bamaga and areas north of the Jardine River. It is advisable to ring and book ahead to ensure a vehicle is available.

Weipa Rent-A-Car (☎ (070) 69 7311, fax 69 7435), Evans Landing, Weipa, has 4WD vehicles available for touring around Weipa.

Motorcycle Rental

It is very difficult to hire a motorcycle to take up to the top of Cape York. However, for riders travelling to Cooktown or Chillagoe, 2 Wheel Adventures (☎ (070) 31 5707) can arrange motorcycles from 250cc to 600cc for $60 to $75 per day, which includes 300 free km in each day of hire.

Tour operators such as 2 Wheel Adventures and Cape York Motor Cycle Adventures can rent a motorcycle to you for use on one of their guided tours to Cape York. For more information, see the Organised Tours section.

Thursday Island & Torres Strait

No visit to the top of the Cape would be complete without a visit to at least Thursday Island, or 'TI'.

There are a number of islands scattered across the reef-strewn waters of Torres Strait, and they exhibit a surprising variety in form and function. There are three main types: the rocky, mountain-top extension of the Great Dividing Range that makes up the western group that includes TI and Prince of Wales Island; the central group of islands that dot the waters east to the Great Barrier Reef are little more than coral cays; while the third type of islands are volcanic in origin and are in the far east of the strait, at the very northern end of the Great Barrier Reef. These Murray Islands are some of the most spectacular and picturesque in the area.

While TI is the 'capital' of Torres Strait, there are 17 inhabited islands, the northernmost being Saibai and Boigu islands, a couple of km from the New Guinea coast.

HISTORY

There were often bloody tribal conflicts across the islands before the Europeans arrived, but inevitably the Islanders came off second-best against the weaponry of the Whites.

When pearl shell was discovered in the waters of the strait during the 1860s, it led to an invasion of boats and crews in search of this new form of wealth. It was a wild and savage industry with 'blackbirding', a form of kidnapping for sale into slavery, and killing being common. Being on the very edge of the frontier, the strait and all those who worked in it and plundered its resources were out of reach of the law.

Around the same time, the missionaries arrived and they were obviously successful, as the Islanders are still one of the most church-going populations in Australia.

During the first half of this century the pearling industry was the lifeblood of the area. It was a dangerous job as there was little knowledge of the physiological aspects of deep diving, and death from the 'bends', or decompression sickness, was common. Poor equipment and the odd storm or cyclone were also perils that the divers and crews faced. In fact, it was a cyclone in March 1899 that caused the biggest loss of life and devastated the industry. That cyclone struck Bathurst Bay where 45 boats from the TI pearling fleet were anchored, and in the following hours only one boat survived and over 300 men were killed.

While a number of nationalities made up the working population, the Japanese were considered by many to make the best divers. The price they paid for their expertise is evident in the TI cemetery where over 500 are buried.

In WW II Torres Strait and the islands were part of Australia's front line in the battle against the Japanese. Horn Island, in essence TI's airport, was bombed a number of times in 1942, but TI never had a bomb dropped on it. Some say that was due to the legend that a Japanese princess was buried on the island, but it was more than likely the fact that there was a large population of Japanese living on TI.

After the war, plastics took over where pearl shell left off. A number of cultured pearl bases still operate around the waters of

TI, but the 100 or more boats that once worked the beds have long since disappeared.

In 1975 Papua New Guinea became independent. Though there was some dispute over international boundaries, all the islands up to two km off the New Guinea coast remained Australian.

Today much of the wealth of the area still comes from the sea in the form of prawns from the Gulf, for which TI is a major port, and crayfish from the reefs of the strait. Tourism is also playing its part in this region of Australia that is so vastly different to the mainland.

THURSDAY ISLAND

The island is little more than three sq km in area, with the town of TI being located on its southern shore. The population is less than 2500.

There are a few stores, including a general store, chemist, takeaways and a branch of the National Bank (with full banking facilities). There are also four hotels, three with accommodation as well as a cold beer. There is intense but friendly rivalry between the hotels, with each supporting a local Rugby League football club. TI also has a police station (☎ (070) 69 1520) and a hospital (☎ (070) 69 1109).

Things to See

The **Quetta Memorial Church** was built in 1893 in memory of the *Quetta*, wrecked three years earlier with over 130 lives lost. The TI **cemetery**, with its Japanese graves and the more recent Japanese Pearl Memorial for those who lost their lives diving for shell, is a poignant place. **Green Hill Fort**, on the west side of town, was built in the 1890s when the Russians were thought to be coming.

While there are places of interest around TI, it is the atmosphere of the island and the people that set it apart from the rest of Australia.

Festivals

The Torres Strait Cultural Festival is held

AIDS poster on Thursday Island (TW)

Thursday Island pub (TW)

THE TROPICS

annually in May and numerous activities are organised such as art exhibitions, traditional singing, ceremonial dancing and cooking, along with a colourful procession. Visitors can also wander through the many stalls set up during the festival, many of which have local art & craft displayed. For further information, telephone ☎ (070) 69 1698, fax 69 1658, or write to PO Box 42, Thursday Island, Qld 4875.

Accommodation

The *Federal Hotel* (☎ (070) 69 1569) is on the beach front at Victoria Parade. The *Torres Hotel* (☎ (070) 69 1141) is back one street from the water on the corner of Douglas and Normanby Sts, while the more up-market *Jardine Hotel* (☎ (070) 69 1555) is on the corner of Normanby St and Victoria Parade. Prices range from $30 to $120 for a single.

There are also a couple of centrally located hostels on TI, the *Jumula Dubbins Hostel* (☎ (070) 69 2212) and the *Mura Mudh Hostel* (☎ (070) 69 1708). Prices range from $15 a bed to $40 a single with full board.

Food

Each of the hotels have counter meals. In the evening, most have a better class of meal in their respective restaurants.

In the main area of Douglas St you will find a number of milk bars and takeaway places, if that is your taste. Don't expect these to be open outside business hours – this is TI!

Getting There & Away

You can either fly to TI or catch the local ferry that runs between Seisia and TI. Even if you fly you will still be up for a ferry ride as the plane lands on Horn Island, separated from TI by the 1.5-km-wide Ellis Channel.

Australian, Flight West and Sunstate Airlines have regular flights to TI. For flight details and reservations, contact Australian Airlines (☎ (070) 50 3711) in Cairns, or the TI office (☎ (070) 69 1264); Flight West Airlines (070) 35 9511) in Cairns, or the TI office (☎ (070) 69 1325); and Sunstate (☎ 13 1313).

The most popular way to get to TI is via Peddell's Ferry Service which leaves the mainland from the jetty at Red Island Point, adjacent to the camping area at Seisia. For details, see Boat towards the end of the earlier Cape York section.

Getting Around

To see the island, you can grab a local taxi (☎ (070) 69 1666) or join any of the tours that generally meet the ferry from the mainland, such as Peddell's Wongai Isle Bus Tours and Willie Nelson's TI Tours. You can book the Peddell's tour through the TI office (☎ (070) 69 1551) or at the Seisia Camping Ground (see Seisia under Facilities in the earlier Cape York section). For bookings and details for Willie Nelson's tour, phone ☎ (070) 69 1588.

Alternatively, you can hire a car from TI Travel (☎ (070) 69 1264) or R & F Self-Service Store (☎ (070) 69 1173).

OTHER ISLANDS

The other inhabited islands of the strait are isolated communities wresting a living from the surrounding reef-strewn sea. The Islanders who inhabit them are fiercely proud of their heritage, with a separate identity to the Aborigines.

Outside of TI the largest group of people are found on Boigu, close to the New Guinea coast, where the population numbers less than 400. Most of the inhabited islands have populations between 100 and 200 people, while Booby Island in the far west of the strait is home to just a couple of families who look after the lighthouse.

Getting around and staying on the other islands of Torres Strait is really for the adventurous traveller. To visit any of the islands you need a permit, and as these are issued by the local council they may not be easy to get. Contact the Islanders Community Council (☎ (070) 69 1446) at the office in Summers St, Thursday Island.

Accommodation & Food

Accommodation on these islands is very limited. The community on Yorke Island,

THE TROPICS

110 km north-east of TI, runs a small, self-contained *guesthouse*. Cost is $25 a single or $30 with meals. Intending visitors should first write to the community council stating details of their visit. It will then be put before the chairperson for approval. For further details, contact the Yorke Island Community Council on ☎ (070) 69 4128.

Accommodation is also available on Horn Island at the *Gateway Torres Strait Resort* (☎ (070) 69 1902) and the *Wongai Tavern* (☎ (070) 69 1683).

Getting There & Away

Once you have a permit you have a choice of flying or chartering a boat. Flying may be quicker and easier, but the essence of Torres Strait is somehow lost. Air Cairns and Falcon Airlines operate regular flights servicing the islands. For further information and reservations, contact the Air Cairns agent on TI at the Flight West office (☎ (070) 69 1325), or Falcon Airlines at its Horn Island office (☎ (070) 69 2777) or in Cairns (☎ (070) 35 9359).

Matilda Highway

Outback Queensland is a place where dinosaurs once roamed, the inspiration for Waltzing Matilda, the birthplace of Qantas and the home of the Stockman's Hall of Fame. It has many attractions for travellers with a sense of history and an appreciation of nature's delights.

The Matilda Highway takes you north from the vast open plains of south-western Queensland into the tropics, where gold and other minerals reign supreme, to the Gulf of Carpentaria and the prawn capital of Australia.

This all-bitumen route, which begins in Cunnamulla and ends in Karumba, 1674 km further north, is one of the best, quickest and most enjoyable routes from the populated southern areas of Australia to the remote, romantic north of the country.

The Matilda Highway is in fact the name given to a route made up of a number of roads and highways. Sections of the Mitchell Highway, the Landsborough Highway and the Burke Developmental Road make up what is now called the Matilda Highway.

HISTORY

Aborigines inhabited this country for thousands of years, and saw the comings and goings of animals that are now preserved only in the stones of Riversleigh, a monumental deposit of bones and other palaeontological finds near Lawn Hill National Park, north-west of Mount Isa, and easily accessible from this route.

Dutch navigators were the first Europeans to sight this land, when Willem Janszoon sailed the Gulf coast in 1606. Others followed but found little to interest them, and it wasn't until the great British navigator Matthew Flinders sailed along the Gulf coast, careening his ship on Sweers Island in November 1802, that the British crown showed any interest in this region.

Ludwig Leichhardt crossed the Gulf plains on his way to Port Essington in the Northern Territory in 1844. Over the next 20 years, some of Australia's greatest explorers, including Thomas Mitchell (later knighted for his exploration achievements), Burke and Wills, William Landsborough, Augustus Gregory and John McKinlay, crisscrossed the vast plains and the low rugged ranges of outback Queensland. In the process they opened up this land to the sheep and cattle graziers who quickly followed.

INFORMATION
Tourist Offices

Travellers will find tourist information centres in most towns along the route. In addition, information is available from the following tourism bodies, which also publish some very good, readily available booklets:

Gulf Local Authority Development Association, PO Box 2312, Cairns, Qld 4870 (☎ (070) 31 1631, fax 31 3340)

Inland Queensland Tourism & Development Board,
PO Box 356, Mount Isa, Qld 4825 (☎ (077) 43
7966, fax 43 8746)

Matilda Highway Marketing & Development Committee, PO Box 295, Blackall, Qld 4472 (☎ (076)
57 4255, fax 57 4437)

Outback Queensland Tourism Authority Inc, PO Box
295, Blackall, Qld 4472 (☎ (076) 57 4222, fax 57
4726)

For information on any of the national parks,
contact the Department of Environment &
Heritage in Brisbane (☎ (07) 227 8186) or
Mount Isa (☎ (077) 43 2055).

Books & Maps
The Queensland Tourist & Travel Corporation has produced the excellent book *The
Matilda Highway*, which is readily available
in good book/map shops or from branches of
the automobile clubs in each state. The
Queensland state mapping authority has also
produced a map called *The Matilda
Highway*, which can be purchased from
Sunmap centres or agencies, as well as from
good book/map shops.

THE ROUTE
Cunnamulla
The southernmost town in western Queensland, Cunnamulla (population 1700) is on
the Warrego River 120 km north of the
Qld/NSW border. This outback town lies 805
km west of Brisbane via St George and 1034
km north-west of Sydney via Bourke (the
next major town south, 254 km away).

The town was gazetted in 1868, and in
1879 Cobb & Co established a coaching
station here. In the 1880s, an influx of
farmers opened the country up to the two
million sheep that graze the open plains
today. The train arrived in 1898, and since
then Cunnamulla has been a major service
centre for the district; in good years it is
Queensland's biggest wool-loading railyard.

For information on Cunnamulla, contact
the tourist information centre (☎ (076) 55
1777) at the civic centre.

The town has two hotel/motels, four
hotels, one motel and one caravan park, as
well as a number of service stations, supermarkets and the like.

For sightseers, there's the **Historical
Society Display**, telling the story of the
pioneers of the district, and the **Robbers
Tree**, a reminder of a robbery that was
bungled back in the 1880s. Another tree at
the civic centre takes some importance from
the fact that it is a yapunyah tree, floral
emblem of the Paroo Shire – and this one was
planted by royalty!

In late August the town celebrates the
Cunnamulla-Eulo Festival of the Opal, a
week-long festival with arts & crafts, a
parade and ball. Another major event is the
annual Show, held in May.

Cunnamulla to Augathella (281 km)
From Cunnamulla you can head east along
the Balonne Highway to Brisbane, or go
west to Thargomindah and the hotel that is
the town of Nockatunga, past the Jackson
Oil Fields to Cooper Creek, South Australia, and on to the outback destination of
Innamincka.

Eulo, 64 km west of Cunnamulla, is on the
Paroo River close to the Yowah opal fields.
In late August/early September the town
hosts the World Lizard Racing Championships, beside the Eulo Queen Hotel and the
Destructo Cockroach Monument. Erected
in memory of a racing cockroach who died
when a punter stood on it, this granite plinth
must be the only cockroach memorial in the
world. Don't let this, or the lizard-racing
competition, put you off visiting Eulo – the
people are really quite friendly.

Our route from Cunnamulla lies north
along the Mitchell Highway, paralleling
the Warrego River (which is off to the
west). The railway follows a similar route
northwards, and a couple of railway
sidings, the odd station homestead and the
small community of **Wyandra**, with the
obligatory hotel and general store, make
up the habitation profile of the 197-km trip
to Charleville. For the most part, the
mainly flat country is clothed in mulga, a
low tree of the wattle family.

Carnarvon Gorge (MA)

Charleville One of the largest towns in outback Queensland, Charleville is 760 km west of Brisbane and situated on the Warrego River. Edmund Kennedy passed this way in 1847, and the town was gazetted in 1868, six years after the first settlers had arrived. By the turn of the century the town was an important service centre for the outlying sheep stations.

Cobb & Co began building coaches at Charleville in 1893, and these coaches, especially designed for Australian conditions, were built here until 1920. The last official service by coach was performed nearby (from Yuleba to Surat) just four years later.

Aviation history was being made at the same time. In 1922 Qantas (Queensland & Northern Territory Aerial Services) was founded in this town; the carrier's first regular flight was between Charleville and Cloncurry, further north on our trip to the Gulf.

The Mulga Tourist Association (☎ (076) 54 1307), or the local tourist information centre (☎ (076) 54 3057) in the town hall, can provide information on points of interest and things to do in and around Charleville.

The town has a couple of hotel/motels, two motels and two caravan parks, as well as service stations, general stores, supermarkets, chemists and butchers – in fact, everything a traveller (or a remote outback community) needs.

Apart from its links with the stagecoach days and the birth of Qantas, Charleville offers history buffs the **Historic House Museum**, the **Steiger Vortex Gun** (invented in an attempt to break the great drought of 1902) and the **Landsborough Tree** (marked by the explorer William Landsborough in 1862, a few km south of town on the edge of the river).

The **RFDS base** (☎ (076) 54 1341) and the **School of the Air** (now called the School of Distance Education) are located in Charleville, and interested people can check these vital outback facilities. Another important office is that run by the National Parks & Wildlife Service. At their **research centre** (☎ (076) 54 1255) on the east side of town, they have set up a breeding programme for the endangered, strikingly beautiful Australian marsupial the bilby, sometimes called the rabbit-eared bandicoot.

A number of events are held at Charleville during the year. In May the annual Show takes place, and in September there is a rodeo, and the Booga Woongaroo Festival, with historic displays and a fishing competition part of the festivities.

North of Charleville From Charleville you can head east to Brisbane via Roma, or west to Quilpie, Windorah and Bedourie via the Diamantina Developmental Road.

Our route, however, continues northwards along the Mitchell Highway, paralleling the Warrego River. The river offers anglers a number of opportunities to dangle a line for Murray cod, yellowbelly, golden perch (one of the tastiest freshwater fish in Australia) or catfish.

Augathella

Eighty-four km north of Charleville is the town of Augathella. It lies at the junction of the Mitchell Highway and the road southeast to Morven and the route to Brisbane. South-east Queensland travellers heading north to Mount Isa, the Gulf or the Northern Territory often join the Matilda at this junction.

Surveyed in 1880, Augathella began as a bullock team camp beside the Warrego River. Today it services the sheep properties that dot the surrounding countryside.

This small country town has one hotel, one motel and a caravan park, with fuel and supplies from the shops in town. Tourist information can be obtained from Russell's Roadhouse (☎ (076) 54 5255).

Augathella to Barcaldine (324 km)

At Augathella you change highways, continuing north-west on the Landsborough Highway; 116 km north of Augathella you pass through the small township of **Tambo**, on the banks of the Barcoo River.

Tambo is surrounded by perhaps the best grazing land in western Queensland, and this small hamlet also has some of the earliest historic buildings in the region. In the main street are timber houses that date back to the town's earliest days, in the 1860s, while the 'new' post office has been operating since 1904. The **'old' post office**, built in 1876 and at that time the main repeating station for south-west Queensland, is now a museum.

The town has a couple of hotels and motels and a caravan park. It can supply all you require, including LPG. The information centre is at the shire council chambers (☎ (076) 54 6133).

The town promotes itself as 'the friendly town of the west', and each year races are held at the local track, a tradition dating back to the formation of the Great Western Downs Jockey Club, in 1865.

From Tambo you continue northwards on the Matilda Highway, but if you're looking for a good excursion, there is access to the **Salvator Rosa** section of Carnarvon National Park. The Salvator Rosa park is 120 km east of Tambo and is accessed via the Dawson Developmental Road and Cungelella station, generally a 4WD route.

Discovered and named by the explorer Thomas Mitchell in 1846, the same year he discovered the downs on which Tambo is situated, Salvator Rosa's 26,000 hectares protect a maze of sandstone escarpments and gorges. It's a spectacularly rugged area with few facilities, and you need a permit from the national parks to camp. Try the park office in Charleville (☎ (076) 54 1255) or Longreach (☎ (076) 58 1761) for more information.

Continuing northwards along the Landsborough Highway, it's a pleasant run of 101 km to the town of Blackall. The **Barcoo River** is crossed 59 km north of Tambo, and there is an excellent spot to stop and camp on the east side of the road. You can even get back a bit off the road, away from the traffic noise.

The Barcoo is one of the great rivers of western Queensland, and must be the only river in the world that in its lower reaches becomes a creek! The Barcoo initially flows north-west past Blackall, then swings south-west

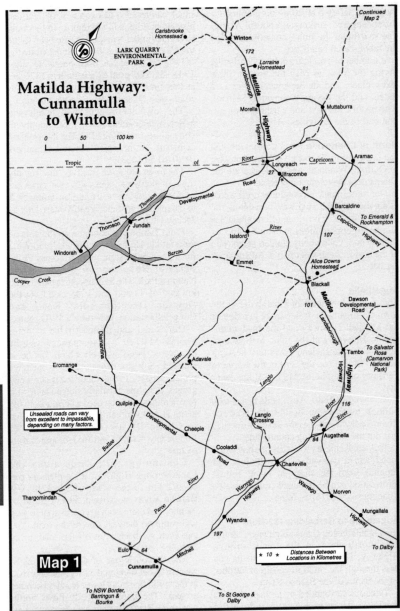

Carisbrooke Homestead

Winton

LARK QUARRY ENVIRONMENTAL PARK

Lorraine Homestead

172

Matilda Highway: Cunnamulla to Winton

Morella

Muttaburra

0   50   100 km

Tropic   of   Capricorn

River

Longreach

Aramac

27   Ilfracombe

81

Road

Developmental

Barcaldine

To Emerald & Rockhampton

Thomson

Thomson   Jundah

Isisford

River

107

Windorah

Barcoo

Emmet

Alice Downs Homestead

Blackall

Dawson Developmental Road

101

Cooper   Creek

Diamantina

River

Adavale

To Salvator Rosa (Carnarvon National Park)

Tambo

Eromanga

Langlo

River

Langlo Crossing

116

Unsealed roads can vary from excellent to impassable, depending on many factors.

Quilpie

Developmental

Cheepie

Nive   River

River

84   Augathella

Cooladdi

Bulloo

Road

Charleville

Warrego

Morven

River

Warrego   Highway

Mungallala

Thargomindah

Paroo

Highway

To Dalby

River

Wyandra

197

★ 10 ★   Distances Between Locations in Kilometres

Eulo   64

Mitchell

Cunnamulla

Map 1

To NSW Border, Barringun & Bourke

To St George & Dalby

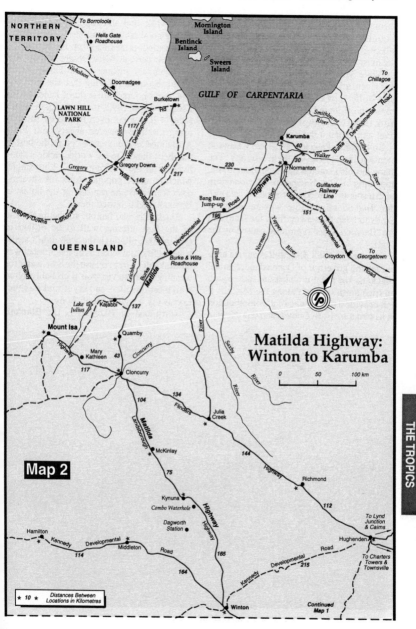

Matilda Highway: Winton to Karumba

Map 2

Continued Map 1

through Isisford and into the Channel Country of south-western Queensland, where it becomes Cooper Creek, probably the most famous of Australia's inland rivers.

While Mitchell had waxed lyrical about this river in 1846, thinking it was a route to the Gulf, it was left to his second-in-command Edmund Kennedy (later of Cape York fame) to discover the real course of the river and to call it the Barcoo in 1847.

Both Banjo Paterson and Henry Lawson mention the Barcoo in their writings. The name has also entered the Australian idiom, appearing in the *Macquarie Dictionary* in such terms as 'Barcoo rot' (basically scurvy), the 'Barcoo salute' (the waving about of hands to keep flies away from the face) and the 'Barcoo spews' (vomiting caused by the heat).

Gazetted in 1868, **Blackall** is named after the second governor of Queensland, Samuel Blackall. The town is a pleasant spot to stop on trips north or south along the Matilda. It can provide a wide range of accommodation in its two motels, five hotels and one caravan park, while fuel and supplies are available from a good range of outlets.

The town prides itself on the fact that it was near here, at Alice Downs station, that the legendary shearer Jackie Howe set his world record of shearing 321 sheep in less than eight hours, with a set of hand shears! Established in 1892, the record still stands today – it was not even beaten by shearers using machine-powered shears until 1950. Acclaimed as the greatest 'gun' (the best in the shed) shearer in the world, Jackie's name lives on in the working man's blue singlet which he made popular. After his shearing days were over, he ran one of the hotels in Blackall, and is buried there.

Blackall is also famous for being the site of the first artesian well to be drilled in Queensland, although the well didn't strike water at first and when it did the product was undrinkable. After you use the bore water for washing or whatever, you'll probably agree with most travellers and say it stinks a little. Locals say it's got a bit of 'body'.

North-east of Blackall is the **Blackall**

Cattle on the 'long paddock' north of Winton (R & VM)

Woolscour, the only steam-driven scour (wool-cleaner) left in Queensland. It stopped operating in 1978, but guided tours of the operation are run by the local tourist office.

Annual events in Blackall include the Claypan Bogie Country Music Festival (in March), the Show (in May) and the Jackie Howe Run shearing competition (in October). In October every even-numbered year, the Barcoo Rush Festival takes place.

For more information on Blackall, contact the Blackall Community Tourist Office (☎ (076) 57 4637/4255).

From Blackall you can travel into the Channel Country of south-west Queensland by heading out to Isisford or Windorah (115 km and 337 km west of Blackall, respectively). Our route, though, lies north along the Landsborough Highway.

North of Blackall Travelling these roads at night is not recommended. Kangaroos often reach plague proportions out in western Queensland, and the edge of the bitumen is a place where water gathers from any rain and where green feed is more readily available. Kangaroos often come out beside the road to feed in the evening, and at night in one 100-km section of this road, you can see in excess of 1000 animals. At times like this it becomes impossible to miss all of them, as they become dazzled by the lights. It's best, for your sake and the animals', not to drive unless you really have to.

An hour's travelling on the bitumen across flat, lightly treed plains brings you to Barcaldine, 107 km north of Blackall.

Barcaldine

Barcaldine lies at the junction of the Landsborough and Capricorn highways, 575 km west of Rockhampton via Emerald, surrounded by sheep and cattle stations. It's known as the 'Garden City of the West', with good supplies of artesian water nourishing orchards of citrus fruits – Barcaldine was the first town in Australia to realise its underground bounty, in 1887.

Established in 1886 when the railway arrived, Barcaldine gained a place in Australian history in 1891 when it became the headquarters of the historic shearers' strike during which over 1000 men camped in and around the town. That confrontation saw troops called in, and the formation of the Australian Workers' Party, the forerunner of today's Australian Labor Party. The **'Tree of Knowledge'**, near the train station, was the meeting place of the organisers, and still stands as a monument to workers and their rights. The **Australian Workers' Heritage Centre**, opened by the prime minister in 1991, also commemorates the struggle.

Barcaldine's other attractions include the **folk museum**, the historic **Beta Farm** (dating from the 1880s) and a number of National Trust buildings. The annual Show is held in May.

A good range of accommodation is available in Barcaldine's six hotels, four motels and two caravan parks. There's also the normal range of stores and outlets for fuel, food and other supplies and facilities. Tourist information is available from the information centre (☎ (076) 51 1724) in Oak St.

Barcaldine to Winton (280 km)

From Barcaldine you can head east to Rockhampton and the coast, or you can head north through the small but interesting towns of Aramac and Muttaburra to Hughenden, 357 km north of Barcaldine. The unsealed road from Muttaburra to Hughenden passes through flat country and can be a bit rough in places, but is usually quite manageable in a conventional vehicle with sufficient ground clearance, driven with care. From Hughenden, you can head east along the sealed Flinders Highway to Charters Towers and Townsville, or continue up the Kennedy Developmental Road to the bitumen at the Lynd Junction and on to Cairns – an interesting route that takes you past the stunning Porcupine Gorge. This road is rocky and rougher than the previous section, but is usually OK in a conventional vehicle driven with care.

Our route from Barcaldine, however, lies west along the Landsborough Highway, across the wide open plains towards Longreach.

Ilfracombe is a small hamlet 81 km from Barcaldine, and it contains several historic buildings and a good folk museum. The local hotel offers accommodation and camping, while the general store provides fuel and takeaway food. You can't get lost here, as all the places are scattered along the highway. The shire council office (☎ (076) 58 2233) is the place to contact for tourist information.

Longreach Longreach, 27 km further west, is on a 'long reach' of the Thomson River. Apart from Mount Isa further north, it's western Queensland's largest town, with a population of around 3500.

The surrounding region was explored by Augustus Gregory in 1858 and 1859, and though the area was settled in the 1870s, the town was not officially gazetted until 1887.

It was in 1870 that Harry Redford stole 1000 head of cattle from Mount Cornish, an outstation of Bowen Downs, north of Longreach, and drove them down the Thomson River and its continuation, Cooper Creek, to the present site of Innamincka. From there he followed the Strzelecki Creek south, finally selling his ill-gotten gains to a station owner north of Adelaide. His exploit opened up a new stock route south, and when he was finally brought to justice, in Roma in 1873, he was found not guilty by the adoring public!

The railway arrived in 1892, and during the early years of the 20th century, the wool boom made Longreach into the town you see today.

In February 1921 the first **Qantas** flight left here for Winton, and the following year Longreach became the operational base for the fledgling airline founded in Charleville. The first seven aircraft built in Australia were constructed here, between 1922 and 1930.

Located in the heart of Queensland's outback and at the crossroads of some of the great cattle stock routes, it is no wonder that Longreach is the site of the **Australian Stockman's Hall of Fame**. Opened in 1988, the brainchild of artist Hugh Sawrey, it is one of the finest museums in the country, honouring the explorers, stockmen, shearers, pastoralists and everyday folk who helped open up outback Australia. It's a place that should not be missed.

A number of events are held in Longreach during the year. The Thomson River Campdraft and the annual Show take place in May, and during July there are shearing championships, as well as the Stockman's Hall of Fame Endurance Ride, run between Winton and Longreach. Every even-numbered year the Starlight Stampede Festival is held, in September.

There are also a number of other points of interest in and around the town and, of course, the river provides an opportunity for canoeing and fishing. A number of tours are available to historic or scenic attractions in the surrounding area, and there are enjoyable cruises on the river as well. Most of these are for two or three hours; try the 'Sunset Cruise'.

As is to be expected in such a large and important town, there is everything a traveller needs. Accommodation-wise there is a wide choice, with five hotels, five motels, two caravan parks and a backpackers' hostel. For local information on Longreach, contact the shire council (☎ (076) 58 4111) or Qantas Park (☎ (076) 58 3555).

Longreach to Winton From Longreach you can head south along the Thomson Developmental Road to Windorah and places further south along Cooper Creek. Northwards you can head to Muttaburra and to Hughenden, 380 km west of Townsville.

For those travelling the Matilda, head north-west out of Longreach along the Landsborough Highway; just out of town you cross the Thomson River.

The turn-off to **Lorraine station** is on the right, 125 km north of Longreach. This sheep property has opened its doors to tourism, and between April and November offers accommodation, station activities and good food.

The township of Winton is entered nearly 48 km further on, 172 km north of Longreach.

Winton

At the crossroads of the Landsborough Highway and the east-west Kennedy Developmental Road, Winton was settled in 1875 and now services the surrounding sheep and cattle stations.

This outback town has its fair share of claims to fame, with Banjo Paterson and Qantas figuring prominently. Back in 1895 the original North Gregory Hotel in Winton was the venue for the first public performance of Paterson's *Waltzing Matilda*, which he had written after a visit to Combo Waterhole on Dagworth station (where a local shearer had committed suicide), 140 km north-west of Winton. Since then the song has become the country's unofficial anthem, recognised around the world as pure Australian. An annual bush-verse competition, The Bronze Swagman Award, attracts interest from all over Australia, keeping alive the Banjo Paterson tradition and celebrating its influence on Australian literature.

Australia's major airline, Qantas, began in Winton – the first board meeting occurred in the Winton Club in 1921.

With those two events in mind, it's no surprise that the local museum is called **Qantilda Pioneer Place**, and it's worth more than a cursory look. As with any country town that has been around for over 100 years, Winton has its fair share of country architecture, with the open-air Royal Theatre testimony to the fine weather and just one of the interesting buildings in town.

South-west of the town is **Lark Quarry Environmental Park**, where fossilised footprints testify to a stampede of small dinosaurs 100 million years ago. It's a trip of 115 km each way on dirt roads to the site, which has no facilities other than a toilet and a rainwater tank. Well signposted from Winton, the site now sports a raised walkway and a sheltering tin roof to protect this unique find from the elements and from people.

Visits can also be made to **Carisbrooke station**, 85 km south-west of Winton. A wildlife sanctuary, the station also has an old opal mine, spectacular escarpment country, Aboriginal paintings and bora rings (circular ceremonial grounds).

With a population of 1200, Winton has three motels, four hotels, two caravan parks, a good selection of stores for supplies, and a choice of fuel outlets. The Gift & Gem Centre (☎ (076) 57 1296) in Elderslie St is the local tourist information centre.

Winton to Cloncurry (344 km)

Heading north-west out of town on the Landsborough Highway, the country is rolling native grassland dotted with the occasional mesa or patch of breakaway country. The wide thoroughfare is a recognised stock route, and it's not unusual to see cattle and drovers wandering the 'long paddock'. In those cases where there are sheep or cattle spread all over the road, you should slow down to a crawl, stopping if necessary, and let the people and dogs handling the stock work their way around you. Enjoy the passing parade – it is a way of life that brings back images of Australia's pioneering past.

The turn-off to Paterson's Combo Waterhole is signposted, 145 km north of Winton, and 20 km further along the Landsborough Highway you come to the small settlement of **Kynuna**.

There are a couple of buildings in Kynuna, and you can get fuel and limited supplies, but for most travellers it is the **Blue Heeler Hotel** that dominates the place, to the exclusion of almost everything else. The large neon sign perched on top of the pub is the latest touch to this 100-year-old watering hole. It's a top spot for a cool beer, and the pub also offers meals and accommodation.

McKinlay, named after the explorer who passed through this region in the 1860s after searching for Burke and Wills, is a little bigger than Kynuna, but that is not saying much! However, this small outback community 75 km north of Kynuna can supply fuel and limited supplies. It also has a top pub that you need to turn off the main highway to visit; once it would rarely see any passing traffic, but since it became **'Walkabout Creek Hotel'** in the quintessentially Australian film *Crocodile Dundee*, life has never

The Purple Pub on the main road in Normanton (R & VM)

been the same. It's an inviting place, dispensing cold beer, good meals and friendly banter. The pub also offers accommodation, and there is a small caravan/camping ground just out the back.

The country begins to change north of McKinlay, the flat plain giving way first to low rolling hills and then to ever more rugged country. By the time the road crosses the railway to Cloncurry and Mount Isa and then, soon after, joins with the Flinders Highway just 14 km east of Cloncurry, you are surrounded by low, craggy hills, scoured with veins of bare rock and cut by narrow, convoluted creeks that tear out the earth after any heavy rain.

The country remains the same for the run into Cloncurry, 344 km north of Winton.

Cloncurry

Cloncurry traces its European heritage back to the days of the ill-fated Burke and Wills expedition, which passed this way in 1861 and named the Cloncurry River, on whose banks the town was built. There are a number

of monuments to these explorers in and around the town.

Founded a few years later, Cloncurry had one of the world's biggest copper mines, ensuring its early prosperity. The **Great Australia Mine**, just a little to the south of town, operated until the early 1920s. Visitors can wander over the old workings and around the ruins.

As you come into town, it's hard to miss the **Mary Kathleen Memorial Park & Museum** on the left. Here a project was developed to preserve some of the relics of the uranium-mining town of Mary Kathleen, now just a spot on the map about 60 km west towards Mount Isa. The park is a beauty, and the museum has many relics of the region's interesting history.

Apart from the museum, Cloncurry's major attraction is **John Flynn Place**. This museum tells the history of the RFDS, which was founded in this town by the Reverend John Flynn, a minister of the Presbyterian Church working for the Australian Inland Mission (which he also helped set up). In

1928 the first flight of the RFDS was from Cloncurry to Julia Creek, 134 km to the east. Just a couple of years earlier, Alfred Traeger, an Adelaide radio engineer, had developed a 'pedal wireless', with Flynn's support, and with such technology the 'mantle of safety' Flynn wanted for the pioneers in the outback was about to be put into place.

There's also an **RFDS Historical Museum** in the town, and an original Qantas hangar. The **Afghan and Chinese cemeteries** here are a little different from the more commonly seen Christian ones, and are testimony to the area's rich cultural heritage. The town is also noteworthy for having recorded the highest shade temperature in Australia: 53.1°C (more than 130°F) in 1889. As in much of the north, the best time to visit is in the cooler winter (dry) season.

With a population of around 2000, and catering for a vast pastoral and mining region, Cloncurry can meet a traveller's every need. The town has a couple of hotel/motels, a motel and a caravan park, and good choices of fuel outlets and places to buy supplies or takeaway food. Cloncurry also has a tourist information centre (☎ (077) 42 1361).

Tours are available in the local area and as far afield as **Kajabbi** (100 km north-west of Cloncurry) and **Lake Julius** (40 km west of Kajabbi). For the do-it-yourselfer, there is fishing in the river and trips to the old mining areas dotted through the ranges. In effect the town is a good base, and a friendly one, from which to explore the surrounding area or even take a day trip to Mount Isa.

Cloncurry to Karumba (445 km)

While the Matilda Highway continues northwards just outside town, Cloncurry is a major stepping-off point for those heading further west to the mining town of Mount Isa and the outback of the Northern Territory. Eastwards, the Flinders Highway stretches all the way to the coast at Townsville, 770 km away.

Once across the Cloncurry River and its new bridge, resistant to high-level floods, the Matilda Highway breaks away from the Flinders Highway and takes to the narrower Burke Developmental Road. It's not long before you realise that you have left the gentle pastoral country well and truly behind.

Quamby, just eight km north of the tiny hamlet of Urquhart, is a total of 43 km north of Cloncurry. Once a Cobb & Co coach stop and a centre for the gold mining that helped develop the region, Quamby now has nothing but the historic Quamby Hotel. You'll enjoy a beer here, and fuel is also available.

Continuing north across the rolling hills dotted with low, spindly gums, you reach the turn-off to **Kajabbi** 29 km north of Quamby. Once the focus of the area, Kajabbi has been all but forgotten. The town was once the railhead for this part of the Gulf's cattle industry and the nearby copper mines, but all that has long since disappeared. The Kalkadoon Hotel is the focal point for locals and visitors alike. From here there is much to explore, including the Mt Cuthbert Mine site, and the site of the last stand of the local warlike Kalkadoon people, who resisted the White invasion in bloody battles during the 1880s.

Just before you get to the Burke & Wills Roadhouse along the Burke Developmental Road, 180 km north of Cloncurry, the Wills Developmental Road from Julia Creek joins the road you are on from the right.

Nearly everyone stops at the **Burke & Wills Roadhouse** (☎ (077) 42 5909) where there's a little shade, some greenery at any time of the year, ice creams to buy from the well-stocked store and, if you really need it, fuel. Accommodation and supplies are also available.

From the roadhouse you can strike northwest along the Wills Developmental Road to the fabulous Gregory River and the equally famous **Gregory Downs Hotel** (☎ (077) 48 5566). From there the reasonable dirt road leads to friendly Burketown.

For those travelling the Matilda, the route continues in a more northerly direction towards the Gulf. The country remains reasonably flat, but once you get to **Bang Bang**

Jump-up and descend the 40-odd metres to the Gulf plains proper, you really know what 'flat' means. This near-sheer escarpment vividly marks where the high country ends, 80 km north of the roadhouse.

From this point the road stretches across vast, billiard-table-flat plains covered in deep grass, which in the Dry is the colour of gold. Dotted here and there are clumps of trees, and wherever there is permanent water or shade there are cattle. In this country the cattle stand out – during the day. At night, as everywhere in outback Queensland, they can make driving on the roads very hazardous. If you have to drive, do so with extreme care; if you make a habit of it, invest in a good set of driving lights.

Normanton On the Norman River 375 km from Cloncurry, Normanton marks the end of the 195-km stage from the roadhouse. The most important town in the Gulf region, Normanton was established in 1868, and really boomed during the 1890s gold rush to the Croydon gold fields, 150 km inland. So rich were these fields that the railway which was supposed to be built from Normanton south was eventually pushed through to Croydon. Today, **the Gulflander**, as it is called, is an isolated offshoot of the main Queensland railway network and caters more for tourists than for locals. Every Wednesday it leaves Normanton at 8.30 am on the trip to Croydon. It leaves Croydon the following morning, getting back to Normanton in time for lunch. It's a beauty – don't miss it.

Since the heady days of gold ended, the town has existed as a major supply point for the surrounding cattle stations, and as the shire centre. Today more and more travellers pass through Normanton on their way to the Gulf or Cape York.

The town has a couple of hotel/motels and a caravan park. It is well supplied with fuel outlets and places to stock up on supplies. Take note of some of the historic buildings still in use; these include the shire offices and the large Burn Philps store, down towards the river end of the town. The Carpentaria Shire Council in Normanton (☎ (077) 45 1268) can help you with information on the area.

Travellers may also be interested in the Normanton Rodeo & Gymkhana held in June, the area's biggest social and sporting event of the year. In August the Races and a ball take place.

As a base for fishing, Normanton is hard to beat, with the Norman River producing some magic-size barramundi. From here it's just a hop, step and jump across the plains to the Gulf port of Karumba.

Normanton to Karumba Heading out of town, the Burke Developmental Road soon crosses the Norman River and, less than 29 km up the road, a major tributary of the river, Walker Creek. At the 30-km mark from the centre of town, you come to a major intersection. Veer left here, sticking to the bitumen, and the road quickly swings almost due west.

Traversing these great plains, it is not hard to imagine that during the torrential rains of the wet season, this area becomes one huge lake. At times, with king tides backing up the waters of the rivers, the floods isolate towns like Normanton for weeks at a time.

The bird life is rich and varied – this region is the best in Australia to see the stately brolga and the very similar sarus crane – a recent natural invader from South-East Asia. Another large bird which you'll see is the magpie-coloured jabiru, certainly one of the most majestic birds of the tropics.

Karumba

Karumba is entered quickly, 70 km from Normanton, and lies right beside the Gulf of Carpentaria and the Norman River. Originally established as a telegraph station in the 1870s, it became a stopover for the flying boats of the Empire Mail Service in the 1930s. The discovery of prawns in the Gulf in the 1960s brought Karumba alive, and today that industry keeps the town humming. You certainly can't miss seeing the boats as they sit beside the jetty, draped with nets, just a stone's throw from the pub and the centre of town.

There's a hotel/motel here and a couple of caravan parks; the former can really be jumping when the boats come in for a short break or for resupply. There are also a number of holiday cabins available. The town can supply basic travelling requirements like fuel and food, as well as near everything for the fisher.

Festivals held during the year include the Snake Creek Turnout (in July), the Barra Ball (in November) and the Fisherman's Ball (in December).

The town lives and breathes fish and fishing, prawns and prawning. If you aren't interested in these things, you won't stay long. Sure, you can actually get to the sea at Karumba – one of the few places around the Gulf that you can – but once you've checked the town, been to the beach at Karumba Point and enjoyed a prawn or two at the pub, there is not much else to hold your attention. Of course you could always fly to Mornington or Sweers islands out in the Gulf, but once again, these are favoured fishing haunts and you need to love fishing to fully appreciate these wild, remote places.

If you don't have your own boat, you can hire one from Karumba Boat Hire (☎ (077) 45 9132) at Karumba Point. There are also a number of boating and fishing tours run from Karumba, and Air Karumba (☎ (077) 45 9354) has flights to Mornington and Sweers islands, as well as further afield around the Gulf. Contact the Carpentaria Shire Council in Normanton (☎ (077) 45 1268) for full details.

Karumba marks the end of the Matilda, and if you have been travelling it from its humble origin in Cunnamulla, 1674 km south, you have experienced one of the best bitumen trips in Australia. Like anything fine, it is to be savoured slowly – take your time and enjoy!

ORGANISED TOURS

Contact the various tourism bodies and regional tourist information centres for details of local tour operators.

FACILITIES

Cunnamulla

There is a range of accommodation to choose from at such establishments as the *Billabong Hotel/Motel* (☎ (076) 55 1225) and the *Corella Motel* (☎ (076) 55 1593). There is also the *Jack Tonkin Caravan Park* (☎ (076) 55 1421), where dogs are allowed (under control).

The Commonwealth, National Australia and Westpac banks have branches in Cunnamulla. The local RACQ depot is Bill's Auto (☎ (076) 55 1407).

Eulo

Travellers can stay at the *Eulo Queen Hotel* (☎ (076) 55 4867) or at the caravan park (☎ (076) 55 4890) – pets are allowed.

Charleville

Accommodation is obtainable at the *Charleville Motel* (☎ (076) 54 1566), *Victoria Hotel/Motel* (☎ (076) 54 1720) and *Warrego Motel* (☎ (076) 54 1299). On-site vans are available at the *Bailey Bar* (☎ (076) 54 1744) and *Cobb & Co* (☎ (076) 54 1053) caravan parks. Pets are allowed at both parks.

The Commonwealth, National Australia and Westpac banks have branches in Charleville. The local RACQ depot is Bert's Body Shop (☎ (076) 54 1733, after hours ☎ 54 1214).

Augathella

Travellers can stay at the *Augathella Motel/ Caravan Park* (☎ (076) 54 5177). Dogs are allowed (on a leash) in the park.

There is a branch of the National Australia Bank in Main St.

Tambo

A choice of accommodation is available from the *Club Hotel/Motel* (☎ (076) 54 6109), the *Royal Carrangarra Hotel* (☎ (076) 54 6127) and the *Tambo Mill Motel* (☎ (076) 54 6466). The *Tambo Caravan Park* (☎ (076) 54 6463) caters for campers and also has overnight vans.

There is a National Australia Bank branch in Arthur St.

THE TROPICS

Blackall

There are a number of hotels and motels offering accommodation, such as the *Barcoo Hotel* (☎ (076) 57 4197), the *Blackall Motel* (☎ (076) 57 4611) and the *Coolibah Motel* (☎ (076) 57 4380). Cabins are available at the *Blackall Caravan Park* (☎ (076) 57 4816), as are on-site vans and caravan and camping sites. Pets are allowed only on application.

Banks represented in Blackall are the Commonwealth, National Australia and Westpac. The local RACQ depot is May's Machinery Sales & Repairs (☎ (076) 57 4100, after hours ☎ 57 4347).

Barcaldine

There is a wide range of accommodation to choose from, including the *Barcaldine Motel* (☎ (076) 51 1244), *Globe Hotel* (☎ (076) 51 1141), *Stalin Units* (☎ (076) 51 1353) and *Lee Garden* (☎ (076) 51 1488). There are also two caravan parks: the *Showgrounds* (☎ (076) 51 1211) and the *Homestead* (☎ (076) 51 1308). Cabins are also available at the Homestead, and pets are allowed (on application only).

Banks to be found in Barcaldine are the Commonwealth and Westpac. The local RACQ depot is Barcaldine Engineering Works (☎ (076) 51 1337, after hours ☎ 51 1544).

Ilfracombe

You can choose to stay in the *Wellshot Hotel* (☎ (076) 58 2106), or in an on-site van at the *Teamster's Rest Caravan Park* (☎ (076) 58 2295), which also has camping sites.

Longreach

The town has a large choice of accommodation, ranging from the *Longreach Motor Inn* (☎ (076) 58 2322), *Longreach Motel* (☎ (076) 58 1996) and *Starlight Motel* (☎ (076) 58 1288) to the *Longreach Swaggies Backpackers & Family Accommodation* (☎ (076) 58 3777). The Swaggies offers family and twin-room accommodation, a laundry and a barbecue area, and meals. The *Gunnadoo Caravan Park* (☎ (076) 58 1781)

The Gulflander (R & VM)

has all camping and caravan facilities, and pets are allowed. Cabins are also available.

All the major banks have branches in Longreach – ANZ, Commonwealth, National Australia and Westpac. The local RACQ depot is Mobil Midtown Service Station (☎ (076) 58 1747, after hours ☎ 58 1080).

Winton

Travellers can stay in the *Outback Motel* (☎ (076) 57 1422), *Matilda Motel* (☎ (076) 57 1433), *North Gregory Hotel* (☎ (076) 57 1375) or *Banjo's Motel/Cabins* (☎ (076) 57 1213). Both caravan parks, the *Matilda Country Caravan Park* (☎ (076) 57 1607) and the *Pelican Fuel Stop Caravan Park* (☎ (076) 57 1478), have on-site vans, along with normal park facilities. Pets are allowed (on application).

The National Australia and Westpac banks have branches in Winton. The local RACQ depot is Winton Fuel & Tyre Service (☎ (076) 57 1305).

Kynuna

The *Blue Heeler Hotel* (☎ (076) 46 8650) has motel and hotel rooms available, as well as a caravan park with an on-site van, powered sites and a camping area. The *Kynuna Roadhouse & Caravan Park* (☎ (076) 46 8683) has an on-site van and cabins, along with normal park facilities. Pets are allowed. Meals are available in the roadhouse from 6 am to 9 pm daily.

McKinlay

The *Walkabout Creek Hotel* (☎ (077) 46 8424) provides accommodation. You can stay in the camping area at the back of the hotel or in the cabins nearby. Pets are allowed, under control.

Cloncurry

The *Cloncurry Motel* (☎ (077) 42 1268), *Oasis Hotel/Motel* (☎ (077) 42 1366), *Leichhardt Hotel/Motel* (☎ (077) 42 1389) and *Wagon Wheel* (☎ (077) 42 1866) offer a range of accommodation. Cabins and on-site vans are available at the *Cloncurry Caravan Park Oasis* (☎ (077) 42 1313), as are powered and unpowered sites. No pets are allowed.

The National Australia and Westpac banks have branches in Cloncurry. The local RACQ depot is Nevs Auto Repair (☎ (077) 42 1243).

Normanton

Accommodation is available at the *Albion Hotel* (☎ (077) 45 1218), *Central Hotel* (☎ (077) 45 1215), *Gulflander Motel* (☎ (077) 45 1290) and *National Hotel* (☎ (077) 45 1324). The *Council Caravan Park* (☎ (077) 45 1121) has on-site vans and all facilities, including a heated pool. Pets are allowed.

The Normanton Travel Service (☎ (077) 45 1200) can help with information and can organise tours and flights. The Westpac Bank has full banking facilities in Normanton, while the Commonwealth Bank agency is at the post office. The local RACQ depot is B & J Fischle (☎ (077) 45 1306).

Karumba

Accommodation is available at the *Karumba Lodge Hotel* (☎ (077) 45 9143). Cabins are available at the *Gulf Country Caravan Park* (☎ (077) 45 9148) – where pets are allowed, on a leash; campers and caravanners can also choose to stay at the *Karumba Point Caravan Park* (☎ (077) 45 9277). There are also quite a number of holiday cabins for rent at Karumba and Karumba Point – contact the Shire of Carpentaria in Normanton (☎ (077) 45 1268) for a full listing.

B & B Supermarket (☎ (077) 45 9242) has just about everything you may need, and its Westpac EFTPOS machine handles all credit cards. A cafe serves meals 24 hours a day.

The Westpac Bank in Karumba is open only on Tuesdays and Thursdays, and there is a Commonwealth Bank agency at the post office.

ALTERNATIVE TRANSPORT
Air

Flight West Airlines (☎ 008 019 104, in Mount Isa ☎ (077) 43 9333) has flights servicing Charleville, Blackall, Barcaldine, Longreach, Winton, Normanton and Karumba.

There are also a number of air charters available, such as Longreach Air Charter (☎ (076) 58 9156) and Crossroads Aviation (☎ (076) 58 2181). Air Mount Isa (☎ (077) 43 2844) does mail runs and supply flights to isolated mines, and takes tourists for negotiable fees. Contact the tourist information centres for a comprehensive list of all air charters.

Bus

Graham's (☎ (076) 30 4188) services all towns on the route between Toowoomba, Dalby, St George and Cunnamulla.

Greyhound (☎ 008 88 2779) and McCafferty's (☎ (077) 72 5100) both service all towns on the Warrego, Landsborough and Capricorn highways between Brisbane and Mount Isa, as well as Rockhampton and Longreach.

Cairns/Karumba Coachlines (☎ (070) 51 8311) runs a service between Cairns, Normanton and Karumba.

Campbell's Coaches (☎ (077) 43 2006), based at Mount Isa, travels once a week from Mount Isa to Cloncurry, Quamby, Burke & Wills Roadhouse, Normanton and Karumba.

Train

Queensland Railways (☎ 13 2232, in Townsville ☎ (077) 72 8211) operates a rail service from Brisbane to Cunnamulla and Quilpie via Charleville, and from Rockhampton to Winton via Blackall. The wonderful *Gulflander* runs between Normanton and Croydon. Twice weekly, the *Spirit of the Outback* runs between Brisbane, Rockhampton, Emerald and Longreach. For more information contact the Queensland Rail Travel Centre (☎ (079) 32 0297).

Car Rental

Offices of Avis and Hertz can be found in the larger towns, such as Charleville, Longreach, Winton and Cloncurry.

THE TROPICS

Gold Fields & Ghost Towns

Gold – when driving through the outback you begin to imagine what lured thousands to seek it in the gulleys, along river banks and underground. The dust that now covers this exciting part of history bites into your nostrils. The history, the remnants of the rush that never ended, the ghost towns (some rejuvenated and others not), are all still there to explore.

As you drive off the beaten track, chances are it is to a Hill End, Just in Time, Old Halls Creek or Palmer River. More than likely the road you are following is there as a direct result of the search for gold. And if you are off-track and *lost*, think of Harry Lasseter in search of his elusive reef.

Our 4WDs are a far cry from the wheelbarrows that Russian Jack pushed, our burden is much lighter than the heavy swags the miners carried, and the metal detectors are a great deal more sophisticated than pick, shovel and cast-iron gold pan. Today, in

Gold Fields & Ghost Towns

THE GOLDFIELDS

remote places, only the gravestones and ruins of the gold rushes protrude through encroaching sand and weeds.

History of the Rushes

The first recorded find of gold in Australia was in 1823 in New South Wales, but it was not until early 1851, when Edward Hargraves vigorously promoted his meagre finds at Ophir, near Bathurst, that the first real rush started. By May that year there were over a thousand diggers in the creeks around Ophir. A licensing system was introduced whereby each person paid 30 shillings, both to limit the diggers and to encourage unsuccessful ones to return to their jobs.

When the gold at Ophir ran out, diggers had already found more on the Turon (Sofala), and soon there were six or seven thousand miners there. The area around Bathurst teemed with hopefuls toiling in rugged creekbeds.

The drift of the population northwards to the gold fields of New South Wales prompted the Victorian government, on 9 June 1851, to offer a £200 reward for the discovery of a payable gold field within 200 miles of Melbourne. Early in the following month the finds of James Esmond at Clunes were made public. In August, diggers were flocking to Ballarat, later to be one of the greatest sources of gold. In September the rush was to the shallow fields around Mt Alexander (later Castlemaine). By December there were 20,000 diggers spread out around there and as far north as Bendigo.

Prospectors had been working at Bendigo during October and November. Lack of water prevented development, but by May the following year there was a rush to the rich discoveries in Eaglehawk Gully. A small rush to the largely inaccessible creeks around Omeo, in Gippsland, followed. The year 1853 saw minor rushes to other regions, including the Buckland River on the rugged Ovens field and, in 1854, Maldon, Avoca, Maryborough and Ararat were opened up.

The diggers came from all parts of the world and their numbers included examples of all professions. There were people from England, continental Europeans (especially Germans), veterans of the Californian gold fields (the '49ers') and impoverished Chinese from Kwangtung province.

Melbourne was the new San Francisco, teeming with diggers infected with a golden wanderlust. Between Princes Bridge and the bay beaches, Canvas-Town, a sea of tents,

Lasseter's Lost Reef

The gold prospector Lewis Hubert (Harold Bell) Lasseter (1880?-1931) is immortalised as one of Australia's great hopefuls. We still know of him today because of Ion Idriess's *Lasseter's Last Ride* (1931); otherwise he would probably have faded into the red dust of the Petermann Range. But Lasseter claimed to have found, sometime between 1897 and 1911, the richest gold reef in Australia, some 23 km in length. The diminutive Lasseter had supposedly been looking for rubies when he stumbled upon gold as thick as 'plums in a pudding'. It was in the remote, arid Petermann Range in central Australia on the NT/SA border.

In 1930 the Central Australian Gold Exploration Company was formed, with Lasseter as a guide. The expedition was well equipped with an aeroplane, trucks and wireless. But things started to go wrong: the aircraft crashed near Ayers Rock, and Fred Blakeley, the expedition leader, abandoned it at Ayers Rock. Lasseter, after an argument with another hopeful prospector, Paul Johns, headed out alone to look for the reef.

Lasseter died of starvation in January 1931 near Shaws Creek and his body was found by Bob Buck in March; his diaries were retrieved and in them he claimed to have pegged the reef. Idriess used these diaries to write the above-mentioned book.

Subsequent attempts to find Lasseter's lost reef have been unsuccessful. His name is perpetuated in the Lasseter Highway, which runs from the Stuart Highway to Uluru (Ayers Rock). ∎

Remains of the Old Halls Creek post office (JW)

was established to accommodate the influx of migrants before they began the hazardous journey to the gold fields.

The introduction of the licence fee on the Victorian fields had always been met with resentment. This flared up after a visit to the Ballarat gold fields by the new governor, Charles Hotham, who resolved to strictly enforce the collection of fees with biweekly licence hunts. After a number of niggling incidents which inflamed the predominantly Irish miners of the Eureka lode near Ballarat, two mass meetings were held on Bakery Hill on 11 and 29 November, and licences were burned at the second meeting.

The following day, the authorities, in a show of force, went on a licence hunt. The diggers resolved to make a stand, and erected Eureka Stockade as a symbol of their own protection. Peter Lalor led the diggers' oath of allegiance to the flag of the Southern Cross. There were about 120 diggers in the stockade on 3 December 1854 when it was attacked by soldiers and police. In the ensuing melee about 30 miners and five soldiers were killed; Peter Lalor had been shot in the shoulder and Captain Wise of the 40th Regiment was mortally wounded. None of the protesters were convicted and the diggers' stand hastened reform on the gold fields. The following year 'miner's right' was introduced.

In 1858 diggers were being transported north to the Tropic of Capricorn, to Rockhampton (also called Fitzroy, or Canoona). In the autumn of 1860, Victorians crossed the border and climbed high into the Snowy Mountains to the alpine rush at Kiandra. Winter snows forced the diggers to look elsewhere, which they did with success – Forbes and Young became rich fields.

Queensland's turn for such frenzy came in 1867 when the white quartz reefs of Gympie were uncovered. Four years later it was the rich fields of Charters Towers, then the steamy tropical forests of the Palmer River and the fields on Cape York, which lured only the desperate.

THE GOLDFIELDS

Discoveries in the Northern Territory followed, and a workable gold field at Pine Creek was announced in August 1872. Isolation, the high costs of mining, and marauding Aborigines were problems. Coolie or indentured labourers were brought in to work the fields, and when the work stopped, they went over the alluvial deposits for a second time. At about this time, interest in gold-mining began to decline for a while.

A resurgence of interest came in 1886, and the Croydon field was opened about 500 km north-west of Charters Towers. Gold was discovered at Halls Creek in the remote Kimberley in 1885, and in 1886 diggers on the Queensland fields made the anticlockwise trek to the new riches. The terrain in the Kimberley was inhospitable, and the track from the wharves at Wyndham and Derby was the most ferocious that miners in Australia had yet negotiated. Still they pushed across it and, unbelievably, miners walked to it from the Queensland fields.

The Pilbara was next to reveal its riches. The year 1888 saw diggers pouring over Pilbara Creek and fanning out through the dry gorges to Marble Bar, Nullagine and the Ashburton River. Despite the intense heat, the lure of gold held them fast and some diggers were rewarded with finds of huge nuggets.

Inland from Geraldton, gold was found near Nannine in 1890. The Murchison field now bloomed and Cue, Day Dawn, Payne's Find, Lake Austin and Mount Magnet joined the huge list of gold towns in the outback.

There followed more discoveries, especially around Southern Cross in Western Australia's Yilgarn district, first opened in 1888. Major strikes were made in 1892 at Coolgardie and nearby Kalgoorlie, but in the whole Western Australian gold-fields area, Kalgoorlie is the only large town left today.

Coolgardie's period of prosperity lasted only until 1905 and many other gold towns went from nothing to populations of 10,000 then back to nothing in just 10 years. Western Australia profited from the gold boom for the rest of the century. It was gold that put the state on the map and finally gave it the population to make it viable in its own right,

rather than just an offshoot of the east-coast colonies.

Depressions and unemployment often attracted fossickers back to the gulleys and rivers, especially during the Great Depression in the 1930s. In other places mining never actually stopped, such as along the Golden Mile in Kalgoorlie-Boulder.

GOLDEN GHOST TOWNS
Western Australia
Old Halls Creek This is a fascinating reminder of the Kimberley gold rush. All that is left are heaps of broken bottles where the pub used to be, the crumbling walls of the old post office, cemetery and a failed tourist venture – the modern building that sits forlornly at the top of the hill. This ghost town is about 14 km east of modern-day Halls Creek, actually on the banks of the creek. In the new town is a statue of Russian Jack.

Gwalia This twin town of Leonora, 237 km north of Kalgoorlie, is another ghost town worth visiting. Gold was discovered here in 1896 and mined until 1963 in the Sons of Gwalia mine. It was the largest mine outside the Golden Mile of Kalgoorlie-Boulder. The 25-metre headframe still stands; its construction in 1898 was supervised by the first mine manager, Herbert Hoover, who became president of the USA in 1929. The town was once so prosperous that the state's first electric trams ran here.

Many of the mine buildings are still intact and there is an interesting museum. Gwalia is a good example of a modern ghost town.

There are many more ghost towns in the area – Ora Banda, Niagara, Menzies, Kanowna and Broad Arrow. Get a copy of the *Gold Rush Country* pamphlet from the Kalgoorlie tourist centre.

Northern Territory
Pine Creek This town, 245 km south of Darwin, has been a ghost town, but in recent years has had a new lease of life because a large open-cut mine has opened nearby. It is in the centre of a number of Top End ghost towns, including Yam Creek, 40 km to the

---

Russian Jack

The gold fields and the rushes threw up many heroes: successful speculators, the 'lucky' who found nuggets or struck it rich, Peter Lalor and the diggers of Eureka Stockade, the knucklemen, the Mountain Maid and the extremely odd and unusual.

Russian Jack was the Kimberley's hero, renowned for his feats of strength and endurance. He is believed to have carried a sick friend over 300 km in his rough-and-ready wheelbarrow. He had originally pushed his barrow, with its two-metre Derbyshafts and extra wide wheel for the sandy tracks, all the way from Derby loaded with food, tools, blankets and water.

His loyalty to his mates and the job became legendary. One day he fell to the bottom of an open pit at Mount Morgan in Western Australia, about 23 metres down. After lying there injured for three days his only comment when they pulled him out was, 'I've missed a shift.' ■

---

north. Pine Creek, surrounded by mullock heaps, has many reminders of the gold rushes. There are many corrugated iron buildings. The old train station has been restored as an information centre, there is a museum on Railway Parade, and Ah Toy's store is a reminder of the time when Chinese outnumbered Europeans on these gold fields.

Arltunga Probably the most isolated of gold fields was centred around Arltunga, on the Hale River north-east of Alice Springs, in the MacDonnell Ranges. Gold was struck at Paddy's Waterhole in 1887, but mining petered out by 1908. All supplies for this field had to be hauled 650 km from Oodnadatta over a dangerous track.

Queensland

This state is replete with abandoned gold-mining towns. Once all the gold was taken, there was often no reason for a town's existence.

Croydon This town, 500 km north-west of Charters Towers, was proclaimed a gold field in January 1886 but gold had been discovered there three years earlier. In its day it was one of the richest fields in Australia and the centre of Queensland's north-west. It even boasted two newspapers, the *Golden Age* and *Mining News*. All that is left now is a pub (the Club Hotel), general store, courthouse, mining warden's office and a tin railway shed. Not much is left of the fabulous Golden Gate mine, except for a few rusting remains. See the Matilda Highway section in

the Tropics chapter for details about the *Gulflander* train between Croydon and Normanton.

Palmer River The Palmer River gold fields hide many once-thriving towns. At the start of the rush the diggers got to these towns from **Cooktown**, itself a great example of gold-fields architecture, via a rugged packhorse road. Later, **Laura**, the railhead of the line from Cooktown, handled 20,000 passengers a year. Today it only has a few houses, including a pleasant pub, a general store and a small museum. Many people come to the area today to see the Quinkan Aboriginal paintings west of Lakeland, believed to be 15,000 years old. There are ruins at **Maytown** and **Palmerville**, south of Laura, about 70 km west of the Palmer River crossing on the Cairns-Cooktown inland road.

New South Wales

The countryside of New South Wales is littered with the remnants of its many gold rushes. Probably the most intact of the ghost towns is **Hill End**, now a picturesque restored village that is classified as a historic site and administered by the NSW Parks & Wildlife Service. Only a few tin shacks remain in the twin town of **Tambaroora**. At the height of the rush, which commenced in 1851, there were 30,000 people here. Not far away are Hargraves, Junction Reefs and Sofala.

More remote, truly outback settings for ghost towns are the two in the far north-west of the state, Milparinka and Tibooburra. **Milparinka**, 315 km north of Broken Hill, was alive in 1880 after the first nugget had been found near Mt Poole, a few miles west. Once it was the main town in the centre of the field but it is now a beleaguered place, the very epitome of a ghost town.

About 40 km north is **Tibooburra**, which became part of the 1880s rush in this region. The lack of water militated against success and the fields had a short life. Tibooburra is today a centre for tourists visiting Corner Country – Cameron's Corner (where New South Wales, South Australia and Queensland meet) and Sturt National Park.

South Australia

The South Australian gold rushes are probably the least known, copper being the main metal sought. **Waukaringa** is about all that is left of the 1880s gold rush. The rush commenced in 1886, when miners flocked to the Teetulpa gold fields. The town is eerie, isolated out on the wide, open plain. To get to the mine ruins, turn north at the town of Yunta on the Barrier Highway, between Broken Hill and Peterborough.

Victoria

Victoria, the smallest mainland state, hardly qualifies as outback. Many of its former ghost towns from its golden era have become popular weekend retreats for city-dwellers in their scratchless 4WDs. Some have been preserved in much the form they had in their heyday and now house galleries and craft shops run by alternative-lifestylers.

The drive from Moe north to Mansfield takes in some of the dense mountain country the miners had to traverse. You pass Walhalla, Woods Point, the A1 Mine Settlement and Gaffneys Creek. **Walhalla** is a particularly good example of a ghost town and there are many buildings left from its mining days.

Checklists

The following checklists should contain the most important bits and pieces for an outback trip.

Before You Go

- Pre-plan – Where, time of year, time needed, distance, fuel range.
- Research – Things to see and do, history, fuel availability, resupply, road conditions.
- Make an itinerary – and use it as a guide only. Keep it flexible to allow for breakdowns, advice or ideas you receive while underway, and places you fall in love with.
- Apply for permits – to national parks and Aboriginal land. Some parks operate on a ballot system in the busy seasons so it's wise to enquire about bookings well in advance. Restrictions are also placed in parks such as Gurig in the Northern Territory, where bookings must be made at least 12 months in advance because only 15 vehicles are allowed in at any one time.
- Book accommodation – If you want to stay at a popular spot, for instance Monkey Mia in Western Australia over the school holidays, you may want to book. Remember that if you book too many places, your flexible itinerary will go out the window.
- Let someone know your itinerary – If you change it greatly, let them know so they don't hit the panic button. Keep in touch with someone at home at prearranged intervals.

Always Carry

basic recovery gear (see below)
first aid kit plus manual (see the Health section in the Facts for the Visitor chapter)
fire extinguisher
CB Radio and possibly an HF radio if you're heading to remote country
vehicle tools and spare parts (see below)
plenty of water (at least five litres' drinking water per person per day)
good maps – the more the better, as they regularly contradict one another
matches
compass
torch (flashlight)
knife
space blanket

Camping & Personal Gear

tent, swag and/or stretcher (camp bed)
sleeping gear
mosquito net
hat (maybe with fly net)
sunglasses
wet-weather gear
portable light
portable fridge or ice chest ('Esky')
folding chairs
folding table
toilet paper
toiletries bag
clothes (including sweater)
camera, film and spare batteries
insect repellent
sun cream
paper and pencils
string
plastic sheet
tarpaulin
poles, ropes & pegs
bucket
shovel
axe (or bow saw)

Campfire Cooking Equipment

medium to large camp oven – pack carefully so it doesn't bounce around and crack
cake rack or similar to place in the bottom of your camp oven
two or three saucepans of varying size, with lids. Choose saucepans that will fit inside one another for better packing
billy (with lid) or kettle
large, sturdy frying pan
oven-proof casserole dish – for use inside your camp oven (helps to keep it clean)
jaffle iron
toasting forks
metal fire grate with legs (preferably adjustable)
steel barbecue plate (optional with fire grate)
lightweight metal shields – to act as windbreaks
long-handled barbecue utensils
heat-resistant gloves
natural-fibre brush – to brush coals off camp oven lid
metal bucket – for boiling water
fire starters

General Cooking Items

gas stove (or similar)
eating utensils
plates, bowls, cups
sharp knives
kitchen table (and chairs)
mixing bowls
flat plastic grater
sieve
chopping board
can opener, bottle opener, corkscrew
peeler
small measuring cup
small plastic funnel
large mixing spoons
aluminium foil
plastic food-wrap
snap-lock plastic bags
rubbish bags
tea towels
dishwashing detergent
pot scourer
water container

Car Tools

repair manual
set of ring and open-end spanners (to suit your
    vehicle)
adjustable spanner
plug spanner
wheel brace, jack and jacking plate (30 cm square x
    2.5 cm thick board)
screwdrivers (standard and Phillips)
Allen keys (if applicable)
hammer, chisel
hacksaw and spare blades
file, including a points file
thread file
pliers and wire cutters
tie wire, nylon 'zip-ties'
Araldite epoxy resin
feeler gauges
tyre levers
tyre pump and pressure gauge
tube/tyre repair kit
battery jumper leads
WD40, or similar
funnel and hose
rags

Car Spares

radiator hoses
heater hoses
fan belts
fuses
globes
electric wire
electrical insulation tape
thread sealing tape
spark plugs (petrol engine)
plug leads (petrol engine)
points (petrol engine)
coil (petrol engine)
condenser (petrol engine)
tyre tube, valves and caps
bolts, nuts, self-tapping screws, washers etc
grease
gasket cement

It's always wise to carry some extra fuel and
engine oil. On longer trips, you could include
a more comprehensive range of tools and
spares, such as a socket set plus any of the
commonly needed special tools for your
vehicle, exhaust sealant, wheel bearings, air
filters and gear oil. It's easy to carry too
much, though, so be critical. If there are
similar vehicles in your group, save weight
by sharing.

Car Recovery Gear

snatch strap
two 'D' shackles
shovel
axe
jack and jacking plate

The above are the basics. Depending on the
nature of the trip and the problems likely to
be encountered, you could add:

Tirfor (or similar) hand winch, or power winch
tree protector strap
winch extension straps
snatch-block
extra 'D' shackles
high-lift jack and base plate
air-bag jack (particularly good in sandy areas)
chainsaw (with fuel, spare chain, chain file etc)

Glossary

amber fluid – beer
ankle-biter – small child, *tacker*, *rug rat*
arvo – afternoon
avagoyermug – traditional rallying call, especially at cricket matches
award wage – minimum pay rate

back o' Bourke – back of beyond, middle of nowhere
backblocks – *bush* or other remote area far from the city
bail up – hold up, rob, earbash
bail out – leave
Balmain bug – see *Moreton Bay bug*
banana bender – resident of Queensland
banker – a river almost overflowing its banks (as in 'the Cooper is running a banker')
barbie – barbecue (BBQ)
barra – barramundi (prized fish of the north)
barrack – cheer on team at sporting event, support (as in 'who do you barrack for?')
bastard – general term of address which can mean many things. While mostly used as a good-natured form of greeting ('*G'day*, you old bastard!'), it can also denote the highest level of praise or respect ('He's the bravest bastard I know!') or it can be the most dire of insults ('You lousy, lying *copper* bastard!')
bathers – swimming costume (Victoria)
battler – hard trier, struggler (the outback is full of 'great Aussie battlers')
beaut, beauty, bewdie – great, fantastic
big bikkies – a lot of money, expensive
big mobs – a large amount, heaps
bikies – motorcyclists
billabong – waterhole in dried-up riverbed, more correctly an ox-bow bend cut off in the dry season by receding waters
billy – tin container used to boil tea in the bush
bitumen – asphalt, surfaced road
black stump – where the *back o' Bourke* begins
blaze – (a blaze in a tree) a mark in a tree trunk made by cutting away bark, indicating a path or reference point; also 'to blaze'
bloke – man
blowies – blowflies, bluebottles
bludger – lazy person, one who won't work and lives off other people's money (originally, a prostitute's pimp)
blue (ie **have a blue**) – to have an argument or fight
bluey – *swag;* also nickname for a red-haired person
bonzer – great, *ripper*
boomer – very big; a particularly large male kangaroo
boomerang – a curved flat wooden instrument used by Aborigines for hunting
booze bus – police van used for random breath testing for alcohol
boozer – pub
bottle – 750 ml bottle of beer
bottle shop – liquor shop
bottlo – bottle shop
bowser – fuel pump at a service station (named after the US inventor S F Bowser)
brumby – wild horse
bruss – brother, *mate* (used by central Australian Aborigines)
Buckley's, Buckley's chance – no chance at all ('Across the Tanami? They've got Buckley's in that *shitbox').* The origin of this term is unclear. Maybe it derives from the Melbourne department store of Buckley's & Nunn; or from the escaped convict William Buckley, whose chances of survival were considered negligible but who ended up living with Aborigines for 20 years; or from the Sydney escapologist Buckley, who had himself chained-up in a coffin and thrown into Sydney Harbour, with dire results
bug – see *Moreton Bay bug*
Bulamakanka – place even beyond the back o' Bourke, way beyond the black stump (see *never-never*)
bull bar – outsize front bumper on car or truck as ultimate barrier against animals on the road

bull dust – fine, powdery and sometimes deep dust on outback roads, often hiding deep holes and ruts that you normally wouldn't drive into; also bullshit

bunfight – a quarrel over a frivolous issue or one that gets blown out of proportion

bungarra – any large (1.5-metre-plus) goanna, but specifically an Aboriginal name for Gould's goanna, prized as food

bunyip – mythical bush spirit said to inhabit Australia's swamps

burl – have a try (as in 'give it a burl')

bush – country, anywhere away from the city; *scrub*

bush (ie **go bush**) – go back to the land

bushbash – to force your way through pathless bush

bushranger – Australia's equivalent of the outlaws of the American Wild West (some goodies, some baddies) – the helmeted Ned Kelly was the most famous

bush tucker – food available naturally

BYO – Bring Your Own (booze to a restaurant, meat to a barbecue etc)

caaarn! – come on, traditional rallying call, especially at football games (as in 'Caaarn the Blues!')

cackle-berries – eggs; also 'hen-fruit', 'chook-nuts' and 'bum-nuts'

camp draft – Australian rodeo, testing horse rider's skills in separating cattle or sheep from a herd or flock

camp oven – large, cast-iron pot with lid, used for cooking in an open fire

cask – wine box (a great Australian invention)

Chiko roll – vile Australian junk food

chocka – completely full (from 'chock-a-block')

chook – chicken

chuck a U-ey – do a U-turn

chunder – vomit, technicolour yawn, pavement pizza, curbside quiche, liquid laugh, drive the porcelain bus, call Bluey

clobber – clothes

cobber – *mate*

cocky – small-scale farmer; cockatoo

come good – turn out all right

compo – compensation such as workers' compensation

cooee – shouting distance, close (to be within cooee of...)

cop, copper – policeperson (not uniquely *strine* but very common nevertheless); see *walloper*

counter meal, countery – pub meal

cow cocky – small-scale cattle farmer

cozzie – swimming costume (New South Wales)

crook – ill, badly made, substandard

crow eater – resident of South Australia

culvert – channel or pipe under road for rainwater drainage

cut lunch – sandwiches

cut snake – see *mad as a...*

dag, daggy – dirty lump of wool at back end of a sheep; also an affectionate or mildly abusive term for a socially inept person

daks – trousers

damper – bush loaf made from flour and water and cooked in a *camp oven*

Darwin stubby – two-litre bottle of beer sold to tourists in Darwin

dead horse – tomato sauce

deli – delicatessen; milk bar in South Australia

digger – Australian or New Zealand soldier or veteran (originally, a miner); also a generic form of address assuming respect, mainly used for soldiers/veterans but sometimes also between friends

dijeridu – cylindrical wooden musical instrument played by Aboriginal men

dill – idiot

dingo – indigenous wild dog

dink – carry a second person on a bicycle or horse

dinkum, fair dinkum – honest, genuine ('fair dinkum?' – really?)

dinky-di – the real thing

distillate – diesel fuel

divvy van – police divisional van

dob in – to tell on someone

Dog Fence – the world's longest fence, erected to keep dingoes out of south-eastern Australia

donga – small transportable hut; also the

bush, from the name for a shallow, eroded gully, found in areas where it doesn't rain often, so people don't go there

donk – car or boat engine

don't come the raw prawn – don't try and fool me

down south – the rest of Australia, viewed from the Northern Territory or anywhere north of Brisbane

drongo – worthless person

droving – moving livestock a considerable distance

Dry, the – the dry season in the north

duco – car paint

duffing – stealing cattle (literally: altering the brand on the 'duff', or rump)

dunny – outdoor lavatory

dunny budgies – *blowies*

earbash – talk nonstop

eastern states – the rest of Australia viewed from Western Australia

Esky – trademark name for a portable ice box used for keeping beer etc cold

fair go! – give us a break!

fair crack of the whip! – *fair go!*

feeding the ants – being in a very deceased condition out in the *donga*

FJ – most revered Holden car

flagon – two-litre bottle (of wine, port etc)

flake – shark meat, often used in fish & chips down south

floater – meat pie floating in pea soup – yuk

flog – steal; sell; whip

fluke – undeserved good luck ('they had three flat tyres, no spare, no puncture kit, no water, but they fluked a lift into town on the monthly mail truck. Otherwise they'd still be there *feeding the ants'*)

fossick – hunt for gems or semiprecious stones

from arsehole to breakfast – all over the place

furphy – a misleading statement, rumour or fictitious story, named after Joseph Furphy, who wrote a famous Australian novel, *Such is Life*, then reviewed the book for a literary journal of the time and criticised it; the public bought it by the ton. Or maybe this is a furphy and the term instead derives from the water or sewerage carrier made by his brother's company in Shepparton, Victoria; in WW I these carriers were places where the troops met, swapped yarns and information, and no doubt construed a few furphies

galah – noisy parrot, thus noisy idiot

game – brave (as in 'game as Ned Kelly')

gander – look (as in 'have a gander')

garbo – person who collects your garbage

gibber – Aboriginal word for stone or boulder; gibber plain – stony desert

gidgee – a type of small acacia

give it away – give up

g'day – good day, traditional Australian greeting

good on ya – well done

grade – (to grade a road) to level a road, usually by means of a bulldozer fitted with a 'blade' that scrapes off the top layer and pushes it to the side

grazier – large-scale sheep or cattle farmer

Green, the – term used in the Kimberley for the wet season

grog – general term for alcoholic drinks

grouse – very good, unreal

homestead – the residence of a *station* owner or manager

hoon – idiot, hooligan, *yahoo;* also 'to hoon' or 'hooning around', often in a vehicle – to show off in a noisy fashion with little regard for others

how are ya? – standard greeting – expected answer: 'Good, thanks, how are *you?'*

how ya goin'? – *how are ya?*

HQ – second-most revered Australian car

Hughie – the god of rain and surf ('Send her down, Hughie!', 'Send 'em up, Hughie!'); also God when things go wrong ('It's up to Hughie now')

humpy – Aboriginal bark hut ('it was so cold, it would freeze the walls off a bark humpy')

icy-pole – frozen *lolly water* or ice cream on a stick

jackaroo – young male trainee on a *station*

jaffle – sealed toasted sandwich
jerky – dried meat
jillaroo – young female trainee on a *station*
jocks – men's underpants
joey – young kangaroo or wallaby
journo – journalist
jumped-up – arrogant, full of self-importance (a 'jumped-up petty hitler')
jump-up – escarpment

kiwi – (also 'kay-one-double-you-one') New Zealander
knackered – exhausted, very tired
knock – criticise, deride
knocker – one who *knocks*
Koori – Aborigine (mostly south of the Murray River)

lair – layabout, ruffian
lairising – acting like a *lair*
lamington – square of sponge cake covered in chocolate icing and coconut
larrikin – a bit like a *lair;* rascal
lay-by – put a deposit on an article so the shop will hold it for you
lemonade – Australian Seven-Up
lock-up – *watch house*
lollies – sweets, candy
lolly water – soft drink made from syrup and water
lurk – a scheme

mad as a cut snake – insane, crazy; also insane with anger
mallee – low, shrubby, multi-stemmed eucalypt. Also 'the mallee' – the *bush*
manchester – household linen
March fly – horsefly, gadfly
mate – general term of familiarity, whether you know the person or not (but don't use it too often with total strangers)
Matilda – *swag*
middy – 285 ml beer glass (New South Wales)
milk bar – general store
milko – milkman
mob – a herd of cattle or flock of sheep while *droving;* any bunch of people (group, club, company)
Moreton Bay bug – (also known as *bug* or

Balmain bug) an estuarine horseshoe crab closely related to the shovel-nosed lobster (good *tucker* with an unfortunate name)
mozzies – mosquitoes
mud map – map drawn on the ground with a stick, thus any rough map drawn by hand
mulga – arid-zone acacia; the *bush*, away from civilisation (as in 'he's gone up the mulga')
Murri – Aborigine (mostly in Queensland)
muster – round up livestock
mystery-bags – sausages

never-never – a place even more remote than *back o'Bourke*
no-hoper – hopeless case
northern summer – summer in the northern hemisphere
north island – mainland Australia, viewed from Tasmania
no worries – *she'll be right*, that's OK
nulla-nulla – wooden club used by Aborigines

ocker – an uncultivated or boorish Australian
ocky strap – octopus strap: elastic strap with hooks for tying down gear and generally keeping things in place
off-sider – assistant or partner
on the piss – drinking alcohol ('they're on the piss tonight')
O-S – overseas (as in 'he's gone O-S')
outstation – an outlying *station* separate from the main one on a large property
OYO – own your own (flat or apartment)
Oz – Australia

pad – animal track ('cattle pad')
paddock – a fenced area of land, usually intended for livestock (paddocks can be huge in Australia)
pal – *mate*
pastoralist – large-scale *grazier*
pavlova – traditional Australian meringue and cream dessert, named after the Russian ballerina Anna Pavlova
perve – to gaze with lust
pineapple, rough end of – *stick, sharp end of*
piss – beer

pissed – drunk
pissed off – annoyed
piss turn – boozy party
plonk – cheap wine
pocamelo – camel polo
pokies – poker machines, found in clubs, mainly in New South Wales
pom – English person
pommy's towel – a notoriously dry object ('the Simpson Desert is as dry as a pommy's towel')
possie – advantageous position (pronounced 'pozzy')
postie – mailman or -woman
pot – 285 ml beer glass (Victoria, Queensland)
push – group or gang of people, such as shearers

quid – literally: a pound, $2. Still a common term in the *bush* for a non-specified amount of money, as in 'can you lend me a quid?' (enough money to last me until I'm not *skint*)

rapt – delighted, enraptured
ratbag – friendly term of abuse (friendly trouble-maker)
rat's coffin – meat pie of dubious quality
ratshit (R-S) – lousy
razoo – a coin of very little value, a subdivision of a rupee ('he spent every last razoo'). Counterfeit razoos made of brass circulated in the gold fields during *two-up* sessions, hence 'it's not worth a brass razoo'
reckon! – you bet!, absolutely!
rego – registration (as in 'car rego')
ridgy-didge – original, genuine, *dinky-di*
ripper – good, great (also 'little ripper')
road train – *semi-trailer*-trailer-trailer
roo bar – *bull bar*
root – have sexual intercourse
ropable – very bad-tempered or angry
rubbish (ie **to rubbish**) – deride, tease
rug rat – small child, *ankle-biter*, *tacker*

salvo – member of the Salvation Army
sandgroper – resident of Western Australia
sanger – sandwich

scallops – fried potato cakes (Queensland), the edible muscle of certain molluscs (north Queensland), shellfish (elsewhere)
schooner – a 425 ml beer glass in New South Wales, or a 285 ml glass in South Australia (where a 425 ml glass is called a 'pint')
scrub – stunted trees and bushes in a dry area; a remote, uninhabited area
sealed road – tarred road
sea wasp – box jellyfish
sedan – a closed car seating four to six people
see you in the soup – see you around
seismic line – *shotline*
semi-trailer – articulated truck
septic tanks – (also 'septics') rhyming slang for Yanks
session – lengthy period of heavy drinking
shanty – pub, usually unlicensed (proliferated in gold-rush areas)
sheila – woman, sometimes derogatory
shellacking – comprehensive defeat
she'll be right – *no worries*, it'll be OK
shitbox – neglected, worn-out, useless vehicle
shonky – unreliable
shoot through – leave in a hurry
shotline – straight trail 'hrough the bush, often kilometres long and leading nowhere, built by a mining company for seismic research
shout – buy round of drinks (as in 'it's your shout')
sickie – day off work through illness or lack of motivation
singlet – sleeveless shirt
skint – the state of being *quidless*
slab – package containing four six-packs of *tinnies* or *stubbies*, usually encased in plastic on a carboard base; also called a 'carton' when packaged in a box (Victoria)
sleep-out – a covered verandah or shed, usually fairly open
sling off – criticise
smoke-oh – tea break
snag – sausage
sport – *mate*
spunky – good looking, attractive (as in 'what a spunk')

squatter – pioneer farmer who occupied land as a tenant of the government

squattocracy – Australian 'old money' folk, who made it by being first on the scene and grabbing the land

squiz – a look (as in 'take a squiz')

station – large sheep or cattle farm

stick, sharp end of – the worse deal

stickybeak – nosy person

stinger – box jellyfish

stoush – fist fight, brawl (also verbal)

stretcher – camp bed

strides – daks

strine – Australian slang (from how an *ocker* would pronounce the word 'Australian')

Stubbies – trademark name for rugged short shorts

stubby – 375 ml bottle of beer

sunbake – sunbathe (well, the sun's hot in Australia)

super – superannuation (contributory pension)

surfaced road – tarred road

surfies – surfing fanatics

swag – canvas-covered bed roll used in the outback; also a large amount

swaggie, swagman – itinerant worker carrying his possessions in a *swag* (see *waltzing Matilda*)

ta – thanks

table drain – rainwater run-off area, usually quite deep and wide, along the side of a road

tacker – small child, *ankle-biter*, *rug rat*

takeaway – fast food, or a shop that sells it

tall poppies – achievers (*knockers* like to cut them down)

Taswegian – resident of Tasmania

tea – evening meal

terrorist – tourist

thingo – thing, whatchamacallit, hooza meebob, dooverlacky, thingamajig

thirst you could paint a picture of – the desire to drink a large quantity of foaming, ice-cold, nut-brown ale

thongs – flip-flops

tinny – 375 ml can of beer; also a small aluminium fishing dinghy

Tip, the – the top of Cape York

togs – swimming costume (Queensland, Victoria)

too right! – absolutely!

Top, the – the tip of Cape York

Top End – northern part of the Northern Territory, sometimes also Cape York

Troopie – Toyota Landcruiser Troopcarrier (seats up to 11 people)

trucky – truck driver

true blue – dinkum

tucker – food

two-pot screamer – person unable to hold their drink

two-up – traditional heads/tails gambling game

uni – university

up north – New South Wales and Queensland when viewed from Victoria

ute – utility, pickup truck

vegies – vegetables

waddy – wooden club used by Aborigines

wag – to play truant ('to wag school')

wagon – station wagon, estate car

walkabout – lengthy walk away from it all

wallaby track, on the – to wander from place to place seeking work (archaic)

walloper – policeperson (from 'wallop', to hit something with a stick)

waltzing Matilda – to wander with one's *swag* seeking work or a place to settle down (archaic)

washaway – washout: heavy erosion caused by running water across road or track

watch house – temporary prison at a police station

weatherboard house – wooden house clad with long, narrow planks

Wet, the – rainy season in the north

wharfie – dockworker

whinge – complain, moan

willy-willy – whirlwind, dust storm

woof wood – petrol used to start a fire

woolly rocks – sheep

wowser – spoilsport, puritan

wobbly – disturbing, unpredictable behaviour (as in 'throw a wobbly')

wobbly boot – (as in 'to put on the wobbly boot') to have consumed too much alcohol

woomera – stick used by Aborigines for throwing spears

yabby, yabbie – small freshwater crayfish

yabby, to – to catch yabbies, a relaxed activity often involving *mates* and a *slab* or two ('they're going yabbying this *arvo*')

yahoo – noisy and unruly person, *hoon*

yakka – work (from an Aboriginal language)

youse – plural of you (pronounced 'yooz')

yobbo – uncouth, aggressive person

yonks – ages, a long time

yowie – Australia's yeti or bigfoot

Index

MAPS

TEXT

PLANET TALK
Lonely Planet's FREE quarterly newsletter

We love hearing from you and think you'd like to hear from us.

When...*is the right time to see reindeer in Finland?*
Where...*can you hear the best palm-wine music in Ghana?*
How...*do you get from Asunción to Areguá by steam train?*
What...*is the best way to see India?*

For the answer to these and many other questions read PLANET TALK.

Every issue is packed with up-to-date travel news and advice including:

- *a letter from Lonely Planet founders Tony and Maureen Wheeler*
- *travel diary from a Lonely Planet author - find out what it's really like out on the road*
- *feature article on an important and topical travel issue*
- *a selection of recent letters from our readers*
- *the latest travel news from all over the world*
- *details on Lonely Planet's new and forthcoming releases*

To join our mailing list contact any Lonely Planet office (address below).

LONELY PLANET PUBLICATIONS
Australia: PO Box 617, Hawthorn 3122, Victoria (tel: 03-819 1877)
USA: Embarcadero West, 155 Filbert St, Suite 251, Oakland, CA 94607 (tel: 510-893 8555)
TOLL FREE: (800) 275-8555
UK: 10 Barley Mow Passage, Chiswick, London W4 4PH (tel: 081-742 3161)
France: 71 bis rue du Cardinal Lemoine – 75005 Paris (tel: 1-46 34 00 58)

Also available: Lonely Planet T-shirts. 100% heavyweight cotton (S, M, L, XL)

Guides to the Pacific

Australia – a travel survival kit
The complete low-down on Down Under – home of Ayers Rock, the Great Barrier Reef, extraordinary animals, cosmopolitan cities, rainforests, beaches ... and Lonely Planet!

Bushwalking in Australia
Two experienced and respected walkers give details of the best walks in every state, covering many different terrains and climates.

Bushwalking in Papua New Guinea
The best way to get to know Papua New Guinea is from the ground up – and bushwalking is the best way to travel around the rugged and varied landscape of this island.

Islands of Australia's Great Barrier Reef – Australia guide
The Great Barrier Reef is one of the wonders of the world – and one of the great travel destinations! Whether you're looking for the best snorkelling, the liveliest nightlife or a secluded island hideaway, this guide has all the facts you'll need.

Melbourne – city guide
From historic houses to fascinating churches and from glorious parks to tapas bars, cafés and bistros, Melbourne is a dream for gourmets and a paradise for sightseers.

New South Wales & the ACT
Ancient aboriginal sites, pristine surf beaches, kangaroos bounding across desert dunes, lyre-birds dancing in rainforest, picturesque country pubs, weather-beaten drovers and friendly small-town people, along with Australia's largest and liveliest metropolis (and the host city of the year 2000 Olympic Games) – all this and more can be found in New South Wales and the ACT.

Sydney – city guide
From the Opera House to the surf; all you need to know in a handy pocket-sized format.

Victoria – Australia guide
From old gold rush towns to cosmopolitan Melbourne and from remote mountains to the most popular surf beaches, Victoria is packed with attractions and activities for everyone.

Fiji – a travel survival kit
Whether you prefer to stay in camping grounds, international hotels, or something in-between, this comprehensive guide will help you to enjoy the beautiful Fijian archipelago.

Hawaii – a travel survival kit
Share in the delights of this island paradise – and avoid some of its high prices – with this practical guide. It covers all of Hawaii's well-known attractions, plus plenty of uncrowded sights and activities.

Micronesia – a travel survival kit
The glorious beaches, lagoons and reefs of these 2100 islands would dazzle even the most jaded traveller. This guide has all the details on island-hopping across the Micronesian archipelago.

New Caledonia – a travel survival kit
This guide shows how to discover all that the idyllic islands of New Caledonia have to offer – from French colonial culture to traditional Melanesian life.

New Zealand – a travel survival kit
This practical guide will help you discover the very best New Zealand has to offer: Maori dances and feasts, some of the most spectacular scenery in the world, and every outdoor activity imaginable.

Tramping in New Zealand
Call it tramping, hiking, walking, bushwalking or trekking – travelling by foot is the best way to explore New Zealand's natural beauty. Detailed descriptions of over 40 walks of varying length and difficulty.

Papua New Guinea – a travel survival kit
With its coastal cities, villages perched beside mighty rivers, palm-fringed beaches and rushing mountain streams, Papua New Guinea promises memorable travel.

Rarotonga & the Cook Islands – a travel survival kit
Rarotonga and the Cook Islands have history, beauty and magic to rival the better-known islands of Hawaii and Tahiti, but the world has virtually passed them by.

Samoa – a travel survival kit
Two remarkably different countries, Western Samoa and American Samoa offer some wonderful island escapes, and Polynesian culture at its best.

Solomon Islands – a travel survival kit
The Solomon Islands are the best-kept secret of the Pacific. Discover remote tropical islands, jungle-covered volcanoes and traditional Melanesian villages with this detailed guide.

Tahiti & French Polynesia – a travel survival kit
Tahiti's idyllic beauty has seduced sailors, artists and travellers for generations. The latest edition of this book provides full details on the main island of Tahiti, the Tuamotos, Marquesas and other island groups. Invaluable information for independent travellers and package tourists alike.

Tonga – a travel survival kit
The only South Pacific country never to be colonised by Europeans, Tonga has also been ignored by tourists. The people of this far-flung island group offer some of the most sincere and unconditional hospitality in the world.

Vanuatu – a travel survival kit
Discover superb beaches, lush rainforests, dazzling coral reefs and traditional Melanesian customs in this glorious Pacific Ocean archipelago.

Also available:
Pidgin phrasebook.

Lonely Planet Guidebooks

Lonely Planet guidebooks cover every accessible part of Asia as well as Australia, the Pacific, South America, Africa, the Middle East, Europe and parts of North America. There are five series: *travel survival kits*, covering a country for a range of budgets; *shoestring guides* with compact information for low-budget travel in a major region; *walking guides*; *city guides* and *phrasebooks*.

Australia & the Pacific
Australia
Australian phrasebook
Bushwalking in Australia
Islands of Australia's Great Barrier Reef
Outback Australia
Fiji
Fijian phrasebook
Melbourne city guide
Micronesia
New Caledonia
New South Wales
New Zealand
Tramping in New Zealand
Papua New Guinea
Bushwalking in Papua New Guinea
Papua New Guinea phrasebook
Rarotonga & the Cook Islands
Samoa
Solomon Islands
Sydney city guide
Tahiti & French Polynesia
Tonga
Vanuatu
Victoria

South-East Asia
Bali & Lombok
Bangkok city guide
Cambodia
Indonesia
Indonesia phrasebook
Laos
Malaysia, Singapore & Brunei
Myanmar (Burma)
Burmese phrasebook
Philippines
Pilipino phrasebook
Singapore city guide
South-East Asia on a shoestring
Thailand
Thai phrasebook
Vietnam
Vietnamese phrasebook

North-East Asia
China
Beijing city guide
Cantonese phrasebook
Mandarin Chinese phrasebook
Hong Kong, Macau & Canton
Japan
Japanese phrasebook
Korea
Korean phrasebook
Mongolia
North-East Asia on a shoestring
Seoul city guide
Taiwan
Tibet
Tibet phrasebook
Tokyo city guide

Middle East
Arab Gulf States
Egypt & the Sudan
Arabic (Egyptian) phrasebook
Iran
Israel
Jordan & Syria
Middle East
Turkish phrasebook
Trekking in Turkey
Yemen

Indian Ocean
Madagascar & Comoros
Maldives & Islands of the East Indian Ocean
Mauritius, Réunion & Seychelles

Mail Order

Lonely Planet guidebooks are distributed worldwide. They are also available by mail order from Lonely Planet, so if you have difficulty finding a title please write to us. US and Canadian residents should write to Embarcadero West, 155 Filbert St, Suite 251, Oakland CA 94607, USA; European residents should write to 10 Barley Mow Passage, Chiswick, London W4 4PH; and residents of other countries to PO Box 617, Hawthorn, Victoria 3122, Australia.

Indian Subcontinent
Bangladesh
India
Hindi/Urdu phrasebook
Trekking in the Indian Himalaya
Karakoram Highway
Kashmir, Ladakh & Zanskar
Nepal
Trekking in the Nepal Himalaya
Nepali phrasebook
Pakistan
Sri Lanka
Sri Lanka phrasebook

Africa
Africa on a shoestring
Central Africa
East Africa
Trekking in East Africa
Kenya
Swahili phrasebook
Morocco, Algeria & Tunisia
Arabic (Moroccan) phrasebook
South Africa, Lesotho & Swaziland
Zimbabwe, Botswana & Namibia
West Africa

Central America & the Caribbean
Baja California
Central America on a shoestring
Costa Rica
Eastern Caribbean
Guatemala, Belize & Yucatán: La Ruta Maya
Mexico

North America
Alaska
Canada
Hawaii

Europe
Baltic States & Kaliningrad
Dublin city guide
Eastern Europe on a shoestring
Eastern Europe phrasebook
Finland
France
Greece
Hungary
Iceland, Greenland & the Faroe Islands
Ireland
Italy
Mediterranean Europe on a shoestring
Mediterranean Europe phrasebook
Poland
Scandinavian & Baltic Europe on a shoestring
Scandinavian Europe phrasebook
Switzerland
Trekking in Spain
Trekking in Greece
USSR
Russian phrasebook
Western Europe on a shoestring
Western Europe phrasebook

South America
Argentina, Uruguay & Paraguay
Bolivia
Brazil
Brazilian phrasebook
Chile & Easter Island
Colombia
Ecuador & the Galápagos Islands
Latin American Spanish phrasebook
Peru
Quechua phrasebook
South America on a shoestring
Trekking in the Patagonian Andes
Venezuela

The Lonely Planet Story

Lonely Planet published its first book in 1973 in response to the numerous 'How did you do it?' questions Maureen and Tony Wheeler were asked after driving, bussing, hitching, sailing and railing their way from England to Australia.

Written at a kitchen table and hand collated, trimmed and stapled, *Across Asia on the Cheap* became an instant local bestseller, inspiring thoughts of another book.

Eighteen months in South-East Asia resulted in their second guide, *South-East Asia on a shoestring*, which they put together in a backstreet Chinese hotel in Singapore in 1975. The 'yellow bible' as it quickly became known to backpackers around the world, soon became *the* guide to the region. It has sold well over half a million copies and is now in its 8th edition, still retaining its familiar yellow cover.

Today there are over 140 Lonely Planet titles in print – books that have that same adventurous approach to travel as those early guides; books that 'assume you know how to get your luggage off the carousel' as one reviewer put it.

Although Lonely Planet initially specialised in guides to Asia, they now cover most regions of the world, including the Pacific, South America, Africa, the Middle East and Europe. The list of *walking guides* and *phrasebooks* (for 'unusual' languages such as Quechua, Swahili, Nepali and Egyptian Arabic) is also growing rapidly.

The emphasis continues to be on travel for independent travellers. Tony and Maureen still travel for several months of each year and play an active part in the writing, updating and quality control of Lonely Planet's guides.

They have been joined by over 50 authors, 90 staff – mainly editors, cartographers & designers – at our office in Melbourne, Australia, at our US office in Oakland, California and at our European office in Paris; another five at our office in London handle sales for Britain, Europe and Africa. Travellers themselves also make a valuable contribution to the guides through the feedback we receive in thousands of letters each year.

The people at Lonely Planet strongly believe that travellers can make a positive contribution to the countries they visit, both through their appreciation of the countries' culture, wildlife and natural features, and through the money they spend. In addition, the company makes a direct contribution to the countries and regions it covers. Since 1986 a percentage of the income from each book has been donated to ventures such as famine relief in Africa; aid projects in India; agricultural projects in Central America; Greenpeace's efforts to halt French nuclear testing in the Pacific and Amnesty International. In 1993 $100,000 was donated to such causes.

Lonely Planet's basic travel philosophy is summed up in Tony Wheeler's comment, 'Don't worry about whether your trip will work out. Just go!'.